Retail Marketing

Drs. F.W.J. Quix
Prof. drs. R.P. van der Kind

First edition, 2014

Noordhoff Uitgevers Groningen | Houten

© Noordhoff Uitgevers bv

Cover design: G2K Designers, Groningen/Amsterdam
Cover illustration: Frank Quix
Translation by: TRANSENTER B.V.

For any comments about this or other publications, please contact: Noordhoff Uitgevers bv, Higher Education Division, Reply Number 13, 9700 ED Groningen, e-mail: info@noordhoff.nl

This edition was created with extreme care. The author(s), editorial staff and publisher accept no liability in the event that any information is incomplete or incorrect, despite this care. They are always open to possible improvements of the herein contained details.

MIX
Papier van
verantwoorde herkomst
FSC
www.fsc.org   FSC® C118189

0 / 14

ISBN 978-90-01-80792-4
NUR 802

Preface

This first English edition of *Retail Marketing* once again demonstrates how rapidly things evolve in our field. Within the last months the landscape changed heavily. We are in the midst of the second big shift in retail. After the introduction of self service some 50 years ago, today the digital physical mash-up is taking place.

We spent a great deal of attention on determining retail trends towards the year 2020. Our thanks in this regard goes mainly to the HBD and Inretail, who gave us permission to use a modified version of the Re'structure Retail 2020 vision report as our new chapter 4.

Nowadays it is impossible to disassociate the internet from everything that consumers do. It has become a part of our lives, which is why we have decided this time to give internet a more prominent position in the book. We were fortunate enough to use a study by ABN AMRO and Inretail in the cross channel retail field, for which we are very grateful. We updated the lost sales area. We would like to thank student-assistant Aron Lewis for this. We opted for new graphic material. Here, in particular, our thanks to the companies of the Foundation Anton Dreesmann Leerstoel for their assistance. We would also like to thank all the members of this foundation for their support from the Leerstoel in Amsterdam and Groningen.

Our special thanks go out to several people for their contribution in various subjects: Wouter Haasloop Werner, John Terra as co-author of chapter 4 and the Cross Channel Report and Chantal Riedeman as co-author of chapter 22. The data have been updated and we have added research data to the book. We also applied some extra focus points in the area of market research. The book is therefore topical, which is very important in a field as turbulent as retail.

Retail Marketing is first of all intended for students at universities and higher economic schools, preparing for a career in retail. To them this is an opportunity to not only gain factual knowledge on retail, but to also understand the industry in which they will be working. In addition, the book is intended for managers in retail. Although in principal these people no longer need to be taught how to do retail and why they develop certain activities, the content might help them to develop a better view of the overall picture.

Drs. F.W.J. Quix
Prof. Drs. R.P. van der Kind
Amersfoort, June 2014

Contents

Part 6
Internal marketing mix 475

Part 7
Control 537

Introduction

Most textbooks treat the retail sector based on the question: what is retailing? Although this question is certainly also discussed in this book, the focus lies on answering the question: how do I do retailing? After all, entrants to the industry will only rarely find themselves in a situation where they are directly involved in the creation of entirely new retail formulas. They are more likely to work in existing companies, where the formulation of the problem is focused more on improvement and optimisation of the existing operations, both in terms of the market approach and in terms of internal procedure. This is why this book pays much more attention to operational applications of the theory.

In this book the retail concept implies 'the sale of goods to consumers, whether or not through stores'. In general, the retail concept has a much wider application: it may include the sale of services to consumers. For example, the office network of a bank (strongly focussed on the marketing of financial services to individuals) may be included in retail. The term 'retail banking' speaks for itself. The same applies for travel agencies and independent insurance agents. The term retail therefore includes 'all purchases of goods and services by the consumer from his (free) disposable income', we shall, however, limit ourselves in this book to physical goods.

Experience shows that the techniques that were initially developed for applications in goods retail, can also be applied successfully in other branches of retail. We can even say that goods retail has lead the way, from which 'other' retail can learn much.

PART 1

Description of the industry

In part 1 we discuss the structure (and specifically the development of this structure) of the retail sector. In chapter 1 we discuss what exactly is to be understood under retail and which changes have occurred through the course of time in the interpretation of the concept of retail.

Chapter 2 discusses some frequently used classification criteria of retail. In chapter 3 we discuss the significance of retail for the European economy, in particular retail. The chapter is supplemented by a comparative analysis of retail in different countries. We also look at the differences between retail marketing and industrial marketing.

In chapter 4 we discuss the retail trends towards 2020. Here we use a method to determine the potency of trend bundles.

1
Retail marketing

The positioning of retail marketing is the central topic of this chapter. Before discussing the concepts of marketing and retail marketing, the definition of retail will be explained in detail. By defining retail, it is important to reflect on the changing function of retail over time. Furthermore, it is important to determine the position retail occupies in the economic theory.

∎ 1.1 The concept of retailing

Retailing

With *retailing* we mean 'all business management activities that focus on direct sales of goods and services to consumers, provided that the goods and services are paid out of the net income of the consumers'.

Direct marketing

With *direct marketing* we imply the direct deliveries to the consumer. Companies that make use of brokering in order to deliver products to the consumer do not participate in retail marketing, but in trade marketing. Unilever does not deliver directly to the consumers and therefore participates in trade marketing. The Body Shop, which does deliver its products directly to the consumer, does retail marketing.

The expenditures should come from the net income, in other words: from the gross income following deductions of social security contributions and (income) tax. Compulsory pension insurance is not included in the retail expenditures. A private investment account, intended for a rainy day, is however included in the retail expenditures. The cost of a business trip (tax deductible) does not apply as retail expenditures, but the cost of a leisure trip does.

Retail expenditures

Retail expenditures can roughly be divided into:
- expenditure on services by consumers, such as banking services, insurance, medical services and leisure trips;
- expenditure on goods by consumers.

Since the sale of consumer goods to consumers takes place primarily through retail, the totality of that expenditure is also called *retail expenditure*.

Retail expenditures

The goods sector is contained within the retail sector, and thus the retail, the clearest in terms of structure. The reason is that retail businesses often only sell to individuals, while suppliers in the services sector – in addition to selling to individuals – are almost always selling to businesses as well. The distinction between private and business is not always used clearly. Selling to the so-called business sector is always much more important to banking companies and insurance companies than selling to individuals. Add to this that production and retailing often take place in the service environment within the same organisation (where the retail function is considered secondary to the production function), it becomes clear why service retail is a much less clearly demarcated area than the products sector.

Retailing

Although the concept of *retailing* implies much more than just goods retailing, the two concepts are often used interchangeably in practice. This is understandable due to the indistinctness described above. In this book, the retail sector of the Dutch economy will largely be explained from the merchandise sector, thus predominantly from goods retail. However, examples from the services sector will be used regularly. Not in the least because of the emergence of mixed forms. Goods retailers are more and more often including service packages in their product ranges, such as insurance, the possibility to draw money and to purchase mobile telephony and internet subscriptions. In late 2013, HEMA announced that it would be teaming up with health care insurer Menzis. The purpose of the

cooperation was to create an affordable insurance in combination with
10% discount on all purchases at HEMA. Also other services were added
by HEMA such as notary services and training and educational programs.

1.2 Retail

Defined in the simplest of terms, *retail* is 'that part of the total economic   **Retail**
activity that deals with the sale of goods directly to consumers'.
Economic textbooks usually classify the activity using the business chain.
Retail will always be located at the bottom of the business chain and is
therefore the final link in the process of supplying goods to the consumers
(figure 1.1).

FIGURE 1.1 The business chain in general

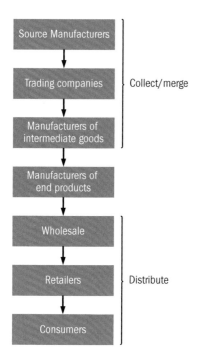

The immediate environment of retail within the business chain is formed by
both the *customers* (the consumers) and the suppliers. The *suppliers* may   **Customers**
be manufacturers of end products that supply directly to the retail. As the   **Suppliers**
concentration and the size of the retailers increase, this will occur more and
more often (figure 1.2). This may also be wholesale dealers, as was
predominantly the case in the past: peddlers that tried to bridge the
imbalances that originated between the large manufacturers and the small
storekeepers.

FIGURE 1.2 The immediate retail environment

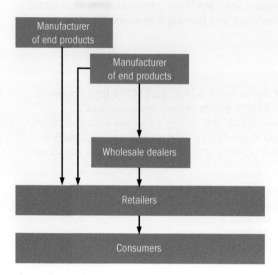

The problem with using the business chain – in order to explain the function of the retail – is that the supply process is generally very much product determined. You can draw up a business chain for the product 'CD's', or for the product 'books'. At the bottom of this business chain you will always find one or more forms of retail that have or will include the specific product in the product range. But does the description of retail as the final link in the production process also imply that retail has been described in all its complexity?
If that were true, the retail form 'department stores', which has both books and CD's in the product range, would be quite comparable with the retail form 'record shop' or 'bookstore' from its position in the market. As we all know, this does not really correspond with reality.

The description of retail as the final link in a production process that propels the goods from the manufacturer to the consumer is therefore incomplete. The conceptual understanding of retail as part of a single product oriented business chain dates from the time that retail was compared to 'the art of distribution'. The old function of retail was 'redistributing the flow of goods from the manufacturer to the consumer by time, by location and by quantity'. This redistribution was necessary since the industrial revolution caused the rise of mass production. Therefore production and consumption no longer coincided, in contrast to the previous period.

Redistribution in time The *redistribution in time* involves the stock function of retail: bridging the period between completion of the production by the manufacturer and the date of purchase by the consumer, often caused by the occurrence of irregularities between demand and production (for example due to seasonal fluctuations).

The *redistribution to location* involves the geographic distribution function: the place of production is rarely the same as the place of consumption. The goods must therefore be delivered to the final place of 'demand'.

Redistribution to location

The *redistribution in quantity* involves solving the differences between the 'output quantities' with the manufacturer and the 'input quantities' with the consumer. From a cost perspective, the manufacturer creates large quantities at the same time, while consumer demands only relate to one or a few products. The output quantity of the manufacturer should therefore be divided into a number of smaller quantities.

Redistribution in quantity

1.3 Changing function of retail

The old distribution concept dates back to the period when the power in the business chain was still found with the manufacturers. In this concept, retail was considered to be part of a *goods producing process*. In fact, we are therefore dealing with an industrial approach to distribution. At the time, retail consisted primarily of product specialty stores: relatively small stores that specialise in a relatively small product range, with strong similarities in terms of product characteristics, like the hardware specialists, the timber trade, the grocer, the milk man, the greengrocer and the pharmacist.

Goods producing process

The change of function that has occurred over the last few decades, is due to the fact that the power has gradually shifted from the retail suppliers (the manufacturers of consumer products) to retail customers (the consumers). With the transition from a *seller's market* to a *buyer's market* an oversupply is created which is offered to increasingly more discerning consumers using a variety of outlet channels. In such a situation it is no longer the manufacturer that determines what is offered when and through which channels, it is the consumer who determines what, when and through which stores he wants to buy. It is the wishes of the consumer and how the retailer responds to these wishes that currently determine the success of retail businesses, and no longer the degree of efficiency in the distribution of products and/or services. In fact, this change in function corresponds with the general shift from an industrial economy to a service economy: retail is no longer a box mover for the industry, but a service provider for the consumer.

Seller's market Buyer's market

The essence of the change is that the function no longer primarily consists of the redistribution of a production flow from current sections of the business chain, but much more from meeting the demand of the underlying sections of the business chain: the consumers. Distribution aspects should indeed be implemented in this new function of retail (*supply on demand*), but they are no longer the only aspect of the business operations. They are still essential, but no longer a sufficient condition for a successful business operation. With an increasing number of retail companies we even see that the physical distribution function is outsourced. As a result, the function of retail has changed from 'redistributors in time, location and quantity of a

Demand supply

product (range)' to 'supplier/maker of the consumer based demand related product ranges in an appropriate supply environment'.

The element with which the retailer responds to the consumer needs is

Marketing mix   called the *marketing mix*. We will discuss this in more detail in part 5 and 6 of this book. The method in which the elements of the marketing mix are compiled, leads to a supply formula: a consistent and weighed composition of the marketing mix elements, leading to a recognisable and logical proposition for the target group. The supply formulas therefore follow the consumer need, and not reversed. It is from this latter opinion that retail, and in particular the retail, is illuminated in this book. In doing this, we will be faced with the diversity of the phenomenon of retail. We look to both pull oriented strategies (demand-driven) that are successful, and to successful companies with a push or partial push strategy, such as the Etam group, which uses a push strategy. Control is central here. We will also return to the mixing forms later in this book.

1.4 Consequences of the changing function of retail

Changing from 'product distributor' to 'demand supplier' has had far-reaching consequences for the modern retail. It resulted, amongst other things, in a considerable expansion of the degree of difficulty of the retail: success factors no longer consisted of only product knowledge and distribution skills, but should have been supplemented with knowledge of the consumer needs, insight into the trends, knowledge of purchasing methods, knowledge of methods to communicate with the consumer and sometimes even – in situations where the manufacturers do not wish to participate in satisfying the needs of the consumer – knowledge of developing own production lines. Evolving from product redistributors into demand supplier in its most extreme form can be illustrated with a comparison between the old and new business chain. The example relates to the Do It Yourself (DIY) sector (figure 1.3 and 1.4).

In the old business chain, retail was found mainly in one column, namely the product line in which one specialises. Consumers who wanted to do DIY had to go to a large number of stores: from the paint dealer to the hardware store, followed by the lumberyard and so on. In each of these stores the consumer once again had to wait for assistance and had to pay separately. All in all, a rather time consuming process that was also – due to the low efficiency in the operation – rather expensive. Because the stores were small, the goods could rarely be ordered directly from the manufacturer:

Wholesale dealers   a brokerage originated (between the *wholesale dealers*). The wholesale dealer made an additional translation between the quantities that were received from the manufacturer and the quantity that an individual retailer could purchase at a time. Therefore, this wholesaler also worked as a distributor.

FIGURE 1.3 Old business chain (example of the DIY industry)

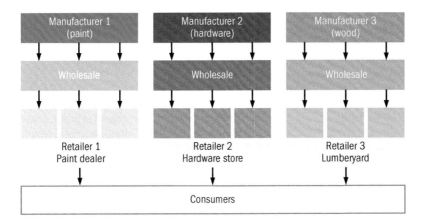

FIGURE 1.4 New business chain (example of the DIY industry)

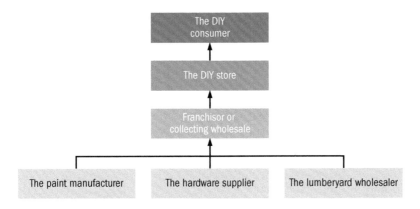

In the new business chain, the need of the consumer is central. Retail offers a product range tailored to the consumer's demand. That product range is generally much wider than before and can come from very different product lines. The supply of products is therefore in the hands of manufacturers from various business chains. It is the retailers' task to combine the products from the same business chains in such a way that a *demand related* product range (a product range tailored to the broad consumer needs) arises.

Demand related

Therefore, it no longer revolves around selling products that are present in the market, but also providing products that the client demands, if needed by developing and producing own retail brands. The latter is also referred to as *private labels,* or house brands. For as far as the retailer cannot comply with the requirements of the new business chain, for example because it is too small or because the expertise is lacking, the retailer can – as in the old business chain – be assisted by wholesale dealers or purchasing organisations. But these wholesale dealers have been given a different function than the wholesale dealers in the old business chain:

Private labels

their job is to presort for the demand-related retail product ranges. Their function is therefore more of a 'collecting' function than a 'distributing' function. The franchisor is the ultimate form of such collecting wholesale: a retail supplier that is not only restricted to supplying a (part of) the product range, but that also takes over other components of the marketing mix of the retailer, such as promotion, store layout, display plans and possibly a complete formula.

The function changes in retail are explained here in the form of two extremes. In practice we see all kinds of mixed forms: manufacturers that take over parts of the detail function through forward integration and retailers that take over parts of the wholesale dealers, or manufacturers who function through backwards integration (figure 1.5).

FIGURE 1.5 Mixed forms in function change of retail

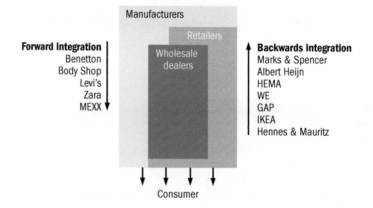

Forward **integration** **Backwards** **integration**

Examples of *forward integration* from manufacturers to retailers are Benetton, The Body Shop (currently owned by L'Oréal), Levi's, Mango, MEXX, Rituals and ZARA. Examples of *backwards integration* of retailers in the manufacture sphere, or at least in the sphere of the prescription of production specifications, are Albert Heijn, GAP, HEMA, Hennes & Mauritz, IKEA, Tesco and WE. Incedentally, these phenomena also appear with wholesale dealers: Schuitema (presently called C1000) was a supplying wholesaler to independent companies in the food sector, but has since become formula administrator of the supermarket formula C1000 and will disappear in time due to the takeover by Jumbo. Intergamma in turn is a franchisor of the DIY store formulas Gamma and Karwei. Example 1.1 with regard to Benetton and example 1.2 with regard to the Body Shop will relate to forward integration. An example of backwards integration will then be given (example 1.3).

EXAMPLE 1.1 FORWARD INTEGRATION: BENETTON

Benetton started in 1965 as manufacturer of knitted products in a number of 'back room workshops' in Italy. Because Benetton had developed a procedure in which knitted products could be coloured much later in the production process than in the paint procedures of the competitors, a competitive advantage was created. After all, in a buyer's market situation where it becomes clear at a very late stage which colours the consumer wants, such a procedure is much more capable of meeting consumer needs than competitors who have to colour their materials six months in advance. However, the existing retail was not yet ripe for this manner of turbo distribution, which is why Benetton developed its own stores, followed by a sizeable franchise organisation later on.

Source: Palermi, Benetton,
After Internationalization
we work for Diversification. In: *International
Trends in Retailing*, vol. 4, no. 2, p. 27-30)

EXAMPLE 1.2 FORWARD INTEGRATION: THE BODY SHOP

The Body Shop was established in 1976 in the pantry behind the house of founder Anita Roddick in Brighton. She was dissatisfied with how existing products in the field of body care were manufactured and presented to the consumer by the existing suppliers (large cosmetics manufacturers such as Estée Lauder, Elisabeth Arden, Chanel and Revlon): 'We sell hope.'). This is why Roddick started to experiment with a number of environmentally friendly and animal friendly substances. The results were not only interesting for her, but also seemed to fill a niche (void) in the needs of other consumers, a niche that was not noticed by the existing suppliers. The result is well-known: a global chain of specialist body care companies, responding to two underlying trends in the current consumer needs: health and caring for the environment. It is interesting to note that one of the recent successes of the Estée Lauder group, shaken up by the success of The Body Shop, is 'Origins', a store formula set up entirely around the idea of caring for the environment.

On 18 March 2006 *de Volkskrant*, amongst others, reported the sale of The Body Shop to L'Oréal. Founder and environmental activist Anita Roddick denied to have gone against her own principles. Animal protection organisations in Great Britain had a different opinion and called for a boycott of The Body Shop, because L'Oréal used animals for testing their cosmetics. The Body Shop became successful because they rejected animal testing. The consumer organisation Ethical Consumer feared that the takeover would have negative consequences for The Body Shop, because L'Oréal placed commercial considerations above idealism. Anita Roddick rejected all criticism. They called the takeover the best gift that The Body Shop could ever have gotten for its thirtieth birthday. 'L'Oréal displayed visionary leadership and is a convinced advocate of our values. They understand that Body Shop is an outsider in the world of the international business community.' In 1984 the company was taken to the stock exchange. In the nineties, the success story was spoiled. The expansion in the American market was a lot less subtle and in its own country other chains also started offering natural products. Roddicks famous peppermint foot lotion was overshadowed by new, more exotic products. In 1998, Roddick stepped out of the daily management of the company and four years later she also gave up her position as President. Roddick denied switching the enemy. According to her,

L'Oréal is prepared to take over the principles of The Body Shop. 'If the largest cosmetics company in the world can learn about small family farms and women's cooperatives, then we should be happy.' For the time being, L'Oréal will manage The Body Shop remotely. The Body Shop remains an independent chain with its own head office.
On 10 September 2007, Anita Roddick passed away due to a cerebral haemorrhage at the age of 64.

Source: Anita Roddick, *Body and Soul*, 1991, Ebury Press, London (printed on recycled paper); *de Volkskrant*, 18 March 2006; *de Volkskrant*, 10 September 2007)

Forward integrated: ZARA

EXAMPLE 1.3 BACKWARDS INTEGRATION: MARKS & SPENCER

Michael Marks was a Polish immigrant. He initially earned a living in England as a market vendor. Later he worked as a market trader. During this period he developed the penny concept: all products were sold for a penny. His slogan read: 'Don't ask the price, it is a penny'. The successful approach quickly led to regular stores that were rapidly expanding. In 1894 he stared a partnership with Tom Spencer in order to strengthen the management: Marks & Spencer was born. However, the actual development of the current concept began with the appointment of Simon Marks, son of the founder, as chairman in 1917. Simon Marks was convinced that – in order to maintain the low price policy – it was necessary to proceed to a modified distribution method, where the manufacturer is the direct supplier. The wholesaler must be eliminated.

However, this meant that the supply volumes per product would have to be considerably higher than it was with the wholesale dealers. A significant reduction of the product range was therefore decided on in order to increase the volume per article. The criteria for this was the success of the products with the public: the products with a high sales rate and large volumes were given extra space at the expense of the products that did not perform as well. The internal competition between product groups for the available space and the connected clean-up of a large number of product ranges resulted in a product line with a completely unique character. This unique character was also appealing to the public: although a large number of products had disappeared, the sales of the remaining products increased much more than the lost sales. Marks & Spencer could no longer be characterised in the then customary supply formula terms: the company was not a department store, nor was it a specialist company. A new phenomenon originated: a store that specialises in a purchase situation for the consumer, namely the purchase moments for simple, quick purchases in the 'many and often range', where the convenience and the price quality ratio is central in the purchase behaviour.

The strategy that was followed therefore led to a limited product supply that could be sold in very large volumes, and therefore lead to an over demand on suppliers. This over demand was used to develop a private brand (Saint Michaels) that was produced entirely according to the product specifications of Marks & Spencer. Marks & Spencer thereby strived for long term coopera-tion relationships (co-makerships) with its suppliers, where Marks & Spencer employees cooperated with the factories as quality controllers. Marks & Spencer still follows this policy very successfully. The company is also known as the 'manufacturer without factories'.

The first years of the twenty first century – from a British point of view – things suddenly went extremely bad for Marks & Spencer. In 1998 the profit amounted to a record amount of over £1 billion, several years later (2001) this was down to £145 million. Marks & Spencer had lost sight of its core values that endeared the company to the British public in the previous century. The problems were also noticed in Europe (including the Netherlands), because the company withdrew from almost all European markets to completely focus on problems on the domestic market.

The decline of Marks & Spencer was due to various developments. Their own brand Saint Michaels, which was the only brand that Marks & Spencer sold for a very long time, perfectly reflected the value-for-money philosophy. However, during the nineties of the previous century there was a sudden expansion of sub-brands, of which very few acquired any client supporters of note. Because the style of the products had become outdated and the product quality declined, Marks & Spencer had a record stock of £3 billion in 2004. While Marks & Spencer was busy expanding, specifically outside the United Kingdom, the domestic market was rapidly changing. Emerging competitors such as NEXT and Topshop, but also supermarkets that had added clothing to their range, such as ASDA (of Wal-Mart), won more and more customers from Marks & Spencer. The problems were still somewhat hidden by the upward trend in retail in general. But the biggest problem was that management had no idea what they actually wanted and what it was that did not work. There were no structural changes implemented to change the tide. Products were placed in the store in the hope that they would sell a strategy that was guided mainly by supply rather than demand. Furthermore, many stores were stuffy and outdated and also much too dark and too crammed. The personnel were also not really motivated by the relatively low wages. Under guidance of CEO Stuart Rose, Marks & Spencer crawled up from the depths, applying a sharp reorientation of the company. The company was put back on the map by focussing on the core values that had made the company so successful. This happened based on three cornerstones: *improve the product, improve the stores and improve the service.*

The product range was tackled by taking important brands back into their own hands, such as the ladies fashion brand Per Una that was bought from the creator.

Backwards integrated: WE

All personnel received extensive training and their salaries were increased, making salary increases dependent on performance. The most visible part for customers was the refurbishing and restyling of the stores. Behind the screens the *supply chain* was de-cluttered, on the one hand by improving the cooperation with suppliers and on the other hand by opening various buying offices globally (*sourcing offices*) to be able to make better decisions across the entire chain, from buying to distribution of the products. Finally, to make it obvious the pioneering role that Marks & Spencer had fulfilled before was fully restored, a large eco plan was introduced in January 2007. In this way Marks & Spencer wanted to manufacture as sustainably as possible, CO_2 neutral resulting in a healthier life for customer

and staff. The company has made it their goal to excel on all these points in 2012. This statement was supported by the introduction of a large number of healthy and organic lifestyle products that could be purchased nowhere else.

Due to all the above measures, Marks & Spencer has returned to the elite British retail division and it can rightfully be called the 'manufacturer without factories' again.

Source: Marks & Spencer: a manufacturer without factories. In: *International Trends in retailing*, vol. 6, nr. 2, p. 23-35; Back in Fashion: How we're reviving a British icon. In: *Harvard Business Review*, May 2007

▮▮ Position of retail in economic theory

Modern retail as we know it only developed after the industrial revolution. Prior to this time there was trade with individuals, but not in the form of institutionalised retail. In the food sphere, surpluses of food produced for own use was traded on the market. In the non-food sphere, valuable products were ordered from craftsmen and produced according to individual specifications. This in fact, in modern terms, involved one-on-one marketing. Only with the emergence of the industrial revolution and the resulting decoupling of the time of production and consumption did the imbalances mentioned above start to take place. Retail arises when the costs of the newly added link (retail) are less than the *economies of scale* of the industrial mass products. From this point of view, the emergence of retail as a separate section in the business chain can thus be linked back to the economic transaction cost theory (Williamson, 1975 and Coase, 1934).

Economies of scale

The above described function changes from retail (from the *goods producing process* to the *demand satisfying process*, respectively from moving boxes to service provision) can be explained using the transaction costs theory: due to the shift of power from the manufacturer to the consumer it is no longer about minimising the cost within the business chain from the view of the manufacturer, but to minimise the find or search problems of the consumer. The search costs of consumers consist of two parts: on the one hand the 'hassle' associated with buying products (such as relocation, the price of the product and finding the product, or the cost of shopping), on the other hand the pleasure that one can derive from shopping (the proceeds). The consumer will choose the store where the balance of the costs and proceeds is the most favourable (Haasloop Werner and Quix, 2010).

Demand satisfying process

Retail only arises if the transaction costs involved with the direct supply from manufacturer to consumer is higher than the sum of the costs that are involved with the supply from manufacturer to retailer on the one hand and the supply from retailer to consumer on the other hand (see figure 1.6).

FIGURE 1.6 Transaction costs

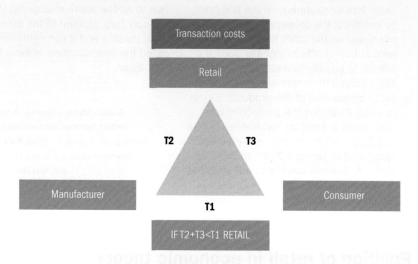

In formula: retail has the right to exist if;

$$T1 > T2 + T3$$

T   = costs involved in the direct distribution from the manufacturer to the consumer
T2 = costs involved in the supply from the manufacturer to the retailer
T3 = costs involved in the supply from the retailer to the consumer

The maturing of the internet paved the way for some manufacturers to supply directly to consumers. Costs directly attributable to distribution can in some cases already be much lower for direct supply to the consumer. Still, some manufacturers will be reluctant, because they are still greatly supported by the retail network. This could be due to the fact that today a large part of the products can be sold via traditional channels, where after sales also takes place via retail. This ensures that the transaction costs theory still turns out positive for the retail sector, but not only because of the direct distribution costs. An evaluation of the transaction costs for each sector within the retail will have to take place in the coming years. As we already noticed, for music, books and travel this will be faster than for other branches.

Online retail within the transaction cost theory
Starting from the Transaction cost triangle and the assumption that internet could lead to a completely different composition of the distribution costs in retail, the possible new combinations will be weighed in the transaction cost matrix of Sarkar, Butler and Steinfield. On the horizontal axis there are the

two options in the 'old' economy, before the existence of the internet, the vertical axis contains the situations in the new economy, after the internet was born (see figure 1.7). Each quadrant will be addressed in more detail.

FIGURE 1.7 Transaction costs matrix

The upper right quadrant: the threatened established retail (bricks and mortar)
Before the internet era, transaction costs benefitted existing stores. With the arrival of the internet, the transaction costs are beneficial to the e-tailers. This is the situation where the established retail should be the most apprehensive. It means that these stores see their sales decrease in the long term in favour of the market share of the e-tailers. In fact, this is already the case: book stores, record stores and especially travel agencies notice the impact of the internet. At the moment, this last category is also the biggest with regard to online sales.

The upper left quadrant: strengthening direct marketers
Before the internet, transaction costs were beneficial to direct marketers and this is still the case. This quadrant forms no immediate threat to retail. After all, these sales were never with the retail to begin with. It will however be clear that the relative position and the technical possibilities of the direct marketers will become stronger thanks to the internet. Dell Computers is an example of a direct marketer that utilises the options of the internet to the full extent. However, Dell also has its eye on retail locations. Dell has kiosks in many shopping malls in the United States to make direct contact with the shopping public.

The lower left quadrant: the area of the pure players (clicks and order)
The transaction costs before the internet were beneficial to direct marketers, nowadays they are beneficial to retail. This means that there are new opportunities for retail distribution systems that offer goods via the internet, to fine tune supply and demand respectively. Amazon, Marktplaats, Zalando, Bol.com and eBay are examples of these so-called *cyber mediairs* or *pure players*.

Example 1.4 illustrates that things could also go wrong with a pure player.

EXAMPLE 1.4 ETOYS

eToys, an American pure player toy e-tailer, is perhaps one of the best examples of a failed online operation. Retail and e-tail are more than a website with many visitors and buyers, the goods also have to reach their final destination. eToys went to the stock exchange in May 1999 for twenty dollars per share. After the first day of trading the share was already over 85 dollars and thus had a market capitalisation of more than ten billion dollars, much higher than the established Toys"R"Us. The company 'invested' tons in marketing. It also invested significantly in the supply chain and the infrastructure, with the intention of cashing in on its achieved first mover advantage.

Business was good: sales increased from 1 million dollars in 1997 to no less than 150 million dollars in 1999. eToys was celebrated as one of the internet heroes and examples for the industry. But in 2000 it became clear that the company had moved miles away from being profitable. The problems piled up. The share price collapsed and in early 2001 they had to apply for bankruptcy, the share price dropped below ten dollar cents and the company had no money left to keep it operational.

Source: *Retail Shopping, 2007: Net versus the Mall*, Harvard Business School, 2007

The lower right quadrant: the multichannel or crosschannel providers (clicks and bricks)

This involves either hybrid companies that start up an internet sales channel from the established retail, or pure players who also build fixed retail from an existing internet channel. Examples are HEMA, H&M and ZARA. While Apple, actually a manufacturer, or rather a brand, which sells directly through the internet, has its own stores and distributes primarily through conventional and online retailers. Coolblue and Pixmania.com are examples in the opposite direction. They are some of the first e-tailers that opened physical branches. In the future we may even see branches of Bol. com appear although they have their physical presence via Albert Heijn.

Analysis of the developments based on the transaction costs matrix
Various studies, including a study by Forrester in the US, which was based on a clustering of retailers according to the transaction costs matrix, indicated the following:
- The established retail (the upper right quadrant) in certain industries will suffer market share loss in favour of internet providers. Although the share of internet providers is still small, the growth rate of sales via the internet is much higher than that of the established retail. The choice is then: stay where you are and eventually experience sales pressure, or join the market share race at the expense of high investments (and therefore pressure on yield) in an internet channel.
- The pure players (the lower left quadrant) do not have it easy either. Their sales have grown considerably, but not all of them are able to make sales profitable. There are two major causes for this:

Marketing
costs
  – *The marketing expenses.* Due to the unfamiliarity of the consumer with (new) pure players, it takes a great deal of time, effort and money to attract visitors to the internet site. As a result, the marketing expenses, and

therefore the break-even point, are extremely high. Because the reliability aspect weighs so heavily, these internet providers also have to advertise relatively much to gain the trust of consumers. Major brands generally have a higher degree of trust compared to lesser known brands. It often happens that the 'per order' marketing costs of a pure player exceed the margin that is earned on the order, and obviously this is of no help at all. In short, selling over the internet requires a rather substantial investment in the brand of the seller and building a new strong brand takes a great deal of money. Companies like Amazon.com, Bol.com and eBay will manage, but many other companies will not make it or have already disappeared.

– *The fulfilment costs.* It often appears that new pure players are indeed able to organise the internal store systems. But when it comes to dealing with the external operations (home delivery etc.), they nevertheless appear to often misjudge the matter: the lack of fulfilment and the high costs that can be involved, often prove to be an obstacle on the road to success. This is certainly the case where these costs cannot be passed on fully to consumers. Where the pure player is able to minimise the inventory costs, by either having no inventory or by having a very limited inventory with good and fast replenishment systems, this will have a positive impact on performance. In the near future this may lead to better scores on the performance indicators.

Fulfilment costs

- The *multichannel*, providers, or rather the *cross channel* providers, appear to be the winners for now. In all instances their *key performance indicators* appear to be more favourable than those of the pure players, at lower costs, although the efficiency of the internet operation is often still lower than that of the store operation. The marketing costs are significantly lower than those of the pure players, because the cross channel providers are able to profit from the brand value and the trust that they have already earned in the market with their existing store operation, while they can usually rely on the support of their existing infrastructure for fulfilment. The latter applies specifically for multichannel providers who already have a 'home delivery infrastructure'. In the early years it was specifically the mail order companies that were able to benefit most from the new marketing methods, but most of them have already become pure players.

1.6 Marketing and retail marketing

This paragraph will first discuss the concept of marketing. We will then immerse ourselves in consumer marketing as part of marketing.

1.6.1   The marketing concept

Marketing is that part of the business process that deals with the marketing or sale of products. There are many definitions of the term marketing, often quite different in nature. Kuhlmeijer (1990), the founder of the commercial economy in the Netherlands, defined *marketing* as follows:

Marketing

> Marketing involves all activities of organised economies which serve to satisfy the needs, desires, aspirations or expectations of individuals by preparing and effectuating the exchange process effectively and efficiently.
> Source: H.J. Kuhlmeijer and B.A. Bakker, *Commercial policy*, Stenfert Kroese, 1990, p. 4

Kotler defined marketing as follows:

> Marketing serves as the link between a society's need and its pattern of industrial response.
>
> Source: P. Kotler *Principles of Marketing*, Prentice Hall, 2007

Thus, both definitions depart from a completely different angle, where Kuhlmeijer's definition seems to fit in with the old business chain, in the sense that the process is seen from above (marketing as *goods producing process*), while Kotler's definition seems to fit in more with the new business chain, in the sense that the process is seen from the consumer (marketing as *demand satisfying process*).

We see the very same movement with the American Marketing Association: after more than twenty years, the definition has changed. The old definition was:

> Marketing is the process of planning and executing conception, pricing, promotion and distribution of goods, ideas and services to create exchanges that satisfy individual and organisational goals.
>
> Source: American Marketing Association, 1985

The new definition is:

> Marketing is an organisational function and a set of processes for creating, communicating, and delivering value to customers and for managing customer relationships in ways that benefit the organisation and its stakeholders.
>
> Source: David L. Kurtz, *Principles of Contemporary* Marketing, 2008

Despite these clear differences, the definitions do have something in common: marketing is equated to the process control of the flow of goods from the manufacturer to the consumer and no specific function is assigned to retail in the production process. With Kuhlmeijer, retail functions act as an aid for the manufacturers with the distribution of goods (retail = outlet channel of the manufacturer). With Kotler, retail mainly serves as conduit of information from the consumer to the manufacturer (retail = information supplier for the manufacturer).

In practice we see that this passive interpretation of retail is incorrect. Retail plays an increasingly more independent role in the process management of the flow of goods from the manufacturer to the consumer, as such that in some cases the production process already begins with retail. HEMA (see example 1.5) began as one of the first retail companies with its own product development.

EXAMPLE 1.5 HEMA

In imitation of the English Marks & Spencer, HEMA started its own product development at a very early stage: the company developed its own production line according to its own specifications. These specifications were always aimed at creating high quality products that could be sold at low prices. In other words, HEMA instructed the manufacturers how they had to manufacture, and at what price the products should be provided to the consumer. Nowadays, HEMA (basically) does not sell any 'known' brands, though some manufacturers of these known brands were not afraid to deliver to HEMA, given the sales that were involved with deliveries to HEMA. As a result, HEMA was one of the first retail companies in the Netherlands that did retail marketing independently. HEMA sold its store as an 'integrated product' and not as a place where a number of brand products were collected. The name HEMA acquired its own brand recognition: it was the first retail company of which the store name was also the brand name.

At the moment there are many examples of retailers who fully or partially develop their own product range. An important part of the sales at Albert Heijn is realised through its own brand. Albert Heijn even opted for a threefold division of its own brand portfolio: in addition to its own brand, AH Basic (previously called Euroshopper) is positioned at the bottom and AH Excellent at the top. The latter brand is often positioned above or equal to an A-brand. The total product range of Aldi consists of own fancy brands (manufactured under responsibility of the parent company Albrecht GmbH). Fashion stores like M&S Mode and C&A at the bottom of the market, and ZARA, WE, Hennes & Mauritz and Claudia Sträter in the middle and higher segment develop their product range in-house using their own styling and product developments, and deliver all their products under their own label.

This development shows that the supposed passivity of retailers in process control is no longer consistent with reality and that the two definitions discussed do not do justice to the role played by retail in the practice. In many cases, retail has taken control of the chain. The Institute for Marketing Studies uses the following definition for marketing:

> Marketing is the management process responsible for identifying, anticipating and satisfying customer requirements profitably.
> Source: UK, Chartered Institute of Marketing, 2002

This definition is different from the previous definitions, because marketing is regarded as a management process and no longer as a flow of goods process. Marketing in this concept therefore involves all parts of the production process and not just an individual function. In the concept of the Institute of Marketing Studies, it is also possible for the location of the marketing function to shift in the business chain, for example from manufacturers to retailers. Finally, it is explicitly included in the definition that it is all about profit.

For retail, with a low added value, this is a useful addition to the previous definitions.

1.6.2   Consumer marketing

Today we recognise several specialisations within the overall field of marketing, such as industrial marketing, business-to-business marketing, service marketing, non-profit marketing and consumer marketing. For the topic of this book, it is mainly consumer marketing that is important. A brief definition of terms follows below. We will then elaborate on the differences between trade marketing and retail marketing.

Definition of terms

Consumer marketing

With *consumer marketing,* we mean all marketing efforts aimed at the satisfaction of the final consumer. Following the philosophy of the business chain, but duly taking into account the specific nature of marketing in the various sections of the business chain, we distinguish within consumer marketing between trade marketing (focused on sales from manufacturers to the middleman and retailers in the merchandise sector) and *retail marketing* (focused on the sales from retailers to the final consumer) (see figure 1.8).

Retail marketing

FIGURE 1.8 Consumer marketing

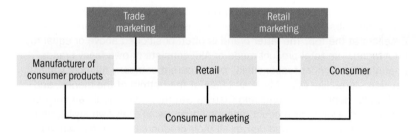

Differences between trade marketing and retail marketing

Although trade and retail marketing both fall under consumer marketing, there are several significant differences (table 1.1). Several of these differences, mentioned in table 1.1, are discussed in more detail below.

TABLE 1.1 Differences in retail marketing and trade marketing

Characteristic	Retail marketing	Trade marketing
Supply chain	Horizontal	Vertical
Business process	Demand driven	Product driven
Target group	Anonymous	Known
Product range	Wide/Very wide	Small
Demand relationship	Assortment driven	Product driven
Place	Consumer leading	Costs leading
Expansion	Once-off	Rearrangement

TABLE 1.1 Differences in retail marketing and trade marketing (continued)

Characteristic	Retail marketing	Trade marketing
Price	Surcharge calculation	Cost price calculation
Promotion	Store oriented	Product oriented
Marketing mix	8 P's	4 P's
Purchase	Primary activities	Support activities
Time horizon	Short term	Long term
Marketing function	Purchase	Sale
Returns criteria	Return on sales	Return on investment

Supply chain
A manufacturer of consumer products can generally only manufacture a limited product line. For example, a coffee manufacturing industry can manufacture espresso coffee beans, ground coffee, coffee pads and instant coffee, but cannot manufacture magazines using the same production machines. The supply from manufacturers to retail therefore always involves small product lines, of which the range is determined by the production process technique. In order to ensure its sales, the manufacturer will try to give these small product lines image components that appeal to certain target groups under the consumers. This results in the image of the seductive Nespresso drinker George Clooney, the 'be yourself' Kanis & Gunnink coffee, the warm feeling that comes with Douwe Egberts (you will find each other while drinking Douwe Egberts) or the passionate Nescafé drinker dancing the tango in her mind.
But a retailer needs more than just Douwe Egberts, or Kanis & Gunnink or Nescafé in its product range. He needs various different brands, because the people living in his catchment area are attracted to both the warm image and 'be yourself' image. In fact, the product line in the coffee shelf in the supermarket, even within such a limited product group, is so much wider than the product line of the individual suppliers.
The supermarket does not try to attract just one type of customer, but a multitude of types. And that is also necessary; otherwise he would not generate a profitable sales volume. The marketing of the retailer is therefore horizontally focussed, in the width, while the marketing effort of the supplier is vertically oriented (see figure 1.9).

FIGURE 1.9 Marketing horizontal/vertical

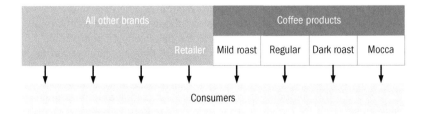

1

Business process
Consistent with the above, the business process in retail – other than in industrial businesses – is generally more driven by demand. This is logical, because industrial companies, once they have selected a specific product and the relevant production process, are stuck with it for a very long time. In retail, because of the relatively low investment associated with changes in the product range, it is much easier to follow consumer demands.

Product and product range
In general, a manufacturer of consumer products will not have any difficulty in defining his product line: Campina is in dairy, Douwe Egberts in coffee and Heineken in beer. When manufacturers speak of expanding the product line, this often takes place through other brands: Under the brand name Pickwick, Douwe Egberts is a tea supplier. In retail, this is not quite as easy: the product supplied by retail cannot be defined as a single product. In its most limited sense, the product supplied by retail consists of the product range and, as we know, that always consists of a multitude of different products, grouped around a specific consumer demand. This customer-driven product range is what gives retailers their added value for the consumer. Even Aldi, with a very limited product range in terms of retail-trade, still carries a product (in the limited sense of range) that is composed of more than nine hundred products. That is much more than all types of Douwe Egbert's coffee put together. This means that the retail product can never be described in simple terms, but that there are always aspects of a 'portfolio' in play. The art is to build up the product range portfolio as evenly as possible. This requires constant attention from the retailer: the product range consists of a mix of products that all have their own operational characteristics with regard to sales rate, margin, laborious nature and service. Controlling this mix is exactly what makes retail so difficult, yet so fascinating.
In addition to these operational aspects of the product range control, technical market aspects also play a role in the control of the product range portfolio: consumer preferences change over time and this should be responded to by adjusting the portfolio. If it remains constant, it eventually becomes contaminated, because products slip in amongst the product range that are good for sales, but it negatively affects the store concept because certain parts of the product range do not catch on with the public and are left on the shelves for too long.
It is important to ensure that the lead in the sorting of the product range is maintained with regard to the competition.

Sorting per range

The *sorting per range* is therefore an extremely important element of the marketing mix of the retailer. Sorting per range traditionally takes place through buying. This is why (as crazy as it may sound) the marketing function in retail is often incorporated in the purchase function and not, as is normal in trade marketing, in the sales function.

Store concept

In the broader sense, one should understand the retail product as the retail formula or the *store concept*. This refers to the balanced composition of the marketing mix, as such that a distinctive store image originates for the consumer. This is clearly a much broader understanding of the product term than just the product range: a beautifully composed product range can go entirely wrong if the presentation principles are not completed, the wrong location is selected for the store, an incorrect price level is set or an incorrect advertising method is used.

Location
An industrial entrepreneur will only occasionally have to make location decisions. In making this choice he is, moreover, primarily guided by cost considerations. Once he has chosen a location he will be stuck with it for a long time, given the high investments associated with production facilities. This is different in retail. First of all the necessary investments for opening a store are relatively small compared to the investments for industrial businesses. This allows a retailer to change its location much faster and with less divestment. In practice this also happens: retailers are constantly busy rearranging their establishment, expanding and reorganising, depending on the developments in the catchment area of the stores. When choosing the location, the retailer would rather base his decision on sales maximisation than on cost minimisation (although the latter also plays a role). Finally, trade marketers tend to interpret the L of location not only as a once-off location decision, but often also as the *outlet channel*. However, retail itself is the outlet channel and this difference in interpretation leads to a very important difference in marketing approach.

Outlet channel

Marketing mix
As stated, trade marketers tend to interpret the L of location as the outlet channel. Once they have supplied to the outlet channel (often retail), they have realised their sales. The big difference is that retail itself is the outlet channel. The goods that the trade marketer has already sold must then still be sold by the retailer to the consumers.
In trade marketing, a customer is a customer. In retail, this is not always the case: visitors who walk into the store do not always walk out as customers (as a visitor that purchased something). Especially in the area of recreational shopping, it often happens that the visitor comes for a look around, but buys nothing. This is why, in retail, the marketing mix consists of two parts: *external marketing mix*, aimed at generating interest for the formula, and *internal marketing mix*, aimed at converting the generated interest into actual purchase behaviour.

External marketing mix
Internal marketing mix

The external marketing mix focuses on the (brand) reputation and image of the formula. It is focussed at generating interest. The external marketing mix consists of the P's and L from Public (target group choice), Product (product range), Location (location), Price and Promotion.
The internal marketing mix focuses on the effectiveness of the outlet as a selling machine. It is thus an attempt to realise a transaction. The internal marketing mix consists of the P's from Presentation, Physical distribution, Personnel and Productivity.

Pricing
A very important difference between trade marketing and retail marketing lies in the way the price is established. Pricing should preferably take place by means of *cost price calculation*, where a profit margin, which can vary depending on the market situation, is imposed on the calculated cost price. Most suppliers of retail therefore apply cost price calculation. They can do this because the products produced are often supplied for an extended period of time and the number of products produced (the product line) is limited. But this is not the case in retail. The number of products here is often exceptionally large. De Bijenkorf, for example, carries about three hundred thousand different products, while the product range also changes very quickly. In this case, cost price calculation per product is very difficult. That is why, in retail,

Cost price calculation

Surcharge calculation

surcharge calculation is generally used instead of a cost price calculation: the purchase price is accepted as given and a surcharge is applied to this purchase price, again varying depending on the market circumstances. Multiplication of the purchase price with the surcharge factor results in the *sales*

Sales price

price. A purchase price of €10, on which a surcharge of 100% is applied, results in a sales price of €20. The margin (calculated on the sales price) then amounts to 50% ((20 – 10) / 20 = 50%). The interesting part now is that the retailer does not know in advance whether the applied surcharge will be sufficient to cover all his costs: if the surcharge is too high, it can mean that the company's prices are too high in the market when compared to competition. If the surcharge is too low, it can mean an anticipated loss.

Conclusion
It can be concluded that most of the differences mentioned above between the trade and retail market can, with further consideration, be traced back to the difference in the size of the product range. This applies for the vision on the business chain, the target group approach, the pricing, the dual marketing mix etc. It is therefore not surprising that precisely the size, structure and composition of the product range are the most commonly used criteria with which a great variety of retail forms can be classified. In this classification one distinguishes between the range (how many different consumer needs are covered by the product range?) and the depth (how much choice does the retailer offer within a single category of need?). By comparing width and depth to each, you get a matrix as in figure 1.10a and b.

Depositary

The lower left side of the matrix contains the *depositary* or agencies, often companies that offer a limited product line from a single supplier. Actually, this is more of an extension of the producer than 'real' retailers, for example the brand dealers from a car manufacturer.

FIGURE 1.10a Retailing: the forms

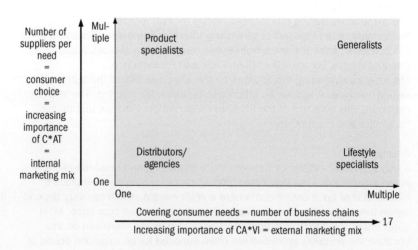

FIGURE 1.10b Retailing: the suppliers

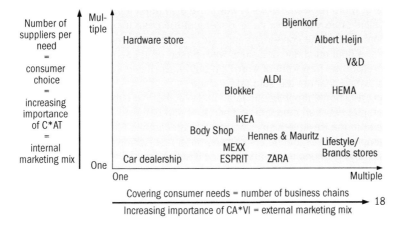

Top left shows the product specialists: multiple choice in usually one or only a few product categories, for example the shoe store, the bakery or the hardware store.

The bottom right shows the businesses that cover a (large) number of different needs, with only a small choice within the needs. Often, these are businesses that try to fill the needs of a particular target group with only a few selected suppliers. They are also known as lifestyle specialists, because the brands of the selected suppliers represent a specific lifestyle, for example Gucci (sunglasses, handbags, clothing, shoes, watches etc.). Finally, the top right shows businesses that offer both a very wide and very deep product range. These are called the *generalists*. In the non-food sector, these are department stores and for the food sector, these are supermarkets.

Generalists

From e-commerce to e-strategy

Many traditional retailers succeed only with difficulty in properly developing their e-commerce activities. These are often barely profitable activities, or even projects. Especially in the early years of Internet, the e-commerce activity started as a project of either the IT-department or the marketing department. Sometimes this still happens today, fifteen years after the first internet bubble. We believe, however, that the impact of the rise of the internet is much larger. E-commerce is neither the beginning, nor the end of this. The internet changes 'customer journeys', the journeys made by consumers from incentive to purchase. Consumers are increasingly drawn to online offers and special deals. Once online, they head to the store where they like to see, try and experience the product. Purchasing follows on site or once again online. The consumer does expect service in the store. This 'customer journey' finally ends back on the net by giving feedback on the product or the service provided by the seller. Just a transaction based e-commerce strategy is no longer sufficient for a retailer. E-strategies are therefore important for two reasons: (1) any retailer that does not actively use an e-strategy, runs the risk of losing the customer to a competitor that does use one, and (2) successful e-strategies lead to lasting customer relationships and customer value. Successful e-strategies address the need for efficiency and convenience.

For example, choice, convenience and speed are increased by reducing search effort. In many branches, online purchases are preceded by consulting one or more reviews. Online reviews are also used more and more often for physical store visits, this is no longer just the case for online stores. More than half of the consumers indicate that, for both online and offline stores, the final purchase decisions were based on these reviews. Reviews are therefore the new form of word of mouth advertising, regardless of through which channel the sale takes place.

Providing additional propositions is another source of customer value.

For example, between products and services and between online and offline channels. In the travel industry, consumers can compile full packages online. For example, when an airline also makes hotel reservations and car rental possible, and provides information on local activities, and all of it automated. If one still prefers advice, there is always the travel agency. Consumers seek information and reduced uncertainty in their purchase process. Online, products cannot be grasped and tested. Well performing e-strategies therefore leave much room for product features. In doing this, they enter the purchase funnel of the consumer for the actual conversion and do not linger on influencing awareness. Later in this book we will come back to this new purchase funnel (see paragraph 19.3).

Finally, a successful e-strategy locks-in customers. For example, by creating switching costs for loyalty programs, or by customisation and creating a valuable network of customers. With a good e-strategy and database marketing, large groups of customers are once again individuals or become known and accessible in small segments. Some companies engage customers in online communities active in their brands and propositions. Mooney and Rollins (Mooney and Rollins, 2008) also call these brands 'open brands'.

Other companies pass product development on to the customers. Last, but not least, companies can engage their customers in word of mouth advertising through review marketing. Lego is a good example of an 'open brand'. Lego involves customers with its products by having them put together their own sets. In addition, Lego customers can join a network of likeminded users. They assess each other's works and designs, which Lego can ultimately take into production. Lego also offers the possibility to order even the smallest missing pieces, through to missing building instructions.

In short, an e-strategy changes consumers from large amorphous groups in shopping streets back into known and accessible individuals with whom you can maintain a valuable relationship. However, developing a successful e-strategy is not an easy task. Successful e-strategies require a fully coordinated multichannel and multi-perspective approach, in other words an actual cross channel approach.

Only if the propositions and brand experience across all channels are coordinated and if all business disciplines work together smoothly, will an e-strategy realise its maximum value.

From multichannel to cross channel management

In literature, we use the term multichannel in two capacities. On the one hand, in the situation where a retailer has different sales channels, such as stores, a website and a catalogue (door to door).

This variation with three channels is often seen in the US. On the other hand, we use the term multichannel in marketing. Multichannel marketing is described as the development and implementation of marketing strategies to interact with customers in more than one channel. However, we prefer using the term cross channel management as an overarching concept of strategy formation, through branding and marketing communication to actual sales, after sales service, sharing and finding information and giving feedback in different channels. Cross channel management is a young part of the field. But at the same time, cross channel management is quickly gaining relevance. Research indicates that by 2015, most consumers will be so-called 'cross channel buyers' (see sub-section 2.6.5). It also appears that cross channel buyers will spend significantly more than single channel buyers. With cross channel management, a well-considered strategy is determined for the channels that you want to use for the biggest impact on the top and bottom line, the performance of the company. For one retailer this would mean online sales, for other retailers this would mean communication and interaction with the end user. To anticipate this correctly, it is necessary to understand the customer journeys of the target group, but also the current and future supply chain and the business model. As with all other strategies, the chosen strategy should regularly be assessed and adapted if necessary. Cross channel management is considerably more complex than classic marketing. It requires integration of strategies and implementation, integration of systems and coordination across all channels that previously functioned relatively independently. Many traditional retailers struggle with the use of a real cross channel approach. This is because their existing strategies are based on branding and creating traffic and conversion in physical stores. In an environment dominated by purchasing and logistics, the introduction of a cross channel strategy, also called e-strategy, is a major operation that affects almost all parts of the company. Therefore a successful cross channel strategy is not only multichannel, but also multi-perspective.

Multiple perspectives are essential for successful cross channel management.
Sometimes the e-commerce team is housed at commerce, or at IT, in a separate department or even as temporary project. The risk of housing the cross channel strategy at commerce is an overreliance on sales and numbers. A correct focus, but without a smooth operation and cost efficient delivery and IT, quickly leads to an unprofitable e-commerce practice as a whole, and therefore not to a successful e-strategy. Especially traditional retailers that practice e-commerce in this way, often stumble into this pitfall. Housing at IT may solve integration issues of e-commerce in the overall IT landscape for purchasing, logistics and reports. The IT department should be strongly commerce oriented, in order to offer the correct mix of flexible development, costs and maintenance. E-commerce as a separate project seems especially attractive to e-commerce starters. Set a fast pace and we will later see where the activities lead. This can work well, except that 'we will see later' can be very disappointing and still lower or destroy the returns of the quick start.
Due to its transparency, lots of e-commerce is associated with relatively low margins. As a result e-commerce and large investment programs do not mix well. The investments in marketing communication, IT and intricate logistics with return flows have to be compensated for by margin growth combined with lower than average operational costs. Successful e-strategies also require an intricate and transparent financial monitoring.

In a cross channel strategy, logistics is fundamentally different than in traditional retail. The traditional model is based on large-scale purchases and transporting large volumes from production locations, through distribution networks to individual stores. In the store, the products are removed from the shelves by consumers individually. E-commerce is based on direct distribution from central locations to individual consumers. In addition, different varieties are often ordered online, of which one or more are returned. A part of the stock and the operating capital invested therein is therefore out in the market. Finally, the logistics should be designed for returns, which traditional retail logistics is not.

In many cases, the staff component within a cross channel strategy is also underestimated. In traditional retail, the purchasing discipline is dominant. It is still said that retail makes its money on purchasing. In a cross channel world the customer comes first, and thus marketing and commerce. In practice this results in interesting frictions between different disciplines in the organisation.

A cross channel strategy can only reach its maximum value in a double integrated approach: integration of all channels (multichannel) for customer touch points and integration of all relevant business disciplines in the organisation (multi-perspective). Moreover, the introduction of a cross channel approach in organisations is a relevant change and requires change management (adaption article Haasloop Werner and Quix, 2010).

Summary

Under retail marketing we understand all business management activities that focus on the direct sales of goods and services to consumers, provided that these are paid out of the net income of the consumer.

The goods sector of retail expenditures is generally equated to retail expenditures. In retail, under the influence of environmental changes and the associated shift of power in the business chain, there has been a change of function: from goods producing process to demand satisfying process. Partly because of this, there was a division in the consumer marketing. This involved, on the one hand, marketing by manufacturer to retailer (trade marketing) and on the other hand marketing by retailer to consumer (retail marketing). In practice there seem to be big differences between trade marketing and retail marketing. An important second aspect of the change in the business chain is control. In many branches the retailers have taken over control in the chain, in which they do not necessary produce themselves, but simply control the chain.

After a hesitant start around the millennium, internet has acquired a permanent place and should be fully embraced by retailers.

To a retailer, internet means a lot more than just e-commerce and should be taken up fully within a cross channel strategy.

2
Goods retail: the classification criteria

Goods retail is characterised by a high degree of diversity that we find in the different classification criteria used in relation to retail. Some of these classification criteria will be treated here, as advocated in the book in a sequence corresponding with the increasing importance for commercial operations.

2.1 Statistical classification criteria of goods retail

The most important statistical classification criteria for goods retail are firstly the criteria for functional and institutional retail, and secondly the criteria for types of goods.

2.1.1   Functional and institutional retail

Functional retail expenditures

The concept of *functional retail expenditures* is a concept that is defined from the demand side (namely the private consumption of households). Under functional retail expenditures we understand that part of the total private consumption that is sold through companies with a full or partial retail function. Private consumption falls into three main categories:
- food;
- non-food and other goods;
- services.

TABLE 2.1 Consumer retail expenditure (including VAT), 2012

	Expenditure (bn)	Per household	Per head	Share
Total	€83.2	€11,040	€4,970	100%
Food and beverages	€39.4	€5,220	€2,350	47%
Durables and other goods	€43.9	€5,190	€2,340	53%

TABLE 2.1 Consumer retail expenditure (including VAT), 2012 (continued)

	Expenditure (bn)	Per household	Per head	Share
Daily purchases	€44.1	€5,850	€2,630	53%
Non-daily shopping	€39.1	€5,190	€2,340	47%

Source: HBD (updated 5 November 2013)

In 2012 total consumption expenditure, according to the industry associa-tion (HBD) amounted to 275 bn. The food category is good for 47% of total expenditure per household per year. The category of durable and other goods accounts for 53% of all spending in the retail sector. The services category, now the most important category of consumer expendi-ture, is expenditure largely outside the retail category. A frequently used categorisation is also that of 'daily and non-daily' goods/purchases. Food and beverages make up a large part of such daily purchases, but the category also includes non-food products sold in a supermarket. Examples are fabric detergents and toothpaste or other personal products. Much of our daily expenditure is thus channeled via supermarkets.

Institutional retail includes all businesses of which the principal activity consists of operating retail. The principal activity is thereby defined as 'the activity in which more than half of the sales is realised'. It is a concept that is determined from the supply and is intended to define the size of the industry. A good example would be a car dealer who, in addition to his retail activities, performs repairs or installation activities. If more than half of his sales realised in the repair sector, the company cannot be included in the institutional retail. However, if more than half of his sales is realised from selling to individuals, it may be included.

Institutional retail

Under *institutional retail expenditures* we understand the total sales of all companies belonging to the institutional retail, thus including non-retail sales. The institutional retail expenditures are significantly lower than the functional retail expenditures. This is because many businesses that cannot be included in the institutional retail still fulfil secondary activities to a significant extent in the retail environment.

Institutional retail expenditures

For example a garage that also sells car parts to individuals, or a plumber that also provides plumbing supplies, or a gas station that also runs a store. Conversely, it occurs much less often that institutional retail companies realise considerable sales outside the merchandise sector. According to figures from the HBD and the Statistics Netherlands, the institutional retail expenditures in the Netherlands comprise only 31% of the total consumption expenditure of households. In 2011 this was approximately €83 billion excluding VAT.

TABLE 2.2 Development Dutch retail as percentage of the total consumption expenditures

	2003	2004	2005	2006	2007	2008	2009	2010	2011	2012
Retail	33.0	31.8	31.2	31.5	31.2	31.3	31.4	30.9	30.7	30.3
Non-retail (services)	67.0	68.2	68.8	68.5	68.8	68.7	68.6	69.1	69.3	69.7
Total	100.0	100.0	100.0	100.0	100.0	100.0	100.0	100.0	100.0	100.0

(Updated 15 November 2013)

The concepts functional and institutional are clearly statistical in nature and have relatively little commercial significance. Nevertheless, it is useful to keep the two concepts apart when using statistical material. When we refer to 'retail sales' below, this always relates to the institutional retail expenditures, unless indicated otherwise. The classification discussed below also relates to the institutional retail expenditures.

2.1.2   Classification of goods retail by types of goods

Classification by types of goods is used by the Statistics Netherlands (CBS) in the [Monthly Retail Trade Statistics] *Maandstatistiek Detailhandel*. This is the classification as handled in the Netherlands, in Europe an increasing trend towards the same classification can be noticed. That statistic gives an impression of the developments of the sales (*nominal development*), the price and the sales (*volume development*) in the main categories: Food and beverages and Non-food and other goods, or 'food' and 'non-food'. The food sector is further divided into ten product groups and the non-food sector into seven product groups. Statistics are an indispensible tool in keeping track of short term developments in retail.

Nominal development

Volume development

Food (food and beverage) is divided into ten product groups (source: CBS, 2008):
* potatoes, vegetables and fruit;
* meat and meat products;
* fish;
* dairy products;
* bread, biscuit and bread products;
* other food;
* ice-cream;
* confectionary;
* beverages;
* tobacco.

The non-food sector (non-food products) is divided into seven product groups (CBS, 2008):
* textile and clothing;
* leather products and shoes;
* furnishing;
* household appliances;
* household products;
* vehicles;
* other non-food products.

2.2 Classification of online and offline goods retail

Although the prospects looked fantastic in the mid-nineties of the previous century, the development of online retail was launched less energetically. Retail sales are considered a benchmark for online sales, but we should focus more on the future than on the past. In 2012 more than 3.4% of all goods retail in Europe went through the online channel, the supposed e-tail sales (Source: Global e-commerce summit 2012).

TABLE 2.3 Development of retail and e-tail sales in the Netherlands (in billions of euros)

	2006	2007	2008	2009	2010	2011	2012
Total retail sales	78.7	82.0	84.0	82.2	82.7	83.0	83.2
E-tail sales total	1.6	2.3	3.1	3.7	4.3	4.5	5.0
Percentage e-tail of retail	2.0%	2.8%	3.7%	4.5%	5.2%	5.4%	6.0%

Source: HBD, Thuiswinkel.org (own adaption 2014)

In 2012 6% of all goods retail in the Netherlands went through the online channel, the supposed e-tail sales. If we also consider that supermarkets have a small share in the online expenditures (0.8% according to ABN AMRO, February 2012), but account for 45% of all retail expenditures, we see a very different picture. Food and personal care account for less than two percent of the total online expenditures in the Netherlands. Now, if we look at the impact of online expenditures on the non-food retail, we see the following. Of the €83 billion euro retail, €45.7 is non-food retail. The online expenditures are 99% related to non-food good retail and represent more than €4.46 billion. This results in a share of more than 9.8% of the annual sales for the online channel in the non-food retail.

Even if we look at the growth rate, we see the power and potential of online retail. In recent years, online retail has produced strong growth rates, where the sales in physical stores have pretty much stagnated. In ten years time, the Dutch online goods retail grew with an average of 30% per year, compared to an average growth of the entire retail, thus including online retail, of merely 1.6%. For comparison, the inflation for the same period was well above 2%. The growth of the physical retail remained well below the inflation and therefore cannot keep up.

TABLE 2.4 Growth rates e-tail versus retail in the Netherlands (increase compared to the same period in percentages)

	2002	2003	2004	2005	2006	2007	2008	2009	2010	2011	2012
Retail total	1.9%	−1.4%	−2.1%	−0.3%	5.4%	4.2%	2.4%	−2.1%	0.3%	1.0%	0.2%
E-tail total	69.0%	24.0%	31.0%	23.0%	26.6%	37.9%	26.4%	16.9%	14.6%	4.7%	11.7%

Source: HBD, Thuiswinkel.org, CBS February 2012 (own version 2014)

The prospects for online shopping are definitely positive. The growth may level off, or rather, fall back to more normal proportions due to the extent it has already reached, but remains well ahead of the total retail. Online shopping is experiencing enormous growth in the Netherlands. In 2001 just over half a billion euro was realised through online sales. In 2005 this already increased to more than €2.8 billion according to Dutch Home Shopping Organisation and it continues to grow up to €9.2 billion in 2012. The majority of the sales that were made online were, however, associated to travel, insurance and tickets. This has come around in recent years, as shown in table 2.5. In 2005 the sales of online goods retail, or e-tail, amounted to 42.8% of the total e-commerce, in 2012 this had already grown to 51.4%.

TABLE 2.5 Development of e-commerce and e-tail in the Netherlands (in millions of euros)

	2007	2008	2009	2010	2011	2012	Index 2007-2012
E-commerce total	4,970	6,325	7,415	8,213	8,980	9,754	1,96
Online goods retail (e-tail) total	2,108	2,933	3,430	3,983	4,490	5,016	2,38
Percentage of e-tail of e-commerce	42.4%	46.4%	46.3%	48.5%	50.0%	51.4%	1.21

Source: HBD, Thuiswinkel.org (own adaption 2014)

As indicated, the growth of online retail over recent years has occurred primarily in non-food categories. E-tail has also exceeded maturity in these categories. For consumers, the online purchasing of books and music is already a matter of course, but the same applies for fashion and shoes. It may sound strange to the young generation who grew up with it, but the management of many traditional (physical) retailers is still getting used to the ease with which clothing is purchased online. Basically everything can be purchased online

TABLE 2.6 Development of e-tail in various categories (in millions of euros)

	2007	2008	2009	2010	2011	2012	Index 2007-2012
Electronics and household appliances	453	554	634	730	762	765	1.69
Clothing	285	353	465	555	630	730	2.56
Books, CD, DVD, games	313	419	481	514	575	620	1.98
Other	1,262	1,752	2,030	2,884	3,343	3,786	3.00

Source: HBD, Thuiswinkel.org (own adaption 2014)

EXAMPLE 2.1 BOL.COM

Bol.com started its activities in 1999, in the middle of the internet bubble. It was an initiative of media group Bertelsmann, which was already a world market leader in the area of distance selling with its book clubs, CD clubs and DVD clubs, and was therefore well positioned for creating a global online store of books and CD's. The name 'Bol' was an abbreviation for 'Bertelsmann On-Line', a twist to the successful partnership with AOL in Europe, which yielded billions for Bertelsmann. After the internet bubble burst, Bertelsmann gradually closed branches of Bol.com throughout the world and in 2003 the Dutch branch, which had become the most successful in the global Bol.com-network, was disposed of. The new owner of Bol.com was a joint venture between two international media companies: Holtzbrinck Networks, part of the publishing group Georg von Holtzbrinck, and publishing and bookselling group Weltbild, the largest bookseller in Germany. In 2009 Bol.com was taken over by NPM Capital and Cyrte Investments. This made media man John de Mol long-distance co-owner. Even more remarkable was the investment of NPM Capital, because they were owners of Selexyz Bookstores, which they sold in the same period. In May 2012 Ahold purchased Bol.com for €350 million. As a result, a physical retailer became owner of a pure player.

Over the years the internet book store became the largest online media store of the Netherlands, with a wider product range than just books. The company has been selling CD's, DVD's, English and Dutch books, electronics, laptops, mobile telephones, games, software and PC accessories, and also second-hand books since 2007. This addition is a new model for the Netherlands, because this actually makes Bol.com just another market place where supply and demand are brought together. The company makes it possible for consumers to offer their books to others and to be found quickly and easily. With every search, the consumer can also see the second-hand offer.

Moreover, the payment is also made through Bol.com, which is a big advantage in comparison with marktplaats.nl at that time. Before Sinterklaas (Saint Nicholas) and Christmas, in the autumn of 2009, the company very successfully added toys to the product range. In the spring of 2011, Bol.com opened the doors for competitors. Sellers of electronics were allowed to offer their products through the platform of Bol.com. Although Bol.com is often referred to as 'the Dutch equivalent of Amazon.com', and there are indeed large similarities, there are also clear differences in the strategy of the two companies. For example, Bol.com is limited to the Dutch language. Bol.com is also limited to a smaller number of product categories, although we have seen an expansion here in recent years. Amazon.com wants to sell everything that people may want to buy online and is active in several (large) countries in the world. Amazon.com starts with the channel – online – and Bol.com focuses on the markets. Daniel Ropers, Managing Director of Bol.com, explained this in 2007: 'Bol.com's strategy not to consider themselves an internet store, but rather a media store that uses the internet to supply buyers of media products to the best of its ability, is motivated by the fact that the customer sees no logical connection between books and washing machines.

Synergies for webshops are therefore rather found in the underlying business processes. However, we believe that most consumers' demands begin with the need, which translates into a product group, and then leads to a visit to a retailer through the "evoked set" of known stores, where the final product choice is made.

A customer therefore thinks: 1. I am going on vacation and need something to keep me busy in the relaxing hours. 2. I need books for this. 3. At which stores can I buy books? 4. Which store is the easiest or best for me? 5. Once I am at the store: can I find and discover the right books to fill my needs? The art is therefore to end up at the top of the mental list of the Dutchman in step 3 and 4, and to live up to the promise and exceed the expectations in step 5. We use the many benefits of the internet to ensure that we score highly in step 4 and 5 when compared to other (traditional) stores. We then use a rather traditional media mix of TV, radio, print and online marketing to highlight these benefits for the consumers, which determines our position in step 3 and 4.' It shows how quickly the world can change, even for a pure player. In the autumn of 2011, Bol.com added household appliances to its product range. It may be assumed that the customer journey of the consumer was central in making this choice. Opening a platform for third parties is driven by the enormous traffic that the online retailer has. By 2013 Bol.com becomes the largest DIY online player.

With the growth and the shares in the various categories in mind, a traditional retailer cannot do without a sophisticated cross channel approach. We expect that, towards 2020, the share of online sales in many non-food categories will lie between 25 and 30% and, in some categories, more than 50% is even possible. When we look at the results of the study performed by Q&A Research &Consultancy in 2011, commissioned by ABN AMRO, it appears that 62% of consumers made their purchases through a physical store in 2011. The study was conducted in seven main industries, sectors, namely: DIY; electronics; Kitchen; Fashion; Shoes; Sport and Housing. Within every category, consumers were asked how they made their purchases in the relevant category over the past twelve months. The same study indicated that, in 2015, 51% of consumers are expected to purchase online. This means that online purchases will increase by 50% in less than five years time. The most striking result from this study of ABN AMRO is that the combination of cross channel purchases will increase in importance. While, in 2011, over 35% of consumers indicated that they use this form in the studied categories, this is expected to be almost 55% in 2015. The cross channel growth will partly be at the expense of the pure players when we approach things from market shares. This development will play into the hands of the retailers that are best able to combine e-commerce, in all its forms, with physical locations. At the same time the pure players, parties that only sell through a webshop, should reconsider moving their beacons at the beginning of this new decade. Having physical stores is a clear success factor in the new internet age: the cross channel era (Quix and Terra, 2011).

EXAMPLE 2.2 COOLBLUE

Coolblue is a pure player with physical stores

Coolblue was established in 1999 by Pieter Zwart, Paul de Jong and Bart Kuijpers. The three started from the idea that specialisation counts. In 2000 this resulted in the launch of Mp3man.nl, which was quickly followed by a series of webshops in the Netherlands and Belgium, such as PDAshop.nl, Digicamshop.nl, Mp3man.be, PDAshop.be, Digicamshop.be. Coolblue's success did not go unnoticed and in 2003 the company was nominated for the Public Award of the Thuiswinkel Awards 2003 and the Jury Starters Award 2003.

Coolblue seems to have invented cross channel thinking. They were probably way ahead of the troops when they opened the first 'stone' store in Rotterdam in 2003. In 2005 Coolblue was one of the first major webshops in the Netherlands that started offering iDEAL. In 2006 Coolblue was able to go the extra mile in the area of service by enclosing an agreement with TPG, making it the fastest delivering internet company in the Netherlands: orders placed up to 19.30 pm, were delivered the next day.

Over the years, the number of specialised webshops in the Netherlands and Belgium grew quickly. In 2011 the company had no less than 51 specialised shops under one roof, with a shopping basket and a checkout. In 2007 they took a step further with regard to delivery: the customer could place an order until 21.00 pm and received his goods the very next day. In 2008 the order time was extended even further to 22.00 pm. The first physical store also opened in Antwerp and in 2008 the stores in Eindhoven and Groningen followed. It then remained rather quiet in terms of opening physical stores. The big question is at what point Coolblue is going to go further with this. In 2011 various studies indicated that a strategy where online and offline is combined will be the winning strategy. In 2012 Coolblue added the same day delivery service and increased once again the time window for orders.

In 2009 Coolblue.be won the BeCommerce Awards 2009 in the categories Overall and Consumer electronics. In the same year they added no less than 26 webshops, followed by another 20 in the year thereafter. In 2010 Coolblue won the jury price in the 2010 Website Awards and the Award in the Telecom category with the 2010 Thuiswinkel Awards. Coolblue.be also won the Award in the Electronics category and the Jury Award in the B2B category. In 2011 Coolblue invested on further growth by opening a new distribution centre with a floor surface of 5.000 m^2. In Belgium, Coolblue was the big winner of the election of the BeCommerce Awards 2011 and in the Netherlands Coolblue won the Thuiswinkel Awards 2011 for Telecom for the second consecutive year. In 2012 and 2013 they once again were among the winners.

The need for the combination approach of online and offline is also evident from several studies. A study by GFK in 2009 in Germany showed that 48% of the offline buyers at H&M had oriented themselves online in advance. A study from 2009 by Macy's in the United States indicated that cross channel buyers spent twice as much compared to the customers that buy through a single channel. Remarkable enough is that one dollar spent online leads to almost six dollars spent physically within ten days. A study conducted in 2011 among retailers in Europe indicated that the online sales had specifically increased for retailers that also have physical stores. In other words, the online proposition does not have a cannibalistic effect, but adds additional sales. These results are reinforced by the findings among retailers that still have gaps in their catchment areas. When opening stores in new catchment areas, they notice specifically that their online sales in these areas increase more than in the areas where they are not yet physically active. Naturally this observation requires additional research, but also leads to the conclusion that cross channel retail requires another look at retail from the perspective of catchment area and sales. Research in 2013 among physical retailers showed that their online sales grows with over 40% conquered to the 12% growth of online in total.

2.3 Classification based on the size of the company

Chain stores

Medium enterprise

Small enterprise

The most important division of the volume in retail is that between the chain stores and small and medium enterprises. A *chain store* (CS) is defined as a businesses with more than a hundred employees, a *medium enterprise* is a business with ten to a hundred employees and a *small enterprise* is a business with less than ten employees. Both of the latter categories are often grouped under the name small and medium enterprises (SME).

Compared to most industries in the Netherlands, retail can be characterised as an industry in which small and medium enterprises (emphasis on small enterprises) are strongly represented. 93% of the businesses fall under the category small enterprise and represent 27% of the sales in the retail. But strong shifts occur within the sub-division. In particular, the market share of small enterprises is greatly reduced. Medium enterprises are able to maintain themselves reasonably well, while chain stores have been gaining considerable market share for decades (see table 2.7).

TABLE 2.7 Developments of sales shares for SME and CS 1980/2010 in the Netherlands

	1980 Sales (in %)	1990 Sales (in %)	2000 Sales (in %)	2010 Sales (in %)
CS	27	36	44	60
SME	73	64	56	40

Source: *Yearbook retail*, HBD/EIM, 1999, p. 9; HBD, 2011 and own version

The question, however, is whether the classification of SME and CS is really a relevant criterion from marketing considerations, because the distinction between the SME and the CS becomes unclear as the SME unites in cooperation accords (see paragraph 2.3).

Yet it is still a commonly used criterion, although perhaps more from the perspective of (political) interests representation than from actual commercial significance.

In the Netherlands large businesses and medium and small enterprises have separate industry associations. This also applies to the retail, with the Dutch Retail Council representing large retailers and many, smaller organisations representing small and medium-sized organisations. The largest organisation for small and medium food category businesses is the Vakcentrum Levensmiddelen (food industry association). These businesses represent, moreover, the largest share of retail sales, largely due to the fact that many supermarkets are owned by independent entrepreneurs.

2.4 Classification based on legal form of cooperation

More important than the classification in chain stores and small and medium enterprises is the classification based on legal forms of cooperation. The most important forms of cooperation that we distinguish within retail are those of purchasing associations, voluntary chain store and franchising.

2.4.1   Purchasing association and voluntary chain store

Purchasing associations are organisations of independent retailers, often on a cooperative basis, who are seeking a condition improvement for their members by bundling purchasing volumes. They were created in the Netherlands in the period around 1930 as response to the price aggressive chain store, primarily in the food sector, such as Spar, Vivo and Sperwer, and later also in the non-food sector, such as St. Homobonus, De Faam, Samen Sterk and Inkoopcombinatie Nederland. The purchasing associations initially worked on a voluntary basis: one could buy through the association, but was not obliged to. The independent member companies often presented themselves to consumers under their own name. So there was no question of 'formulation'. This neutrality diminished at a later stage, particularly in the food sector. The purchasing associations evolved into the *voluntary chain stores* (VCS), where independent entrepreneurs committed to purchase from one specific wholesaler and where the member companies presented themselves using a single formula name. The member companies remained independently operating stores, where the contribution of the umbrella organisation was initially limited to the product range.

Purchasing associations

Voluntary chain stores

Forced by the competition of the chain stores that continuously developed tighter, more centralised formulas, the umbrella organisations also tried to influence the formulas on parts of the marketing mix other than just the product range.

One example is the development of the VCS company Schuitema, currently C1000. The organisation has grown to formula administrator of the C1000 supermarkets, where entrepreneurs have found shelter. But the organisation also has a limited number of own stores. Until 2008, almost three quarters of C1000 was owned by Ahold, the parent company of Albert Heijn. In the course of that year, ownership was transferred to private equity firm CVC. In November 2011, Jumbo purchased the supermarket chain and suddenly became number 2 in the market. C1000 will disappear as a brand. Nowadays, there is a strong mix of the various legal forms. Example 2.3 is an example of this.

EXAMPLE 2.3 ENTREPRENEURS PARADOX
Chain stores seem to be getting bigger but strangely enough, there are now more opportunities than ever before for independent entrepreneurs. Provided that the regulations are properly regulated, many retailers predict a wave of consolidation in which many chains will be purchased by foreign players. These players are indeed on the lookout for purchasing power and a larger market. The question that remains: is there any chance for the small, independent entrepreneur? About a quarter of the interviewed retailers wholeheartedly answered 'no' and predicted the end of small retailers. According to these retailers, it is impossible for a small independent retailer to continue to exist. An important argument here is that these small retailers always lack the competitive edge to implement a good and economical procurement. They indicate that large, global organisations are able to buy at low prices. Moreover, these large retailers have extremely high sales rates, making it possible for them to frequently change their product range. Small independent retailers simply cannot compete on that level.

Attention
But the question is also whether these small independent retailers should even want to play that game. These super specialists would be wise not to look at the big players; they will never be able to win. With them it is all about personal attention, a remarkable product range, service and of course customisation. While chain stores generally experience customisation as a hassle, this is core business for super specialists. And for that matter, the tide seems favourable too. Because of the increase of individualisation, there is more need for customisation than ever before.

Retail service organisations should not forget about buying
There is room for small entrepreneurs. But these are mainly entrepreneurs that are able to specialise or are looking for a niche market. They provide variation in the store image that is largely dominated by chains. These specialists are able to remain independent. Their uniqueness ensures sufficient customers. They do not necessarily need an A1-location, nor is purchasing power a requirement. But those who are less able to specialise will be in much greater need for cooperation. For these entrepreneurs it is indeed important to have a good location and to buy at lower prices. Retail service organisations can play an important role. Their role, however, is not just important on the front lines of the store, but also on the background! A trend seems to be developing in which such clubs are increasingly more concerned about the selling side. That is logical, because there is clearly much to gain. But independent entrepreneurs are particularly concerned about the purchasing power. Due to their service and personal attention, they can afford having a price difference compared with their competitors; but if the price gap is too large, consumers may still pull out.

Powerhouses

Independent retailers feel that there are not enough of these vigorous purchasing clubs. For this reason various sectors have initiatives where independent retailers from different regions can combine forces and purchase collectively. This cooperation is not only limited to purchase: here and there are signs indicating that retailers from different regions also cooperate in the area of sales. For example, they collectively create websites where they sell excess stock. Such initiatives ensure that independent retailers tap into a much larger market area. This also enables them to change their product range at an increased frequency.

Miracle cure?

Franchisees are typically more driven than branch leaders. Research indicated that, in comparable store sizes, franchisees produce an average of ten to fifteen percent more sales and have seven to eight percent less expenses. Good franchisees also require much less guidance than branch leaders. Is franchising then the miracle cure? No. Franchising is not equally suitable for every organisation.

It is an especially ideal model for an organisation that only pursues growth with own brands. But concepts that depend on known A-brands, for example, will benefit less. Franchisees are usually like water; they always seek the lowest point. This means that they want to organise their purchases outside the franchise organisation and get 'a bargain' elsewhere.

Guaranteed income

Foreign retailer organisations call on different forms of cooperation.
There are constructions in which branch managers become co-owners of the company. Media Markt is a good example, where every branch manager has almost 10% share in the profit. With this form of participatory entrepreneurship, chain stores try to get the best out of their stores and employees. By giving them share in the profits of success, the chain itself also grows.

Source: adaption from Mark Hemmer and Frank Quix,
10 Retail paradoxes, HBD, 2005

In the non-food sector, the development of purchasing combination into voluntary chain store is not yet underway. This is due to the increasing diversity of consumer demand, where the purchasing based on the 'greatest common denominator' of the members started to work more counterproductively than beneficially. In some cases, buying combinations in the non-food have not yet developed to a form similar to the VCS: the *purchasing and sales organisation*. The characteristic here is not only the collective purchasing, but also the fact that they present themselves under a common name and often advertise together. Examples of such organisations are the Expert Group (electrical products) and the Topform furniture stores. But in general it is clear that the impact of these types of cooperation accords on the Dutch market was extremely limited and cannot really be called successful.

Purchasing and sales organisation

Today we can see that the phenomenon of purchasing association (or purchasing combination) no longer plays a significant role, except in a few relatively small market segments. The purchasing associations have disappeared; they have evolved into independent retail organisations or retail service organisations, or have joined larger retail groups. In the non-food sector, purchasing associations have evolved into retail service organisations. A large non-food retail service organisation is Euretco (used to be Euretco and Intres). It primarily represents entrepreneurs in fashion, housing and sport. Purchasing is still an important task, but organisations have also started to play a more facilitating role for entrepreneurs. This partly deals with a form of formula management, but far less than with franchising. There is a particular focus for supporting tasks, including payment transactions. In fact, we can say that the function of the purchasing association, especially in the non-food sector, but also in the food sector, either will be or has been taken over by the phenomenon of franchising. Even the retail service organisations use franchising with some of the formulas that they use, for example Intersport with Euretco.

2.4.2   Franchising

Franchising
Franchising can be characterised as an intermediate form between the chain stores and the voluntary chain stores. It is a form in which independ-

Franchisor
ent entrepreneurs can join a central formula administrator: the *franchisor*, often an existing chain store, such as Pearle, Formido or Halfords, but sometimes also a so-called marketing organisation without its own facilities, such as Gamma.

Franchising is also characterised as a growth strategy. The franchisor is able to expand the chain with a relatively smaller capital. The independent

Franchisee
entrepreneur (*franchisee*) is personally responsible for the investments of his own branch.

A second argument for the growth strategy theory is the so-called span or control. Various studies, amongst others by Harvard (Bradach, 1998), have shown that the span or control in a franchise environment is much larger compared to a chain store situation.

The franchisee that joins a franchise organisation is obliged to abide by the rules that the franchisor considers necessary to maintain the marketing concept. Depending on the severity of these requirements, this is referred to as *soft franchising* and *hard franchising*. In those cases in which the franchisor imposes such severe requirements on every part of the marketing mix (such as 100% product range purchasing, specified store layout and one uniform and specified price level) that the consumer is unable to determine whether he is in an own branch or a franchise establishment

Hard
upon entering the store, is called *hard franchising*. Incidentally, this is the

franchising
most common and fastest growing form of franchising. This form of franchising is often applied from existing chain stores with proven formulas, such as HEMA, Blokker, Hunkemöller and Albert Heijn.

One of the methods that are used by chain stores to apply franchising within their organisation is conversion franchise. Through this method, company owned and operated stores are converted into franchise stores. In this way, chain stores often give a store manager an opportunity to become an independent entrepreneur. Conversion franchise can help to increase the market share. A case study of various Dutch chain stores has shown that, in the situation of conversion franchise, the entrepreneur is able to get up to 10% more sales from a catchment area. Due to the lower cost levels, the entrepreneur is also able to generate better returns (Quix, 1996).

In cases where the franchisor imposes less strict requirements, for example at least 70% product range purchasing and no specified store layout, or only imposes requirements on some parts of the marketing mix, it is called *soft franchising*. This form often originated from suppliers (and sometimes even from the old buying combinations) that saw their markets being placed under pressure, and therefore developed formulas for their customers. The movements in the market seem to suggest that more and more soft-franchise organisations are switching over to hard franchising.

Soft franchising

The benefits for the franchisee is that he can join a renowned formula at a relatively low cost and that he no longer needs to spread his focus over the many areas of attention associated with retail. He can also remain independent. He can focus entirely on managing his store and his personnel, and leave other activities to the franchisor, such as purchasing, promotion and store concept. The franchisee pays (a *fee*) for the efforts of the franchisor for keeping the concept up to date and the services that are provided by the central management organisation.

Fee

The benefit for the franchisor, in addition to the direct revenue from the fee, is that the formula can be expanded even faster and with less private investment. On the one hand this leads to a faster coverage of the catchment area, which can, for example, make the external promotional program more efficient in terms of costs per contact. On the other hand, it leads to an increase of the purchasing volume, and therefore to an improvement of the purchasing conditions (either in terms of a lower purchase price, or in terms of the opportunities to develop own brands).

In the Netherlands franchising in food and non-food retail really started to develop strongly in the beginning of the nineties. In 2010 the total consumer sales by franchisees in the food and non-food retail represented €22.4 billion, nearly 27% of the total retail sales in the Netherlands (see table 2.8).

TABLE 2.8 Developments of sales for franchise stores 1985-2010 in millions of euros

	Retail food	Retail non-food	Total
1985	€234	€1,674	€1,908
1990	€583	€1,900	€2,483
1995	€2,500	€3,775	€6,275
2000	€3,385	€5,365	€8,750
2005	€8,700	€8,300	€17,000
2010	€12,592	€9,775	€22,367

Source: NFV, 2011

Franchising is not only a very important factor for the development in sales, but also for employment. Especially the number of franchise stores showed significant growth in the past 25 years. In 1985 there were about 6,000 retail franchise stores in the Netherlands, in 2010 this number increased to over 16,000, according to the Dutch Franchise Association (NFV). Two thirds of all branches can be attributed to non-food retail. All retail franchise stores provided work for 171,809 people in 2010 (see table 2.9).

TABLE 2.9 Developments in employment in franchise stores 1985-2010 numbers of people including part-timers

	Retail food	Retail non-food	Total
1985	5,280	17,219	22,499
1990	9,046	37,535	46,581
1995	23,500	30,000	53,500
2000	38,000	47,000	85,000
2005	70,000	62,000	132,000
2010	101,853	69,956	171,809

Source: NFV, 2011

Franchising is also an important factor in the food service, also known as hospitality retail, in the neighbouring branch of sport. As a general rule we do not include this type of company within the definition of this book, yet it is becoming more and more a part of the streetscape and thus often of the retail DNA. Think of companies like McDonalds, KFC or New York Pizza. These organisations also make frequent use of franchise. According to the Dutch Franchise Association, 2,160 franchise stores were active within hospitality retail in 2010. Together they represented a sales of almost 1.7 billion Euros.

2.5 Operational classification criteria

The best known classification of retail from the operational point of view is:
- logistics oriented retail;
- sales oriented retail;
- purchase oriented retail;

However, this classification is not very clear. Indeed, in all cases logistics, sales and purchase belong to the primary functions of retail. If you fail to monitor and control all three aspects as retailer, you will have little success in the long run. Nevertheless, the classification does have realistic value, in the sense that it indicates where the focus of the commercial activities will be. After discussing the three components, we will briefly discuss the drawbacks and benefits of this classification.

2.5.1   Logistics oriented retail

Logistics oriented retail

Logistics oriented retail is involved when the focus of daily business is the organisation of the flow of goods. It often involves retail companies where we deal with product categories with a time-stable product range and consumer purchasing behaviour that is characterised as 'routinely purchasing well-known products'. In such a situation, the purchasing process will be more focussed on *availability* (ensuring a constant presence of the product range) than on *innovation* (ensuring a constant upgrading). The daily activities will therefore primarily consist of agreeing on longer term conditions and ensuring that the *external logistics* (the flow of goods from supplier to central warehouse and/or the stores) are in order. Even so, the sales procedure will strongly focus on ensuring an optimal presence and findability of the products in the shelves: indeed, when routinely purchasing well-known products ('shopping'), the presence of the desired goods is very important. If this presence is not guaranteed, the customer's efforts were in vain. He will then find another seller that does stock the item, and therefore most likely shift his purchasing orientation in the future. The first retailer has lost a customer. The daily activities of the sales in such companies are therefore focussed on keeping the *internal logistics* (the flow of goods from central warehouse and/or store warehouse to the sales shelf) well-organised.

Marketing in logistics oriented companies is focussed primarily on the presence of a product range that is known to consumers. Yield optimisation in logistics oriented retail therefore benefits particularly from the optimisation of the flow of goods, both externally and internally. Logistics oriented retail is found primarily in those companies that focus on supplying the daily necessities: supermarket organisations, such as Albert Heijn, Jumbo and Plus, are almost always logistics oriented.

Characteristics of logistics oriented organisations are:
- high sales rates;
- stable product range;
- low margins;
- self-service;
- efficient, comprehensible presentation;
- many customers who often come from small market areas;
- big visiting frequency;
- small catchment area.

2.5.2 Sales oriented retail

Sales oriented retail is involved when the focus in the business process is organising and pacing the flow of customers. This often (but not always) involves retail companies where one has to deal with relatively low frequency purchased product categories, (partially) unstable product ranges and a consumer purchasing behaviour which is accompanied by a limited orientation.

Marketability is central in the purchasing process of such companies. The purchasing department will be willing to make concessions to the product range philosophy (for example by purchasing goods that are foreign to the sector) if one would be able to 'trade' with it, or if it would attract extra customers. The purchasing culture will therefore be mainly product oriented (instead of product range oriented).

The sales procedures in these companies will focus mainly on a series of promotional approaches and a great deal of attention for external advertising. The advertising pressure is often extremely high. This is necessary, because it involves low frequency purchased products, of which the consumer has not developed any routine behaviour with regard to the store choice. If a consumer buys a new television on average once every

Availability
Innovation

External logistics

Internal logistics

Sales oriented retail

2

ten years, there is little point for him to keep track of which suppliers have which special offers in the period in between. It is therefore important for the seller to regularly maintain a prominent presence in public to inform the buyers who just happened to be in the market for his products at that time, of his offer.

Marketing in sales oriented companies therefore exhibits characteristics of aggressive sales techniques, in the sense of the more or less forcing products onto consumers. In the current situation in the Netherlands, where there are empowered consumers who are confronted with an excess of supply, this 'push marketing' has relatively little sense. It is therefore understandable that predominantly sales oriented retail in the Netherlands hardly ever occurs any more, although exceptions to the rule always manage to rise. A traditional example of a sales oriented retail company has always been Kwantum, who used to sort their product range primarily based on bulk supply. Today, however, Kwantum is more of a purchase oriented retailer (on the price aggressive side of the market) than a sales oriented retailer. Action, on the contrary, is a sales oriented retailer pur sang. In only a few years, the West Frisian company has grown into an international retailer in bulk goods. In 2011 the company was taken over by venture investor 3i to enable further international expansion of this formula. In 2012 the company almost reached the €900 million sales.

Factory outlet centres

As already indicated, it is difficult to be successful as a sales oriented retailer in current times, just think of the so-called *factory outlet centres* that have only been active for a mere decade. Two of these centres were opened in 2001, where brands could sell their 'outdated or excess' products, often clothing, at lower rates. Incidentally, stores themselves are also active in this form of retail, for example Miss Etam which has its own outlet stores. Characteristics of sales oriented retail companies are:
- discount type approach;
- relatively low frequency purchased product package;
- (partly) changing product ranges;
- relatively high sales rates;
- relatively low margins;
- self-service;
- limited problem solving behaviour;
- simple store layout;
- high and sharply promotional oriented advertising efforts.

2.5.3 Purchase oriented retail

Purchase oriented retail

Purchase oriented retail is involved when the focus of the daily business is the constant renewal of the product range. This often involves product categories in which one has to deal with fast, fashionable trends and consumer purchasing behaviour associated with extensive orientation: one is tempted to visit many stores before purchasing something.

The purchasing process in such companies focuses mainly on predicting and estimating fashion trends (short term) and developments in consumer behaviour (long term). Since the preparation time for a new collection can be considerable (fashion companies are already working on the collection that has to hit the stores in two or three seasons), this is a risky and difficult process – a process that not only requires great insight into the (future) needs of consumers, but also requires highly specialist product knowledge. The expertise that is obtained in the purchasing more often results in the purchasing department evolving into a *sourcing*-function:

Sourcing

they do not purchase what manufacturers (coincidentally) release on to the market, but rather the retailer purchases production capacity for what he feels that he can sell over a year. This is often accompanied by strict product specifications from the retailer. The final result may be a store in which products are only sold under the own retail brand, created according to their own specifications. It is clear that, in purchase oriented companies, the marketing is primarily the responsibility of the purchasing department.

The sales process in such companies focuses mainly on providing more insight into the product range philosophy on the store floor for the selected target group: the sales mix does not focus on forcing products on consumers, but on attracting prospective customers or visitors and creating such an attractive store image, that the prospective customers are inclined to include the store in their list of stores to be visited. Marketing in purchase oriented companies is therefore primarily focused on building a recognisable supply formula that is not based solely on supplying products, but on supplying a total concept for a target group. Predominantly purchase oriented retail companies are becoming more common, especially – but not exclusively – in the fashion industry, for example Hennes & Mauritz, WE and ZARA. But companies like The Body Shop and, to a certain extent, Halfords also fall under this category.

Characteristics of purchase oriented retail companies are:
- medium frequency and low frequency purchased product package;
- stable product ranges, yet very variable content of the product ranges (fashionable);
- pleasant store atmosphere;
- relatively low sales rates;
- relatively high margins;
- thematic advertising;
- large catchment area.

Hennes & Mauritz is a predominantly purchasing-oriented retailer

2.5.4   Drawbacks and benefits of classification based on operational characteristics

As indicated, the classification of logistics oriented, sales oriented and purchase oriented retail cannot be clearly defined. In reality, the distinction will often have a gradual nature. Indeed, in all cases logistics, sales and purchase belong to the primary business processes of retail. Yet the distinction still has practical value: depending on what focus is placed on one of the three primary business processes, expertise and culture differences develop in the organisation. These culture differences are the reason why it is especially difficult for people in a logistically organised operation to manage product ranges that have to be sold through a purchase oriented approach. Dealing with product ranges with a low sales rate, which have to be renewed often, has proven to be an entirely different story in the practice than working with stable product ranges with a high sales rate. This is why, as yet, most attempts at selling simple clothing items in supermarkets have basically failed.

2.6 Classification based on the shopping behaviour of the consumer

In the daily practice of retailing, we use several concepts that are aimed making a marketing relevant classification in the shopping behaviour of consumers. The distinction is important because, depending on the behaviour of the customers, the retail offer should exhibit various characteristics. One of the problems with the used classifications is that they often overlap considerably, but do not fully cover one other. This is because the consumers behaviour is very diverse and cannot be captured be a simple definition. Another problem is that the classification is almost always explained from the extremes, while in practice there is usually a continuum. We will treat several of the most commonly used concepts. We should however realise that the behaviour of the consumer is increasingly difficult to classify and that marketers are very clever in constantly inventing new criteria for consumer behaviour. The last word has not yet been spoken.

2.6.1   Fun shopping/run shopping

One widely used distinction in shopping behaviour, for example, is the distinction between fun shopping and run shopping. *Fun shopping* is recreational shopping, which consumer do for fun. *Run shopping* is purchasing necessary products, something that consumers often hate doing. The extremes are obvious: if someone hates doing the daily grocery shopping, it will be called run shopping; if someone absolutely loves buying new clothing, the purchase of a new outfit will fall under fun shopping. But where should we place the purchase of socks or pots? Obviously, depending on the degree of interest in the product for the person involved, somewhere between fun shopping and run shopping. In view of optimising the consumers search costs, we can define fun shopping as 'the consumer's purchase moments in which the shopping pleasure exceeds the trouble of shopping'. Run shopping relates to the opposite: 'the moment in which the troubles exceed the shopping

Fun shopping
Run shopping

pleasure'. The rise of the internet has drastically changed the nature of fun shopping. Consumers orient themselves increasingly more online before actually going shopping. A share of run shopping will also migrate to the internet. We will get back to the changing purchasing processes as a result of the internet. This does raise the question of how important the current classification still is. The fact is that the footfall (number of passers-by in shopping areas) has decreased over the last ten years. It would appear that consumers are now more rational and aware when heading out, even for that which used to fall under fun shopping.

2.6.2   Daily/non-daily purchasing behaviour

Consumers have a different attitude to the daily purchasing behaviour than when it comes to purchasing items that are not purchased daily. The *daily purchasing behaviour* is often focused on purchasing consumables: goods that are lost during use. The *non-daily purchasing behaviour* refers mainly to consumer goods, also known as 'consumer durables'. These are goods than can be used several times in a row. They are subject to wear, but are not used up. The purchase process of consumer durables has changed drastically as a result of the internet. The degree of orientation in advance has increased greatly, especially when it comes to categories such as electronics. Consumers very often start their search online. We will come back to this new search and purchasing process later on.

Daily purchasing behaviour

Non-daily purchasing behaviour

We often use this classification to indicate the difference between the buyer of food and the buyer of non-food, or the difference between 'grocery shopping' and 'shopping'. However, this is too simple: there are situations where a consumer buys food from a non-daily attitude, for example when he or she is giving a birthday party or a dinner for the boss. It is certainly not excluded that, in such a case, one could choose a different purchase location than the supermarket which one visits for the daily necessities. There are also situations where items are purchased with a high frequency in the sphere of non-food products, such as socks, paper and washing products.

One characteristic of daily purchasing behaviour is that consumers base the store selection on habit. In such a case we speak of called 'fixed' store orientation. Purchasing daily articles is usually associated with few complicated selection processes: *routine purchasing behaviour*. Consumers know the product range, can properly assess the price level of the products and often know in advance which products they need. There is little comparative shopping. Again, the internet has contributed to the changing purchasing process. There still is not any comparative shopping, but comparative orientation has become much easier. Even for daily purchases, consumers can use price comparison on websites and through Apps on their mobile telephone. A chain like Tesco even offers such service on its own website, making it possible for customers to compare Tesco's prices with its competitors.

Routine purchasing behaviour

The store forms that meet the need for daily grocery shopping are usually stores with a logistic orientation. The store layout is often focused on the ease (a much-used term in retailing is *convenience*) for the customer: the proximity of the store, the ease of navigation (fixed product locations in the store) and the speed of the checkout all play an important role. With the AppieApp, Albert Heijn offers customers the convenience of being able to find the products in the store quickly.

Convenience

2.6.3   Low involvement/high involvement purchase moments

The distinction between *low involvement* and *high involvement*, which is widely-used in professional literature, refers to the degree of involvement of the consumer when purchasing products. The classification is partially parallel to that between daily and non-daily. It is clear that daily grocery shopping for people who run the household, is not a hobby, or for whom cooking is a challenge, is associated with low involvement-purchase behaviour. For cooking enthusiasts, however, or for people who greatly appreciate the daily contact of the supermarket, very regular grocery shopping may be accompanied with high involvement-behaviour. Nor is it correct to assume that buying non-daily products is always associated with high involvement purchase behaviour. For men who are not interested in fashion, the purchase of a new suit is an absolute disaster, which is not exactly associated with a high degree of involvement. High involvement is often associated with extensive problem solving behaviour (Verhage, 2010).

Low involvement

High involvement

2.6.4   Convenience, shopping, specialty and preference goods

The classification of *convenience*, *shopping*, *specialty* and *preference goods* is a classification of consumer goods based on the purchase behaviour of consumers.

Convenience goods
Convenience goods are products in the daily product package, which purchase is accompanied by a low involvement. This often involves a slight brand preference. These products are purchased in the store that is 'easiest' or nearest.

Shopping goods
Shopping goods are products where consumers shop very comparatively. These are often products with a relatively low purchase frequency or a strong alternating fashion trend, as a result of which the ready knowledge of the attributes of the product is not available. The purchase of these kinds of products is also associated with extensive problem solving behaviour and the consumer visits many stores before purchasing something.

Specialty goods
Specialty goods are products for which the consumer has a very clear brand preference. This generally, involves low frequency purchased products. The purchase of these types of products is associated with a very high degree of involvement and consumers are prepared to put much effort into purchasing the relevant brand product.

The classification of consumer goods in convenience, shopping and specialty goods is used frequently in general marketing. From a retail marketing point of view, however, it is not yet complete. It appears that there is yet another category of goods that could not be placed under this classification: so-called *preference goods*. This involves high frequency purchased, daily products, of which the purchase is indeed associated with low involvement purchase behaviour, but for which the consumer sets higher than average requirements. This may be brand products, but it may also be a preference for a certain store, either due to the service offered, or due to the quality offered, for example the high-quality neighbourhood specialty stores.

Preference goods

Over the next few years, this classification will also be influenced in the search and purchase process through the use of the internet. Not so much because products can no longer be classified into these four groups, but rather because they will take up a larger online component.

2.6.5   Classification based on channel use

The most important development for the future is probably the classification on how we shop. We come from a world that consisted of buying
through one channel. Channels were added over time, but all of them were
rarely ever used by one organisation at the same time. In the Netherlands,
it was certainly not common to combine stores and catalogues, although
single foreign retailer did try. With the rise of the online channel it was
reluctantly tried, but, in the early years, the pure players appeared to be
better equipped, or maybe they just had more perseverance. The next step
in retail seemed to be a multichannel approach. As we already indicated,
we believe that this approach is also outdated. Retailers should build their
orientation completely around the customer, and the customer assumes
cross channel. This suggests that the time has come for a new classification from the consumer perspective based on the channel use. The
previously cited research commissioned by ABN AMRO, has brought
forward the following classification: online buyers, offline buyers and cross   **Cross channel**
channel buyers. Consumers were asked how they made their purchases   **buyers**
within the seven main categories, over the past twelve months. Based on
how the purchases were made, the classification was made based on the
type of buyer, as indicated in figure 2.1.

FIGURE 2.1 Distribution of buyers in the Netherlands online-offline
and cross channel

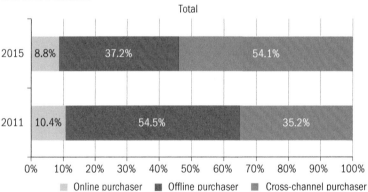

As suggested, online buyers are consumers that have only purchased online
within the answered category over the past twelve months. Over the past
twelve months, offline buyers have only purchased products in physical
stores within the answered category. Cross channel buyers have indicated
that, within the answered category, they have purchased both online and in
physical stores. A total, the so-called average was also mentioned in this
study. This was chosen to be able to identify and compare the various
groups of buyers. This average can also be used to compare the various
sectors to the average score. In order to achieve a good average, the
results of this study were assessed, in which the various sectors were
assessed based on the relative sales share of every sector.

Own research among 118 non food retail chains showed the score of online
sales by these physical retailers. These developments show that cross

channel players are moving faster with average online sales growth of over 40%, whereas the online market stores youth notes of 12%.

2.7 Synthesis of supply and demand

Sub-paragraph 2.5.4 discussed the difficulties of a clear categorisation of the various forms of consumer retail behaviour. The classifications outlined seemed, at first, to show strong similarities, yet on closer consideration they reveal an array of differences. In any event, it is important to realise that the needs driving each form of consumer behaviour must be met by some aspect of the retail offer – if a store is to be successful. Supply and demand are inextricably linked. One of the most relevant examples of integration between supply and demand characteristics was developed by the IPM (the Institute for Psychological Market Research). Figure 2.2 categorises retail according to two, main criteria. Firstly by the size of the store (the *supply criteria*), and secondly by consumer behaviour, which broadly corresponds to what was discussed above (under *demand criteria*). Four quadrants are the result, which enable a broad description of consumer behaviour, supply behaviour and retail formula behaviour.

Supply criteria

Demand criteria

FIGURE 2.2 High/low involvement in large/small stores

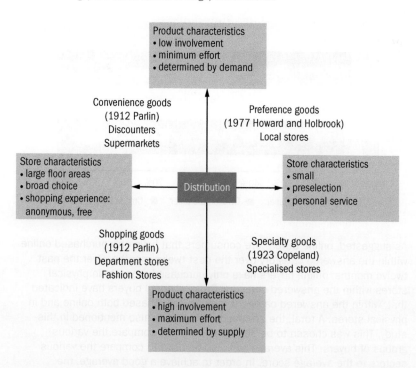

It must be repeated that the industry is hard to categorise. This classification is no more than an approach, but one that does have the advantage of dealing with the related issues on an integrated basis. We also demonstrate that, in practice, both extremes and every variation between them can occur: the assortments of medium-sized stores, for instance, commonly range from high involvement to low involvement. It is, however, noteworthy that – viewed in the longer term – this middle segment seems to be shrinking, whereas growth in retail formula supply is largely taking place in the corners of the matrix, in the more extreme positions. The reasons for this development obviously lie in the increasing complexity of consumer demand and the retailer's reaction to this.

2.8 Retail – supply side

The retail in the Netherlands is not only a complicated industry, it is also a large one, consisting of more than 80,000 businesses with approximately 108,000 establishments and a sales of approximately €83 bn (2010). These businesses provide employment to approximately 680,000 people. This makes retail the largest employer in the Netherlands. Within the European Union retail employs approximately 31 million people in 6.2 million retail businesses with total sales of approximately €2,273 bn. We will look at developments in this environment, in retail, in the underlying dynamics of supply and demand and in the proliferation of outlets in the Netherlands.

2.8.1   Environmental developments

At least 864,000 businesses were active in the Netherlands in 2010 according to the CBS. This number has grown considerably in recent years. Between 1995 and 2010 the number of businesses in the Netherlands grew by 45% (although there is a gap in the relevant CBS data, as one of the basic series was discontinued in 2008). The overall growth picture contains differences in growth rate per category: banking, insurance and business services grew very rapidly; industry, construction industry and the retail, on the other hand, lag behind the general rate of increase. The total number of ventures in the Netherlands has mainly grown in recent years as a result of the increase in one-man businesses. In 2010 the total increase in the total number of companies is due to the growth of this 'sole trader' category. For our purposes, growth in the category' trade and repair businesses ' is particularly significant. This is by far the largest category identified by the National Statistics Office and constitutes the most important part of the retail category. The growth rate of this category does, however, continue to lag behind the national growth rate for all forms of business.

2.8.2   Developments in retail

Table 2.10 clearly illustrates development of the retail category relative to total business activity in the Netherlands.

TABLE 2.10 Retail growth in relation to all forms of business

	Number of businesses in the Netherlands	Retail share
1995	596,365	85,325 (14.3%)
2000	679,565	85,720 (12.6%)
2005	719,405	83,400 (11.5%)
2010	864,000	80,000 (9.3%)

Source: HBD/CBS, 2011

We will now look at a number of businesses and the employment situation and then discuss contribution to national income.

Businesses numbers and employment opportunities

The number of businesses in the Netherlands has grown over the years and this trend continued after 2000. The total number of retail businesses gradually decreased in the period before 1990. But after 1990 a change took place and the number of retail businesses once again slowly grew, though at a much slower rate than the increase in the total number of businesses. This trend continued up to 2000, whereafter a slight fall is seen in the number of retail businesses. Retail's share of total business fell by 14.3% in 1995, to 12.6% in 2000 and 5% in 2005. The number of p.73 businesses ended up, according to an HBD estimate, at 80,000 in 2010. This means that retail in 2010 comprised less than 10% of all businesses in the Netherlands. Although retail is still one of the most important industry categories in the Dutch economy, in terms of number of businesses and certainly in terms of number of employed people, we must note what appears to be a decreasing trend of importance of the category. The impression of relative stagnation changes if it is viewed from the perspective of employment – in which there is clearly an upward trend (see table 2.11).

TABLE 2.11 Growth of employment in the retail sector (employees)

Year	Years of employment (× persons)
1990	461,000
1995	521,000
2000	617,000
2005	625,000
2010	680,000

Growth 1990-2010: 53%

Source : HBD, 2011

The retail sector accounts for 10% of the number of jobs in the Netherlands. This includes the above-mentioned 680,000 employees and another 142,000 entrepreneurs and employed family members, giving a total of at least 822,000 people working in retail.

On the basis of the data in table 2.11, in combination with the growth in the number of businesses, we can conclude that significant retail growth is taking place.

Growth in the number of e-tailers

There has been enormous growth in the number of webshops in the Netherlands. In 2000 there were 800 registered online stores according to the HBD. Ten years later there are 7,100 businesses active in retail, according to the HBD. And many more webshops are active in categories other than retail. According to Thuiswinkel.org there are at least 37,500 webshops in the Netherlands. Barriers to entry for online businesses of course seem low. This partly explains the explosive growth.

But success on the internet demands as much professionalism as required in the physical marketplace. Online also presents barriers to entry, for example the ease with which the consumer can find the online store on the web.

Contribution to national income
There are very few figures available on the added value provided by the retail in total. Estimates assume a percentage between 4.5% and 5% gross at factor cost. The impression exists that this (in itself small) percentage is currently under pressure as a result of tightening margins. Based on the figures, we see that the retail is still a category of relatively small-scale businesses. Average retail business size is small in comparison with the total average business size in the Netherlands. On the other hand, trends in the data indicate that retail is rapidly catching up: the growth in the number of retail employees paired with the reduction in share of total number of businesses, means that the size of the remaining retail businesses is growing. At the same time we note that retail profits, in any event expressed as a contribution to gross national product (GNP), is (very) low. One way or another, this will lead to a situation in which inefficiently managed companies, or those unable to leverage scale advantages, will fall away. This process will accelerate, especially in periods of economic decline. This process of acceleration was seen in the recession following the financial crisis of 2007. In the Netherlands, companies such as It's and Hans Textiel – both large chains – succumbed. The phenomenon of concentration and increase in the size of operations are trends that will be further reinforced by this situation. In this, retail has clearly shown the characteristics of a maturing industry category – developing from an old-fashioned segment of extremely small-scale operations into a category characterised by trends towards concentration, increase in business size and increasing professionalisation.

2.8.3   Underlying dynamics of supply and demand
This is made clearer if we look at the underlying dynamic of supply. First we must note that evaluation of the retail supply side on the basis of the number of businesses in the category only takes one dimension into account. Eurostat thus observes that the Netherlands qualified in 1993 as one of the 'under-serviced' countries in terms of retail outlets, with just 64 (50 in 2006) retail businesses per 10,000 inhabitants. (The average for Europe is 96).
Far more important than the number of businesses (in any event for the consumer) is the number of establishments operational in the retail. Euromonitor's 1992 outlet count presents a totally different picture: the Netherlands, now with 10.7 establishments per thousand inhabitants, is (after Belgium) the country with the highest store density in North-Western Europe (for which the average is 7.6 per thousand inhabitants). This is a result of a single business having many *subsidiaries* or branches. This **Branch** heavily branched structure is particularly prevalent in the Netherlands. It is **proliferation** therefore important to take the number of outlets into account, in addition to the number of businesses.
Between 1960 and 1990 there was, in total, a very sharp reduction in the number of selling establishments. This reduction took place primarily in the food sector, where the increase in average business size has been very marked. However, the non-food sector also experienced reductions. This often concerned old-fashioned, artisanal, product-oriented, specialist

businesses – which succumbed to competition from the specialised, large retailers. During the 1980s the situation seemed to stabilise. In the beginning of the 1990s, the trend changed and the number of outlets started to grow. Between 1995 and 2005 the situation seemed to stabilise again, with only a few, smaller variations in the number of locations. A very important development in the long run for the retail is the increase in the number of square metres of retail floor space. This has increased enormously in recent years. In the last ten years the number of retail square metres increased by almost 27%. In the same period between 2000 and 2010, retail sales increased by almost 14%. This meant that productivity decreased considerably per square metre – by more than 10%. We will return to the importance of growth and the positive development of the productivity of the retail sector, but it is obvious that negative growth of sales per square metre is not good for the retail sector in the long run. One of the issues in relation to this productivity decline per square metre is to be found in the increase in store size researched by Locatus in various categories. Figure 2.3 shows how DIY and garden centres in particular have grown enormously in square metres between 2003 and 2013. A striking aspect of the increase in the number of square metres is especially in the growth of non-food retail floor areas, which has exceeded that of food retail in recent year (see table 2.12). This is all more striking when we look at sales growth in both sectors from 2003 to 2010. During this period sales increased in food retail by 10%, to more than €36.7 billion, while non-food retail grew by 9% to €45.5 billion. This means that productivity per square metre showed particularly poor development in the non-food sector.

FIGURE 2.3 Percentage increase in average store size 2003-2012

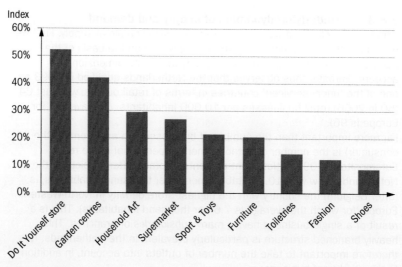

Source: Locatus 2010

TABLE 2.12 Growth in total retail floor area* in millions of sq. metres

	2005	**2010**	**Growth**
Food retail	4.5 m^2	4.7 m^2	+4.4%
Non-food retail	21.2 m^2	22.9 m^2	+8.0%
Retail total	25.7 m^2	27.6 m^2	+7.4%

* The store floor surface is the publicly accessible floor space in the store.

Source : HBD, Locatus, 2010

2.8.4　Proliferation of outlets in the Netherlands

The Dutch retail landscape has become one of increasingly similar stores. The complaint is also heard that even shopping streets are becoming the same. Chain stores increasingly dominate shopping precincts, though they are frequently operated by an individual entrepreneur, as franchisee of a large retail chain.

There has been a slight decline in the number of businesses in the period between 1960 and 1990. This is mainly attributed to the decline of the number businesses with no branches. In the period between 1960 and and 1990 this category reduced by more than 38%. Only after 1990 is a slight recovery seen in the number of establishments, with a small dip visible at the turn of the last century. We see a completely different picture in relation to branches. Here an enormous increase takes place in the period from 1960 to 1995: the number doubles. After the peak in 1995 the number of outlets shows a drop, with a small rise again in 2007. Apparently there has been a reversal of the trend of the last thirty years: the increase in the number of outlets now lags behind the increase in the number of businesses with one establishment. There seems, therefore, to be a revival in the fortunes of the SME. In any event, the current supply side of the Dutch retail is one that is still dominated by the strong presence of branches. This trend is also apparent abroad, though the rate of change varies by European country.

We must also take into account that statistics give a considerably diluted picture of reality. HBD statistics only show owned outlets, excluding the establishments of affiliated businesses such as franchisees, voluntary associations and members of group marketing organisations. As stated in sub-paragraph 2.3.2, in the period under consideration the cooperation of independent entrepreneurs within *umbrella organisations*, and (especially) in terms of franchising has grown strongly. In the rapidly shrinking category of businesses with only one establishment there will therefore be many businesses which are legally independent businesses but which, from a marketing point, must be viewed as branches. This includes franchisees of branched companies and businesses seen as members of an umbrella organisation from the consumer's point of view. If we look at the sales of franchise organisations, including the sales of their own branches, we see in table 2.13 that the 2010 sales of this combined form of retailing amounted to at least €37 bn.

Umbrella organisations

TABLE 2.13 Sales of franchise organisations in 2010 in € millions

	Franchisees	Own outlets	Total
Food retail	12,960	11,072	24,032
Non-food retail	9,670	4,236	13,906
Total	22,630	15,308	37,935

Source: NFV, 2011

This shows that franchise organisations, including retail organisations in which some outlets are franchised operations, comprise at least 45% of total retail sales in the Netherlands. A warning on the interpretation of statistics therefore seems in order. If we look at the official registration of the trading entity, i.e. to the legal structure of the supply side business, then we must conclude that Dutch retail still consists of approximately 80 to 90% independent SME businesses. But if we look at to their marketing approach, i.e. at their marketing structure, then we reach a totally different conclusion. Seen from the consumer's point of view, approximately 70 to 80% of the Dutch detail trade belongs to large, cooperative organisations. And this trend seems set to continue into the future. The increasing degree of cooperation in the approach to the consumer is a function of the need for recognisable retail formulas in the market. We therefore see a remarkable and powerful development which also characterises the Dutch retail: an extreme and still increasing proliferation of outlets. This is true for both real branches (= extension of owned establishment) and synthetic branches (= affiliation of self-employed persons to an existing formula). Synthetic branches are mainly franchisees and, in particular, members of 'strict' franchise groups.

Retail also continues to provide room for new entrants. Real, like for like growth in terms of number of businesses in retail has grown since 2001. (See table 2.14.) Of course the low entry threshold plays a role in this, as no particular obstacles exist in the retail sector. These thresholds to entry are even lower in relation to online stores.

TABLE 2.14 Number of 'starters' and 'stoppers' in retail

	Number of starters and other business formation	Number of deregistrations	Net growth
2008	17,600	13,100	+ 4,500
2007	18,300	12,600	+ 5,700
2006	18,100	11,700	+ 6,400
2005	17,600	11,500	+ 6,100
2004	16,000	10,500	+ 5,500
2003	13,600	9,700	+ 3,900
2002	11,900	9,000	+ 2,900
2001	11,800	10,000	+ 1,800

Source : KvK (Dutch chamber of commerce) company dynamics (updated 12 January 2010)

2.9 Demand side in retail

We will now deal, successively, with individual expenditure and trade spend.

2.9.1   Individual expenditure

The purpose of retail marketing is to satisfy consumer demand. In fact, each time a consumer makes a purchase of either a service or good using net disposable income, we can say that retail activity has taken place. The demand side of the market must therefore be described from the point of view of development in private consumption in family households.

Consumer spending is measured by National Statistics Office and published In the *National Accounts*. Consumer spending amounted, in 2009, to €262 bn. This falls into three main categories (after some processing by the authors):
- Food and related products (FRP): about €36.7 bn.
- Durables and other goods (DOG): approximately €84.9 bn.
- Services: approximately €140.4 bn.

Each of these categories is divided into a number of sub-categories, making it possible to obtain information at a detailed level. We will first look at consumer consumption and retail, thereafter at the growth of consumer consumption over time.

Consumer consumption and retail

Although, in the broadest sense, all household consumption expenditure falls under retailing, we usually only include *expenditure of disposable income* as retail spend. That is, all expenditure of net income after deducting fixed expenses. Fixed expenditure items are mostly fixed, monthly, financial commitments such as home rental or mortgage repayments, insurance and healthcare premiums and expenditure on (means of) transport. This distinction is not absolute: the decision to buy a house and finance the purchase with a mortgage is clearly a freely-made decision of the consumer. This is also clear from how this purchase decision takes place: extensive problem-solving behaviour occurs, involving many house inspections and many mortgage proposals. But, once the transaction is concluded, the purchaser is tied to the resulting, monthly payments for many years and the expenditure then falls under fixed charges. These payments are, according to the usual interpretation, no longer retail expenditure.

Consumer expenditure of disposable income

This limited definition of retail spending results in very large portions of consumer expenditure not being included in the broader context of retail, although such spend is linked to decision processes which are very similar to retail purchase decisions from a consumer point of view. The decision to enter into a private insurance contract or to temporarily invest unspent funds in a bank account hardly differs from the process applied in purchasing a wide variety of the goods available in retail outlets. The fact that many consumer services are not counted as retail purchases is related, in turn, to the fact that the retail sector is mainly limited to sales of goods. It has, moreover, led to an even more limited application of the expression 'retail expenditure' in common usage – in which retail expenditure is normally equated to *expenditure by the retail itself*. Although the retail

Retail spending Retail expenditure

the main supplier of goods to consumers, this is also a simplified representation of the actual situation. This is illustrated in table 2.15, which shows the distribution channels through which consumer spending takes place, in relation to a number of important categories. We have used data from 2008 in this example. Food, beverages and tobacco have had an average VAT rate of 12% applied as two tariffs are normally applied to this category, 6% for foods and 19% (since October 2013 21%) for all other items.

TABLE 2.15 Household purchases by distribution channel, for a number of goods categories

Category	Retail (%)	Remaining channels (%)
Food and related products	73	27
Furniture	90	10
Domestic equipment and electronics	89	11
Clothing	95	5

Source: HBD, 2008-2011; CBS, 2011 (own version)

Table 2.15 shows that although most of the spending on goods takes place in retail outlets, significant spend also takes place with the consumer utilising channels other than (traditional) retailers. So we see, for example, that spending in the food sector is channeled via retail (75%) but also via channels such as foodservice (25%).

Growth of individual consumption over time
Individual consumption has developed over the last few decades, as shown in figure 2.4.

FIGURE 2.4 Development of consumer expenditure

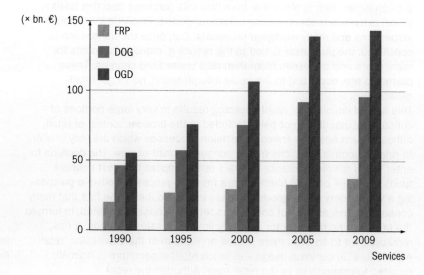

Each of the three main categories showed positive growth, albeit to different degrees. FRP showed the smallest increase (in line with Engel's law, which states that an increasingly smaller proportion of necessary items – including food – are purchased from a growing income. DOG shows somewhat stronger growth, while the service category exceeds all others. In relative terms this means that the share of goods purchased by consumers is falling sharply relative to total retail consumer spending. It is striking, however, that FRP has shown stronger growth over the last five years, almost doubling the consumer expenditure on DOG. The reasons for these developments become clear if we look at the underlying components. If we introduce a separation between fixed charges and disposable income, the share of free spending appears to be reduced by the increase in the share of essential services. Free spending consists almost entirely, but not exclusively, of expenditure on goods – but also on non-fixed services such as leisure and holidays. Further analysis also shows that the reduction in expenditure of freely disposable income is only partly due to volume issues. This is more pronounced than in the goods sector, price changes in the past being the reason for growth of the service category. Price increases in this sector have, in recent years, been more than twice has high as in the goods sector.

Moreover the phenomenon of heavy price increases in the service category seems less pronounced in recent years. The reason is the increasing privatisation of public services and, as a result, increasing competition within the service sector, as a result of which cost increases can no longer be automatically passed on in the consumer price. The flattening of the growth curve in DOG also has to do with limited growth or even decline in the underlying prices of many product categories. Volumes have continued to increase, but prices have often decreased. This trend seems to have reversed by the end of 2010 and early 2011 and, for the first time, businesses like fashion companies are being faced with rising inventory purchase prices. Rising energy prices, with ongoing demand for energy for production and transport, will have the effect of driving these prices upwards.

2.9.2   Development in retail expenditure

As mentioned in sub-paragraph 2.8.1, not all spending on goods takes place via the traditional retail channel. Table 2.16 shows how consumer retail spending has developed as a share of total consumption over the past thirty years.

TABLE 2.16 Retail spending 1970-2010 as share of total consumer expenditure

Year	Retail spending (× € 1 billion)	Individual consumption (× € 1 billion)	Share (in %)
1970	18.5	32.3	57.3
1980	41.1	93.5	44.0
1985	42.3	112.4	37.6
1990	53.6	137.6	39.0
1995	59.0	172.0	34.3

TABLE 2.16 Retail spending 1970-2010 as share of total consumer expenditure (continued)

Year	Retail spending (× € 1 billion)	Individual consumption (× € 1 billion)	Share (in %)
2000	73.0	207.0	35.2
2005	76.8	246.0	31.2
2010	82.7	268.0	30.9

Source: HBD (updated 15 November 2011)

We can therefore conclude that the Dutch retail, although still a growth market in absolute terms, is faced with a decreasing market share. There are exceptions though. Firstly, in the period from 1985 to 1990, in which there is a slight recovery of market share. This probably arose as a result of the catch-up effect related to the crisis in 1980 when consumers delayed purchases, notably of high ticket items. When this effect had ebbed, however, market share continued to decline rapidly until the period of 1995-2000, in which a light recovery again took place. After 2000 the decline set in again, but seemed to stabilise on its way towards 2010, hovering around 31% and falling just below this magical threshold for the first time in 2010.

Summary

Retail is a very diverse industry. It is therefore difficult to use one exact classification. Depending of the problem, we often have to deal with various criteria. We can approach these classifications from various angles: statistically, by the size of the company, legally and by the form of operation. Classifications by the purchase behaviour of consumers are more important for marketing. In this case we distinguish between fun shopping or run shopping, between daily purchasing behaviour or non-daily purchasing behaviour, between low involvement or high involvement purchase moments, and finally between convenience, shopping, specialty and preference goods.

3
The retail in international perspective

The global retail environment has changed quickly in the last decades. Internationalisation is at the order of the day in retail. This has led to consolidation in various markets in the form of takeovers, but also to the entry of new players in already established markets. The shopping streets in Europe seem to have become uniform, they seem to be more similar internationally. The Media Markt, H&M's, ZARA's, IKEA's, Vero Moda's and Jack & Jones's of this world are expanding their networks. In addition, global players are searching for new markets in Brazil, China and Russia, the so-called BRIC countries.

We will successively focus on the European retail and its international ambitions. This paragraph is followed by a paragraph on European integration and concludes with a look at the world as a global retail marketplace. We will show some large countries with the largest local players.

3.1 Internationalisation of Dutch retail

In contrast to the countries around us, the Dutch retail sector is characterised by an unusually fine detailed texture – the result of relatively
small-scale stores (density, expressed in number of outlets and square
metres of floor space is high). However, these stores belong to relatively
large businesses (density, expressed in number of businesses, is low).
This indicates that the degree of proliferation of branches is further
advanced than in surrounding countries. The development of branches
per business confirms this. It also appears that the degree of cooperation between independent businesses with only a single establishment
is unusually high. The result is a dense, small scale but extremely
professional infrastructure on the retail supply side. This supply structure faces a demand situation that may be described as growing slowly
in absolute terms and shrinking rapidly in terms of relative market share
– also when compared to neighbouring countries. In addition, absolute
expenditure per head of population is low. This combination of supply
and demand factors should lead to a strongly competitive situation and,
as a result, relatively low margins and profit levels. In general, this also

**Return on
sales**

appears to be the case. The average *return on retail sales* in the Netherlands is between 1.5 and 2%. In other countries this margin is, generally,
considerably higher – especially in England, where margins are extremely
high in comparison.

This leads, on the one hand, to a difficult operational situation for the
Dutch retailer: profitable business management is not easy in this
market environment. On the other, it indicates a Dutch retail strength:
those who survive the unusually competitive Dutch retail market have an
advantage over foreign companies who attempt to penetrate this market
without being used to its low margins, small sales and dense, finely-wo-
ven market structure. It is therefore no surprise that internationalisation
of the Dutch retail was quite a difficult process in the period up to the
end of the 1990s. In contrast, the export of Dutch retail formulas
(mainly to Belgium but also increasingly to Germany, England and France)
has seemed to be more successful.

Hyperstore

The *hyperstore*, formula, while it enjoys wide-ranging success in many
countries has, despite various efforts, never obtained a foothold in
the Netherlands. Albert Heijn, with its AH-XL store formula version, is
actually the only chain with big enough stores to offer competition to
hyperstores, though even they are not able to face up to Carrefours and
Auchans in France. Stores of this type do not yet appear achievable in
the Netherlands. A worldwide formula like Toys"R"Us, that has booked
huge successes in many countries failed to make it in the Netherlands.
The Dutch stores were eventually sold to the Blokker group and are now
re-named Toys XL, this signalling the final curtain to the American's
Dutch venture.

Foreign businesses like Hennes & Mauritz, IKEA and Media Markt, that
have indeed been successful in the Dutch market, often have a similar
philosophy to local retailers. These successful retail formulas had
specialised assortments, were heavily branched and had an aggressive

approach to pricing. And there have also been successful ventures in partnering franchise-type approaches such as the formulas of the Danish Bestseller group like Vero Moda and Jack & Jones.

As a result of the unification of the European market, which caused the traditionally strongly regionalised European market to evolve into one huge, integrated market, there is currently an increasing degree of penetration by foreign companies in the Netherlands. As opposed to previous situations, this not only involves companies from neighbouring countries doing 'border hopping' but includes companies from other continents engaging in 'distance jumping' precisely because Europe looks like it is becoming an integrated, opportunity-rich, consumer market.

Border hopping

Distance jumping

The most striking example is Wal-Mart, the largest retail company in the world, with a sales of almost $410 billion in 2010. In 1998, Wal-Mart took over the German Wertkauf, followed by the large branches of the German Spar in the same year. In 1999 they continued their European march by taking over Asda in the UK. But Wal-Mart was not the only company to take this leap. Costco (one of Wal-Mart's most important competitors in the USA) is now strongly represented (and successful) in England. Wal-Mart soon discovered that Europe, and in particular Germany, was not the same as the United States. In 2006, Wal-Mart pulled out of the German market and sold its branches to German retailers, including Real. Wal-Mart, just as several European retailers, underestimated the specificity of Germany. At the end of September 2010, Wal-Mart placed a bid on the South African Massmart, to take a step on a new continent.

IKEA is aiming arrows towards the Middle East. Mid 2011, the Swedish company announced to the world that they would be opening a Flagship store in Dubai. In late 2010 the British Marks & Spencer (M&S), with the Dutch Bolland at the helm, also announced that they were again looking at the European mainland. For M&S this would be a return after a long absence, the British retailer is negotiating the reacquisition of branches that it used to own in both Spain and France. M&S closed all stores in Europe in 2001. But ten years later the company appears to be returning. The Netherlands become a part of that plan.

Primark, the Irish fashion chain, opened its first store in the Netherlands in 2008. For the moment it seems like every opening of this stylish price buster is a success. The British fashion chain New Look followed in 2009, they not only followed the strategy of opening own stores, but also that of 'store in stores' in, amongst other, V&D branches. The British chain also immediately added an online store. In a very short time, this chain opened webshops in countries where they were not even physically active yet. Some American chains also made the crossing to Europe. Abercrombie & Fitch, Hollister, Banana Republic, GAP and Victoria's Secret opened stores in Europe, not only in the UK, but also on the mainland. The lingerie chain Victoria's Secret opened a store in, among other places, Schipol, but surprisingly enough this was not for lingerie, but for cosmetics.

Country strategy

Global strategy

The big difference between Internationalisation attempts in the past is that the current wave is not based on a *country strategy* (penetrating country by country, making it profitable and then continuing), but on a *global strategy*: the goal is not to be represented in one country, but in Europe. The exploitation of the Dutch market is therefore no longer a standalone exercise with an independent yield strategy, but part of conquering Europe. The fact that some Dutch establishments can only be made profitable with difficulty is no longer that important. It is therefore expected that Dutch retail, despite the often difficult start of foreign companies, will eventually face increasing competition from large and strong foreign retailers. The Dutch retail is subsequently preparing for this through intensive cooperation, merging and in general increasing volume.

The consolidation will also continue in the years ahead, in which the Dutch food retail sector will once again lead the way. Super de Boer changed ownership and a decent player disappeared from the playing field. The consolidation in food was actually heralded with the transfer of the Schuitema share ownership of Ahold, to venture investor CVC. The end is not yet in sight for food. The cards will be shuffled and dealt again. In recent years Sligro has made several moves, but there are still many regional players. Further consolidation will also take place within non-food retail. The first set here is the merger between the two buying combinations. But the economic circumstances are also chipping in. This is why It's in Electronics disappeared and Dixons in the Netherlands was taken over by the parent company of Mycom. Free Record Shop filed for bankruptcy and it launched with a smaller number of outlets, but again had to file for bankruptcy another time in 2014. Block Electronics closed down as some fashion and shoe retailers.

Global internet strategy

Internationalising will also occur more and more often through a *global internet strategy*. The internet provides an excellent opportunity to quickly be present in many markets at relatively low costs. None of this happens by itself and it is certainly not the case that there are no costs involved. Language barriers remain an issue in Europe, because the customer contact will have to take place in the local language. The logistic costs are also considerable. Local partners may be used in this, but this also adds costs to the products.

International cross channel strategy

In recent years, however, we see that both internet retailers and physical retailers are moving to a growing number of countries. For physical retailers this is even a method to see if the physical presence is useful and feasible. Some international physical retailers even do the opposite. They open some physical stores in European capitals or favourite shopping destinations and use this to attract attention to their (local) webshops. In other words, an *international cross channel strategy*.

3.2 The European integration

First we discuss the implications of the further unification of Europe. Then we discuss the forms of internationalisation. Finally we will extensively discuss the geographic differences within Europe in terms of consumer behaviour.

3.2.1   Implications of the further unification of Europe

The implications of the further unification of Europe are of increasing importance for the retail in the Netherlands. The European integration is gradually creating a domestic market of about 500 million residents in 28 EU countries. This does not mean that this domestic market is already homogenous. There are still very large differences between the Southern and the Northern countries, and between Anglo-Saxon and Rhineland culture. This does mean that the ability to grow beyond borders is getting bigger, and we can see this happening all around us. There is a wave of consolidation taking place in Europe, with major implications for the future retail structure. Within Europe, big players from different countries are taking over retailers in other countries. Some retailers enter a country by opening new branches and using the fact that others are going under and carrying on in these locations.

A second implication of the integration is the fact that Europe, with a consumer potential of almost 500 million residents, is now also becoming interesting for retailers from other continents. Admittedly some companies still misjudge the fragmented nature of the European market segments, which often results in significant teething problems, but still: Wal-Mart and Costco (both from the US) have already built up a considerable market share in England. Nevertheless, Wal-Mart had to acknowledge its superior in Germany and this is partly traced back to the difference between the abovementioned Rhineland and Anglo-Saxon culture. In addition, Wal-Mart entered the UK with a price aggressive formula in a market where the prices for foodstuffs were the highest in Europe. In Germany, Wal-Mart took over an operation in a country that has always been known for the phenomenon hard discount from Aldi and Lidl.

3.2.2   Forms of internationalisation

Although internalisation as a growth strategy basically falls under 'market development' in the terms of Ansoff (see paragraph 7.2), there appears to be a wide variety with regard to the strategies used. We cannot explain all of this in these specifications. The most important choice that we have to make if we want to expand our companies abroad, is the choice between *formula export* or *formula takeover*.

Formula export
Formula takeover

Formula-export
Formula export means that one exports a formula that works well in the domestic market, unchanged, to foreign countries. A study conducted under Dutch retailers in cooperation with Rabobank in the fall of 2011 indicated that formula export is the best method. This strategy does not take into account the fact that the foreign market, with regard to consumers and competition, can sometimes vary from the domestic market.
The method seems easy and simple, certainly if it is accompanied with *border hopping* (spreading like wildfire from the domestic market to nearby regions, where the existing logistical infrastructure can be used). The same study indicated that this is the most suitable method. The idea here is specifically that a formula that works in Breda and Nijmegen, should also work in Antwerp, Wijnechem, Keulen or Oberhausen. However, each time it appears that formula export is much more difficult than one would initially think. Borders within Europe are

Border hopping

still formidable barriers, both physically and psychologically. One eventually comes to the conclusion that some adjustments are required to make the formula successful in foreign countries. Although it was thought that they were busy with market development, they actually got caught up in diversification. Formula export will be more successful as the formula becomes more focused and more responsive to universal needs, and less successful as the formula becomes less product focused, or various needs are covered at the same time. From this perspective it can be explained that specialty stores with a pronounced lifestyle approach (Hennes & Mauritz, ZARA, and IKEA) will be successful, while department stores will rarely succeed. This seems to be changing where department stores either take the path of lifestyle approach, for example HEMA, or of the mini shopping centre with many little store-in-stores. The pioneer in this field is the British Selfridges, owner of de Bijenkorf in the Netherlands since 2010. V&D is specifically and successfully following this last path now. Several examples of successful formula export: Hennes & Mauritz, The Body Shop, IKEA, ZARA, Mango, M&S fashion and Hunkemöller, all speciality stores with focus. Several examples of failed formula export: Marks & Spencer, Marktkauf, Argos and Toys"R"Us, predominantly warehouse style companies, without clear focus. Applying focus within a department store concept contributes to the internationally successful rollout.

A second threat to the formula export is the success of the first location abroad. For Germany, the shopping centre CentrO in Oberhausen is almost always chosen. Ample time is taken for the first finger exercises and the establishment appears to be successful. Then four or five new branches in Keulen, Neurenberg, Hamburg, Berlin and Munich follow. Then Germany appears to be more diverse than ever imagined and Oberhausen turns out to be not very German. Moreover, management attention is required in five to six places rather than on that one spot.
Successful export to one country is not a guarantee for another country. Blokker is successful in Belgium, but not in the German market, while Zeeman is an example of a Dutch retailer that has exported its formula to various European countries in a practically unaltered form.

The most appealing and successful formula exporters in fashion is the Swedish H&M, the Danish Bestseller (Vero Moda, Jack & Jones) and the Spanish Inditex (ZARA). In housing, the Swedish IKEA has expanded successfully in a segment where very little other formulas are active. The Dutch WE fashion is active in multiple European countries. Since the beginning of 2010, this company has also made a cautious start in China. At the beginning of 2012, WE already opened twenty branches in China. Another large Dutch retail group is ERB, active in multiple countries with M&S fashion, America Today and Coolcat. Hunkemöller, established in 1886, is a powerful player in lingerie. This company is successful in various European countries, both offline and online. A market leader in the Benelux and Germany. Media Markt is an example of formula export in electronics, where the company takes over almost everything, from the original concept to the advertising. Media Market had to retract from France in 2011. The strategy of the Germans focuses on becoming at least number one or two in a country. If the number one position is in sight, they will try to get the number two position with the second formula. In late 2010, Media Markt also started its Chinese adventure in Shanghai, but pulled out late 2012.

Formula takeover
Formula takeover means purchasing well functioning formulas in the countries where you want to expand. This strategy explicitly takes into account the fact that the market circumstances abroad vary from those in the domestic market. This strategy is often chosen when the internationalisation is associated with *distance jumping*, where one cannot use the existing logistical infrastructure and back-office in the domestic market. This method does not appear to be very risky (why would a formula that has always been successful, no longer be successful after takeover?), but in practice this is often just the case. Remote management is often difficult, the difference in management style is often a problem, portfolio management of various brands or formulas in various countries is complicated and the statutory directives vary per country, whereby control is often quite difficult. The developments at Ahold in 2003, which for many years was the textbook example of a company that was very successful abroad through formula takeovers, speak for themselves.

Distance jumping

3.2.3   Geographic differences within Europe
Although European integration leads to a domestic market of 500 million consumers, one still cannot speak of 'European Consumers'. Various studies, amongst others conducted by the World Bank, Usunier in 1993 and by Helfferich, Hinfelaar and Kaspar in 1997, indicate that there are multiple clusters within Europe, between which very different consumer behaviour occurs (see figure 3.1) and which often runs right through countries. We will now look more closely at these clusters. The subjects of choice criteria and collection changes are also discussed.

Clusters of Usunier
Usunier recognises a total of four clusters. According to this theory, the Netherlands is parts of two clusters: the so-called Nordic cluster and the Anglo Saxon Europe. It should be stated that the Netherlands is still mainly associated with the Nordic cluster. According to the model of the World Bank, the Netherlands belongs to the so-called *northern cluster*, along with regions like the Flemish part of Belgium (the Walloon part of Belgium belongs to the French cluster), the north-western part of Germany and the Scandinavian countries. According to the model of Usunier, Belgium belongs to the Central European cluster.

Northern cluster

It is clear that Dutch retailrs that want to expand abroad will primarily focus on companies in their own cluster. Based on the model of the World Bank, the first stop would be Belgium, Germany and Scandinavia. Only in the second instance will one think of expansion to countries with different consumer behaviour. In practice we also see this happen. WE (Germany, France, Switzerland and Belgium), Hunkemöller (Belgium, Luxemburg, Germany, Denmark and France, but nowadays also in the Middle East and Eastern Europe), M&S fashion (Belgium, Luxemburg,

FIGURE 3.1 European clusters on consumer behaviour

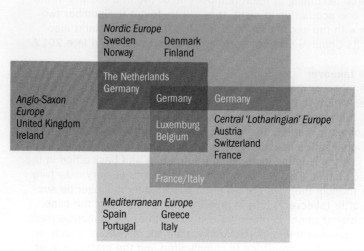

Source: *Usunier*

Germany and France) limit their attention predominantly to the northern cluster. We also see the reverse happening. Leroy Merlin, one of the largest French suppliers of DIY products, was actively expanding to Belgium up to 2000, with very little success. The company has since ended its Belgium exercise and has sold the stores to Praxis Netherlands.

Southern cluster

It is now focusing on the *southern cluster*, consisting of Italy, Spain and Portugal.

The fact that the differences are also present within clusters is indicated by a study that was conducted at the beginning of 2008 (Van der Kind and Quix, 2008). In thirteen European countries they investigated amongst other

Store choice criteria

store choice criteria, in other words the reason why a consumer chooses a particular store. Obviously the latter cannot just be explained culturally, but, to a certain degree, also involves the already existing store infrastructure. However, the differences in this level are often big and sometimes remarkable. Moreover, this study also examined the extent to which consumers want the collection in a fashion store to change and how often they purchase fashion items.

Store selection criteria
The study eventually provided a list with more than 25 criteria that would be important for a consumer when choosing a particular store. Ten of these 25 criteria, on average, account for almost 57% of the total in Europe. Incidentally, the difference is big; in France, the ten aspects together account for 50% of the decision making and in Finland, for example, it accounts for almost 65% of the decision making. The results are summarised in table 3.1. An excellent price-quality relationship is an important aspect for choosing a particular store in almost all countries. In Finland, this aspect weighs 12%, followed by Belgium, France and Austria with 11%. Most European countries are around an average of 8%. In most countries the

Hunkemöller now has operations in Europe and the Middle East

price-quality relationship is also the most important criterion. The Netherlands and the United Kingdom values the size of the product range much more.

Collection changes
Fashion is a special branch of sport within the retail, especially since it is also culturally determined how fashion is viewed and how this is purchased. In recent years the collections have been changing more rapidly. In this light it is interesting to know how often consumers feel that collections should be changed. In chapter 7 we will return to the reversal of the value column and the power of consumers in relation to the success of the so-called vertically organised companies like ZARA and Hennes & Mauritz. Our research shows that European consumers believe that fashion should change in stores at least 10.4 times per year. In other words, they expect new items in the collections of fashion retailers on average every five weeks. When asked how many times a year one purchases fashion, the reply was 9.4 times per year. If we calculate an index based on these two numbers, it would be 90.
This means that consumers expect the retailer to change more often than they would purchase. The variation in the desired number of collection changes in Europe is quite large (see table 3.2).
Swedish consumers, perhaps already used to the speed of H&M, expect something new every 3.5, while Finnish consumers expect something new just over four times per year. French consumers indicate that they want new collections approximately six times per year. Austrians have the highest purchase frequency of fashion, with almost fourteen times per year, followed by the Swedes. The French only buy new clothing six times

TABLE 3.1 Store selection criteria in Europe

	DK	G	F	SF	I	ES	P	GB	S	N	NL	B	A	Total
Good price-quality	8%	9%	11%	12%	8%	8%	8%	6%	8%	9%	8%	11%	11%	8%
Large product range	6%	8%	5%	11%	8%	7%	9%	7%	7%	6%	9%	9%	9%	8%
Good product range	7%	8%	6%	5%	6%	7%	6%	7%	9%	7%	7%	4%	10%	7%
Low prices	6%	6%	7%	9%	5%	5%	4%	4%	8%	10%	7%	7%	8%	6%
Good price promotions	8%	5%	3%	11%	7%	6%	7%	4%	10%	4%	2%	3%	5%	5%
Friendly staff	6%	5%	4%	4%	4%	5%	3%	4%	5%	5%	6%	5%	5%	5%
Good service	5%	4%	3%	8%	5%	5%	5%	5%	5%	6%	4%	4%	5%	5%
No pushy sales people	6%	5%	3%	0%	3%	4%	4%	3%	4%	6%	5%	7%	6%	4%
Pleasant atmosphere	3%	3%	4%	1%	5%	3%	5%	5%	3%	5%	5%	6%	3%	4%
Location	3%	5%	3%	4%	4%	5%	2%	4%	3%	1%	4%	6%	2%	4%
	58%	58%	49%	65%	55%	55%	53%	49%	62%	59%	57%	62%	64%	63%

Source: Frank Quix and Rob van der Kind, 2008

per year. The index for the number of times that new items are expected and the number of time that items are purchased in France is almost 100 and in Italy exactly 100. The index is most positive in Finland with 154, followed by Austria and Portugal with respectively 121 and 118. In Germany the index is the lowest with 72; here consumers expect frequent changes, but they make relatively less purchases.

Even within the clusters of corresponding consumer behaviour there still seems to be big differences (see example 3.1).

TABLE 3.2 Product range changes and purchase frequency for fashion in Europe

	How often do you buy clothing per year?	How many times per year must a fashion store introduce new clothing ranges?	Index
Austria	14.3	11.8	121
Belgium	9.0	9.8	92
Denmark	7.8	8.1	96
Finland	6.5	4.3	154

TABLE 3.2 Product range changes and purchase frequency for fashion in Europe (continued)

France	6.2	6.3	99
Germany	7.3	10.1	72
Italy	10.4	10.4	100
Netherlands	10.6	9.3	115
Norway	10.0	9.7	103
Portugal	10.2	8.6	118
Spain	8.2	10.1	81
Sweden	13.2	14.5	91
UK	7.9	10.1	78
Total	9.4	10.4	90

Source: Frank Quix en Rob van der Kind, 2008

EXAMPLE 3.1 M&S MODE

M&S Mode was one of the first companies that expanded abroad from the Netherlands. The company established branches in Belgium/Luxemburg and Germany. It opted for the strategy of formula export, in other words unaltered transposition of the domestic market concept to other countries. Although the expansion was successful, market research showed that in each of the three countries where M&S Mode was represented, the perception of the formula by the consumer was different. In the relatively fashionable Netherlands, M&S Mode was perceived as a rather stiff store in the middle segment of the market where older women with figure problems shop. In Belgium, where fashion is sold in relatively expensive, independent specialists, M&S Mode is perceived to be a discounter. In Germany, with a classic taste pattern and an extremely price sensitive public, M&S fashion is perceived as an expensive store in the classic fashion sphere. At the end of 2010, M&S Mode was purchased by ERB, the company of retail entrepreneur Roland Kahn, founder and owner of Cool Cat, but also of America Today and, since 2011, the lingerie brand Sapph.

3.3 The retail market in Europe

Table 3.3 indicates the ten largest countries with regard to retail sales in Europe (2009). The five largest European markets together account for 60% of retail sales across all of Europe. The top ten accounts for 80% of all sales, versus 20% for the other 25 countries in Europe. The growth rates within Europe are enormous. Most countries do not get further than a growth of 2 to 3% per year. This means that it takes extreme pain and effort to keep up with inflation. If we look at the underlying trends, it appears that in most countries food retail takes up the bulk of the growth and non-food often cannot keep up with inflation. This means that, in the mature Western European retail markets, there is an actual slight decline of non-food every year. Naturally this does not affect all market players, because there will always be retailers that grow above the market. But it does ensure that parties will lose out on markets that do not actually grow.

TABLE 3.3 Retail sales, excluding vehicles, per country

Position	Country	2005	2010	Share 2010	Growth 2005-2010
		(€1 mld)	(€1 mld)		
1	France	380.8	412.4	14.2%	8.3%
2	Russia	168.8	403.3	13.9%	138.9%
3	United Kingdom	287.5	334.3	11.5%	16.3%
4	Germany	328.7	328.5	11.3%	−0.1%
5	Italy	217.3	216.5	7.5%	−0.4%
6	Spain	193.8	198.3	6.8%	2.3%
7	Turkey	59.3	130.0	4.5%	119.2%
8	Poland	75.4	98.7	3.4%	30.9%
9	Switzerland	78.5	89.6	3.1%	14.2%
10	Netherlands	74.7	83.0	2.9%	11.1%
11	Belgium	55.4	63.5	2.2%	14.6%
12	Sweden	49.2	61.8	2.1%	25.6%
13	Austria	46.6	53.3	1.8%	14.4%
14	Greece	45.8	45.8	1.6%	0.0%
15	Norway	35.6	45.2	1.6%	27.0%
Share of top 15 countries of total Europe				88%	

Source: National bureaus of statistics, Credit Suisse, Eurostat, Deloitte, PWC, Reuters (processed by authors, 2011)

The estimated retail sales in Europe, including Eastern Europe and Turkey, was €2,900 billion in 2010. All amounts have been recalculated at exchange rates at the end of 2011, including the figures from 2005, the growth in Europe is therefore realistic. Turkey and Russia are rapidly developing countries in Europe. Not only do both countries show strong growth figures in retail, but they also have a second communal factor: a huge population that is relatively young. Turkey especially has a very young population. Further economic growth in both countries and the relatively low starting position make them attractive retail countries.

3.4 Online retail in Europe

Internet penetration

The underlying factor for the success of online retail is internet penetration. The development of this is often the explanation for the differences in the world. The number of internet users has quickly increased throughout the years. According to a study by GFK Intomart, 6% of the Dutch households were connected to the internet in 1997. In 2011 this had increased to 88%; the Netherlands is thereby one of the leaders in Europe. The growth of the online population in the Netherlands in the period 2000-2011 was no less than 281%. The average internet penetration in Europe is already over 67%

and had a growth of almost 260% between 2000 and 2011. If we look at the large online markets and thereby the favourable markets in Europe, then this would be Germany (19%) the UK (15%) and France (13%). Together they account for almost half of all internet users in Europe.

TABLE 3.4 Internet users in the European Union

EUROPEAN UNION	Population (2011 Est.)	Internet Users, Latest Data	Penetration (% Population)	User Growth (2000-2011)	Users % EU
		Internet			
Austria	8,217,280	6,143,600	74.8%	192.6%	1.8%
Belgium	10,431,477	8,113,200	77.8%	305.7%	2.4%
Bulgaria	7,093,635	3,395,000	47.9%	689.5%	1.0%
Cyprus	1,120,489	433,900	38.7%	261.6%	0.1%
Czech Republic	10,190,213	6,680,800	65.6%	568.1%	2.0%
Denmark	5,529,888	4,750,500	85.9%	143.6%	1.4%
Estonia	1,282,963	971,700	75.7%	165.1%	0.3%
Finland	5,259,250	4,480,900	85.2%	132.5%	1.3%
France	62,102,719	45,262,000	69.5%	432.5%	13.4%
Germany	81,471,834	65,125,000	79.9%	171.4%	19.2%
Greece	10,760,136	4,970,700	46.2%	397.1%	1.5%
Hungary	9,973,062	6,176,400	61.9%	763.8%	1.8%
Ireland	4,670,976	3,042,600	65.1%	288.1%	0.9%
Italy	61,016,804	30,026,400	49.2%	127.5%	8.9%
Latvia	2,204,708	1,503,400	68.2%	902.3%	0.4%
Lithuania	3,535,547	2,103,471	59.5%	834.9%	0.6%
Luxembourg	503,302	424,500	84.3%	324.5%	0.1%
Malta	408,333	240,600	58.9%	501.5%	0.1%
Netherlands	16,847,007	14,872,200	88.3%	281.3%	4.4%
Poland	38,441,588	22,452,100	58.4%	701.9%	6.6%
Portugal	10,760,305	5,168,800	48.0%	106.8%	1.5%
Romania	21,904,551	7,786,700	35.5%	873.3%	2.3%
Slovakia	5,477,038	4,063,600	74.2%	525.2%	1.2%
Slovenia	2,000,092	1,298,500	64.9%	332.8%	0.4%
Spain	46,754,784	29,093,984	62.2%	440.0%	8.6%
Sweden	9,088,728	8,397,900	92.4%	107.5%	2.5%
UK	62,698,362	51,442,100	82.0%	234.0%	15.2%
European Union	502,748,071	338,420,555	67.3%	258.5%	100.0%

Source: InternetWorld Stats.com, 2011

It may have taken a little longer than was hoped for or expected, but today the internet is on the agenda at every retailer. It may not be the top priority for every retailer to sell over the internet, but with such internet penetration rates, it is already a must for any retailer to be findable on the net for the orientation process alone. The availability of internet will only increase, especially with the further rise of mobile internet. The next generation is growing up with computers and tablets, we should therefore rather refer to

Screenagers them as *screenagers*. In 2020, these screenagers will be between 25 and 30 years old and are entirely screen oriented and not afraid of technology.

Internet generation The generation before them (the *internet generation*) is currently between 25 and 35 years old and, in 2020, will be around 35 to 45: a group that has much purchasing power and consists of young families. These developments alike, it is important that retailers are preparing for a world in which internet is an integral part.

An additional aspect of the role of the internet is that of a source of information. In 2007 the National Internet Research of TNS/Nipo revealed that consumers are increasingly considering the content of companies as reliable information. However, this seems to be changing quickly; consumers are depending more and more on the opinions of others. Information generated by users is becoming ever more important when making choices in the purchas-

Reviews ing process. Consumers find reviews about products, services and stores. In 2010, one in every six consumers stated that they based their store choice on a store review. By 2011 this had increased to one in five, and consumers expect this to continue to increase to one in three. Retailers should be aware of the role that the internet plays. They should therefore consider how they can use reviews in their own internet strategy.

The composition of the population that is active on the internet is becoming more like that of the Netherlands. The gender distribution is already entirely consistent with that of the Dutch population between 16 and 65 years. Regarding the level of education, the less educated are still slightly underrepresented. This is approximately 30% of the Dutch population and 22% of the active internet population. In terms of age structure, the distribution of the online population is quite similar to that of the Dutch population. However, the figures of Blaauw Research and the Dutch Thuiswinkelorganisatie [Home Shopping Organisation] have a classification ranging from younger than 25 years to older than 44 years. Since the class of 44 years and over involves a considerable part of the population and the deviating internet behaviour is established here, this part of the population is slightly more difficult to verify.

The number of Dutch people that purchase online has increased since 2002. In that year, 3,3 million people had made one or more online purchases. According to the Home Shopping Market Monitor of Thuiswinkel.org, this number increased to 9,6 million in 2010 and will exceed 10 million in 2011. This means that 87% of the Dutch population between age 15 and 65 will have made an online purchase. This is in line with online purchases, as measured by Nielsen, in different parts of the world. In Europe an average of 85% of the population made an online purchase in 2010. The only area of the world that remains significantly behind is, not surprisingly, Africa. Actually, online retail has become a very mature business in all corners of the world.

TABLE 3.5 Online goods retail in Europe

	Online retail sales billions of euros	Growth percentage
2005	40.5	
2006	50.0	23.5%
2007	63.6	27.4%
2008	76.1	19.6%
2009	94.9	24.6%
2010	108.8	14.7%

Source: Data monitor (processed Q&A Research, 2011)

The online goods retail in Europe has reflected a so-called *double digit* growth for years. In five years time, the sales in online retail has more than doubled. In 2010, this yielded more than 108 billion euro. This is indeed less than 4% of the entire retail sales in Europe, but online retail is still showing a strong growth, while the entire retail in most countries shows a stagnating growth. The outlook for online retail in the coming years is indeed that it will level off in terms of growth. However, online retail will still be developing much more rapidly than physical retail.

Online retail

TABLE 3.6 Online goods retail in Europe in 2009

	Online retail sales billions of euros	Share
France	20.7	21.80%
Germany	15.5	16.30%
Italy	7.3	7.70%
The Netherlands	3.7	3.90%
Spain	5.6	5.90%
United Kingdom	26.7	28.10%
	79.4	83.70%

Source: Data monitor (processed Q&A Research, 2011)

The largest online markets in Europe are, not surprisingly, also the large traditional retail markets. The six largest online retail countries account for almost 84% of all online sales in Europe. In comparison, to achieve a comparable percentage for the entire retail sales in Europe, one needs the sales of at least twelve countries. The United Kingdom is far ahead in this area. This country not only has the largest share within the European market, but also has the highest online share of retail sales.

3.5 Retail markets in the EU in detail

Several retail markets in Europe are discussed below.

France

France is one of the largest retail markets in Europe. The country has almost 63 million residents. The population, just as in many other countries in Europe, is relatively old, with a complicating factor being that people are going on pension at a relatively young age. In recent years, the retail has had to deal with stagnating growth and sometimes even with declined expenditure. In the early nineties, an average household con-sisted of 2.6 persons, the expectation for 2020 is that this will decrease to almost 2. The total retail expenditure in 2010, according to Mintel, was 403 billion Euros. Food retail in France accounts for 52% of all expendi-tures, the other 48% is spent on non-food. France is the country of the hypermarkets. They also account for a considerable part of food retail. Carrefour is the largest food retailer of the country, followed by E. Leclerc and Intermarche. In the Netherlands, both of the latter would be defined as voluntary chain store. Large non-food players in France are Galeries Lafayette, including Monoprix, the most important rival for the Dutch HEMA, and PPR, amongst other chains such as Conforama, Fnac and Printemps. Darty is the big electronics retailer, but the departure of Media Markt-Saturn, who sold their branches to Boelanger, ensures that Darty remains a formidable competitor. IKEA is also one of the largest retailers, however only active with less than thirty branches. Other large French retailers that are also active abroad are companies such as Leroy Merlin (DIY), Sephora (perfumery) and Décathlon (sport).

United Kingdom

In the online field, the UK is ahead of the other large retail markets in Europe. The economy is under a lot of pressure due to the financial crisis. For the consumers, there was also an increase of VAT in the beginning of 2011. In 2011 it also became clear that the Euro crisis would not leave the United Kingdom unaffected. The stagnating growth in combination with increasing inflation will also get a grip on expenditures. With nearly 62 million residents, the United Kingdom is one of the largest markets, but even here the population is ageing. The number of single households is already a third of all households and this is growing rapidly. This is manifested especially in the larger cities. Retail sales, despite the poor economic circumstances, have managed to be maintained and have been able to keep up with or remain slightly above inflation in general. The growth is especially due to food retailers. Until 2009, they managed to achieve very good annual growth rates averaging nearly 5,5% per year. On average, non-food realised a growth of 2% per year, in which some categories significantly underperformed. In 2010, the total sales in retail amounted to 334 billion euros.

Nearly 49% of all expenditure was spent on food. The largest food retailers in Great-Britain are Tesco, followed by J Sainsbury and ASDA Group, part of the American Wal-Mart. Tesco is the biggest player in the British market and has almost just as much sales as the next two competitors combined. Big non-food retailers include Alliance Boots, Arcadia Group (amongst other TopStore), Argos, B&Q, DSGi (owner of the British Dixons, but also many other electronics chains across Europe),

John Lewis, Marks & Spencer and Next. But foreign parties are also big in the UK, such as the American Amazon, certainly not inferior to many physical retailers. The Irish Primark is a big player, almost four times as big as the Swedish H&M in sales, with much less stores. The other Swedish player, IKEA, is still relatively small considering the size of the country, with less than twenty branches. Superdrug, part of AS Watson, is the third player in drugstores.

Germany

Although German retail has recovered slightly, retail has fallen from being the biggest market in Europe in terms of sales, within fifteen years, to the third position behind France and the United Kingdom. The German retail is dominated by hard discounters (almost 40%) in the food segment. In other sectors within retail, more and more players who maintain low prices as a principle appear to be winning. Germans have become extremely price sensitive in recent years, partly due to the hard discounters in food retail, and demand price aggressiveness from the other retailers. Many foreign retailers consider Germany to be a very attractive market. High income, excellent job opportunities and many residents. But how much does this market vary from any other market in Europe? Most foreign chains either need a great deal of time to adjust to German consumers, or do not make it in the end.

The German population may be the largest within the EU, but it has been decreasing since 2002. Towards 2050 it is expected that the population will decrease by 15 to 20%. The population decline is caused by considerably low birth rates. Because of this, age categories up to 45 have been declining for years. As a result Germany does not just have a rapidly ageing population, but fewer children are also being born into the population. This has implications for retailers who want to settle in this market. Single households almost have the upper hand in Germany. In 2011 they accounted for 40% of all households. If we also consider the two-person households, just under 35% of all households, this means that three quarters of all households in Germany consist of a family of a maximum of two people. The total retail sales in 2010 was almost 329 billion euro, of which around 40% consisted of food sales and the other 60% of non-food retail. The biggest German international retailer is Metro Group, which houses the wholesale trade establishments of Metro, and in some countries Makro, but also for example Media Markt-Saturn and the Real supermarkets in Germany. Other famous big retailers of German origin are obviously the discounters Aldi and Lidl. In addition to these players Edeka, Rewe and Tengelmann are the other big food retailers in Germany. Dm-Drogerie is a big player in the drug store sector and is active in many countries, as well as Rossmann which is part of AS Watson. Germany also has big players that are active internationally in the DIY segment, like Bauhaus and Hornbach. Amazon.de is a big online player in Germany and, as a pure player, was able to claim a place in the top fifteen of all retailers. Zalando is the fast growing new giant as pure player.

Italy

The Italian economy has experienced a very meagre growth in recent years, especially in relation to inflation. Since 2005, consumer prices have increased more rapidly than the economy has grown. The financial crisis has even turned the limited growth into a declining market, where consumer prices also continue to rise. With more than 60 million residents, Italy is one of the largest consumer markets in the EU. In 2010, the retail sales amounted to almost 217 billion Euros, according to ISTAT. 46% of this was due to food retail sales, and the other 54% was from non-food retail. The Italian population is increasing slightly, while the family size is showing a slight declining trend. This seems to deviate slightly from the general trend in the EU. But a closer analysis shows that the number of children is indeed declining. The slight decrease in the family sizes can be explained by the greater extent in which other family members (grandmothers, grandfathers, or brothers and sisters) continue to live within one family. The Italian population is ageing rapidly. In 2010, 20% of the population was already 65 and older and by 2030, this should be far above a quarter of the population. The Italian retail is still largely dominated by independent entrepreneurs, especially in comparison with other Western European retail markets. This is partly explained by the protection that independent entrepreneurs often receive, but also partly from cultural aspects. Foreign chains are gaining ground. French chains especially have in recent decades sought to gain market share in Italy, where, it should be pointed out, they were a little more successful than the others.

As mentioned, retail is still very fragmented in Italy. This is also visible with the big players. In Italy, food retail is still divided over a large number of parties that are often regionally dominant, but have no national coverage. In addition to Co-op, the biggest player, we see many players like Conad, Carrefour, Esselunga and Auchun. The biggest non-food player is MediaWorld, the Media Markt label in Italy. Other big non-food parties are purchasing organisations such as Euronics and Expert. IKEA was the first major retail chain in terms of sales, followed at a distance by Coin department store and fashion group, the French Adeo (DIY) and the Italian Benetton.

3.6 Attractive markets for expansion

The United States still has the most interesting retail market, as this market is the largest individual market in terms of sales, but also because of the low risk that this market brings with it and the relative high growth in expenditures in this market. The growth is always a relative concept and highly dependent on the economic developments and expectations. The United Kingdom is also a lucrative retail market, with a low risk and above average growth. The fastest growing retail markets are China, India and Russia. The risk in these new or emerging markets is higher, compared to the already mature European markets.

Attractiveness   Retail Forward, an American research agency that specialises in retail and is now part of Kantar Retail, has reflected this attractiveness schematically (see figure 3.2). The countries are indicated according to sales, risk and growth.

Retail Forward has made a ranking of thirty retail markets based on an index figure. The higher the index, the more attractive the country is for starting a retail operation. The ranking is based on a weighted index of three measuring units. The first measuring unit is the expected actual

FIGURE 3.2 Best Opportunity Quadrant

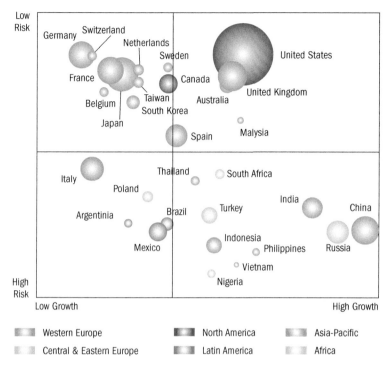

Source: *Retail Forward Inc.*

growth of the retail in 2008. The second measuring unit is the risk involved with trading in the relevant market; this often depends on the economic and political situation in a country. The third measuring unit for the index is the size of the retail market. The weightings are applied as follows: the growth of the market accounts for 55% in the index, the risk of de market for 25% and the market for 20%. This leads to the ranking as shown in table 3.7. In this list, the Netherlands can be found in the fourteenth position, just above Germany. The low positions of Belgium and Switzerland, at respectively 25th and 26th position after Vietnam, Mexico and Brazil, are very remarkable.

TABLE 3.7 Ranking list Retail Forward attractive retail markets

Rang	Land	Regio	Index
1	United States	North America	79
2	China	Asia-Pacific	78
3	Russia	Central-Eastern Europe	76
4	United Kingdom	Western Europe	74
5	India	Asia-Pacific	73

TABLE 3.7 Ranking list Retail Forward attractive retail markets (continued)

Rang	Land	Regio	Index
6	Australia	Asia-Pacific	64
7	Canada	North America	55
8	Malaysia	Asia-Pacific	55
9	Spain	Western Europe	51
10	Japan	Asia-Pacific	50
11	Sweden	Western Europe	49
12	South Africa	Africa	49
13	France	Western Europe	48
14	Netherlands	Western Europe	47
15	Germany	Western Europe	46
16	Turkey	Central-Eastern Europe	46
17	Philippines	Asia-Pacific	44
18	Indonesia	Asia-Pacific	43
19	South Korea	Asia-Pacific	42
20	Taiwan	Asia-Pacific	41
21	Thailand	Asia-Pacific	38
22	Vietnam	Asia-Pacific	38
23	Mexico	Latin America	37
24	Brazil	Latin America	35
25	Belgium	Western Europe	33
26	Switzerland	Western Europe	33
27	Nigeria	Africa	32
28	Poland	Central-Eastern Europe	30
29	Italy	Western Europe	29
30	Argentina	Latin America	19

Source: Retail Forward inc.

Summary

Retail has become a global game. Many retailers look for their growth somewhere else when their domestic market threatens to become too small. There are many different considerations to be made when it comes to where a retailer should or should not branch out. Only allowing yourself to be guided by figures and statistics is certainly not the wisest choice, but you should definitely consider the figures and statistics when making your decision. An expansion plan is not just for today and tomorrow, but it is a medium long and even long term operation. The expectations for market developments are extremely important. It nevertheless remains that the best prospects should also beat the cultural aspects. In retail, a perfect formula in the wrong country can be very costly, especially when you want to begin with a larger number of branches after the first finger exercises.

Due to the small internal market, retailers will at some point have to choose where to go if growth is no longer possible in the domestic market. The expansion question should be answered based on market size, market developments and demographic developments. But softer cultural aspects also play a role. A fascinating process, but necessary in the global game that is retail.

3

4

Trends in retail towards 2020

Towards 2020, retail will change enormously. Together with our colleague's at Q&A Research & Consultancy, we conducted a retail vision study in 2010 for the HBD and Inretail. We are very grateful to both organisations for allowing us to use the results of this study in its edited and updated form. In this chapter we outline why ten important mega-trends will impact retail and why, this time, it will happen much faster than in all the previous periods.
First we will discuss Re'structure (paragraph 4.1). This paragraph explains that five gaming rules, designated by us as 5 R's, have changed definitely and irreversibly. We will then briefly explain the method developed by us, the trend bundle methodology, to perform a trend analysis, with attention to trends, needs and competences. In paragraphs 4.3 through 4.11 we will discuss the ten trend bundles in more detail. All chapters follow the structure of the trend bundles. The developments do not stop today; we will continue to update these trend bundles. We specifically want to ask everyone to support us with this, for the newest trends

visit www.qanda.nl. We finish this chapter by explaining exactly what 5 R's, in combination with the trend bundles, will mean for retail in 2020.

4.1 Re'structure

Retail is constantly subject to change. This certainly does not mean that everything is always thoroughly reorganised, but in the next few years a number of fixed values will change permanently. We are standing on the verge of major changes.

Re'structure has two meanings in English, one is restructuring and the other is retail structure. These two meanings give the best impression of what will be taking place in the next few years. The retail structure in the Netherlands, but certainly also far beyond our national borders, will change. These changes demand a response from retailers. On the one hand, this means an adaption of the retailers' current way of working to the new situation. On the other hand they will have to find another way of dealing with, or even have to adjust themselves to the new retail structure. In this chapter we show that the ten outlined trends will change the retail world more than ever and that the retailers will have to change with it. Obviously not all trends are new and many of the outlined matters are already present everywhere. But are they already acting to these trends? 'No!' is the answer that is given by many retailers, immediately followed by: 'It won't happen that fast! We have already been through this and it didn't happen then either!' This may be true, but five of the most important gaming rules have changed, the building

Restructure

blocks for restructure. We call them 5 R's:

@: Reach
©: Resources
#: Repopulation
€: Revenue
m²: Reshaping

Each item of the 5 R's has changed irreversibly and cannot be compared with the situation ten years ago. As a result, the next ten years in retail will change more than it has in past twenty years! The basics behind the irreversibility of 5 R's lie in the control. The customers, the consumer has taken charge of an increasing portion.

4.1.1   @: Reach

Everyone is online

Reach

In a short time, the internet has gained enormous coverage in the Netherlands. Data from the World Bank shows that the internet penetration in the Netherlands has increased from 44% in 2000 to 93% in 2012 (International Telecommunication Union). For comparison: in the same period, Germany and the United Kingdom have grown relatively fast as well. However, in France, the internet penetration only reaches a level of 83% of the whole population (see figure 4.1).

FIGURE 4.1 Development of internet penetration in Europe

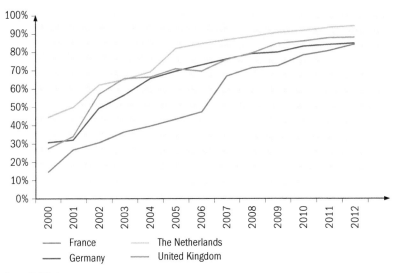

Source: World Bank

In 2010, 70% of the Dutch were online every day (TNS Nipo 2010). The number of access points to the internet (fixed and mobile) is growing. The Dutch currently have 1,7 telephone and internet subscriptions per capita (World Bank, International Telecommunication Union).

Classic and New Internet Time
Over the years, our internet use has changed drastically. We currently distinguish between two forms of internet use: Classic Internet Time, traditional surfing and email use, and New Internet Time, used amongst other social media. In 2010, the Dutch spent 65 minutes per day on Classic Internet Time and 28 minutes on New Internet Time. In two years the internet use in the Netherlands has increased by almost 30%. However, this is entirely benefiting from the New Internet Time. Compared with 2008, classic surfing even declined by 24% (Spot.nl).

New Internet Time

Mobile internet
In 2012, the Dutch population had 1.18 mobile telephones per capita (see figure 4.2). At the end of 2013, the Netherlands was positioned on the fifth place of countries within Europe with the most frequently mobile internet use. The number one is Sweden, where people are as well at home as on their way the most frequently online compared to the rest of Europe (Statistics Netherlands). In 2013, 56% of the Dutch population between 16-75 years old used their mobile to go online. Since Wi-Fi is available on an increasingly number of locations, also the use of laptops on the way increased.

Mobile internet

FIGURE 4.2 Number of mobile telephones per 100 residents

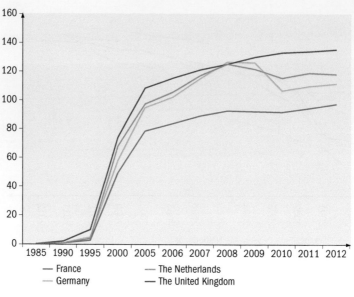

— France — The Netherlands
— Germany — The United Kingdom

Source: World Bank,

Instant internet

Instant
Internet

With the arrival of new communication products with *instant internet*, the world is kicking it up a gear. Instant internet means immediately switching on and going online instead of starting up and waiting. The arrival of the iPad in 2010 was just the beginning of instant internet, with the announced arrival of tablet computers from many other brands. Apple and the parties that use Google's Android as an operating system make it possible to go online with a single click. There will be a permanent change in the communication methods of consumers and thus customers. In late 2010, it was already predicted that the iPad would be the fastest-established consumer electronics product ever and would thus overshadow the DVD-player. According to research agency NPD, the iPad, as a single product, was already considered as the fourth category of electronics in the United States in 2011 (see figure 4.3).

In 2020, online coverage will be instant. You will have access to the world through the internet, always and everywhere. This will create an entirely new situation, which will ensure that the earlier described trends where the internet and communication play a role, are irreversible. While trends in this field have already been mentioned in the past, the situation now is that the matrix is 100% present for the trends to prosper. In addition, the internet phenomenon is growing very rapidly. In 2005 there was no Twitter; today it is being used by more people than there are living in the EU. Barely anyone had heard of Facebook in 2005. In 2005 it was almost a year old and only used by some students. In 2013 it was the largest network site in the world, with more than 1 billion users.
From 2014 Google Glass will be launched widely and makes internet access more instant and interactive then ever before.

FIGURE 4.3 Expected expenditures for electronics in 2011 in the US (in billions of dollars)

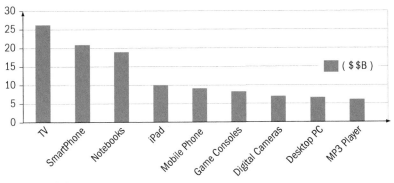

Source: NPD 2010

From WWW to MOA

The newspaper NRC Next opened September 2010 with the following message: 'The world wide web is dead, the newspaper opened with three-week old news'. *NRC* gives a prominent position to one of the most important authors in the area of the internet: Chris Anderson, chief editor of the magazine Wired and author of The longtail (2006). Anderson clearly states in his essay that the World Wide Web (WWW) is on the brink of its final end. The use of the browser will continue to lose ground and this will be in favour of (web)apps. Apps are applications, small programs for mobile telephones and tablet computers. Apps are often based on easy use of information that is available on the internet. The big advantage is that information is available quickly and easily, but with a pre-selection of those who made the (web)app. They made their debut with the arrival of the iPhone a few years ago. According to Anderson, more and more users choose their own personal little web of apps instead of searching through the browser. Internet consumers choose speed instead of the flexibility of the world wide web. We will therefore go through a transformation from WWW to MOA, an internet world that consists of My Own Apps.

(Web)apps

Communication starts with the customer

Consumers, retailers' customers, choose when to take which information and especially if they want to share it. Communication and promotion is a marketing process in which the customers are closely involved and in which they themselves help shape. Increasing transparency has a role in this. The internet has opened up the world and it demands the same from retailers. Consumers will start using social networks more and more often. In 2010, one in six Dutch placed a review about a store and one in three Dutch read such a review. Almost half of the Dutch indicate that their store selection depends on a store review. What is striking when asking about giving reviews is that when a retailer actively requests customers via email to give a review on the store, up to two thirds are willing to do this. Review marketing is also not scary: 70% to 85% of all reviews are positive!

Review marketing

4.1.2   ©: Resources

The world is finite

Resources

The increased information supply and the greater transparency in the internet world have made the finiteness of the world more visible than ever before. The natural resources are limited and that has become increasingly clearer in recent years. Despite the economic recession, we have seen increasing energy prices. Alternatives are indeed being used, but for the time being our demand exceeds the supply. Rising energy prices therefore have a significant influence on the cost of merchandise, not only due to the transport costs, but also due to the manufacturing process.

Commodities crisis

In addition, we also need other commodities to manufacture products. The economic crisis has caused the commodities crisis to slide into the background, but it still plays a role. The global population growth in combination with the economic growth in rising markets will permanently increase the pressure on commodities. This goes further than just oil or iron ore, for example. Even products that we rely on for agriculture and stock breeding is experiencing shortage because of the growing world population. This will gear up inflation in our part of the world, which will have irreversible implications on margins and sales in retail.

Think differently, act differently

The end of the infinite world is irrevocable and affects so much more than just the prices. This will change the way we think about how we are to deal with commodities and waste. In the European Union, the annual e-waste, waste of small electronic and household appliances, devices such as mobile telephones, computers, televisions et cetera, deliver twenty kilos of waste per capita. This waste consists of extremely hazardous substances, which are also very scarce. Up to 2020, the e-waste in China will expand by 400% and in India even up to 500%. While we are trying to create some awareness of this, it should be demanded from the entire world. The heap of rubbish that is also caused by other industries, is considerable. Especially with our urge to try and shorten the product life cycles, hoping to increase the sales rate. The fashion, shoes, sport and housing industry will also have to think about recycling. Not just for the flow of packaging, but also for the products that are sold.

Energy as nagging factor

Energy consumption in stores has increased rapidly in the past few decades. The best excuse is obviously the changing climate; it is getting warmer, and thus more air-conditioning is required. This may be the case, but if we do use air-conditioning, the goal is not to cool the entire street. Environmental awareness starts by ingeniously trapping heat inside the store. There is also a lot to be gained in the area of lighting. In every investment for renovations that is made over the next few years, one should consider the impact of energy consumption. Retailers can save money. At some point, there will be an energy label for every retailer, whether or not visible to the customer. Today, one may think that nobody pays any attention to this, but in 2020 it will be quite different.

Labour is also a resource
Not all resources will decrease on a global scale. Labour will always exist with a further growing world population, but the low-paid labour will continue to move. The urge to always manufacture cheaper, causes these movements. The increased transparency, faster and easier availability of information and the possibility to easily share information, demands additional efforts from retailers. Consumers will be more likely to ask how and where something was manufactured. The 2013 Bangladesh issue was a sad but best example of the transparency and awareness.

4.1.3   #: Repopulation

From pyramid to biscuit barrel
The world population is growing, especially at the bottom of the new markets. Dutch residents are mostly ageing fast as in the rest of Western Europe. In the Netherlands, there was exactly the same number of people over and under 40 years in 2010. Over the next 10 years, this trend will rapidly move up to more than 50 years. The population pyramid with a relatively small group of older people at the top and a large inflow of young people at the bottom is something of the past. The pyramid is replaced by a biscuit barrel, a more and more evenly accumulated population. Over the next 10 to 20 years, we will first have to deal with a much larger group of older people at the top of our population structure, after which the population structure will be distributed evenly.

Repopulation

4

65-plus is growing fast
According to the SCP, the Dutch population will consist of 17 million residents in 2020, of which 10 million will be between the age of 20 and 65. To our current standards, this group is our potential labour force. The group over the age of 65 is growing incredibly fast. Between 2010 and 2020, this group will increase by almost 33% to 3,3 million. For comparison, in this 10 year the entire Dutch population will grow by only 3%. 80% of the growth of our population is also accounted for by its non-Western Dutch citizens (SCP).

The number of young people remains the same
The good news, on the other hand, is that the number of young people hardly decreases, while their composition is rapidly changing. This could mean that retail still has a pond to fish from in terms of labour force. Yet it is not inconceivable that the shortage of staff, and especially qualitative staff, will increase rapidly. The increasing demand for labour forces to take care of the elderly alone will increase more and more, and thus place enormous pressure on the available capacity. On the other hand, the rapidly growing level of education will also take a bigger slice of the cake. In 2020, 30% will have completed college or university training. Is retail then still attractive as an employer?

The number of households is growing
The evolution of the number of households, but especially its composition, will have an effect on retail. According to the SCP, the number of households will increase by more than 7% (see figure 4.4) between 2010 and 2020. The reason for this increase includes the increased number of older people living alone. But the cohabitation of young people later on

Single person households

also plays a role. The number of people that live alone after a period of cohabitation also plays a role, but certainly does not predominate. More households are basically an opportunity for retail, but the supply should match this. Smaller households naturally mean smaller residential environments. The SCP even predicted in 2011 that, by 2050, a point will be reached where the Netherlands will have as many single person households as multi-person households.

FIGURE 4.4 Composition of households in the Netherlands 1960-2020

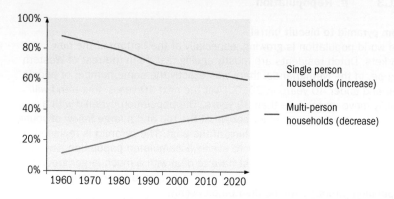

Source: CBS, SCP, 2010

In 2020, four out of ten households will only consist of one person. This means more than three million households.

Urbanisation

Urbanisation

This trend is also reflected in the on-going *urbanisation*. In the last twenty years, the percentage of Dutch that have moved to urban areas has increased from less than 70% to almost 85% (World bank). Especially the 'rural areas', particularly on the Dutch-German border, will show a decre-ase in population in the next 10 to 20 years (CBS). This will have an enormous impact on retail in these areas, since no people equals no trade.

The old entrepreneur

The age structure of the entrepreneurs is ageing even faster in compari-son to our population. In 2010, the average age of entrepreneurs in retail was already 45 years and thus 5 years above the average age of the Dutchman (see figure 4.5). Many retailers are from the baby boom generation. More than 35% of the entrepreneurs is 50-plus. Research by Inretail shows that about 30% of the SME members want to stop between 2010 and 2015. Successors for this group are hard to find. The young generation of entrepreneurs within these families are more and more often making different choices. Buyers for these stores are very hard to find. These SME's often sign up to chain stores, but in the most favoura-ble case they are only interested in the location and not in the company. The lack of succession will be reflected in lower retail space to operate in 2020.

FIGURE 4.5 Composition of entrepreneurs in retail according to age

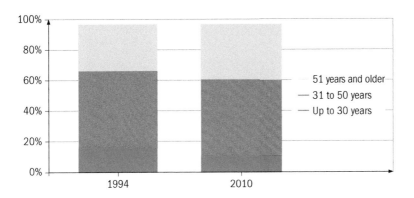

4.1.4   €: Revenue

Stagflation is not a doomsday scenario

Since 2000, expenditures in the non-food retail have shown only a very   Expenditures
limited growth. In thirteen years, this part of retail realised a decrease of
7% in the entire period. In the same period, inflation increased with 29%.
Food retail managed to keep up with inflation in the first period. From
2006, sales in food retail has grown faster than inflation. There are a few
dips, but ultimately food beats inflation. As a result, the doomsday
scenario of stagflation in non-food retail has been a reality for more than
ten years (see figure 4.6).

Moderate outlook

The forecasts for economic growth are very moderate and this even leads
to a decrease in retail sales in the Netherlands. The fear for a so-called
double dip, also known as the W-shaped recession, sounded the alarms in
the summer of 2011. These outlooks follow a period that has shown a
barely rising trend since 2000. In early 2012 the time had come; the
Netherlands ends up in a recession and there are signs of the dreaded
double dip scenario. It is expected that the first five years towards 2020
will show a similar development. There will be hardly any growth in the
retail (stagnation). This combined with the further rise in prices (inflation).
Consumers will be cautious in their purchases and much more price
sensitive, or rather, more so than they were before. They will be more price
sensitive due to the price promotions, especially from food retailers. In
addition, a whole other price realisation arose due to the emergence of
price competitors in several sectors.

FIGURE 4.6 Value development of food and non-food with regard to inflation

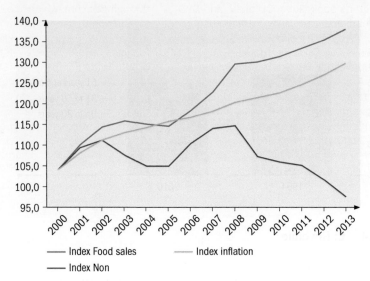

——— Index Food sales   ——— Index inflation
——— Index Non

Source: CBS, HBD, own adaption April 2014

From consumption economy to a user's economy

Is the end of the consumption economy in sight? There seems to be a second movement that plays a role in the development of expenditures. There is a growing group of consumers who feel that enough is enough. While status was derived from materialistic things up to 2007, that seems to have permanently been replaced by buying only what you need. This changing purchasing behaviour is reinforced by the ageing society. The fact that we grow older may be considered beneficial because we have the opportunity to spend for even longer. Moreover, this group has an even higher disposable income, but the big question is how this will develop with the growing problem of the sustainability of pensions. And yet it seems that this group already limits its expenditures in the retail. On the odd occasion that this group spends money, it is more likely to spend it on goods and services that fall outside of the retail sector, such as travelling and health (wellness).

Decreased demand and opportunities in emerging markets

When we look at the housing sector, for example, we see that expenditures in the past decade have actually shown a downward trend (index 96, source: Woonmonitor Inretail). There is a decreased demand and it is not limited to only this sector. In the retail sector in Europe and the United States, the supply has grown too rapidly and the consumer demand has been surpassed. In the West, there are too many stores, too many retailers and too many shopping areas. This means that mainly large retailers in Europe and the Netherlands are going to rethink their investment opportunities. For the time being, Europe will experience stagnating growth in the retail, but simultaneously emerging markets like China and India offer most retail sectors double digit growth rates. International retailers, or retailers with this ambition, can only invest their Euros once. The choices are then obvious to do this in markets that are still growing.

This means that, in Europe, investments will be more conservative and reinvestments will not be made as rapidly. This, in turn, provides opportunities to the local heroes who can better distinguish themselves from chain stores in the domestic market.

4.1.5 m²: Reshape

Too many stores

Over the years, the Netherlands has been cluttered with too many stores. There seemed to be no limit to the number of square metres of stores that we could absorb in our country. This is how different the playing field has become since the financial crisis. Everyone is waking up and facing a world with way too many metres. This financial crisis may not have been the cause of the surplus of stores, but does make the harsh reality clear in no-time. In twelve years, the number of square metres of stores has increased with almost 33% from 21.8 million square metre in 2000 to 28.9 in 2012, and the end is not yet in sight with several millions of square metres in the planning (see figure 4.7).

Reshape

FIGURE 4.7 Development of retail floor space in the Netherlands (in millions of square metres)

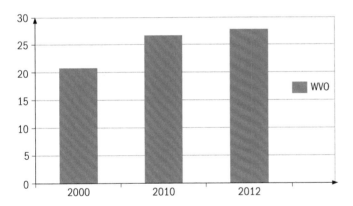

Source: Locatus HBD, 2012

Sales in retail failed to keep pace with this development. Although there was talk of an increase in sales, this was very limited. In addition, this was mainly accountable to food retail. This has several implications. Firstly, this resulted in a lower floor productivity for retailers. In 2000, an average sales of almost €3,340 per square metre was recorded, in 2012 this has dropped to almost €3,100 (see figure 4.8). This trend of declining floor productivity appears to be ongoing, the decline in floor productivity keeps on growing.

In addition to the already existing vacancy, this situation can lead to even more empty space, or lower rent, so that the empty space can at least become profitable again. The floor productivity in the housing sector may not

FIGURE 4.8 Development of floor productivity in 2000, 2010 and 2012 in euro

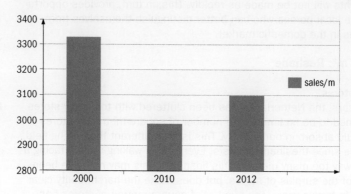

have declined, but a sales of €800 to €900 per square metre in furniture stores for example (one of the lowest in the retail), show exactly how little room there is when there has not been any increase in sales for several years.

Retail mix to be thoroughly reorganised

The idea that segment classifications are relevant to consumers, is an outdated concept. Blurring, or rather the phenomenon that we want to think and do in designated segments, is an idea that is based on the fact that the supply side plays a leading role. That time is permanently behind us. We can anxiously hold on to this, but the consumer does not think in terms of segments, as the supply side may wish. Well before 2020, shopping centres will be composed based on purchasing motives, store needs and target group.

Property owners become retailers

This will also affect how we compose a shopping centre. Shopping centre owners are also kind of retailers. Their product range mix consists of the retail mix of their centre. The product range mix also includes margin mix. Every retailer knows that not every product will leave the premises with the same margin and the same will happen with rental prices in the future. In addition to the composition of segments, there will also be a variation in rental income. There will be more flexibility in determining the rent per square metre than is possible today. Parties who barely pay any rent, but ensure traffic, are certainly not unimaginable. Small independent retailers as local flavour in a shopping centre, but also as someone who can increase the length of stay. A long length of stay ultimately means more sales for the centre and those who realise that, will be rewarded. Sales related rent fits in very well in such a scenario. The Rent Act already provides opportunities for differentiated rent for small independent entrepreneurs, but it is hardly used in the real estate sector.

The retail

Suburb

As mentioned, the retail landscape will change quickly and drastically. The suburb, retail, is detached from the retail mix issues and will continue to develop towards target groups and purchasing motives.

This suburb (peripheral shopping areas) will especially be able to develop better when, for example, it is classified based on lifestyle. Create shopping centres where everything comes together to match a target group: from housing to mobility, and from fashion to sport. Supplemented with qualitative catering and services appropriate to its target group. The opportunity for pure players to launch their physical locations here. Where their extensive range can be physically seen and experienced in combination with the ability to collect products purchased online. After all, the suburb combines accessibility and affordable parking space with large shopping areas.

Prime highstreet locations
The town centre will also undergo a metamorphosis with the further maturation of the internet. When a fifth, a quarter or even more of all retail purchases find their way to consumers over the internet in 2020, this will be reflected in the number of stores. After all, you do not need more stores for less trade. Compared to today, this may easily mean that you need about 20% less stores in a town centre. This will not provide the ghost image of every fifth store in the shopping street being locked. This image will not unfold to us, but the approach routes will drastically change in appearance. Is this new? No, stores have been changing shape in these approach routes for many years, some of these places are not even considered as such any more. The most important thing now is that this will happen much faster than in the previous periods. In addition, the chains will further advance and claim everything that is called A1. Every town centre will then look exactly the same.

Neighbourhood and community centres
This is probably the most interesting of all. In fact, the stores that are closest to the consumer. The interpretation of these shopping areas may change because of this proximity effect, or in other words be close. These are ideally places where new forms of retail services will be presented as a result of internet purchases. After all, where else can we collect the products that are purchased online? Obviously you can have them delivered at your home, but we are never there, certainly not when deliveries are made. The office is another alternative, but in the future this will no longer offer a solution (see the cross channel trend). Retail concepts where we can collect our online purchases will emerge in these neighbourhood shopping centres. Especially fashion retailers can thus become advanced outposts for fashion brands or pure players. It is no longer necessary to have everything in stock, but it is possible to have everything for sale.

City centre

Channel conflict is worth a solution
Actually a combination of coverage and store setup, but appropriate to this game rule, because the channel conflict is all about the old supply-driven thinking. Many traditional retailers and manufacturers still steer clear of cross channel thinking due to channel conflicts. After all, if the manufacturer processes directly to consumers, retailers will boycott this manufacturer. And vice versa, if the retailer goes online with the manufacturer's brand, he will no longer be supplied. This is due to the selective distribution that is basically broken by presenting brands online. Manufacturers want to avoid this at all costs. This way of thinking predates 1990 and no longer fits in the present time. The customer determines where and how he purchases and if a retailer fails to comply, there is always someone else that will play the game following the new game rules.

Channel
conflict

Considerably less metres

By 2020, the number of square metres of stores will decline with at least 20 to 35%. This is partly due to the influence of a loss of sales of at least 20% for the non-food retail to online, but also due to the abundance of retail space. Retail, especially in an environment with very limited growth, cannot afford sub-optimisation of sales per square metre. By definition, retailing means wanting to become more efficient and effective and the same applies for floor productivity. This restructuring will partly occur due to the disappearance of SME entrepreneurs. This also means that the retail landscape will change drastically for the SME and that up to half of the current entrepreneurs will disappear from the scene.

4.1.6   Trend bundle methodology

Trend bundle methodology

To determine the impact of trends on a company's strategy, we used the so-called 3 forces model (see figure 4.9). The 3 forces model consists of the following forces: (macro)trends, consumer needs and competences. Together they are a trend bundle.

FIGURE 4.9 The 3 forces model

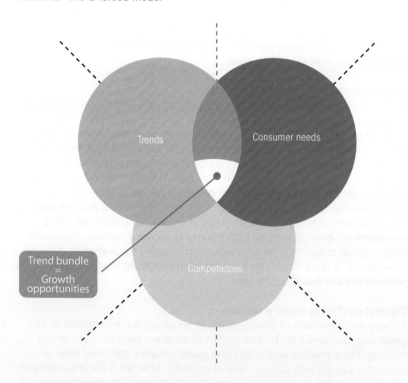

Trend bundles are used to arrive at a vision or strategy for a retail company. Every trend bundle consists of the three forces and the cutting edge of every trend bundle indicates the growth opportunities. The bigger the cutting edge, the bigger the opportunities for growth.

When performing a vision or strategy for a retail organisation or for the entire retail, the forces will always have to be viewed from the model. Trends are not independent, they are meaningless if there is no relationship with consumer needs and if a connection cannot be made with what companies can or should do with them in their business process. The following paragraphs approach the matter every time from the (macro)trend. We then looked at the consumer needs involved in this trend and finally at the accomplishments of retailers. However, with the last macro trend we abandoned this path, because this trend has no immediate impact on consumers and retailers. The consumer needs are briefly outlined and the underlying research data can be found on the website of this book.

4.2 Trend bundle 1: individualisation

Every consumer is an individual with specific demands and needs and wants to be treated as such. Consumers experience 'more of the same' from retailers, while they are clearly less sensitive to mass communication. They seek customisation, they want to help decide. They also want to be able to contribute to what retailers have to offer. They want to have the feeling that the supply was created especially for them. They want to be personally approached with products, facilities and services tailored to their personal requirements.

Individualisation

4.2.1   Sub trends
4.2.1.1 Micro segmentation
Consumers differ with respect to what they buy, where they buy and why they buy. Based on these differences, they have been classified into different target groups. This segmentation of the market is timeless. The way that this is given substance clearly changes under the influence of individualisation. It calls for the recognition of specific needs and require-ments. It is becoming more and more difficult to compartmentalise consum-ers and if this is successful, the groups are becoming smaller and smaller. There is a clearly a trend to 'many markets of one'. In other words, many markets with individuals or small groups of individuals that require their own treatment or approach. This means that there is more room for so-called 'niche players' who choose to operate in a small part of the market.

Micro segmentation

4.2.1.2   Mass customisation
Consumers are becoming increasingly demanding. With their individual preferences and needs, they require more and more customisation, or products or services that are customised to their individual preferences and living conditions. However, the majority still has a uniform taste. Retailers respond to this development by delivering mass customisation They are thereby able to deliver customised mass production to the consumer. Or rather, to create the feeling that customisation is being delivered. It is possible to create a basic product that is suitable for large groups and simultaneously, through minor adjustments based on personal wishes and needs, present this as customisation. This is already being applied in many industries. In the fashion industry, Suitsupply is an example of delivering affordable mass customisation. Designonstock applies this in the housing sector. At Sparta it is possible to design your own personal limited edition bicycle.

One-to-many approach
Individualisation has accelerated under the influence of technology and automation. In addition, consumers are becoming less sensitive to mass

One-to-many approach

communication. These developments contribute to the fact that it has become essential to use a personal approach for consumers. They no longer want to be bothered with the offers in which they are not interested. An important role for an online retailer is getting to know consumers based on their behaviour and responding to this by offering relevant products and services. It is about creating a feeling among consumers that they are being given a one-on-one treatment. In practice this comes down to a one-on-many approach. Customers are communicated with based on groups with corresponding characteristics.

4.2.1.3   The consumer as manufacturer

A product is an extension of a person's personality. Consumers want to add a personal touch to the product. They want to be more and more like a manufacturer, where they can indicate how a product should look or taste. In the fashion industry one can increasingly compile clothes or shoes based on personal preferences. Nike ID is a successful example of this as is Converse with your own customised All Stars. 'Design your own life' from IKEA is a good example within the housing sector. In the food industry, consumers can produce their own chocolate at Rittersport and Lays has involved its clients in the development of new flavours. Consumers can compile their own fragrances at Rituals. This trend which is already visible, will continue developing in the coming years, especially with the rise of 3D printing solutions. As HEMA and Media Markt are offering.

4.2.1.4   Service demand

Service demand

There is a growing demand for service and attention. The notion of personal is central. This may relate to a product range that is tailored to the individual, but it is mainly about the personal approach. Hospitality and hostmanship are very important. It's all about hospitality, giving people a feeling that they are welcome and that they are special. An example is the use of stylists in furniture stores that advise individuals in decorating their homes. In the fashion industry, WE uses a style advisor in several stores. Hereby freeing time for the individual and giving the customer individual advice. In addition, special shopping evenings are organised on which special style advisors are present. The customer is the centre of attention and feels special. Rituals also applies the personal touch in the store by creating small personal moments. For example, Rituals has polarising scents among which consumers can almost certainly find something for themselves. In the housing sector, design programs are being used increasingly more often. Kitchen stores and interior decorators use a projection screen so that the decor of the room or kitchen can be designed directly with the client.

4.2.2   Consumer needs

4.2.2.1   Need for customisation

Consumers need an individual approach. On the one hand this is possible by offering products that are tailored to their wishes and needs and, on the other hand, through a personal approach.

Customisation consists of the ability to personally customise products according to personal taste and style. In addition to this need for customisation, there is a clear willingness to pay extra for such products (see table 4.1).

TABLE 4.1 Need for customisation

	Total
Need for products that are tailored to wishes and needs	60%
Willingness to pay extra for these products	52%
Importance of product customisation according to personal taste and style	75%
Willingness to pay extra for these products	49%

The personal approach consists of receiving relevant information tailored to the needs of the customer. Nearly half of consumers are willing to reveal some of their background in exchange for such information supply. With the rise of the smartphone, it will be much easier for retailers in the future to give substance to this customer need and the customer can be personally approached.

4.2.3   Competences individualisation

Responding to the trend towards individualisation is often simpler than that retailers think. The competences that are necessary to make maximum use of this trend are usually already present in the organisation. For example, information required to know the customer is often already present, but still has to be used and recorded correctly. Customer segmentation and customer provenance research are very important and useful methods. Based on this, one can then choose smaller target groups or niche markets. A second development that comes from this main trend is the demand for service. Making customers feel welcome should actually be the core competence in retail. Hospitality, a personal approach and offering service should be core values of every retailer. The process of properly assisting a customer begins by listening carefully. Some industries even take this a step further by having a customer assist in designing and creating new products. The consumer is then co-producer, also known as prosumer. Retailers can also involve customers in what should be purchased or what should be placed on the shelves. In the spring of 2012, Wal-Mart started the program getonthe-shelf.com where customers could decide which products they wanted in the product range. Giving customers the opportunity to add a unique touch to mass products, by personalising products, is also very close to the trend towards individualisation. One step further in meeting individual customer requirements is offering 'Made to measure'-customisation, in other words mass customisation.

Developing competences or continuing to use them to fulfil individual customer demands will be more important in a displacement market where the consumer has the choice and information on where to get it.

4.3 Trend bundle 2: cross channel

The internet as sales channel offers many new opportunities in retail. Internet is an important motive for traditional (offline) sales channels when they are able to properly coordinate the online and offline sales channels that are available. An important game rule is that consumers have an

Cross channel

increasing desire to purchase products at any time and through every channel.

4.3.1   Sub trends

4.3.1.1   Everything, everywhere and always

Everything, everywhere and always: that is what today's consumers want. This has accelerated through the internet. The channel is no longer important. A store is a store, whether it is online or offline. Consumers want to be able to buy always and everywhere. This is an enormous challenge for the traditional offline retailers, because a cross channel strategy will win from online stores in the future. Retailers should offer many ways of selling in order to respond to consumer needs.

4.3.1.2   Mobile purchasing

In the United States, the number of mobile internet users exceeds the number of internet users over the computer. Morgan Stanley (www.morgan-stanley.com) predicts that this will be the case within five years. Under the influence of the increasing use of mobile internet, mobile purchasing will expand tremendously. Applications are or will be designed accordingly. Kieskeurig.nl offers consumers an iPhone application that allows them to scan or enter barcodes. This shows them prices, product characteristics and reviews of the product. In a few simple steps, they can buy the desired product at the best price using their mobile telephone. The mobile smartphone also offers opportunities for new forms of marketing. When passing or entering a store, consumers can receive deals or information on behalf of this store. The smartphone is becoming an increasing part of the orientation and purchasing process.

Mobile payment
At the moment, most mobile payment systems are still small-scale. Examples are SMS Cash or My Order. This will automatically open a bank account into which the consumer should then deposit an amount. The mobile telephone can be used to deposit money in this account. The telephone can also be used to execute payment orders. In a few years, mobile payment will be available for many more consumers. Major banks introduce mobile payments, and PayPal is introducing mobile wallets as in Google. NFC payment systems will be introduced. The goal here is that you can hold your mobile telephone against a payment terminal at the checkout and that the payment is then processed.

4.3.1.3   The conversion takes place elsewhere

Consumers visit the stores to see, feel and experience the product and decide at a later stage whether or not to purchase the product. If the transaction does not take place in the store and they continue their purchasing process online or elsewhere, the store runs the risk of losing them permanently. In other words, the store is the showroom, but the transaction takes place elsewhere. The role of the store is changing under the influence of the internet. Stores are becoming more of a platform than a place for holding stock.

4.3.1.4   Convenience while shopping

The convenience factor is becoming increasingly important when shopping. This is a trend that has been going on for years. The importance of convenience is increasing by the lack of time that consumers have to store. They do not have enough time for everything that they want to do. The increasing use of internet also plays a major role within that convenience. Business models need to be increasingly more adapted to the convenience factor. This will be a huge challenge for both online and offline retailers over the next few years. Some online retailers, including Wehkamp, have already invested on the convenience factor. They realise that the internet market has matured. Internet stores have developed from an ordering channel into actual stores that are able to inspire consumers and allow them to expe-rience. A good combination of technology, convenience and emotion are important for an online store to be successful.

4.3.2   Consumer needs

Almost 90% of consumers make online purchases. When we look at the visitors' frequency of online stores, we see that this has increased in recent years and that it will reflect a further increase towards 2015. The same applies for the online purchase frequency. Since the majority of consumers already purchase online, the online growth potential is found especially in the number of orders. However, this varies greatly per industry, for the underlying data please refer to the website of this book. For consumers, the channel selection is not as relevant. Almost half indicated that it is not important whether they buy from an online or offline store. In 2015 the channel discussion will be entirely obsolete, customers will visit and purchase cross channel and will not think in terms of channels (see table 4.2).

TABLE 4.2 Development of the various channels

Visit preference	2010	2015
Offline	29%	27%
Online	23%	25%
Not preference	48%	49%
Purchase preference	**2010**	**2015**
Offline	31%	25%
Online	20%	24%
Not preference	49%	51%

There are other motives to purchase online and offline. The most impor-tant motives to purchase online are mainly based on convenience and price. Consumers mainly want to shop when it suits them. The most important motives to purchase in a physical store include the desire to see and experience the product. In addition, both the delivery and shipment charges and the need to take the product right away with them plays an important role.
Consumers need to be able to buy smoothly and easily from retailers, where the channels are no longer separated, but integrated. The next big challenge for retailers is already lurking, namely mobile commerce. At the moment, only a small portion of consumers have made a purchase through via mobile telephone. This will grow tremendousy in the coming years. This

applies for both consumers that already have a mobile telephone with internet, as well as consumers that have a mobile telephone without internet (see table 4.3). More than half of all consumers will purchase via mobile telephone and it is expected that this will be considerably higher than indicated below, since the penetration of smartphones is growing much faster than the forecasts have indicated.

TABLE 4.3 Mobile commerce

	Total
Purchased via mobile in 2010	12%
Purchased via mobile in 2015 (no mobile internet yet)	52%
% Purchased via mobile in 2015 (already mobile internet)	64%

4.3.3   Competences

Customers do not think in terms of channels, they do not buy in a channel, they buy from a brand. Consumers orient and buy cross channel. Retailers should be aware that channels are secondary to the fulfilment of the information and buying needs of a customer. Consumers are always and everywhere online everywhere and always have access to all information. This means that consumers can also gain access to information indepen- dent of the platform, using their mobile telephone, tablet or PC. It is Any Time, Any Where, Any Device (AWATAD), and this means information is also available on mobile websites and apps. Retailers should also respond to the commercial part of this cross channel trend. This means offering purchasing options through all channels, making it possible without barriers to the customer. All possible combinations of purchasing and collection should be possible. Online ordering and collection in the store, ordering in the store (from a larger online product range) and delivery to your door, ordering mobile and collecting at a click-and-collect point from the local shopping centre. This can be done everything by yourself, or by working together with other market participants that offer solutions for a cross channel approach.

Cross channelling also leads to a new look at the conversion, the percent- age of visitors that eventually buy. As a result of the internet it is not only the actual conversion, also known as expenditure conversion, that plays a role, but also the step before: the decision conversion. The decision conversion is the first step towards a paying customer. Being visible in this first phase of the purchasing process is of vital importance in a world where internet is almost by definition the start of the search process for a consumer. From TOMA (*Top of Mind Awareness*) we move on to TOIA (*Top of Internet Awareness*). Name recognition has always been important in a crowded market, but now name findability is important. Those who are placed at the top of the search engine based on relevance also have a chance to participate in the remainder of the purchasing process. Especially in a world where the number of entrants continues to increase, it is very important to be found. Retailers have several opportunities to increase their findability, but there is one that will become more important and should be incorporated in the business process: review marketing. When consumers go on social media in an increasingly growing number, retailers will also

AWATAD

TOIA

have to incorporate these 'channels' in their cross channel approach. In some cases this may be for commerce, actually selling goods, but usually this is limited to informing customers or personally following information given by customers about the retailer. Especially young people up to 30 years make frequent and intensive use of the new media. Therefore, it can be very useful to give young people the opportunity within a retail organisation to get the most out of this development. The question for the cross channel trend is whether retailers should personally develop these competences, or whether they should work with parties that already have them. Many of the competences will eventually have to be located within the retail organisation, because the entire retail will develop as cross channel. However, scale plays an important role.

4.4 Trend bundle 3: digital super consumer

The orientation and search process of the consumer has changed completely under the influence of the internet. The consumer has become a well-informed expert in more and more areas. Online and offline information sources are used in combination in order to find the correct information. The increasing use of social media, forums and review sites reflect this. Consumers give their opinions, listen to others, learn from each other and look for likeminded people with similar characteristics and/or needs. The impact of the use of social media is increasing. In the past, 40 people would hear about a bad experience with a store at a birthday party. Now, thousands of consumers see this opinion because it is shared via internet. We are about to face a generation of consumers that are fully accustomed to communicating with each other and obtaining information using this kind of media. The next generation, the fifteen-year-olds of today, cannot be compared to the current forty plus generation. We have to deal with the pre-internet and post-internet era in which consumers use an entirely different way of orientation and information. For retailers, this means ingeniously using both old and new forms of media.

Digital super consumer

4.4.1   Sub trends
4.4.1.1   Multi channel search process
Consumers use the internet increasingly more often to orient themselves, and this trend will continue in the coming years. They pay a visit to Marktplaats, search on Google, compare products on choosy.nl, visits the website of a manufacturer or brand, or go to an online store. Simply paying a visit to a physical store is still possible. They use many information sources. To what extent they use them and in which order this happens, varies per consumer and per purchase. Internet is and will be a very important mean of communication for retailers and should also be considered an extension of the store. The retailer should make sure that he is visible in both worlds. For offline retailers this is a way into the online world, for online retailers this is a way into the offline world. This does not mean that online stores have their own physical store. They may also choose to be visible in a store by working together with brands and retailers. Or simply traditionally through the mailbox. The Wehkamp magazine is a good example. With the magazine they are able to reach offline consumers through the mailbox.

Multi channel search process

4.4.1.2   Word of mouse

Word of mouse

'Word of mouth' is or will be replaced by 'word of mouse'. Consumers used to share their experiences about products and stores with each other through physical contact, for example during birthday celebrations. Thanks to the internet there are no more geographic barriers and consumers from all over the world can exchange information with each other whenever they want to. By a simple click at the mouse from your computer, hence the term 'word of mouse'. The traditional circle during birthdays still exists, it has just grown significantly and is accessible at any time of the day.

Infobesitas

Infobesitas

The internet has resulted in an overflow of information for the consumer. There is so much information available that it is becoming more and more like an impossible task to find what you are looking for. A simple search in Google shows that there are more results. In short, there is too much information for consumers. Retailers can help consumers filter this information in their search. Google is dominant in the area of filtering and searching. And Google continues to develop in this area. The more Google grows, the more specific search engines are born. After all, bigger means even more information, which means that 'infobesitas' is just around the corner. There are parties that are responsive to the need for specific information. Such parties already exist and more will follow. A hotel can be found on TripAdvisor. Wikipedia is the free encyclopaedia that is often used. A store can be found in a flash on Wugly.nl or Yelp.com.

Reviews

Consumers are looking for certainty and confirmation that the choice for the product or the store is the right one. A review on a product, store or service is an ideal tool. Despite the need for information, consumers still do not share their experiences enough with others. In this regard, the 80-20 rule applies to reviews. Many people read them, very few people post them. At present, reviews are still very product-oriented because this is efficient and easy. New applications such as Yelp (www.yelp.com) and Foursquare (www.foursquare.com) show that this is also heading more and more towards suppliers or locations. So far, these are mainly hotels and restaurants, but this will definitely also be applied to stores. On Wugly.nl consumers can already leave reviews and gather information about stores. This gives them insight in the performance of the stores. It also gives retailers insight in their own performance. In addition, reviews can also be used by retailers and brands to build confidence among consumers who have no experience with them.

4.4.1.3   Social, online networks

The need to belong to something is part of being human. That in itself is nothing new. But the way that this is done has changed completely with the rise of social, online networks. This rise is taking place faster than it was ever anticipated. Within a few years' time, more than 1 billion consumers joined Facebook. The number of Twitter-users is increasing very rapidly at the moment. WhatsApp is beating each month its own record of number of messages. Such social networks affect that way that consumers communicate with each other. They also support group behaviour. They are especially fun for consumers when they use it in groups and are thus mutually engaged. Consumers with similar needs and interests find each other here. National and international virtual networks of groups, which influence one other at a distance, are created. Consumers will choose more and more with whom they want to get in touch. 'Unfriending' is a trend where they decide for themselves with whom interaction is or is not interesting. This relates to people, but also to stores and brands. Networks are also self-created. For example, there is a very popular Facebook page about Action that was created by consumers themselves.

Branded social networks

The initiative for creating social networks was at first mainly that of consumers. This is now used more and more often by brands and stores. Consumers can join, share information and ideas with each other and ask and answer questions. Starbucks (www.mystarbucksidea.force.com) is a good example. The idea is that the customer knows best of all what they expect from Starbucks. Starbucks invites the customer to share this with them. It is also possible through Facebook. IKEA launched a successful Facebook campaign in Sweden. The first person to see a new showroom model in a store and post the photo on Facebook, was given that showroom model. Not only did this result in more visits to the store, but also in more advertising. Such networks and campaigns created by brands and stores will be much more common in the future. Administrators of such networks should be critical when it comes to the question with whom they come into contact. This does not mean that any random person can join a network. People have to meet certain characteristics or conditions. Thus forming groups of link minded people. Retailers want to come into contact with their target group, which is not everyone.

Branded social networks

Social shopping

Shopping is often a social affair. Shopping with others is just so much more fun than doing it alone. Social interaction while shopping is now also possible online. Consumers can meet each other online, come up with ideas and exchange opinions. A new argument for why it is not necessary to hit the streets. Facebook enables consumers to store online with others. For example, Levi's integrated Facebook into their website. Visitors to the website can indicate whether they like a product through a 'like'-button. This information is shared with other visitors, including the Facebook friends of the relevant person. Storewithyourfriends.com is another good example of applying social interaction while shopping online. In three steps, you can start an evening of online shopping.

Social shopping

4.4.1.4   Augmented Reality

Consumers have an increasing need to see what things look like in real life. Does this couch even look right in my living room? Does this kitchen really fit in my house? Does this coat really match my outfit? Do I look good with these glasses? Through Augmented Reality, or added reality, retailers and brands are increasingly more capable of answering such questions. Through the use of the internet and mobile internet in particular, the application and the use of Augmented Reality has accelerated.

Augmented Reality

This combines real pictures with virtual pictures. IKEA created an Augmented Reality application for the iPhone. Consumers can use it to see if a piece of furniture really looks good in their living room. In the fashion industry, Augmented Reality is implemented in combination with photos or a webcam. Ray Ban developed the Virtual Mirror, making it possible to try on and view a pair of glasses at home. Zugara enables consumers to virtually try on clothing. Holition creates tools for all kind of retailers to see how bracelets, rings or watches would look like. Which means that, instead of two worlds, we now have to deal with three. Offline, online and virtual.

4.4.2 Consumer needs

Nearly two out of three consumers currently use the experiences and opinions of others in determining the product selection. To determine the store, this applies for one out of two consumers. Despite the frequent use, only 32% of the consumers indicate that they also share their experiences and opinions on products with others. This is even slightly lower for stores (see table 4.4).

TABLE 4.4 Importance of reviews

Use of experiences and opinions of others online	Total
Determine product selection	61%
Determine store selection	49%
Share experiences and opinions with others online	**Total**
On products	32%
On stores	26%

With all the information that is available online, especially in combination with the start of many shopping trips online, there is a certain oversupply of information. Consumers have to deal with an overload of information. Nearly half of the consumers indicate that they often cannot find what they are looking for because of the large quantity of information online. The challenge for both offline and online retailers is to lower the search cost of consumers and to help them in making decisions.

Despite experiencing information overload, we see that many consumers have joined a social network (see table 4.5). Based on consumer expectations for the future, it appears that all networks are growing except for Hyves – where the number of accounts will clearly decline. In addition, new online networks that we do not even know yet or that do not even exist yet, will emerge, for example, in 2010 Google+ had no users while it is now a rapidly growing network.

TABLE 4.5

Social networks	2010	2012	2015
I have a Twitter account	14%	18%	28%

I have a Hyves account	51%	38%	26%
I have a Facebook account	30%	49%	53%
I have a Google+ account	-	24%	33%

Consumers need information and they happily share this with others. Consumers also trust this information more than that from, for example, the retailers themselves. However, the quantity of information is difficult to process and the consumer needs help to quickly and easily make the right choice.

4.4.3 Competences
The digital super consumer is better informed than ever before and is online for almost every shopping trip, whether this is to purchase fashion, electronics or furniture. How should retailers respond to the information need of consumers? And how can retailers help make useful information accessible to their customers?

The customer journey of consumers has changed. Indeed, the search often starts online, where consumers are simultaneously confronted with an overload of information. For the retailer it revolves around using the right mix of information sources, such as printing, the store, radio, TV and the internet. Every industry has different characteristics per medium for each phase in the purchasing process. Properly understanding the characteristics and following them in time ensures that the retailer always has the best media at the start. The retailer should help the customer in his search process and thus do nothing more than that which was always done in the store. In an environment where information is present in abundance, this means applying infodising. Organising information, just as merchandising is organising the supply in the store. In other words, retailers should also make pre-selections online by filtering and offering options. The ability to quickly filter the selection based on logic search criteria is indispensable.

Being found online has become very important and will only increase in importance. Search engine optimisation has become an important competence, as well as review marketing. Reviews help consumers in the search and purchasing process. Retailers should make their customers ambassadors. Allow customers to tell you what they think of the products and of the retailer too. Reviews are especially good content for the website. The retailer helps his customers to easily make the right choices. Moreover, the customers help the retailer and his suppliers to improve the products and to compile the ideal product range. The chain is thereby reversed. The customer guides the retailer when it involves the question of which products should be removed from the product range. Customers do not only filter on the website of the retailer; they often use review sites and comparison sites for the filtering process. Gathering product reviews and posting them on comparison sites increases the findability on the internet. Actively asking for reviews on the stores and having these comments posted on review sites also increases the findability. In most cases, the reviews are positive, but sometimes improvements will also be suggested. Being open for criticism and converting it into an opportunity for improvement will lead to an improvement of the performance of the retailer. Getting started with optimising the search and purchasing process of the customer is becoming increasingly more important. In part, this means developing new competences in the area of infodising, but these are in fact an extension of one of the core competences of retailers merchandising. It may be sufficient to purchase competences or techniques, yet individual new functions should still be ensured when purchasing.

4.5 Trend bundle 4: the end of the pyramid

End of the pyramid

The composition of the population is changing. The number of older people are increasing and this generation of 'new elderly' forms the largest retail target group in the coming decades. They are affluent elderly, who feel and act younger. They have new demands and require other products, services and facilities, where a single solution is not enough. They divide their time differently. It is not wise to consider them as a homogenous group. Their expenditure pattern is partly determined by their age, health, income and amount of free time. The 'one size fits all' as a solution for older people is a thing of the past. In addition to older people who are acting younger, we also have younger people who are acting older. They mature faster and become independent much faster. Partly because of this, the number of households is increasing while households are also getting smaller. Finally, the development in the number of immigrants also affects the composition of the population.

4.5.1   Sub trends
4.5.1.1   Shift of gravity
The Netherlands is dealing with an ageing population. The population concentration shifts elsewhere. 2010 is the pivotal year. In 2010, the Netherlands had exactly the same number of residents older than forty as residents younger than 40. This is illustrated in figure 4.10. Until 1970, there was still a population pyramid. The centre of gravity of the population was at the bottom. This centre of gravity shifts and therefore we can no longer speak of a population pyramid. In 2010, the population peak starts at 32 years and runs through to 50 years. In 2020, the peak will start at 42 years and run through to 60 years. Therefore, the centre of gravity of the population in 2020 is 10 years older than today.

The same trend is visible in all Western European countries, in some even faster than in the Netherlands.

FIGURE 4.10 Age structure of the Netherlands 1970, 1990, 2010 and 2020

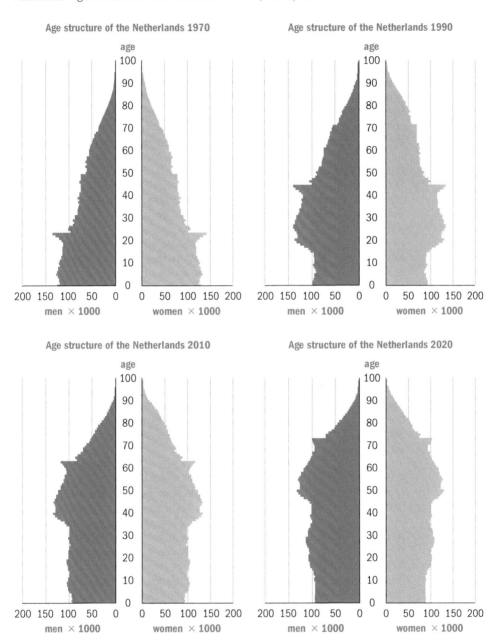

Multicultural society

The Dutch population is growing. In 2020, the number of residents will exceed 17 million. This growth is largely accountable to immigrants. In 2010 20% of the population consisted of immigrants. This increases to 23% in 2020 and 29% in 2030. This is evident from the population forecast of the CBS. An immigrant is someone who has at least one foreign-born parent. The growth is mainly caused by Non-Western immigrants. These immigrants are younger than the Western immigrants and natives. A trend seen in many other Western Countries. Because the immigrant population is growing, this is becoming an ever more interesting target group for retailers. Therefore, good insight into the behaviour and preferences of immigrants is very important. Responding to this demand often requires an adjustment of the product range. This is implemented in the food sector. Jumbo supermarkets, for example, have a fresh meats product range of Marhaba Halal Food in forty of their stores. By doing this, Jumbo wants to cater better to the needs of the Muslim consumer. The immigrant population also affects the composition of the retail landscape. More and more immigrants are starting their own stores. They focus mainly on the immigrant target group.

Calendar age is history

We are indeed getting older, but we are not behaving older. Older people often feel younger for longer and this is reflected in their purchasing behaviour and lifestyle. Older people exercise more regularly, are less traditional than the last generation and also purchase products that are trendier. On the other hand, some young people are behaving much older or are more mature. They leave home earlier, live independently and have to make adult decisions much sooner. In the future, the living mentality of consumers will be decisive and not the calendar age.

4.5.1.2   Smaller households, smaller living

The number of households is increasing. But the households are getting smaller and consist of fewer people. People wait longer to live together or do not do it at all. People are waiting longer and also having fewer children. People also tend to live much 'smaller'. This applies especially to the cities. Small space living is therefore also an important development. For the housing sector, probably even more important than ageing. Smaller households and smaller living requires corresponding products. Small, snug and sociable. The single person household becomes the new norm in all urbanised area's in Europe.

4.5.1.3   The end of the 'one size fits all' mentality

Older people need other products. Being fit and healthy is becoming more and more important for older consumers, and stores and product developers will have to respond to this even more. More attention to sport, wellness and leisure. One single product that is suitable for all older people is a thing of the past. Older people need specific products that suit them in terms of age, but also suit their (younger) age feeling in terms of appearance and design. Within the housing sector, there is a need for homes and products that can withstand the life-cycle changes over time. This relates to, amongst others, height adjustable products. But recreation, comfort, relaxation and ergonomics are also becoming increasingly more important. With regard to clothing, it involves products of which the style is adjusted, but corresponds with the current fashion. Retailers and designers will respond to this.

Service demand

Service demand

The demand for service and attention is increasing. Luxury, comfort and ease are important for the older target groups. Keywords are hospitality and hostmanship. It's all about hospitality. Giving people the feeling that they are welcome and that they are receiving personal attention. Service demand does not only relate to stores. Shopping areas can also provide in this. For example parking opportunities. The Netherlands can look at countries such as Italy for a good example. There, parking garages have broader paths and lights indicate where an open space is available. Quite simple, but very effective. It is not about the measure of service that is offered. But rather the quality of the service. Older target groups have a greater need for accessibility, safety, high-quality stores and good personnel. The town centres will therefore become somewhat less favoured by this group. Smaller and regional district centres are becoming more attractive to this group. And not only older people have this need. This also applies for younger people. However, in most cases the definition of service will be quite different. With them, it will be based more on speed and knowledge.

4.5.1.4   New and old elderly
The elderly people at present are an important target group for retail. Older consumers now have a lot of free time, low financial costs and a lot of money to spend, making them interesting. The generation of older people will be very different. Future older people have a very different lifestyle and demand pattern compared to presently older people. They have much less savings, have more credits and therefore also have much less to spend than the current older generation. In addition, they are more modern than the current older people and grew up in an entirely different information world. Both the old elderly and the new elderly cannot be approached as a single group. Available time, life stage and lifestyle determines what people find important. This requires a different approach.

Older employees
Ageing not only affects consumers, but also the workforce of the retailer. Employees are older, cost more and have to be replaced eventually. Especially the latter is an exceptional challenge for retail in the coming years. Furthermore, many entrepreneurs are reaching retirement age. The problem of succession then comes into play. If there is no succession, certain gaps will develop in the market. It is likely that this will be filled by chain stores. As indicated, succession is a problem, but the recruitment of new entrepreneurs is also a problem. The youth of today do not see the retail sector as an interesting sector to make a career. 'It is perfect for a part time job, but not for 'real' work'.

4.5.2   Consumer needs
According to consumers, it's not about their actual age, but rather about their emotional age. Half of consumers feel younger than they actually are. This has tremendous implications for determining how to communicate with target groups.
On average, the perceived age (feeling age) of the target group is ten years less than the actual chronological age. For research data, please refer to the website of this book. Therefore, determining target groups based on actual age is not the most logical approach. Yet we see that purchasing behaviour is adjusted to age and that the need for service, improved accessibility and private parking increases.

4.5.3   Competences
The changing population structures calls above all a changing mindset. The retailer can no longer determine the actual age of his customers based on

the behaviour and attitude of his customers. Young people may act older and older people may act younger. This means that the retailer should let go of the traditional way of segmenting and selecting boxes. It is all about mentality and lifestyle. The retailer should address his potential customers based on that.

The retailer should immerse themselves in the product use of his customer; older people require different product features than young people. The composition of the population, more single households, will also affect the size of the living space and therefore also the products that are used in those houses. Product range composition will therefore be affected by the target group.

Different target groups will also have different service needs, especially the older target group will have a greater demand for services and this means that retailers who want to focus on this group, will have to respond to this with their staff. The further urbanisation will cause the average age in large cities to decline, resulting in more single households and resulting in the development of a larger multicultural mix. All these developments contribute to paying more attention to the composition of the store staff. Retailers should ensure that the store team is a good reflection of the customers. The changing composition of the population in Western European countries will differ more greatly within the countries. This requires adjustments in store teams, product range compositions and to offered facilities and services.

4.6 Trend bundle 5: glocalisation

Glocalisation

Glocalisation stands for the combination of global and local. There are increasing opportunities for retailers to purchase and manufacture products globally. Retailers are more and more active in different countries. More and more global strategies are being developed in terms of efficiency and effectiveness. In addition, people are aware that there are local differences and needs, and that consumers want them to respond to these. This means a global strategy with room for local adjustments.

4.6.1 Sub trends

4.6.1.1 Local shopping

Local shopping

Consumers want to shop locally and close by. This applies to both daily grocery shopping and a shopping trip. The willingness to travel is greater for a shopping trip. Due to a lack of time and the need for convenience, consumers do not want to travel far in order to shop. This trend will continue in the coming years. Smaller shopping destinations are becoming more attractive to consumers. They can easily park there, they feel safe and it takes little time to reach the shopping area. In addition, online shopping imposes other requirements for shopping. The senses have to be stimulated; consumers want to be surprised. Social interaction is also becoming more important. And what better place to find this than in a store.

Consumers also need smaller stores that offer a product range that they need. Preferably, this product range should also be unlike the others. The time aspect also plays a role. Shopping at large stores that have too broad a selection takes too much time. These developments offer many opportunities for the small and medium enterprises.

Local stores

Close and local are still important elements for customers. This partly relates to local stores, but also to local products. This is a reaction to the dominance of the chain stores. We will see the rise of the local hero. Consumers need authenticity, craftsmanship and personal contact. This is mainly found at the local independent entrepreneurs. They also need variety and experience. This is one reason why smaller shopping destinations are becoming more attractive. They offer the right mix of local stores and national formulas. Local heros no longer believe in the mass and a shopping street with the same chains. They are convinced that customers love shopping with a local hero. This has more added value to them than a shopping street where all the stores look alike.

Local needs

Responding to local or national needs is becoming more important. This is strengthened by the importance of responding to personal needs and preferences. Social and cultural differences also demand this. This relates to, for example, the dimensions of products and the selection of products from the collections. In some countries, fur sells very well. In other countries, there is no need for fur or it is prohibited. Countries where the average woman is taller need longer lengths. Gerry Weber takes such differences into account. If necessary, HEMA adjusts the product range to the composition of the catchment area. The baby clothing department is larger in areas where many young mothers live.

In terms of product origin, consumers have increasingly more local needs. This is clearly visible in the food industry. Under the name 'joining forces locally', Jumbo collaborates with local farmers and entrepreneurs to work together to strengthen the product range. Local also has to do with quality and reliability. In the housing sector, Scandinavian design is associated with quality and reliability. Which is why Jysk, for example, shares with consumers that their mattresses are manufactured in Denmark.

4.6.1.2   Globalisation

Globalisation or fragmentation? The big question is which way towards the future we are heading. Towards one large market and will markets become more and more integrated? Or will retailers go back to the basic and choose smaller markets in order to respond to local needs? The second scenario is more likely to occur. ZARA is a good example of globalisation. In terms of dimensions, they adapted the collection to fit the Spanish consumer. This company uses a single collection for the entire world. Not every woman will find what they want at ZARA, but due to uniformity and high volumes, it achieves tremendous efficiency benefits. Rituals is another example of a concept that opted for one type of approach. Rituals wants to reach a certain group of consumers and this group can be reached in several countries. If you start a good thing, it can be done the same elsewhere. Starbucks is yet another example of this. globalisation is becoming more important for retail. Retailers use this to create scale benefits that are necessary to properly operate and perform. An implication of globalisation is that we encounter more eastern influences in collections. Retailers partly adapt their collections to new emerging markets (see paragraph 4.12).

Globalisation

4

4.6.1.3   Near sourcing

Innovation and speed are becoming more important. Consumers want to be surprised and inspired with every visit to the store. Collections or parts thereof have to change more quickly. In addition, consumers want to have the product in their home as quickly as possible. At IKEA, you can take a couch home with you immediately. Another retailer will then have to explain why the delivery of a couch purchased from him, takes 10 weeks. Innovation, quick response and quick delivery forces retailers to manufacture locally or nearby. Italy, Portugal, Spain, Turkey, Morocco and Eastern European countries are becoming increasingly popular. This is at the expense of production in the Far East. Within the housing sector, this applies mainly for decoration and home accessories. For large products, this is a different story. Couches and cupboards can easily be manufactured as semi-finished products in the Far East. They can then be adapted to the specific demands and needs of the customer in factories that are closer by. Delivery within one to two weeks is then possible.

The balance between speed, quality and price should be considered every single time. Choosing for the price often means the Far East and this is at the expense of the delivery time. Retailers who respond to trends and developments want flexibility and are increasingly opting for manufacturing nearby.

4.6.1.4   Borders are fading

Borders are fading and barriers are disappearing. Under the influence of globalisation, more international companies are emerging on the Dutch market. Primark started with stores in Rotterdam and Hoofddorp, and expanded with new stores rapidly. In 2006, the Danish Jysk opened its first stores in the Netherlands and at the moment it has more than twenty sales points.

Chinese retailers have also found their way onto the Dutch market. The Chinese furniture maker, Kuka, currently has seven stores in the Netherlands. Dutch retailers are also crossing the border more and more often. Rituals plans on opening stores in Italy, Sweden and Brazil. Borders are fading increasingly more. Barriers are also disappearing. This applies mainly to the online market.

Online retailers are opting to enter new markets evenmore often. Amazon. com is a good example. This company focuses specifically on the Dutch market. This requires more than simply having a website translated, but there are obviously far fewer barriers online than in the offline world. And the same applies for consumers; they buy more from foreign websites. Is there a product not yet available in the Netherlands? Simply import it from China or the United States.

4.6.2   Consumer needs

4.6.2.1   Importance of the country of origin

Consumers (about half) find it important that stores provide information about the country of origin or production. Despite this importance, it is the general opinion that this information supply is inadequate. When we look at the store selection when it involves local products in the product range, we see that almost half of the consumers prefer stores that provide local products.

When choosing products, people also take into account the country of origin when this is specifically required per situation. With an identical price and quality, the European product is preferred over the non-European product and the Dutch product is preferred over the European product.

Price and quality clearly affect the preference. If the price of the Dutch or European product is higher, the non-European product is often chosen. If the price is higher and the quality is better, mass preference goes to the Dutch or European product.

Dutch consumers shop locally. 69% almost always choose the nearest shopping area. Local shopping has increased in recent years and will continue to increase towards 2015. In addition to proximity, parking costs and accessibility also play an important role.

4.6.3   Competences glocalisation

Responding to local needs of the customers is as old as retail. In addition, the retailer should consider the size of the actual shopping world of his customers on a daily basis. This often does not extend further than his nearest competitors. Naturally the whole world is within grasp thanks to the internet, but the own shopping centre is the frame of reference for most purchases.

Under pressure from the eternal desire for efficiency, products have to be purchased on a global scale, not in the least to respond to the price competition. This global purchasing competence is countered by the adaption to local circumstances. Tastes differ and have to be responded to. Adapting product ranges to local circumstances will grow in importance, especially for large, global retailers. This applies to most sectors in retail, whether it be food or non-food retail such as fashion, DIY, sport or electronics. In the area of manufacturing, local manufacturing can also help a retailer to be more effective. Local is easily referred to as being manufactured in Europe. Shoes and fabric from Italy, Spain or Turkey. 'Made in Holland' or 'Made in EU' may also be a marketing argument, consumers will pay more attention to this in the future. In order to respond to the local taste, one can also opt for manufacturing in the Far East, while the design is created by a local designer. Responding to the glocalisation trend will not involve very large adjustments in competences, because most retailers already purchase globally because of the efficiency-effect and purchase local or regional for the effectiveness effect.

4.7 Trend bundle 6: priority time (Einstein Time)

Lack of time demands that consumers are smart when dealing with limited time. Priorities have to be set. Work and free time are getting mixed up more and more. Work is now possible everywhere. Consumers can store both quickly and slowly; the available time and the need is crucial. For the same purpose, consumers can sometimes decide quickly and other times they approach shopping as a fun pastime and take more time.

Priority time

This leaves room for fun shopping and run shopping. Buying online and offline is also becoming more varied. Convenience and speed are important with online purchasing. Enjoyment and experience are desired in the offline world.

4.7.1   Sub trends

4.7.1.1   It is now 24/7

Opening hours of stores are changing. It's not about more hours, but about different hours. Stores that are open longer, also open their doors later. We are still too traditionally accustomed to opening hours from 9.00 am to 18.00 pm. Sometimes we have Sunday shopping or extra shopping evenings. Some formulas are open longer, like IKEA and Media Markt. You see this often in some sectors, like DIY markets and supermarkets. The starting point should primarily be the needs of the consumer. Online retailers realise that. Most of their visitors come around when the physical stores are closed. They know that consumers appreciate it if they can still be reached after 18.00 pm. The opening hours of the future require a new way of thinking. Being open at times that best suit the customer. Not 24 hours per day, but at the times that correspond with the needs of the target group. A consultation on a new interior design is more logical on an evening during the week than during office hours. There will be more appointments outside of shopping hours. The 24-hour economy will not be as extreme as in America, but consumers want to be increasingly more in control about when they go shopping. Sunday plays an important role in this.

4.7.1.2   Acceleration and deceleration

The time that consumers spend on shopping is becoming a paradox. Sometimes they want to shop quickly, other times they take a lot of time. If time is scarce, decisions can be made quickly. While Christmas shopping, customers can be in and out of a store within five minutes. Stores like Rituals realise that and respond accordingly. During the holidays, popular products are already gift wrapped. Rituals enables consumers to quickly run in and do their shopping. At other times, Rituals is there for them when they want to relax and enjoy.

The sales argument also accelerates or decelerates the behaviour of the consumer. During the World Cup, they buy a TV within a day. Usually they would take much more time. The investment also determines how quickly they decide. Buying a car or kitchen may be a long process. Small purchases are often more impulsive and require little time. Consumers can be both fun shoppers and run shoppers. Stores also respond to this. A cup of coffee and an employee who provides detailed advice are already waiting for the fun shopper. Custom fitting a suit within fifteen minutes is possible for the run shopper.

4.7.1.3   Enjoy and experience

In general consumers have everything that they need. They can eat and drink, they have a furnished house and a well-stocked wardrobe. Based on what they have, there is no further reason for them to visit a store. Consumers have no further needs and demands, they have desires. For retailers, it is increasingly more important to awaken these desires. Creating a pleasant shopping environment is becoming more and more important. Shopping should be an experience. Consumers should fall in love with a store or a shopping area. As retailer, you should create reasons for them to come to you, that is what it is all about. The Apple brand has shown that this is possible. Many consumers with different backgrounds walk around in their stores and often buy nothing. They enjoy the product, the environment. They love the brand and sooner or later they will buy the product that they desire. What applies to stores, also applies to shopping centres. Theme-oriented shopping centres and recreational shopping centres should offer a total experience. Consumer entertainment, offering them an accommodation feature. A natural environment will become more important. Using trees, natural light, open terraces and the link with water. This will also be seen more often in stores.

Convenience

Consumers have a growing need for convenience. This is often related to saving time and effort. Time is growing more and more scarce for consumers. If time is available, they want to use it as efficiently as possible. This does not necessarily mean that they want to spend less time on shopping, for example. They simply want to be able to use the time as efficiently as possible. And then the convenience factor comes into play. An easily accessible store or shopping area saves on time. A carefully selected product range that meets the demands and needs of the customer, that is convenience. And what about an interior decorator that sees customers at their homes. Shopping at the moment that best suits the consumer, that is also convenience. This is also the reason why the online market has expanded in recent years, and why it will continue to grow. Online shopping saves time and effort. Many retailers, online and offline, are aiming at the convenience factor over the next few years. The interpretation will be diverse. As long as it responds to a need of the consumer.

Convenience

4.7.1.4 Lack of time and quality time

Consumers have less and less free time available and are becoming more selective in filling this free time. On a 24 hour basis, consumers had an average of 3.8 hours of free time in 2010 (see table 4.6). It turns out that, if you add up all the consumers' activities, you come to a total of almost 30 hours per day. This means that the consumer of today, is a multitasker. He does multiple things at the same time. The amount of free time is scarce. The consumer has to make choices and set priorities for many uses of this free time. Shopping therefore has to take it up against, for example, gaming, going out and exercise. Consumers are becoming more and more selective in how they spend their free time. Their phase of life has an influence. Senior citizens with a lot more free time continue to shop, but do so selectively. They will avoid busy days. Consumers with little time (the working generation), want to spend this time as best as possible. It is especially within this group that shopping has to compete with other forms of leisure activities.

Work life balance

Time is dynamic and consumers are no longer thinking in blocks of 3×8 hours. Work and free time keep them busy 24 hours a day, or they could be busy with it for 24 hours a day. The distinction between work and time off is no longer as clear. Personal business is being done more and more during working hours and work related business is being done more and more

Work life balance

TABLE 4.6 Time allocation of Dutch

Time distribution in main categories per day	2010
Media	6.9
Sleep and personal care	11
Housekeeping	3.4
Work and study	3.6
On the road	1.2
Free time	3.8
Total	29.9

in private time. Consumers buy products during the day and check their business e-mails during their free hours in the evening. Work is often being done on Saturday or Sunday as well. The so-called 'new work' is also important in this context. This relates to dealing with more flexible working hours. An hour in traffic must not be at the expense of working time, but also not free time. Consumers are becoming increasingly more outcome and output-oriented. It does not matter when the tasks are performed, as long as they are completed at an agreed time. But there is also a counter movement visible: consumers who turn off their business telephone on Friday evening and turn it on again on Monday morning.

4.7.1.5 Creating scarcity

Deliberately creating scarcity is implemented increasingly more often in retail in order to encourage consumers to decide more quickly. Scarcity creates an urgency. An urgency to make a quick purchase decision. Exclusive items with a limited circulation create a sense of urgency. The Viktor&Rolf collection at H&M is a good example of this. Many consumers wanted a piece of clothing from this collection and rushed to visit the H&M stores. The sense of urgency is increasingly generated by so-called pop-up stores. These are stores that often only exist briefly. These stores are usually found in the large shopping destinations. Because they only exist briefly, consumers know that they have to act quickly. The store can be gone as soon as tomorrow. Scarcity can also be created in the form of time. This involves, for example, offers with a limited duration. Or offers that are only applicable to the first hundred visitors of a store or website. You have to make sure you are there, you do not want to miss out.

4.7.2 Consumer needs

The consumer wants to shop when it suits him best and that means that Sunday shopping has an added value, without all the stores having to be open every Sunday. Half of the consumers that find Sunday shopping to be an added value indicate that once a month or a few times a year is sufficient. A specific desire with regard to opening hours is that the stores remain open later. The current closing times of the stores are clearly not of this time. On average, a store should only close between 19.30 and 20.00 pm. Shopping on appointment meets a need of one in three consumers and can also meet the desire for extended opening hours.

4.7.3   Prioritisation competences

On average, consumers spend almost twice as much time on media consumption than working. Media use has therefore become one of the biggest competitors of shopping. How can retailers win the favour of the time conscious consumer?

Most Dutch retailers close their stores at 18.00 pm. Not because they have to, but because they can. However, online shopping is often attributed to the price aspect, and yet many studies have indicated that the ability to buy whenever you want to is at the very top of the list. New and other opening hours seem to be the best remedy for physical stores, not in the least for the ability to collect the products purchased online. The best advice seems to be adjusting the opening hours, including Sunday shopping, to the specific target group. In doing this, one can work on appointment during the regular opening hours but also offer the customers the ability to come by outside the standard opening hours. For those sectors where it is possible, the choice can also be offered to visit the customer. This does not require any new competences, only flexibility from the retailers and the use of techniques that enable working on appointment.

Giving the best customers priority seems to be something that does not need much consideration; however, this is not often thought of in retail. Being assisted sooner at the checkout, being able to make an appointment outside office hours, etc. Because of the perceived time pressure, consumers want instant satisfaction of their buying needs increasingly more often. Traditional industries sometimes find it difficult to follow the speed of the customer. Same day purchases of custom suits and furniture off the shelves seemed impossible to these industries, but are now possible because some retailers have implemented competences to make this possible. Sometimes customers need time to think about a purchase, especially if it concerns a large purchase. Retailers such as Apple offer consumers enough time to experience the product, other retailers choose to offer their customers catering accommodation where they can think about their upcoming purchase. Once the choice is made, Apple picks up speed again and quickly offers the product without requiring that you go through the checkout, by paying with an employee in the store.

Another phenomenon that benefits online shopping is going to the store for nothing. Consumers do not mind going to a store if they are sure that the product in question is present. Online reservation or online buying and collecting is an outcome for the consumer. Perhaps the greatest challenges for the retailer is on the level of having the correct employee at the correct moment. Throughout the years, under economic pressure, we have often had to choose cheaper, and therefore often much less experienced, employees on busier and therefore more expensive hours. The consideration that should be made each time is what the extra expenses and extra income will yield.

4.8 Trend bundle 7: transparency

The possibilities of the world are limited. This should be handled responsibly. Consumers are becoming more and more aware of what they buy and what they consume. Quality of life for the next generations, nature, environment, social equity, sustainability and social responsibility are becoming

Transparency

increasingly more important. Retailers are expected to deal with this consciously. They have to be honest and open and inform consumers of their actions. They must be transparent. Transparency is not just about corporate social responsibility. Under influence of the internet, consumers are becoming ever more informed on products and stores. This for example relates to the price, the quality and the service. The world has become more transparent because of this. Consumers are increasingly aware of what they can expect from a brand of store. They also become more critical and give their opinion more often.

4.8.1 Sub trends
4.8.1.1 Open and honest
Customers want to know who or what the retailer is and what they do. The retailer is expected to be open and honest. This has two sides. On the one hand, customers want more information on where the retailer gets his products and on how they are manufactured. This means that the retailer will have to share this. Consumers appreciate the fact that the retailer is, in any way, responsibly busy. For this reason, many retailers are sharing more and more on what they are doing. The downside is that the retailer is also open and honest when he has done something less responsible. The media is paying more and more attention to the mistakes of the retailers in the area of production. Consumers expect the retailer to respond to this openly and honestly. This is becoming even more important under the influence of internet and social media. An individual can make a difference. If one person establishes a mistake, this can be spread over the world through various media. Everyone has the right to speak, every-one can be found and everyone may give an opinion. Therefore, the retailer will have to work in a responsible and therefore open and honest manner.

Corporate responsibility

Corporate social responsibility

Consumers are environmentally aware and pay more and more attention to how organisations deal with this. The future of the following generations is important. The pressure on the production methods of organisations is also increasing from stakeholders. They should be responsibly manufacturing by using the correct materials. Sooner or later corporate responsibility will be a precondition, whether or not under the pressure of social organisations. At the moment there are still too many companies that are irresponsible with regard to nature and the environment, for example in their use of wood, pollutants and CO_2 emissions. In the future there will be ever more water-marks and brand names that ensure sustainable production methods. An easy example is that, for every tree that is chopped down for furniture, a new tree must be planted somewhere else. In the fashion industry, more and more companies are opting for bio-cotton. C&A only uses bio-cotton for its cotton clothing. H&M has indicated that they intend to do the same from 2020. Apart from using materials, sustainability also relates to energy consumption. The big question is how online players will respond to this. The delivery of packages causes much energy consumption and CO_2 emissions. Physical locations where consumers can collect products are becoming more important for the future.

4.8.1.2 Responsible prices
Corporate responsibility is at odds with the interests of 'Value for money' for the consumer. Corporate responsibility is important, but not at any price.

A balance must be found. The question is how consumers will handle the choice between being responsible and a profitable price. Furthermore, consumers want to invest in sustainability, but there should often be a reward in it for them. In that sense they are ecoists who unite ecological and economic motives.

4.8.1.3   Integrity and trust

Choices that organisations make in the area of Corporate Social Responsibility (CSR) should not be made for them to win. They should be made because it is something that a retailer as an organisation wants and which they also support. At this moment, corporate social responsibility is still a bit of an 'obsession' for organisations. It must be an intrinsic motivation for organisations to be involved with this and not a so-called 'look at us' principle. It's no longer about what you sell, but about who you are as an organisation. Consumers want an organisation that they can trust. Corporate responsibility is becoming an increasingly more important element within this trust. Consumers give more and more preference to an organisation that they feel good about. Corporate social responsibility should be a precondition for organisations and not a means to use in the marketing strategy.

Working together and contributing together

Corporate responsibility is not just for organisations. It is a process wherein consumers and organisations cooperate more and more often to realise this. Initiatives in the area of contributing together are applied increasingly more often by retailers. Such initiatives are increasing in numbers. Excellent examples are retailers where consumers can return their old products and get a voucher in return. The old products are recycled or donated to consumers that can use these products. Levi's applied this principle. There are also initiatives where consumers can support charities through retailers. Mumsmarket.nl is a good example. Consumers can buy children's clothes and toys here and, at the checkout, consumers can specify which charity should be supported by this purchase.

4.8.1.4   Green programs

Corporate responsibility is applied more and more often within organisations. Project developer and investor Redevco is an excellent example of this. Along with its tenants, this company has drawn up a green lease contract. The contracts contain agreements on the energy consumption and measurement thereof. The idea is that tenants share their details so that a summary of the energy consumption of the tenants can be acquired. Based on this, it is possible to see which buildings and possibly tenants require attention in the area of energy consumption. Another example is the development of the most sustainable lighting plan at retailers. In corporate responsibility, small amounts can often help.

Green programs

Everything will be transparent

Transparency goes beyond corporate responsibility. Thanks to the internet, consumers are better informed on all aspects of the retailer's store. This involves sales prices, product features, services and staff performance. This has resulted in an increase in competition and price pressure. Customers are negotiating more about the price. They have more knowledge on the product and are therefore critical on what they do and do not want to buy.

The consideration between price and quality can be improved more. Consumers also give their opinions on products, stores, services and employees more often. In doing so, they also contribute to a more transparent world. The retailer is also part of this. If everything is in order, the retailer has no need to worry about his/her position in the transparent world.

4.8.2   Consumer needs

Consumers are looking for stores that are open and honest regarding products that they sell and the circumstances under which they are manufactured. Stores still have a long way to go in this area. Only 42% feel that stores are currently open and honest about this.

Approximately 30% of consumers have decided not to visit a store because they had heard bad news regarding poor working conditions or the use of certain raw materials. Over the next five years, this percentage will double. More than two in three consumers are willing to pay (slightly) more for a responsibly manufactured product. It seems that, in the near future, consumers will make such assessments more often and will be willing to pay a bit more for products that are good and socially responsible.

4.8.3   Competences

The world has opened up. Consumers can find all kinds of information on retailers online. Is all the information correct? No, not always. This is suggestive and placed by external parties. Consumers realise that and correct one another more and more often. A piece of openness on the part of the retailer is in place. The world has changed. Consumers expect more openness from the retailer. This requires a different mentality. Corporate social responsibility is not a trend, it is the most natural thing in the world. It should obviously be a natural component in all procedures. It is not an advantage if one does this, but rather a disadvantage if one does not do it. It is not a mean to show how good a retailer is, but rather a mentality on how good the retailer is doing. A way to demonstrate the impact of a product in an accessible way is the 'Global footprint'. Timberland imported this footprint to the United States and Canada a few years ago. All products are provided with a label indicating the impact to the environment. With such an initiative, a retailer gives his/her custom-ers a choice.

One of the ways in which a retailer can contribute very actively to a better society is by opening the market for third world products. The basic thought behind many initiatives such as Fairtrade/Max Havelaar and Return to Sender is that, by buying these products, we help entrepreneurs in the third world in building a better existence. Giving products a second life or reusing them in another way is also a way to contribute to a better environment. In the United Kingdom, M&S offers consumers a voucher of five pounds when they return old clothing. M&S then ensures that the useful clothing finds its way to a new user via Oxfam. Similarly, the use of green energy is also something that can be shared easily with the client and the reuse of materials fits in with the renewal of the corporate identity, the formula or the concept fits in exceptionally well with the new era. Moreover, corporate social responsibility does not necessarily have to cost money, but it can contribute just as well to the result.

New competencies needed are certainly needed to meet the trend of transparency, but much of this is also a question of a new mindset, using the existing competencies.

4.9 Trend bundle 8: the new middle market

The middle of the market has changed. The competition field has therefore also changed for many retailers. The traditional bottom of the market has slowly moved up to the middle under the influence of price/value retailers. This results in a new definition of the middle. Price has become more important. Retailers cannot serve the entire market and have to choose whether to be a price/value retailer or choose for a position on the top. It is only possible for big players to operate both the top and the bottom of the market.

New middle market

4.9.1   Sub trends
4.9.1.1   New generation discounters
Customers are more than ever considering the price-value ratio. This is also the matrix for what we call the new middle. These are retailers that want to serve the masses. From the industry point of view, these are retailers that we probably consider as the bottom. These new generation discounters are retailers that combine a competitive price proposition with a good shopping environment. The retail landscape will be defined and dominated by chain stores that are most successful in playing the 'no compromise game', and in 2020 they will occupy the A1-locations in the town centre. Primark is a very good example of these new generation discounters. This is an Irish clothing formula that offers fashionable clothing at low prices in a good shopping environment. Such formulas encourage consumers to learn how to shop at low cost in a nice, proper and trendy environment. Consumers are no longer punished for low cost shopping and new generations are growing up with this. The accession of such discounters has or may have significant implications for the current distribution of the market shares within an industry. What has IKEA done with the housing sector? The 'I'm not crazy'-feeling (the theme used by Media Markt to shake up the Netherlands) is dominant in the electronics industry.

Value for money
Value for money, consumers are more concerned with this than ever before. Price has become a precondition to them. This has changed the purchasing behaviour. Not only does this apply to consumers with an average or below-average income, but also for consumers from the higher segment. They are also price conscious and base their choices on that. The 'value for money'-principle is more and more applicable to certain product groups. Furniture is a good example of this. Furniture has converged from exclusive products to products for which the consumer wants value for his money. Such movements are influenced by the accession of the new generation discounters. As a result of their accession, the price consciousness of the consumer has been downgraded. This price consciousness is also affected by the change of life expectancy of products. When trends and innovation become more important, the life expectancy of products is shortened and one is not prepared to continuously pay the highest price for it. It happens more and more often that products are not sold at the normal sales price.

Value for money

Every week, a product is on sale somewhere. And if it's not on sale, a discount is negotiated more and more often.

Price communication

Price
communication

Last but not least. Price is back as marketing P, but especially in communica-tion. The customers will be more price sensitive, not in the least because of the increased supply in the new middle. For retailers in the traditional middle, this means that price will become an important marketing P. The retailer will have to show that he also has attractive prices. This can be achieved, amongst others, with strong opening price points. He can also use his price stretch. In times of economic recession, it is useful with the composition of the product range mix to take into account the customers wallets. One should add some brands and products to the bottom, where it is necessary.

The best form of price communication is of course that where a separation occurs with the product itself. HEMA is very successful in doing this with the slogan 'What can you buy for so little'. Developing a concept in such a direction and applying that to the situation of the retailer is obviously the best.

4.9.1.2   The new middle market

The combination of the rise of the new generation discounters and the price conscious consumer has ensured that conventional market classification of low-middle-high, no longer exists. The bottom of the market has become the new middle: stores and formulas with a clear luxury or value proposition at an affordable price. ZARA and H&M are excellent examples in fashion, IKEA in housing, Media Mark in electronics and Rituals in luxury cosmetics. Such formulas form the new middle, but clearly with a lower price level than the old middle. They use fun and good concepts that can be innovative and extremely affordable. The top of the market is formed by luxury and design. This is a segment that is struggling somewhat with the rise of the new middle. This does not apply to the very top. It specifically relates to the brands that are just below the very top.

It is not either/or, but both/and

The consumer determines for himself from which store a product is purchased. They purchase from stores at the bottom and top of the market. Therefore, it is not either/or, but both/and. Either you look for fashion products by famous designers and therefore make a conscious durable purchase, or you choose less costly products that require replacement sooner. Therefore, the motivation to purchase or use a product plays an important role in this choice. A consumer can easily combine a luxury designer couch that has to last many years, with trendy chairs or pillows from IKEA that have to be replaced once every two or three years. Customers that purchase from the high segment, also buy from IKEA and ZARA. Whether a product is a demand, need or desire, also determines the choice.

Demands and needs are especially price sensitive and the choice is therefore based on this. The price plays a less dominant role with desires. This is all about the 'wow effect' around stores and products.

Design for the masses

Design is or will become available to the masses. Luxury designer brands have collections that are attractive to the mass in terms of price.
Retailers also collaborate with designers to compile collections, making design available to the masses. H&M is a good example of this. This fashion chain works with designers such as Karl Lagerfeld and sells collections designed by him in the stores. Admittedly this is done at a higher price level than the H&M consumer is accustomed to, but still very afforda-ble. Another example is Jan des Bouvrie at Gamma. Or the website of GOOI design (www.gooidesign.nl).
This company sells hip, trendy and affordable designer furniture, making it available to the masses.

4.9.2 Consumer needs

The middle still dominates the market. Consumers mostly choose retailers in the middle segment. This varies from 40% in shoes to 47% in sport (see table 4.7). Yet the middle has changed over the years. Price/value retailers are classified as middle. The retail offer in the higher segment is also larger than that in the lower segment.
This is especially visible with the housing and sport sectors.

TABLE 4.7 Distribution of the market based on price level

Distribution of the market based on price level	Fashion	Housing	Sport	Shoes
Low	26%	24%	21%	28%
Middle	42%	41%	47%	40%
High	31%	35%	33%	32%

What is of influence in the selection of products and stores? Price, quality or a mixture of both? The consumer is very clear in this. It is the mix of price and quality that is offered. Value for money, that is what it's all about for the consumer.

4.9.3 Competences

The middle always contains the most people and that is why it is such an interesting market segment. Many retailers have always pursued this, because it was the basis for success. But what about the middle market? Is it still the most attractive part of the market? Where do the masses buy today and in the future? It is up to the retailers to assume their position in the market and to secure their market share. Retail is polarising. The premium brands are flourishing more than ever and new concepts are being introduced at the bottom, causing a shift of the middle segment. The new middle market, where the masses are, is claimed by new players at the bottom of the market. These retailers, like Primark and Newlook, can offer very attractive propositions in great shopping environments. Due to the volume that they get, especially from high turns, they are capable of putting down a competitive price proposition. They opt for quick changes and short life cycles. Fresh fashion, perhaps perishable, but perfectly appropriate for the target group. This means that the supply chains of the new middle market players should respond perfectly to speed and mass. One of the answers to make a difference in the new middle is accessible design. This can be filled with famous designers or artists as filled by C&A and H&M. Each in its own way, with personalities that match the brand and the target group. Only a small part of the collection is filled in this manner, but it reflects on the entire brand. Especially chains that are positioned in the middle segment can use this to create some distance with regard to the new entrants to the bottom. The luxury brands, super premium, have experienced good years despite the recession. The blows fall just below this segment. The premium brands do everything they can to remain premium. They create more scarcity in order to remain luxurious. Is it real scarcity? No, if it was, they would not grow as much as they are today. Their growth is specifically in volume. They create the feeling of scarcity. The LVMH-group (Moët Hennessy - Louis Vuitton) have opted for the stores of some of their brands to close half an hour earlier. Also, the number of products per customer is limited. All this to promote the sense of scarcity and to increase the urge to want to have a product. Ultimately, it's all about value for money. Customers are no longer prepared to pay much, but want real value for money. Value retailers will dominate the market in the so-called 'no compromise game'. Customers want maximum service in combination with the best prices. Retailers that have already had success with this, are the winners in consumer satisfaction. For example, a super-market chain such as Jumbo, Lidl, Essalunga. Low prices, good service and a wide product range. But companies like Media Markt, Decathlon, HEMA and Hornbach, each promise the customer the same thing.

4.10 Trend bundle 9: affluenza

Affluenza

There is a growing realisation that there is a limit to the unlimited (financial) possibilities. Driving forces behind this realisation are the global economic slowdown, the problems in the housing market, unemployment, inflation and high costs. There is a prospect of a period of limited growth with inflation and uncertainty. This leads to cautious purchasing behaviour of consumers (affluenza). In addition, retailers have to deal with high commodity costs and more and more ageing employees. But despite the fact that the prices are under pressure, consumers expect high performance from the retailers.

4.10.1   Sub trends
4.10.1.1   Stagflation

Stagflation

Inflation continues to increase but the expenditures stagnate. The golden age of easily buying is over and it is questionable whether this period is ever going to come back. In the period of 2000-2007, the sales in many businesses witnessed a positive development year after year. From 2007 it stabilised and since 2008 the retail sales has decreased. The retail industry is sensitive to economic fluctuations. The expenditures are clearly influenced by the expectations of consumers in respect of economic developments. The housing market in particular has been hit hard since 2008. The sales in the kitchen industry in 2009, for example, was 20% lower than in 2008 and many companies disappeared in 2009. The cake that is distributed in the retail has been smaller since 2008 and will remain small the coming years. In 2011 the Euro Crisis also came into the picture. This means that it is highly likely that Europe is facing a period of stagnation in combination with increasing inflation. This combination of both phenomena is called *stagflation*. The result of this development will be a drop in demand in the retail.

Rising costs
For the first time in 10 to 15 years, fashion prices are going up. Various costs such as transportation, labour and commodities are going up. Additionally, volumes are declining. Only by implementing efficiency improvements retailers are able to keep the prices from rising under the influence of these developments. If that is not possible, margins are placed under pressure or retailers must opt to increase selling prices.
In addition, costs are rising under the influence of the importance of durable and responsible manufacturing. This causes the manufacturing costs to increase, but this increase in cost cannot be fully passed on to consumers. Furthermore, the Netherlands is confronted with higher costs for healthcare. This will also have an impact on retail.

4.10.1.2   Conscious spending
Consumers are becoming more conscious about their money. A euro can only be spent once. In times when the economy slows down, this feeling is strengthened. But it is also a development that comes from the consumers themselves. They realise that they have been living beyond their means for quite some time, everything and anything was allowed. This time is over. Consumers buy carefully and conservatively. Buying is once again a rational consideration. Some product groups are affected more by this than others. For example, this applies more to housing than to fashion or electronics. With housing, it involves higher amounts and investments and it is often chosen to use certain furniture for a longer time. With electronics and fashion, this applies much less because the investment is smaller, but especially because there is more renewal and innovation.
Conscious spending also influences the store selection. Stores with a proposition of good value for money are often chosen.
Especially in times when the economy is slower. When the economy recovers, spending is likely to increase, but this level will never go back to the level during the period 1995-2000. The consumer is and remains conscious, even if the crisis subsides.

Price transparency
The fact that consumers are price sensitive and spend consciously has been strongly influenced in recent years by the increasing price transparency. The tremendous increase of price transparency is mainly a result of the internet and the use of technology while shopping. Nowadays, consumers can often find a supplier that is cheaper and use this increasingly more often as a sales argument or in negotiations with the seller. This price transparency will take off even more. There are no more surprises. Google currently has product feeds. A store can upload all its products, including the sales price, to Google. If a consumer is looking for a specific item, Google can show them which stores sell the relevant product. Often also at what price and whether the product is in stock. For retailers, this means that they have to legitimately argue why they are sometimes slightly more expensive. It then comes down to distinctiveness.

Price
transparency

4.10.1.3 No compromise game

Conscious spending does not mean that the consumer chooses the lowest price. They expect retailers to perform well on both price and quality. This is also called the 'no compromise game'. Consumers do want to pay a lower price, but this may not be at the expense of other aspects, such as service and quality. They are using their money more consciously, but they certainly benefit from good service. Investing in well-qualified personnel can therefore also benefit in times of crisis. Additional service and attention can actually help a doubting consumer to make a large purchase. Consumers spend money, but they do so more and more consciously and with retailers that can offer them the best compromise between price and quality.

4.10.1.4 Second-hand

Second-hand already plays a large role, and this role will continue to increase. Consumers buy used products mainly based on the price and not so much based on being conscious or responsible. The acceptance for used products is huge, especially for furniture. Many furniture have a second life cycle. Consumer activities on Marktplaats of eBay prove this. In addition to housing, bicycles and baby products are also examples of products for which second-hand is fully accepted. For retailers, the second-hand market is only interesting when the article value is interesting. This is the case with housing, for example. Other than that, second-hand will mainly be something that takes place between consumers, possibly supported by parties such as Marktplaats. This does not mean that websites like Marktplaats or eBay are not interesting for retailers. More and more furniture companies, for example, successfully sell their excess stock through such websites.

4.10.2 Consumer needs

Consumers have become conscious and will remain conscious. 51% indicate that they can spend less. As many as three quarters indicate that they deal with their money more consciously. These are not only the people that have less money to spend. Therefore, being conscious does not only relate to having a smaller budget. Consumers will also remain conscious in the future. This is partly fuelled by the expectation that they will have less to spend in 2015 compared to today. Consumers that have less money to spend mainly purchase cheaper products or fewer pieces. Major purchases are postponed under the influence of the economic situation. This applies to almost half of the consumers. They will continue to do this in 2015. Products with a high purchase value will therefore be purchased less. Generally, consumers are simply prepared to continue using products for longer. Moreover, stores with lower prices are clearly visited more frequently than other stores. Incidentally, a low price may not be at the expense of the quality.

4.10.3 Competences

Consumers spend less. Partly because they feel like they have less money to spend, and also because they have developed a sense that enough is enough. The end of consumerism presents itself and almost everyone is convinced that the first years of the millennium were extraordinary. The trend of conscious spending seems to have been primarily motivated by the consumers themselves. In addition, consumers are well informed about selling prices, promotions and offers. Both developments are strengthened by the economic circumstances. The new, conscious consumer will not easily be seduced. To do that, retailers will have to devise approaches. Consumers do downtrading in bad economic circumstances. This means that they move to cheaper products in times of crisis. In order to hold on to his own customers, he will have to go along with the customers in the downward movement. This is possible by paying attention to opening price points and by stretching the product range. Price as marketing weapon always rears its head when things get tighter in the market.

The method chosen by HEMA is therefore also interesting. HEMA goes back to its genesis years, the crisis of the last century, with fixed round prices. It is mainly an appeal to the fact of what you can still get for 2 or 3 Euros. In this way, the attention is drawn away from the actual product-price combination. Nobody knows the reference prices of the products, but when such a big deal is made about the round price, the consumer must be forgiven for thinking that it is a good deal. Price communication is mainly a matter of communication and less of the price itself. Another way to avoid the erosion of margins by rising prices is joint purchasing or joint collection development with other retailers in other market segments.

Another method that will bring results is by increasing the share of private label. This requires a certain scale size, but this can also be achieved within buying combinations for independent entrepreneurs. The share of private label will continue to increase in many sectors in the coming years, if only because of maintaining the margin mix.

The urge that customers have for used products may also be an opportunity. Retailers can create their own market sites. This is certainly possible in markets where the product value is high enough and the product life is longer than the economic life expectancy. The advantage of a market place created by the retailer, is that the customers can offer goods through his website and that the retailer takes care of the payment process.

He actually provides the store-window (virtually or possibly physically) for the goods to change ownership. One can compare it with the second-hand books of Bol.com.

In line with the marketplaces, we have the phenomenon of 'trade ins', the retailer is the formal owner of the traded products. In the video game world, it's a business model used by various chain stores.

Apple has the market for refurbished Macs in various countries. Officially inspected and repaired Apple computers with a limited guarantee. In this way, Apple is able to avoid a price drop in its products in its largest markets.

In times of crisis, the temptation is great to use the staff as a closing entry. Based on cost considerations, one would like to cut down on the capacity. A dangerous decision, but certainly understandable. However, when we look at the other trends, it is wise to make regular evaluation. In the end the proof of the pudding is in the eating. In times of crisis the number of visitors in stores may decrease, but not always the number of potential customers. The spectators generally remain home. The capacity may not and cannot only be based on the flow of visitors, but should be based on the purchase intention of the visitors. This requires regular calibration, not only of the visitor numbers but also of the purchase intention.

4.11 Trend bundle 10: new markets

New markets

Underlying global economic procedures are very powerful, especially in developed countries like America and Japan, and developing countries like China and India. More than 4 trillion consumers in emerging markets see their income triple over the next twenty years. This new middle class offers tremendous profit and growth opportunities for international retailers. In the coming years, the focus will lie on expansion to these growing markets. Even under the influence of the stagnating European economy. This trend stands apart and has a major impact on retail in general.

4.11.1 Investing in emerging economies

During the National Retail Federation Congress in the United States, economists indicated that the United States and countries in Europe had managed to avoid a further recession by increasing the global trade. This increase was due to the economies in the emerging countries. Retailers in the United States and Europe also realise that, for the time being, the purchasing power in the current markets will not return to the level of the first years of this century (see table 4.8). Growing economies in Asia and South-America are completely open to international retailers and many of them have their sights set on these countries for the next few years. The growth opportunities for brands and retailers can rather be found there. Some retailers even dare to say that Europe will be the third world or old world in the area of retail. In respect of investments we lag behind Latin America, India and China.

TABLE 4.8

Population: top 5 (in millions)	2010	Population: top 5 (in millions)	2025
China	1,354	India	1,459
India	1,215	China	1,417
United States	318	United States	404
Indonesia	233	Pakistan	335
Brazil	195	Nigeria	289

Largest economy: top 5 BNP* in $ billions	2010	Largest economy in purchasing power: top 5 BNP PPP in $ billions	2010
United States	14,587	United States	14,587
China	5,927	China	10,170
Japan	5,459	Japan	4,299
Germany	3,281	India	4,195
France	2,560	Germany	3,059

TABLE 4.8 (continued)

Highest economic growth (selection)	2000-2010	Lowest economic growth (selection)	2000-2010
China	10,5	Italy	0.4
India	7.5	Japan	0.7
Indonesia	5.2	Germany	0.9
		France	1.1
		The Netherlands	1.4
Highest economic growth (selection)	**2000-2010**	**Lowest economic growth (selection)**	**2000-2010**
		United States	1.6
		England	1.7

Source: Pocket World figures 2011/2012, the Economist

* BNP = Gross Domestic Product, also abbreviated as GDP

** PPP = Purchasing Power Priority, is used to normalise the mutual of differences based on the currency rates with a statistical exchange rate based on a 'store coin' in the relevant country.

4.11.2   Custom retail concepts

Retailers that are geared towards expansion into new markets will customise their retail concepts. Consumers from emerging countries are different from the average European consumer. They have a different physique, different taste, different lifestyle and especially a different culture. In order to be successful, it is very important for retailers that they adjust their retail concepts. The same applies to manufacturers. Within the fashion industry, there are already examples of brands involved in this activity. They do not make products for Europe, but for Russia and China. Piet Boon is a good example; they only develop products for China and Russia. The counter trend is that large international players invest less in stores in the Netherlands and Europe. Consequently, retail concepts have to do longer with this. For retailers who continue to focus on the Netherlands and/or Europe, this means more opportunities to distinguish themselves.

4.11.3   Needs and competences

Even with this trend bundle, there is indeed a relationship with the two other two forces, although this was less relevant in the context of the research carried out for the HBD and Inretail. The increasing prosperity in emerging markets creates a need among consumers for new forms of retail. Growing prosperity, by definition, leads to an increase of disposable income. Moreover, this growing prosperity also leads to the consumers desire to purchase new products. Food expenditures are increasing, even if this increase is basically still moderate. Expenditures on durable and other goods are increasing more rapidly. The food consumption remains in line with what they were used to. But especially the desire to own prod-ucts of western origin offers opportunities for western retailers. They also appear successful in the emerging markets. It is remarkable that many of these products are manufactured in the Far East, in this case often in the country where they are now being purchased. For example, clothing from brands such as Jack & Jones, H&M or products from Apple.

With regard to the competences, having operations in China, for example, has quite a few implications. Firstly because of the fact that a collaboration is required with a local partner so as to even do business.

Summary

The environment of the retail has changed drastically. The five gaming rules – Reach, Resources, Repopulation, Revenue and Reshaping – have changed permanently. Conversion is in need of adjustment. There are two types of conversion: the decision conversion and the expenditure conversion. Decision conversion is the first step towards a paying customer. From TOMA (*Top of Mind Awareness*) we move on to TOIA (*Top of Internet Awareness*), in other words from brand recognition to findability.
Retailers have several opportunities to increase their findability, but there is one that will become more important and should be incorporated into the business process: review marketing. The basic idea behind review marketing is that customers are able to share experiences about the retailer and his products. This is the new way of word-of-mouth advertising.
Because of online searching the number of visitors will decline, but potential customers will be better prepared. In other words: the purchase intention of the visitors will increase.
We have seen that awareness and transparency will further increase, in this respect retailers will have to answer to their customers.
The changing composition of the population will affect where a retailer will settle and in what format. Big cities will grow larger because of the ongoing urbanisation, these big cities will also contain more and more young people and single households. On the outskirts we will see signs of shrinking and, more significantly, ageing.
We also discussed a period of stagflation, the combination of very moderate growth and inflation. This situation leaves room to value retailers, organisations that combine a competitive price combination with a good shopping environment. We self-labelled this as the new middle.
The retail landscape will be determined and dominated by the chain stores that are most successful in playing the 'no compromise game'. Low prices, good service and an attractive store.
The P of Price is back as marketing P, but especially in communication. For retailers in the traditional middle, this means that price is important in the marketing mix in order to reach the price sensitive consumer.
Ultimately, all these developments affect the composition of the retail landscape. We need fewer stores, shopping centres will have to adapt to the needs of the consumer and the world will become a cross channel world. Eventually, the number of square metres of stores will decline by at least 20 to 35% by 2020. Partly due to the rise of online shopping, but also due to the abundance of retail space. By definition, retailing means wanting to become more efficient and effective and the same applies for floor productivity. In the end the survivors are those concepts which are able to adapt to the new market conditions.

PART 2

The market strategic process in retail

In part 2 we focus on the processes that need to be followed in order to achieve a balanced retail strategy. In chapter 5 we briefly discuss the structure of the strategic process in general. The process is explained using examples in the retail. In chapter 6, we focus on the specific aspects of the strategy formulation in retail, where we specifically discuss the relationship between the elements of sales, margin and costs. Chapter 7 is devoted to the dynamic aspects of retail and the influence on the strategy formulation.

5
The strategic process in retail

Retailing is an industry that is very tactical by its nature. The changing circumstances, developments and dynamics in retail require a strategic approach within the retail sector. In this chapter we will discuss the concept of strategy, the relationship between strategy and tactics, the functions of a strategy and the way in which strategy creates a context for the implementation of the policy in the long term. Strategic procedures, the various phases within these procedures and strategy formulation such as 'rolling process' are also discussed.

⬛5.1 The concept of strategy

Strategy

Under a *strategy* (Verhage, 2010) we understand 'the expressed and applied collective pursuit of an organisation'. In other words, the description of the end situation (and of the road leading there) that the company wishes to reach in the long run. The concepts indicated in the definition mean the following:

- *Expressed*: in other words that the strategy must be accessible and comprehensible to everyone in the organisation. This can be done, for example, through a *strategy statement* or through a very clear code of conduct provided by management. If this is not the case, it could still involve a strategy, but this will very rarely lead to a common objective.

Strategy statement

- *Applied*: it must be clear to the people in the organisation that they work according to a strategy. An expressed strategy which is constantly deviated from is not an effective strategy. After all, when the organisation realises that the strategy is not followed, they will no longer stick to the strategic considerations.
- *Collective*: all parts of the organisation must work together to achieve the objectives of the strategy. If not, a situation could arise where parts of the organisation work against each other.
- *Target*: a strategy describes a target situation. A primary objective of a strategy is not so much the realisation of a number of quantitative key figures in the distant future (although these may not be lacking in a good strategy). Rather, the aim to achieve some fairly broad principles that collectively indicate what one wants to be and what position one strives for in the market, even with regard to competition. This is how a strategy determines the procedure and the culture of the company.

⬛5.2 Strategy and tactics

Retailing is an industry that is very tactical by its nature. This is because most of the activities are of a daily nature: stocks in the store should be replenished every day, the store has to be put in order again every day, the tills are cashed-up and the orders are carried out. The demand side also knows daily fluctuations. The purchasing behaviour of the customers is different on a Saturday than on a Monday. Customers behave differently in good weather than in bad weather. All of this means that, in the operation of retailers, there is a lot of emphasis on short term aspects of the business operations. This does not have to be an issue if there is a stable environment. However, part 1 of this book has shown that the current environment is everything but stable: the consumer, the competition, the economic environment and other factors are changing at an ever increasing pace. In such a situation we cannot be satisfied with a 'next' or a 'responsive' policy, where we act from day to day. A strategy is therefore required. A strategy should lead to a framework for the implementation of the policy in the longer term.

5.3 Functions of a strategy

A strategy has the following functions:
1 Identity;
2 Differentiation;
3 Criteria for the result;
4 Framework for planning and daily actions;
5 Motivation.

1 Identity
A strategy should lead to a description of the identity or the personality of
the company. People will often try to summarise this identity in a so-called
mission statement: a brief, concise representation of what the company   **Mission**
stands for (see example 5.1).   **statement**

EXAMPLE 5.1 HEMA-MISSION

A good example is the mission that
HEMA is currently using. Throughout the
years, this mission has been adjusted
in terms of wording, but the content
remains the same. Since 1926, HEMA
has aimed to show that a fun and comfortable life does not have to be expensive and is therefore accessible to all
sections of the population. HEMA's mission can be summarised in two words:
exceptional simplicity.

HEMA should be recognised as a single
formula, whether the establishment is
located in Amsterdam, Brussels, Leeu-
warden, Maastricht, Neuss or Paris. This
does not mean that HEMA has to stock
the same product range to the same
extent everywhere. It means that the
consumer should always get the 'HEMA
feeling' at any random HEMA establishment. The USP (unique selling proposition) of HEMA is an ideal combination of
price, quality and design. The focus here
does not lie on the cheapest, the best
quality or the best design, but on the
best combination of these three in the
markets. This is why HEMA opted for the
house brand (private label), even before it
existed. In its marketing approach, HEMA
specifically opted to cover the normal,
daily needs of the consumer.

HEMA's purchasing mission is:
'We purchase the products that consumers need "frequently" and "often".'
Exceptional simplicity also stands for
daily products with a somewhat different
styling, where the brand name is less
relevant than the price-quality relationship.
'Exceptional simplicity' also means that
the price plays an important role for the
consumer, but above all revolves around
the usefulness.
HEMA is a centrally managed company.
After all, this is the only way that it is
possible to achieve the same formula
principles throughout the Netherlands
and abroad. The HEMA formula requires
active and consistent work. It is not
about maintaining the status quo, but
further 'proactive' action is needed for
the further development of the formula.
With a wide range and a relatively low
sales area, this also means that choices
should be made continuously: HEMA
chooses for the consumer by making it
easy to find. With different formats, this
means even more choices, but in such a
way that the customer will understand.
Alignment with the immediate catchment
area is central.

The combination of the own store brand and a good price-quality relationship requires control over the production process: HEMA has outposts in the factories of its suppliers (prior checking). Moreover, the company has its own laboratories where quality checks are performed before the goods enter the store (subsequent verification). If something still goes wrong, HEMA has a 'satisfied or your money back' guarantee. Because of these stringent inspections, HEMA was able, for example, to build up a market share of 30% in a custom sensitive market like foundations without having fitting rooms available in store: the consumer knows that HEMA's sizing is always perfect. Yet HEMA introduced the first fitting rooms in Amstelveen in 2011, something which had already happened in international establishments.

Finally: *particular simplicity* is also about how the store operation is performed. For consumers, who after all do not want too much difficulty involved in the purchase of 'regular things', this means a clear insightful store where one can quickly find all the required products: fixed locations in the store, a high visibility rate and a clear presentation. To the internal organisation this means an operation that has very little associated cost, otherwise one cannot realise the low prices. For example: self-service in a pleasant, but not too expensive store atmosphere, on a limited floor space.

Unique selling propositions

2 Differentiation
A strategy should clearly indicate what *unique selling propositions* the company has. A unique selling proposition (USP) is a consumer relevant product characteristic that distinguishes from the characteristics of competing products and which cannot easily be imitated. Examples from retail: HEMA's house brand, the knock-down furniture in IKEA, the animal friendliness at The Body Shop and the EDLP (Every Day Low Price) at Jumbo.

3 Criteria for the result
Although a strategy basically represents a target situation, one should identify the objectives and, where possible, quantify. In a strategy for retail companies, we have to distinguish between hard and soft objectives. Under the *hard objectives* we generally understand the key figures that are also used in the financial budgeting, such as sales, profit, cost and productivity figures. With *soft objectives* it involves the realisation of perceptions to the customer. A retail company that wants to evoke the image of 'the problem solver for the small starter' (IKEA) with its consumer should actually verify that this image becomes anchored over time.

Hard objectives
Soft objectives

4 Framework for planning and daily actions
It is through the daily nature of the procedures in retail that we must ensure that the short term activities (tactics) fit into the long term framework. A strategy ensures that this framework can arise:

an office supply store, with a product range aimed at the establishment of
the home office, that includes stuffed animals in the product range to boost
sales is wrong.

5 Motivation
A strategy can play a very important role in motivating an organisation. If we
do not simply know what we have to do (work routines and procedures), but
also know why we have to do it (strategic plan), we generally work in a much
more motivated manner and – perhaps this is even more important – we
often are much more motivated to work together as well.

5

5.4 A closer look at the strategic process

The strategic process can be reflected as in figure 5.1.

The strategic process can be classified in the following phases:
- Phase 1: analysis.
- Phase 2: SWOT.
- Phase 3: strategy formulation.
- Phase 4: translation from policy to implementation.
- Phase 5: control of the implementation.

After discussing these phases, we will discuss strategy formulation such as a 'rolling process'.

FIGURE 5.1 The position of environmental exploration in the strategic process

5.4.1 Phase 1 Analysis

The process begins with an analysis phase. In this analysis phase, we investigate all the factors that are important when preparing a strategy. Roughly, we can arrange them in the external analysis and the internal analysis.

External analysis

The external analysis consists of:

Environmental exploration
- *Environmental exploration.* Environmental exploration covers those factors that affect the company from the outside. These may be economic factors (such as the spending limit of consumers, the general economic developments and the wage developments), but also demographic factors (such as the age of the population, the family composition, the

training level and the urbanisation) or (mass) psychological factors (such as psychological trends, lifestyles and attitudes).
- *Competitor's analysis.* In fact, competition is a factor that affects the company from outside. As such, the competitor's analysis actually belongs to the environmental exploration. Since competition is exceptionally strong in retail and in particular in retail, and develops rapidly, it is customary to consider the competitor's analysis as a separate part of the analysis phase.

Competitor's analysis

Internal analysis

The internal analysis consists of:
- *Strength-weakness analysis.* The strength-weakness analysis covers factors that can affect the company from the inside. Because we generally know much more about our own company than that of the competitor or the environment, it is actually expected that this is the simplest part of the strategic analysis. In practice, however, it seems that this is not usually the case. The reason is once again the strong daily activity oriented attitude of retail, where an overall view is sometimes lacking.
- *Prevailing vision.* The prevailing vision in itself is not as important for the objective analysis. It is conditional for the acceptance of the results of the analysis and therefore for the ability to implement the strategy. The vision especially plays a role in the situations in which there were adjustments to the strategy of long-established companies.

Strength-weakness analysis

5.4.2 Phase 2 SWOT (strengths, weaknesses, opportunities, threats)

The strategic analysis generally results in a large number of findings that are not always consistent with each other. Suppose that the analysis leads to the conclusion that the price level of the retailer is too high, while it was also found that competing stores should rather be assessed on the 'service' component. Both of these 'weaknesses' seem impossible to align. After all, increasing the service level will generally also involve an increase in cost and therefore an increase of the price level. Add to this the finding that, in retail, the increase in labour costs per hour is generally higher than the increase in sales (threat, see paragraph 6.4) and we have a combination of external and internal factors that could form a serious problem.

The *SWOT-analysis,* also known as situation analysis or strategic audit, aims at combining these findings from the strategic analysis in such a way that it generates a clear picture of the current situation in which the company finds itself. Often, they are accompanied by a straightforward itemised list of opportunities, threats, strengths and weaknesses. Much more powerful, but also much more difficult, is the compilation of the SWOT in such a way that opportunities, threats, strengths and weaknesses can be directly combined. We refer to this method as a *dynamic SWOT*. In this compilation the SWOT results in a matrix consisting of four fields, where each field of the SWOT matrix once again implies a special meaning for the policy (see figure 5.2). For a more exhaustive treatment of the SWOT, see Verhage, 2010.

SWOT-analysis

Dynamic SWOT

5

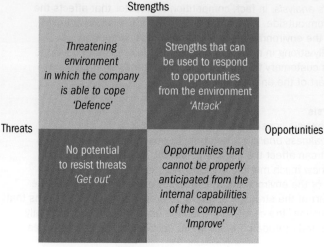

FIGURE 5.2 The meaning of the quadrants in a SWOT-matrix

Strengths

| Threatening environment in which the company is able to cope 'Defence' | Strengths that can be used to respond to opportunities from the environment 'Attack' |

Threats   Opportunities

| No potential to resist threats 'Get out' | Opportunities that cannot be properly anticipated from the internal capabilities of the company 'Improve' |

Weaknesses

5.4.3   Phase 3: Strategy formulation

A business strategy and a function strategy are necessary for the development of the strategy formulation.

Business strategy

Business strategy

The next step in the process is to define which policy will be implemented over the next few years, using the results of the SWOT analysis. Where does the company want to be in a few years, given the market conditions and the individual possibilities? Which weaknesses have to be solved, which threats need to be addressed, which opportunities need to be exploited and which strengths need to be developed to achieve this goal? In short, what is the *business strategy*?

Function strategy

Function strategy

After examining the business strategy, all parts of the company should determine what the statements in the strategy mean for the individual functions and how they should interpret the stated objectives from their own performance. The result of such a reflection is called a *function strategy*. Function strategies in retail include the purchase strategy, the sales strategy and the logistics strategy.

If the business strategy of the retailer indicates that the formula focuses on the lower-earning population groups, this implies low costs for sales so as to apply a price level that only covers the cheapest 25% of the price

Cost leadership

structure in the market (in short, one chooses a strategy of *cost leadership*). This strategy has implications for all functions in the company.

For purchasing, this means amongst others that a choice should be made between buying far away in lower-wage countries (resulting in long supply lines, while maintaining margin) or buying nearby (resulting in short supply lines, but with a margin sacrifice).

For example, this could mean that sales will have to make a choice between cheap – yet decentralised – locations for the store or more expensive, central locations, where they will have to save on other cost entries than just the rent.

For the logistics function, this may mean that they should aim for high sales rates in order to reduce inventory costs. One should then choose whether to have a central warehouse (to optimise the internal logistics process) or not to have a central warehouse, but just-in-time delivery proce-dures (to optimise the external logistics process).

A good strategy not only includes the overall business strategy, but also the specification of this business strategy into sub-functions. Obviously these function strategies have to be assessed for their suitability in the business strategy, hence the feedback loops in figure 5.1.

5.4.4   Phase 4: Translation from policy to implementation

The strategic process is often considered as terminated on the time that the business strategy is adopted and communicated to the organisation. However, determining what the target is ('expressing') and the actual realisation of this target ('applying') are two very different things. To apply the strategy, it is essential that the strategy is complemented by periodic planning: short term plans that are aimed at gradually bringing the pursued target closer. For support functions in retail, we call these action plans *function plans* and for the primary commercial functions, we call them *marketing plans*.

Function plans
Marketing plans

The structure of the marketing plan is discussed in detail in parts 5 and 6. These short term action plans also have to be assessed for their suitability in and consistency with the functional strategies and the business strategy.

5.4.5   Phase 5: Control of the implementation

The last – and maybe even most important – phase in the strategic process consists of the *control on the implementation*. The concept of *control* is not only intended to mean checking on the compliance of agreements, but also – and especially – in the sense of control and management of the process. After each period for which the action plan applies, it must be checked whether the agreements that were made in the plans have actually been executed, whether they have had any results and whether any adjustments have to be made in the next action plan. Due to consistency, it is advisable that the control instruments are the same as those which have been used in the analysis phase. Part 7, which focuses on the control phase, will show that this is possible.

Control

5.4.6   Strategy formulation as a 'rolling process'

The above is a description of how the strategy process should actually proceed. However, in practice we find that this ideal situation is only rarely achieved in retail. First of all, it is already a fact that long-term in retail is fairly short, compared to the industry for example. The lifecycle of retail formulas is growing increasingly shorter under the influence of the rapidly changing environment: nowadays, we assume that a formula has to be revised every three to five years. Compared to the industry, where long term still implies a period of five to ten years, this is very short. This creates a tendency in retail to interpret the strategy based on short term plans, rather than vice versa, as it should actually be done. Secondly, we find that, in practice, the process is often not fully completed: the strategy is indeed pre-pared, sometimes even provided with partial strategies, and communicated

5

through internal circulars of video sessions, but the translation into action plans often leaves much to be desired. Let alone that one should add to the control of the implementation which exceeds the financial control of budgeting.

Rolling process

In response to these practical shortcomings, more and more retail companies – especially the larger, professionally managed businesses – go to strategy formulations such as the *rolling process*: a process where an annual strategic audit is carried out, sometimes very extensive, sometimes less extensive, but always focused on adequately responding to the increasingly faster changing external environment. These strategic audits do not always result in changes in the strategic considerations. It can however be established that, due to the strategic audit, the manner in which the strategic objectives are to be achieved is often changed from year to year. The process therefore has a larger influence on the action plans than on the business strategy. Obviously such a process requires a high degree of flexibility from the organisation. It seems worthwhile to note that, in the current environment, flexibility is one of the most important conditions for survival, especially within the retail sector.

Summary

The rapidly changing environment of the retail and the strongly moving competition necessitates constant reflection. The development and maintenance of a strategy may be helpful in this. Under a strategy we understand 'the expressed and applied collective pursuit of an organisation'. The strategic process consists of the following components:
- the pre-analysis, consisting of the external and internal analysis;
- the synthesis of the pre-analysis in a SWOT or a strategic audit;
- the translation of the SWOT into a strategy, including the preparation of a mission;
- the translation of the strategy into function plans or policies;
- the realisation of the function plans into action plans;
- the control of the implementation.

Not all stages are always completed in practice. That is why more and more (especially larger) companies in retail are starting to make annual adjustments, giving the strategic approach the character of a rolling process.

6
A closer look at the strategic process in retail

In principle, retailing seems to be a simple business: one tries to generate returns by making sales, in which one tries to achieve a certain margin.
But the reality is much more complex and unmanageable, and therefore difficult to reduce to a static 'basic formula'. In this chapter we focus on the basic principles, formulas, the connection between the components of the main formulas, the mechanisms at play and the dynamics within these mechanisms.

6.1 Formula in retail

Return (R)
Sales (S)
Margin (M)
Costs (C)

In principle, retailing seems to be a simple business: the objective is to generate *return (R)* by making *sales (S)*, on which one tries to achieve a certain *margin (M)*. In order to make these sales, one has to incur *costs (C)*. In an equation, it appears as follows:

$$R = S \times M - C$$

Strategies in retail are basically developed to optimise the above objective function for the long-term. This means that R should be continuously enforceable, that the growth of S should be resistant, that M should be acceptable to consumers and that the operational process should be under such control that C does not get out of hand. In short, the strategy should result in a formula that is attractive to consumers and can be maintained for a long time.

Concept
Technical
development

A formula in retail always consists of two parts: the *concept* (the qualitative vision) and the *technical development* thereof (the actual translation). If a good concept is not properly translated, it will eventually fail. Nor will a well-conducted store that has no underlying concept have any chances of survival.

The problem that arises when handling this simple equation is two-fold:
- All elements on the right side of the formula affect each other: increasing the costs can lead to the need for a margin increase (and therefore possibly to an increase of the price level). This will almost certainly influence the sales level. Therefore, we cannot suffice with a single approach to a part of the formula, but we must always apply the formula as a model in which interactions between the variables occur.
- Sales, margin and costs are fairly unambiguous concepts. In practice, however, this is more complicated. Sales in retail is realised in a different way than in an industry, for example, where one often deals with a *mono-product situation*. In a mono-product situation, you can express sales as price times volume ($P \times V$). A characteristic of retail, however, is that we deal with a wide variety of products, that we use different versions with different prices within a product group, and that different margins often have to be used for the respective product groups. Therefore, the simple view of sales as the product of volume and price does not apply in retail. Sales and margin in retail are the results of using a product range mix and a margin mix.

Mono-product
situation

Table 6.1 reflects the sales shares and the margins of the partial product ranges of two formulas that both move in the same market segment. For convenience, the margins for the partial product ranges in both formulas are equal, although this may not always be the case in practice. The product range in both cases consists of groups: books, magazines, stationery/office supplies, greeting cards, tobacco products and candy. It is evident that the product range mix and, as a result thereof, the margin mix of both companies, varies greatly. The first formula is comparable to, for example, Bruna or AKO, and the second is comparable to a convenience store with an additional convenience product range, such as Primera.

TABLE 6.1 Related sales mix, margin mix and formula

Partial product range	1 Sales mix per formula (in %)	2 Sales mix per formula (in %)	3 Margin (in %)	4 Gross profit magazine store (in %)	5 Gross profit convenience store (in %)
	Magazine store	Convenience store	Product group	1×3	2×3
Books	20	12	20	4	2
Magazines	30	15	30	9	5
Newspapers	10	4	45	5	2
Paper /office supplies/ stationery	30	10	40	12	4
Greeting cards	3	12	60	2	7
Tobacco	5	39	15	1	6
Confectionary	2	8	25	1	2
Total	100	100		33	28

Therefore, the sales and margin (and thus the return) in retail do not just depend on volume approaches ('selling more!'), but can also be influenced by selling in another mix ('selling differently!'). As a result, sales analysis in retail is always associated with portfolio-like approaches.

Something similar applies to the cost structure. Not only is this fairly complex in retail (see paragraph 13.2), but we can also achieve the same result using another cost mix: labour costs (such as advice) can sometimes be replaced by cost of product information. Cost of external promotion can sometimes, with the same result, be replaced by cost of internal promotion. Space cost (stock on the shelf) can sometimes be replaced by labour cost (replenishing shelves more frequently). This is different to an industry, where, once a particular production process has been chosen, we are stuck with the cost structure of this process for a long period.

We therefore have to deal with more than the fact that the components of the formula $R = S \times M - C$ affect each other. It also shows that various combinations are possible within all formula components to achieve the set objectives. The objective function of retail is indeed easy to imagine, but optimising that function in practice is extremely complicated. It requires constant alertness to changing consumer preferences (the need to adjust the product range mix), changing price sensitivity (the need to adjust the margin mix) and changing efficiency opportunities (the need to adjust the cost mix).

6.2 Frictions

Frictions

The rather complex situation described in paragraph 6.1 is even more complicated because the objective function has to be optimised, while two opposing forces or *frictions* are constantly at work. On one hand, we have to deal with the previously mentioned contradiction between short-term (tactical) and long term (strategy). It will be clear that this contradiction in retail, basically present in every company, is more acute than elsewhere as a result of the above described mix approaches: the sales mix that has optimal profitability today may vary from the sales mix that is optimal for the long term. The same applies for the margin mix and the cost mix. On the other hand, we have to deal with the situation that the return in retail (especially in retail), expressed as percentage of the sales (return on sales), is lower than in many other commercial branches. This was also demonstrated by the figures in chapter 2, where it was found that the added value of retail is low. On average, retail in the Netherlands makes about one or two percent profit on every euro. This low profit percentage implies that we constantly have to make considerations between the sales opportunities that arise in the market and the costs that are involved in using these sales opportunities. In other words, there is constant friction between the external market position and the internal efficiency. In retail, it is possible to generate huge sales in a way that was not profitable. Therefore, the approach in retail marketing cannot be separated from efficiency aspects.

6.3 Friction matrix

Friction matrix

If we position both frictions opposite one another, the so-called *friction matrix* is created (see figure 6.1).

FIGURE 6.1 Friction matrix: frictions in retail

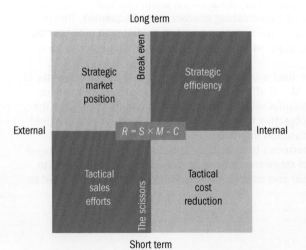

The objective function is central in the matrix. The upper left quadrant relates to *external market position* for the long term and is the actual

External
market position

subject of this book. In this quadrant we are busy with strategic marketing. For retail, this means the development of concepts and formulas:
product development.

The upper right quadrant relates to the *internal structure* of the company.   **Internal**
In this quadrant, we are occupied with strategic efficiency. This often   **structure**
involves building comparative, operational advantages over the competi-
tion. It is possible that increasing the cost is associated with improved
profitability, namely, if the extra costs C lead to a more than proportional
revenue $S \times M$.

Effectiveness is more important than productivity: process development.

The lower left quadrant relates to the *short term market position*, such as   **Short term**
sales promotions and responding to the seasonal demand. This quadrant   **market position**
is less about strategic aspects of the marketing approach and more about
the tactical aspects: merchandise.   **Tactical cost**

And finally, the lower right quadrant relates to the *tactical cost aspects*.   **aspects**
This is more about boosting productivity than increasing the effectiveness:
productivity development. The question in this quadrant usually is:
how can we reduce costs while maintaining the sales level?

The matrix is an important tool in the analysis phase of the strategic
process. Because both the key points and the instruments to be used per
quadrant are different, it is important to know where the centre of gravity
of the problems lies. Figure 6.2 reflects the matrix in more detail: the
outer ring indicates the key points; the inner ring indicates the most
important instruments. Most of these instruments will be treated in more
detail later on.

FIGURE 6.2 A closer look at the frictions in retail

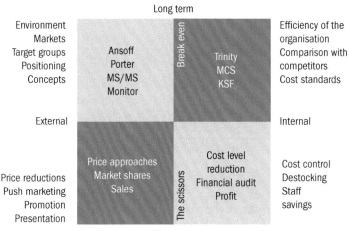

6.4 The scissors

The so-called *scissor mechanism* is active on a short term basis between   **Scissor**
the external and internal aspects of the retail operation. The effect of the   **mechanism**
scissors is one of the reasons why, in retail (particular in retail), particular

attention is paid to the sales development from day to day. The effect of the scissors is illustrated in figure 6.3.

FIGURE 6.3 The effect of the scissors

	Total	Food	Non Food	Labour cost*
2000	100	100	100	100
2001	105	107	104	105
2002	107	111	105	109
2003	106	112	102	114
2004	104	109	99	118
2005	104	108	97	123
2006	105	110	96	127
2007	105	111	97	132
2008	109	117	97	136
2009	108	119	98	141
2010	110	120	98	145
2011	113	122	99	149
2012	115	123	100	152

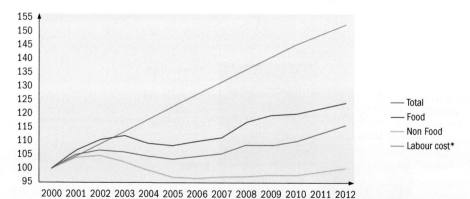

* average cost increase of labour

Figure 6.3 describes the price development of the consumer expenditures in the period 2000 to 2012, where the baseline (2000) is set as 100%. It is evident that, in this period, the prices of consumption increased with an average of 15%. But if we look at the two major categories that make up consumer expenditures, it appears that inflation varies considerably per category. Inflation was low in the non-food sector, namely 0%. It was higher in the food sector, 23%. In the same period, the increase in hourly labour costs in trade was approximately 52%. Labour costs are the largest cost entry in the retail sector. In retail, the labour costs are often 50% to 60% of the revenue or gross margin (S × M).

FIGURE 6.4 The Gap based on sales development and labour cost development

	Total	Food	Non Food	Labour cost*
2000	100	100	100	100
2001	106	107	106	105
2002	109	111	108	109
2003	107	113	104	114
2004	105	112	101	118
2005	105	111	101	123
2006	110	115	107	127
2007	114	119	111	132
2008	117	126	112	136
2009	113	126	105	141
2010	113	127	103	145
2011	110	133	102	149
2012	112	131	98	152
2013	110	133	94	154

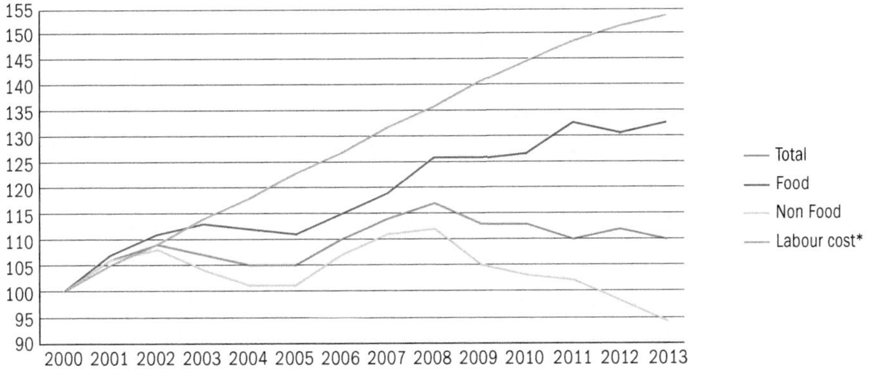

*average cost increase of labour

As we have seen in figure 4.6, the sales in both food and non-food have increased over these past eleven years. For non-food, this means that the marginal growth of 1.2% is explained entirely by volume growth.
It is clear that a situation where the major cost entry increases much more rapidly in price than the sales will eventually lead to an unsustainable situation: this causes profit erosion, illustrated in figure 6.4 by the formation of a gap. If we want to maintain profit levels, we need to ensure that every year we make more sales volume than the previous year or that we reduce the costs every year.
Without significant structural changes in the operation, cost reductions are finite. The short term solution to the dilemma of the scissors is therefore sales growth: growth must!

6

The scissors have been working almost constantly during the post-war period, with two exceptions. The first exception was during the severe recession of the early eighties of the last century. Due to the soaring unemployment, the labour costs development lagged behind on inflation. The second exception was in 2001, during the introduction of the euro, which was accompanied by strong price increases. In periods of a favourable economic climate, the effect of the scissors is not always noticeable, because the positive developments of the consumer expenditures may exceed the negative effects of the scissors. However, in times of economic downturn, the scissors are a retail killer of the highest order.

6.5 The break-even mechanism

Break-even mechanism

Break-even point

The long term translation of the scissor mechanism is the *break-even mechanism* (BE mechanism) (Verhage, 2004). The break-even philosophy was originally developed from financial management and this is why, in literature, it is also generally treated with the financial key figures. The *break-even point* indicates at what sales level, given the budgeted cost structure, initial losses turn into profit. From this point of view, it is a static tool for investment decisions. However, the mechanism can also be used the other way. It is a code that indicates to which point the current sales can drop before the company finds itself in a loss situation. In this respect, it is a dynamic tool for the calculation of the resistance or the safety margin of the company against recessions or attacks from the competition.

In this paragraph we discuss the effect of the break-even mechanism, the calculation of the break-even point and the influencing capabilities thereof.

6.5.1 Effect of the break-even mechanism

The effect of the break-even mechanism (BE mechanism) may be illustrated using the graph in figure 6.5, in which the horizontal axis represents the sales level and the vertical axis represents the revenue, respectively the costs. We will then discuss the fixed costs, the variable costs and the revenues.

Fixed costs

Every retailer has to begin with some necessary costs for the business operations, even if no sales are made, such as rent or the purchase of a store, and the purchase of material and equipment for the store. These costs are independent of the sales to be achieved. These are fixed costs. The graph (figure 6.5) reflects these costs using the horizontal line FC (= fixed costs).

Variable costs

Once the retailer starts making sales, the costs that do in fact depend on the sales are added to the fixed costs. For example, the retailer has to hire staff, purchase packaging materials and organise the incoming

FIGURE 6.5 The break-even mechanism

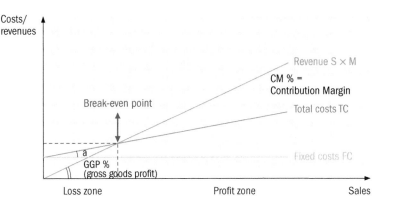

transportation of the goods. All these costs will increase as the sales increases. They are thus variable with the sales, and are therefore *called variable costs*. The higher the percentage of variable costs in relation to the added sales, the greater the angle of inclination (a) of the variable cost line will be. The steepness of the variable cost line therefore indicates the cost dependency of the added sales.

The fixed costs and the variable costs collectively form the *total costs*. They are represented by the TC (= total costs) line in the graph (see figure 6.5). This line actually reflects the variable C in the model $R = S \times M - C$.

Called variable costs

Total costs

Revenues

If you do not have any sales, then you do not have any revenue either. The revenue line will therefore always pass through the origin. With a margin of M % you will have a revenue for every hundred euro sales of M % × 100. In retail, you call this the *profit on goods*. Therefore, the angle of inclination of the revenue line actually indicates the margin: the higher the margin, the steeper the revenue line extends. The revenue line is shown in the graph by the line starting at the origin S × M (see figure 6.5). And with that, the circle is complete again: the break-even mechanism is in fact a reflection of the previously discussed objective function of the retail $R = S \times M - C$.

It should be clear that the angle of inclination M of the revenue line S × M should preferably be larger than the angle of inclination a of the variable cost line. If this is not the case, there will not be any intersecting point of the total cost line TC with the revenue line S × M, and the company will never find itself in a profit situation. To the left of the intersecting point of the revenue line S × M and the total cost line TC, the company incurs a loss; to the right of the intersecting point, it makes a profit. The figure clearly indicates that increase in sales will lead to a more than proportional growth in profits, because the revenue line S × M has a steeper gradient than the cost line TC. We call this phenomenon the *leverage effect* or *leverage*. The problem is that the reverse is also true: decreases in the sales lead to a more than proportional reduction of the profit, something that retailers tend to forget after a period of relative prosperity.

Profit on goods

Leverage effect
Leverage

The intersecting point of both lines is the break-even point. It is character-ised by the situation that costs and revenues are exactly equal to each other, or, in terms of the model: $S \times M = C$.

Given the high volatility of the elements S, M and C in the objective function of retail and given the fact that the BE-graph (break-even graph) is in fact nothing more than a reflection of this objective function, the BE-mechanism in retail, more than in other commercial branches, has become a widely used tool for the daily monitoring of the state of affairs. However, it is exactly because of this volatility, that a number of problems arise in the application of the system. The biggest problem is determining the fixed costs. In the industry it is generally not a problem to determine the fixed costs. But how should you determine the fixed costs in retail if the costs of real estate (rent and/or depreciation of buildings, generally considered one of the fixed costs) can be replaced by personnel costs (generally considered to be variable costs) as indicated in the previous examples? An additional problem is that the interpretation of fixed and variable may vary per level in the organisation. For the management of a chain store, the cost of renting a branch may be variable: after all, these costs vary with the total sales of the company. However, for the manager of the relevant branch, the real estate costs of his branch will be fixed. In practice it will often come down to making agreements about which entries will be considered 'fixed' and which will be considered 'variable'. And it is usually done at each level of responsibility in the company.

6.5.2 Calculating the break-even point

The break-even point is where $S \times M$ is equal to C. The margin (M) in retail can generally be expressed directly and proportionally in sales terms: a margin of 30% means that a gross profit of goods of 30 Euro is made on every 100 Euro. The costs are divided into fixed costs and variable costs. The fixed costs are independent of the sales and are therefore a constant C. In the (simplified) assumption of a straight, proportional relationship between sales and variable costs, you can express the variable costs as fraction (a) of the sales. In other words, variable costs = a × S. The value $S \times M = C$ can then be converted into:

$$M \times S = C \times a \times S$$
$$M \times S - a \times S = C$$
$$S(M - a) = C$$

and therefore applies to the point where the value $S \times M = C$ increases (the break-even point):

$$S(be) = C / (M - a)$$

Resistance

Thus, once we have determined the break-even point, we can determine the *resistance* (or the safety margin) of the company or the establishment. The resistance is defined as 'the percentage that a company can fall back in sales, without resulting in loss.' It is therefore the relative distance of the actual sales level to the break-even sales level. It is clear that the company with the highest resistance will be able to sustain itself the longest in the competition, respectively in an economic recession.

The resistance (R) is determined as follows.

$$R = \frac{(\text{actual sales} - \text{break-even sales}) \times 100\%}{\text{actual sales}}$$

or:

$$R = \frac{\{S(a) - S(be)\} \times 100\%}{S(a)}$$

The formula shows that there are only two ways to increase the resistance (and thus competitiveness) of a company: either by increasing the actual sales, while maintaining the level of the break-even sales, or by downward influence of the break-even point, while maintaining the actual sales level.

6.5.3 Influencing capabilities of the break-even point

The location of the break-even point (and hence the degree of resistance) is not a constant feature, but it is constantly subject to influences from both outside and inside the company. If a proactive policy is not provided, these influences (including the effect of the scissors) will often cause the break-even point to rise (and hence reduced resistance). We will first discuss the external factors, followed by the internal factors that influence the break-even point.

External factors

Earlier in this book, we established that the environment of the Dutch retail is highly competitive. This is partly caused by the structure of the Dutch retail, and thus by the supply side: intricate, professionally organised and small-scale. But the demand side also contributes to the survival of the fittest. Dutch consumers, like the German consumers, and more than in the other European countries, display a frugal attitude: the German and Dutch buy according to price. Yet, throughout the years, we see a picture emerging where both extremes seem to do very well. The extreme luxury brands at the top are also able to claim their place at the top, but the proverbial middle that used to be the best position, seems to be an increasingly difficult position.

The price sensitivity is partly reflected in the strong price competition between Dutch retailers. There is a constant tendency to pressure margins in Dutch retail operations, especially during periods where there is a lack of demand (for example in the period 1981-1983, the period 2000-2003 and most recently in the period of the financial crisis 2008-2009 and the Euro Crises from 2011). In terms of the break-even mechanism, this means that the angle of inclination of the revenue line S × M drops. On the other hand, we noted in the discussion of the scissor mechanism that the price development of the labour costs in the Netherlands is structurally higher than the price development of the retail sales. In terms of the break-even mechanism, this means that ceteris paribus, the angle of inclination a of the variable cost line, rises.

Strategic gap

6

Figure 6.6 reflects the consequences of these changes, brought about by external causes: relatively small drops in the angle of inclination of the revenue line (the margin) and relatively small rises in the angle of inclination of the variable cost line lead to very substantial shifts of the break-even point, and thereby to a drop of the resistance if the sales remains the same. This creates a *strategic gap* that must be filled in order to avoid profit erosion. The consequence is that the entrepreneur should either ensure that his break-even point remains low through productivity improvement (maintaining sales at a lower cost), or he should ensure that he realises such an increase in sales that the shifting break-even point is compensated.

FIGURE 6.6 The dynamics of the break-even point due to external factors

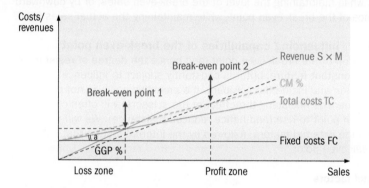

Internal factors

From the internal operation there are countless possibilities that can influence the position of the break-even point, for example:

- We can increase the margin. This means that the angle of inclination of the revenue line increases and the break-even point shifts to the left. We run the risk of pricing ourselves out of the market in relation to the competitors, resulting in a decrease of actual sales and, therefore, possibly the resistance too.
- We can try to influence the angle of inclination of the variable cost line downwards, also causing the break-even point to shift to the left. This means productivity improvement or providing less service. In the last case, we run the risk that sales is influenced, with potential consequences for the resistance.
- We can try reducing the fixed costs, such as searching for cheaper locations. This causes the fixed cost line FC to drop and the break-even point to shift to the left. Even in this situation, repercussions may still be expected: cheaper locations are usually a synonym for less favourable locations, with possible implications for the sales.

Not every approach for reducing the break-even point is wise. Short term solutions, such as increasing the margin across the board with 1% for instance (hardly noticeable to consumers) or by reducing the level of service by not temporarily replacing a sick employee, do contribute to the profit, but not to maintaining the formula. From a strategic point of view, it is therefore rather about influencing the cost structure than influencing the cost levels. In terms of the friction matrix: the position of the break-even point should preferably be influenced from the upper right quadrant and not from the lower right quadrant. Table 6.2 contains a detailed example illustrating this statement.

TABLE 6.2 The influence of a different cost structure, with equal sales and profitability

	Situation 1	Situation 2
Sales	€3,000,000	€3,000,000
Margin	30.0%	30.0%
Fixed costs	€500,000	€300,000
Variable costs	10.0%	16.7%
Revenue	€900,000	€900,000
Total costs	€800,000	€800,000
Profit	€100,000	€100,000
Break-even sales	€2,500,000	€2,250,000
Resistance	16.7%	25.0%

Situation 1 is a company with a sales level of €3 billion per year, which realises a margin of 30%. The total revenue is therefore €900,000. The level of the total costs amounts to €800,000, of which €500,000 are fixed costs and €300,000 are variable costs. The profit therefore amounts to €100,000, a return on sales of 3,3%.

Situation 2 describes a similar company, with the same sales, the same margin and the same total costs and, therefore, the same profit. However, the structure of the costs is different. Unlike company 1, company 2 makes much more use of part-time staff that are flexible in use.
The result is that this company has lower fixed costs, but higher variable costs.

The effect of this difference in cost structure becomes clear if we calculate the break-even point and the resistance of both businesses: although the overall profitability is the same, the break-even point of company 2 is 10% lower than that of company 1 and the resistance is 8.3% higher. Situation 2 is, ceteris paribus, as seen from the competition situation, clearly superior to situation 1.

This does not mean that you, as a retailer, should always works on variability of your cost structure: if you are certain that, due to the economic circumstances or otherwise, your sales will increase in the future, then it may make sense to actually seek to replace variable costs with fixed costs. After all, the increasing sales will automatically reduce the relative cost pressure of fixed costs in the future. However, if you are not certain if future sales increases (there is a recession, or there are new strong competitors in the market), it is always advisable to seek a more flexible cost structure. Ultimately, the choice between fixed costs and variable costs therefore remains a business decision.

6.6 Pricing and costs of e-tailing

Surcharge calculation

The pricing within the e-tail infrastructure will often occur in a totally different manner than in the traditional retail structure. Pricing in the traditional retail takes place by means of *surcharge calculation*: a surcharge percentage is applied to the purchase price of the products. This may vary depending on the competitive structure, sales rate and risks of going out of fashion. This surcharge (the gross profit percentage of goods) then counters all costs excluding the so-called cost of goods sold. Therefore, this includes the personnel costs of the company, the logistics costs of the flow of goods and the rent for the store premises. Because these costs may be high, the surcharge factors are often considerable.

But what about a virtual store? We mention the following aspects:
- The analogy in the virtual store for the service staff is the *search engine* or at least the search structure within the website. This can no longer be dismissed with a single investment. Instead, this requires constant attention, because this is one of the success factors for conversion on a website. The term conversion indicates when a person converts from a visitor to a buyer. This is often indicated with a percentage. A conversion of 10% means that 10% of all visitors become customers. However, the cost advantages here in the online environment are greater than in the physical environment.
- The analogy for the 'merchandisers' is keeping track of the content of the search structure. In a virtual store, this will be associated with significantly less costs than in a real store: after all, the single introduction of an item in a database is cheaper than constantly replenishing shelves with physical products. However, it is important to remember that every customer wants something else. Reviews (content generated by other customers) play an important role.
- The analogy for the store location is the website itself. In traditional retail, the retailer makes the establishment available to his customers 'for free' in the hope that enough money is spent to be able to finally pay rent: it is extremely rare for a retailer to charge an entrance fee for the store. With most virtual retailers, the website is also made available 'for free'. However, the sales needed per visit to cover the 'rental costs' will be much lower than in a store on the Kalverstraat for example. On the other hand, the marketing costs per visitor will be different. In this case, the cost for attracting traffic through other sites is obviously an important example. These are often calculated per CPC (*Cost per Click*) or CPM (*Cost per Mile*). In the first scenario, one pays for the actual visitor, in the second scenario, per indicated impression. The latter form obviously does not guarantee a visit, but it is a guarantee for every 1,000 views of the message. The internet is evolving and people are prepared to pay increasingly more for the added value. In recent years, two models have been added: CPL (Cost per Lead) and CPS (Cost per Sale). Both are based on the principle that, the further one moves into the purchasing process and the closer one comes to the transaction, the more one is prepared to pay. The CPL in particular can be used for services, but also for the sale of cars, for instance. The CPS will be used in more and more online environments and is already widely used through so-called affiliate

programs. With these programs, websites with many visitors can join to offer their advertising space, for which they are paid depending on the method (CPC, CPM, CPL or CPS) that they choose to use. The more someone ends up on a certain website at the end of his purchasing process, the more attractive it becomes to choose for a CPS method.

- The analogy with the logistic costs (in the traditional retail that includes all costs involved with the physical flow of goods from supplier to the shelf – generally the consumer will cover the last part: from the shelf to their homes) does not apply with the virtual store. The prices of the products probably do not include shipping charges, because – depending on the physical address of the consumer – this cannot be calculated in advance. In general, consumers will have to pay for the delivery. This means that they will personally pay for a large part of the logistic costs, including the part that they used to do themselves. This also means that the part of the margin that traditional retailers have to use for the logistics becomes clear with the virtual store and disappears from the margin. The consequence is that the price level perceived by the consumer in virtual stores is likely to be lower than in traditional stores, even if the other operational costs were equal.

All these aspects can cause the operational cost structure of the e-tailer to be significantly lower in the long run than that of the traditional retailer. The entire cost structure should be viewed primarily from the perspective of the fixed and variable costs theory, where the e-tailer has an advantage over the retailer that uses a multi-channel approach. In the most extreme form, the costs of stocking is passed on to manufacturer, there are no costs for maintaining an establishment, there is no risk of the stock going out of fashion and the personnel costs are minimal. What remains are the costs of the *information mediation*. The matching of supply and demand when purchasing a couch (very high receipt price) basically should not be more expensive than matching the supply and demand of a tin of cat food (very low receipt price). So there is a chance that the margins in e-retailing can be much lower than in traditional retailing, causing a reduction of the consumer price level. This will then cause pressure on the margins for the established retail, making survival in traditional retail, as a result of the effect of the scissors (the phenomenon that the price of costs rise faster than the sales), much more difficult than it had already been in the past.

Another important consideration for e-tailers relates to the right diagnosis and control of the marketing costs by type of purchase. The best online shoppers are in fact those who have been active and buying longest. However, the annual Forrester study in the United States indicates that e-tailers commit more than 50% of their marketing efforts into acquiring new customers and less than a quarter of all efforts are aimed at retaining existing customers. Actually, e-tailers need to monitor what their marketing costs are per processed order and they should also keep track of these costs with regard to *first time users* and *returning users*.

Various studies have indicated again that the cross channel companies achieve the highest contribution margin, and ultimately also the highest operational margin. This once again supports what we explained before. In table 6.3 we compare two anonymous examples.

TABLE 6.3 Added value of the online retail

	Pure player	Cross channel
Sales	100%	100%
Cost of goods	51%	50%
Fulfilment costs	11%	8%
Customer service costs	3%	2%
Contribution margin	34%	39%
Marketing costs	6%	6%
Development and technology costs	3%	3%
Content costs	0.5%	1%
General and administration costs	3%	3%
Operational margin	21%	27%

Despite the constant growth of the internet, the online sales of the goods retail is still limited to about 4.5% of the entire retail sales. This is obviously also caused by a large part of sales on foodstuffs with a small online part. However, the online sales will increase rapidly over the next few years. Depending on the sector within the non-food goods retail, this may rise to about 25% in one sector, and even above 50% towards 2020 in another sector.

But ultimately it is not only about the actual online sales, but also about the online related or influenced sales. Websites of retailers are increasingly popular, even with the initial orientation and in the purchasing process. Consumers do not think in terms of channels, as retailers are traditionally used to. The internet must be an essential part of every retail strategy. Not so much from the perspective of the number of transactions online today or over five years, but from the perspective of how the consumer makes his or her customer journey (see paragraph 19.3).

6.7 Effect of measures on the profits from the formula $R = S \times M - C$

The previous section indicated that there are many options to influence the position of the break-even point. However, not every measure has the same effect. Figure 6.7 indicates which measures have what effect.

FIGURE 6.7 The 'drivers' of the return R

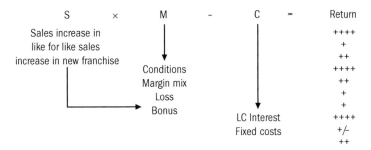

We discuss the measures in the following parts using the formula
1 S = Sales.
2 M = Margin.
3 C = Cost.

Ad 1 S = Sales
An increase in sales generally has a direct influence on the profitability
of a retail company through the effect of the previously discussed
leverage. However, there are different ways to realise an increase in
sales. Some of them are associated with more costs and investments
than others. The most profitable way to realise an increase in sales is
like for like growth. In other words, growth of the sales from existing
stores. To realise this growth, there is no need for investment and it will
generally not be necessary to significantly expand the workforce. Due to
these low growth costs, the return of like for like growth is higher than
for example the return from growth by adding new branches (expansion).
There is a slightly lower return with *growth through franchising* than with
like for like growth. After all, just as with like for like growth, there is no
need for investing in new stores (the investment costs are born by the
franchisee), but it will be necessary to spend more money on monitoring
the operation of the franchisees. Moreover, the franchisee also has to
live from the sales made by him.
A portion of the margin should therefore be sacrificed to satisfy the
franchisee.
Not directly as profitable, but sometimes necessary to maintain the
market position of the company, is *growth through expansion*: we need to
invest in new stores. It will involve initial losses and growing-pain effects,
as a result of which, especially in the first years, the returns of new
stores may even be negative. The more difficult the expansion (by
expanding abroad for instance), the longer the period of negative profit
may be.
With the arrival of the internet and especially by fusing all the channels,
a new challenge is created in the area of sales. Where we always used
to look at sales from establishment's perspective, in future we will have
to look at it from the customer's perspective. Our motto is to combine
the entire sales that is realised by a customer, online or offline. But how
can we do this if there is no customer identification system? A simplification of the model may be helpful: attribute all sales (online and offline)

Like for like growth

Growth through franchising

Growth through expansion

that is realised in the catchment area of an establishment to that establishment. We will come back to this later on.

Ad 2 M = Margin

The most effective way to influence the profitability from the margin is by *improving the purchasing conditions*: when we can buy cheaper without needing to change the sales price level, the condition improvement translates directly into profitability. However, to take advantage of the possibility of improved conditions, it is necessary to achieve a certain predominance over the supplier. That predominance is easier to build up if we have large sales volumes and can show positive growth. Therefore, there is a positive relationship between margin and growth potential.

Another way to improve the profitability from the margin is *optimisation of the margin mix*. By improving the sales in product groups with high margins and the relative slowing down of the sales in the product groups with low margins, the average margin of the entire store increases 'in the mix'. However, this form of margin increase is associated with a cost, and that can be quite high. To be able to implement this margin mix control, it is indeed necessary to change the layout of the store, and that can be expensive. The best known example of this type of approach in the supermarket is to place the most profitable products at eye level and the worse performing products in the bottom shelves. Products at eye level are bought more quickly than products for which you have to get down on your knees. The analogy in department stores: products on the right side of the isle are noticed (and therefore purchased) more quickly than products on the left side of the isle, because of the customers 'tendency to look right'. This only applies to countries where they drive on the right side of the road.

Yet another way to increase the profitability from the margin, is the realisation of *contributions by the supplier* (bonuses, such as promotional campaigns in the store supported with money from the supplier, or advertising contributions) respectively *reducing loss* (reducing theft, breakage and administrative stock errors). Although in the latter case, it often involves large amounts in absolute terms, it produces relatively little compared to the sales: for example, with a loss of 1.5% of the sales (for a company like V&D with a sales of €1.2 billion, this is still an amount of approximately €18 billion that simply slips through the cracks), reducing the loss by 10% would 'only' produce 1.8 billion, while improving the margin mix by 1% will easily produce 12 billion.

Ad 3 C = Costs

The most effective way to increase the returns of a retail company based on the cost environment, is *reducing labour costs*. Labour costs are the largest cost entry for the retail. Roughly 50% of the total earned gross profit (M × S) in the Dutch retail is spent on wages. If we manage to reduce the labour costs by 1%, without sacrificing the sales or the margin (on average 30% of the sales in the Dutch retail), we will realise a profit improvement of 1% as a percentage of the sales × 50% × 30% = 0.15%. With an average 'bottom line' return of the Dutch retail that

---

6

Improving the purchasing conditions

Optimisation of the margin mix

Contributions by the supplier
Reducing loss

Reducing labour costs

moves around 2% of the sales, 1% labour cost savings will produce 2.15% / 2% = 7.5% profit improvement.

Reducing the fixed costs can basically also be very rewarding. The most important part of the fixed costs is formed by the real estate costs (rent, depreciations etc.). These can easily amount to (especially for A-locations) 10% of the sales. However, reducing these costs by half is sometimes associated with considerable investments, such as relocation of the store.

As discussed above, the cost structures for online operations are drastically different from that of offline operations. Although the costs of the rent of the location are reduced, there are many other costs that are taken into account in the discussed formula.

Finally, we can reduce the costs by reducing the investments in the stock. This generates interest earnings, but this potential profit is relatively small compared to the previously discussed methods. Suppose a company with a sales of €90 billion has a sales rate of 3. In other words, an average of €30 billion in stock is present in the company at a market value. With a margin of 50%, this means that it has a purchasing value of €15 billion. Halving the stock (which is a huge task) produces €7.5 billion less capital investment. At an interest rate of 6%, this means a cost reduction of €450,000, which is not much. However, there are other reasons – not so much from the cost thought, but from the marketing thought – that make it necessary to work with low stocks with respectively high sales rates. We will discuss this in more detail in chapters 7 and 21.

Summary

Retailing is a simple affair that can be represented by the formula R = S × M − C, where R = Return, S = Sales, M = Margin and C = Cost. The problem is that, in practice, all the elements of the formula are interrelated and influence each other. Moreover, the simple-looking concepts like sales, margin and cost seem to consist of a mix of factors. Through these relationships and mix aspects, retailing is easy to reflect in the form of a formula, but the practical implementation is rather complex. The addition of the internet channel has made the world more complex, because the cost structures differ completely, while the purchasing and margins remain equal. It is important to take into account, when using the formula, that the formula is interpreted differently with a pure online operation and in a cross channel operation than compared to the traditional store situation.

The objective function R = S × M − C actually appears to be the reflection of the break-even mechanism. An analysis of the factors over time shows that there is a gradual upward pressure on variable costs (the effect of the scissors), combined with downwards pressure on the margin (increasing competition). As a result, break-even point – if we take no action – gradually shifts upwards, resulting in the possibility of profit erosion. This is why constant attention is required for the development of the resistance: the relative distance between the actual sales and the break-even sales. If the resistance decreases, the competitiveness of the company decreases.

We can avoid a decrease of the resistance by either making the actual sales grow (growth must!), or by lowering the break-even point (thus constant focus on the cost structure).

7
Dynamics of retail

Both the effect of the scissor and the effect of the break-even mechanism lead to the fact that increase in sales has an important role to play in the survival of a retail formula. Growth is the most important instrument that we have at our disposal to overcome the strategic gap.

The haunting effect of the strategic gap is the reason why every true retailer continuously compares the sales of the current sales period, with the sales that he achieved in the same period last year. There are huge retail companies where the director receives SMS messages about the sales figures on his telephone every Saturday evening, or he sits glued to his computer screen to constantly receive sales reports from the branches via e-mail. If the sales progression is positive, the atmosphere in the company is cheerful and happy. However, if there sales is reduced – especially when reductions have occurred during several consecutive periods –, the atmosphere in the company is depressing.

The danger with such an attitude is that one seizes every opportunity to achieve an increase in sales, even if they are contrary to the long term policy. Precisely because of this strategic analysis, it is important that we take a closer look at the phenomenon 'growth'. We will do so in this chapter.

7.1 Strategic gap

Strategic gap

With a passive policy, the effect of the scissors and of the break-even mechanism both result in a deviation developing between the actual and the desired return development. This gap is known as the *strategic gap*. This gap can be bridged in several ways. We discuss these ways in this paragraph.

Consolidation of the market position

7.1.1 Consolidation of the market position

First, we have the possibility to *consolidate the market position*, coupled with an increase in productivity, to improve returns. This approach involves relatively little risk. After all, we know the market and have already built a position. The point is to maintain the current sales at lower cost: do better with the same!

7.1.2 Repositioning

Repositioning

A second possibility to bridge the gap is to modify the formula as such that a new growth impulse arises. We continue to serve the same target group with basically the same product range, but we do this in a different way. This is known as *repositioning*: doing the same thing differently! This situation has more risks involved. After all, we are never certain whether the renewal will lead to better results. In practice we see that repositioning in retail companies is often performed with extreme caution.

7.1.3 Product development

Product development

The third possibility is to add new product ranges that fit closely with the already implemented product ranges. This is known as *product development*. The situation does not seem very risky. After all, what is wrong with adding a range of fresh items to the range of dry groceries? Nevertheless, it appears in practice that there are indeed risks associated with the strategy of product development. First, the new product range will often require new expertise that is not always present. We then run the risk of shooting past our objective: the new product range, that initially enters the store unprofessionally, has a negative effect on the old product range, causing the consumer appreciation for the formula to decrease. Secondly, product development often involves blurring. After all, one includes products in the product range that had previously been carried by other companies. The formula therefore has to deal with more competitors then before, while, moreover, the distinctive character of the product range may decrease. Product development should therefore always be associated

USP

with building new distinctive USP's (Unique Selling Proposition) in the added product range relative to the competition. If we do not take care, we are only concerned with imitation and blurring of the industry. The phenomenon of blurring is increasing significantly at the moment, not just in

Banc assurance

retail, but also in the financial sector, the *banc assurance*, although it appears that the tides are turning in the latter sector ever since the financial crises broke out. More banks seem to be going back to their core business: banking.

7.1.4 Market development

Market development

The fourth possibility is attracting new target groups or markets that have not yet been served: *market development*. This strategy also involves risks: by addressing new target groups, we may have to take measures that alienate the old target group from the formula. In addition, we are much less familiar with the needs and desires of this new target group than with those of the old group, who have been coming to the store for many years.

7.1.5   Diversification

The fifth – and most risky – approach to 'close the gap', is that of *diversification*: including new products and product ranges to approach new target groups. This strategy involves both the risks that are associated with product development, as well as the risks that are associated with market development.

Diversification

7.2 Generic growth matrix

It is clear that the methods discussed in paragraph 7.1 involving the ways in which a gap can be closed are closely connected to the theory that forms the basis of the *generic growth matrix* of Igor Ansoff (Verhage, 2010). Ansoff states, based on an existing situation, that 'only' four strategies are possible from the perspective of growth. These strategies are formed by developing new product-market combinations from an existing product-market combination. The message from the Ansoff model is that a common concept like 'growth' is in fact uncommon. Even at a high level of abstraction, there appear to be four 'core strategies' for growth.

Generic growth matrix

The interpretation for retail is the following:
- *Market penetration*: the further and better deepening of existing product-market combinations (old product/old market). In retail we call this 'like for like' growth, in other words, the growth within stores that have been open for more than one or two years, excluding the expansion. Like for like growth is a very important variable within retail, because it shows how the strength of the formula develops. For example, a company that has good growth rates due to strong expansion, but has a negative development on a like for like basis, will eventually have serious problems. Alternative terms for 'like for like' growth are 'organic growth', or 'growth on existing surface'.

Market penetration

- Through *cross channelling* existing customers are given the opportunity to make their purchases through different channels. The experience of many case studies shows that customers who use multiple channels make more purchases from the company. For instance, Macy's reported that cross channel buyers spend twice as much at Macy's than the buyers that only buy from the physical store. In 2011, Real determined that those who also make online purchases with this German supermarket chain, spend a total of 8% more at the chain compared to those who only visit the physical supermarket. The company also indicates that it has only recently started online on a broad scale.

Cross channelling

- *Product development*: providing new products or product ranges to the existing target group (new product/old market). If this is done by adding to existing product ranges in the same store, it is known as *product range expansion*. If this is done by serving the existing target group from a new store with an entirely new product range, it is known as *formula development*.

Product development
Product range expansion
Formula development

7

Upgrading

Downgrading

Filialisation

Internationali-
sation

Cross
channelling

Diversification

- *Market development*: offering the existing formula in new markets or to new market segments (new market/old product). If the new market segments involve higher income groups than before, market development is often accompanied by *upgrading* the formula. If it involves attracting lower income groups, market development is often accompanied by *downgrading*. If it involves new regional market areas in which the same target group as before is attracted, it is known as expansion or *filialisation*. If it involves foreign markets, it is known as *internationalisation*. We must conclude that internationalisation often starts off as market development, but eventually often takes the form of diversification. Besides, under the influence of European integration (see chapter 3), internationalisation is increasing by leaps and bounds.
- Adding new channels (*cross channelling*) gives consumers another way to make purchases, over the internet or by phone. Adding new channels is one way of market development. This allows new customers to be reached. Using affiliate partner programs may offer support in this, but so will cooperating with pure players who open their platform to third parties, like Amazon, Zalando, Bol.com and in a slightly different manner Neckermann, Otto and Wehkamp.
- *Diversification*: entering a new market with a new product. This is the most difficult and risky form of a growth strategy, because we do not know the new market, nor do we have the expertise for the new product. Diversification in retail is therefore only rarely successful.

The essence of the growth matrix is that every growth strategy requires a different approach. Growth through market penetration (old market/old product) requires a different approach than growth through market development (old product/new market), and that, in turn, requires a different approach than product development (new product/old market). In the first case, the organisation should be focused on optimising the formula. This requires an attitude that is strongly focused on the management of existing stores and the maintenance of the product range. The strategic objective is often: 'improving the profitability per existing metre of retail floor space'. The implementation of this strategy is often a mattre for the local branch manager.

In the case of market development (for example expansion through filialisation) the organisation must focus on creating technical opportunities to open new stores. An external, thematic orientation of the organisation is necessary: we must consult with project developers, municipalities and real estate agencies. We must have executors in the implementation phase: individuals with a DIY culture who can quickly reproduce an existing concept. The strategic objective is: '(profitable) expansion of the total market share or increase in sales, rather than by existing metre of floor space. In retail, the implementation of the growth strategy through market development often ends up in the (central) sales function. What is remarkable here is that when it boils down to a strategy to which the internet channel is added, it often ends up with the marketing staff department or IT. However, if you look at the objective of a cross channel strategy, you would say that this is a strategy of market development and would therefore be the responsibility of the sales manager or the general director. The use of the website within the marketing mix should naturally fall within the responsibility of the marketing manager.

An externally oriented attitude is also necessary with product development, but with a different focus than in market development: the challenge now is to properly assess the desires of the customers and to
provide them with a creative solution in return. We need developers rather
than executors. The strategic objective is usually expressed in 'obtaining
new market shares'. In retail, the implementation of this growth strategy
often ends up with the purchasing department.

The fact that the conditions for developing the various growth strategies
are so different, also means that it is very rare in practice for all growth
strategies to be implemented at the same time. It is generally necessary
to make choices: doing everything at the same time divides the attention
and may be at the expense of the effectiveness. However, there are
examples of retail companies that do indeed attempt to implement
various growth strategies at the same time. These are often companies
where the need has become extremely high. A clear example of a combination of growth strategies in retail can be found in the history of de
Bijenkorf (see example 7.1).

7

EXAMPLE 7.1 DE BIJENKORF

In the early eighties of the last century,
de Bijenkorf was in an extremely difficult
position. The target group on which de
Bijenkorf focused (the 'better off') moved
away from the big city and settled in the
suburban areas. Moreover, there was talk
of income equalisation which meant that
the income growth of the target group of
de Bijenkorf was significantly lower than
that of non-customers. Increasing sales
growth of de Bijenkorf was therefore
pressured in two ways: the target group
became smaller and the expenditures of
the target group grew slower than the
total retail expenditures. To make matters
worse, in 1981 a serious recession took
place which mainly had implications for
the sales of luxury product categories,
which covered most of the product range
of de Bijenkorf. Expenditures on luxury
products decreased by 30% in volume
within a year. The 'scissor' was especially
hard at work. In this period, de Bijenkorf
made a million loss and even threatened
to drag the parent company KBB down
with them. In order to reverse this
situation, they developed a major
approach that became known as 'strategic reorientation' and which contained
elements from every quadrant of the
Ansoff matrix:

- Market penetration: encouraging the
  remaining loyal customers to spend
  more money is addressed with the
  development of a loyalty card: a kind
  of *preferred-client* approach of de
  Bijenkorf which had accompanying
  benefits, such as discounts on
  promotions, notification of sales and
  credit facilities. The approach turned
  out to be very successful: currently, a
  major part of the sales of de Bijenkorf
  is realised by customers with a loyalty
  card (the Bijcard).
- Product development: the product
  range was completely re-launched.
  Rather than covering the entire
  range of needs of the top layer of
  the population of the catchment
  area, a product range was developed
  to focus on the needs of everyone
  (including the lower-earning part of the
  population), but still specialised in the
  area of living environment and fashion.
  The mission of de Bijenkorf was
  changed from: 'de Bijenkorf has it all',
  implying that you could find everything
  in de Bijenkorf (as long as you could
  afford it), to 'The marketplace for
  good looking and good living', implying
  that de Bijenkorf had all kinds of nice
  (good!) things for living and fashion,

in a lively atmosphere and at a reasonable price level (market!). The development of the Bijenkorf Home Collection fits in well in this mission: high-quality product ranges that could endure being compared to the major fashion brands, at a price level that was considerably lower.

- Market development: the abovementioned activities resulted in a trend towards a reversal of the sales developments, mainly because existing customers were buying more. However, this was not enough to solve the entire problem. They also needed more customers. Therefore, a manifestation was developed that was aimed at the large number of people that even considered to no longer visit de Bijenkorf because of the 'high cost image', to have them get reacquainted with the revamped and popularised Bijenkorf. In 1984 they started with the Three Crazy Days (Dolle Dwaze Dagen - DDD), an approach where high-quality branded products were sold at extremely competitive prices for a period of three days. The intention was explicitly to attract new target groups – at least once – to de Bijenkorf in the hope that the introduction would lead to repeat visits. The Three Crazy Days were so successful (not only in terms of attracting new customers, but also with regard to sales), that the action

has since been repeated every year and has become a kind of national celebration.

In 1999, KBB and Vendex merged to form the new organisation VendexKBB. This brings all large department stores in the Netherlands under one roof. In 2004 the newly listed retail giant was delisted by a private equity consortium. From 2006 the company changed its name to Maxeda, where it has been known from the beginning that the underlying businesses will eventually change hands. A part of the underlying businesses was already separated.

De Bijenkorf continues to develop itself within the group and is the last of the chains to find a new owner: not a private equity party, but a strategic buyer. In January 2011, the British department store operator Selfridges, which was ultimately owned by a Canadian investor, became the owner of de Bijenkorf. The strategy implemented at de Bijenkorf already seems very similar to the success formula that the new owner has implemented already for several years and everything seems to indicate that this strategy will continue. With the new owners, de Bijenkorf's opportunities of reaching brands and shopping possibilities have increased significantly. The same applies in the area of cross channel retail.

7.3 Dynamics of retailing in the recent past: the post-war period

As we discussed in chapter 1, the emergence of modern retailing can be explained by the economic transaction cost theory. Traditionally, the function of retail was to lower the total costs in the business chain by solving imbalances of time, location and quantity, initially mainly in favour of the manufacturers/suppliers. This connection with the suppliers was also evident from the type of stores that emerged. Until the Second World War, the store base consisted mainly of product oriented specialty stores, a type of store that, from the product range, was clearly tied to a specific business chain. After the Second World War, there was a tremendous acceleration in the dynamics of the types of stores and the relevant operational approaches. We will discuss the implications that these dynamics have on the formula development (the 'outside' of the operation) and on the process development (the 'inside' of the operation) using the theory of the *value chain* of Michael Porter. We will then discuss the developments in various periods after 1945.

7.3.1   Value chain

The basic principle of the value chain (Porter, 1985) is that every company consists of several interrelated sub-systems, with the main breakdown:

- *Primary activities*: the sub-systems that are directly related to the actual transformation process. Due to the nature of the transformation process (activity 2 cannot take place if activity 1 is not ready), the primary activities are always connected in 'series' within the value chain.   **Primary activities**

- *Secondary activities (support activities)*: the sub-systems that have no direct impact on the transformation process, but which are conditional to this. We often see that these secondary activities play a role with each of the parts of the primary process: therefore, they are not only connected in 'series', but also parallel.   **Secondary activities**

Each of the sub-systems adds revenue (values) and costs to the total of the value chain. By analysing these values and costs per sub-system, even – or especially – with regard to the performance of the competition, we can identify the core competences per sub-system. The latter allows us to better utilise the *competitive advantage*.

In assessing the totality of the value chain, it is important that the sub-systems are also 'dovetailed': excellent logistics can be useless if it does not match the sales activities. This dovetailing of the sub-systems it what makes it possible to collect the potential competitive advantages. In other words, the added value within a company will be greater as we have more core competences within the chain and as these core competences are better coordinated. The analogy within retail is the development of formulas instead of simply implementing activities of purchasing, sales and logistics. The value chain for the retail is shown schematically in figure 7.1.

FIGURE 7.1 The value chain of retail

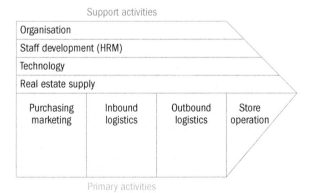

7.3.2 Phase 1 1945 tot 1960: seller's market

The environment in which the retail operated in the period 1945 to 1960 can be outlined using the details in table 7.1.

TABLE 7.1 Development of key figures for retail in the Netherlands*

	Phase 1, 1960
Private consumption	€11 billion
Share of retail	55%
Sales in retail	€5.9 billion
Number of branches	188,500
Sales per branch	€31,300
Share of chain stores	15%
Share of franchise	n.i.

*All amounts have been converted into Euros for the sake of comparability.

Source: HBD, CRK, CBS (own editing)

In 1960, the total private consumption in the Netherlands was €11 billion, of which 55% came from retail, resulting in a sales of €5.9 billion for the retail. These sales were made by over 188,500 branches, which means sales of approximately €31,300 per branch.

The environment was further characterised by an excess in demand and a supply surcharge. It was therefore a *seller's market*: the power was with the suppliers. They also used this power, for example, by establishing and maintaining a vertical price maintenance, as a result of which the marketing mix variable price could not be applied by retail, under penalty of exclusion of deliveries. The size of retail companies was too small to be able to circumvent this sanction by developing own brands. This meant that the buying side of the retail company was actually very simple: it was possible to order products from the package that suppliers offered (the P of product range was therefore specified, the only degree of freedom was not purchasing certain products: *product marketing*). Price negotiations did not occur: the P of price was not an impressionable variable.

Seller's market

Product marketing

Even on the sales side, the operation was actually very simple. Because there was an excess of demand, everything could be sold, as long as it was in stock. Even stores in relatively bad locations (the L of location) could achieve reasonable sales. The mix of impressionable factors in the marketing mix in this period also explains the large number of businesses. There was no real need yet to develop formulas (or distinctive concepts compared to the competition). The sales would be achieved either way, the P of promotion was not really important. The only P's from the marketing mix that could or had to be influenced from retail, were the P's of personnel and of physical distribution. In this period, the retail was designated with the term 'retail distribution engineering', which in fact was largely the reality. The value chain in this period reflected the image as in figure 7.2: a strong internally oriented operation, where the main activity was the logistics, often managed from a hierarchical organisational structure. The companies were

relatively small. Purchasing, sales and logistics were controlled from a
central point: the director/owner. Staff were easy to find. The information
flow was strongly focussed on the distributive aspects of the operation.
Locations were not hard to find and not difficult to select: every store
performed well.

FIGURE 7.2 The value chain of retail, phase 1: to 1960, sales market

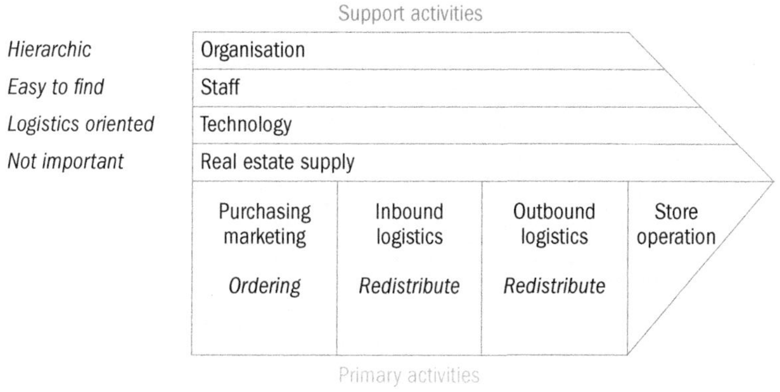

7.3.3 Phase 2 1960 to 1980: buyer's market

In the period 1960 to 1980, the environment in which the retail operated
changed dramatically, as we can see in table 7.2. There was a very significant growth of the private consumption. This growth was accompanied by a
significant loss of market share for the retail. Yet, in absolute terms, sales
in retail grew from €5.9 billion to €41.1 billion. This period was also
accompanied by a radical change of the retail structure: the number of
branches declined from 188,500 to 143,000, mainly due to a reduction of
the old product specialty stores. This often involved the disappearance of
businesses with only one branch, the so-called 'mom and pop stores'.

TABLE 7.2 Development of key figures for retail in the Netherlands, Phase 1 and 2

	Phase 1 to 1960	Phase 2 to 1980
Private consumption	€11 billion	€93.5 billion
Share of retail	55%	44%
Sales in retail	€5.9 billion	€41.1 billion
Number of branches	188,500	143,000
Sales per branch	€31,300	€283,700
Share of chain stores	15%	27%
Share of franchise	n.i.	3.8%

Source: HBD, CRK, CBS (own editing)

The combined result of the growth in retail expenditures and reducing the supply is an extreme increase in sales per store: from approximately €31,300 to €283,700. Staying ahead of the scissors (the phenomenon where costs increase more rapidly in price than sales, also see paragraph 6.4) was never a problem in this period. Good sales were realised.

In the period 1960 to 1980 there were also major changes in the demography of the Netherlands (see chapters 4 and 8). First, there was a drastic levelling of the income situation. The income growth of disadvantaged groups was much higher than the income growth of the wealthy. This resulted in new target groups that, due to the improved income situation, mirrored their buying patterns on the consumption patterns of the previous top tier. Obviously this is also one of the reasons for the huge increase in private consumption. In addition, there was also a public authority controlled redistribution of the population that could be described as a combi-

Concentrated deconcentration

nation of losing the rural character of the countryside and urbanisation. This planning policy was called *concentrated deconcentration*. The result of this policy was the development of a large number of moderate sized independent centres, too small for large-scale developments like hypermarkets, but big enough for an adequate supply of relatively small chain stores. In this period we also see the development of the typical Dutch retail form of small-scale franchised businesses, with a price competitive market approach, such as Blokker, HEMA and Zeeman on the non-food side. But the Dutch supermarkets also became concentrated in this period. Companies were turned into very large companies, despite their small-scale store formulas, due to the multiplication factor.

The growth of the retail companies in this period resulted in the original seller's market changing into a buyer's market: the power in the business chain started to shift from the manufacturers to the retailers that had significantly increased in size. The vertical price maintenance was abolished, allowing the retail to include the pricing tool in the marketing mix. At the same time we see the rise of the horizontal price maintenance, because the retail companies that originated also applied more and more forms of cooperation. Examples here are franchising, but also voluntary chain stores and the continued growth of buying combinations.

The increased volume of retail companies also enabled them to develop own brands in those cases that the manufacturers failed to meet the product range requirements (and that lasted for a very long time). The supplied product range was henceforth composed by the retailers and no longer by the manufacturers. However, this meant that the retail was no longer a simple reseller, but had to assess the consumers demand at own risk and cost and had to develop a fitting product range. We were in the

Product range marketing

middle of *product range marketing*. Especially in the non-food sector, where it often involves *lead times* of six months or longer, this meant that predicting the demand became the most important success factor. Those who could adequately respond to what consumers wanted in the store over six months (or later), were lucky: the sales was guaranteed in that case. It was therefore possible to build adequate *cash flow* from sales, which was further strengthened by the fact that, in this case, the sales rate was high and the logistic costs were low. The released cash flow could be used for rapid expansion to the increasingly more common growth centres on the urbanised countryside. Figure 7.3 shows which image the value chain reflected in this period.

FIGURE 7.3 The value chain of retail, phase 2: 1960-1980

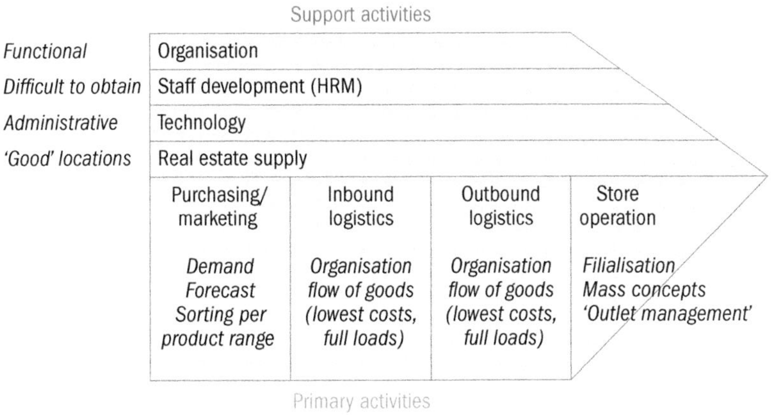

Support activities

Functional	Organisation			
Difficult to obtain	Staff development (HRM)			
Administrative	Technology			
'Good' locations	Real estate supply			
	Purchasing/ marketing	Inbound logistics	Outbound logistics	Store operation
	Demand Forecast Sorting per product range	*Organisation flow of goods (lowest costs, full loads)*	*Organisation flow of goods (lowest costs, full loads)*	*Filialisation Mass concepts 'Outlet management'*

Primary activities

The hierarchal organisational structure of the previous period could no longer be maintained in this situation of rapidly growing companies: a functional structure emerged where purchasing, logistics and sales were separated. Purchasing was no longer simply filling in checklists based on the order books provided by the manufacturers, but it became *marketing*: predicting and responding to the needs of consumers. Sales was no longer simply filling the shelves, but it became *outlet management*: managing a multitude of branches. Logistics, formerly the primary function of retail, became a cost entry: the lower the logistic costs, the higher the cash flow, which is why they drove as much as possible with 'full' loads. The information was strongly focussed on managing branches. The process was mainly externally focused: on the purchasing side on the development of purchasing markets, on the sales side on the demands of the consumer. In short, despite the fact that the structure of the value chain in its entirety was the same as in the previous period, we see that – under influence of the altered environment – the procedures that take place within the value chain had a completely different content.

Marketing

7.3.4   Phase 3 1980 to 1990: stabilisation
In the period from 1980 to 1990, compared to the previous one, there were considerable changes in the external environment in which the retail had to operate. In the early eighties, there was a significant recession that had profound implications for retail. The reorganisation of the establishment database was accelerated by the elimination of weak companies. The chain store, with its more favourable cost structure and its greater formula power, jumped in and filled the vacant places. But the recovery after 1984-1985 did not lead to an increase of the supply: the number of branches decreased slightly to 138,500. The majority consisted of the branches from chain stores or independent businesses that joined commercial organisations for support, where franchising particularly seems to be gaining popularity. In terms of quality, however, there were indeed changes in the supply: the

Formula marketing

share of formula companies increased and represented more than a third of the sales. We were in the middle of the *formula marketing* (table 7.3).

TABLE 7.3 Development of key figures for retail in the Netherlands, phase 1, 2 and 3

	Phase 1 1960	Phase 2 1980	Phase 3 1990
Private consumption	€11 billion	€93.5 billion	€137.6 billion
Share of retail	55%	44%	39%
Sales in retail	€5.9 billion	€41.1 billion	€53.6 billion
Number of branches	188,500	143,000	138,500
Sales per branch	€31,300	€283,700	€387,000
Share of chain stores	15%	27%	36%
Share of franchise	n.i.	3.8%	4.7%

Source: HBD, CRK, CBS (own editing)

There were also changes on the demand side. The Dutch consumer, who already had a tight-fisted expenditure pattern (the retail expenditures per capita are lower in the Netherlands than in the neighbouring countries), underwent a *culture shock* as a result of the recession. Consequently, the consumer developed a variety of savings strategies. After the recession, this was partly continued and thus resulted in a change in the buying patterns of consumers. One of the implications was that the growth of the retail started to decline: the sevenfold expansion in the twenty year period between 1960 and 1980 fell back to a growth of approximately 36% in the ten years between 1980 and 1990. Target groups started to blur, the consumer became individualistic and, in response, the retail converted from target group marketing to *purchase time marketing*. Where the target groups of HEMA and de Bijenkorf used to be clearly identifiable and distinct in composition, HEMA decided to focus on the daily non-food purchase time for everyone (run shopping), while de Bijenkorf focussed on the recreational purchase time (fun shopping), which even the less fortunate have need of from time to time. Everyone visited every store within their store horizon.

Purchase time marketing

The effect of the scissor was very noticeable in this period. It was therefore no surprise that there was a significant *efficiency drive*: *Direct Product Profitability* came up, larger companies started to apply sales occupancy schedules, full-time employees were replaced by part-time employees and space-management programs were introduced. In the previous period, the focus in the operation was aimed on the development of new formulas, causing a significant degree of dynamics to occur in the supply. This focus shifted to strengthening existing formulas and develop-ing new internal, cost-effective processes. At the end of this period, the Netherlands had become a country of branch managers and managers, with a fairly uniform, but efficient structure. The Dutch retail was able to work with margins that were much lower than the foreign margins, with low sales per store, for consumers with a tight-fisted attitude. These character-istics formed a solid barrier to foreign suppliers who wanted to come to the Netherlands. We also see that the internationalisation in this period took place mainly from the Netherlands to other countries (especially to Belgium), while the opposite occurred much less and was rarely success-ful. Halfords (acquired by Macintosh and sold in 2013) and Dixons (acquired by Vendex and later sold by its successor Maxeda) are examples of foreign companies that gave it a go in this period, but were ultimately unable to keep up with the pace. In this period of stabilisation, the value chain showed little change. At most we can say that much attention was paid to the supporting activities necessary to achieve the cost savings in the primary activities. During this period, the establishment regulations were also adapted. It was the beginning of the first out-of-form shopping areas. The Netherlands had its own interpretation of large-scale and peripheral retail.

7.3.5   Phase 4 1990-2000: vertical integration and scaling

We already saw that, in the previous periods, retail in the Netherlands showed a high degree of dynamics in response to changes in the environ-ment; in the bygone period, these dynamics were strengthened even more. The filialisation that was initiated in the eighties was further strengthened. The chain stores continued its march further, but even franchising started to take off. In 2000, the sales share of all franchise stores increased to 12%, tripling in just twenty years. However, in the first five years of the nineties, the number of stores increased sharply. A real turning point seems to be development; there was even enthusiastic talk of a break in the trend. In 1995, the Netherlands had 156,000 stores. Several experts predicted that the trend of fewer stores had finally turned.

TABLE 7.4 Key figures for retail in the Netherlands, Phase 1, 2, 3 and 4

	Phase 1 1960	Phase 2 1980	Phase 3 1990	Phase 4 2000
Private consumption	€11 billion	€93.5 billion	€137.6 billion	€207 billion
Share of retail	55%	44%	39%	35%
Sales in retaill	€5.9 billion	€41.1 billion	€53.6 billion	€73 billion
Number of branches	188,500	143,000	138,500	149,500
Sales per branch	€31,300	€283,700	€387,000	€488,300
Share of chain stores	15%	27%	36%	44%
Share of franchise	n.i.	3.8%	4.7%	12%

Source: HBD, CRK, CBS (own editing)

Despite the increasing consumer expenditures (booming behaviour in an incipient recession), there is an extremely unstable situation in the retail: companies like Peek & Cloppenburg, C&A and V&D are having a very difficult time, Kreymborg and Amici even falling away, while companies like Hennes & Mauritz, IKEA and Cool Cat are flourishing. It seems like there is a revolution at play: the old established order is dying and being followed up by fast, nimble newcomers. Vertically integrated companies are able to accelerate achieving market share. The new 'vertical' players are characterised by keeping control over the entire value chain. Retailers, especially in fashion, were used to purchasing from manufacturers who put together collections. In fact, it was mainly collections and making selections from the range. Many (fashion) retailers still see the world like this, but for retailers that have implemented the vertical integration, this works differently. These retailers have their own design departments. They may have outsourced their manufacturing, but they are in full control. An important feature of these retailers is the relatively high turnaround speed that they show compared to the traditional competition.

A second development that retail has to deal with are the new shopping hours. After Germany, the Netherlands had the most restrictive trading hours act in Europe. Meanwhile this restrictive store closing law (you have to be closed from 18.00 pm to 09.00 am) was replaced by a store opening law (you may be open, at your own discretion, between 06.00 am and 22.00 pm) in 1996. Especially entrepreneurs in chain stores consider, in majority, that the trading hours act has a positive effect on their sales, but also on the total employment in the retail. Smaller store owners are less positive about the new policy, although the trading hours act also creates opportunities for these entrepreneurs. Interestingly enough, most stores remain closed in the evenings after 18.00, unlike our eastern neighbours who are now open everywhere until 20.00. Not so long ago, stores in Germany had to be closed after 14.00 on Saturday afternoon. Our environment has changed in terms of working hours and labour participation. In addition, the internet has been added as a time independent channel. How do retailers respond to the new consumer demand? Availability to consumers will determine future transactions.

Just before the internet bubble, e-commerce made the world shake in its foundations. Forecasts regarding the online sales, but especially the rate at which this should happen, ensured that a real internet hype was created. The new mechanism of buying at home from behind your computer seems to be causing physical shopping to disappear.

Although the number of stores has increased over the years, a slow downwards trend was already visible before 2000. But not the number of square metres of stores; this is constantly increasing further. Stores are bigger, they offer a wider range and they are totally focused on the customer. This development is one of the main *drivers* behind the vastly increased sales per establishment.

In 2000 this had already grown to €488,300, an increase of more than 26% in ten years and an increase of more than 72% since 1980.

EXAMPLE 7.1 VERTICAL AND TRADITIONAL SUPPLIERS COMPARED

In 2007, the extent to which the performance of so-called 'verticals' (retail companies largely work according to the above described processes of demand tracking) and more traditional suppliers (who still work with the old method of demand forecasting) differs from one another with regard to margin and sales, was examined based on an annual report analysis.

The null hypothesis was that the verticals focus on a high sales rate and a relatively low margin (resulting in a high $GMROI$ = sales rate × margin), while the traditional suppliers focus on high margins with a relatively low sales rate. And then we also have a group of exclusive designers that focus on an extremely high margin in combination with an extremely low sales rate (see figure 1).

FIGURE 1 Graph of sales rate

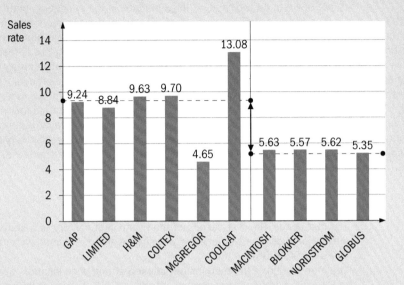

Indeed, the analysis shows that the sales rate of the verticals is on average one and a half to two times as high (5 to 9 in comparison to 3 to 6) as that of the traditional suppliers. Translated in commercial terms: a customer of a vertical seller encounters a new, current collection almost every month, whereas that of a traditional supplier encounters the same collection for three to four months. Let it be clear that, in a situation where the consumers behaviour changes from 'wardrobe marketing' (buying a new wardrobe every six months) to 'collection marketing' (buying something every month to go with that which they already have in their wardrobe), the verticals will be at an advantage.

FIGURE 2 Graph of margin

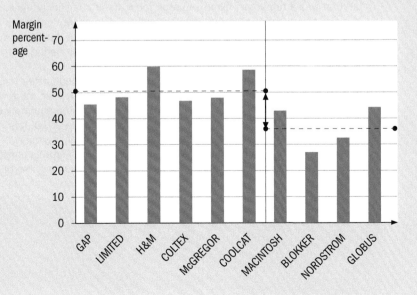

Though the null hypothesis was confirmed, this does not seem to be the case with the margin (see figure 2). In contrast to the expectations, the margin of the verticals was even unexpectedly higher than that of the traditional suppliers (with the exception of GAP). Further analysis revealed the cause of this. We are dealing with an annual report analysis here. As opposed to budgeting, in which one works on *input* margins, these annual reports work with *output* margins. The cause of the phenomenon seems to be that traditional suppliers do indeed use high margins in the budgeting, but that they have to mark down more due to the relatively low sales rate during the season because of 'being out of fashion', causing the ultimately realised margin to be lower than that of the verticals. The lesson: short lead times and high sales rates do not just lead to low inventory costs and high topicality, but ultimately to high profits, because the percentage markdowns are greatly reduced.

Phase 5 to 2010

The last period, the first decade of the twenty first century, is a series of difficult periods. The Netherlands were in the grip of a recession for several years (2002-2005).

The introduction of the euro initially caused strong price inflation, specifically in food retail. Prices increased by up to 6%. In 2003, after declining market shares (and accounting fraud at Ahold parent company), Albert Heijn launched a large price offensive, the starting point for the price war. As a result prices in the supermarket sector had virtually no increase or even decrease for several years. Laurus lost the battle, leading to the disappearance of the formulas Konmar and Edah (where the name Laurus expires and becomes Super de Boer N.V.). The foreign supermarket companies still have not managed to enter the Dutch market, the French Casino made an attempt, but left again in 2009 when Jumbo took over Super de Boer.

The financial crisis followed in 2007. This did not immediately affect the actual economy of the public consumption, this was still increasing in 2008, but that was a temporary climax. Europe found itself in a second recession in a short time and the Netherlands certainly had its share. In 2010 a new problem emerged, but we had to wait until deep into 2011 before the Euro Crisis showed itself in its full extent. Economists predict a period of stagflation that may just continue for one or two decades.

The share of retail in the total private consumption dropped further to 31% and the number of branches shows another decrease, but once more with the knowledge that branches have become larger again. The summary of table 7.5 shows the developments of the key figures up to 2010. It is striking how the filialisation has continued to push through, certainly supported in this by the growth of the sales in franchise. Formula concepts now dominate the shopping streets and retail is turning into a game of big players.

TABLE 7.5 Key figures for retail in the Netherlands, Phase 1, 2, 3, 4 and 5

	Phase 1 1960	Phase 2 1980	Phase 3 1990	Phase 4 2000	Phase 5 2010
Private consumption	€11 billion	€93.5 billion	€137.6 billion	€207 billion	€265.6 billion
Share of retail	55%	44%	39%	35%	31%
Sales in retail	€5.9 billion	€41.1 billion	€53.6 billion	€73 billion	€83 billion
Number of branches	188,500	143,000	138,500	149,500	108,000
Sales per branch	€31,300	€283,700	€387,000	€488,300	€768,500
Share of chain stores	15%	27%	36%	44%	60%
Share of franchise	n.i.	3.8%	4.7%	12%	27%

Source: HBD, CRK, CBS (own editing)

This is also the period in which the so-called *category killers* grow in Europe and in the Netherlands. Category killers are companies that opt for a very wide product range and competitive pricing. Additionally, they preferably establish themselves on a low-cost location which has lots of parking. These are retailers that apply supermarket principles to non-food categories. High turnaround speeds with lower margins. European examples are Castorama (DIY), Decathlon (Sport), Hornbach (DIY), Leroy Merlin (DIY), IKEA and Media Markt-Saturn. IKEA has been operating in the Netherlands for many years and will expand considerably in the first years of the new decade. Media Markt started in the Netherlands in 1999 and, within a decade, became market leader in its sector. Companies like Hornbach and Decathlon also settle down in the Netherlands, but they clearly need more time in order to settle on many places.

The initially stringent PRE (peripheral retail establishment) policy was made more flexible, becoming the much more liberal LRE policy (which included large-scale peripheral stores). This was followed by the Nota Ruimte 2005 in 2006, under which municipalities could decide, in consultation with the province, whether retail premises may be established outside urban areas. The freedom of municipalities has not yet lead to large landslides and many new branches. The question is how this will develop because of the economic situation, the vacancy on furniture boulevards and the development of e-commerce. The time may come to develop an ERE-policy (electronic retail establishment). In doing this, new store concepts may emerge on today's furniture boulevards and LRE-locations, for example, shopping areas where online purchases can be collected offline. This may solve one of the most expensive and perhaps most complicated parts of the online logistics. After all, we still combine a very limited part of all our purchases. We do not aggegrate them and if we buy on five different websites, there is no way to indicate that they can be delivered at the same time, by a single party, at home or at work. The ERE locations may offer the solution. These are places with lots of parking and generally easily accessible. Pure players could establish pickup centres here.

Traditional retailers could also establish themselves here, offering the possibility to collect online purchases. Additionally, lockers could be installed on these locations to collect online purchases. Amazon.com has similar pickup points in the United States and Ahold also started with such points. The development of online shopping is gigantic in this period. In 2005, the online sale of products only amounted to 1.2 billion, while this increased to 4.3 billion in 2010. Where traditional retailers immediately walked away from e-commerce after the internet bubble in 2001, they all started to come back in the second half of the decade. Online retailing is no longer the magic word, but *multichannel* or *cross-channel*. Retailers believe that it is no longer up to them to choose the channel, but that they have to simplify matters for the customer. Customers do not think in terms of channels and they want to buy anytime and anywhere. The growth rates may be levelling off online, but with percentages over the last few years of around 10% to 12%, this is still much higher compared to the limited growth of the entire retail of around 1%.

The first outlet centres were introduced to the Netherlands in 2000. It took a few years for them to prove themselves, but the first two centres seem to be doing well now. Nevertheless, there is still a lot of resistance in the Netherlands against opening more of these so-called *outlet centres*, shopping areas where brand manufacturers sell various models at lower prices. But these centres seem to provide in a need and the cannibalisation on the existing retail is not always as evident as claimed.

Private equity discovers retail as domain for achieving their goals. In 2002, CVC became the first private equity firm that made a large scale deal with the so-called six pack. They purchased six specialised store formulas from VendexKBB. The six formulas are known together as Retail Network Company. After revitalisation, each of the formulas is later sold to new shareholders. VendexKBB also had a turn in 2004. A consortium around KKR removed the fusion product of Vendex and KBB from the stock exchange. The organisation was renamed and, after a while, was known as Maxeda. The objective of this exertion was not for the long term, but optimisation and resale. Throughout the years, Maxeda has sold almost all companies. In 2007 HEMA was sold, again to a private equity firm. The British Lion Capital took over the Dutch party. In 2011, this resale was temporarily taken off the market. In 2008, CVC returned to the front and Schuitema, the owner of C1000, removed the company from the stock exchange. The sale to a new owner, Jumbo, was realised by early 2012. In 2009 V&D also ended up in new hands and, once again, this was a private equity firm, Sun Capital partners, which became owner of a Dutch retailer. In 2011, the private equity firm 3i seized the North Holland retail company, Action. Despite the financial crises, the private equity firms still seem to believe in retailers and it seems that not only the financing model has room for improvement, but also the business model of the retailers themselves. In retail, the return on sales (ROS) is relatively low and the return on investment (ROI) is relatively high. This makes it particularly interesting for private equity. The optimisation of businesses and achieving scale benefits by accelerated growth seems to be paying off.

These remain challenging times for retailers. V&D seems to be doing better, but comes from a very difficult period. This company has drastically adjusted its business model. It is clear that the company is building, but also that it is facing difficult market conditions. The same applies for many other retailers, including C&A. There are implications for traditional retailers that do not move quickly enough. In 2004, Megapool was the first victim of traditional retailers. Their rival, It's, has been able to hold on for a few years longer, but expanding category killers and online retail in the electronics branch were too powerful, even for this company. In the books industry, Selexyz had problems during the course of 2011, and Free Record Shop in the music industry in 2013.

Both industries are affected by the rise of internet retailers. Many traditional retailers were too late in implementing changes. In the fashion industry a large chain also experienced problems and Hans Textiel had to close their doors.

7.4 From product push to demand pull: consumer central

Predicting the trends in demand (the core competence of the past) is increasingly more difficult and, in some categories of goods (like fashion), perhaps even *de facto* impossible. This probably means that the old processes within the value chain will (have to) change again. Which direction can that go?

Let us make the extreme assumption that it would really be impossible to predict demand, even in the short term. In fact, this will never be the case. But as working hypothesis to determine what we should prepare ourselves for, it makes sense to work out such a hypothetical situation, even if it is only as a *worst case scenario*. The only option in such a scenario to determine how the product range should be composed is to try out the product range in the sales. This is the only way to determine whether or not a product is successful. In other words, the demand forecasting (*product push*) is replaced by demand tracking (*demand pull*) and the relevant market research function shifts from purchasing to sales. In recent years, this field has also been called *effective consumer response (ECR)*. The development that lies behind this and which was strengthened by the arrival of the internet is that we evolve from a *B2C (Business to Consumer)*-market to a *C2B (Consumer to Business)*-market, also referred to as a customer centric environment. It may appear to be just words, but it has a huge impact on businesses and means that customer satisfaction is the factor in question. However, establishing the fact that a product is successful, is of little help if it is not possible to store enough stock in order to meet the demand. This means that the long lead-times of the past, caused by the actual production time and the logistic processes, are no longer manageable. We need to move forward to a situation where the lead time is shortened to the extreme. In other words, the logistics, which in the previous period were considered a cost entry, are becoming more and more a marketing instrument.

It is no longer about low-cost supply, but about rapid supply of the branches, even if this is at the expense of the margin. This need does not necessarily have consequences for the profitability. If we are able to achieve an increased sales rate by shortening the lead time, the net result may even be

Product push
Demand pull

Effective consumer response

Continuous replenishment

better than before. The use of *continuous replenishment* (*CR*) is required, in other words: ensuring that the right amount of products is always present in the right place. From the perspective of returns, it is more favourable to make a margin of 30% six times a year than to make a margin of 40% three times a year. The critical control variables for the future are therefore no longer just margin, sales, or floor productivity, but should also include *gross margin return on inventory* (*GMROI*) defined as margin multiplied by sales rate. We will discuss this method further in paragraph 13.4. If we want to follow this method, it is necessary to be assured of a fast, flexible supply and production of goods. Depending on the findings in sales, it should be possible to quickly adjust product specifications. We must therefore create the possibility to quickly rearrange the production with our suppliers in the short term. In short, purchasing will have to deal less with sorting per product range and more with capacity management and process control. To make this work, a good relationship with suppliers is necessary. Using

Supply chain management

supply chain management (*SCM*), it is possible to make this coordination with the suppliers. Where vertically organised companies like H&M and ZARA already take care of this by themselves, it also applies to other retailers that *chain integration* is not a luxury, but a necessity. If one wants to reduce the stocks in the chain and therefore minimise the capital requirement of goods in the chain, then cooperation is of great importance. It is also essential to share information with each other.

Much has changed in the area of the information flows. We cannot wait until the end of the season to analyse the sales results, but need to do this all

Direct product profitability

year round, every day, week and per period, during which different key figures are central. *Direct product profitability* (*DPP*), scanning data and *activity based costing* (*ABC*) should be available to the capacity manager (the

Activity based costing

old buyer) from day to day, in order to implement rapid control. Again, sharing information with suppliers allows you to make the chain more efficient. If lead times can be shortened and thus also the stock days in the chain, a lot of money and therefore margins will be available.

It is clear that this makes the process much more complicated than it used to be. This requires a lot from the organisation. Instead of the functional responsibilities of the past (where purchasing was responsible for the (inflow)margin, sales for the costs and purchasing and sales collectively for the sales, with all the consequences), we are moving towards control where the overall responsibility for margin, sales, logistics and costs per product range group are managed from a central point. We are moving from a functional control to a divisional structure, where the product range groups (category) will effectively operate as separate *strategic business units*. We

Category management

call this organisation philosophy *category management* (*CM*) (Munneke, 1998). See also sub-section 20.2.2.

The value chain for the retail that goes with such a process might look like figure 7.4a.

FIGURE 7.4a The value chain of today

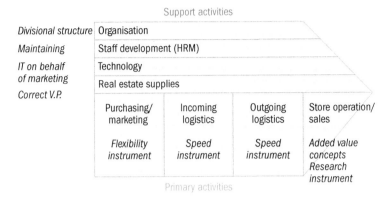

Figure 7.4b also shows the relationship with the supplier.

FIGURE 7.4b The value chain of today: the process

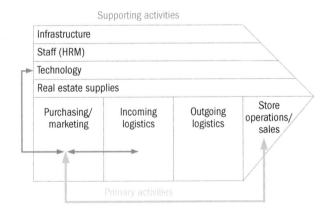

7.4.1   The new interpretation of the transaction cost theory

In paragraph 1.5 we already determined that the ratio of retailing can be found in the transaction cost theory: in those cases where *economies of scale* were realised through the mass production and where it was cheaper in terms of transaction fees to *outsource* the distribution, retailing emerged. In the original situation, where there was clearly a seller's market, retail formed a part of a *goods producing process*, or an extension of the manufacturers. We then saw a development in which the original function of the retail as part of a goods producing process, gradually shifted to that of retail as part of a *demand satisfying process*. This does not mean that the ratio of the retail (reducing costs in the business chain) is no longer relevant. We simply have to interpret the transaction cost theory from another point of view. Where is the power currently in the business chain? It is evident that it largely ended up with the final consumer. Admittedly, the retail thought that they had the power for some time, but it is becoming more and more apparent that this was actually only derived power. If this is true, we have to interpret the transaction cost theory in the new situation from the most powerful factor: the consumer. In this perspective, we should really say that the ratio of the retail is no longer to reduce the actual tangible costs in the business chain, but to reduce the (tangible and intangible) 'search costs' of the consumer. Search costs should thereby be interpreted in a broad sense: they form the balance of positive costs in terms of time, money and displacements, and of negative costs (revenue) in terms of shopping pleasure. The consumer will then prefer to use this transaction place, physical store or webshop, where the search cost balance is more favourable. With that we have the explanation as to why it is so important to have a clear and consistent formula within the current retail, both online and offline. After all, a consistent formula is nothing more than insurance for the consumer that his expectations of the brand will be met. Moreover, the formula thereby reduces the need to search elsewhere (so it reduces search costs).

With that we also have the explanation of why supermarkets compete increasingly more on product range, promotions and services, now that the prices are very close together due to competition (with price reductions it is no longer possible to reduce the search costs for consumers) and where the branches have been positioned very close to each other (another supplier can always be found in the vicinity of any Albert Heijn, making it increasingly more difficult to reduce the search costs via network densification of branches). After all, this is the only way that it is still possible to reduce the balance of the tangible costs and the (intangible) revenues.

In some non-food categories, the process has already changed completely. With access to the internet, reducing the search costs in the electronics industry has certainly changed in favour of the consumer. Consumers can compare performances, prices and suppliers. The step to buying online is a very small step. We also see that the online share in this industry is already considerable. Entirely new industries have emerged to reduce the search costs of consumers, just think about the (price) comparison sites.

Social media has added a dimension to this in the last few years. Not so much because everything that happens is new, because it is in fact word-of-mouth advertising, only through the digital highway. After the product comparison sites, following the example of travelling (Zoover, Tripadvisor and Booking.com) and restaurants (Iens and Yelp), there are now also store comparison sites like Wugly and Yelp. Within online retail it has long been customary for suppliers to get reviews. Initially this was also done on (price) comparison sites, like Kieskeurig, but now this is also done on shopping websites such as Wugly.

Facebook has grown fast over the last few years and by the time that we wrote this book, already had 1,23 billion users over the world. This medium is typically used by brands to bind consumers to them. The so-called 'like' makes it possible for very many connections to see at a single glance what someone likes. Google did not stay behind and started its own network: Google+. This social media is used to bundle the opinions of others. They give retailers the advantage of being able to see the comments and personally respond. In this context we should also specifically mention Twitter, which can be used to communicate with the customer. However,

retailers are faced with the challenge of how to manage the endless
information flow, especially when they represent a bigger brand and will
therefore also evoke many opinions. The emergence of new media requires
an adjustment of at least the communication and marketing strategy of
every retailer. We will come back to this later in the discussion of the
customer journey of the consumer (see paragraph 19.3).

7.5 Development theories in retail

In the literature on retail, we distinguish four development theories:

- The theory of the *Wheel of Retailing* of Malcolm P. McNair (McNair, 1958)   **Wheel of**
  assumes that every innovation in retail is caused by the accession of   **Retailing**
  price aggressive specialist newcomers. Newcomers who subsequently,
  forced by rising costs (the mechanism of the scissor!), firstly commit
  product range expansion, secondly apply upgrading and finally specialise
  in the more expensive segment. The development of department stores
  like de Bijenkorf and Maison de Bonneterie are good examples of this.
  They both started off as specialist suppliers of (household) textile. This
  was followed by a period of parallelisation in the segment of bulk goods.
  In the period after the First World War, there was a clear upgrading
  from neighbourhood stores to elite department stores and, finally, a
  period of relative specialisation emerged. In the case of Bonneterie,
  this specialisation led to the creation of a fashion store. In the case of
  de Bijenkorf, this led to a fun shopping department store, focussing on
  fashion and living.
- The *harmonica* of Stanley Hollander (Hollander, 1966) is based on   **Harmonica**
  alternating cycles of specialisation and parallelisation, creating a kind of   **theory**
  wave motion in the marketing approach of formulas.
- The *dialectical theory* of Thomas Maronick and Bruce Walker (Maronick   **Dialectical**
  and Walker, 1975) is based on the assumption that there is a continuous   **theory**
  process of thesis (luxury downtown department stores) and antithesis
  (in response: cheap hypermarkets), from which a synthesis eventually
  develops (high-quality hyper stores like Carrefour).
- The *evolutionary theory* of Anton Dreesmann (Dreesmann, 1968) is based   **Evolutionary**
  on the Darwinian evolutionary theory of the creation of sub-types, types,   **theory**
  specialisation, fanning out and finally displacement. Based on the idea
  that a retailer has to adapt to the environment, the Dreesmann theory is
  very interesting. Especially when we perceive that consumers are quickly
  able to adapt to the new environment.

We have to conclude that none of these theories fully comply in practice. We
often have to combine elements of the four theories to (*ex post*) reach a
reasonable explanation of the developments. The best known theory is that
of the 'Wheel of Retailing', which did indeed give an adequate explanation
for the situation immediately after the Second World War, but which seems
to be outdated now. Specifically the fact that not all formulas begin as
downgraded, price aggressive specialists, undermined the philosophy. We
increasingly see formulas arise precisely at the other end of the spectrum:
high-quality, lifestyle-like specialty stores, like ZARA, Next and Benetton.

7

Summary

In this chapter we tried to make two things clear. First of all, there are
several possibilities to increase sales. Using the product market matrix of
Igor Ansoff and the strategic-gap analysis, we wanted to make it clear that
this is possible, namely by:
- Market penetration: do better with the same;
- Market development: do the same, but for a bigger target group or in new
  regions;
- Product development: do new things for the same target group as before;
- Diversification: do new things for new target groups.

Each of these growth strategies requires an individual approach, both with
regard to organisation and process. Market penetration is the least risky,
followed by market development and product development. The most risky is
the diversification strategy. We often see that diversifications in retail fail.
Secondly we wanted to show that, in the post-war period, considerable
changes took place in the dynamics of retail. These dynamics in retail
basically consisted of gradual changes, but over time we see that these
changes continued to accelerate. Due to the changes in the environment, we
have seen amongst others the development of product marketing, via
product range marketing to formula marketing. This was accompanied by
significant changes in the internal processes within retail. At the moment we
can see these changes occur at an accelerated rate. Not in the least
because of the extent to which the internet has become a part of our daily
lives, with the result that the internal processes within retail continue to
change. Increasingly, there will be a reversal of the value chains: from
product push to demand pull: in other words, the true reversal retailers of
the future are not Business to Consumer companies, but real Consumer to
Business companies.
The chapter concludes with a brief summary of a number of growth theories
in the area of retail, the most common of which is the 'Wheel of Retailing'.

PART 3

External analysis

Effective functioning in society requires knowledge on the one hand (what am I doing?) and skill on the other hand (how am I doing?). In the previous two parts we tried to provide some insights into the structure and composition of the retail sector in the Netherlands, and the peculiarities of the strategic process in retail. These parts are aimed at imparting knowledge and understanding retail. In the following, we shift the focus more to a combination of 'knowledge' and 'skill' aspects: how do we implement retail strategies? Which details are necessary for this? And above all, how do we interpret these details and how do we translate the results into action?

In this part, we pay particular attention to the influences of the external environment of retail. The analysis of the external environment provides insight into the opportunities and threats that we have to take into consideration when determining our strategy. A part of the external exploration also relates to the trends (see chapter 4).

8
Environmental exploration

Retailing is typically an industry that is closely related to its environment. This environment is constantly subject to change. The relationship between retailing and environment is also highly dynamic in nature, as we have seen in chapter 7. In this chapter we specifically discuss the relationship between retail and an ever changing environment. Which environmental factors play an important role and how do these factors evolve? What are the most important environmental factors ('opportunities and threats') for retail and what role do they play in the strategy formulation? What is the influence of the economy? In this chapter, we give an answer to these questions.

8.1 Rapidly changing environment

Retailing is an industry where we have to deal with a continuous and very direct interaction between what is happening in society and the answer to this that we, as retailers, have to develop. In the past, when society had a more static character, a retailer could suffice with gradual adjustments to the concept: the changes in society unfolded so slowly that the frequency of the technical maintenance of the concept was enough to keep up with the developments. In the current turbulent environment, this is no longer possible: the *product life-cycle* of the formula is often shorter than the maintenance cycle. In economic terms: the economic life expectancy of a concept is shorter than the technical life expectancy. The reason for this is the rapidly changing environment. It is therefore important to know the environment well in order to quickly recognise the developments relevant to the retail and to take corresponding action. Therefore, this requires an analysis of the *environmental factors*: those factors (opportunities and threats) that affect the retail company from the outside and of which the development cannot be influenced by the retailer.

Environmental factors

FIGURE 8.1 The position of the environmental exploration in the strategic process

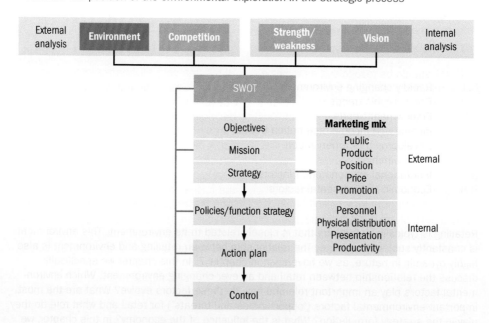

Environmental exploration

Environmental exploration can be subdivided into three main groups:
• analysis of trend developments;
• analysis of institutional frameworks, such as legislation;
• analysis of economic environmental factors.

The position of the environmental exploration in the strategic process is shown schematically in figure 8.1.

A number of key environmental factors that are important to retail are discussed below. We have to note that the treatment cannot be exhaustive and that there is no set rule to be given for the identification of environmental factors: the relevance of previously identified environmental factors may change from year to year, while new factors constantly emerge (see chapter 7).

8.2 Demographic trends

Retail, as the last link in the production process, serves the consumer directly. The developments in the composition, geographic distribution and lifestyle of consumers (summarised under the term *demography*) are therefore an important factor for the retailer.

Demography

The relevance of demographic developments to retail is often extremely direct, as demonstrated by the following examples:

- Older people feel more insecure and less able to cope regarding the increasing insecurity than younger people. Increase in the proportion of older people in the population should therefore lead to a shift of the product ranges in retail, such as more security equipment and other forms of insurance. In practice we already see this happening. For example, DIY markets in older neighbourhoods carry a wider range of security than in new neighbourhoods. Insurance companies develop special products for older people, such as 'reverse mortgages' and senior investments.
- Single households need smaller packages than multi-person households. Supermarkets will have to respond to this when the portion of single households increases (already doing this: Albert Heijn's product range in the centre of Amsterdam, which has many single households, has a larger share of small packages than in Almere, which has many families with younger children). But it also affects how we live. IKEA has responded well in showing how to design a home with very few square metres. HEMA responds to the changing demography with mini-supermarkets in town centres.
- The owner of a newly purchased home with garden, living in a small town, seems to spend a lot more on DIY activities than residents of a rented apartment in an old quarter of the city. DIY organisations therefore keep an eye on where these developments take place and then choose their location so that accessibility from such neighbourhoods is optimal.

This paragraph focuses on the developments in the age structure of the population and on the family composition and the number of households.

8.2.1　Developments in the age structure of the population

Figure 8.2 shows how the development of the age structure of the population evolved over the past century and how it is expected to develop in the future. It is clear that significant changes have occurred, not only by the increase in the population itself (the pyramid is wider), but also in the distribution over the age groups (the pyramid deforms from a pure cone to a kind of biscuit barrel). In common parlance, this development is also known under the term *ageing*.

Ageing

8

Declining birth rate

Birth surplus

Baby boom

However, further examination of the pyramid shows that there is a high incidence of ageing (the relatively heavier representation in the pyramid in the older age groups). In the Netherlands there is only a limited extent of a *declining birth rate* (the relatively lower representation at the bottom of the pyramid). Incidentally, this trend is much stronger in other European countries and requires attention when one opts for international expansion. The cause of the ageing population and declining birth rate must be sought in the sudden increase of the *birth surplus* (the difference between the number of new births and deaths) after the Second World War, the so-called *baby boom*. This is partly reflected in the age structure of 1950, where we experienced a strong increase in the number of children aged 0-4 years. After 1950, the birth surplus decreased, in a trend-like manner. The decrease continues for several decades (1950: 3.1 children per woman; 1970: 2.6 children per woman; 1990: 1.6 children per woman), but by 2000 the birth rate recovers slightly to 1.7 children per woman, and by the end of the first decade of the new century, the number of births per woman increased again to 1.8 children. At the same time, the children born during the baby boom are growing older and shifting to the middle age classes, which explains the pot-bellied shape of the population pyramid in 2000 and 2010. With a glance at the more distant future, the belly will always continue to move up and in 2020 the baby boomers will already be 75 years old. By 2030, the shape will resemble a cylinder that is capped slightly at the top on both sides.

This has the following significance for retail:
- The age structure of the population has implications for the retail operation. The age structure of employees in retail differs significantly from the overall age structure of employees. The employment in the Dutch business community consists of more than 11% of young people aged 15-24 years. In retail, this figure is approximately 30%. It is clear that a relative decrease in the number of available young people has a far greater influence on retail than on the business community as a whole. One of the consequences may be that retailers have to hire more older people, respectively have to appoint returners. In general, older employees are more expensive than younger employees. This trend may therefore be an additional boost to the effect of the scissor (see chapter 6). The question, however, is how long we have to maintain this situation. The new situation in terms of age structure requires a new approach to salaries in retail. We will have to work with all relevant social partners to come to a new salary structure if we want to keep retail accessible to all consumers.
- Older people exhibit expenditure patterns and behavioural patterns that deviate rather strongly in parts from that of younger people. The combination of an increasing portion of older people and a decrease of the portion of younger people may therefore have implications for the development of market segments. Retail must prepare for this by adjusting the product range and sometimes adjusting the retail formula.

FIGURE 8.2 Age structure of the Netherlands 1960, 1980, 2000 and 2020

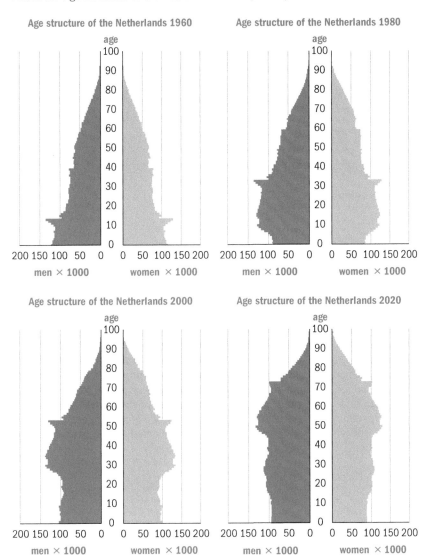

An example of the first one: table 8.1 shows the result of a study on the expenditure pattern per age group. It is clear that the patterns differ substantially. Table 8.1 should be interpreted as follows: per capita, younger people spend 20% more than average on mobile telephones, including subscription fees, and older people spend 13% less than average.

The figures indicate that, if the expenditure behaviour per age category would remain the same (which is unlikely), significant market dynamics can occur simply through the ageing population and declining birth. The mobile market may become much smaller, while the markets for furniture may grow

TABLE 8.1 Expenditure patterns of age groups

Item	Relative expenditure per capita compared to the average	
	Age 15-34 year as index	Age > 55 year as index
Clothing	102	92
Jeans	104	87
Mobile telephones	121	77
Tablets	108	99
Laptops	99	97
Jewellery, watches and trinkets	76	106
Furniture	79	121
Care, medical products	92	99
TV's	80	111

Source: Frank Quix, Q&A Research & Consultancy, 2011

significantly. What makes this analysis much more important is that it indicates that the age groups have very different purchase patterns for some product groups, while the purchase patterns of these age groups do not or barely differ from other product groups, even if this was expected, for example when it involves medical healthcare products.

The described development of a simultaneously ageing population and declining birth rate is expected to continue for the time being. Table 8.2 shows the expectations of the population structure by age group in 2015 and 2025, where the trend that started is clearly reflected in the structure of the population.

TABLE 8.2 Population structure by age group, history and prognosis

	1990 (in %)	2000 (in %)	2010 (in %)	2015 (in %)	2025 (in %)
< 45 years	67	62	57	54	53
> 45 years	33	38	43	46	47

Source: CBS StatLine, 2011

8.2.2   Family composition and number of households

Table 8.3 shows how the number of households in the Netherlands has developed over the past few years. It is very clear that significant changes have occurred in the composition of the households: the number of single households increased by 134% from 1980 to 2007, while the increase in the number of multi-person households was only 19%. This is associated with a reduction of the average number of persons per household from 2,78 in 1980 to 2,25 in 2007. According to the prognosis, this development is still far from over: in 2025, 41% of all households will be single households, while this percentage was only 22% in 1980. This means almost twice as many in less than fifty years' time.

TABLE 8.3 Development of number of households, history and prognosis

	Single households (× **1,000**)	Multi-person households (× **1,000**)	Total (× **1,000**)	Persons per household maximum
1980	1,085	3,921	5,006	2.78
1985	1,556	4,057	5,613	2.54
1990*	1,794	4,318	1,662	2.41
1995	2,109	4,360	6,469	2.35
2000	2,272	4,529	6,801	2.30
2005	2,449	4,642	7,091	2.27
2010	2,670	4,717	7,387	2.22
2015	2,904	4,697	7,601	2.16
2025	3,275	4,717	7,992	2.09

* Household series: calculated figures based on Housing Needs Survey 1985/1986, Population statistics, statistics of the housing stock and survey of Uninhabited Houses.

Source: CBS, Households Prognosis 2002-2050, Andries de Jong, CBS, StatLine, 2011

The increase in the number of single households is often attributed to the increase of young single households. But in fact there are two effects at work. On the one hand, there are increasingly more 'incomplete' single households among the older population, in other words, divorced people, widows or widowers. Since women live longer than men, this specifically relates to the female part of the population. On the other hand, we see a growth of young single households; there seems to be a trend developing where young people continue to live longer alone. This trend may directly affect the further development in the future of multi-person families, because having children at an older age is increasingly less likely.
But not only is the development of the portion of singles relevant; we also see developments occur in the category of multi-person households (see table 8.4). The portion of families without children is increasing significantly: from 26.6% in 1960 to 45.6% in 2010.

We provide the following examples of the possible significance of these developments to retail:
• The number of households will increase significantly more than the number of consumers. For retail, this means that a shift may occur to costs related to the household (such as furniture and household items) at the expense of the expenditures related to the person (such as fashion, personal care and books). After all, every house has at least one TV and, based on the fact that a Euro can only be spent once, expenditures in one category may be at the expense of another. As for food, the development in terms of money may even turn out to be more favourable. Smaller packages and more convenience products at higher prices, such as ready-to-eat meals.

TABLE 8.4 Development of the number of families without children

| | Couple with | | | | One parent with | | Total | % |
	O children	1 child	2 children	3 or more	1 child	2 or more		without children
1995	1,843	784	926	402	218	142	4,315	42.7
2000	2,016	768	908	406	229	155	4,482	45.0
2005	2,062	755	932	400	262	182	4,593	44.9
2010	2,127	742	929	377	293	193	4,661	45.6

Source: CBS-publication Monthly Statistics of the population, CBS StatLine, 2011

- The increase in the number of single households and the number of families without children may negatively affect the sales developments in product categories that are related to children, such as toys, baby clothing and children's bikes. On the other hand, the development of families without children and single households means that more disposable income is available for non-essential expenditures.
- Changes may also occur in the service sector: singles, and to a lesser extent, two-person households without children, generally have less concern for dependant relatives than families with children. Regarding the sorting of the product range pertaining to life insurance, this may for instance lead to a reduced relevance of risk insurance (insuring that dependents are not at risk) and an increased importance of capital insurance (insuring that policyholders themselves are not at risk in the future).

8.3 Employment trends

In the development of employment, two trends are very important for retailers. The first is the growing proportion of working women (table 8.5). This often involves the middle age and older age categories that work part time: returners. The growth of female employment by more than 60% over 40 years is an important development for retail, especially in the view of the store opening.

The significance for retail: on one hand, this development can absorb the previously described 'declining birth rate', which makes it increasingly more difficult to find young employees. On the other hand, it means that there will be more available income per family (which is favourable for retail). At the same time, there is less time available to spend this higher income (which is unfavourable for retail). We therefore have to deal with an increase of the portion of consumers with relatively much money and relatively little time. The objective of retailers to have longer opening hours for the stores is thus clearly affected, but definitely needs to be developed further. The closing times that we were used to in the past were therefore established in a time where the female employment rate was very low. We are heading towards the 50% employment rate and will therefore require a further reorientation of opening hours. The majority of Dutch retail still opens its stores once most of the Dutch people are already several hours

TABLE 8.5 Persons employed in the Netherlands

	Total (× 1,000)	Of which woman (× 1,000)	Share (in %)
1970	5,451	1,563	28.7
1980	5,955	2,022	33.9
1990	6,695	2,593	38.7
2000	8,115	3,544	43.7
2005	8,251	3,760	45.6
2010	8,644	4,039	46.7

Source: CBS StatLine, 2011

at work and closes the doors again before the typical employee has emerged from the afternoon commuter traffic. German retailers (known for years as the most conservative of Europe and even closing their stores on Saturday afternoons) generally open their stores every day until 20.00. Not linking the opening hours to the working hours of the labour force plays right into the hands of online retailers. The enormous growth of online sales is certainly associated with the conservative point of view of many retailers regarding the opening hours.

8.4 Income and income distribution trends

The sales in the retail sector are highly dependent on the expenditure possibilities of consumers. The development of the income situation of the Dutch population is therefore an extremely relevant environmental variable. An increase of income generally leads to an increase of expenditures in retail. The ratio, however, is not one on one: the income elasticity varies per product category. An increase in income will generally have less effect on the primary expenditures (such as food, basic products and risk insurance) than on secondary and tertiary categories, such as luxury products, fashionable clothing, leisure trips and investments. The opposite also applies: in times of recession, for example, the sales in the food sector are better maintained than in the luxury sectors. This is illustrated in table 8.6, in which the development of the growth rates of a number of product categories is displayed during the only real major post-war recession that we have known in the Netherlands, namely that of 1981-1983. It is clear that the decline in growth rate of the luxury product categories is much stronger and more dramatic than that of the basics.

TABLE 8.6 Relapse of growth rate of product categories during the recession of the early eighties of the last century in terms of volume development

Items with a primary character	Trend progression 1977-1979	Growth rate	
1 Groceries	1	4	+3
2 Milk and dairy	12	8	−4
3 Stockings/socks (excluding pantyhose)	−4	−4	0
4 Household items	2	−6	−8
5 Office supplies/Stationary	14	8	−6
6 Underwear	+5	−3	−6
Items with a secondary/tertiary character	**Trend progression 1977-1979**	**1980-1982 Relapse growth rate**	
1 Women's tops	14.0	−8	−22
2 Shoes, including sport shoes	22.0	−3	−25
3 Home textile	26.0	−4	−30
4 Furnishings	−6.0	−17	−11
5 Furniture	−5.0	−18	−13
6 Leather goods	12.0	−3	−15
7 Toys	13.0	0	−13

In the recent crises years, we also see that food and non-food retail sales do not develop equally (see figure 8.3). Especially striking, particularly in the latest crisis, is that food retail showed a growth in value. In the last ten years, food retailers only experienced a slight decline in value in 2004 and 2005. It is important to note that, in 2005, the supermarkets only recorded a minor decline of 0.4%. Recessions affect non-food retailers more than food retailers. Actually, this is not really surprising; consumers always need to eat and if they only have a limited income growth, they will save on non-food purchases.

Possibly even more important than the average income trend, is the income distribution trend. The income distribution of the Dutch population has significantly levelled out from the fifties to at least the late nineties. This means that the income in the lower income categories increased more than that of the higher income categories. This is in strong contrast to the image that is often sketched in discussions on bonuses and high salaries of executives. Here too, it applies again: pay attention to the numbers behind these facts. How many people are involved? Incomes in the Netherlands have experienced a strong levelling and the proverbial

FIGURE 8.3 Value Development of Dutch Retail 2000–2012

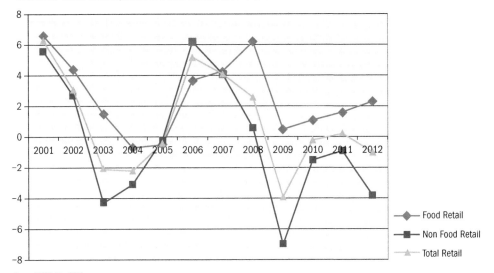

Source: CBS Statline 2014

Balkenende norm is probably the best example of this. The levelling of the income situation had a direct impact on retail. Because the income of the lower income groups grew much faster than that of the higher income groups, *mass consumption* became possible: items that used to be reserved for the high-earning top tier of the population, came within reach of the entire population. This promoted amongst others the strong expansion of chains, mainly in the lower price segment, which is one of the characteristics of the Dutch retail infrastructure. The levelling of incomes also has a great advantage: in times of crises it is less likely for everything to fall apart, because a levelled income distribution can better absorb economic blows.

Mass consumption

Furthermore, we must conclude that the government policy in the new millennium exhibits traits of unlevelling. This could lead to a division of society into *haves and have-nots* and to a distorted income distribution. This may have substantial implications for retail. On the one hand, the financial retail will for example be able to survive: provisions that were previously provided by the state (pensions, benefits), now have to be provided increasingly more by consumers themselves. This may lead to a shift from the collective to the private sphere. Alternatively, it may cause the market of the retail merchandise sector to stagnate completely, or grow less quickly, partly because money that is spent on pension premiums can no longer be spent on goods, and partly because popularisation of new markets is less likely to occur.

8.5 Development of urbanisation

Urbanisation

**Suburbanisa-
tion**

**Concentrated
deconcentra-
tion**

The development of *urbanisation* in the Netherlands has taken place along different lines than abroad. Abroad, a very strong urbanisation took place first, a migration from the countryside to the cities. In the second phase, a movement of *suburbanisation* occurred in response: fanning out from the cities to related areas, which nevertheless remained dependent on the nearby cities for their provisioning. The result was the emergence of very large agglomerations with a generally strong central provisioning.

Instead of large agglomerations, the Dutch planning policy led to a simultaneous development of 'de-villaging' and 'urbanisation'. This policy was characterised by the term *concentrated deconcentration*. As a result, a large number of medium sized municipalities, independent of the agglomeration, originated: the urbanised countryside, whereby every municipality had a personal – albeit limited – provisioning. The urbanisation structure, which was established by the policy of concentrated deconcentration, is one for the main causes of the small-scale retail infrastructure that is typical for the Netherlands. The catchment areas of the centres in the urbanised countryside were in fact too small to maintain large-scale developments in the retail as they occurred abroad. They were however an ideal breeding ground for the multiplication of small-scale formulas. In the period in which this played out (1950 to 1990), the strong expansion of most Dutch stores took place (see table 8.7).

Table 8.7 also shows that several other developments took place from 1990. First of all, it is striking that especially the number of residents in municipalities with less than 5,000 residents and 5,000 to 20,000 residents decreases strongly. The explanation lies firstly in the municipal reclassifications (predominantly groupings of municipalities) in this period.

TABLE 8.7 Long term developments in the Netherlands

	1950	1960	1970	1980	1990	2000	2005	2010
Number of residents	10 billion	11.4 billion	13.0 billion	14.1 billion	14.9 billion	15.9 billion	16.3 billion	16.6 billion
Residing in:								
Municipalities with < 5,000 residents	14.7	11.6	8.2	5.0	2.3	0.4	0.2	0.1
Municipalities with 5,000 to 20,000 residents	28.8	28.4	30.0	30.1	28.8	22.4	16.6	13.1
Municipalities with 20,000 to 50,000 residents	15.6	15.6	18.0	24.4	26.1	31.4	34.3	35.9

TABLE 8.7 Long term developments in the Netherlands (continued)

	1950	1960	1970	1980	1990	2000	2005	2010
Municipalities with 50,000 to 100,000 residents	9.5	11.4	14.5	13.7	17.5	14.9	17.5	18.4
Municipalities with 100,000 or more residents	31.4	33.0	29.3	26.8	25.3	30.9	31.4	32.5

Source: CBS StatLine, 2011

Many of the smaller municipalities were absorbed by municipalities that currently have 50,000 and 100,000 residents. In addition to this administrative scaling, urbanisation also takes place: the population in municipalities with 100,000 residents shows a strong increase between 1990 and 2000. In the years following the turn of the century, the increase levels off slightly, although there is still a relative growth. Between 1990 and 2000, this development seems to be at the expense of municipalities with 50,000 to 100,000 residents, because the number of residents in this group declines in the years after 2000, returning to the level of 1990, and even appears to increase again towards 2010. The population in towns with between 20,000 and 50,000 residents continues to grow after 1990 to nearly 36% in 2010.

The impact of these developments on retail is that larger retailers settle with smaller sizes in smaller catchment areas. Take HEMA for example, who settles in municipalities like Best and Someren with a slightly smaller size store, in smaller neighbourhood shopping centres, but also on high traffic locations. The retailer follows his customer with a matching product range.

A consequence of the urbanisation combined with the ageing, is the depopulation in some areas of the Netherlands. There is already evidence of shrinking in some corners. The *shrinking* areas are located in De Achterhoek, East Groningen, Zeeland and South Limburg. A city like Heerlen already has the fewest births, the oldest population and the most deaths. In the mentioned areas, the classes are growing smaller and the number of residents is slowly decreasing. The long term implication of this development is that fewer stores are necessary. But heading towards the future, this means adjusting product ranges. Back to School promotions are not very useful if nobody has to go to school.

8.6 Trend watching

In addition to the quantitatively observable shifts, qualitative shifts also occur in the vicinity. This often involves changes in the attitudes of consumers. The big problem with detecting changes in consumer attitudes is that one never knows in the early stages whether it involves a *hype* (short-lived change in consumer attitudes) or a *trend* (lasting changes in consumer attitudes, often in response to structural changes in the social perception).

Hype

Trend

Trend watching

Trend watching is a way to give direction to the biggest unpredictable factor that exists: the future. There are frequent publications, of varying quality, incidentally, engaged in the inner life of the consumer. But not all detected trends are actually important to retail. In chapter 4, we extensively discussed the developments of importance towards 2020 according to the *Re'structure* report by HBD and Inretail (Terra and Quix, 2010). Furthermore, we refer to reports and websites, such as *10 Retail para-doxes* of the HBD (Quix and Hemmer), *2020: four scenario's for the future of retail*, HBD, *The New Shopping*, HBD (Quix, Terra, Hamann and Wortel) *The Popcorn report* (Popcorn), *Generations* (Strauss and Howe) *Megatrends Netherlands, New Netherlands* (Bakas) and the websites Frankwatching.com and Trendwatching.com. Using trend information correctly starts with the fact that multiple sources should be used. It is very important that you also look at who made the prognosis and whether this person has been correct with his prognoses in the past. It is also good, in addition to the qualitative trend reports, to see if these are supported by quantitative data.

One way to get started on trends and on what they can mean for a retail operation is the 3forces model (see paragraph 4.2). Within this model, we start by identifying trends as the first force. The second force is to identify consumer needs and the third force is to identify competences. The combination of the three forces is called a trend bundle. The growth path is found where the three forces intersect. The bigger the cutting edge, the bigger the opportunities for the company (see paragraph 4.2).

8.7 Institutional environmental factors

Institutional environmental factors

Under *institutional environmental factors,* we understand the legal and legislative frameworks within which the company should operate. In a small and densely populated country like the Netherlands with a strong regulation, there are many, such as licensing systems for exercising professions, dismissal law, wage systems (including statutory minimum wage regulation), liability regulations, price regulations and establishment legislation.

The institutional environment is generally fairly stable. Once legislation exists, it remains in effect until the law is changed. However, if such a law is changed, the impact of that change is often very direct and abrupt. This is an important difference with the previously described environmental factors, where trend changes actually take place gradually. Changes in the institutional factors may well be important for the industry as a whole and for individual companies. A historical example of such an abrupt change in the institutional frameworks with profound implications for the industry as a whole is the prohibition of vertical price maintenance, regulated by the Law on Economic Competition.

Before the ban on vertical price maintenance came into effect, retail suppliers were allowed to make price agreements with their customers. In fact, this meant that a large number of branded product manufacturers determined the consumer price bypassing the retail, under penalty of exclusion of supplies. This made it impossible for the retail to use the price instrument in the mutual competition. Letting go of the vertical price maintenance meant that the retail had more grip on the overall marketing mix, and also used that. Discount formulas became possible and the battle for market share erupted. From the consumers' side, this meant that it was worthwhile to 'shop around': more stores were visited prior to making a purchase, the usual store loyalty decreased and the consumer gained more insight into the formula selection.

We will discuss two institutional factors below: the trading hours act and the policy on retail warehouses.

8.7.1   Trading hours act

The previous Dutch trading hours act (Strauss and Howe, 1991) that dates back to 1930 was slightly modified in 1976, and finally, in 1993, changed once more. This law had a highly restrictive nature: stores could be open for a maximum of 52 hours per week, but never after 18.00. A shopping night was allowed once per week. All other opening hours were exceptions and had to be exempted case by case. The revision in 1993 eased restrictions somewhat: stores could now be open 56 hours per week, the closing time was extended to 18.30 and a limited number of Sunday openings were allowed.

Compared to neighbouring countries, those rules were still extremely inadequate: in 1996, the average operating time of stores in Europe was 87 hours per week. Compared to the 56 hours allowed in the Netherlands, this was significantly more. A large number of countries (France, Sweden, Ireland, Spain and Portugal) did not even have regulations. Even Germany, that had a rather restrictive system, had longer opening hours than the Netherlands.

For many years, there has been a heated debate in the Netherlands on the liberalisation of the opening hours. The arguments in favour of longer opening hours focused on the statement that developments in society compelled further liberalisation, such as the increasing number of two-income households, the flexible working hours in general and the increased employment of women. The arguments against were related to the social disruption that could occur in the private lives of employees and independent entrepreneurs in the retail.

In any case, after years of wrangling, a new law on opening hours was established in 1996 with a much more liberal signature. In fact you could say that we went from a store closing hours law (you had to be closed from ... pm to ... am) to a store opening hours law (you may be open whenever you want to, on condition that ...). The new legislation created a number of new consumption opportunities for the shopping public. On one hand, the law created the possibility to be open longer every day than before (extension of the daily operating time) and on the other hand, the law indicates a sharp increase in the number of days (Sundays and holidays) that stores may be open. Municipalities may allow retailers to be open a maximum of twelve Sundays per year. In tourist centres, it is even allowed to be open every Sunday. There was some debating in 2007 regarding the last clause, because more than a third of the Dutch munici-palities determined that they were such a tourist destination and that the stores could be open (much) more often than twelve Sundays a year: the fourth Balkenende government wanted a stop to the 'misuse' of this tourism clause. However, a majority of the municipalities are of the opinion that the shopping hours are their own, local responsibility. Moreover, a study in late 2007 indicated that the majority of the Dutch population find that twelve open Sundays per year are more than enough, while a quarter would like to be able to shop every Sunday.

In 2011 another attempt was made to expand the Sunday opening. With a new seating of Parliament and a new government in which the VVD has governmental responsibility, it seemed as though the expansion actually had a chance of success. However, another bill floundered in the spring, this time because the Groen Links, CDA, PVV and the entrepreneurial minded VVD voted against it. Limiting the Sunday opening and the still traditional opening hours of many retailers, continued to play into the hands of online retailers and online activities of traditional retailers. Some retailers did however use the opportunities offered, such as Media Markt, with late night shopping every day.

In the spring of 2012, the city of Amsterdam announced a trial for 24 hour opening of stores. Stores in two districts of Amsterdam could participate in the trial. If it is successful, it could be expanded to the rest of the city. The significance of extending and expanding the opening hours/days, is illustrated in examples 8.1 and 8.2.

EXAMPLE 8.1 EXTENDING THE DAILY OPENING TIME

Extending the daily trading hours will primarily influence the everyday expenditures. There seems to be a shift from the sales of the morning to the evening. Several large Dutch supermarket organisations have therefore opted to have all their branches open until 20.00 at night. Albert Heijn has even gone as far as having an increasing number of branches remain open until 22.00 at night.

Figures show that organisations that extend their opening hours (often larger retail businesses) win market share from organisations that choose not to do so (often the slightly smaller, independent organisations).

Another positive aspect for the retail of the extension of the daily trading hours is the fact that a portion of the market share lost to fast-food businesses in the past may be recovered. The strong growth of the fresh ready-made meals and meal components in supermarkets' product range indicates that the attempt is also successful.

EXAMPLE 8.2 EXPANDING THE NUMBER OF OPENING DAYS

Expanding the number of opening days turns out to be especially important for suppliers of non-daily goods in the larger town centres. For example, it is known that the Dutch department store organisations owe a large portion of their sales growth in 1998 and 1999 to the sales of the additional Sunday openings. There is some debate about the additional sales that is earned on Sunday. A study by the Dutch Retail Council shows that retailers earn 20% of the weekly sales on a shopping Sunday, but entrepreneurs in smaller (neighbourhood) centres are often less enthusiastic (which may also be related to the very occasional Sunday opening in these centres, which means that many consum-ers are not aware of the opening).

It should also be noted that they have less time to shop during the day on week days due to the rising female employment. In the past the housewife would run the household and do grocery shopping, while the man was the sole breadwinner. However, over the past few decades there have been strong changes in this area (see for example table 8.5 in paragraph 8.3).

8.7.2 Policy on department stores

The Dutch government used to have a conservative policy with regard to the admission of department stores outside the direct retail agglomerations. This policy was designated as 'the policy on *peripheral retail outlets* (PRO, in Dutch PDV)'. The *PRO-policy* was based on the following two principles:

- maintaining the retail function of the inner cities and other existing retail concentrations;
- promoting the dynamics in retail.

In the past, especially the first objective received much attention. This resulted in a policy where peripheral department stores were only allowed in cases of exception. The exception categories were named and shamed. This related to the retail in flammable and explosive substances, and retail formulas that required a large surface for display due to the nature and size of the carried products, such as companies for cars, boats, caravans, gardening equipment, (bulky) building materials, kitchens, plumbing and home furnishings (including furniture).

The assessment of the policy (by the province) was strict. Businesses that wanted to settle on the outskirts had to prove that there was distributive space for their formula. This means that the new peripheral establishment may not cause the floor productivity (the sales per metre) of the already established retail to drop beneath a certain, government-imposed standard value. Theoretically, this meant that peripheral branches were only possible in case of relocation (as in the case of furniture stores that flocked to the new furniture malls) or in case of clearly inadequate supply (as was the case in the rapidly growing market for do-it-yourself products). The research method was prescribed and was known as *distribution planning research* (DPR). Despite the strict policy there were still loopholes in the law, allowing companies outside the exception categories to establish themselves on the 'green pastures': both fashion stores (Superconfex, Marca, Kien) and department stores (Maxis, Miro, Famila) appeared in peripheral locations. It became clear that the dynamics in retail would not be stopped by conservative policies. In 1993, this ultimately necessitated an expansion of the old PRO-policy.

This expansion of the PRO-policy is referred to as the *LRO-policy*, where the abbreviation refers to concentrated *large-scale retail outlets*. The LRO-policy includes the possibility for a bundling of large-scale retail formulas outside the immediate core shopping areas and with an industry pattern that is much broader than the categories applicable in the PRO-policy. The following conditions have to be met:

- The locations should not be competitive with existing retail concentrations.
- The locations should be near urban hubs.
- The locations should be easily accessible with public transport.

The interpretation and the assessment of the policies were decentralised: from now on, it will be up to the municipalities to decide whether they want to proceed with the allocation of a LRO-location. They will also establish the allowed industry pattern.

(margin notes)

Peripheral retail outlets
PRO-policy

Distribution planning research

LRO-policy
Large-scale retail outlets

**Environmental
Memorandum**

A new expansion of the settlement policy took place in 2006, with the *Environmental Memorandum*. It stipulates that municipalities may personally determine whether or not they want to allow stores on the outskirts. The province has the final word and looks at how these plans affect the region. In 2011, the Space Memorandum was replaced by the *Structural Vision Infrastructure and Space (SVIS)*.

The LRO-policy and the new responsibilities of local authorities will undoubtedly lead to an increase of the dynamics in Dutch retail. This will partly be because existing Dutch formulas that were previously held back in their development by the PRO-policy are given new opportunities. In addition, it is expected that formulas from the existing small-scale structure will develop into large-scale. Finally, it is already apparent that new suppliers are emerging, partly from abroad where the scale is already well developed, and partly from the Netherlands itself.

In the years immediately following the introduction, there were no major changes in the Dutch retail landscape. Municipalities and provinces were still rather hesitant about the possible consequences of stores and shopping centres outside the existing centres. The plan for a huge shopping mall at Geldermalsen with 150,000 m^2 of stores and leisure activities was rejected by the Provincial States of Gelderland. Other plans, such as a mega American style shopping mall in Tilburg, were met with considerable resistance and were eventually voted against in a referendum by the population of Tilburg, this last one to the great disappointment of the College of Aldermen of the municipality. Yet different agencies, such as the Spatial Planning Office (SPO) and the Rabobank, expected that large shopping centres outside the city would eventually appear in the Netherlands.

However, there is a downside to the development: liberalisation, coupled with the decentralisation of policy to the municipalities, may result in an abrupt expansion of the overcapacity being created in the already cluttered Netherlands. The varied industry pattern to which the new policy opens up the possibility, combined with good accessibility by car, may cause the sites for large-scale retail to develop superregional traction. So municipalities that are capable of supporting large shopping centres within their borders, will receive purchasing power.

The poor economic conditions in the first decade of the new century led to a withering of retailers on residential boulevards. The first vacancy is already a fact and the question is when the first municipalities will make use of their powers to allow other sectors to these retail locations. Moreover, it is advisable to also consider to what extent there are opportunities for so-called C&CO-policy. C&CO refers to Click & Collect Outlets, shopping areas where online retailers allow consumers to collect products that they purchased online. The current LRO- and PRO-sites are characterised mainly by accessibility and availability of parking space, an ideal combination, even for an C&CO-site. Moreover, the sites are large, making it possible to offer the possibility of storing large quantities of goods and displaying the product range in an attractive manner, relative easy and with minor adjustments. The advantage for municipalities is that, in this way, a shopping area can be revitalised. And for consumers it offers an answer to a need.

8.8 Economic environmental factors

In practice, expenditures in retail appear to be strongly influenced by consumers' expectations of economic developments. Unfortunately we must conclude that, in the Netherlands, only a relatively small number of details that could offer any insight into the actual relationships between economic developments and consumers are published. This is due to the open nature of the economy of the Netherlands. The Dutch export of goods and services is roughly as large as the domestic consumption. In a country like the United States, the export is only 15% of the domestic consumption. Most macroeconomic models used by the Dutch government are therefore aimed at explaining the competitiveness compared to other countries, and not to explain the domestic demand.

Private expenditures in the Netherlands are therefore almost always a result of *output* of the models and are not used as input. In the United States, for example, where the export ratio is of much less importance, this is completely different. The expected development of *private consumption* is used as input of the economic models and *retail spending* is one of the most widely used indicators to measure the state of the economy. This means that we are hardly able to rely on official publications to predict the private demand. Nevertheless, there are some indicators that help us in assessing the influence of economic developments on private expenditures. We discuss a few below.

8.8.1 Index of consumer confidence

The *index of consumer confidence* is actually the only data which attempts to explain the consumer perception on the economic developments and responses to this in the form of purchase plans. The index of consumer confidence is compiled by the National Statistics Office based on five questions that are partly related to the overall consumer perception on the development of the economy, and partly on an assessment of their own financial situation. One of the questions is whether the consumer plans on making a large purchase over the next twelve months. For every question, the percentage of negative and positive answers is netted. This gives a number of sub-indices, such as: the economic climate index, the index on willingness to purchase and the index for their own financial situation. Finally, the sub-indices are averaged and that results in the index for consumer confidence. The index itself is a meaningless number. Only in relation to previous measurements it creates a meaningful interpretation: it is the fall or rise of the index that warns us when something is about to happen.

Studies in the relationship between consumer expenditures and the development of the index of consumer confidence seem to suggest that the relationship between the index and the actual expenditure behaviour of consumers (that was at least present in the past) are becoming weaker over time. The value of the index as a predictive variable for planning in retail is thereby considerably weakened. Only the sub-index of willingness to buy seems to provide a decent explanation. At least, the degree of correlation between the position of the index and the development of consumer expenditures is reliable. At the same time we see that the *regression coefficient* (the extent to which the expenditures respond to changes in the index) varies widely and mainly decreases (see example 8.3).

Index of consumer confidence

Regression coefficient

EXAMPLE 8.3 CONSUMER INTEREST

Should de Bijenkorf, kitchen centres and car dealers fear the worst because the National Statistics Office announced a considerable drop in consumer confidence several weeks ago? Not necessarily. On Friday it was shown that consumption increased by 2.1% in August. This when the newspapers were already full of the credit crisis, there were already banks in trouble, NIBC had already issued a profit warning. There was no lack of bad news on the economy. Nevertheless, consumers con-tinued to buy at will.

The figure on consumer confidence published monthly by the National Statistics Office is composed of several sub-questions. The researchers ask for an opinion on the overall economic situation of the Netherlands in the coming year and about the willingness to buy, including a question on whether it is a favourable time to make large purchases. It seems logical that frightened citizens that predict a sinking economy do not feel that now is the time to purchase a car or washing machine. Indeed, there is a connection in recent history between these two opinions. But even more striking is the often considerable discrepancy between the two. The opinion of the economic situation appears to be rather sensitive to the economy throughout the years. Dutch people are easily deterred by a few newspaper headlines in the economy attachments.

For example, in the spring of 1996. The economy was just recovering after a dismal start of the decade. The opinion on

the economy and about the willingness to buy increased hand in hand. Then the national pride, the NV Fokker Aircraft Factory, went bankrupt. As a result, the attitude towards the economy fell into a deep hole. But almost nothing changed in the willingness to buy. The negativity about the economic climate was merely of a short duration and soon consumers rushed to the shopping paradise.

In late 1998, something similar happened: the Currency Crisis in Asia! Confidence in the economy plummeted again, and the willingness to buy, again, only suffered marginally.

Would the same happen again? In September, consumer confidence made an unprecedented fall. This was mainly due to the negative opinion about the economy, which had changed from plus 16 to minus 18. The pessimists were once more in the majority. But the same gloomy people still found it a convenient time to make large purchases. The index only dropped from plus 12 to plus 10. As long as consumers only read about the bad news in the newspaper, they will keep on spending. Only when the bad news lasts long, like between 2002 and 2005, will consumers keep a hold on their wallets.

Source: Bartjens, The Financial Daily,
22 October 2007

8.8.2 Indicator of cyclical movement: the economic clock

Economic clock   Since 2005, the CBS has been using *the economic clock* as an instrument to see the current state of the economy and which way it is heading at a single glance. The hands of the economic clock consist of fifteen indicators:
- producer confidence;
- orders;
- consumer confidence;
- large purchases;
- interest rate;
- consumption;

- export;
- investments;
- manufacturing;
- gross domestic product (GDP);
- labour volume;
- unemployment;
- vacancies;
- temporary jobs;
- bankruptcies.

The discussed index for consumer confidence, as one of the most important sub-indices, recognises the index of consumer attitudes regarding the economic climate. The opinion of consumers about the economic climate is influenced by reports in the press (reading the economic page is therefore also a form of environmental exploration) and these, in turn, are derived from the official publications about the development of the economy. The periodically published development of the economic clock is therefore also one of the data from which we can derive the economic environmental temperature (see figure 8.4). The interactive economic clock of the National Statistics Office can be found on the website of this book.

FIGURE 8.4 Economic clock for March 2012

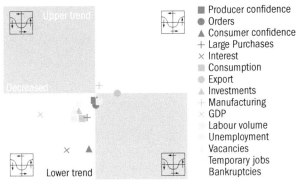

Producer confidence
Orders
Consumer confidence
Large Purchases
Interest
Consumption
Export
Investments
Manufacturing
GDP
Labour volume
Unemployment
Vacancies
Temporary jobs
Bankruptcies

Source: CBS.nl

Summary

The environment in which the retail operates is subject to increasingly rapid changes. As a result, the life cycle of retail formulas are getting shorter. It is therefore important to always keep watching what happens in the environment, at the risk of developing a wrong concept.
Within the environmental exploration, we can distinguish three main groups, each of which in turn can be divided into a number of subjects.
- Trend developments: in this chapter we discussed a number of demographic trends, as well as employment trends, income and outcome distribution trends and the development of urbanisation. We also discussed trend watching.

- Developments in the institutional frameworks: often abrupt in changes and thus often more important for the short term than the trend developments. We discussed the liberalisation of the settlement and environmental policy (LRO, PRO, C&CO), as well as the implications of the new trading hours act.
- Economic environmental factors: we discussed the index of consumer confidence and the economic clock. We concluded that consumer confidence is less important as a predictor for retail expenditures.

It is not possible to give an exhaustive summary of all factors impacting on the retail. The environment is subject to constant change. Depending on the problem and the time, we must constantly examine which factors are important.

9

Competitor analysis

Competition plays a major role in retail: 'retail is war'. In this chapter, we discuss concepts such as competitor's analysis and the levels therein, as well as the force fields and dimensions that play a role here. Who is the competitor? We give a few examples of competitor's analysis and the application thereof on various levels and of the competitive positions.

⬛9.1 Levels of competitor analysis

Displacement market

Competitive environment
Competitor's analysis

Competition in the retail industry is quite fierce. A *displacement market* is referred to especially in the goods sector of retail. The services sector of retail has not yet come this far, but even there the effects of the increasing number of suppliers and the blurring is becoming clearly visible. So there is every reason to pay separate attention to techniques that are aimed at better identifying the *competitive environment* (all of the existing and potential competitors in their interrelationships). The purpose of the analysis of the competitive environment (the *competitor analysis*) is to gain insight in that part of the overall competition that belongs to the relevant competition, namely the suppliers that compete directly with their own formula. Identifying the relevant competition can lead to identifying the direct competitor, namely the supplier whose own formula suffers the most, or the enemy.

We therefore have to deal with three levels in the competitor analysis:
1 the macro level, focusing on the strategic analysis of the competitive environment and the possible movements that occur therein;
2 the meso level, focused on identifying and analysing the current relevant competition;
3 the micro level, focused on identifying the most important direct competitor and analysing the strengths and weaknesses of this party.

The position of the competitor analysis in the strategic process is shown schematically in figure 9.1.

FIGURE 9.1 The position of the competitor's analysis in the strategic process

9.2 Michael Porter's theory

The American marketing guru Michael Porter has made an important contribution to 'lifting' competitor analysis above the tactical level. While there is much criticism of his theories (specifically since the handled concepts are not clear) (Hendry, 1990), we must conclude that his ideas have had a major impact and that the application of his ideas into practice has actually helped improving the developments within the competitive environment. We will now briefly discuss and illustrate Porter's theory with several applications in the area of retail.

9.2.1   Five Forces Model

Businesses that already have an established position within their market tend to view the competitors based on existing competition. They only look at the current market participants in their own sectors. Porter points out that this is a dangerous and limited vision, because there are four other – mainly externally determined – forces acting on the current competitive environment which may, on the long term, be of strategic significance. In fact, he warns against the possibility that the current competitive environ- **Five-forces** ment is subject to change as a result of these four externally active forces. **model** He illustrates this with the so-called *five-forces model* (see figure 9.2).

FIGURE 9.2 Porter Five Forces Model

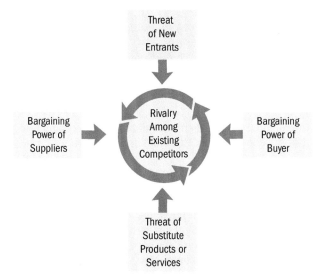

The four external influencing forces are:
• Power shifts in the relationship between the existing suppliers and their suppliers. The shift in power between manufacturers of consumer products and the retail, already described in chapter 7, is a good example of this.

9

The Supermarket Jumbo sometimes competes directly with hard discounters Aldi and Lidl

- Power shifts in the relationship between the existing suppliers and their buyers. The shift from seller's market to buyer's market is an example of this.
- The risk of new entrants. There are many examples of situations in which existing suppliers do not or are too late in realising that there is a new supplier. A good example is the 'encirclement attack' of the German Aldi in the UK. The high profitability of the English supermarkets was proverbial. In 1990, Aldi quietly started opening establishments across the UK. The company chose sites that were not (no longer) interesting to existing suppliers, often in relatively small suburbs in a circle around a large city. Because of the low overheads, Aldi was still able to function profitably. Due to the low prices, according to English standards, these Aldi establishments were quite successful and pulled many customers away from established suppliers. These establishments only discovered this much later. Today the profits of the large English supermarket organisations are under considerable pressure because they have to adapt to the price level of Aldi, while they are not (yet) able to match the cost structure of Aldi.

The still rather unexpected entry into Europe of the largest retailer in the word, Wal-Mart, with the acquisition of the British Asda, may also be classified under this chapter. In any case, this has led to an acceleration of the concentration trends of the major retailers within Europe.
- Threat from replacement products. There are also examples of this. In the food sector, for example, the phenomenon occurred that consumers made increasingly more use of fast food concepts such as McDonald's. This was at the expense of the traditional eating occasions for which the consumer would previously visit supermarkets. The fact that now, as a result of the altered shopping hours, the tide has turned and the supermarkets are regaining market share, illustrates the point. This is also partly motivated by the range of convenience food and ready-to-eat meals in the supermarket.
There are also examples in the financial services sector. Banks are starting to offer products that can serve as a substitute for the pension insurance or endowment insurance, such as single premium and investment accounts.

The warning of Porters five forces model (figure 9.2) is clear:
Do not limit yourself in the analysis of the competitive environment to the established order, but also analyze the other, potentially threatening forces.

9.2.2 Yield curve

Porter researched a large number of industries and companies during the empirical testing of his theory in the context between the level of profitability and the size of the company. The background of this testing was his doubts about the theory of the concept of the scale benefits handled in the business economics: the bigger the marketing volume of the company, the lower the cost per unit, the higher the profit. Porter's findings, however, led to an entirely different conclusion: companies with a relatively small market share were often more profitable in terms of *return on investment* than companies with a fairly large market share. Therefore, the *economies of scale* do not always seem to work. On the other hand, he established that these scale benefits did appear to be present in very large companies. He attributed the result of these findings to the so-called *yield curve*.
Further analysis showed that the apparent contradiction between the regularity of the economies scale and the findings of Porter was due to economies of scale based on perfect competition with homogenous products. Porter's empirical analysis shows that this assumption is rarely correct. The reason of the course of the curve was found to be attributable to the fact that the smaller suppliers, at least in the perception of consumers, offered better quality products than the large and the major suppliers. The smaller suppliers were often *niche marketers* who either focused on specific target groups, or were able to somehow bring 'added value' (differentiation) in their overall product concept. This allowed them to charge a higher price than their larger competitors. This *differentiation premium* compared to the average price was the cause of their high yield. The major companies at the other end of the spectrum were often focused on the mass market. Due to their large volume they are able to benefit from the economies of scale and could therefore offer at lower cost than

Yield curve

Niche marketers

Differentiation premium

Mass merchandiser

Niche player

Stuck in the middle, bad strategy

their slightly smaller colleagues. This cost *leadership* advantage was the reason for their high yield. Porter's conclusion was that it was necessary to make choices in situations where there is no complete and homogenous competition (and in which consumers' market does this still exist?) either strive towards cost leadership and become a *mass merchandiser*, or strive towards added value concepts and become a *niche player*. If the company does not make a choice, a situation may arise where we as suppliers are not clearly profiled and where we need to 'be' all kinds of things. Porter characterised this position as *stuck in the middle, bad strategy*.

9.2.3   Competitive strategy-matrix

Competitive strategies

Cost leadership

Differentiation leadership

Focus strategies

Cost focus

Differentiation focus

Building on the above described findings, Porter developed the philosophy of *competitive strategies*. In his vision there are only three general competitive strategies:

- *Cost leadership*: this is when the company applies a 'broad' market methodology with a price aggressive approach.
- *Differentiation leadership*: the marketing approach is broad, but the interpretation takes place by supplying added value.
- *Focus strategies*: Porter recognises two strategies, namely:
  - *cost focus*: a narrow marketing approach is pursued, but the approach is price aggressive;
  - *differentiation focus*: here you can also see a narrow marketing approach, but the interpretation takes place with added value.

Thus Porter comes to an assessment of the competitive environment using a four-field matrix (see figure 9.3).

FIGURE 9.3 Porter-matrix for the competitive environment

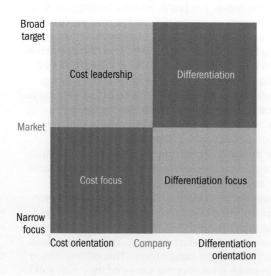

Competitive environment matrix

9.2.4   Conversion of the matrix into retail concepts

In practice, the *competitive environment matrix* seems to be readily applicable in retail. However, a number of translation steps need to be taken. It should be clarified what we understand by the terms *broad target* and *narrow focus* in retail. In general, we interpret this with application to retail in terms of 'the width of the need coverage for the consumer'. Retailers that cover many different needs are arranged among the broad-*target suppliers*. Retail formulas that focus on one or only a limited number of specialised needs are arranged among narrow focus. In fact, this can be translated back to the product range width. Broad-target suppliers are suppliers with a parallelised product range (supermarkets and department stores), narrow-*focus* suppliers are speciality stores. Similarly, we must clarify what is meant by *cost orientation* and *differentiation orientation* in retail. In general this is translated in terms of *price suppliers* (or discounters) versus *quality stores* (or luxury stores). This interpretation fits well with consumer behaviour: in a situation where there is an established retail structure and a given distribution of the population, there are two main factors that lead consumers in their store selection behaviour:

- *Width of the range*: if the consumer has no distinct idea of what products he needs to satisfy his needs, he will choose a store with a wide range of choices. If the consumer knows exactly what he needs, he will choose a store with a specialist range of choices.
- *Expenditure possibility*: when consumers have little money (or are only prepared to pay a small amount for the product: low involvement), they will basically choose discount stores. If consumers have a large budget (or are prepared to pay much for the product: high involvement), they will basically choose a high-quality supplier.

The resulting retail competition matrix shows the image as displayed in figure 9.4.

Broad target
Narrow focus

Cost orientation
Differentiation orientation

Discounters
Quality stores

FIGURE 9.4 Porter retail matrix

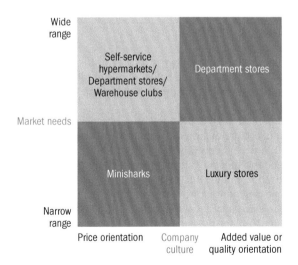

A warning is in order. There were two main objections raised against Porter. First, it is not clear how he defines the competition when handling the matrix. When analysing the competitive environment on which for example KLM operates (international passenger transport), should you also involve the Dutch Railways and cars? Or just competing airlines? This objection also applies for retail. If we try to evaluate the combined retail in the Netherlands using a Porter-matrix, the DIY store will probably end up in the lower left quadrant. After all, DIY stores specialise in the low price segment with only DIY products. However, if we would evaluate the DIY market, the DIY stores will probably end up in the upper left quadrant. After all, within this market, they are the seller with the widest range. The results of the matrix therefore depend on the chosen market definition. When using the matrix, it is important that you use a proper definition of the market. The second objection involves the fact that Porter believes that a combination of differentiation and cost leadership is not possible. In practice, however, this certainly does occur: there are cost leaders that use a part of their efficiency premium to improve the quality of supply. According to Porter, they are therefore both cost leader and differentiation leader. In order to keep to our own range: is HEMA a quality supplier or a price supplier? Although it is agreed that HEMA is not expensive, this company does supply *value for money*, a relatively high quality for the asked price. The reviews by consumers (and organisations) on the HEMA range are also generally positive. It is therefore important, with the positioning of suppliers, to estimate the primary USP of the supplier on the price-quality axis. In HEMA's case, given the previously discussed mission, it is likely that if the desired quality level would make the offering price too high, HEMA would still opt for the lower price. HEMA therefore is positioned in the price supplier segment.

9.3 **Application at the macro level: the retail structure of France and the Netherlands compared**

The historical development of the competitive structure of the Netherlands, in combination with the effect of the scissors, eventually led to an intricate, relatively price aggressive retail supply, with the following characteristics (see figure 9.5):
- An extremely well presented segment in the lower left corner: there is no sector, or there is a price aggressive, small scale, franchised supplier. It is partly due to this development that the 'traditional' segment (the independent specialty store: the 'mom and pop' store) has almost disappeared from the Dutch streets.
- A very weakly occupied segment in the Netherlands in the upper left corner: price aggressive parallelised suppliers. The self-service department store is much more prevalent in other European countries. It is obvious to assume that there is a relationship with the segment in the lower left corner, which is strongly occupied in the Netherlands. Why would one travel to a remote location if there is a small scale supply in the neighbourhood that can provide the same price level in the market?

- A reasonably occupied segment in the upper right corner: traditional department stores.
- A relatively weak occupied segment in the lower right corner: luxury specialty stores. This is also a less occupied segment in several other European countries, with some exceptions in the cosmopolitan cities, where there is purchasing power for this segment and the associated tourism.

FIGURE 9.5 Porter-matrix the Netherlands

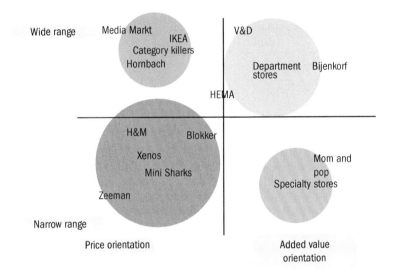

If we draw up such a structure matrix for a country like France, we get an entirely different picture (see figure 9.6):
- A weakly occupied segment in the lower left corner: although this segment has seen several new developments kicking off in recent years, it is still minimal compared to the Netherlands. This is partly why the mom and pop segment is not yet properly represented in France.
- A very strong segment in the upper left corner: the department store tradition was not adopted by the franchised specialty stores in France, but by the peripheral self-service department stores such as Carrefour, Auchan and Casino. This is partly due to how urbanisation developed in France, and partly because of the liberal policy towards peripheral branches.
- A relatively weakly occupied segment in the upper right corner: actually there are only two suppliers left in this section, namely Lafayette and Printemps. Both, with exception for their head offices in Paris, are experiencing difficulties with their formulas. A large part of the income is also from HEMA-like subsidiaries such as Monoprix.
- A fairly strong segment in the lower right corner: luxury specialty stores, including designer stores of big names, but also luxury shopping streets.

FIGURE 9.6 Porter-matrix France

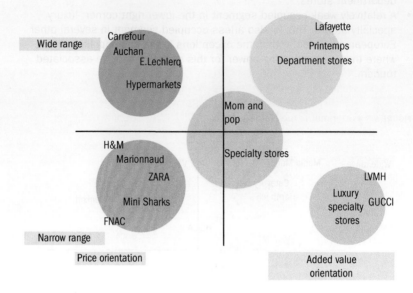

The resulting matrix gives an entirely different picture of the Netherlands. It will be clear that it is important to make such an assessment of the competitive environment, before deciding to proceed in entering a new market. Not only does this apply for internationalisation, as in the example, but also for entering new regions. Even in a small country like Belgium or the Netherlands, the local competitive environment can often be very different.

9.4 Application at the meso level

The assessment of the competitive environment gives an overall picture of the structure of the competition. We often have to deal with a variety of store types and store formulas. Not all identified competitors are relevant competitors. A formula such as Leen Bakker (part of the Blokker group) clearly manifests itself as a supplier in the furniture sector. The company focuses on the less expensive mass segment of *knock-down furniture*. Given this positioning, Leen Bakker is a competitor for the furniture department of de Bijenkorf, but not a relevant competitor. However, Leen Bakker is a relevant competitor for IKEA.

Hereafter, we will use the supermarket channel to explore how we can identify the relevant competition and the strategic movements to which this may give rise. We will gradually build the case from the perspective of the market leader, Albert Heijn.

When drafting a Porter-matrix, the following steps must be taken:
1 Defining the market and label the axis.
2 Determining from which point of view you want to fill the matrix: from the consumer or from their own (commercial) assessment of the competition.

3 Determining which 'players' are involved, starting with the market leader.
4 Positioning the players relative to the market leader.
5 Based on the empty spaces in the matrix, check if no suppliers were
   left out.

9.4.1   Defining the market and determining the viewpoint

The supermarket channel in the Netherlands consists of (in statistical
terms) parallelised suppliers in the area of food and beverage. This
implies that we do not look at the specialised suppliers: the baker, the
milkman and the butcher. Within this channel we call suppliers that offer
many SKU's (*stock keeping units*) *broad-range suppliers* and those offering
a more limited selection, *narrow suppliers*. We consider the competitive
environment from the consumer: 'expensive' suppliers are therefore
suppliers who, in the eyes of consumers, ask high prices. Economical
suppliers, in the eyes of consumers, are the price busters.

Stock keeping units
Broad-range suppliers
Narrow suppliers

9.4.2   Identifying the market players

In practice it is often difficult to exhaustively identify the market players.
In our case, it is clear that Albert Heijn, Aldi, Jumbo, Plus and C1000 in
any case belong to the players. They are often mentioned first, which
means that this involves profiled formulas with a high TOMA (*Top Of Mind
Awareness*). You then start looking for other suppliers. It makes no sense
to search too long for additional suppliers. The first four formulas that
come to mind are usually enough to start filling in the matrix.

Top Of Mind Awareness

9.4.3   Perception of the matrix

It is clear that almost everyone will place Albert Heijn in the upper right
quadrant because of the width of the range and the high cost image. It is
equally clear that Aldi, with only nine hundred SKU's and an evident low
cost image, will end up in the extreme lower left corner. Dirk van den
Broek, with a narrower product range than Albert Heijn and a relatively low
cost image, is generally placed at just about half of the width axis and to
the right of Aldi on the low cost axis. C1000 is perceived to be cheaper
than Albert Heijn, with a slightly narrower product range. C1000 therefore
ends up in the upper left quadrant, slightly lower on the width axis than
Albert Heijn. C1000 is perceived to be more expensive than Aldi, and ends
up on the expense axis to the right of Aldi. Jumbo, in turn, is perceived by
consumers as having a wider range and also has a better review on price
compared to Albert Heijn. The initial positioning of these formulas leads to
an interpretation as in figure 9.7.

9.4.4   'Check' the perception of the matrix

Especially in a highly competitive channel as supermarkets, it is almost
impossible for the matrix to not be fully perceived. An examination of the
first perception shows that there are several 'white spots'. Firstly, the
extreme upper left corner is blank. The 'very broad-ranged, very cheap'
seller obviously does not have a high TOMA. AH XL plays a partial role in
that quadrant, although the supply is smaller compared to a real hyper
market. However, AH XL still has a better position on product ranges than
competitor Jumbo.

FIGURE 9.7 The initial perception of the matrix

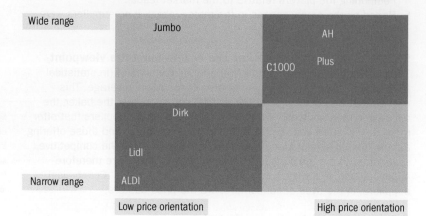

An outlet of the convenience formula of AH to Go

Secondly, the lower right quadrant is blank. Apparently the Netherlands also has few high quality, narrow product range suppliers. This often involves independent entrepreneurs that have been able to survive and earn a good living by providing extra quality or extra service: the night stores (where the extra service is the opening times) and delis, but nowadays also, and increasingly, the convenience stores at gas stations and formulas such as *AH to Go*. As the latter formulas expand more, the lower right quadrant will also be filled with an initial perception.

Finally, the centre is hardly filled. This is also logical, because the formula in 'the centre' – at least in Porter's opinion – are *stuck in the middle* and therefore by definition not strongly profiled. They do not have a high TOMA and do not quickly come to mind. This centre contains all formulas that are not really broad-range, but also not really narrow, and not really expensive, but not really cheap either. The result of the exercise is the total matrix of figure 9.8.

FIGURE 9.8 Porter-matrix of the supermarket channel

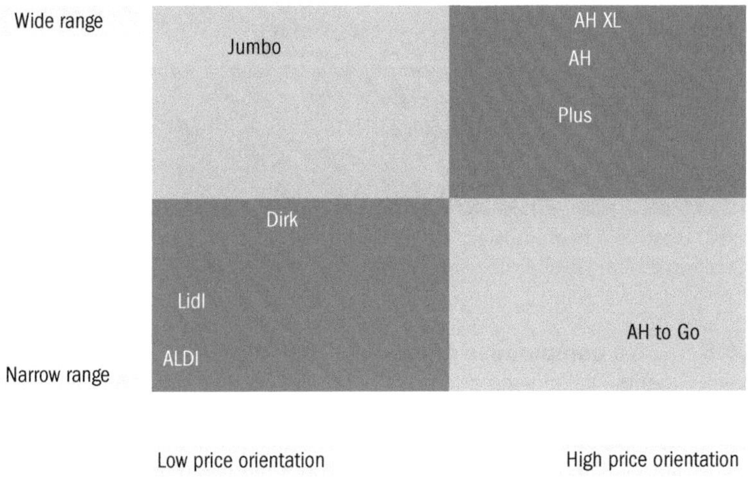

Wide range

Jumbo

AH XL

AH

Plus

Dirk

Lidl

ALDI

AH to Go

Narrow range

Low price orientation   High price orientation

Still, there are interesting options if we look more closely at the perception of the matrix. Take Jumbo for example, the second player on the Dutch market following the acquisition of C1000. A formula that represents a price orientation and an added value orientation, combined with a wide range. Within the matrix, this formula should occupy two positions, namely in the upper right corner and in the upper left corner of the matrix. It is fair to say that Jumbo has both smaller stores (with a more limited range) as well as very large stores with a very wide range. From this perspective, they would also hold a position in the lower quadrants. Compared to Albert Heijn, we should indeed be able to distinguish between two types of Jumbo's, but the combination of price and added value continues to exist. The strategic question for this family business after acquiring C1000 is what to do next? They could opt for the 'two formula approach', whereby each formula could take a unique position in the market. Or it could opt for the Ahold strategy, one name, but different formats with their own sub label. The preliminary choice is one name which makes sense based on the C1000 position. Probably Jumbo will opt for the one formula multi funnel strategy.

9

Jumbo, amongst others, is doing its best to deliver added value, in this case by providing free parking to customers visiting the supermarket

9.4.5   No compromise game

Eysink Smeets' vision seems to be at odds with Porter's vision, but is certainly not less interesting. Eysink Smeets' axis system is similar to Porter's, but is powered entirely by how the customer experiences and desires something. Eysink Smeets believes that the customer is looking for the ultimate combination of low cost and high added value. In other words, low prices, great selection and great service. Porter's approach that is most in line with this is that of *cost leadership*, although we have rather confronted Porter's theory at this point, by speaking of a 'broad' marketing approach. In

No compromise game

fact, Eysink Smeets says that, in the *no compromise game* model, no concessions were made to the pricing or to the supply. This means that an ordered cost structure is a basic condition for retailers.

On the axes of the matrix, the price is set on the vertical axis and the added value is set on the horizontal axis (see figure 9.9). This creates four quadrants. The upper left quadrant is the area where all concessions are met. In the eyes of the customer this is the least desirable location. The lower left and upper right quadrants are the quadrants where concessions are made on one of the two aspects. The lower left quadrant is where retailers make concessions related to added value. The upper right quadrant is the location where concessions are made related to price. The players that are positioned here are experienced as more expensive.

When we look at European food retailers that perform excellently in the eyes of consumers, these are Colruyt (Belgium), Esselunga (Italy), Jumbo (the Netherlands) and Lidl (Germany and Spain). These are all retailers that combine EDLP (Every Day Low Prices) with a wide and full range, except for Lidl. For the latter it also applies that the range has expanded in recent years.

All indicated companies are family companies. The example of Essalunga in Italy is also evident for the application of this approach. The owners of Esselunga only opted for the EDLP in combination with offering extra added

FIGURE 9.9 No Compromise matrix

Source: Eysink Smeets

value in 2005. In only a few years, this company has grown into one of the most valued supermarket chains in Italy. It has even been crowned as the best retail company in Italy, twice.

The model works for both food and non-food retailers. The basic positions that were traditionally taken within the axis system, are the following: Hard Discounter (HD); Soft Discounter (SD) and Full Service (SF) (see figure 9.10).

FIGURE 9.10 No compromise matrix perceived

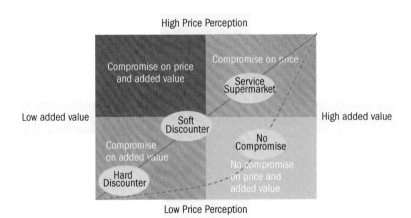

Source: Eysink Smeets

The *Hard Discounters* have a limited product range; especially or even exclusively own brands and low prices. In the supermarket world, these are the Aldi's, Penny's and to a lesser extent the Lidl's of this world too. In fashion, these are companies like Zeeman, Kik, Ernstings Family. The *Soft Discounters* use lower prices, but certainly not the lowest and have less

Hard Discounters

Soft Discounters

added value compared with the Full Service-players. In food, these are parties such as Dirk, C1000 and Rewe. In fashion we would traditionally have positioned companies here like C&A, Peek & Cloppenburg, V&D, HEMA, Kaufhof, Upim and Oviesse. Department stores often fall under this category and we also see that, in course of time, they choose to move up. They either choose for considerably more added value in combination with higher prices, or for slightly more added value in combination with a slightly better price perception.

Full Service-players

The *Full Service-players* are those that offer a very high added value in combination with prices that they feel should accompany them. The question is clearly whether the latter is still true in the eyes of the consumer. Players in food in this domain are companies like Albert Heijn, Carrefour, Sainsbury's and Real. The price perception of these companies is often seen as relatively higher than that of the competition, but they also offer a lot of added value, certainly compared to the competitors. In fashion, we often think about the independent local heroes and the more luxurious department stores such as de Bijenkorf, Galeries Lafayette, La Rinacente and Selfridges.

FIGURE 9.11 Shifting playing field

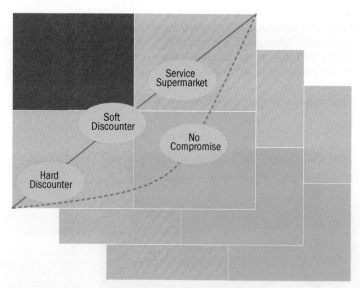

Source: Eysink Smeets

In the new way of thinking, a new position was added, namely that of the No Compromise (NC). These are the companies that are able to combine the best of both worlds. We already named those in food, but such players can also be distinguished in fashion. At the beginning of the new millennium, companies like H&M, ZARA and to a lesser extent C&A had managed to claim this position. At the end of the first decade of this century there were several newcomers on this front, such as Primark and New Look. These new retailers set a new benchmark regarding the price and are thus among the competition. The environment in which they sell their products is in no way

inferior to that of the already existing players. With the growth of these players, the entire playing field shifts, so to speak (see figure 9.11). However, this takes the theoretic approach of this model a step further than the relatively static approach of Porter. Although, even in Porters' model, nothing remains as it is, it is based on a type of status quo. While Eysink Smeets' model is based on ever-present dynamics. According to Eysink Smeets, a retailer that has been able to take up a certain position, should constantly keep improving on both axes. If he does not,
the playing field will slowly start to shift and if he is not careful, he will eventually fall outside the playing field.

9.5 Identifying the relevant competition

From the overall picture of the competitive environment, we can now derive the relevant competition for Albert Heijn. It is clear that, given the position- ing, Aldi and Lidl are not relevant competitors of Albert Heijn. The buying opportunity that Aldi or Lidl focuses on is completely different to that of Albert Heijn. Both cover the (non-daily) buying opportunity for low-cost bulk purchases, without pretending to have everything that one may need. They will therefore only rarely be the 'primary supermarket' for the consumer. In addition to Aldi and Lidl, one always needs another seller to complete the total required package. It should be noted that Lidl is more and more eager to claim the role of primary supermarket. The company does this by gradually expanding their product range. Albert Heijn specifically aims at being the primary supermarket for the consumer: the supplier where you can get everything that you may need on a daily basis. But this does not mean that Aldi is not a serious threat for Albert Heijn. Aldi's presence has resulted in a change in what consumers consider to be daily purchases: if cat food is bought in bulk once a month from Aldi, cat food will disappear from the definition of the 'daily package' and will therefore be purchased less from AH. In contrast, C1000 is a direct competitor for Albert Heijn. After all, C1000 also focuses on the total provision for the daily buying opportunities. The USP that positions C1000 in the market compared to Albert Heijn is *the price image*. In recent years this fact has however clearly been subject to erosion, since the price war of 2003. Similarly, the middle segment is also relevant competition for Albert Heijn: after all, it also serves the daily buying opportunity. The middle segment is less complete and less expensive than Albert Heijn, but not very profiled. Finally, the deli stores compete with Albert Heijn in the area of quality. The USP that Albert Heijn uses with respect to these suppliers is the fact that Albert Heijn is cheaper. The conclusion is clear: the relevant competition is largely formed by the formulas that are positioned closest to the own formula in the Porter matrix.

9.6 Determining the direct competitor

The most important competitor is then selected from the relevant competi- tion. There are various ways and criteria to identify the most important competitor. Sometimes this happens instinctively, sometimes it happens based on externally available data on the development of the competitor (strong growth or strong gains of market share) and sometimes it happens

Benchmarking

with more advanced market research techniques or techniques such as *benchmarking* (a method to analyse the critical success factors of the competitor using a systematic process). We will now immerse ourselves in the market for alcoholic beverages and in the fashion industry.

9.6.1   Market for alcoholic beverages

Gall & Gall is market leader in the area of liquor stores. Gall & Gall is part of Ahold. The formula was created as a result of a merger between the old, rather small, but reputable Gall & Gall and the much larger, but less reputable Alberto. Alberto was not created as a formula, but as a result of the institutional constraint that supermarkets are not allowed to sell spirits. Ahold opted for a pragmatic solution by separating a part of the supermarket (or by buying a property right next to the supermarket) and setting up a liquor store there. Alberto was actually an extension of Albert Heijn and also used the sales flow that was generated by the supermarket. In the new situation, Gall & Gall was appointed as individual SBU (*strategic business unit*) with a large number of *stand-alone* sites. A private marketing approach was now necessary and that includes competitor's analysis (see table 9.1).

TABLE 9.1 The suppliers (chain stores) in the area of liquor stores 2010

	Number of branches	Market share (in %)	Market share per store (in %)
Gall & Gall	540	31.1%	0.058%
Mitra	320	14.8%	0.046%
Dirck III	63	4.2%	0.067%

Source: websites retail chains 2011; Nielsen, 2010 (own editing)

The assessment showed the following:
- The most important competitor in absolute terms for Gall & Gall, is Mitra: with 320 branches and a market share of 14.8%, this company is (remotely) the second supplier in the market. However, Mitra is not as important per store: the market share per store is only 0.046%.
- The third party in the market is Dirck III. From the number of branches this company does not mean much with only 63 branches. Nevertheless, it still realises a market share of 4.2%. The reason for this is the very high market share that every store realises: 0.067%. It therefore appears that, where Gall & Gall meets Dirck III, this is a more important enemy than Mitra.

The message is that, depending on the used criteria, we can come to different conclusions regarding the enemy. Calculated from the number of branches and the overall market share, Mitra is the enemy. Calculated from the strength of the formula (expressed in the market share per establishment), Dirck III is the enemy.

9.6.2   Fashion industry

Destination store

The example of Gall & Gall relates to a so-called *destination store*, in other words a store where you go with a specific intent to purchase. It barely ever happens that you shop on a comparative basis for a bottle of cognac. In the fashion industry, shopping on a comparative basis is very common. Even though you have preferred stores, other stores are very often visited to see what they have to offer. Fashion stores are 'express stores'. The criterion for determining the direct competitor is not which competitive seller achieves the highest sales, but which competitor is visited most in addition to our own store. To determine this, you will generally have to conduct a market research (see table 9.2).

TABLE 9.2 Absolute and relative competition for company X

Supplier	Visit percentage Dutch women	Visit percentage company X-visitors	Relative 'attractiveness' for company X-customers
V&D	37	32	0.86
Miss Etam	26	42	1.62
C&A	47	35	0.74
De Bijenkorf	20	33	1.65
WE	16	22	1.38
M&S Mode	27	20	0.74
H&M	49	34	0.69
Zeeman	23	15	0.65
Didi	12	15	1.25
Benetton	7	13	1.86

Table 9.2 clearly establishes that:
- H&M is the most visited store in the area of fashion: 49% of Dutch women sometimes visit H&M.
- H&M is indeed an important competitor, but not a direct competitor for company X. While an average of 49% of the Dutch women sometimes visit H&M, this is 'only' 34% of the visitors of company X. The relative competitive strength of H&M compared to company X is therefore 0.69 (namely 34%/49%). The most important direct competitor for company X appears to be Benneton. Benneton is not a big player in the overall competitive environment: only 7% of the Dutch women visit this formula. However, the percentage of the visitors of company X is 13%.
- The relative competitive strength of Benneton compared to company X is therefore 1.86.

9.7 Analysis of the direct competitor

Identifying the direct competition does indeed indicate who the competitor is, but not why he is a competitor. In order to respond adequately to the competition, we need to know more. A relatively easy method that is used in retail is *mystery shopping*: anonymously visiting the competitor as a customer, followed by an analysis based on a checklist. Incidentally, mystery shopping is more than just visiting and assessing the competition.

Mystery shopping

Many retailers use this methodology where one uses anonymous customers to objectively observe how processes are run on the store floor, even for their own organisation. Important in mystery shopping is that the actual working procedure is compared to the intended working procedure.
Based on a predefined questionnaire and a predefined scenario, where all target elements are discussed, the mystery shopper visits a location, runs through the scenario and records the findings in the questionnaire.
Generally a score structure is included in the questionnaire, so that the results of the survey can be expressed in percentages. This gives you a clear picture of the state of affairs and you can compare the results, identify trends and assess where improvement is needed. Obviously, you also gain insight into what is actually going very well on the store floor. When own branches and competitors are visited, it is possible to set clear benchmarks and the potential for improvement can be identified.
We will discuss the various forms of mystery shopping below. We will see what you can measure. Finally, we will list the conditions for a successful mystery shopping program.

9.7.1   Various forms of mystery shopping
Mystery shopping is used as measuring and benchmarking tool and as a tool for improvement.

Measuring and benchmarking tool
Mystery shopping can be used for the following:
- Eyes and ears on the store floor for the management: this is the most original application. Results are mainly used as management information and to understand how it works in practice on the store floor.
- Competitor's analysis: mystery shopping is often used as competitive research. An assessment is made of the working procedure, prices, products and services. You have to remember that the results of the survey are based on the working procedures and processes of the own organisation. The results therefore only provide insight into how the competitor operates, measured by your standards.
- Reseller evaluation: mystery shopping research is also used by producers/manufacturers to identify and make agreements on the positioning of the products. It can also be used to verify that agreements on the point-of-sales material and the information supply are observed by the reseller. These results are used in evaluation sessions with the retail chain and the manufacturer.

Tool for improvement
Mystery shopping can be used for the following:
- Reflective moment for the employees on the store floor: a mystery shopping report serves as a mirror to the employees on the floor. This makes mystery shopping an immediate tool for improvement.
- Identification of training needs: the results of a mystery shopping survey can instantly provide clear insight into the question of where the training needs of an organisation is located. Should the emphasis lie on service, product knowledge or sales techniques?
- Motivation tool/training on the job: if a mystery shopping program is communicated correctly, it has a direct impact on the store floor. The

employees are once again reminded of the intended working procedure and encouraged to act accordingly.

9.7.2 What can be measured with mystery shopping

Mystery shopping is a tool that is an extension of *audit*. An audit generally measures 'hard values'. Mystery shopping is mainly about 'soft values', or aspects on which an employee has an influence. Mystery shopping, as a tool for improvement, only uses aspects on which an employee has an influence. When measuring 'hard values', it is more a matter of an audit. When directed at competitors, it will be secret and will fall under mystery shopping and not under audit.

We will briefly discuss the measurement of 'soft values' and we give the questionnaire of the mystery shopper.

Audit

Measuring soft value

To illustrate, we give an example of questions for mystery shopping as a method of evaluating employees.

What is not a good question: 'Is there a fire door present?' The employee has no influence on this.

What is a good question: 'Was the fire door clear of obstructions?' The employee does have an influence on this.

Elements that are often included in retail are:
- care for the location/first impression;
- service;
- point-of-sales materials;
- sales techniques/up-selling;
- product knowledge;
- employee presentation;
- finalisation.

9.7.3 The conditions for a successful mystery shopping program

We will list the following conditions for a successful mystery shopping program:
- *Objectivity*: since mystery shopping is a measuring instrument where one must be able to compare the results, an objective rating is of the utmost importance. If there is room for interpretation by the mystery shopper, the generated data is not comparable.

  Objectivity
- *Impressionable aspects*: mystery shopping is all about improvement. It is therefore important not to evaluate an employee on aspects on which he has *no* influence, for example, the state of the ceiling in the store.

  Impressionable aspects
- *Fast feedback*: in order to use a mystery visit survey as a tool for improvement, it is necessary for an individual report to be fed back within a few days. This way, a visit can be recognised and relived by the employee.

  Fast feedback
- *Positive*: acceptance of the results can only be guaranteed with a positive approach. Therefore, it is important that the questions and the program structure are positive. The method is primarily focused on what works well rather than on everything that needs to be improved.

  Positive

9.8 **The Net Promoter Score**

One of the methods developed in order to measure own performance and very suitable for comparing with the relevant competition is the *NPS*, the *Net Promoter Score*. This method, developed by Reichheld in 2003 (Reichheld, 2003), is a simple measuring method and was partly developed because existing loyalty metrics were insufficiently effective, but often also proved to be complex. This is mainly why they were not useful to managers and thus functioned poorly. Reichheld also believes that a traditional customer satisfaction survey is a poor predictor for profit growth, and therefore a bad steering instrument. According to Reichheld, the Net Promoter Score gives the answer to the question of what contributes to profitability and it can predict. The NPS-method is based on asking one central question to customers: how likely is it (on a scale of 0 to 10) that you would recommend a company to a friend or colleague? Within the NPS method, we distinguish three different groups of respondents: Promoters (9-10), Fence sitters (7-8) and Detractors (0-6). The percentage of Detractors is deducted from the percentage of Promoters. The thus acquired result is the Net Promoter Score (NPS). The NPS is a percentage that defines the customer loyalty of a company. Various studies have shown that this strongly correlates with the organic growth of a company. According to Reichheld, the best scoring organisations, such as eBay, Dell and Amazon, have an NPS between 50% and 80%. Companies generally achieve an NPS of approximately 5%-10%. The strength of the method is that, by allocating a single score, one can clearly indicate how an organisation performs and what their potential is for customer loyalty and sales growth. This also makes it such an interesting steering instrument for management. It is certainly also interesting as benchmarking tool, because all companies are evaluated with the same method. Later in the book, we will come back to the importance of the NPS in relation to the retail waterfall.

The basic idea behind the NPS-method is that promoters ensure an increase in the added value. Studies have shown that this group provides recommendations to others. Especially in light of the increasing importance of social media and review marketing, the NPS seems to have become a more important benchmark for retail companies. Promoters are responsible for 80% of all recommendations. The causes of a decrease in added value, the Detractors, are also an interesting phenomenon in view of reviews and social media. They are for more than 80% responsible for the negative word-of-mouth advertising. The influence of reviews will become increasingly more important, in 2010 one out of six Dutch people based their purchase location on a review, while it is expected that, by 2015, this will be one in three. *Word of mouse*, the digital version of word-of-mouth advertising, is and will remain an important factor for every marketer. The big advantage of the digital version is that this can be followed and a certain degree of control be introduced, which was not possible before. It is now possible to conduct review marketing from behind the screen. It is possible to follow the consumer's opinion through various digital platforms such as Ekomi, Trustpilot, Yelp and Wugly, but also through specially developed filters for Facebook and Twitter.

Table 9.3 illustrates what the NPS means to electronics retailers in the Netherlands in mid-2014. It is clear that the scores are significantly lower than the values of the best performing companies in Reichheld's study. Apparently the electronics retail in the Netherlands do not have all that many fans yet, and perhaps the entire industry is in need of investment. Since the method is not only to be used absolutely, but especially for a relative benchmark, it is good to look at the average NPS for the entire sector. We calculated these based on all companies included within this sector and by averaging the NPS. This brought us to an average NPS of −37. It is remarkable that none of the companies have a positive NPS. Even companies like BCC or De Harense Smid, who claim that they pay a lot of attention to service and to the customer, remain stuck on a negative NPS.

TABLE 9.3 NPS in the Dutch electronics retail 2014

	NPS	Detractor	Fence sitters	Promoters
Kijkshop	−68	70%	29%	1%
Scheer & Foppen	−35	46%	43%	11%
Blokker	−60	64%	32%	4%
Dixons	−54	61%	31%	8%
BCC	−20	33%	53%	13%
De Harense Smid	−37	47%	44%	9%
Electro World	−36	51%	34%	15%
Media Markt	−22	36%	50%	14%
EP	−29	40%	48%	12%
Expert	−30	46%	39%	16%
Saturn	−14	30%	54%	16%
Total/average	−37	48%	42%	11%

Source: Q&A Research & Consultancy, 2014

The supermarket sector creates the image as shown in table 9.4. A lot of consumers have given their opinions regarding the supermarkets that they visited in 2014. Again, the relatively low scores are remarkable; apparently retail still scores significantly lower compared to other sectors. Only five out of eighteen food retailers have a positive NPS. The best scoring chain, Deen, has an NPS of 19.

TABLE 9.4 NPS in the Dutch food retail 2014

	NPS	Detractor	Fence sitters	Promoters
Spar	−50	60%	30%	10%
Poiesz	−29	44%	40%	16%
Coop	−28	45%	39%	16%
PLUS	−23	37%	48%	14%
Aldi	−20	39%	43%	18%

TABLE 9.4 NPS in the Dutch food retail 2014 (continued)

	NPS	Detractor	Fence sitters	Promoters
C1000	−20	38%	45%	18%
Deka Markt	−15	33%	49%	18%
Vomar	−15	33%	48%	18%
EMTÉ	−13	32%	49%	19%
Boni Supermarkt	−8	27%	54%	19%
Jan Linders	−7	34%	40%	27%
Dirk	−5	28%	50%	23%
Albert Heijn	−2	27%	47%	26%
Jumbo	1	28%	43%	29%
Hoogvliet	7	22%	49%	29%
Nettorama	9	25%	41%	34%
Lidl	12	20%	48%	32%
DEEN	19	17%	47%	36%
Total/average	−10	33%	45%	22%

Source: Q&A Research & Consultancy, 2014

9.9 The Net Loyalty Score

The previously discussed Net Promoter Score developed by Reicheld is an interesting score for measuring loyalty, but measures only the dimension of recommendation. The NPS is an important score since it gives one of the two dimensions that are important for evaluating the loyalty of the current customer base. Since we believe that retention, the fact that customers return themselves, is maybe even more important there was a need for a second measure. At Q&A Research & Consultancy we developed in 2013 the Net Loyalty Score (NLS) (Quix & Terra, 2013). We used the likewise methodology for the NLS as Reicheld did for his NPS. Our central question for the NLS to the current customers: How likely is it on a scale from 1 to 10 that you would visit this company again? We also distinguish the three different groups of respondents: Promoters (9-10), Fence sitters (7-8) and detractors (0-6). Since we used the same scale, we used also the same method for calculating the scores for the companies we measured. We deducted the percentage of the Detractors from the percentage of the Promoters. The score that we retrieve is a measure for the retention and in our vision the other important factor for measuring loyalty towards a brand or company.

If we relate the NLS to the lower footfall in the inner city centres the retention score is even becoming more important for retailers. Keeping existing customers over a longer period of time is becoming an as important asset as getting new customers. Attracting those new customers is basically partially measured by the NPS, because this factor is representing the likely hood that somebody promotes a company or brand.

9.10 The Loyalty Matrix

As mentioned earlier from our perspective loyalty is not a one dimensional aspect. We believe that two factors determine the loyalty of a customer toward a brand or company: the likelihood to recommend (NPS) and the likelihood of retention (NLS) By plotting both the scores on two axis the loyalty matrix is created. On the x-axis we state the NPS and on the y-axis we state the NLS. We will let cross the axis at the averages of all the plotted scores, because we create in this way a relative measure to position the competing against each other.

FIGURE 9.12 The Loyalty Matrix

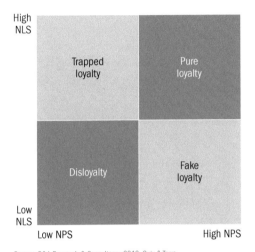

Source: Q&A Research & Consultancy 2013, Quix & Terra

Every quadrant represents a level or state of loyalty of customers towards the company or brand.

The lower left corner is obviously the most unattractive quadrant of disloyalty. Companies plotted here have a relatively low NPS and low NLS and against competition lose on both ends.

Fake loyalty, the quadrant at the lower right side with a high NPS, but low NLS. At the first evaluation this seems to be an odd quadrant and maybe it is hard to believe you could find companies or brands here. There are quite some companies positioned in this quadrant. Their strategy is based on switching behaviour of customers. You will find companies like telco operators, energy service companies, internet providers and in the old days newspaper or traditional media companies. The offer to new customers, acquisition, is always better than to existing customers. Resulting in customers that recommend the company to others, but themselves are more likely to switch to a competitor for the better offer they can get there themselves.

The upper left quadrant is the so called trapped loyalty, a high NLS combined with a low NPS. Why will customers go to stores they don't recommend to peers? This is typically the vision we used to have on loyalty, the lack of something better. Trapped loyalty is seen with retailers that score extremely well on the factor nearby. They are not generally speaking the best option, but the best available offer due to the lack of something better. A tricky loyalty, because when a better option is entering the market place the customer flow can change easily. And the market place is becoming a relative name, due to the fact that online offer can be reach anywhere, of course if the delivery is fast. Pure loyalty yes it does exist. The upper right

THE LOYALTY MATRIX IN PRACTICE

The assumption within retail is quite often that loyalty is related to the brand or concept. As companies measure their NPS in total they try to convince themselves how well positioned they are. Loyalty is claimed to be created by the brand, the concept, advertising and the loyalty program. In 2013 we have executed a research among 8 DIY stores of one brand, well distribute across the country. At all stores for several weeks customers were asked the NPS and NLS questions. Since we also have done the research on a national level we also had the scores for the total DIY chain. In the graph below we decided to let the axis cross on the national average score for the chain so we could benchmark internally all the DIY stores against the national chain average.

The different stores scored completely different from the national average. None of the stores even scored on the national average. Depending on local competition and the performance of the local teams the scores given by the customers differed. Based on this small study we can show already that there is not something like one general type of loyalty, but is likely to be different even within a store chain. From this study we can derive that loyalty has a local component and even more important loyalty is only local relevant. The combination of the local competitor mix and the state of loyalty towards each of the competitors is crucial for the positioning of each player. From some 200 big retail chains we collected the data which can be segmented towards local communities. We could create un this way the loyalty matrix per shopping area based on active national players in the local arena. Within one matrix the performance of all retailers within one segment are clear. They are positioned relatively from each other

since the axis crosses at the average of all scores of all retailers included in the local arena. One of such exercises resulted in the matrix below for women's fashion retailers.

FIGURE 1 The Loyalty Matrix-DIY

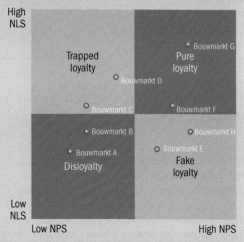

Bron: Q&A Research & Consultancy 2013

FIGURE 2 The Loyalty Matrix-Fashion

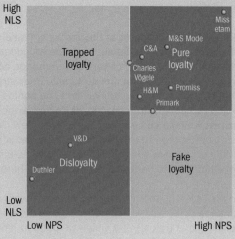

Bron: Q&A Research & Consultancy, Retailranking 2014

quadrant combines a high NLS and a high NPS. Real fans that love to recommend the brand or company and they also return themselves as a customer.

Being positioned in the disloyalty quadrant is a burden that will understand everybody however since it is a relative measure always some players will be positioned here. It is not a real big problem to be positioned in the trapped loyalty quadrant, as long as no new real competitor is entering the market extremely close to this player. Nevertheless it is worthwhile to understand and investigate what these current customers makes real fans. Ask customers feedback and try to find out what makes them happy and your natural promoters and ambassadors. The fake loyalty quadrant asks for immediate action. Most companies that used these strategies of switching when entering markets, understand in the meanwhile that this is not a sustainable strategy in the long run. They understood that high costs accompanied the acquisition of the customers and that they left as soon as they could accept an offer from a competing company. Customers are I the end as loyal as you make them, and they show the attitude that was teach to them. Lowering the cost of acquisition and enlarging the period of the relationship is extremely important and improving long-term profitability. Investigate quickly what makes people choose for a company and even more important why do they stay.

9.11 **Analysis of the competitive position**

A slightly more complicated technique, which often requires separate market research, is the so-called *importance/performance mapping*. Importance/ performance mapping works as follows: interviewing consumers provides you with an *importance scaling* of the aspects that consumers deem important when shopping. In the Retailer of the Year survey, Q&A Research & Consultancy annually conducts such a survey for the retail sector in nine European countries. Some examples of sectors can be found in table 9.5, 9.6 and 9.7. Examples from the Netherlands and some foreign countries were used here. What is immediately noticeable when analysing the tables is that consumers in different countries in Europe find different aspects to be important. Thus we can note that the same aspects are indeed more important for supermarkets (see table 9.5). In Belgium and Germany, value for money is the most important aspect, followed, in the Netherlands and Belgium, by promotions, and in Germany by product range. Although not all differences are very big, they still ensure that retailers have to adjust the marketing mix per country to be in favour of the consumer. Due to the importance of value for money and the product range, no compromise-retailers are greatly appreciated.

Importance/ performance mapping Importance scaling

TABLE 9.5 Importance attached to shopping aspects, supermarkets

Aspect	The Netherlands* Importance	Belgium Importance	Germany Importance
Product range	18.5%	16.2%	22.3%
Customer oriented personnel	11.3%	11.1%	5.5%
Value for money	19.8%	26.1%	23.3%

TABLE 9.5 Importance attached to shopping aspects, supermarkets

Aspect	The Netherlands* Importance	Belgium Importance	Germany Importance
Service	5.5%	4.8%	2.5%
Promotions	19.5%	18.7%	20.4%
Price level	16.8%	13.7%	16.5%
Atmosphere	5.3%	3.1%	5.3%
Innovation	1.0%	2.3%	2.0%
Qualified personnel	2.3%	4.1%	2.1%

Source: Retail Jaarprijs association * and Q&A Research & Consultancy, 2011

With women's wear, the combination of value for money and product range is decisive (see table 9.6). It is striking that in Germany, promotions are significantly more important compared to both other countries. The exchange in Germany for promotions seems to be at the expense of the personnel aspect.

TABLE 9.6 Importance attached to shopping aspects, women's wear

Aspect	The Netherlands* Importance	Belgium Importance	Germany Importance
Product range	21.6%	18.4%	19.1%
Customer oriented personnel	12.2%	12.9%	7.6%
Value for money	20.8%	24.4%	23.9%
Service	3.5%	3.6%	4.1%
Promotions	13.5%	13.4%	19.0%
Price level	11.3%	12.6%	11.5%
Atmosphere	7.2%	4.1%	6.7%
Innovation	2.6%	5.0%	4.4%
Qualified personnel	7.%	5.7%	3.8%

Source: Retail Jaarprijs association * and Q&A Research & Consultancy, 2011

For the electronics industry, value for money is the most important aspect in all surveyed countries; in Italy and Germany, however, it is followed by promotions and in the Netherlands by qualified personnel (see table 9.7). The differences in percentage of the importance for promotions are especially remarkable. This is over 5.5% between the Netherlands and Germany. The Netherlands and Germany are comparable with regard to price level, but Italy differs considerably.

TABLE 9.7 Importance attached to shopping aspects, electronics

Aspect	The Netherlands* Importance	Italy Importance	Germany Importance
Product range	15.2%	17.0%	15.2%
Customer oriented personnel	9.1%	5.0%	6.1%
Value for money	18.9%	20.0%	21.3%
Service	10.9%	5.0%	8.1%
Promotions	15.5%	20.0%	21.1%
Price level	10.6%	15.0%	10.7%
Atmosphere	1.9%	1.0%	2.2,%
Innovation	1.3%	1.0%	3.2%
Qualified personnel	16.6%	16.0%	12.0%

Source: Retail Jaarprijs association * and Q&A Research & Consultancy, 2011

The importance of the various aspects differs considerably from sector to sector, as demonstrated by the three tables when we only look at the Netherlands. For the electronics industry, for example, qualified personnel are greatly valued, where this is the second least important aspect with supermarkets. Value for money is the most important aspect with electronics. Product range is the single most important aspect within the fashion industry. Value for money is the most important for supermarkets, followed immediately by promotions.

The aspects may also vary over the years. Tables 9.8 and 9.9 show the differences in the Netherlands between 2007 and 2011. Price quality has especially increased in importance for both sectors. In turn, the product range increased in importance in the fashion industry, but decreased slightly with the supermarkets. The changes in importance every year are indeed minimal, but significant differences may develop over the years. This means that a retailer should permanently be on guard and should monitor his own environment. Constantly measuring what is important to the customer is of great importance.

TABLE 9.8 Importance attached to shopping factors, supermarkets 2007-2011

Factor	2007 Importance	2011 Importance	Delta Importance
Product range	20.0%	18.5%	−7.5%
Customer oriented personnel	13.2%	11.3%	−14.4%
Value for money	15.5%	19.8%	+27.7%
Service	6.0%	5.5%	−8.3%
Promotions	18.4%	19.5%	+6.0%

TABLE 9.8 Importance attached to shopping factors, supermarkets 2007-2011 (continued)

Factor	2007 Importance	2011 Importance	Delta Importance
Price level	15.3%	16.8%	+9.8%
Atmosphere	5.3%	5.3%	0.0%
Innovation	2.0%	1.0%	−50.0%
Qualified personnel	4.2%	2.3%	−45.2%

Source: Retail Jaarprijs association and Q&A Research & Consultancy, 2011

TABLE 9.9 Importance attached to shopping factors, women's wear 2007-2011

Factor	2007 Importance	2011 Importance	Delta Importance
Product range	19.3%	21.6%	+11.9%
Customer oriented personnel	12.7%	12.2%	−3.9%
Value for money	15.6%	20.8%	+33.3%
Service	6.1%	3.8%	−37.7%
Promotions	13.4%	13.5%	+0.7%
Price level	12.9%	11.3%	−12.4%
Atmosphere	7.0%	7.2%	+2.9%
Innovation	5.6%	2.6%	−53.6%
Qualified personnel	7.5%	7.0%	−6.7%

Source: Retail Jaarprijs association and Q&A Research & Consultancy, 2011

If we know what is generally important to the consumer when choosing a store, we can then ask the consumers how they assess these aspects with regard to their own store and the competitor's store. This gives an assessment of the *performance*. Both observations can be compared against each other, producing the image as shown in figure 9.13.

The following applies with this figure:
- The vertical axis indicates, in order of importance, which aspects consumers find important for a store.
- The horizontal axis indicates, for the same aspects, how the consumer assesses the performance on each of these aspects for a specific store.
- The 45-degree line represents the expectations of the consumer: a store for which all aspect observations end up on the line, scores exactly as consumers actually believe that a store should score.
- Every deviation from the 45-degree line either means a shortcoming (if the observation is to the left above the diagonal line) or an unexpected windfall (if the observation is to the right below the diagonal line).

FIGURE 9.13 Importance/performance mapping

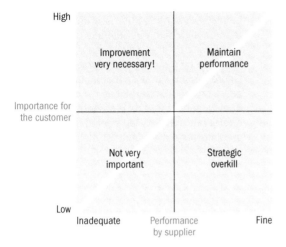

- In the upper left corner of the graph, we find the aspects that the consumer finds very important, but which are simultaneously assessed to score very poorly with the relevant store. Significance for the policy: first priority in the approach.
- In the upper right corner, we find the observations of the aspects that consumers find important and in which the relevant store scores well. Significance for the policy: maintain the performance through *business as usual*.
- In the lower right corner, we find the observations involving *strategic overkill*: aspects that are not particularly important to customers, but which they still find that the relevant store scores extremely well in. Significance for the policy: rather spend the costs associated with the good performance in this quadrant on improving the performance in the upper left corner.
- In the lower left corner, finally, we find the aspects to which consumers do not attach particular importance and which do not score particularly well. Significance for the policy: not very important, first take care of the other priorities.

Strategic overkill

Not only does the importance/performance mapping provide insight into the strengths and weaknesses of the formula, but it also provides immediate prioritisation of the approach. The differences in importance of the aspects per sector are also important to recognise (see examples 9.1, 9.2 and 9.3). The aspects with the highest importance should be addressed first if not properly performed. Where properly performed, the most important aspects will require continuous attention in order to maintain the good scores. In addition to viewing their own scores and those of the competitor, it is advisable to view the own scores from the target groups for instance. The details from both the scores and the interests are often also available by age groups and gender. The result may then be that the scores based on the population are not good, but that those within the own target group are good.

EXAMPLE 9.1 C&A, H&M AND MISS ETAM

Figures 1, 2 and 3 indicate how important consumers find the mentioned aspects and then how they evaluate them for three big competitors in the fashion industry, namely C&A, Miss Etam and H&M. In the three figures, the aspects are equal on the vertical axis, because this indicates the importance for the entire women's wear industry. The horizontal axis shows that there are several differences at store level. Dutch consumers find product range and value for money to be very important aspects in this sector. Miss Etam scores more than enough here but still falls outside of the 45-degree line, which means that there is still room for improvement. Figure 1 shows that C&A does indeed score on the 45-degree line for customer friendly personnel and promotions and offers, but that they lag behind on product range and value for money.

FIGURE 1 Importance Performance Map C&A

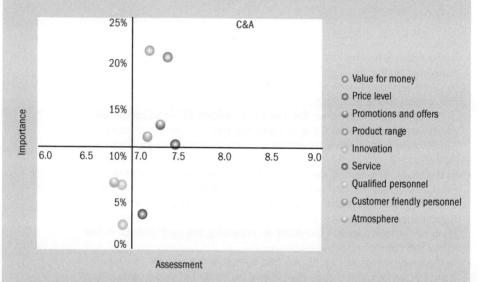

Source: Retail Jaarprijs association and Q&A Research & Consultancy, 2011

All aspects are reviewed to be more than sufficient with Miss Etam. Several aspects are found to be less important, such as the atmosphere, service and innovation. These are also located in the lower right corner, which means that it involves strategic overkill.
The third formula in this comparison has almost nothing in the strategic overkill corner. H&M only has innovation in that corner, but that is also what they want to be known for. Figure 3 shows that the points of improvement for H&M are particularly value for money and product range, but also customer friendly personnel.

FIGURE 2 Importance Performance Map Miss Etam

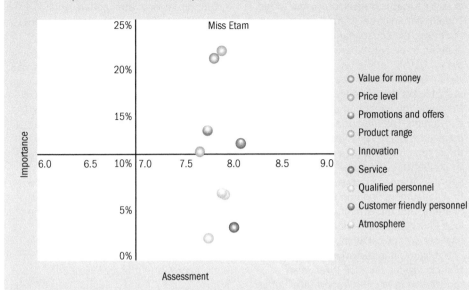

Source: Retail Jaarprijs association and Q&A Research & Consultancy, 2011

FIGURE 3 Importance Performance Map H&M

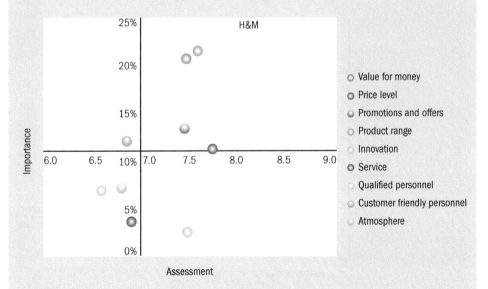

Source: Retail Jaarprijs association and Q&A Research & Consultancy, 2011

EXAMPLE 9.2 ALBERT HEIJN, C1000 AND JUMBO
The supermarket sector seems to be on the move, the consolidation battle appears to be set. Where Ahold had owned C1000 until a few years ago, Jumbo became the new owner of C1000 in 2011. We therefore look at Albert Heijn and the direct competitors C1000 and Jumbo. The *importance/performance maps* have been developed for these three supermarkets (see figures 1, 2 and 3). In the various figures one can clearly see the difference between the aspects that consumers find important in super-markets, and the aspects that they find less important. The less important aspects are far below the 45-degree line in the figure. It is remarkable that Albert Heijn is lagging on price level, even though this is of great importance. Albert Heijn (see figure 3) scores better than

C1000 on service, atmosphere and innovation (see figure 2), but, to consumers, this is less important in a supermarket.

Comparable to C1000, Albert Heijn is able to fill the product range aspect especially well, and even approaches the 45-degree line. Nevertheless, both Albert Heijn and C1000 have to recognise that Jumbo is their superior. The most important aspect, value for money, is actually almost on the 45-degree line. Jumbo scores around the 45-degree line in the four most important aspects (see figure 1), while C1000 scores everything to the left of the line. Albert Heijn only has one product range to the right of the line, but price level is even in the area where improvement is greatly needed.

FIGURE 1 Importance Performance Map, Jumbo

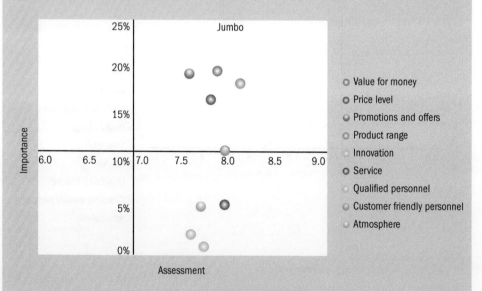

Source: Retail Jaarprijs association and Q&A Research & Consultancy, 2011

FIGURE 2 Importance Performance Map C1000

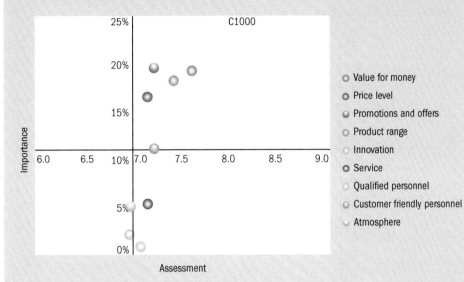

Source: Retail Jaarprijs association and Q&A Research & Consultancy, 2011

FIGURE 3 Importance Performance Map Albert Heijn

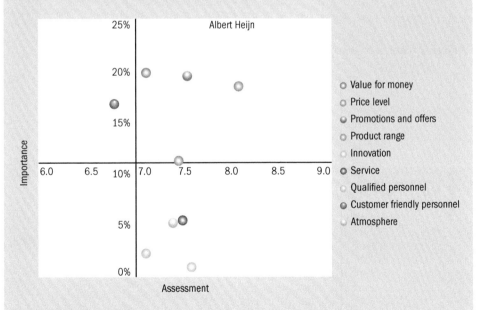

Source: Retail Jaarprijs association and Q&A Research & Consultancy, 2011

EXAMPLE 9.3 MEDIA MARKT AND BCC

FIGURE 1 Importance Performance Map Media Markt

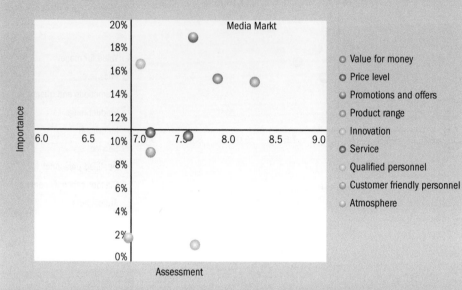

Source: Retail Jaarprijs association and Q&A Research & Consultancy, 2011

FIGURE 2 Importance Performance Map BCC

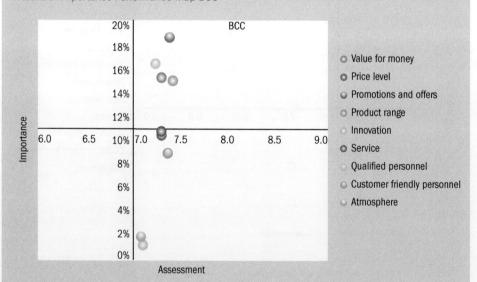

Source: Retail Jaarprijs association and Q&A Research & Consultancy, 2011

The importance/performance maps for the chains in the electronics industry show that qualified personnel and value for money are important aspects (see figures 1 and 2). However, Media Markt's performance on qualified personnel is second worst rated aspect, after atmosphere (see figure 1). This aspect is therefore the first priority, because it is so important. The assessment of BCC's aspects are closer together, but qualified personnel, and especially value for money, are far outside the 45-degree line (see figure 2). With BCC, none of the important aspects are to the right of the 45-degree line, which is the case with Media Markt. That group scores very well on promotions and product range. Media Markt is able to score better on everything. It is important that you not only score as many points as possible on the 45-degree line, but that you also take into consideration the scores of the competition. Media Markt opts for better performance, even beyond the expectation or aspiration level of the scores that are important. In doing this, Media Markt has clearly opted for a mix of product range and price oriented aspects. BCC would in this case be able to opt for more attention to expertise.

9.12 Positioning of competitors

Positioning graphs are often a great way to quickly gain insight into how different retailers are positioned relative to each other, in the eyes of consumers. A good way to position retailers is, for example, to start based on the previously mentioned aspects where consumers choose certain stores. It can also be linked to Eysink Smeets' model, for example, by comparing the value for money and product range aspects against each other (see figure 9.14).

FIGURE 9.14 Positioning graph for electronics industry

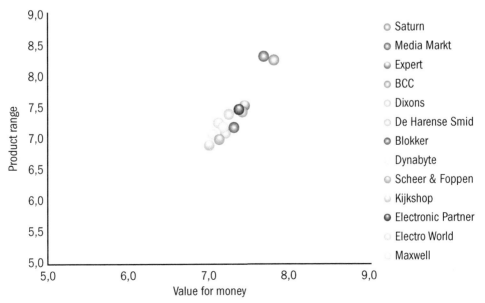

Source: Retail Jaarprijs association and Q&A Research & Consultancy, 2011

Following the example from the previous paragraph in terms of electronics, we can see how the importance performance scores translate into the positioning of companies (see figure 9.14). Media Markt and Saturn are able to distinguish themselves from all the other players with the choices that they make in the area of product range and value for money. Actually, these are the only no compromise retailers in this playing field and that is not surprising for a *Category Killer*.

For example, when we create a positioning graph for electronics chains in Italy, we get a picture as shown in figure 9.15. This revealed that Media World (Media Markt) is perfectly able to distinguish itself from all its competitors on both aspects. Fnac, on the other hand, scores significantly better on product range compared to many of its competitors, but loses on value for money compared to almost all competitors.

Category Killers

In Germany the *Category Killers* are also winning from the specialised retail.

Naturally it is important for a retailer how he is compared to competitors, but, above all, it is important how he wants to be seen by consumers. In other words, does the perceived positioning go with the target group that he wants to serve? Thus, opting for a service and product range with slightly higher than average prices may be a good choice if it matches the target group. Danger of positioning in general is that one could lose sight of his own customers. Therefore, it is also important that you always look at the individual target group of today and the possible target groups of tomorrow.

FIGURE 9.15 Positioning graph for electronics industry in Italy

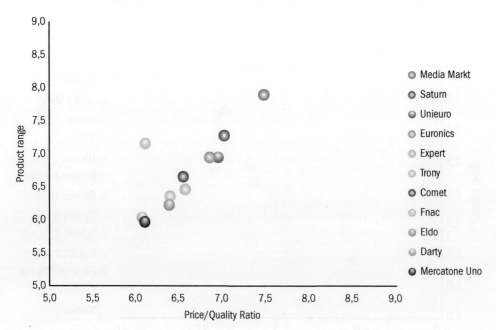

Source: Q&A Research & Consultancy, 2011

FIGURE 9.16 Positioning graph for electronics industry in Germany

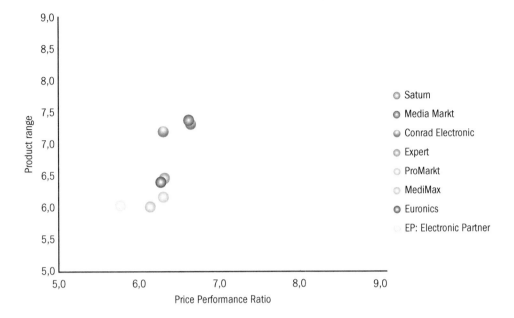

Source: Q&A Research & Consultancy, 2011

It is possible that the positioning of a competitor and its customers may be attractive and that a retailer would therefore want to move his own position respectively. This phenomenon is called a *repositioning*, and can take place more frequently during the life cycle of a retailer. With every change of position, it is important that one always keeps an eye on the current customer group, if one does not want to lose them, and to tap into new groups.

Summary

Many West-European markets have too many stores. It is then important to follow the competition carefully. With competitor's analysis it is important that we not only take into account the existing and identified competition, but also the competition that we have not yet noticed, or who come from other sectors. Michael Porter's five forces model may be helpful here. Porter's theory about the competitive strategies is also an easily applicable, but still rather crude instrument to evaluate the competition on a strategic level. It is not only important to look at the overall competitive environment (macro), but also to separate relevant competition from the overall field (meso). You can then select the enemy within the relevant competitors (micro).
We also discussed Eysink Smeets' theory about the no compromise game to show that retail is not just about the status quo, but especially about

keeping pace with the dynamics in our immediate environment, including our competitors.

Given the 'crudeness' of the Porter-model, a further 'tactical' analysis of the competition is needed. We have a variety of methods at our disposal for this. We discussed the importance/performance mapping, mystery shopping, the competition checklist and, not to forget, the NPS methodology. The first method (the importance/performance mapping) is a particularly good starting point, especially considering the fact that these details are relatively easy to obtain and provide a basis for improvement. Moreover, this data can be viewed from the perspective of the individual target group. This method also provides further insight into what consumers find really important.

Ultimately it is always about satisfied customers; they will return and recommend retailers to others. The NPS method is an easy, simple and effective methodology. A score shows the retailer how he performs and how his competitors perform. In a world that will revolve increasingly around word of mouse, the digital version of word-of-mouth advertising, the NPS is an important measuring instrument for success.

We concluded the chapter with the positioning of retailers in their competitive environment. Naturally it is important how one is compared to competitors but, above all, it is important how one wants to be seen by consumers. In other words, does the perceived positioning go with the target group that one wants to serve?

PART 4

Internal analysis

In part 3, we focused on methods and information that is important to the external analysis. We concluded that the number of external data sources at our disposal, is actually quite limited. For the analysis of relevant external developments, we must therefore often rely on ad-hoc research.

In the following part, we will focus on the internal analysis. The problem with the internal analysis in retail is that one generally already has an extraordinary amount of data: this is known as an information overload. The point of the internal analysis is therefore mainly to collect concentrated, policy relevant information out of this information overload. This part discusses a number of models and methodologies that may be helpful. The treatment in this part will primarily focus on reducing the information overload. The models can also be used at a lower level for more detailed analysis. The tactical applications of a number of these models are discussed in chapter 24. As starting point, we will use the previously discussed formula $R = S \times M - C$ with the treatment of the internal analysis.

In chapters 10, 11 and 12, we discuss the various ways to look at the S of sales.

Chapter 13 discusses several methods that may be helpful in the analysis of R, M and C.

10
The sales concept in the commercial retail function

A simple concept as sales can, in practice, lead to considerable confusion and misunderstandings. This can often be traced back to the situation where you know what is meant by sales in financial terms, but that you do not understand the process through which the sales is achieved.

10

10.1 General definition of 'sales'

Participants in the production process generally tend to define the sales in terms of parts of the production process on which they have the most influence from their function. This certainly applies to retail. For example, a logistics manager of a retail company, who, in view of his function, is responsible for ensuring the most effective flow of the goods, will tend to regard sales from the details involving stock levels and sales rate. He views sales as the product of stock turn and average stock: $S = ST \times AS$.

A human resources manager in retail, who, in view of his function, is responsible for the best possible use of available personnel, will interpret sales from the number of employees and the amount of work that can be done by each employee. He views sales from the perspective of the number of employees (converted into full time-equivalents) and labour productivity: $S = FTE's \times LP$.

As a result, especially in larger retail companies where the various business functions are often split, considerable conceptual confusion may occur. Such differences in perspective when looking at sales may also occur on the commercial side of the retail company.

10.2 The commercial concept of sales in retail

Sales

Suppliers of retail (often industrial companies that can only serve a limited number of closely related markets due to the technical limitations of the production unit), will tend to express *sales* as the product of the average price and the quantity, the volume.

$$Sales = Price \times Quantity$$

This is the sales concept that is used in most economic textbooks.

However, such an approach is less useful in retailing. Indeed, typical retailing is that one operates in many different product markets at the same time. Each of these products has its own price and has its own marketing volume. It is therefore almost impossible to calculate the marketing volume for each of these products individually. With such an approach, even a highly specialised seller as Aldi (with a product range of 'only' about seven hundred articles) would be confronted with seven hundred databases that need to be followed. It is for this reason that we work with groups of similar products in retailing. Such groups are called *product ranges*. Product ranges can be composed of a large number of individual products and brands. The product range of building materials in a DIY market includes both bags of cement and plaster board or insulation material. The product range of animal food in a supermarket includes both dog and cat food, and both the brands Whiskas and Felix, often supplemented with its own brand. The size of a product range is expressed in the number of different variants (or: *stock keeping units*, SKU's) being carried.

Product ranges

Stock keeping units

A single buyer often buys such clusters of similar products. The sales concept of this buyer will therefore be focused on this market: he measures his contribution to the commercial policy of the company as the market share that he is able to realise in this market segment. To him:

$Sales = Market\ share \times Market\ size$

The total sales of the company can then be represented as:

$$S = \sum_{l}^{n} (MS \times MS)$$

In this formula, *n* represents the number of product ranges.

From the perspective of a branch manager, however, sales is achieved in an entirely different way. A branch generates its sales by realising very small market shares in a multitude of product markets. The sales of a single branch is therefore the sum of small market shares in greatly different market segments. The branch manager will therefore be much more inclined to look at how the sum of these small sales are realised from his market area through his outlet.

$Sales = Customers \times Average\ ticket$

The total sales of the company can be represented by:

$$S = \sum_{l}^{n} (C \times AT)$$

In this formula, *n* represents the number of branches.

The fact that the three parties involved (see figure 10.1) in the commercial playing field each view sales in their own way regularly leads to misunderstandings in practice, even within the operation of the retail company. The most important communication problems that occur in larger retail companies are those between purchasing and sales. It is therefore important that both purchasing and sales understand eachothers perspectives. This is particularly so because, in practice, it is relatively rare for a retail company to be either exclusively purchasing oriented, or exclusively sales oriented.

FIGURE 10.1 The sales triangle in the commercial playing field

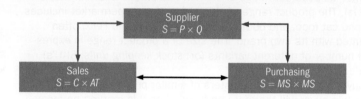

A mix of both elements is almost always involved. A single vision would only suffice on both ends of the spectrum. In all other cases, we have to use both 'sales perspectives' together.

10.3 The like for like sales concept

Like for like sales

Like for like sales is defined as the sales that is made on existing long-term operational floor space. It is in fact the total sales of the company, minus any new launches, extensions of square metres on existing sites, expansion and growing pain effects. The concept is important because the like for like growth is in fact the best benchmark for assessing the formula strength of a retail company. A retailer may have splendid growth rates, but if this is only caused by the expansion while the like for like sales decreases, this means that, over time (especially in a relatively small country like the Netherlands, where expansion quickly comes to an end), the formula will be in trouble. This is building a giant with feet of clay, choosing a (temporary) leap forward. After all, the cash flow that is needed to finance the expansion comes from the like for like performance. If this cash flow runs dry, expansion financing will be more difficult and, moreover, the new branches will soon be in a like for like situation and therefore exhibit negative growth rates. The (negative) scissor effect will then have a duplicate effect.

Summary

The interpretation of the concept of sales often depends on the person who uses it: retail suppliers will be inclined to view sales as the price × quantity marketed volumes ($S = P \times Q$). Sales leaders or branch managers, on the other hand, will be inclined to view sales as the product of the number of customers and the average ticket per customer ($S = C \times AT$), while buyers will be inclined to define sales in terms of the market share that they build in their market segment ($S = MS \times MS$). In all cases we have to take the concept of like for like sales into account, no matter what the perspective. The fact is that the three participants involved in the commercial process will each use a different interpretation of the concept, often leading to communication problems in practice.

10

11
Sales from the perspective of the establishment

In this chapter we focus on the sales from the perspective of the establishment. We discuss the model-based approach of the retail formula: the retail monitor formula. We also discuss the use of the model at a global level, the use of the model for internal strengths and weaknesses analysis, the use of the model in the context of lost sales and the so-called retail waterfall.

11.1 Model-based approach to the retail formula

Catchment area

A manager in a relatively small, well-defined *catchment area* – in the daily products sector – where the purchasing behaviour is habitual (for example a neighbourhood supermarket), will basically suffice with the description Sales = Customers × Average Ticket. His goal will be to ensure that customers from the catchment area come around more frequently and leave with even more purchases, to maximise his sales. It is not without reason that the marketing mix of supermarkets is sometimes represented by MFOF rather than by the four P's: Many, Fixed, Often and Full. This implies that one seeks many fixed customers who often visit the store and leave with a 'full' cart.

In other sectors of retailing, however, the purchasing process has to be further detailed. For example, in the 'furnishings' sector there is no well-defined catchment area (customers are prepared to travel large distances for orientation in these kinds of products). There is also no question of habitual purchasing behaviour (furniture is purchased on average once every ten years). Moreover, because of the high purchase amount, there are significant risks for the consumer. This gives the potential customer the tendency to orient himself with different suppliers before proceeding with the purchase. From the perspective of sales maximisation, it is useful for a number of suppliers to be based together, strengthening the pull from the catchment area (more visitors), even if one runs the risk that the buying percentage of visitors per outlet goes down because of the many purchasing alternatives presented to visitors. Furniture boulevards are the result.

In such low frequency purchased product categories, with a fashion-related trend and a buying pattern that is not habitual, where every visitor to the store is certainly not automatically a customer, we need to refine the insight into the purchasing process. How do we make a resident in the catchment area, a visitor to the store? And then, how do we turn this visitor into a customer for as many possible items from the product range?

Retail monitor formula

This is why we developed the *retail monitor formula*. In process terms, focusing on applications in retail, the formula is as follows:

$$S = CA \times VI \times C \times AT$$

S = sales
CA = catchment area
VI = visitors index (the percentage of residents from the CA that visit the store per period)
C = conversion (the percentage of visitors that actually buy something)
AT = average ticket

The term $CA \times VI$ in the formula represents the number of visits to the store. The term $CA \times VI \times C$ represents the number of purchasing visitors, or customers. From the application in the area of retail marketing, it is important that the formula breaks down into two separate parts. The combination $CA \times VI$ represents the external dominance of the retail formula and shows to what extent one is able to attract visitors to the store with the retail formula. This is known as the *attraction value* of the retail formula.

Attraction value

The combination $C \times AT$, however, relates to all internal store factors and shows to what extent one is able to capitalise on the external pull of the formula. We as retailers have absolutely no use for stores that are fun to visit, but where nothing is sold. The combination $C \times AT$ is known as the *transaction value* of the retail formula.

<aside>Transaction value</aside>

It will be evident that the sales definition in the retail monitor formula $S = CA \times VI \times C \times AT$ is a model-based approach of the process, in the sense of a 'simplified representation of reality'. The breakdown into an external and internal marketing approach, which is specific to retailing and which is, in fact, the underlying reason why we have to deal with a double marketing mix in retail, is essential in the model.

In practice, the external and internal approach will affect each other partly. For example, a successful improvement of the internal marketing mix, such as a logistic approach aimed at reducing the 'out of stock' and thereby increasing the conversion, will eventually lead to an increasing visitors index, because customers who had previously been disappointed by 'out of stock', will start to notice that the situation has improved.

The *monitor analysis*, as we often refer to the use of the model, is an important analysis and should actually be performed regularly by every retailer. The analysis is not only suitable on branch level, but also works on chain level and department level. In the following paragraphs, we will discuss how the analysis and the retail monitor formula can be used.

<aside>Monitor analysis</aside>

11.2 Using the model at a global level

In retail, we have various outlet channels: supermarkets, specialty stores, department stores and mail order companies. Various formulas operate within these outlet channels. It seems to be possible to indicate how the various formulas within one outlet channel generate their sales using a simple approach with pluses and minuses. We use HEMA and de Bijenkorf department stores as examples. Both comply with the technical definition of department stores: relatively large-scale suppliers of parallelised product ranges in predominantly non-food environment. However, interpretation of the formula shows that both department stores generate their sales in entirely different ways. We illustrate this through the following points:

- *Catchment area*: the catchment area for an individual HEMA establishment will be relatively small, partly due to the large number of HEMA branches, and partly due to the offered assortment. Consumers are not inclined to travel large distances for toothbrushes, underwear and clothespins. In contrast, the catchment area of a Bijenkorf, with ten branches in the Netherlands (which will decline to seven) and a product range that consists predominantly out of relatively low frequency purchased products, for which people are prepared to travel large distances, is considerably larger than that of a HEMA.

<aside>Catchment area</aside>

- *Visitors index*: from the smaller catchment area of a HEMA, residents come by relatively often. This is partly connected to the proximity, but more importantly to the offered assortment. Because the product range of a HEMA includes mainly high frequency purchased everyday products which, in terms of price and quality, stand out favourably with the competition. On the other hand, the visitors index of de Bijenkorf will be rather low, at least compared to that of a HEMA. After all, the product sold by de Bijenkorf fall mainly under the low frequency purchased assortment, such as furniture and fashionable clothing of a higher than average price and quality level.

<aside>Visitors index</aside>

Conversion

- *Conversion*: conversion will be very high at HEMA. People mainly visit a HEMA because they need something and not, or almost never, because it is so much fun to spend time in a HEMA. The purchase intention is therefore very high. However, it is not excluded that a large part of the visitors of de Bijenkorf are only there because it is an attractive store, where you can get inspiration and properly orientate yourself on the latest fashion trends. It is expected that conversion in de Bijenkorf will therefore be much lower than in the HEMA.

Average ticket

- *Average ticket*: the average ticket, or the amount spent, in a HEMA will be relatively low, while that in a Bijenkorf will be relatively high.

If we summarise the above in pluses and minuses, we see that both formulas – despite the fact that both cases involve department stores – generate their sales in entirely different ways (see table 11.1).

TABLE 11.1 The development of sales in two formulas within one outlet channel

	CA	VI	C	AT
HEMA	–	++	++	–
de Bijenkorf	++	–	–	+

The HEMA/Bijenkorf example clearly indicates that, when it involves sales problems, we need to look for the solution in various directions. In HEMA's case, we need to find the solution mainly in increasing the average ticket.

Cross-over selling

This requires research towards influencing capabilities for *cross-over selling*: how can we encourage visitors to a HEMA to purchase one more product than they intended per visit?

In de Bijenkorf's case we have two starting points: the visitors index and conversion. Influencing the visitors index requires research into the possibility of further market penetration. Instruments such as external promotion, customer loyalty tools (such as customer cards) and promotions (such as the Three Crazy Days) are obvious answers. Influencing conversion requires, amongst other, product range analysis, research on the impact of the price level and analysis of the visibility rate of goods. Instruments such as de Bijenkorf House collection, innovations of in-store presentations and improvement of the logistic process are obvious answers.

11.3 Using the model for internal strengths and weaknesses analysis

In addition to using the model for global strategic analysis as described in paragraph 11.2, we can also use the model – provided that sufficient data exists – for more specific analyses in the area of product range (see example 11.1).

Department stores are companies which, by offering a multitude of sub product ranges (parallelised), try to provide customers with a complete proposition in the market. The number of different sub product ranges in such a concept can be up to forty or more. Managing such a number of sub product ranges requires quite a lot of attention. It is important to condense the information as such that one can quickly see which approaches are necessary for which sub product ranges. It is possible to create this condensation with the aid of the model. Suppose we have the details for each department, we could then categorise the departments based on the characteristics $CA \times VI$ (the number of visitors that are drawn by the department, or the attractiveness of the department) and C (the percentage of transactions that are realised by these visitors, or the merchandise of the offered assortment in the department).

Such a classification leads to a summary in which you can determine, at a glance, how consumers respond to what is offered (see figure 11.1).

FIGURE 11.1 Segmentation of departments based on $CA \times VI \times C \times AT$

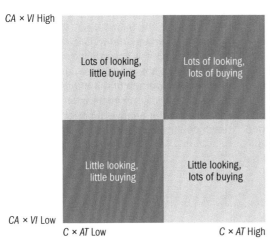

$CA \times VI$ High

Lots of looking, little buying

Lots of looking, lots of buying

By departments:
High $CA \times VI$: nice, attractive department
High $C \times AT$: good purchase worthy product range

Little looking, little buying

Little looking, lots of buying

$CA \times VI$ Low

$C \times AT$ Low $C \times AT$ High

We can make the following classification:
- Departments that are visited more than average and where more than average is purchased contribute disproportionately to the appeal of the department store as a whole. Moreover, they form the basis of the sales, at least for the number of transactions. Such departments are known as *anchor departments*. The policy of such departments can be characterised as: at least maintain, if possible expand. If such departments – measured in time – show deterioration on one of the characteristics, this implies weakening of the strong points of the formula.   **Anchor departments**
- Departments with a high $CA \times VI$, but a low $C \times AT$ are *viewing departments*. These are important for the attractiveness of the department store as a whole, but less important for generating sales. The signal: determine why, despite the fact that so many visitors are walking around the department, so little is being purchased. Is it the price? Or is it the selection?   **Viewing departments**

11

11

<table>
<tr><td>Functional
product
categories</td><td>• Departments with a high $C \times AT$, but a low $CA \times VI$ are generally departments with *functional product categories*. These are products where one goes with a specific intention to purchase, but not really from high involvement. The approach should be aimed at – at least if possible – introducing fun shopping.</td></tr>
<tr><td>Question marks</td><td>• Departments which have both few visitors and where little is purchased are the *question marks*. With these departments, we should determine whether they are actually necessary for the concept. If this is not the case, it would be wiser to close the department and to use the space for anchor departments, for instance.</td></tr>
</table>

We discuss the importance of every department based on example 11.1.

EXAMPLE 11.1 GALERIES LAFAYETTE

Thanks to market research, the French department store Galeries Lafayette is quite capable of determining the extent of its catchment area. From the internal data recording, the department store is able to determine almost exactly how high the average ticket per department is. Two of the four variables are therefore already known: CA and AT. VI and C should therefore be further investigated. Galeries Lafayette does this by means of a periodic random survey among the residents of the catchment area.

The most important questions that are asked are: Have you visited the department store in the past period? If so, which departments did you visit and did you also purchase something from there? By comparing the results per department against the average of the department store as a whole, an impression is obtained of the relative importance of each department (see figure 11.2).

FIGURE 11.2 Product range analysis Galeries Lafayette, based on the monitor model

Galeries Lafayette in example 11.1 used the results in two ways. First in the form of a *timing analysis*: is the result of the measurement consistent with what we want with our concept (see the remainder of example 11.1)?   **Timing analysis**

EXAMPLE 11.1 GALERIES LAFAYETTE (CONTINUED)

The Books department in Galeries Lafayette has a relatively low return. From this perspective, it was considered to reduce costs (space, service) for this group. However, the sales analysis shows that the books department attracts many visitors and also contributes substantially to the success rate of the visitors. In short, it is an anchor. From the perspective of Galeries Lafayette's attractiveness to customers, we come to a completely different conclusion and we should actually consider making more investments in this department (which were also made based on this analysis).

Incidentally, as it applies to all analysis: the results should be interpreted with an understanding of business. The Children's wear department (with a product range of clothing for children up to twelve years) falls under the 'functional' quadrant: a low number of visitors and a high conversion. We need to be aware that in France, as in most West-European countries, only a third of the women have a family situation where there are small children. Under the specific target group 'women with small children', the visitors index for this department is therefore probably three times as high as the image indicates. This is, in fact, yet another anchor, albeit for a limited target group. Something similar applies to the 'Christmas department', a department that Galeries Lafayette only runs for one month of the year. The image relates to the annual situation. Therefore, during the one month that the department is open, the visitors index is probably twelve times as high as the annual plan indicates. During the Christmas period, the department is therefore a super draw card.

Additionally, the details can also be used for *sequential analysis*. Firstly by determining at a collective level whether the conversion respectively the visitors index is subject to change. In the image, this means shifting the crosshairs. If the VI-axis shifts upwards, it means that the department store is increasing its appeal. If the C-axis shifts to the right, it means that the purchase worthiness of the product range is increasing. Secondly, the sequential observations are used to determine whether there are any shifts in the relative position of the departments. Thus, signals can be received quickly and corrective measures can be taken.   **Sequential analysis**

11.4 Using the model in the context of lost sales

The model can also be further operationalised. In the retail sector, much attention is paid to attraction and transaction. Much money is spent to attract as many possible consumers to the relevant store, in other words a lot of promotion is done to increase the visitors index. With regard to transaction, many retailers look at the conversion and the average ticket.

Purchase Intention

The conversion is often measured and reported based on visitor counters, often incorrectly referred to as customer counters. Quite apart from the fact that not every person who enters a store is also an individual buyer or decision maker, part of the visitors have no prior intention to buy anything. It is difficult for a retailer to determine what kind of visitor enters his store. Some visitors intend to make a purchase. These visitors have a *purchase intention*. But not all visitors have entered the store with the intention of making a purchase. The level of purchase intention is quite different from sector to sector. In DIY markets, the number of visitors that enter the store with a purchase intention is much higher than, for example, in the fashion or sports sector. In the last two sectors, we also have many orienting visitors.

Lost sales

Within the retail sector there have not been many studies into the phenomenon of *lost sales*, or unrealised sales. The studies on lost sales that we have encountered in the literature, however, are often from the perspective of the supply chain. Our perspective here is one from the marketing perspective. Or to be more specific: we want to look at lost sales from the transaction perspective. Under lost sales we understand 'the sales that a store in retail has basically missed'. When the consumer did indeed intend to purchase, but ultimately purchased nothing. We define lost sales as follows: the percentage of the visitors that do indeed have a purchase intention, but do not make a purchase.

In order to measure this phenomenon, customers should be classified based on the original purchase intention and the final purchasing behaviour. Based on this classification, store visitors can be divided into four groups (see table 11.2):
- planned purchase: visitors with purchase intention that actually made a purchase;
- unplanned purchase: visitors without purchase intention that still made a purchase;
- lost sales: visitors with purchase intention that made no purchase;
- orientation: visitors without purchase intention that indeed purchased nothing;

TABLE 11.2 Distribution of visitors

		Purchase intention	
		Yes	No
Purchase	Yes	Planned purchase	Unplanned purchase
	No	Lost sales	Orientation

Impulse purchases

In general, unplanned purchases are purchases where the consumer's involvement is low. Purchases in this category are often referred to as *impulse purchases*. In planned purchases, the involvement is much higher. In general, these products are purchased less frequently and are usually preceded by a search process. The sum of the planned and unplanned purchases, or the total purchases by consumers, represents the previously described conversion in the monitor model (see paragraph 11.2).

Therefore, we also look at the transaction part of the monitor model, in which we apply a refinement to the model on the basis of the purchase intention.

$$\text{Value LS} = \text{PI} \times (1 - \text{C}) \times \text{AT}$$

With out-of-stock, lost sales are on the cards

The extent of lost sales can be calculated as follows. Multiply the purchase intention (PI) with one minus the conversion (C), times the average ticket (AT). In this formula, the conversion and purchase intention are still unknown factors and need to be investigated. A retailer knows the average ticket.

Lost sales can only be measured on site. Research through the internet or mail is not suitable because the time between event and interview is often too far apart. This not only affects the fact whether one still remembers if something was or was not purchased. It is also true that a purchase is stored in the memory, while a non-purchase is often not. Much more important is that the reason for the lost sale can no longer be traced. Lost sales relate to situational behaviour and should therefore be measured and investigated directly on site.

To determine the true impact of the lost sales for a retailer, it is useful to determine the missed conversion (MC). The missed conversion is the lost-sales percentage divided by the total conversion (unplanned and planned purchases) and the lost-sales percentage. Realised conversion plus lost sales (consumers with purchase intention) is after all the conversion that one could have realised, but did not realise. In a formula, missed conversion appears as follows:

$$MC = LS / (LS + C)$$

Example 11.2 provides an example of measuring the purchase intention and the final purchasing behaviour.

EXAMPLE 11.2 LOST SALES IN VARIOUS SECTORS

Interesting results have emerged from a large on site survey conducted by the University of Amsterdam and Q&A Research & Consultancy in 2010 (Quix and Bakker, 2010). The lost sales survey was conducted in five sectors (Media, Do-It-Yourself, Electronics, Fashion and Shoes) in 29 chains and in a total of 62 branches. In total, over 6,600 consumers were interviewed on site.

TABLE Retailers lost sales survey 2010

Sectors						
Electronics		**Media**	**DIY**	**Shoes**	**Fashion**	
It's	**Paradigit**	**AKO**	**Hornbach**	**Van Haren**	**Hunkemöller**	**Duthler**
Utrecht	Amersfoort	Amsterdam	Zaandam	Amsterdam	Amsterdam	Hoofddorp
A'dam Osdorp	Amstelveen	Utrecht	Nieuwegein	Utrecht	Utrecht	
Amsterdam						**Purdey**
Nieuwegein	**Dixons**	**Bruna**	**Multimate**	**Ziengs**	**OPEN32**	Amsterdam
	Amsterdam	Amsterdam	Castricum	Hoofddorp	Amersfoort	Utrecht
Prijstopper	Utrecht	Utrecht		Zeist	Zeist	Haarlem
Amsterdam			**Big Boss**			
Utrecht	**Dynabite**		IJmuiden	**Schoenenreus**	**WE**	
Zeist	Amsterdam			Amsterdam 1	Amsterdam 1	
	Utrecht			Utrecht 1	Amsterdam 2	

TABLE Retailers lost sales survey 2010 (continued)

			Gamma			
Media Markt		Utrecht	A'dam Zuid-Oost	Amsterdam 2	Utrecht	
Amsterdam	**T for Telecom**		Nieuwegein	Utrecht 2		
Utrecht	Amsterdam	**Van Leest**				
	Utrecht	Amsterdam	**Karwei**	**Nimco House**	**Houtbrox**	
Saturn			A'dam Noord	**of Shoes**	Utrecht	
Hoofddorp		**Selexyz**	Amersfoort	Almere		
Utrecht		Amsterdam		Alkmaar	**Score**	
		Utrecht		Hoofddorp	Amsterdam	
					Utrecht	
						Total
Chains	8	5*	5**	4	7	29
Branches	19	10	8	14	14	62

* For the analysis, Van Leest was considered part of the Free Record Shop, since these formulas fall under the same holding.

**For the analysis, Big Boss was considered part of Multimate, since these formulas fall under the same holding.

When we look at all investigated sectors we see that, on average, the image as shown in figure 1 is created. Measured by the number of visitors, the average lost sales percentage in the five investigated sectors is 28%. 46% of the visitors convert. These are all visitors that purchased something, planned or unplanned. On average, 26% only orientate themselves in the store. They have no purchase intention and eventually buy nothing.

Fashion industry

Within the fashion industry, consumers were interviewed in Duthler, Houtbrox, Hunkemöller, OPEN32, Purdey, Score and WE.

Based on the variable purchase intention and the final behaviour (whether or not to proceed with a purchase), visitors to stores in the fashion industry were classified into the four previously described groups. This distribution for the fashion industry is found in figure 1. This shows that 58% of the visitors have a purchase intention (the sum of planned purchase and lost sales). This means that 58% of all visitors to the store intend to purchase a product. Compared with the 2007 survey, this has increased.

Back then it was only 42%. This means that, in 4 years' time, specific purchasing has increased by 16 percentage points, thus increased by 38%.

This group with a purchase intention can be further divided into visitors who ultimately purchased something (planned purchase, 28%) and visitors who ultimately did not make a purchase (lost sales, 30%). In 2007, the planned purchases amounted to 23% and, in these four years, this has increased by 5 percentage points. This growth, however, is more limited than that of the purchase intention. The purchase intention showed a growth of 38%, and the purchases showed a growth of 22%. It is therefore clear that retailers have lost out on sales.

In 2007, the number of visitors without purchase intention in the fashion industry was 58%, and in 2010, this decreased to 42%. This group can also be divided further into people who eventually purchased something (unplanned

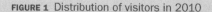

FIGURE 1 Distribution of visitors in 2010

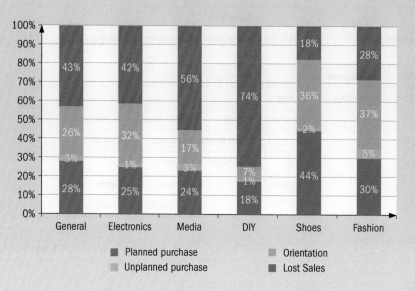

■ Planned purchase   ▨ Orientation
▨ Unplanned purchase   ■ Lost Sales

purchase, 5%) and visitors who purchased nothing (orientation, 37%). It is remarkable that especially unplanned purchases have decreased sharply, from 13% in 2007 to 5% in 2010; they more than halved. The planned and unplanned purchases together form the conversion. In 2010, the average conversion in the fashion industry was 33%. This is a slight drop of 3 percentage points when compared to 2007. However, because of the lost sale, this conversion could have been 30% higher and could therefore have been 58%. The missed conversion, the lost sale expressed in a percentage of the possible conversion, in fashion, is even more than 51% compared to 3 years earlier when that was only 34%. This is a huge increase.

Do-it-yourself sector
Within the DIY sector, consumers were interviewed in Big Boss, Gamma, Hornbach, Karwei and Multimate.
The purchase intention has also increased within the DIY sector. In 2007, this was 85%, while it had already increased to 92% in 2010. This group can be further divided into visitors who ultimately also purchased something and visitors

who ultimately did not make a purchase. The planned purchase group increases by 2 percentage points, to 74%. This seems to be a significant improvement and could easily lead to satisfaction. However, when we look at the lost sales percentage, we see that this increases by 5 percentage points, to 18%. The main reason is the decrease in the number of visitors without purchase intention in the DIY sector. This number dropped from 15% in 2007, to only 8% in 2010, almost halved, where the fashion sector experienced a decrease of less than a third. Within the group with no purchase intention, we see that there is still a group that decides to purchase. This group that makes unplanned purchases is only 1% in the DIY sector. Within this sector, the average conversion was 75% and it dropped by 2 percentage points compared to the previous survey in 2007. The missed conversion, the lost sale expressed in a percentage of the possible conversion, in the DIY sector, is almost 20% compared to 3 years earlier when that was only 14%. Once again we see a significant increase in the missed conversion.
Within retail, lost sales cause a huge loss in sales. Addressing this phenome-

non is therefore important. For this purpose, however, it is necessary to know what precedes a lost sale. In other words: what is the reason why visitors with a purchase intention decide not to purchase anything? The study revealed that, in 84% of the cases, in the eyes of the consumer, the product range was the most important reason not to make a purchase. Three important reasons were mentioned within the product range. The first point was being out of stock (product, brand, colour, size). Out of stock is the underlying reason for sales losses in 41.2% of consumers. The second point was the variation in the product range, this causes 26.2% of the lost sales. And finally, the price level was mentioned by 9.7% of consumers with a lost sale.

The staff are only mentioned as the reason for lost sales in 2% of the cases. But it should be looked at in more detail. Products being out of stock are indeed experienced as such by consumers, yet it appears that most retailers only have a very low out of stock situation. The customer is therefore unable to find the product. The question, however, is whether an employee could have helped. In the situations where the consumer is addressed by an employee in the store, the lost sales appear to be lower than in situations where this does not happen. By showing the customer the correct products, the store employee can also play a role with regard to the variation of the product range.

Our final remark in the context of lost sales involves the trend of the declining number of orientating customers in the various sectors. This is consistent with earlier observations regarding declining visitor numbers in retail. In other words, the visitors index in retail is decreasing.

This is partly attributable to the economy. We believe that the internet also plays an important role in this. Consumers are better informed when they set off and they know what they want and where they can get it. This also explains the decreasing number of unplanned purchases.

This makes it even more important to combat lost sales, after all, not making a purchase also leads to discontentment and could drastically reduce the probability to revisit and recommend to others.

11.5 The new retail monitor formula

We already indicated that the retail monitor formula is a simplified rendition of reality. In many cases, the formula as we have used it for many decades is more than adequate for many analyses. But in light of the decreasing visitors index in the retail over the last ten years, a small update of the formula may not be such a bad idea. The new retail monitor formula is then:

$$S = CA \times VI \times VF \times C \times APC \times AAP$$

S = sales
CA = catchment area
VI = visitors index
VF = visitors frequency
C = conversion
APC = articles per customer
AAP = average article price

11

The new retail monitor formula is more in line with the retail waterfall, because the new formula pays more attention to the number of times that consumers visit a store. This means that the visitors frequency is also part of the attraction strength of a retailer. Naturally the necessary attention is also given to attracting new customers within the external marketing mix. Actually, this is a common tactic, attracting more customers. On balance, this means attracting new customers often. By adding the visitors frequency, we will certainly also play the game to have existing customers visit more often. Repeat visits are important, because these customers already know what they like about us and what they can expect. If they are satisfied every single time, they will not only return, but also recommend this to others. Think of the Net Promoter Score discussed in chapter 9.

A second addition to or extension of the model relates more to the internal marketing mix. In this, the average ticket is split even further into two components to be further operationalised: the article per customer and the average article price. This allows us to add a new performance indicator to our toolbox: the APC (articles per customer). This helps the employees to be more aware of the number of items they sell. In general, this also means higher revenues. The additional sales often have a lower average article price, but they do in turn have a higher margin. For example, when purchasing shoes, accessories are additional sales, or a T-shirt with a pair of jeans, or a belt with a pair of pants in the fashion industry. The APC in the formula

Cross selling

helps the retailer to become more aware of *cross selling* (selling other additional products) opportunities and also makes it possible to measure these. The AAP (average article price) helps the retailer to be more aware of

Up selling

the *up selling* opportunities. Up selling implies selling a different, more expensive product than that for which the customer initially came to the store. The use of the AAP-tool makes it possible to assess, per sales employee and branch, the extent to which people conduct up selling. The more expensive products often provide a better contribution to the eventual profits of a company. Even if the margins are lower, in Euros, the contribution is generally higher, assuming the same cost one makes when selling the slightly more expensive product.

The new monitor formula therefore gives the retailer slightly more tools for steering, where the visitors frequency is obviously difficult to determine without system. Although checking in through foursquare may offer a solution here. Why would a retailer not want something like this to happen in store or in a shopping app? The internal aspects can be measured very easily using the checkout.

11.6 The retail waterfall

Waterfall model

We find a slightly different approach of the same problem in the so-called *waterfall model* (see figure 11.4). The retail waterfall is another schematic representation of reality, but clearly indicates how we eventually get from a market to a customer and from there, whether he will return. Based on this model, a retailer can see what effects his actions have on the attraction value and transaction value.

FIGURE 11.3 Retail waterfall

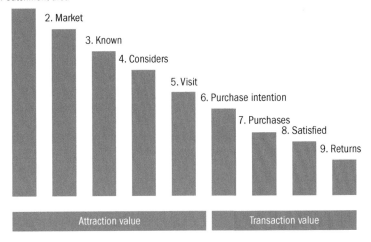

The catchment area is the residential area that a retailer would like to or is able to operate. The opening of a webshop may therefore have enormous implications for the catchment area. The market is the percentage of consumers within the catchment area in need of the products that a retailer sells. For supermarkets, this percentage is extremely high, since supermarkets provide for a daily need. For an optician or a sport store, for example, the market is much smaller, because not everyone wears glasses or is a sports fanatic. It is therefore important to disable the non-relevant target groups (for example households without cars for a car radio supplier), so that we can define the market. Within this market, a percentage is aware of a retailer. This is often referred to as *top of mind awareness*, or TOMA. The TOMA is the percentage of consumers that can spontaneously mention the name of a retailer within a relevant product category. For example, when you mention shoes, consumers spontaneously think about Van Haren (Deichmann), Manfield, Scapino, or a local retailer. Others think about Zalando. With electronics, many consumers spontaneously think about Media Markt, BCC (Darty) or Expert. Another way to measure familiarity is aided brand awareness. In such a measurement, the names of the retailers are shown and consumers can indicate which of the brands they are familiar with. This familiarity is higher than the spontaneous (TOMA) familiarity. Some of the consumers actually take the retailer into consideration. We believe that, in the future, TOIA (*Top of Internet Awareness*) will also play a role. TOIA is the findability on the internet, but then the relevant findability. A consumer searching for shoes or for a shoe store will find the retailer from which he wants to buy products based on his search commands. Some of the consumers who take the retailer into consideration will also actually visit this retailer, be it online or at the physical location. This is therefore the equivalent of the visitors index multiplied by the catchment area. We see, however, that we approach things from the market and not only from the catchment area, because not everyone that lives in a certain area is interested in the products sold by a retailer, or falls under the target group

Top of mind awareness

Top of internet awareness

11

of a retailer. A chain like Score chooses to only serve men with jeans and related products.

Not all visitors to a store who have a purchase intention will proceed with the purchase of a product. The next step in the retail waterfall is purchase intention. Not all visitors of a shopping area have a prior purchase intention and obviously the same also applies to a store. Yet much has changed here in recent years. The great debate within the retail is the issue regarding too many stores with too few visitors. According to many parties, the number of visitors is decreasing, but this is only relevant if the purchase intention does not increase. Because of the growth of the internet and the use of the internet in the orientation and purchasing process of consumers, the purchase intention of the visitors has increased (see example 11.3). Theoretically, the number of buyers can obviously still rise above the next step of buyers if many impulse purchases are made.

EXAMPLE 11.3

Earlier in this chapter, we discussed lost sales. This survey was conducted in both 2007 and 2010, under similar circumstances, with mainly the same chains and with the same questions. We made some additional analyses because we also looked at the foot fall, in other words the number of visitors. If we look at the foot fall of the whole Netherlands, we can see that, while the index for the number of visitors was 100 in 2007, it had dropped to 95 in 2010, which is a drop of 5% in three years' time. In the following tables we show what this means for the purchase intention and for the conversion. Because opinions vary considerably about the decline of the foot fall in recent years and because there are also gloomy reports about the future, we made similar calculations for the case in which the drop in the foot fall would have been as much as 10%.

TABLE 1 Foot fall, purchase intention analysis with a drop of 5%

		2007	2007	2010	2010	Δ
Number of visitors (FF)	Index	100		95		−5%
Purchase intention			Within FF		Within FF	Δ
Fashion		40%	40	58%	55	38%
Electronics		60%	60	67%	64	6%
Do-It-Yourself		85%	85	92%	87	3%
Shoes		34%	34	62%	59	73%
Media		69%	69	79%	75	9%

TABLE 2 Foot fall, purchase intention analysis with a drop of 10%

		2007	2007	2010	2010	Δ
Number of visitors (FF)	Index	100		90		−10%
Purchase intention			Within FF		Within FF	Δ

TABLE 2 Foot fall, purchase intention analysis with a drop of 10% (continued)

	2007	2007	2010	2010	Δ
Fashion	40%	40	58%	52	31%
Electronics	60%	60	67%	60	1%
Do-It-Yourself	85%	85	92%	83	−3%
Shoes	34%	34	62%	56	64%
Media	69%	69	79%	71	3%

TABLE 3 Foot fall, conversion analysis with a drop of 5%

		2007	2007	2010	2010	Δ
Number of visitors (FF)	Index	100		95		−5%
Conversion			Within FF		Within FF	Δ
Fashion		36%	36	33%	31	−13%
Electronics		49%	49	43%	41	−17%
Do-It-Yourself		77%	77	75%	71	−7%
Shoes		22%	22	20%	19	−14%
Media		62%	62	59%	56	−10%

TABLE 4 Foot fall, conversion analysis with a drop of 10%

		2007	2007	2010	2010	Δ
Number of visitors (FF)	Index	100		90		−10%
Conversion			Within FF		Within FF	Δ
Fashion		36%	36	33%	30	−18%
Electronics		49%	49	43%	39	−21%
Do-It-Yourself		77%	77	75%	68	−12%
Shoes		22%	22	20%	18	−18%
Media		62%	62	59%	53	−14%

Not all visitors of a store will buy a product. Within the retail monitor analysis, this is conversion. This is related to the transaction value of the retailer, or the extent to which the retailer is able to transform visitors into customers. Some of the customers are satisfied with a retailer and some of these customers return for a future purchase. The transaction value of a retailer and the experiences that a customer has with a retailer, affect the future attraction value of the relevant retailer. Bad experiences ensure that consumers no longer take a retailer into consideration or visit him.

Good experiences ensure that consumers continue to consider the retailer and visit him, and share these experiences with other parties, which is also why we made a new version of the waterfall. Due to the rise of social media, comparison sites and review sites, the effect of feedback from the experience of the consumer is greater. For the retail waterfall, this means that this feedback will have an effect, positive or negative, on the percent-age of 'known' and the percentage of 'considers' (see figure 11.3).

Due to the changing purchasing process, the rules of the game have changed to influence the steps of the retail waterfall. For a retailer, this means that the new rules should be applied. We will return to the new customer journey in chapter 19.

Summary

Managers working in sales view the sales primarily from the perspective: customers × average ticket. For shopping situations where a visit to a store always involves buying one or more products, such as supermarkets, this is enough. In the majority of the buying opportunities, however, this condition will not be enough. A visit to a store does not always imply a purchase. This is especially true in product categories like fashion, where the purchase is associated with extensive search behaviour. In these cases we therefore have to refine the simple approach customers × average ticket, through the formula $S = CA \times VI \times C \times AT$, where S = sales, CA = catchment area, VI = visitors index, C = conversion and AT = average ticket. Important in the formula is the fact that this consists of an external and an internal part: $CA \times VI$ represents the external appeal of the store: the attraction value. $C \times AT$ is an approach for effectiveness of the internal store factors: the transaction value of the concept.

We also used the model for a subject that is often approached from the supply chain: lost sales, the unrealised sales. We examined the phenomenon on the basis of the monitor model and, even more specifically, from the transaction part. Lost sales focuses on that part of the flow of visitors that had a prior intention to a purchase something from the retailer, in other words consumers with purchase intention. With this, we have applied a refinement to the model, with which we gain insight into the sales that a retailer missed through lost sales. We also showed the impact of lost sales in terms of missed conversion.

Using the retail monitor formula, we can analyse at a global level how formulas generate their sales. In this chapter, we did this for the department store formulas of de Bijenkorf and HEMA.

On a more detailed level we can use the model to measure the reactions of the public on the product range portfolio, as we saw in the example of the French department store Galeries Lafayette.

We saw how the retail monitor formula can be used in the context of lost sales. Retailers are still losing out on a lot of money in the final part of their overall process, namely in the store. This also applies to online retailers, where the conversion is often also disappointingly low. We also showed the new retail monitor formula. This formula is an addition to the existing formula. However, we need additional information to be able to fully utilise the new formula. If a retailer possesses this additional information, he possesses extra tools to optimise and improve the own business operations.

We concluded the chapter with the retail waterfall, where we also discussed the changing environment. The use of internet and the possibilities to find and share information through amongst other social media, ensures that retailers have to take even more notice of the retail waterfall and have to include this in the market movements.

11

12
Sales from product groups

In this chapter we discuss the sales from product groups, such as market share in retail, assortment dominance matrix or BCG-product range matrix, measurement of the product range portfolio, analysis of the development of the portfolio, prioritising the approach, recharging the ADM, goldmine analysis and the connection between GM-analysis and ADM-analysis and the fair-share analysis. Here we answer questions like: How do we calculate the market share? How do we measure and analyse portfolios and what do these results mean to us? Which models can be applied and what do we mean by the fair-share method?
All methods of analysis of the product groups as described in this chapter apply throughout retail, whether you are using online, offline or cross channel.

12.1 Market share in retail

Market share

Market position is, at least from a quantitative point of view, expressed in *market share*. In industrial marketing, calculating and determining the market share is relatively simple: we determine our market, we determine the market size and we divide own sales by the market size. In retail, this is generally not as simple: in retail, market share is realised because many different product markets are operated simultaneously. Calculating, and especially managing market shares within retail, therefore has traits of portfolio management: simultaneously playing a large number of product markets to get the average market share – which is created by the mix of large and small markets and the mix of high and low market shares – as high as possible. It is therefore not surprising that the analysis tools

Portfolio management

used in retail for this purpose, rely on the basic principles of *portfolio management* as developed by the Boston Consulting Group (BCG) (Verhage, 2010).

12.2 Assortment dominance matrix or BCG-product range matrix

Boston Consulting Group-matrix

It is clear that the idea behind the *Boston Consulting Group-matrix* (managing a variety of companies in very different markets by means of a portfolio analysis) is basically very useful for product range management in retail. After all, this also relates to simultaneous management of a variety of product range groups in often very different market segments. However, some adjustments are necessary to make the BCG-matrix suitable for applications in retail. First, we need to replace the entry 'growing market/shrinking market' in the BCG-matrix for the assortment dominance matrix (ADM) with 'large market/small market'. The reason for this is because the growing or shrinking market does not provide any stable information for retail: if the economy relapses, most growth markets for retail turn into shrinking markets within a year. The entry large/small is much more stable: a large market will remain relatively large, even with a relapse due to economic trends. A small market will not immediately be large.

Secondly, the assessment of the market position in the ADM is not so much tied to the relative market shares compared to the competition (as in the BCG-matrix), but to the relative market shares compared to the own average performance. As zero point in the matrix, we therefore use the average market share over the entire product range that is applied by the company on the vertical axis, and the average market size of all market segments in which the company is active on the horizontal axis.

Thirdly, we must realise that market share in retail, other than in the BCG, is not an absolute guarantee for profitability. The distinction between high and low market shares compared to the average in the ADM should rather be interpreted from the recognition and acknowledgement by the consumer. A higher than average market share in a specific sub product range means that the consumer strongly identifies this group with the company and also expresses this by spending more than average on this group. It is therefore a measure for the reputation.

The resulting *assortment dominance matrix (ADM)* is reflected in figure 12.1.

Product range dominance matrix

FIGURE 12.1 Assortment dominance matrix: market share versus market size

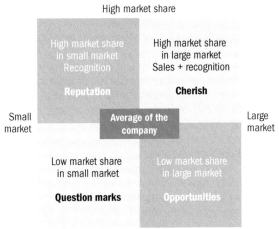

If the company's position were equally strong in all considered market segments and if all market segments were equally large, then all observations would be situated in the centre of the matrix. In practice this never happens and the observations are spread out.

The 'spread in market size' between large market segments and small market segments is a measure for the attractiveness of the market segment pursuant to sales potential. In a large market, small market shares can still represent significant sales. However, the 'spread in

Top of mind awareness

market share' is much more related to the dominance of the product range and the so-called *top of mind awareness* with the consumer: a higher than average market share means that this group, in the opinion of the consumer, is better filled than the average product range. It is a measure for the reputation of the sub product range in the experience of the customers.

The ADM thus leads to a classification of the considered product range into four categories:

- High market share (reputation) and large market segment (good sales): recognition by the customer and the basis for sales. You should cherish this and make sure that you do not lose your position. A declining position in this sub product range means that the formula is weakening.
- High market share (reputation), small market (limited sales): important for the image of the store among consumers, but less so for the sales. Moreover, it is possible to generate significant sales in retail by simultaneously being active in many different parts of the market. HEMA is an example of such an approach.
- Low market share (little reputation, we are doing something wrong), large market (good sales opportunities): opportunity! If it is possible to find the reason for the low market share and if it is possible to work out a few things, you have a significant growth potential. Gaining market share in large markets has a double effect.
- Low market share (little reputation) in small markets (little sales potential). These are the well-known question mark groups: Are they really necessary? Are they worth maintaining? In retail, this often involves the so-called *service product ranges*: groups that are not very attractive from profitability or sales potential, but which cannot be left out from the overall proposition to the consumer. A consumer will not understand if a shoes store sells shoes, but not laces or cleaning products.

Service product ranges

The ADM can be used both for the analysis of the current product range position and deriving improvement opportunities for the future from this analysis, as well as for measuring the developments in the product range position in time and identifying changing market positions per sub product range. The information required to draw up the ADM is limited and generally present within retail companies, namely:

- Own sales figures per sub product range (if these figures are not present, you can also work with figures measured by market research).
- Figures on the Dutch market by product range group. These figures are often available from generally accessible market research. In the non-food sector, we have the so-called GFK survey and in the food sector, we have the Nielsen survey.

It is often thought that these methods are less relevant in the online world, because they use the so-called *longtail* there. This longtail implies that one can offer all imaginable products in the online world because retail space or shelf space is not a limiting factor. Nevertheless, we believe that properly using the ADM can lead to higher profitability. The latter also because increasingly more online players find it important to keep stock of the products in order to ensure the speed that the customer wants. Not only turnaround speeds play a role then, but also how the products from the product range are coordinated.

12.3 Measurement of the product range portfolio

Figure 12.2 reflects the product range position for a men's fashion store. The details were derived directly from the GFK-menswear study, an omnibus survey that most major clothing companies in the Netherlands participated in.

FIGURE 12.2 Product range portfolio for a men's fashion store, period 1

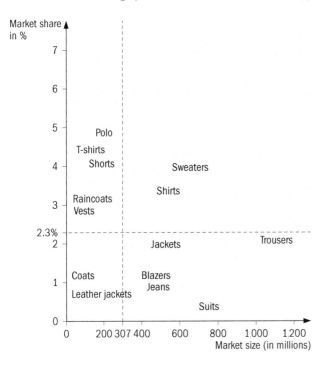

The ADM clearly indicates that the average market share of this company is 2.3% in the total market. In this year, the total market was approximately €2.25 billion. The company therefore had a sales of approximately €52 billion. The average market share of 2.3% is realised because higher than average market shares are achieved in some market segments, and significantly lower market shares in other market segments. The strong groups generally involve relatively high frequency purchased products with low average tickets, while the weaker groups involve large confection: low frequency purchased, high average tickets. The secant lines in an ADM graph are always placed on the average of both value axes (respectively 2.3% and 307 million).

Express store
Destination store

Casual

In terms of store typology, the interpretation reads: the company is more an *express store* (a store that you come across while you are shopping and where you purchase a product in passing) than a *destination store* (a store that you go to intentionally because you need something). In terms of appreciation of the product range, the store seems rather to be identified with the *casual*, leisure clothing habits, than with actual menswear.

If so, the question arises as to why the sub product range 'jeans' (a rather frequently purchased product with a casual association and a market size of €212.5 billion) is positioned so poorly in the matrix. The position can be much better, from both the purchasing behaviour (jeans are often purchased in express stores) and the product range (jeans fall under the category 'casual clothing'). For example, if a better approach of this group would make it possible to increase the market share of jeans from the current 1.1% to the average level of 2.3%, this could possibly represent an additional sales of $(2.3 - 1.1) \times 212.5$ million = 2.55 million, or a sales of approximately 5%, for the relevant company. This is still a nice progression in a displacement situation.

12.4 Analysis of the development of the portfolio

Dynamic measurement

Perhaps even more interesting than the static measurement of the product range position, is the *dynamic measurement*. Figure 12.3 shows the ADM for the same company, but this time for the situation several years later.

The comparison of the charts of both periods clearly shows that there has been a shift in the product range positioning in the company, without this leading to any apparent growth in the average market share. Market shares have grown in sweaters, raincoats, jeans and blazers. Market shares have dropped in shirts, suits, T-shirts and polo shirts. If we limit ourselves here to the large market segments, the comparison of the charts clearly shows that the market for sweaters is dropping, while the market for shirts and suits is growing. We therefore realise increasing market shares in declining markets, and declining market shares in growing markets. It appears that the market opportunities are underutilised. Although the total sales of the company will indeed have grown (the market size of menswear at the time of the preparation of the second chart was approximately €2.6 billion, 2.3% of €2.6 billion is €60 million), we must still ask ourselves whether the product range is not in need of a revision. After all, in retail, with its highly competitive setting, we cannot afford to leave any opportunities unused. For example, if the company had realised the same market share in shirts in the second measurement as with the first measurement, it would have achieved a $(3.5\% - 3.0\% =)$ 0.5% higher market share in the second period in a market that is worth approximately €400 billion, and therefore have generated additional sales of approximately €2 billion.

FIGURE 12.3 Product range portfolio for a men's fashion store, period 2

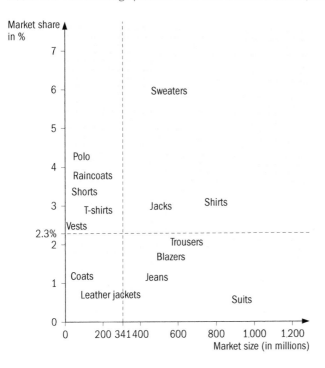

12.5 Prioritising the approach

It is clear that, if we experience sales problems, we should first find the solution in the 'opportunities' quadrant of the product range. After all, these groups offer the biggest improvement in sales, while they are probably the easiest to improve. The second priority will be to further build on existing strengths, thus addressing the 'anchors' or cherish groups. This because it involves large markets, where one already has a high market share. Achieving an even higher market share is more difficult than achieving a slightly better market share in groups where one lags behind. The third priority is the *image-niches*: groups where they already have a high market share (so it is difficult to achieve even more), while the markets are small (so it does not produce much). The lowest priority is the development of the 'question marks': low market share and small market. It likely requires much effort to increase the market share, while it does not even produce much sales. We often see that reorganisation of these groups have a more favourable effect than further development.

Image-niches

12

12.6 Recharging the ADM

It is clear from the above that the ADM can be a powerful tool in the measurement of the development of the product range and the development of corrective measures. The disadvantage of comparing two ADM's simultaneously is that we need to compare observation to observation in order to get an overall picture of the development. In those cases, it is sometimes useful to draw up a Dynamic ADM. Its structure is simple: we divide all results from the second ADM by the results of the first ADM (in other words: we appreciate the results of the first ADM at 100%) and we position the resulting numbers per department in a matrix, of which the crosshairs is 100/100. If all market shares in both years had remained exactly the same, and if all markets had also remained the same with regard to size, all resulting numbers would end up exactly in the 100/100 point. In practice, of course, there will always be a spread and, from this spread, we are able to learn something. Figure 12.4 shows the dynamic ADM. With the help of this summary matrix, it is possible to see at a glance which (and by which) departments caused the change in the average market position.

FIGURE 12.4 The dynamic ADM

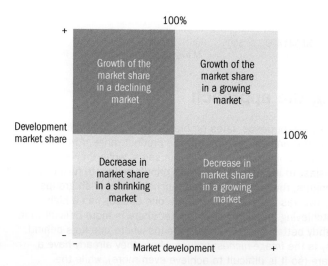

Example 12.1 shows how the market share can fluctuate, where we compare the market share of M&S Mode at two different times.

EXAMPLE 12.1 PUSH FORWARD

M&S Mode initially had considerable success in the Dutch market. The company had built a niche position which covered the slightly older woman with conservative dressing habits and figure problems. It turns out that there was a need for such a concept, which meant that M&S Mode could expand

rather well. The concept also picked up abroad. In 1995, M&S Mode had branches in the Netherlands, Belgium, Germany and France. The development of sales and profitability was positive. There seemed to be nothing to worry about. Around 1995, expansion opportunities in the Dutch home base (which still represented approximately 50% of the sales) appeared to come to a halt. Further growth would therefore only be possible from additional market penetration of existing Dutch establishments or by accelerating the already started internationalisation. The Executive Board examined the possibilities of further Dutch market penetration using the ADM. The results are reflected in figures 1 (ADM year 1), 2 (ADM year 6) and 3 (dynamic ADM year 1/year 6).

FIGURE 1 ADM M&S Mode Year 1

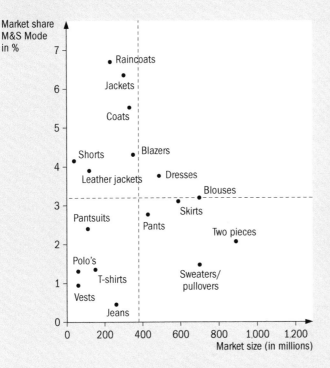

The comparison of figures 1 and 2 clearly shows that, despite the positive development of sales and profit for the company as a whole, the product range position of M&S Mode in the Netherlands is weakening. The average market share drops from 3.1% (with an average market size of €180 billion) to 2.6% (with an average market size of €230 billion). The lovely figures with regard to sales growth and profitability were therefore primarily caused by the expansion abroad. However, the company even realised growth in the Netherlands: the decline in the market share of 16% (2.6/3.1 = 0.84) is lower than the market growth of 28% (230/180 = 1.28).

Figure 3 illustrates more clearly what is going on: the majority of the observations are situated in the quadrant with declining market share associated with a growing market. M&S Mode is no longer able to use the opportunities in the market. Alarming was the phenomenon that this quadrant contained the majority of the anchors (anchors or cherish groups: groups with a high market share in large markets, vital to the concept). The conclusion was clear:

FIGURE 2 ADM M&S Mode Year 6

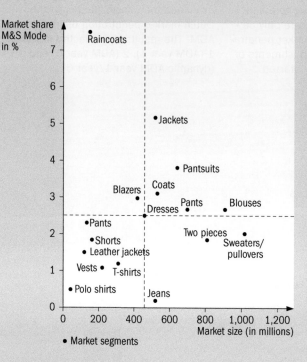

FIGURE 3 Dynamic ADM M&S Mode year 1/year 6

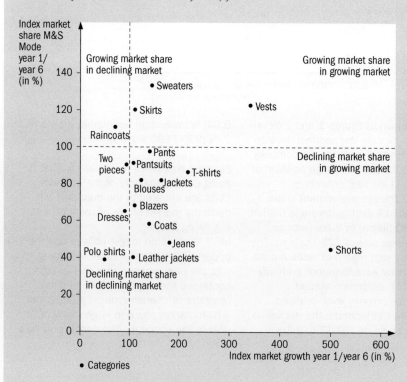

M&S Mode was busy with the push forward. Before the company proceeded with accelerated expansion, it was necessary to first establish the concept on the domestic market. The very rapid expansion in Germany was suspended and even partially reversed. The expansion in Belgium and France was put on the back burner. All attention was focused on improving the sorting per product range and strengthening the formula. The reorganisation cost a lot of money, but it has paid off. Currently, M&S Mode is healthy again.

Example 12.1 explains that it is possible in retail for attractive financial key figures (profit and sales) to be associated with strong negative developments in the market position, either because the decline in market share lags behind the growth of the market, or because the rapid addition of branches conceals the declining market share on a like for like basis.

EXAMPLE 12.2 A CLOSER LOOK AT THE GARDEN INDUSTRY
A large chain of garden centres prepared an ADM and dynamic ADM to gain more insight into the position of product groups and the developments therein. The ADM of the company indicated that the retail chain had a market share of more than 50% in six of the twelve product groups, although this mainly involved product groups in small markets (see figure 1). Only one of these product groups – perennial garden plants – falls in the upper right quadrant, cherish groups (with a high market share in a large market). In addition to perennial garden plants, this applies for the product groups garden furniture, BBQ and major maintenance, which form the most important product groups for the garden centre. There are opportunities in cut flowers/leaves and animals, both large markets. But the garden centre's market share for these product groups is relatively low.

FIGURE 1 Assortment dominance matrix for a garden centre

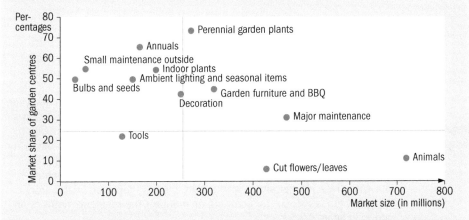

The dynamic ADM of the chain of garden centres shows the developments over a certain period (see figure 2). The garden furniture and BBQ category (one of the cherish groups) shows fantastic developments for the chain of garden centres.

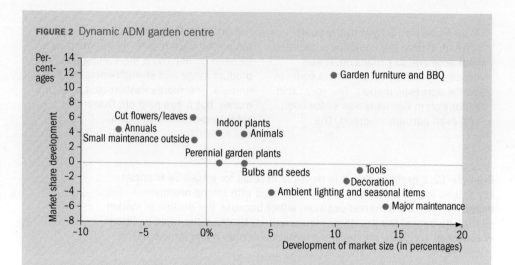

FIGURE 2 Dynamic ADM garden centre

The market is growing by approximately 10%. Additionally, the market share is growing by 12%. Garden furniture and BBQ's are therefore becoming even more important for the garden centre. The animals (opportunity) and indoor plants (recognition/image) product groups also show both market growth and market share growth.

Perennial garden plants and bulbs/seeds are indeed increasing in absolute sales, but the market share remains the same.

For the categories of tools (question mark), decoration (recognition/image), decorative lighting/seasonal items (recognition/ image) and the cherish group major maintenance, the garden centre should be very careful. Due to an increase in market size that is larger than the decrease in market share, the sales are increasing for these groups, but the market shares are decreasing. Such a trend can very well be visualised by analysing the ADM and the dynamic ADM.

12.7 Goldmine analysis

Sometimes it is not possible in practice to collect the data that is necessary to prepare an ADM. This may be due to the market data not being available or not being reliable.

Goldmine analysis

We can still, on the basis of the own business information, use an analysis that is very similar to the ADM. We call this analysis the *Goldmine analysis* (GM-analysis), because it is not focused on analysing the market position, but on analysing the contribution of product range groups to the profitability of the company. The entry 'large market/small market' in the ADM is replaced in this analysis by the entry 'high sales share/low sales share'. The entry 'high market share/low market share' is replaced by the entry 'high/low gross margin' or 'contribution margin'. The resulting matrix is as shown in figure 12.5.

Therefore, the goldmine matrix describes how, in terms of the formula R = S × M − C the product range contributes to R. The ADM describes how S is established in the formula. Both methods may therefore also be used to deepen the understanding of the issues. In the goldmine analysis, by analogy

FIGURE 12.5 The goldmine matrix

	Volume makers • High market share and/or • High sales per m^2 • Low gross profit per m^2 and/or • Low/negative DPP *Policy: profit improvement* • Loss and cost minimisation • Cost-saving measures	**Goldmines** • High market share and/or • High sales per m^2 • High gross profit per m^2 and/or • High/negative DPP *Policy: positional defence* • Confirming authority • Diligence in management

Dominance	**Concerns**
	• Low market share and/or
	• Low sales per m^2
	• Low gross profit per m^2 and/or
	• Low/negative DPP
	
	Policy: elimination or cooling down
	• Loss and cost minimisation
		Profit-makers
		• Low market share and/or
		• Low sales per m^2
		• High gross profit per m^2 and/or
		• High/negative DPP
		
		Policy: dominance improvement
		• Increase sales/
		  market share without
		  generating too much profit

Profit

Source: W. v.d. Ster: product range portfolio in retailing

of the prioritisation with ADM, we can also develop an order of desired approaches. Suppose we want to improve the profitability of a company from the product range mix, the following order is then created:

- Priority 1: *profit-makers*. This regards product range groups that have a low sales share, but a higher than average profitability. Strengthening these groups therefore contributes disproportionately to the profit development.   **Profit-makers**
- Priority 2: *goldmines*. This regards product range groups that have large sales and a higher than average profitability. The further expansion of the sales, considering the already large share in the total sales, will be more difficult than with the profit-makers. But it will contribute disproportionately to the profit development.   **Goldmines**
- Priority 3: *volume makers*. This clearly does not concern increasing sales. After all, increasing sales would more likely cause deterioration of the margin mix than improvement. From profitability, in these product range groups, you would have to work on improving margins, probably even if that is slightly at the expense of the sales. Margin improvement, however, because it concerns volume groups in likely very competitive market segments (hence the low profitability), may prove to be very difficult.   **Volume makers**
- Priority 4: *concerns*. Why would we try to further strengthen less profitable product range groups, which already generate little sales, to improve profitability? It is quite possible that reorganising these groups, if that is possible from the concept, would generate more than further expansion.   **Concerns**

12.8 Connection between GM-analysis and ADM-analysis

We can now connect the results from the profit portfolio analysis (the goldmine) and the sales portfolio analysis (the ADM) together (see figure 12.6). By comparing the desired prioritisation of approach from both analysis, we gain insight into which groups are very important to improve both profitability and the market position. We therefore hit two birds with one stone. We improve profitability while simultaneously strengthening the product range concept. These are the groups that end up in the upper right corner of the figure: attack! We can also see the groups of which it is more or less clear that they will neither contribute significantly to the sales, nor significantly to the profit improvement. These are the groups that end up in the lower left corner of the figure: reorganise!

FIGURE 12.6 The combined GM/ADM

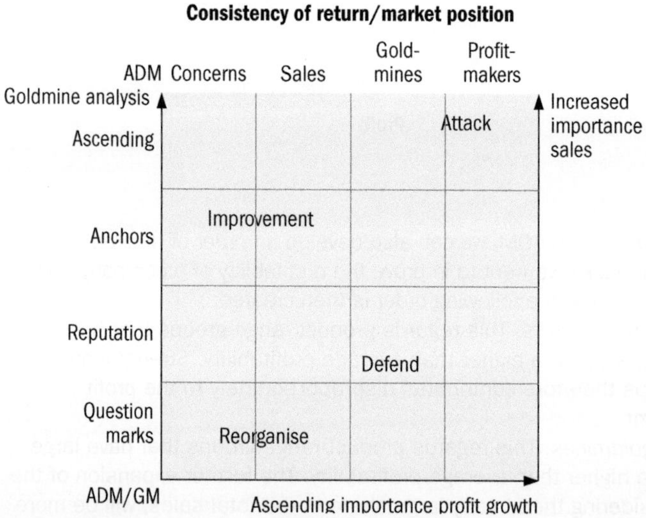

Consistency of return/market position

	ADM	Concerns	Sales	Gold-mines	Profit-makers	
Goldmine analysis						Increased importance sales
Ascending					Attack	
Anchors		Improvement				
Reputation					Defend	
Question marks		Reorganise				
ADM/GM		Ascending importance profit growth				

12.9 Fair-share analysis

In those cases where the market size is fairly stable when measured over time and where there are no large dynamics in the market development, the contribution that an analysis of the market growth/decline provides to the insight (as in the ADM), is rather limited. Because the setup of an ADM is rather difficult and requires the analysis of many market segments, we often have to resort to the approximate, but much simpler methodology of fair shares in these cases.

Fair-share analysis
In the *fair-share analysis,* we always compare the own performance with a predetermined standard. The result is expressed as an index relative to the standard. If the index is higher than 100%, we are performing above the standard. If the index is below 100%, we are performing below the standard.

The standard itself can take various forms. If, for example, we would regard the distribution of the sales in the market as starting point and compare these sales to the sales share that is generated by the product range groups in the own company sales, we get a fair-share analysis that is very close to the results that we also get from an ADM-analysis. The fair share then shows the ratio between the market share of the product range group and the average market share of the company as a whole. In fact, we get a kind of relative market share indicator (SWOT aspects of the ADM), but we lack the market size indicator, the opportunity-threat aspect of the ADM. Figure 12.7 illustrates the fair-share approach based on the example of the men's fashion store used earlier.

FIGURE 12.7 Fair-share analysis of a men's fashion store

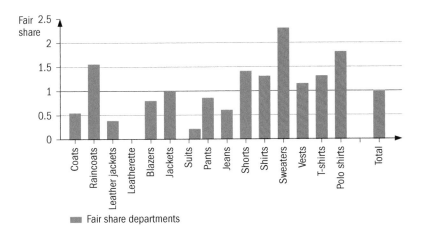

Explanation
In polo shirts, the company has a fair share of 1.75, which means that polo shirts achieve a market share that is 1.75 times as big as the average market share of the company as a whole. In coats, however, the company only has a fair share (or a relative market share) of 50%.
If the average profitability of coats, expressed in margin, is 50%, and that of polo shirts is 35%, then an improvement of the product range concept of coats will not only lead to a sales improvement, but also to a disproportionate profit improvement.

In practice, the fair-share analysis is often used in the food sector. Not so much to clarify the strategic position of the product range portfolio, but also as a method to determine whether – and by which departments – branches deviate from the averages in their sales mix. In this case, we use the sales distribution of the entire company (and therefore not the distribution of sales in the market, as in the example of the men's fashion store in paragraph 12.3, figure 12.2) as standard and we compare this against the sales distribution of the establishment. You then have an indication on which parts of the product range, the relevant establishment deviates from the average of the company. Based on this data, we can take corrective action if necessary. If we can also add the results of the (local) goldmine analysis to the fair-share analysis, we get an instrument at establishment level that is very close to the previously discussed integration mix of goldmine and ADM and which is very useful in doing local marketing.

In example 12.3, we compare two V&D branches, namely in Zoetermeer and in Amsterdam.

EXAMPLE 12.3 V&D

V&D has a large number of department stores in the Netherlands, ranging from the very large downtown branches in major cities, to relatively small branches in provincial towns. For the establishment of the branches, V&D uses a standard floor plan that is indeed distinguished according to the size of the branch, but in which the formula principles with regard to the product range of the V&D-concept, are represented. All product range groups of V&D are therefore, to a greater or lesser extent, present in every branch. It is obvious that the consumers' responses to this product range are quite different. In Zoetermeer (limited size of the branch, relatively weak competition), they respond differently than in the Kalverstraat in Amsterdam (relatively large branch, very strong competition). This is also evident from the fair-share analysis. V&D Zoetermeer scored better than the national average in the groups sound carriers, woman's wear, lingerie and baby/children clothing, and worse in home ware, toys, camping and sport. V&D in the Kalverstraat, on the other hand, scored very poorly for camping, sport and toys, while electronics and fashion accessories, on the other hand, scored extremely well (see table 1).

By combining the results of the fair-share analysis (the *market performance*) with the profitability per department and per branch, we can now develop an instrument that enables the local branch manager to do *local marketing* (see figures 1 and 2).

TABLE 1 Fair-share analysis for Zoetermeer and Kalverstraat (standard: total sales distribution V&D in the market)

Department	Sales share V&D				
	National (in %)	Zoetermeer (in %)	Kalverstraat (in %)	FS Zoetermeer	FS Kalverstraat
Woman's wear	14	16	14	1.17	1.01
Men's wear	10	11	9	1.05	0.90
Baby/children clothing	8	11	5	1.29	0.54
Lingerie	7	9	6	1.26	0.90
Fashion accessories	12	11	20	0.96	1.68
Cosmetics	5	4	5	0.88	0.94
Sport	5	4	4	0.71	0.86
Camping	1	1	0	0.79	0.29
Toys	2	1	0	0.50	0.09
Home ware	2	1	2	0.50	0.63

Department	Sales share V&D				
	National (in %)	Zoetermeer (in %)	Kalverstraat (in %)	FS Zoetermeer	FS Kalverstraat
Household	9	8	7	0.94	0.82
Office supplies/ stationary	7	8	8	1.17	1.04
Books/magazines	4	3	4	0.80	1.03
Sound carriers	7	9	7	1.27	1.00
Electronics	6	3	10	0.44	1.56
Total	100	100	100	1.00	1.00

FIGURE 1 Fair-share/goldmine matrix Zoetermeer

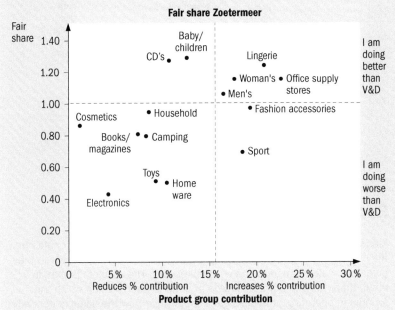

All departments in which the branch scores better than V&D nationally (fair-share branch > 1), are above the line, indicating where the fair share is 100. The departments in which the branch scores worse (fair-share branch < 1), are below the line. The departments in which sales increase leads to a reduction of the average branch contribution in percentages of the sales are to the left of the thick vertical line (representing the average return of the branch). The departments of which the sales increase leads to an increase of the percentage of branch contribution are to the right of this line.

It is clear that V&D in Zoetermeer should pay attention to its local marketing of the fashion accessories and sport departments, while V&D in the Kalverstraat should try to better utilise the local market opportunities of the men's wear, lingerie, sport and home ware departments.

FIGURE 2 Fair-share/goldmine matrix Kalverstraat

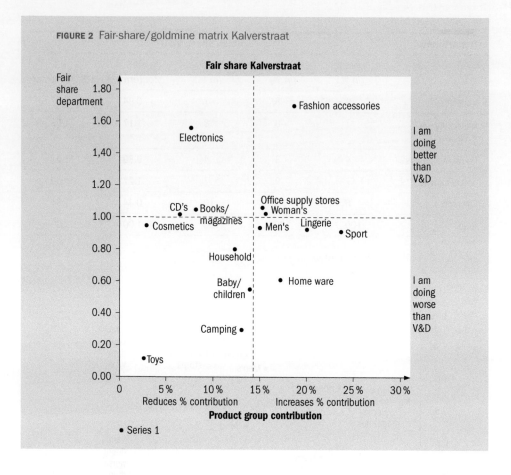

Summary

Managers working in the purchasing department, often consider sales from the market share that they obtained in the market segment for which they purchase: sales = market share × market size. The problem is that, in retail, there is generally a multitude of market segments on which the formula is operating. It is possible to determine how the sales is generated per market segment, but it is more difficult for the overall sales of the formula (MS × MS). We then have to deal with a portfolio of market segments. The method to perform such portfolio analysis on the product range of a retail formula, is the ADM (assortment dominance matrix), an instrument derived from the portfolio matrix of the Boston Consulting Group (BCG). In the ADM, the market size (as a measure of the appeal of the market segment from the perspective of sales) and the achieved market share (as a measure for the strength of the sub product range from the formula) are compared to one another. In cases where data on the market size is missing, we can use simpler models that can often be completed with internal business information, but that provide us with less information. Examples are the so-called goldmine analysis and the fair-share method.

Regardless of the form of retail that is used, online, offline or a mix of both, these analyses are of great importance.

13
Profitability

It goes without saying that, in a book which basically deals with retail marketing methods, it is important to pay attention to the efficiency side of the operation: marketing in the retail sector comprises of more than just building a market position. The idea is to build this market position in a stable, profitable and defensible manner. We shall now consider, in particular using techniques developed within the retail sector, how the strategic profitability of retail organisations can be influenced and controlled from the operation.

13.1 Limited returns

Figure 13.1 shows the position of the strengths/weaknesses in the strategic process.

FIGURE 13.1 The strategic process: the efficiency

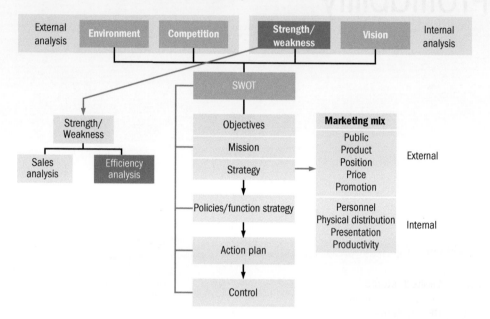

The fact that the returns in the Dutch retail sector are generally rather low, at least in terms of return on sales (ROS), has often been pointed out. This does not only apply for retail (wherein there is an average return of approximately 1 to 1,5% ROS), but also for the leisure sector, like travel agencies, cinemas and restaurants. Increasingly, it also applies to several retail branches where the returns were historically quite significant, but where, due to changing market circumstances, there is increasingly more friction between the sales and the returns. In the insurance sector, for example, it is becoming increasingly more common that suppliers with an outdated (and therefore more expensive) operational structure will have to withdraw from certain product markets because their products can no longer be sold profitably. A very clear example is that of the vehicle insurance. The large traditional suppliers, like Nationale Nederlanden and Aegon, lose market share to relative newcomers like Centraal Beheer. These newcomers have developed a more efficient operation, allowing them to offer cheaper rates than the older suppliers. And, because of the lower offer price, they are able to push these older suppliers out of the market. The same thing is happening in the banking sector. The larger traditional suppliers (ABN AMRO, Fortis, Rabobank, ING-bank) are no longer able to offer simple and therefore price sensitive products, such as current accounts and simple savings products, on a profitable and competitive basis.

They are pushed out of the market by relative newcomers through the system of direct sales or direct writing and Spaarbeleg (product specialisation). Within the largest Dutch bank insurer, the ING-group, which includes both ING Direct and ING bank, this even led to the 'transfer' of low profit clients. In the future, this phenomenon of tightening margins due to stronger competition will manifest increasingly more in all retail sectors, including the government privatised sectors such as public transport, telecommunications and social services. The Wheel of Retailing and the effect of the scissors will also manifest in these sectors.

13.2 Profit optimisation in retail

Within the retail sector, two approaches are currently being used for the optimisation of the cost effectiveness. Firstly, systems that directly target the influence of R in the formula $R = S \times M - C$. These can also be called *top-down systems*. These methods include the techniques of DPP/DAP (*direct product profitability* and *direct assortment profitability*).

Secondly we have systems that focus more on the mutual coherence and influence of S, M and C. An example of the latter method, which is also known as *bottom-up* approaches, is the *trinity model* (also known as: the *strategic retail resource model*) (Lusch, 1986).

Both systems are based on the principle of optimising the use of scarce production resources. The *DPP/DAP*-systems are more rigorous than the trinity model, in the sense that the philosophy behind *DPP/DAP* is that the optimisation should occur to only one production factor, namely the retail floor space (or the shelf space). The reasoning behind this statement is that space is the most inflexible production factor, at least in the Netherlands. In times of prosperity you can never have enough; in times of misfortune, street-front retail space is very much like dead weight. *DPP/DAP* therefore tries to optimise the contribution margin (R) per space unit, whereby the other influencing production factors are considered as more or less a given and cannot be changed. To some extent, the *DPP/DAP* system works as a black box: it provides insight into how R develops, but not why.

The trinity model works reversed (see paragraph 13.4). This model provides no direct connection with profitability. Without additional cost information, this model cannot be used to check whether a company or a product range is profitable. However, the trinity model does show where the causes of any adverse development can be found, because the various production factors themselves – through interim variances – are interconnected.

The trinity model could therefore work as a 'tin opener' for the black box of the *DPP/DAP*.

Table 13.1 reflects the typical cost structure of a retail company. This structure is fairly universal. Almost all retail companies use this setup, with only minor deviations. However, this does not mean that the structure of the costs is also universal.

Margin note:
Direct product profitability
Direct assortment profitability
Trinity model
Strategic retail resource model

Margin: 13

There may be significant differences in the cost mix, both between sectors and between formulas within the same sector, and between various times within a formula. Table 13.2 and 13.3 illustrates a few things.

TABLE 13.1 Typical cost structure of the retail

Sales including VAT
Less: VAT
Net sales
Less: Purchase value
Gross goods profit
Less: discounts
More or less: cash discrepancies
More or less: stock discrepancies
More: bonuses
Net goods profit
Less:
• labour costs
• publicity
• transport costs
• accommodation
• depreciations
Contribution 1 (branch contribution)
Less:
Interest costs
Contribution 2 (branch contribution after interest)
Less:
overheads head office
Contribution 3 (operational result)

The examples in the tables clearly show that the structure of the operation in retail is often more flexible than, for example, in the industry. Once a decision has been made in the industry on the structure of the production process, we are bound to this decision for a long time. In retail, it is much simpler to adjust the processes. Also because some cost categories are mutually interchangeable, without affecting the sales results. Labour costs can be substituted, to some extent, by costs in the area of presentation modes.

Internal and external promotion costs are interchangeable to some extent, while for example inventory costs can be reduced by using more labour (supplementing more often). While such flexibility is enjoyable from the perspective of business operations, it simultaneously – in the competitive situation in which the Dutch retail finds itself – leads to an unpleasant side effect: we must always be alert to opportunities to sharpen the processes. If we do not use the most effective processes, there will always be a competitor who will be doing this and who will, thereby (because of their lower cost structure), be able to push us out of the market.

TABLE 13.2 Comparison of cost mix of two different sectors

In percentages of net sales	Department store (in %)	Computer company (in %)
Sales including VAT	115.4	119.0
Less: VAT	15.4*	19.0
Net sales	100.0	100.0
Less: purchase value	55.0	81.0
Gross goods profit	45.0	19.0
More or less: cash discrepancies	0.1	0.0
More or less: stock discrepancies	1.2	0.3
More: bonuses	0.0	0.0
Net goods profit	43.7	18.7
Less:		
• labour costs	14.5	5.2
• publicity	3.2	2.8
• transport costs/physical distribution	3.1	0.6
• accommodation	8.2	0.6
• general costs	2.5	0.4
• depreciations	4.0	1.5
Total: direct branch costs	35.5	11.0
Contribution 1 (branch contribution)	8.2	7.7
Interest costs	1.4	0.9
Contribution 2 (branch contribution after interest)	6.8	6.7
Overheads head office	5.9	4.7
Contribution 3 (operational result)	0.9	2.0

* Through the combination of food and non-food products and the accompanying different VAT rates of respectively 6% and 19%, the department store has, in this case because of the specific margin mix, an average rate of 15.4%.

TABLE 13.3 Comparison of cost mix on two different times within one formula

	Computer company period 1 (in %)	Computer company period 2 (in %)
Sales including VAT	119.0	119.0
Less: VAT	19.0	19.0
Net sales	100.0	100.0
Less: purchase value	79.0	81.0
Gross goods profit	21.0	19.0
More or less: cash discrepancies	0.0	0.0
More or less: stock discrepancies	2.6	0.3
More: bonuses	0.0	0.0
Net goods profit	23.6	18.7
Less:		
• labour costs	5.9	5.2
• publicity	2.1	2.8
• transport costs/physical distribution	0.5	0.6
• accommodation	0.7	0.6
• general costs	0.5	0.4
• depreciations	2.4	1.5
Total: direct branch costs	12.0	11.0
Contribution 1 (branch contribution)	11.6	7.7
Interest costs	1.4	0.9
Contribution 2 (branch contribution after interest)	10.1	6.7
Overheads head office	5.9	4.7
Contribution 3 (operational result)	4.2	2.0

Therefore, if we want to maintain a once developed, successful formula on the long term, then we must not only be extremely alert to changes in demand, but also to changes in the process-based environment.

13.3 DPP systems

DPP systems
Direct product costs

Under *DPP systems* we understand, in the most general terms, methods where we subtract the (variable) direct costs (DPC = *direct product costs*) that are associated with carrying a product, from the achieved gross margin (see figure 13.2), or:

$$DPP = Margin - DPC$$

Thus we obtain a kind of contribution margin of the product or article that gives a better impression of the contribution of the product to the overall profitability, than just the gross margin.
In fact, by using DPP, we try to achieve a kind of reverse cost price calculation. In the industry, it is common to calculate the sales price of a product through cost price calculation, including the calculated profit margin.

FIGURE 13.2 DPP calculation model

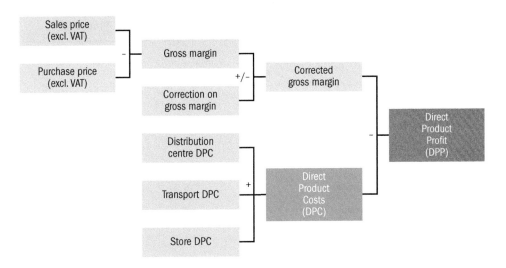

Source: Prodis Brochure 'Wat is DPP?'

Such methods are virtually inapplicable in retail. Even a highly specialised supplier in retail still has a product range that is many times larger than that of the average industrial supplier. It is extremely laborious and not really feasible to obtain a separate cost price calculation for each of the products in the product range. This is why we often use the *surcharge calculation* in retail: to the purchase price, we apply a fixed factor which should basically be enough to cover all costs plus profit. We call this factor the *surcharge factor* (or the *calculation factor*). With DPP we try to determine, assuming an average goods margin, what is left of this margin after deducting the direct attributable costs. This immediately brings forward one of the difficulties in applying DPP: DPP is extremely laborious and time consuming, in fact almost just as laborious as cost price calculation. We will now discuss the application of DPP in the food and non-food sector.

Surcharge calculation

Surcharge factor

13.3.1 DPP applications in the food sector

Table 13.4 is a schematic example of the application of DPP. The example shows two substitutable products, for example, shampoos with the same product characteristics of two different manufacturers.
The setup clearly indicates that, in the 'old' method where one would only be guided on the corrected gross margin, the selection would probably fall on product B.
After all, this product delivers a better gross margin (1.72 rather than 1.56). However, because the manufacturer of product A was better at taking into

account the processes in his supply method within retail (for example by convenient outer packaging, thus associated with less labour and space when filling the shelves) and because the sales rate of his/her product is better (leading to less stock costs in the store), the DPC of product A works out at 50 cents compared to 86 cents for product B. On balance, the DPP of A is therefore higher than that of B. Therefore, based on the DPP-method, product A is selected.

TABLE 13.4 Example of DPP

	Product A		Product B	
	Less:	%	Less:	%
Sales	6.80	100.0	7.00	100.0
– purchasing costs	4.27	62.8	4.19	59.8
– VAT	1.13	16.7	1.17	16.7
Gross margin	1.40	20.5	1.64	23.5
+ payment discount	0.03	0.5	–	0.0
+ other discounts	0.13	1.9	0.08	1.2
Corrected gross margin	1.56	22.9	1.72	24.7
Distribution centre costs				
– labour	0.07	1.0	0.11	1.6
– space	0.05	0.7	0.08	1.2
External transport costs				
– labour/materials	0.05	0.7	0.11	1.5
Store equipment costs				
– labour	0.22	3.2	0.34	4.8
– space	0.09	1.4	0.19	2.7
Inventory costs				
– distribution centre	0.01	0.2	0.01	0.1
	Less:	%	Less:	%

TABLE 13.4 Example of DPP (continued)

	Product A		Product B	
– store	0.01	0.2	0.02	0.3
Direct Product Costs (DPC)	0.50	7.4	0.86	12.1
Direct Product Profit (DPP)	1.06	15.5	0.86	12.6

DPP has become possible thanks to the rapid development of information technology. This allows the retailer to perform a large number of calculations in a short time. But if one can also leave the calculations to a computer, the maintenance of the system remains very laborious. Even in a sector where there is a relatively stable product range, such as supermarkets, one should still take into account the fact that roughly 25 to 33% of the product range is replaced every year. All such changes need to be introduced and processed. For a company like Albert Heijn, with an average number of approximately 12,000 SKU's, this means 3,000 to 4,000 changes per year. It is therefore very rare that DPP systems are continuously used as a management tool. The use, however, focuses more on the incidental measurement of the utilisation of shelf space, in order to maximise the revenue through the development of a standard space plan or shelf layout. Thereby, we use a further refinement of the DPP methodology, where we calculate the DPP per space unit. Products with a lower than average DPP per space unit will then qualify for a reduction of allocated shelf space or for a less prominent space, for example, the bottom shelf. Products with a higher than average DPP per space unit will qualify for an expansion or a better space in the shelf, for example, at eye level.

13.3.2   DPP applications in the non-food sector

The 'real' DPP systems are hardly applicable in the non-food sector. The reason for this is twofold. Firstly, in the non-food- sector it is very uncommon that individual products have a fixed space due to seasonal patterns. The direct space costs could therefore depend on the time differences, which complicate the ability to maintain the system. Secondly, the product ranges change several times per year in the non-food sector. In the fashion sector, there is even a continuous change of the product range. In addition, the product ranges in the non-food sector are often much larger than in the food sector: a company such as de Bijenkorf has a product range that consists of an average of 300,000 SKU's. This means that application of the system on product level in the non-food sector is extremely laborious and needs to be updated very frequently. As a result, the application of this system is often too expensive. A solution was found in the development of the DAP (*direct assortment profitability*), where costs and revenues are not allocated to the space unit per product, but to the space units for entire (sub)product ranges.

DAP

Moreover, this also leads to complications: much stronger than on product level, the phenomenon that consumers appear to respond in their purchasing behaviour to the amount of space that is made available to (sub) product ranges, plays a role on product range level. At least in the non-food sector: the more space, the higher the spending per customer. The following numbers are used as a general rule: 10% more space results in 3% to 5% more sales, in other words a 'space elasticity' of 0.3 to 0.5. The problem, however, is that this general rule relates to an average.

Analyses within warehouse organisations teach that the customers' responses to space changes can vary greatly per sub product range and that the space elasticity can vary from almost 0 to (in exceptional cases) more than 1. Several things are illustrated in figures 13.3 and 13.4.

FIGURE 13.3 Space elasticity of household products

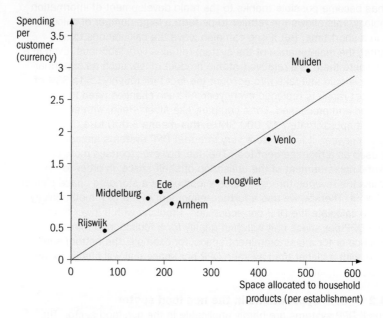

The examples reflected in figures 13.3 and 13.4 relate to several sub product ranges within a self-service department store. The horizontal axis shows the space made available per establishment, per sub product range. The vertical axis shows the average ticket on this sub product range per visitor. It is clear that, in both cases, an increase in space will lead to more spending per visitor. It is also clear that the extent to which this occurs varies per sub product range. The angle of inclination of the regression line is significantly different. The finding that customers respond differently with different product groups to the available space, means that, unlike DPP systems, one should take this space elasticity into account when using DAP systems to optimise profit per space unit. An example of such optimisation is given in table 13.5.

FIGURE 13.4 Space elasticity of curtains and blinds

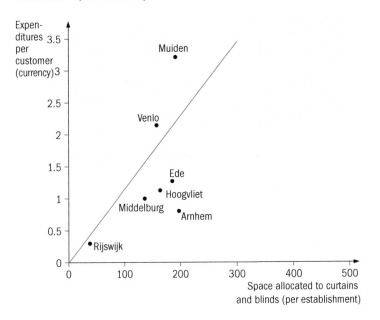

TABLE 13.5 Optimisation using DAP

	Department 1	Department 2	
1 Total sales	182,280	424,560	Sales control
2 Number of space units	12.4	24.4	
3 Sales/space unit	14,700	17,400	
4 Goods profit/space (in %)	38	29	
5 Goods profit/absolute	5,586	5,200	Margin control
6 Direct costs/space unit	2,750	2,300	
7 Contribution/space unit	2,830	2,900	DPP-control
8 Elasticity	0.86	0.43	
9 Extra profit with expansion of a space unit	2,439	1,247	DAP-control

The example relates to the allocation of a limited amount of 'free' space, situated between two departments. This situation occurs very regularly within department stores, for instance, as a result of seasonal variations and product range changes. To which of the two surrounding departments can we best allocate the free space? The example illustrates that, in the 'old' methods, where control was based on sales opportunities in total (the first line in table 13.5), the space would probably be allocated to department 2. If we would not use sales maximisation as starting point, but rather margin maximisation, the space would probably be allocated to department 1 (line 5 in the table). In the newer techniques, in which DPP philosophies are used (line 7 in the table, after deduction of direct costs), it does not really matter much which department is given the space. The DPP values for both departments are at almost the same level (line 7 in the table). But if there is a switch over to the DAP method (line 9 in the table), in which the space elasticity is also taken into account, it is clear that the space would then be allocated to department 1.

13.4 The strategic retail resource model (trinity model)

Dupont model of financial performance

The trinity model is a system that is inspired by the *Dupont model of financial performance*. The Dupont model not only looks at the final *bottom-line* profitability of a company, but also tries – by providing connections between the various financial ratios – to determine which *key success factors* influence the profitability. Robert E. Lusch (Lusch, 1986) applied this philosophy to the operational aspects of retail and developed a model that he named the strategic retail resource model or the trinity model. We discuss the structure, the application and the use of this trinity model.

13.4.1 Structure of the trinity model
Figure 13.5 reflects the structure of the trinity model.

FIGURE 13.5 The trinity-model

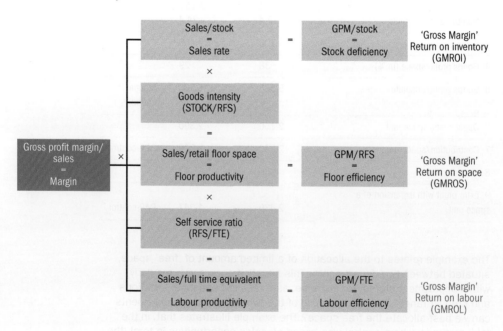

The trinity model is based on the idea that in retail management, one only needs to use three production factors or assets (hence the name *trinity*), namely:
- Variable assets: in retail, this consists mainly out of stocks.
- Fixed assets: the store – to be approached in retail through the retail floor space (RFS).
- Human assets: the personnel – expressed in the model in fulltime-equivalent (fte).

For most retailers, this will be very recognisable. The daily operation in the retail is indeed controlled through sales rate (the productivity of the variable assets: sales/average stock), the floor productivity (the productivity of the fixed assets: sales per space-unit), and the labour productivity (the productivity of the human assets: sales per *fulltime-equivalent (fte)*). However, Robert Lusch argues that, for the long term optimisation, it is not about productivity, but about the efficiency of the assets. He defines efficiency as: productivity × profitability.

Fulltime equivalent

13

The implications of this statement are far reaching. It means that, in the vision of Lusch, it is not about finding the *lowest costs solution*, but rather about finding the *highest efficiency solution*, in other words, finding an optimal balance between the market position on the one hand and productivity on the other hand. Sudden cost increases are allowed in this philosophy, provided that they lead to corresponding improvement in the revenue. Investing in the increase of service (or adding labour) can be useful if it leads to an increase in the floor productivity (improvement of the market position), even if this service increase leads to a relative reduction of labour productivity.

Lowest costs solution
Highest efficiency solution

It is for these reasons that, similar to the financial Dupont model, the trinity model uses interim variables, namely the goods intensity and the self-service ratio. The self-service ratio in the model forms the link between floor productivity (sales per space unit) and labour productivity (sales per fte). The self-service ratio is defined as 'the number of space units that must be maintained per fte': the higher the number, the less service will be offered. The model is thus algebraically correct, because:

$$(\text{sales} / \text{metre}^2) \times (\text{metre}^2 / \text{FTE}) = \text{sales} / \text{fte}$$

or:

$$\text{floor productivity} \times \text{self-service ratio} = \text{labour productivity}$$

The goods intensity forms the link in the model between sales rate (defined as sales divided by the average stock) and floor productivity (defined as sales per space unit). The goods intensity is defined as the stock per space unit. This means that this model is also algebraically conclusive, because:

$$(\text{sales}/\text{stock}) \times (\text{stock} / \text{metre}^2) = \text{sales} / \text{metre}^2$$

or:

$$\text{sales rate} \times \text{goods intensity} = \text{floor productivity}$$

With a high self-service ratio, still try to improve the service level: supermarket chain K-Mart in the US

Goods Intensity

The interesting thing is the fact that an algebraically constructed variable, which is not actually used in practice in retail, is suddenly getting an explanatory value. *Goods intensity*, in retail terms, is a measure for the dominance of the presentation of the product range. The higher the goods intensity, the more compelling the product range appears to the consumer. Analysis carried out on several sub product ranges within the department store sector, indicated that the relationship between goods intensity and sales per metre was very different per sub product range. For some product ranges, such as women's wear and decorative lighting, the sensitivity of the sales per metre for increasing the supply pressure per metre appears to be virtually zero. This corresponds with the practical conclusion that, when purchasing fashionable, trendy products, the consumer has a need for space and clarity rather than many goods. For other partial ranges, the relationship appears to be greatly positive, for example, for stationary and for painting accessories. This leads to the conclusion that the consumer, when purchasing functional products such as stationary and painting accessories, rather has a need for lots of choices and a wide product range, than for space.

Although this outcome sounds quite logical, there is a lesson to be learnt. If, in a situation where we have to consider the costs, but where we also have to work on improving the market position (such as in a situation of displacement marketing), we were to consider achieving our objectives by increasing the stock, we must – in order to obtain the highest revenue from the efforts – differentiate between departments. Increase of supply pressure will generate far more profits in one department than in the other.

13.4.2   Applications of the trinity model

You can use the trinity model in two ways. First, you can use the model for sequential analysis within a formula. You then measure, in fact, the manner in which the operation of the relevant formula develops in the course of time. Second, you can use the model for simultaneous analysis of two different suppliers. Comparison of the variables then teaches us how the performance of the one supplier compares to the other: you then use the model as a kind of benchmarking tool in the competitor analysis.

13.4.3   Use for sequential comparison

In figure 13.6 we have worked out the trinity model for a company that sells radio and TV products. It is a relatively small company with six branches that always made a decent profit, but ended in a loss in the 6th year. The trinity model was used in the SWOT to determine what caused this unexpected loss situation and what corrective measures should be taken to make the company profitable once again.

From this figure, we can draw the following conclusions:

1 A part of the development can be traced back to the margin. In the previous years, it moved at a level of 23 to 22%, but fell back in the last year to 21%. It is therefore necessary, for the recovery of profits, to pay more attention to the margin control.
2 The problem is not caused by incorrect use of the variable assets. The stock sales rate even shows an upward trend, while the goods intensity is developing positively. Therefore, in order to resolve these problems, we need not to look primarily at the logistics.
3 The problem is apparently not caused by the use of the fixed assets. The sales per metre, or the floor productivity, shows significant increases and also moves at a level that is very attractive. Considered from the market position, we are dealing with an extremely healthy operation. However, it is clear that the growth rate of the sales per metre has decreased slightly in the last year. The combination of lower growing floor productivity and decreasing margins then leads to a signal in the model: for the first time in years, the floor efficiency exhibits a decline. This is a clear illustration of Robert Lusch's intention. Although the floor productivity increases (the daily or tactical benchmark), the floor efficiency exhibits (the strategic benchmark) a decline.
4 If the problem is not caused by the use of variable assets and not by the use of fixed assets, the cause must therefore be sought in the human assets. This is clear. The labour productivity shows a strong downward trend and this decrease had actually already started in the previous year. The simultaneously decreasing margin translates into a fairly dramatic decline in the labour efficiency.

13

FIGURE 13.6 Trinity chart Electro inc.

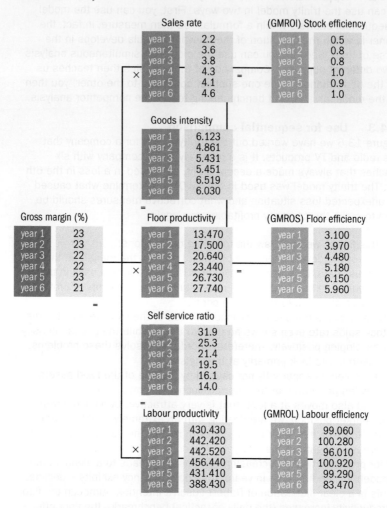

Interesting for the detailed analysis is the relationship between the self-service ratio and the labour productivity. In the good years, the company invested considerably in the service level: the self service ratio decreased significantly from year 1 to year 4. This investment was obviously extremely profitable and led to a very strong increase in the floor productivity, with simultaneous increase of labour productivity, and that is a wonderful combination. Thus, there appears to be no reason not to invest further in the service increase. And this was also done. In both year 5 and year 6, the self-service ratio declined significantly. In both these years, however, it appeared that, unlike the previous years, the increase of service was accompanied by a reduction of labour productivity. The conclusion is clear: they had exceeded the optimum of the service level. The further addition of service in these last two years was not to the benefit of the customer, but rather to the employees. The result of the addition was that, on average, the employees did not have to work as hard. That may be pleasant for the employees, but it could not have been the intention of the retailer.

13.4.4   Using the trinity model as a *benchmarking* tool

This chart contains an analysis of the operation of a number of Belgian supermarket organisations (see figure 13.7). By comparing the core numbers, we get an idea of the strengths and weaknesses of the competition. We will analyze two suppliers as example: Aldi and Delhaize.

FIGURE 13.7 Benchmark Belgian supermarkets

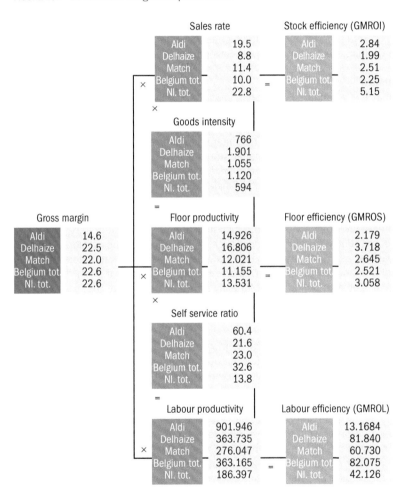

Sales rate		Stock efficiency (GMROI)	
Aldi	19.5	Aldi	2.84
Delhaize	8.8	Delhaize	1.99
Match	11.4	Match	2.51
Belgium tot.	10.0	Belgium tot.	2.25
Nl. tot.	22.8	Nl. tot.	5.15

Goods intensity	
Aldi	766
Delhaize	1.901
Match	1.055
Belgium tot.	1.120
Nl. tot.	594

Gross margin		Floor productivity		Floor efficiency (GMROS)	
Aldi	14.6	Aldi	14.926	Aldi	2.179
Delhaize	22.5	Delhaize	16.806	Delhaize	3.718
Match	22.0	Match	12.021	Match	2.645
Belgium tot.	22.6	Belgium tot.	11.155	Belgium tot.	2.521
Nl. tot.	22.6	Nl. tot.	13.531	Nl. tot.	3.058

Self service ratio	
Aldi	60.4
Delhaize	21.6
Match	23.0
Belgium tot.	32.6
Nl. tot.	13.8

Labour productivity		Labour efficiency (GMROL)	
Aldi	901.946	Aldi	13.1684
Delhaize	363.735	Delhaize	81.840
Match	276.047	Match	60.730
Belgium tot.	363.165	Belgium tot.	82.075
Nl. tot.	186.397	Nl. tot.	42.126

Aldi
Aldi is a discounter with a very limited product range. This is clearly reflected in the core numbers: a very low margin indicates a lower price level, the very high sales rate indicates the limited product range and the high self-service ratio and the very high labour productivity indicates a very low service level, as is expected from a discounter.

The fairly low floor productivity is also striking. We would expect a discounter like Aldi to actually strive for very high sales per metre. Obviously this is not the case and Aldi follows a different strategy, at least in Belgium. The company seems to have opted for relatively low-cost locations, making it possible to still – perhaps as counterbalance to the strongly represented large hyper stores in Belgium (Carrefour) – handle fairly large stores. This seems to be confirmed by the very low goods intensity. Large stores with a limited product range always lead to a low goods intensity.

Gross margin return on space

Gross margin return on inventory

Gross margin return on labour

The combination of the very low margin and the relatively low floor productivity also leads to a lower than average floor efficiency, or *gross margin return on space* (GRMOS). Viewing the efficiency ratios shows that Aldi in Belgium mainly builds profitability from the variable assets (stock) and the human assets. The GMROI (*gross margin return on inventory*) and the GMROL (*gross margin return on labour*) are the highest of all recorded companies, while the GMROS are below average in Belgium.

Delhaize

Delhaize is a nationally operating chain of neighbourhood supermarkets. Unlike Aldi, which covers bulk purchases, Delhaize strives to cover the total daily shopping package. Delhaize's USP is not the price, but the proximity, convenience and selection. This means that Delhaize will have a very wide product range in relatively smaller stores close to the consumer, with an average or slightly above average price level. The core numbers confirm this image: a margin that lies on the Belgian average; low sales rate, lower than the Belgian average; very high goods intensity, which indicates a wide product range in smaller stores; high floor productivity, far above the Belgian average; low self-service ratio, which indicates a high level of service and labour productivity that is almost average. If we look at the efficiency variables, we find that the operational use of the production factors at the neighbourhood supermarket Delhaize is entirely different than the discounter Aldi: Delhaize builds its profitability from a strong use of the fixed assets (the highest GMROS of all formulas), performs on the factor labour average and has a lower than average use of the variable capital.

Finally, from figure 13.7, we can compare the Belgian total figures with the Dutch total figures. We see that the operational structure of supermarkets in the Netherlands are entirely different to that in Belgium. The Dutch supermarkets often work with much smaller product ranges and, partly because of this, with lower stocks than those in Belgium. This is expressed in the high Dutch sales rate and the low Dutch goods intensity. The high sales rate of the Dutch supermarket (average 22,8) means that the financing of the Dutch supermarket is largely done from supplier credit. With a consumer sales rate of 22 and a payment frequency to the suppliers of 12, the retailer already has the revenue of customer, two weeks before he has to pay the supplier. A Belgian supermarket, on the other hand, must finance at least part of its stock self or through bank financing.

The utilisation of the fixed assets in the Netherlands is more favourable than in Belgium. This is because the Dutch supermarkets, on average, are much smaller than those in Belgium. The downside of this favourable performance in terms of floor productivity and stock is found at the 'labour' factor. Achieving a very high sales rate on relatively small floor surfaces takes a lot of manpower. After all, stocks must be replenished very

frequently and store care is very labour intensive. We also see that labour productivity in the Netherlands is significantly lower than in Belgium.
The differences in operational structure can be translated into the efficiency variables: The Dutch supermarkets build profitability mainly from a very strong logical operation and proper utilisation of fixed assets. The use of the 'labour' factor, on the other hand, is on the thin side when compared to Belgium. The Belgian supermarket builds profitability mainly from the 'labour' factor and to a lesser extent, from fixed assets, and performs very weak on variable assets. It is clear that knowledge of these differences in structure is important for Dutch supermarkets to expand to Belgium.

Summary

The high degree of competition and the thereby occurring phenomenon of displacement marketing means that sales and margins in the retail sector are subject to a constant downwards pressure. In such a situation, we cannot and may not consider marketing only from the perspective of generating more sales, but we also have to concentrate of the cost-revenue structure. Sales on which we earn nothing, eventually leads to loss of the competitive position. Within retail we use two groups of models to optimise the cost effective-ness: top-down models that focus directly on the explanation and analysis of R in the formula $R = S \times M - C$, and bottom-up models that focus more on the explanation of the correlations between S, M and C. Within the first group we can classify DPP-models or DAP-models. A representative of the second group of models is the so-called trinity model. The operation of the models is explained based on several examples.

13

PART 5

Translation from analysis to strategy

In part 3 we looked at the external analysis: the threats and opportunities, factors from the outside on which we have absolutely no control. We focused on economic and demographic environmental factors, on trend developments in the consumer behaviour and on competitor's analyses.

In part 4, we described some methods and techniques through which we can determine the internal strengths and weaknesses (factors that we can influence). We did this based on the formula $R = S \times M - C$, where the constituent parts of the formula where are all dealt with separately. The next important issue is to convert the outcome of the analysis phase into a policy.

In this part, we will therefore pay attention to the manner in which the outcomes of the external and internal analysis are integrated into a SWOT and how we can achieve a translation into future policy from this SWOT, through the definition of the desired marketing mix.

14
From SWOT to marketing mix

In this chapter, we explain the route from SWOT to marketing mix and discuss the combination analysis, SWOT-matrix working procedure, the marketing mix of retail and the approach through the Store Compass. We deal with the matter based on the location SWOT in the strategic process, the various phases in the application of the SWOT matrix, the marketing mix variables within retail, the Store Compass and the crucial points therein.

14.1 Dynamic SWOT analysis

Figure 14.1 shows the position of the SWOT in the strategic process.

FIGURE 14.1 The SWOT in the strategic process

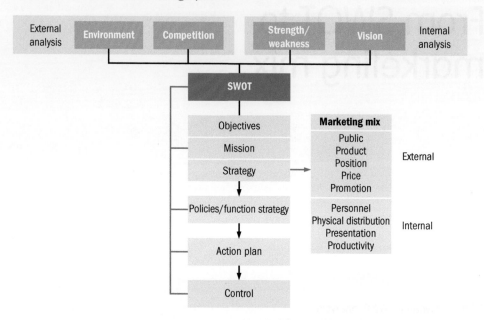

SWOT-analysis Strategic audit	The *SWOT-analysis* (Verhage, 2010), also known as *strategic audit* or situation analysis, focuses on integrating the results of the external and internal analysis in such a way that there is a clear picture of the situation in which the company finds itself. We often suffice with a direct summary of all strengths, weaknesses, opportunities and threats when preparing a SWOT, not really making it clear how the ties are set. It is much better, but also much more difficult, to prepare a SWOT analysis, as such that the components are combined. In such a setup, the result of the SWOT is a matrix that consists of four fields (see figure 14.2).

The advantage of such a combination analysis, the *dynamic SWOT analysis*, is that we can quickly understand the situation of a company.

- If most of the combinations fall in the quadrants 'strengths/opportunities', we have an ideal situation. The world is open and the company is ideally positioned to face the future. An attack strategy is obvious.
- If most of the combinations fall in the quadrant 'weaknesses/opportunities', it seems the time has come for a radical restructuring of the operation. There are countless opportunities for a favourable sales development, but the internal conditions are not suitable to use them. An internal recovery plan is necessary.
- If most of the combinations fall in the quadrant 'strengths/threats', the external circumstances are not favourable. But the company is adequately equipped to deal with this. The aim is to maintain the position until the external conditions improve again. A defensive strategy

is in place. The weaker competitors will automatically fall off as a result of the external threats, and this creates more room in the market for sales growth.
- Finally, if most of the combinations fall in the quadrant 'threats/ weaknesses', the company finds itself in the worst circumstances. We should seriously consider whether it still makes sense to continue the operation. A strategy of retreat seems the appropriate choice.

FIGURE 14.2 The SWOT matrix

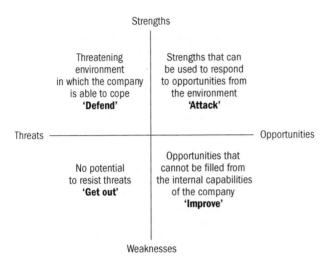

The observations in the upper right corner of the matrix are our strongest offensive weapons in the implementation of our strategy. The observations in the lower left corner are the biggest obstacles in the implementation of the strategy.

14.2 Working procedure of the SWOT matrix

A SWOT matrix is constructed through a number of steps.

Step 1: identification
The preparation of a SWOT begins with the straightforward identification of strengths, weaknesses, opportunities and threats. In practice, this can lead to quite extensive lists, in which old and new are mixed. It is important not to select too much in this phase. A seemingly insignificant strength can, in conjunction with an opportunity that is considered to be less important, suddenly produce a very strong combination and thus form a weapon in the fight.

Step 2: finding the combinations
The second step consists of making the combinations. This is a time consuming matter, because all elements on the list of the first step should be assessed for their possible combination with other elements. In addition, a number of combinations will fall off as 'irrelevant' or 'unimportant'. This

phase therefore leads to a compaction of the outcome. This step actually ascertains in which of the four quadrants the different combinations end up.

Step 3: determining the relative importance

The third step consists of elaborating on the combinations, and the translation of the combinations into a manageable terminology. In effect, this comes down to determining the positioning of the combinations within each quadrant. A combination of intense strength with a very interesting opportunity is positioned in the upper right corner of the first quadrant. A combination of a moderate strength with a nice opportunity is positioned in the lower left corner of quadrant 1, thus close to the centre of the matrix. By adding these weights, you determine which combinations are actually important. This is also necessary, because you often find so many combinations in the second step that you are at risk of losing your overview. It is then necessary to apply a certain degree of prioritisation. It are especially the observations in the furthest corners of the matrix, on which you should primarily focus. These are observations known as the 'issues' (see figure 14.3).

FIGURE 14.3 Zooming-in with the SWOT matrix; determining the issues

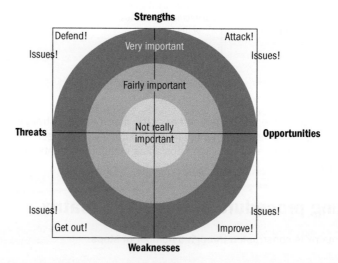

Step 4: clustering the results

The fourth and final step is to cluster the results to focus areas. The clustering aims at isolating SWOT combinations that deal with specific parts of the policy. The clustering to parts should preferably match the elements of the marketing mix. This is the only way that we can obtain a decent translation of SWOT into strategy. We then look, for example, for all the combinations that involve the marketing mix variable 'target group' or the marketing mix variable 'product range'. We are therefore actually trying to implement a separate SWOT on the different marketing mix variables, within the SWOT matrix. The outcome may be that we find three combinations in one subarea in the quadrant 'strengths/opportunities, and two combinations in the quadrant 'threats/weaknesses'.

The distribution of the combinations in the cluster 'target group' then enables us to reflect on the development of policy options in the area of the target group. A (non-exhaustive) example of such clustering is shown in figure 14.4. The figure refers to a SWOT which was carried out for the IADS (the *International Association of Department Stores*) to develop the future policy of the affiliated department stores.

FIGURE 14.4 SWOT for the IADS

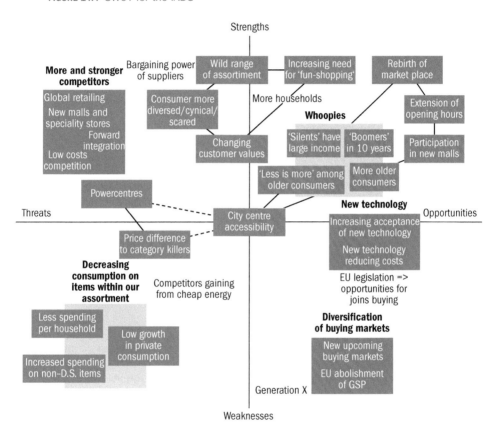

14.3 The retail marketing mix

In the previous section it was explained how a straightforward identification of the results of the external and internal analysis can lead to clusters of combined observations that relate to parts of the policy, expressed in the P's of the marketing mix. Actually this comes down to the translation of the results of the situation analysis or SWOT (the 1st situation) in approaches for the future (the target-situation).

The retail marketing mix differs from the marketing mix of industrial companies by the fact that it consists of more marketing mix variables than the usual four P's of Position, Product, Promotion and Price. The difference is caused largely by the interpretation of the variable 'Position'. In general marketing, we consider this variable as the description of the distribution methods. The variable relates to the choice of the channels and how the logistics from the production site to the outlets is controlled. Sales is considered to have been generated at the moment that the supplies are transferred to the outlets.

However, this does not apply for retail. After all, retail itself is the channel. At the moment that sales is generated for the suppliers (supplier to retailer), the retailer still has to begin generating his sales (supplier to consumers). This last phase in the overall production process requires a completely different approach. On the one hand, the retailer should ensure that there is sufficient interest for what he has to offer, on the other hand, he must ensure that the interest is also converted into actual purchases. The connection with the previously used formula $S = CA \times VI \times C \times AT$ (see chapter 11) is clear. The first part of the formula $(CA \times VI)$, or the number of visitors that one is able to attract, is related to generating interest. How do we get the residents of the catchment area to come to the store to see what we have to offer? It is literally a measure for the attractiveness of the formula that the retailer introduces to the market. We call this the

Attraction value

attraction value. To influence the attraction value, we use the *external marketing mix*.

The second part of the formula $(C \times AT)$, or the final sales that one can generate from this visit, relates to the internal store factors. It is a measure for the effectiveness of the store as a sales machine. We call

Transaction value

this the *transaction value* of the formula. To influence the transaction value, we use the *internal marketing mix*.

The first set (external marketing mix) is used to attract visitors from the catchment area to the store or outlet. This entails the P's of:

- Public: target group.
- Position: choice of the location.
- Promotion: especially the external promotion.
- Product: to be interpreted as assortment or product range.
- Price image: cheap or expensive.

The second set (internal marketing mix) is used to turn visitors into customers. This entails the P's of:

- Presentation: the manner in which the goods in the store are brought to the attention of the public, including the 'internal promotion' and the packaging.
- Personnel: the operating system, ranging from full personal service to self-service.
- Physical distribution: in order to sell goods, they need to be present.

By naming and specifying the marketing mix variables, you eventually get to the interpretation of the formula. Figure 14.5 illustrates the external marketing mix for two forms of retail, both belonging to the outlet channel of department stores, but which lead to other formulas because of the different interpretation of the mix.

FIGURE 14.5 The primary marketing mix of traditional department stores (Bijenkorf, Printemps) and of self-service warehouses (Carrefour, Euromarche, Makro)

Element	Traditional department store	Self-service warehouse
Public	Luxury buying opportunity High involvement	Low involvement
Position	Town centre A1-location	Peripheral
Product (range)	Small and deep	Wide and shallow
Price	Relatively high Style and quality	Discount
Promotion	Glossy	Newspaper

We will deal with each of the mentioned marketing mix variables in the following chapters. It will not be possible to cover it all: books have been written on every mentioned mix variable. We will therefore focus mainly on the aspects that are typical for the retail sector, and there are enough.

14.4 Approach through the Store Compass

Characteristic of the transition from analysis to implementation in the above is the split into external marketing mix variables (aimed at the attraction of the store) and internal marketing mix variables (aimed at the transaction in the store). A somewhat deviating approach, also regularly applied in Dutch retail, is the 'pentagon & triangle' model of D. Tigert and L. Ring of Babson College in the United States. They do not really distinguish between attraction and transaction, but between *back-office* factors and *front-office* factors. The idea behind the Tigert and Ring model is that there are in fact three strategies for retailers to follow: the choice for cost leadership, differentiation or niche player. The first choice is based on operating according to the triangle; the differentiation choice is based on the pentagon. Under *front-office factors*, also known as **Front-office** the front of the store, we understand all elements of the formula that consumers can experience from their own perception. Under the *back-office factors*, also known as the back of the store, we understand all the **Back-office factors** elements that consumers can perceive through direct perception, but which create conditions for the proper implementation of the concept. Tigert represents his conceptual thoughts in a model that is known as the 'pentagon & triangle'.

The pentagon in the Tigert and Ring model, however, has a slightly different thought process than the interpretation of the retail marketing mix. Hemmer and Quix have edited the pentagon, the *Store Compass* is **Store Compass** the result (see figure 14.6).
The so-called Store Compass revolves around five crucial points. Where the marketing mix refers to so-called 'marketing P's' that need to be interpreted, this model refers to the retail W's. The more critical and more demanding consumer is no longer just looking for a product at a certain

price and at a certain location. The consumer is now looking for a complete solution to a problem and taking a different approach may help. Which is why this model refers to the retail W's: where, what, worth, who and why. This might seem like old wine in new bottles, but it is the underlying thoughts that feed the model. The P's from the marketing mix should not be cast aside, but lie under this model.

FIGURE 14.6 Store Compass

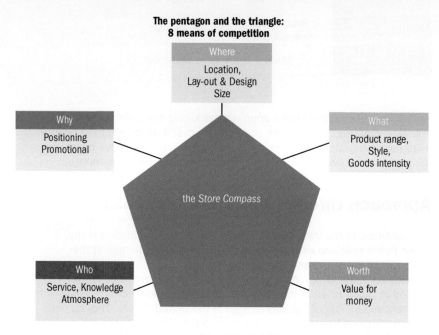

Source: *Quix and Hemmer, 2006*

The Store Compass shows that a store formula can distinguish itself from the competition on these five components. It is much like a mirror in which a retailer can compare his own achievements to that of his competitors. By collecting consumers' scores on the five components of their own formula and that of competitors, retailers can determine their position and decide where they want to make a difference. This way, the Store Compass offers retailers the opportunity to choose in which of the W's they want to excel, as it is impossible to dominate all five W's: in practice, one or two points are more than adequate. Next, one or two other points should score average and two or three may score lower than average. The further a retailer is positioned in one of the corners of the Store Compass, the more pronounced the formula is distinguished from the competition. At the same time, this also means that it is becoming increasingly more difficult for the retailer to take a different route. Aldi and Lidl, for example, are exceptionally dominant on the W of worth. For them it is difficult, if not impossible, to decide an exclusive delicatessen store based on only freshly made products.

We further elaborate on the following retail W's:
1 where;
2 what;
3 worth;
4 who;
5 why.

14

1 Where

'Where' is more than just a good location, as the P of position in the marketing mix perhaps suggests. The W of where also refers to the 'accessibility' and 'lay-out', or how the store is structured. The location is extremely important to retailers, while research shows that, in most cases, location is not one of the most important selection criteria for consumers. This is logical, because most stores are all located together in an A1 location. Moreover, consumers also often opt for proximity. People usually go to the closest supermarket or DIY market. This is a fact on which entrepreneurs have very little influence. But with a new establishment or a relocation of a company, this is a very important choice for a retailer. Once a company is established at a certain location, it has very little influence on the 'location'. Sometimes it is possible to realise more parking spaces. With respect to the lay-out, the possibilities are often somewhat larger through the course of time. Expansions are then not often possible, but through an optimal supply chain over time, storage space can often be drawn to the store so that the sales area can increase.

2 What

A good assortment, much innovation and a good range of brands may be factors that can distinguish the retailer in the area of 'what'. This is not just about the product. Consumers today are looking for the 'what' and seek solutions. They want to know what a product can do, whether it can increase their comfort or save time and whether it fits in their lifestyle. It is therefore no longer just about the product, but it is more than ever about understanding the customer. It is essential to understand what a customer wants, so that the retailer can offer a solution that actually fulfils the customer's needs. Customisation can play a role. In many cases, the W of 'what' will coincide with the W of 'who', because solutions often do not stop at just the product. Providing services may be part of the solution.

3 Worth

The P of price is replaced by the W of worth. The important factor for 'worth' is value for money. Consumer research clearly shows that the orientation of the consumer has shifted from 'the lowest price' to value for money. However, this does not mean that price no longer plays a role: price is always important. Price orientation becomes more important, especially when the economy is experiencing a slump. To positively influence the W of worth, there are two options: either lowering the price or increasing the quality. It is tempting to always go for the lowest price. But it is also very dangerous. Because there are only a few players who can really play this game: these are the so-called cost leaders. They are able to offer the lowest price, because they are constantly improving on the efforts of the previous day. Take a Wal-Mart, for example, that has made this their corporate mission.

Retailers who cannot play this game, are wise to focus on quality. This can be done by, if possible, selling better quality products (thus the W of 'what') or by adding to or improving the service (the W of 'who'). There is also a situation in which a retailer is permitted to reach out for the price weapon. This can be done when the market share is put under pressure. If the market share no longer grows or even decreases, one may choose, if economically justified and in view of improvement, to deploy the price weapon.

Lidl is (just as Aldi) exceptionally dominant on the W of worth

4 Who

The W of 'who' is about more than simply having friendly staff and/or trained personnel. It is also about providing excellent service. The combination of these three factors is decisive for the store atmosphere. Consumer decisions are increasingly influenced by the atmosphere within a store team. The finest store with the best products but with a bad atmosphere or unfriendly staff will never succeed, unless the retailer sells a product that cannot be purchased anywhere else. For most retailers this will not apply. They will have to pay increasingly more attention to the atmosphere in the store. It is therefore very important for a retailer to be very careful about this. In other words: How do employees interact? How do they treat their customers? And how do they respond to their customers? Attention for the store atmosphere will also generate direct returns. Various studies have shown that a pleasant shopping atmosphere has a positive effect on profits. Not only does the number of shoplifting cases decrease, but by paying attention to the customer, there is a much better chance that the customer will say something if he/she receives too much change.

The W of 'who' is closely related to the earlier described W of 'what'. Because consumers want more than just a product, well trained personnel is a 'must'. The consumer is in search of a solution. Training employees is therefore increasingly more important. For the latter, the combination of performance of store personnel and remuneration certainly also applies. With employee performance it is not only the sales per employee that applies, but also how employees are assessed by the consumer. Ultimately, satisfied customers ensure new sales and that begins with a good assessment of the staff.

5 Why
The last W is the 'Why' question. What are the reasons whether or not to buy from a particular retailer? It is a combination of all previous W's, but it also includes additional characteristics. The 'why' question can be influenced by promotion and communication.
External and internal communication play a crucial role. It is important that the expressions correspond with the other W's. An example: if a retailer wants to win on price, then it is not advisable to display expensive looking flat screens to communicate the cheap price. This will immediately create an 'expensive' feeling to the buying public. In short: a retailer should communicate that which corresponds with what consumers can expect when they visit the store. It sounds very easy, but it is often easier said than done. This is why it is important to continuously measure whether consumers still look at the store as it was intended. And when changes are implemented on one of the five points of the Store Compass, it is crucial to adjust the communication accordingly and then to determine whether the consumer also sees and experiences it in the intended way.

In fact, the two approaches, the Store Compass and the 'pentagon & triangle' model, are virtually the same thing: they both use internal and external factors. The difference lies in the fact that, in the Store Compass, direct connection is sought with the behaviour of consumers in stores, whereas in Tigerts approach, the perception of the consumer (which does not have to be the same as behaviour) and operational aspects of the operations are taken into account.

Summary

In this chapter, we looked at the process of translating a SWOT analysis into a proper interpretation of the marketing mix. We demonstrated the benefits of a combination analysis: the so-called dynamic SWOT analysis. This is not just a list of the various components of the SWOT, but they are also placed in a matrix which clearly indicates the combinations.
It also becomes clear what attention is needed. Obviously this is less straightforward compared to a simple SWOT, but it provides much more insight into how to act and how priorities apply.
With regard to the marketing mix for retail, we have shown two approaches, both the traditional approach with the five P's and the use of the Store Compass. This last model is an adaptation of the Tigert and Ring pentagon & triangle model. In the Store Compass we talked about the five W's of marketing. This seems like the same meat with a different gravy, but the approach is reasoned somewhat more from the store formula. Moreover, the idea of the Store Compass emphasises that one cannot excel at all the points and that you have to make the difference on a few points in relation to your competitors.

15
Public or target group

In this chapter, we discuss the various aspects of the general public or the target group and explain the choice of the target group, market segmentation, segmentation strategies and segmentation criteria. We will also elaborate on domain-specific segmentation and segmentation of customers. Based on some case studies and examples, we finally discuss the segmentation capabilities.

15

15.1 Choice of the target group

Although it is becoming increasingly more difficult to identify target groups (see paragraph 8.6), it makes strategic sense to develop, in advance, a clear picture of the group on which we primarily want to focus our retail concept. In the current environment, where we see fragmentation of consumer behaviour (every consumer visits almost all kinds of stores), this is not done to supply only to the selected target group. After all, this would only result in limiting the target group and the market coverage. This is rather done to focus on the concept and to anchor the reputation of the store with the consumer. In the current circumstances, we use *target marketing* to develop a *store personality*. Figure 15.1 first shows the position of the general public (or the target group) in the strategic process.

We will start by discussing the reputation of the target group, followed by the description of the exact target group.

Target marketing

Store personality

FIGURE 15.1 The strategic process: target group selection

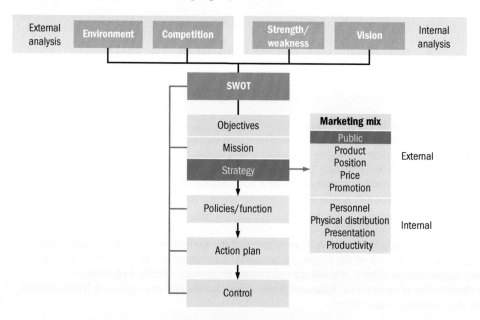

15.1.1 Target group: known or anonymous?

Manufacturing companies generally know who their customers are. The customer places the order and the customer is invoiced. It is clearly very easy to approach the customer in a situation such as this, where all the details of the customers are known. In the retail sector, and especially in retail, such customers do not exist or are very rare. In the vast majority of purchase transactions in the retail sector, the address, personal characteristics and history of the purchasing behaviour are not known: the customer is mostly anonymous. The personal data (name and full address) are unknown. The customer enters a store, looks around, picks up a product of choice from the shelf, walks to the checkout and pays, sometimes even without uttering a single word. This means that, in retail

marketing, you have to find a different way to become aware of the needs
of the customers than in trade marketing. Today, *CRM-systems* solve this
problem partially. CRM is short for customer response management.
Many retail companies have created customer cards, part of such a CRM
system. Due to the automatic processing of the data from these customer cards, it is now possible to learn more about the characteristics
and the behaviour of customers. Customer loyalty systems, such as Air
Miles, basically also make it possible to connect the purchasing behaviour
and customer characteristics. Air Miles enable retail companies to
distinguish good customers from bad customers, but not to learn about
the purchase history of these customers. Due to privacy considerations,
only the frequency of visits and the total average ticket may be registered. It is partly for this reason that Albert Heijn (actually, one of the
initiators of the Air-Miles system) introduced the bonus card in addition
to Air Miles. Participants of the bonus card system declare that they are
willing to share their details, although the privacy aspect was once again
acknowledged. Albert Heijn's customers are free to choose whether or
not to reveal their personal data. Despite the fact that there are sufficient consumers who have given permission, there is a difference
between theory and practice. Although Albert Heijn should theoretically
be able to implement one-on-one marketing to individual customers
using the bonus card, it appears to be unmanageable in practice: the
abundance of information involved in the registration of all transactions
of the millions of AH customers, is so big that Albert Heijn still only have
a limited use of one-on-one marketing. The bonus card functions
primarily as an additional price incentive for good customers (who visit
the store most frequently), and to a lesser extent as a marketing tool.
However, such a system can be used reasonably effective by using a
different concept, namely, one-to-many or one-to-group marketing. This
concept focuses more on groups with similar behavioural patterns.
Information is sent to these groups based on these details. Let us take
young parents, for example: these can be identified by the purchasing
behaviour of amongst others diapers. Or wine lovers based on their wine
purchases. Based on these
purchases, you can provide these groups with information on special
offers that are relevant to their purchasing behaviour. Not everyone gets
the same offer and not everyone gets an individual offer, but they do get
a personalised offer. This significantly reduces the need to know
everything about the customer and makes it possible to better adjust the
marketing to the greatest common denominator per group or segment.
The best practice, when it comes to evaluating as much detail as
possible on consumer groups, is still Britain's Tesco. Within the retail
sector, the Tesco Clubcard is the most successful loyalty program in the
world. Tesco uses the acquired insights of its customers, to serve the
customer. To this day, this translated into more loyalty and higher
returns. Example 15.1 deals with loyalty systems in the Netherlands.

In trade marketing, the manufacturer knows exactly which retailer is his
customer and how often he orders which products. Therefore, he knows
his customer and the overall behaviour of his customer. The retailer only

CRM-systems

15

15

EXAMPLE 15.1 RESEARCH: THE CUSTOMER CARD IN YOUR WALLET

More and more Dutch retail chains are introducing loyalty systems. The goal is to achieve a greater connection between retailer and customer.

The average Dutchman's wallet already contains 4,2 cards from a retail chain. Dutch women have five cards in their purses. In almost 60% of all cases, consumers save for something with these loyalty systems, in the other cases the card simply involves cash discount. Increasing loyalty should primarily be shaped by better responding to the needs of the customer, rather than giving discount or points. With the introduction of such systems, the collection of personal details is often seen as a major obstacle. However, research among more than 24.000 consumers showed that only 18,6% object to the providing personal details. Among women, this percentage is even lower, only 15,5% of women prefer not to provide any information about themselves. Almost two thirds of consumers who prefer not to provide personal details indicate that their own privacy is the most important reason. Other arguments that are used include being telephoned unnecessarily or receiving unwanted mail or e-mail.

Extra service for regular customers

Loyalty can also be increased by pampering loyal customers even more. In aviation, this is already very common, but it appears that space has also been created in retail. 57% of the respondents have indicated that it is only fair that regular customers get priority at an express checkout upon presentation of their customer card. When it comes to parking in the front, more than two third of respondents agreed that this is only fair for regular customers. Although Makro is strictly speaking not a retailer, it is an organisation that already uses such methods.

The harsh reality

Most systems today are very transaction-oriented: discount on the current or a future purchase. The consumer's opinions on the current systems are clear. 61% of the respondents find that one gets discounts on products that one does not want or need.

Source: De klantenkaart op zak [The customer card in your wallet], Q&A Research & Consultancy, February 2008

knows that certain people visit the store at a given moment, but he does not know if these people have ever been in the store before. Actually, the retailer can therefore only register visits and, in this respect, it is not known how many people there are per visit and how often they visit.

After all, the number of people who visit the store, equals the total number of visitors to the store, divided by the average visit frequency per person. This last is only sporadically known, for example if the retailer has done special market research or if he has a customer card system. This never used to be such a big problem: consumer behaviour towards stores was pretty clearly defined. A person that was attracted to de Bijenkorf, would not bother visiting the HEMA. And a person who always purchased from HEMA, would almost never have gone to de Bijenkorf because the price level was too high for their budget. There was a clear, though not exact, separation between various target groups that corresponded rather nicely with store preferences. However, this distinction disappeared as the average income increased, as the 'class difference' became less decisive and as consumers became more assertive. The consumer now shops at HEMA, Zeeman, Claudia Sträter and de Bijenkorf. This means that the relationship between visitors and customers is becoming even less clear than it was in the past.

15.1.2   The second-best-solution within the retail

The retail has opted for a pragmatic approach to the problem: if consumers can no longer be classified into identifiable groups, let's see if they can be divided into groups of similar purchasing situations. For the food sector, this resulted in the concept of the *dual consumer*: one and the same consumer can manifest as two different buyers. A famous example is that of the Jaguar owner, who does his *high-involvement* purchases at the supermarket deli, and goes to the Aldi for his *low-involvement* bulk purchases.

Dual consumer

For the non-food sector, with its much greater diversity of product categories, the dual consumer approach is already too coarse. Here one has switched over to *moment marketing*: responding to purchase situations or use situations which every consumer periodically needs, to a greater or lesser extent. After the blurring of traditional target groups, HEMA, for example, decided to concentrate on the purchase situation focussing on the purchase of daily consumables, while de Bijenkorf has chosen the purchasing situation, focusing on recreational shopping in non-daily goods.

Moment marketing

Just because target groups can no longer be easily defined, it does not mean that the concept of target group can no longer be used as a marketing instrument. Target groups are mainly used as a reference guide in the modern approach: a description of the customer in which the selected purchase opportunity is the most common. The target group therefore became an instrument to establish focus in the marketing concept. We will discuss this further in chapter 15.

Optical Group is one of the retailers that conducted special marketing research that led to segmentation, thus providing the basis for a new positioning (see example 15.2).

EXAMPLE 15.2 CUSTOMER SEGMENTATION WITH OPTICAL GROUP BRINGS FOCUS

About instinct, vision and figures

During the years 2005 and 2006, Optical Group made an important decision. They opted for a more pronounced vision of the formula. The idea of the commercial management is that there is room for a formula in the mid to high segment of the market. In 2006, on initiative of a former optics entrepreneur, a study was started into the segmentation of consumers in the optics market. It soon became clear that the research question is consistent with the needs of Optical Group to further

substantiate the instinct and expert views on the optics market.

In addition to a market segmentation, a customer segmentation was made of Dutch people that wear glasses and of Optical Group customers.

Why segment?

In the optics sector, it has long been the norm for consumers that wear glasses to purchase a new pair of glasses on average every 3.6 years. This study also indicated, once again, that the assumption still holds true. Interestingly, however, was that the average was still standing, but that there were no significant differences between men and woman or between various age categories. Nevertheless, there are clear differences in the dataset when it comes to the average wearing time. These vary enormously.

Domain-specific segmentation was opted for during the study: a form of segmentation that is based on the attitude and behaviour in relation to the purchase of a pair of glasses. The segmentation was applied ex post, afterwards, on the dataset. The applied method of segmentation leads to six segments which are heterogeneous from one another, but homogenous when it comes to the groups themselves. The average wearing time and the average expenditure per group appears to differ significantly.

Six consumer segments in the optical sector

The following six segments are defined based on the ex post segmentation: Price Shopper; Premium Shopper; Value for Money Shopper; Aspiration Shopper; Fashion Shopper and Traditional Shopper. In figure 1, the six segments are compared to each other based on wearing time and average expenditure. When we look at the underlying sociodemographic details of every segment it is immediately clear that gender, age and education are not explicitly explanatory factors to be included in one of the groups.

It is true that, on average, one segment is slightly older than the other, but generally all segments include people of various ages, every gender and every level of education. In addition to the market segmentation, Optical Group also had a segmentation of its own customers made. The segmentation criteria are identical, but the research group is limited to Optical Group customers. The six various segments can all be found at Optical Group, except that they occur in entirely different proportions. Figure 2 shows the distribution of segments in the market and among customers of Optical Group.

The distribution with Optical Group clearly shows that there are three customer segments that are over-represented within the customer base. 85% of customers represent 92% of the sales. It is particularly valuable that Optical Group focuses primarily on three core customer groups. Within this, the groups each have their own dynamics and require an individual approach in terms of communication and product range. The understanding that Optical Group acquired in their customers, ties in nicely with the newly developed vision. The formula, which is still under development, can be further improved on. More targeted marketing activities, campaigns and offers are developed per target group, thus increasing its effectiveness. The combination of offline and online works especially well.

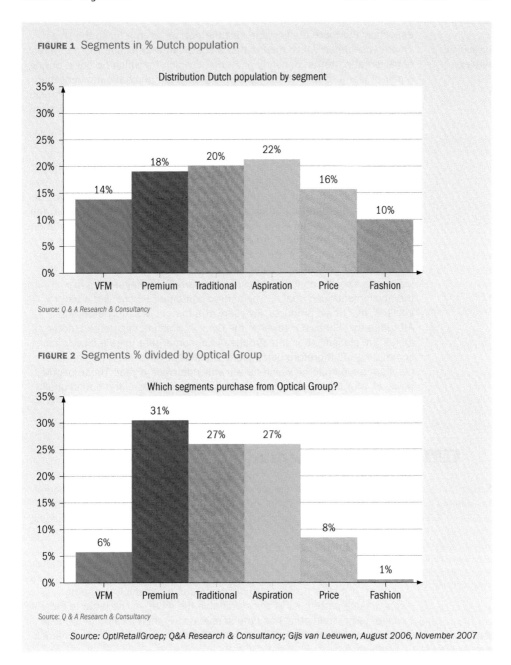

FIGURE 1 Segments in % Dutch population

Distribution Dutch population by segment

Source: *Q & A Research & Consultancy*

FIGURE 2 Segments % divided by Optical Group

Which segments purchase from Optical Group?

Source: *Q & A Research & Consultancy*

Source: OptiRetailGroep; Q&A Research & Consultancy; Gijs van Leeuwen, August 2006, November 2007

15.1.3 Description of the exact target group

The phenomenon of the increasing difficulty to describe the exact target
group is incidentally still growing in importance: where one initially talked
about the 'increasingly individualistic customer' (which implied that there
was more and more diversity in customer segments and that, as a result,
more and more smaller target groups arose), the food sector already talks
about the *dual customer*. This means that a customer can exhibit two
different behavioural patterns at two different times. In the non-food sector,

Dual customer

15

Fragmented customer

especially the more fashionable part thereof, we even refer to the *fragmented customer*, which means that a customer may exhibit many different behavioural patterns, depending on the occasion for which he buys: buying a pair of jeans to work in the garden is a different purchase moment than buying a pair of jeans for the disco. One can even see some schizophrenia where consumers are involved. Think of McDonald's, where consumers buy a Big Mac Menu with a Cola light, or someone who wears a Corneliani suite with a white T-shirt from HEMA. All these different behavioural patterns have resulted in the fact that, in retail, one focuses more on so-called purchase moments or use moments, and less on target groups. Consistency with the known terms *fun shopping/run shopping* (see sub-paragraph 2.5.1) or with the difference between daily/non-daily will be clear: these are different purchase moments. This does not mean that the concept of target group is no longer used at all within retail. Segmentation, or classification into target groups, is no longer possible on the basis of generic classification for the entire market. Target group segmentation in retail can now only be domain-specific. This method of segmentation that looks at a specific domain, also known as product category, fits in well with the abovementioned dual or fragmented customer. Purchasing a pair of glasses, electronic products, jewellery or a bicycle is simply different. Attitudes and behaviour towards the domain which is segmented, determines the classification into groups. A consumer that uses a bicycle for commuting will therefore purchase in a different way than a person who purchases a bicycle on which he will only ride twice a year. These people, however, may be equally appreciative of classical music and sound quality and have some penchant for design boxes. The domain-specific segmentation leads to these opinions, a generalistic method does not.

15.2 Market segmentation

Market segmentation

When choosing a target group, we use *market segmentation*. Under market segmentation we mean dividing the market into more or less homogenous groups of individuals with common characteristics and a similar purchasing behaviour.

A sensible market segmentation must comply with:
- *Heterogeneity of needs*: the 'needs' of the segment (and the derived demand for products) should be distinguished from those of other groups. It makes no sense to define groups that exhibit the same purchasing pattern as everyone outside the group. If the latter is the case, target marketing has little sense: one is then located in the field

Mass merchandising

  of *mass merchandising*. Target group determination is then easy, namely 'everyone'.
- *Measurability*: the criteria on which the segmentation occurs should be measurable. This seems to be a clincher: after all, it makes very little sense to define segments if we do not measure them. Yet it is currently one of the biggest problems in segmentation. As a result of the individualisation of the consumer and the blurring of the demand structure, we increasingly come to the conclusion that it is becoming more difficult to find measurable criteria that describes consumer behaviour.

- *Approachability*: a selected segment must be approachable through promotion and distribution techniques. A well measurable segment that cannot be approached has no operational significance.
- *Size*: the segments should be large enough for economic 'full utilisation'. When target marketing is only used for applying focus, this condition is of less importance. Nevertheless, it is nice when the selected segment is so large that, in itself, it provides sufficient support for a profitable operation.

15.3 Segmentation strategies

According to research by Alsem (Alsem, 2001), two strategies may basically be used to form segments.

- *A priori segmentation*: in this, consumers are classified on the basis of general characteristics and it is subsequently checked whether there are differences in behavioural characteristics between groups. Van Raaij (Van Raaij, 1999) describes this form as backwards segmentation. A disadvantage of this form of segmentation is that the segments are not homogenous with respect to their product requirements, purchasing behaviour and use. The number of segments is hereby known in advance.

  A priori segmentation

- *Segmentation based on behavioural differences*: this is based on groups of customers that exhibit a different behaviour with respect to the product and the basis on which the general nature of the groups can be described is subsequently searched for. This is also known as forward segmentation or *ex post segmentation*. The advantage of this form is that homogenous segments can be formed with respect to product requirements, purchasing behaviour and use. The behavioural analysis is often based on differences in the importance that customers attach to certain product attributes (benefits). This form of segmentation is also known as benefit segmentation. The benefit of this segmentation is that, if segments are found, then at least the requirements of homogeneity and heterogeneity are met and there is a direct relationship with purchasing behaviour. With this form, the number of segments is not known in advance.

  Ex post segmentation

Especially the second form of segmentation is used much currently. There is an increased use of explanatory variables instead of descriptive variables. Classic segmentation based on general variables has increasingly less explanatory power when it concerns consumer behaviour. General variables are also not valid for all areas of consumer behaviour, are descriptive and do not explain how and why consumers prefer certain product attributes and benefits. General classifications are therefore released and we are looking increasingly more at specific domains or products, or domain-specific segmentation. Because consumer behaviour is a multidimensional phenomenon, we now use several variables rather than a few variables as segmentation basis.

In chapter 8, we already discussed various segmentation criteria, but given the increasingly explanatory nature of these variables in the next section, we focus on more behavioural segmentation criteria and, in particular, the link to a specific domain.

15.4 Segmentation criteria

We cannot give a definite criterion for market segmentation: the selected criteria depend partly on the consumer needs that we want to cover with the company. If we decide to market fashion (angle: expression value), we will probably use other segmentation criteria than if we choose to market life insurance (angle: caring for relatives). In the first case, a criterion that is related to the fashion sensitivity of the consumer seems to be the obvious choice, in the second case, a criterion that involves the family situation. An additional difficulty for retail is that, in practice, the subjects from the selected segment cannot be observed as individuals, but often only as anonymous visitors who wish to fill a specific purchase situation. This is why, in retail, in addition to target grouping for applying the marketing focus, we also use *purchase moment segmentation* to further interpret formulas. The concepts explained in chapter 2 as 'daily/non-daily', 'high involvement/low involvement' and 'fun shopping/run shopping' will thereby come back into play. The problem is that, within a clearly demarcated target group with similar spending behaviour, one individual can fill the need through run shopp-ing, while the other individual prefers fun shopping. Below we discuss some of the most common approaches used in the segmentation of the retail market.

Purchase moment segmentation

15.4.1   Geographic segmentation

Geographic segmentation

'All business is local' is a statement that applies even more for retail than for the industry. The statement implies that there will be geographic differences in the composition, behaviour and demand of consumer groups. In situations involving only one branch, this will not be a problem. In situations involving operation in various geographic regions, such as a department store or chain store, this causes problems. Basically, these regional differences, even in the tiny Netherlands, can lead to regional differentiation of product ranges: flans sell easy in Limburg and less well in Friesland. Nevertheless, we note that over the years the regional differences within the Netherlands have become considerably less expectant.

However, the ever increasing internationalisation of formulas in retail once again raises the problem of the geographic segmentation.

A department store formula like Marks & Spencer attracted a different target group in France than in England. In the Netherlands, Marks & Spencer turned out to be a bigger rival to V&D, and to a certain extent even to de Bijenkorf, than it was to HEMA (see example 15.3).

EXAMPLE 15.3 HEMA

In the early nineties of the previous century, HEMA expanded to Belgium. Soon after opening the first branch, the Belgian consumer seemed to respond entirely different to the HEMA range than the Dutch consumer (see figure).

The figure describes the fair shares (see chapter 12) of the sales shares of several departments of the Belgian HEMA branches compared to the sales shares that were achieved in HEMA in the Netherlands. The norm in this

The difference in response of Belgian and Dutch consumers to the same product range

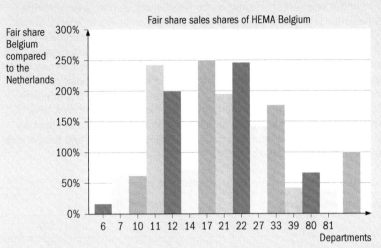

Fair share sales shares of HEMA Belgium

fair-share analysis is therefore the distribution of the sales in the Netherlands. A fair share > 100 implies that the department does relatively better in Belgium than in the Netherlands, a fair share < 100 implies the opposite. It is clear that the sales mix in the Belgium HEMA is entirely different to that in the Netherlands. The departments of cheese (17) and personal care (11) clearly do much better in Belgium than in the Netherlands, while the departments of cakes (6) and electrical items (81) do much worse in Belgium than in the Netherlands.

15.4.2   Demographic segmentation

In the area of demographics, there are a number of important criteria for segmentation.

Age

Age, especially in retail, is a powerful segmentation criterion. The criterion is easily measurable. Age segments are easily approachable, while the needs of age groups vary considerably and, therefore, their purchasing behaviour as well. In chapter 7, with the discussion of the possible implications of the ageing population, it was shown that, with unchanged expenditure behaviour per age group, the increase of the proportion of older people can lead to the need to adjust the sorting per product range. We must realise, however, that even within age groups, there is still momentum in the expenditure behaviour. Because the assumption that the age group 40-50 years exhibited the same expenditure behaviour in 1990 as in 1970, is demonstrably incorrect.

15

Income/social class

Volume component

Even the income, or the approach of the income through the social class, is a powerful segmentation criterion for retail. Income affects expenditure behaviour in two ways. First through the so-called ability to spend, or the *volume component*. It is clear that someone with a higher income can spend more money on goods and services than someone with a low income. This basically applies to all expenditure categories. Secondly, we can see that, with increasing income, changes occur in the relative composition of the purchased goods and services package. This is caused by the effect of Engel's law, indicating that – as the income increases – relatively less is spent on primary goods (such as food and drinks) and more is spent on luxurious product categories, such as fashionable clothing and recreational services (see table 15.1).

TABLE 15.1 Distribution of expenditure according to income

Expenditure category	Income group (in %)	
	< €14,800	> €31,500
Food	18.4	16.3
Home	42.1	31.0
Of which basics:		
• rent	32.1	21.3
• heating	5.7	3.3
Of which luxury:		
• furniture	2.3	4.3
• clothing/shoes	5.7	7.4
• recreation/development	25.3	36.3

Source: Statistisch jaarboek CBS, 2003

Family cycle

In several cases, the family cycle can be an important segmentation criterion. The criterion exhibits a certain degree of correlation with both age and income. With income because – as you progress through the cycle – there is generally more discretionary income that becomes available. With age because the cycles are associated with increasing age. We generally distinguish between the following cycles:

1 young singles;
2 *nestlers*: newly married of cohabiting families, without children;
3 *full nest*:
   a *young kids* < 5 years;
   b *young kids* 5-12 years;
   c *kids* > 12 years;
4 *empty nest*;
5 *retired*.

Home furnishing store IKEA focuses mainly on segments 1, 2, and 3a. In contrast, more expensive suppliers in the same sector (such as

Stoutenbeek) focus more on segment 4: those who refurnish the home once the children have left home and are therefore no longer under budget pressure. Mortgage banks focus mainly on *nestlers*, life insurers especially on the *full*-nest group.

IKEA focuses mainly in segments 1, 2 and 3a

15.4.3 Psychographic segmentation

The phenomenon that makes target groups increasingly difficult to identify using ex ante definable 'fixed' variables, led to a new trend in marketing in the early seventies of the previous century, in which consumers where characterised based on psychographic factors.

Psychographic segmentation

We discuss the bell shaped curve and the De Bock Barometer below. We also provide an example of domain-specific segmentation.

Bell shaped curve

A much used application of psycographical research, in retail and especially in the fashion sector, is the translation of the *bell shaped curve* of E.M. Rogers (Rogers, 2003). The bell shaped curve was originally intended to explain how product innovations gradually penetrate a small trendsetting group of people, to acceptance by the masses, finally ending up in the dying phase. It is the target group translation of the product life cycle. Research has shown that we can also use the curve to describe the fashion sensitivity of consumers. We distinguish between five fashion sensitivity groups (see figure 15.2):

Bell shaped curve

Innovators
1 The trendiest group is that of the *innovators*. One could say that this group is not so much fashion conscious, but rather that they are trendsetters.

2 Fashion trends, developed by the innovators, are taken over by the **Adopters** *adopters*. The adopters have a fashion attitude that can be characterised as 'on trend'.

Early majority
3 After the adopters, the trend is copied by the *early majority*. They can be characterised as trend followers in terms of fashion attitude.

Late majority
4 They are followed by the *late majority*. In terms of fashion attitude, this group is very conservative and values proper clothing more than the right fashion.

Laggards
5 Finally we have the *laggards* or stragglers. They do not care about fashion at all. To them, clothing should be functional, long-lasting and not too flashy.

FIGURE 15.2 The bell shaped curve

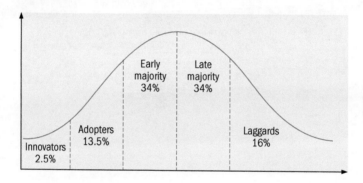

AIO analysis
In the more advanced lifestyle approaches, consumers are analyzed using a so-called *AIO analysis* (activities, interests and opinions). Moreover, statistical techniques clustered into groups with similar AIO characteristics are also used. Thus creating 'consumer personalities'. These are typologies or lifestyle groups that are theoretically manageable as target groups. It will be clear that such segmentations do not always need to match the old segmentation based on age, gender, occupation or income. This immediately **Lifestyle** indicates one of the problems of *lifestyle segmentation*.

segmenta-
Based on research, we can often demonstrate the existence of certain **tion** lifestyle clusters. The measurability criterion has then been met. It can often be observed from the research that different clusters have different needs. The criteria of heterogeneity in the purchase behaviour have then also been met. The approachability of the typologies, however, leaves much to be desired: How do you approach a group of consumers, of which random surveys have indicated that it does exist, which is described as innovative, active in the area of sports, environmentally aware and interested in culture? After all, there are no statistics that classify the population on these criteria. In the practice of lifestyle research, we also see that the groups for the practical applications are translated back into the old segmentation criteria: the ambitious Amsterdam canals occupant, at the beginning of a brilliant career, with an outgoing-activity pattern is known in **Yuppie** the parlance as *yuppie*. The term 'yup' represents *Young* (age) *Urban*

(geography) *Professional* (profession). Other known typologies of this nature include *dinki's* (*Double Income, No Kids*) and *whoopies* (*Wealthy, Healthy Older People*).

Dinki's
Whoopies

Although lifestyle segmentation is therefore fairly difficult to apply in retail, the lifestyle research has significantly increased insight into the behaviour of consumers. Especially in the fashion sector, research in the area of lifestyle is therefore relatively often done. However, this is more about the description of an ideal type of customer based on which one can apply better accents in the store concept (focus), than actually editing the target group.
It is more a guide for the formula development, than for marketing.

15

15.5 Domain-specific segmentation as a good approach

Despite the fact that it no longer seems to be sensible that retailers work with general segmentations and target groups based on socio-demographic details, there is another path that can be followed. We indicated before that segmentation around a specific domain does provide an outcome. Consumers can indeed be clustered based on purchase behaviour, as long as it is linked to a specific domain. Thus, consumers can be segmented for sports articles, foodstuffs, glasses, bicycles or electronics. It is quite conceivable that one purchases a bicycle differently than, for example, a mp3 player or a pair of glasses. Hence the fact that a general segmentation often offers no further solution, where a specific segmentation does. With a *domain-specific segmentation,* the consumer is classified based on attitude and behaviour (purchase behaviour) in respect of the domain for which the segmentation applies. For example, a segmentation can be made for the optics sector as we discussed in example 15.2 with the Optical Group. But this segmentation can also be carried out perfectly for other sectors. In recent years, the HBD has carried out several of these segmentation studies in various branches.

Domain-specific segmentation

Example of domain-specific segmentation
The domain-specific segmentation is basically a variation on the lifestyle segmentation, especially with respect to purchase behaviour regarding the specific domain. This is a useful and workable segmentation method. This segmentation method also identifies different groups of buyers, which can all be described based on their behaviour. Example 15.4 is an example of a domain-specific segmentation for the jewellery industry, commissioned by the HBD and the NJU.

EXAMPLE 15.4 MARKET SEGMENTS IN THE JEWELLERY INDUSTRY
Socio-demographic characteristics have little explanatory power
Analysis of the results shows that socio-demographic characteristics such as gender, age, education and income are not explanatory for consumer behaviour in the jewellery industry. This is an important fact, since target groups are often defined based on these variables. The following examples demonstrate this.

Gender
- Men wear and purchase other jewellery than women.
- Women often purchase more jewellery, but men spend more overall and per purchase.
- However, not all men and women buy in the same way.

Age
- On average, the expenditures increase as one gets older. Especially people between 45 and 60 years spend significantly more in total.
- As one gets older, one buys fewer and fewer pieces.
- The expenditures of the categories 25-34 years and 35-44 years are almost equal.
- However, within all age groups, purchases are not done in the same way.

Education
- Education does not explain the number of times that one buys jewellery, nor the number of pieces that one buys.
- On average, the expenditures increase for higher educated people.

Income
- As income increases, more is spent on average on jewellery.
- People with an higher income buy less often.
- Within the different income groups, the average expenditures varies from one another.

Attitudes and outlooks explain consumer behaviour
Based on attitudes, outlooks and what consumers consider important, it is possible to form clearly defined groups that explain the purchase behaviour and the expenditure pattern of the consumer to a large extent. Thus, the fact that one consumer finds price important and the other attaches more value to quality, may largely explain the behaviour of the consumer. Based on attitudes and outlooks, four target group segments were

identified for the jewellery industry (see figure 1).
Table 1 shows how the various segments are structured with respect to gender, age, education, income and purchase behaviour.

FIGURE 1 Size of segments in % of the total market

■ Traditional buyers
■ Impulse buyers
■ Price buyers
■ Fashion buyers

Traditional buyers
Traditional buyers attach most importance to the quality of the jewellery that they wear and buy. For traditional buyers, the price is secondary to the quality. When buying jewellery, the brand does play a role, but it is not a priority. A piece of jewellery is not considered a fashionable product. Traditional buyers are not easily influenced by people from their environment.

Impulse buyers
Impulse buyers buy jewellery very frequently. 56% of them say that they often buy jewellery on impulse. Impulse buyers also take their budgets into account when making a purchase. With regard to expenditures, impulse buyers are the third segment. Price is a decisive factor in this segment. For the impulse buyer, the quality of the jewellery is not more important than the price. 82% of

this segment consists of females. This explains why impulse buyers often see jewellery as a fashionable product and are interested in trends in jewellery. They also take into account what the immediate environment (friends/acquaintances) thinks.

TABLE 1 Consumer segments in jewellery

	Traditional buyers	Impulse buyers	Price buyers	Fashion buyers
Gender				
Male	40.0%	18.0%	32.1%	38.7%
Female	60.0%	82.0%	67.9%	61.3%
	100%	100%	100%	100%
Age				
15 through 24 years	14.4%	27.9%	15.4%	28.6%
25 through 34 years	23.1%	26.6%	19.7%	19.4%
35 through 44 years	19.7%	22.1%	31.9%	24.0%
45 through 60 years	42.8%	23.4%	33.0%	28.1%
	100%	100%	100%	100%
Education				
Low	19.2%	16.3%	23.0%	18.1%
Medium	51.1%	57.1%	52.9%	51.9%
High	29.7%	26.5%	24.1%	30.0%
	100%	100%	100%	100%
Family income (gross)				
< 25,000	22.7%	29.7%	28.8%	22.6%
25,000-35,000	35.7%	37.8%	35.4%	38.1%
35,000-55,000	33.5%	26.2%	28.8%	29.7%
> 56,250	8.2%	6.4%	7.1%	9.7%
	100%	100%	100%	100%
Purchase behaviour				
Expenditures (2004-2005)*	€397.2	€181.0	€124.4	€457.8
Numbers (2004-2005)*	3.6	9.0	3.4	6.5
Purchase frequency (per year)	2.4	6.1	2.2	4.1

* = 1 January 2004 through 31 August 2005

15

15

Price buyers

For the price buyers segment, it's all about the price of the jewellery. Price is the decisive factor. Quality and brands are not important to this segment. Very little value is attached to staff. Out of all the segments, price buyers purchase jewellery least frequently and they also spend the least amount of money. Despite the fact that price buyers want to spend as little as possible on jewellery, this is not the segment with the lowest income. The segment consists largely of women (68%), yet they have a different image of jewellery than the impulse buyers. Trends and fashion is not important and the environment has very little influence on the jewellery that they wear and buy.

Fashion buyers

Fashion buyers are most interested in fashion and trends, and this is clearly taken into account when buying and wearing jewellery. Their immediate environment has significant influence on them. Fashion buyers find it important that others like their jewellery and they want to impress.

Jewellery, just as clothing, is considered a fashionable product. Furthermore, fashion buyers are quality conscious. When buying jewellery, they attach more value to qualified personnel. 39% of the fashion buyers segment consists of men and is therefore less feminine than often perceived.

A vision for the future of the local jeweller

Results show that it is impossible to serve the entire market because consumers differ with respect to who they are, what they buy, where they buy and why. Jewellers have to make a choice, or they risk losing to the competition. The segmentation in combination with the consumer trends described in chapter 8 will lead to a future vision (see figure 2):

- *Traditional buyers*: this segment has additional purchasing power and provides opportunities to increase expenditures. An increase in frequency is difficult because it does not reflect the behaviour.
- *Price buyers*: it is difficult to increase expenditures. This segment mainly offers opportunities to increase the frequency by increasing the product involvement.
- *Impulse buyers*: it is difficult to increase the frequency because this is already very high. Expenditures may increase as impulse buyers grow older and get more income to spend.
- *Fashion buyers*: especially the purchase frequency of this segment can be increased. Fashion buyers are looking for innovation and this offers opportunities to increase this frequency. This will

also have a positive effect on expenditures.

- *Immigrant buyers:* this segment is very similar to the fashion buyers. Given the disposable income available, this

segment especially offers opportunities to increase purchase frequency.

FIGURE 2 Expenditures and purchase frequency per segment

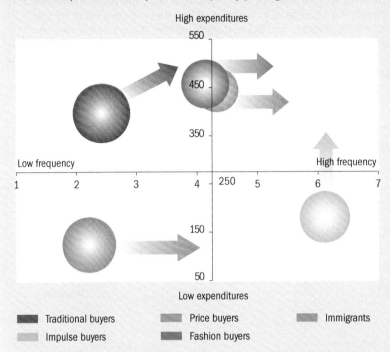

To illustrate this, it could mean the following for the market size:

- A shift of 3% from traditional to fashion, and 2% from impulse to fashion leads to a 2% larger market.
- A higher frequency of +10% with traditional and fashion leads to a 7% larger market.

- A 5% higher average ticket with traditional, leads to a 2% larger market.
- The combination leads to a 12% larger market.

Source: HBD/ Q&A Research & Consultancy

De Bock Barometer
A widely used model in the Netherlands that can be used for segmentation is the *De Bock Barometer* (see figure 15.8). Using the De Bock Barometer, we can classify the market into clusters of user groups. This model is a very handy tool for a domain-specific segmentation. We do this by using a matrix, in which one axis is assigned as the 'fashion sensitivity' (actually the bell shaped curve), while the other axis is assigned a type of measure for 'forceful' behaviour. The upper left corner of the figure contains very forceful, innovative people, the bottom right corner contains the well behaved – also with respect to fashion attitude – conservative people and the upper right corner contains the attackers with a

De Bock Barometer

Mood boards

traditional fashion attitude. The strength of the model lies in the combination of the identification of the groups as well as the translation into product range: using so-called *mood boards*, which reflect the collages of styles and colours, we can determine which sub groups feel attracted to which product range.

The name says it all: this involves a barometer. A barometer measures the weather changes, but is not able to predict the climate changes. It is therefore a short term instrument. It has no predictive value for the upcoming seasons and is basically unstable: the clustering can be different for each year or season. The great advantage of the barometer lies in the internal use within a company. By preparing the matrix and the connection with style preferences, unanimity is created within the company regarding the typology of sub target groups and the associated product ranges.

FIGURE 15.3 De Bock Barometer

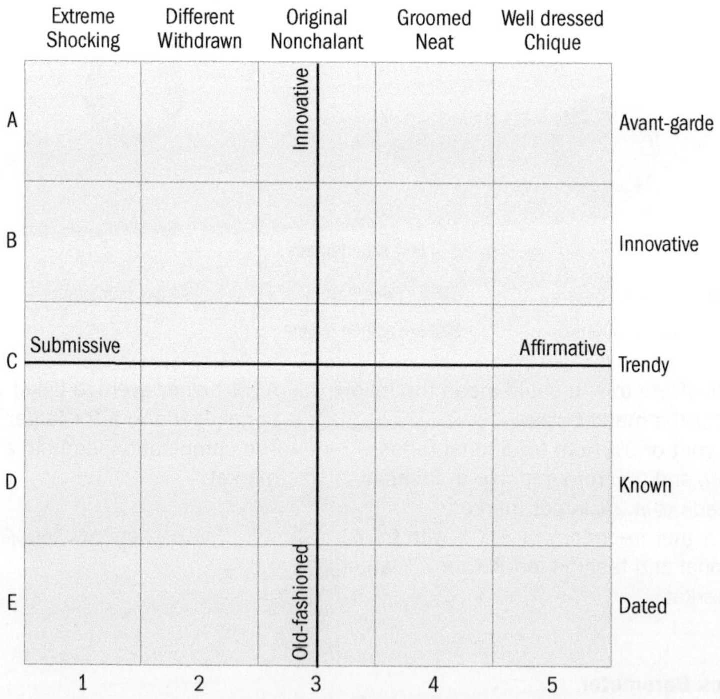

Segmentation as an aid in positioning

In paragraph 9.9, we discussed the positioning of the competitors. The use of segmentation methods, especially the domain-specific method, may be helpful in determining the current positioning of a retailer and what has to be done to achieve the desired future positioning. The starting point for the use of domain-specific segmentation for a positioning problem is to first determine which consumer groups can be identified in the market for electronics or furniture, for instance. We then look at where the interesting groups are. The same segmentation method is then used for the current customers. In this way we can determine which part of the market is covered and where more opportunities or threats are located. If one conducts such research and also includes competitors in the research, it is in fact an excellent positioning based on the potential buyers groups. Subsequently, choices can be made for certain buyer groups and the corresponding positioning of the retailer.

15

15.6 Segmentation of customers

In chapter 6 we discussed the strategic scissors, the mechanism that places people in retail under constant pressure to achieve sales growth. In the competitive situation of Dutch retail, this basically means serving the customer better than the competition. This means that we should know exactly what our customers want. But how do we discover this in an industry in which there is a strongly increasing individualisation of the consumer? Moreover, at least in goods retail, the customer mainly approaches us anonymously. Unlike in the retail service sector (travel agents, insurance or banking), where each transaction is associated with the registration of personal characteristics, we only know the customers visiting times in the goods retail. It is very rarely known whether a visitor is a once-off visitor who accidentally comes along, or whether it is a high-frequency, targeted, big spending, loyal customer.

We will now discuss the following subjects: retention strategies and segmentation of existing groups of customers.

15.6.1 Retention strategies

When we come to the conclusion that, to optimise efficiency, we should constantly be influencing sales, the question arises how we should do this. In retail, there is a tendency, because of the anonymity of the customers, to see sales maximisation as maximising the number of transactions: the more sales transactions, the more sales. Hence the often promotion-oriented implementation of advertising of retail, which is attracting as many customers as possible. The question is whether this is the only and correct way. After all, we run the risk that, with such a blatant approach in which we consider every transaction as equal, we reward the loyal customers who come often and spend a lot, too little, while the bad customers, who do not come often and spend very little, are given too many advantages. Perhaps an approach aimed at retaining the good customers (*retention strategy*) is more useful than the usual approach aimed at attracting new customers (*domination strategy*). American research has shown that, in many cases, it is much more profitable to invest in retaining existing customers than in winning new customers (see example 15.5).

Retention strategy

Domination strategy

EXAMPLE 15.5

If a company was to generate a sales of €100 billion. This sales is generated because the company has a customer base of one million customers, who visit the store on average two times a year. €50 is spent per visit. It was found that repeat visits amount to 80%. This means that, out of every one hundred customers from the customer base, about twenty fall away after every visit (either due to objective reasons, such as relocation or death, or from subjective considerations: one is not satisfied). With a rectilinear extrapolation, this 80% 'retention rate' implies that the original customer base has disappeared completely after about five visits (thus at a visiting frequency of twice a year: after two and a half years). The average 'sales value' of a customer during his lifetime is therefore 250, or rather a revenue value with a margin of 40% of €100 billion.

This company has been trying to increase the 'retention ratio' from 80% to 90%. The involved program (aimed at increasing the customer satisfaction), is accompanied by the significant investment of €50 billion. Assuming that the approach succeeds, we find that only 10% falls away after every visit. With a visiting frequency of twice a year, this means that the customer base no longer disappears after two and a half years, but only after five years. The sales value and the revenue value of the customer have doubled: Instead of €250 sales, it becomes €500 sales per customer. Instead of €100 revenue, it becomes €200 revenue per customer. For the total customer base, this is therefore €200 billion. The proceeds from the investment of €50 billion for increasing customer satisfaction produce revenue of €100 billion in five years: an ROI of 200%.

Loyalty cards from various retailers

Although example 15.2 is a simplified example, the message will be clear. Minor improvements in the retention ratio can greatly improve profitability. The above obviously does not mean that nothing should be done at all about domination strategies. After all, even in the example one should still ensure that the decay of the customer base is supplemented. It does mean that retail should pay relatively more attention to retaining good customers than is currently the case. This requires a more nuanced approach than simply striving for as many transactions as possible.

This is why more and more retail companies are making use of the so-called *loyalty programs*, aimed at identifying customers that are worth retaining. In practice, this often comes down to analyzing the existing customer base. It this case it rather involves a pragmatic segmentation afterwards than a deliberate choice for specific market segments in advance.

Loyalty programs

15.6.2   Segmentation of existing customer groups

Retention strategies are expensive. It is therefore important to use the investments involved with retention strategies correctly. Retain quality customers rather than low value customers. We therefore have to achieve a segmentation of our existing customer base in good and bad customers to know where to invest. A good customer is defined as a customer who contributes a lot of sales during his lifetime, a bad customer is one that contributes little sales.

The model $S = CA \times VI \times C \times AT$ discussed in chapter 11 is a possibility to create a segmentation of the existing customer base in the above described terms of good or bad customers. Supplemented with the details from the loyalty system (it is possible to register how often a customer visits and how much he spends each time), it is then possible to make a classification of the existing customers based on their value to the retailer. If we take the example of the visitors index as an indication for the interest that the visitor has in the relevant store concept, and the conversion as an indication of the propensity to buy, and we rank the visitors according to these two criteria, we get a customer segmentation matrix with four fields, as can be seen in figure 15.4.

The core-customer matrix consists of the following four fields:

1 Core customers: these are customers that visit the relevant store much and often (that are attracted by the concept), but – when they visit – also spend a lot of money (thus they are also attracted by the selection). It is for these core customers that we built the concept and these are the very core customers who qualify for retention strategies.

2 Loyal budget customers: these are customers that visit much and often, but who do not buy very much when they are in the store. These are customers that are attracted by the concept, but – probably due to budget restrictions – cannot buy as much as they may want to. This group is often very similar to the core customer, but have a lower income or still have smaller children. In time, these customers may become core customers. These customers also qualify for retention, but have – at least for the short term – a lower priority than the core customers.

FIGURE 15.4 The core-customer matrix

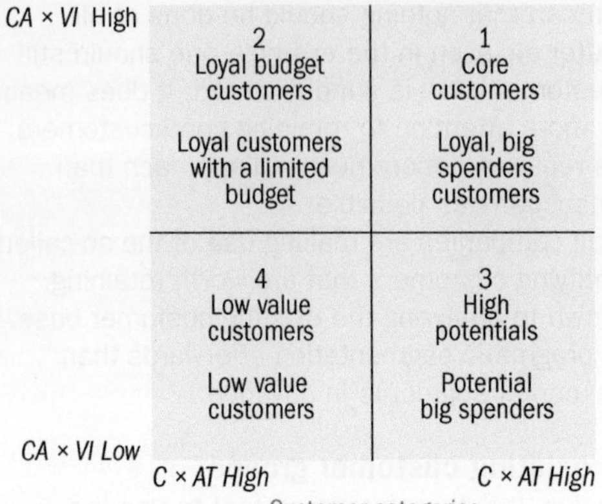

$CA \times VI$ High

2 Loyal budget customers Loyal customers with a limited budget	**1** Core customers Loyal, big spenders customers
4 Low value customers Low value customers	**3** High potentials Potential big spenders

$CA \times VI$ Low

$C \times AT$ High $C \times AT$ High

Customer categories

3 High potentials: these are customers who visit the store very rarely, but – when they do – they buy a lot. These customers probably do not find it an attractive store, but have considerable resources. This is the group on which many retailers focus on with domination strategies. However, if the domination is successful, it is probably a Pyrrhic victory: the high potentials are – as long as the formula is not adapted to their needs – by definition disloyal.

4 Low value customers: these are customers that do not visit often, and – when they visit – also spend very little. This is the group of customers for whom the store formula was in any case not developed. This often involves bargain hunters who constantly 'shop around' and can almost never be hooked, unless it is through a permanent flow of push-marketing-like actions. It is then regrettable to establish that promotions, aimed at winning new customers, often causes this group to grow.

After identifying the four groups, the company should analyse the needs and characteristics of the groups. The earlier described *importance/performance mapping* (see paragraph 9.9) can be helpful here. It will often turn out that this identification of needs and characteristics provides significant differences between the groups.

Example 15.6 uses the model $S = CA \times VI \times C \times AT$.

EXAMPLE 15.6 TRAVEL AND TOURISM

Under travel and tourism, we generally understand two groups of companies: tour operators (manufacturer) and travel agencies (retailers). Travel agencies are in the same circumstances as goods retail: there is strong competition (especially because of the forward integration of the tour operators), the margins are low and the costs increase every year. The effect of the scissor is also felt in this sector. In order to survive, it is necessary for a constant growth of sales. The ANVR (the umbrella organisation) therefore commissioned a study into the possibilities to increase the market share of travel agencies in the total travel sales, which was 30% at the time of the study. The ANVR used the above described model for the analysis. Holidaymakers were classified based on two criteria:

- *Booking behaviour*: the population was divided into people that said that they always use travel agencies when booking holidays (*CA × VI* high) and people that said that they always book their vacation themselves (*CA × VI* low).
- *Holiday frequency*: On the one hand there are people who said that they go on holiday twice per year (*C × AT* high), on the other hand there are people who go on holiday less than twice a year (*C × AT* low).

The analysis shows that the number of loyal, big spending customers of travel agencies is only a limited number of all holidaymakers, namely only 10%. *Loyal budget customers*, who use travel agencies wherever possible, consist of about 25% of all holidaymakers. From this perspective it would certainly be possible to increase the market share of travel agencies in the overall holiday market, mainly by operating the *high potentials segments* (24% of the number of vacationers) and *low value customers* (45% of the number of vacationers). However, further identification teaches us that the four groups showed significant differences in terms of purchase behaviour (see figure 1).

FIGURE 1 The product sales of the customer group

Vacation destinations in Europe

Through travel agency	LBC 21%		10% Core	
	Spain	220	Canary islands	500
	Canary islands	200	Greece	200
	Greece	200	England	200
			Spain	180
	Germany	72		
	France	67		
	Belgium/Luxemburg	77	France	73
	The Netherlands	128	Austria	185
			France	160
	Greece	50	England	125
	Austria	71	Belgium/Luxemburg	110
	France	93		
	Spain	40	Canary islands	50
			Greece	75
			Spain	40
Do it themselves	LVC 45%		24% HP	
	Very little vacation		A lot of vacation	

To customer characteristics

* Read: core customers choose 5 × as often for Canary islands on average

Loyal budget customers and core customers displayed a strong preference for the popular vacation destinations such as the Canary Islands and Spain, while they chose considerably less than average for the closer destinations in Europe. The behaviour of the high potentials appeared to be exactly the opposite:
a relative rejection of the popular vacation destinations and a strong preference for countries like England, France and Belgium. So if we want to look at the growth of the high potentials, this implies a reconsideration of the product offer (product development in the sense of Ansoff). The low value customer, finally, showed an entirely different behaviour, namely a strong preference for camping holidays in the Netherlands, a market that is actually not covered by the Dutch travel agencies at all. The lesson to be learnt here is that the general problem of developing a growth strategy for travel agencies, with further analysis of the customer segments, seems to fall apart in at least three secondary issues. For high potentials, we will have to do product development, for low value customers, will have to do market development and for loyal budget customers, we will have to do further market penetration.

Summary

Target groups are becoming increasingly more difficult to identify. However, this does not mean that one cannot use segmentation in retail. Unlike in the past, traditional socio-demographic segmentation is no longer used to define actual target groups, but rather to apply focus in the retail concept. We can use area-specific segmentation for both target marketing and concept development.
We have discussed two segmentation strategies: the a-priori-segmentation and the so-called ex-post-variation.
Market segments must fulfil four criteria, in order to render the segmentation at least operational:
- heterogeneity of needs:
- measurability of the segment;
- approachability of the segment;
- adequate size.

Segmentation can be done based on different criteria. There is no unambiguous criteria that can be used for all situations: *different segmentation for different needs*. In this chapter, we discussed a number of segment criteria: geographic segmentation, demographic segmentation, psychographic segmentation and domain-specific segmentation. The last form of segmentation, we discussed in slightly more detail, because it offers some pointers for the operation and positioning of a retailer.
In a situation of displacement marketing, it is important to retain loyal customers (core customers). Retention strategies should therefore be used. Using the retail monitor formula discussed in chapter 11, it seems possible to establish a pragmatic segmentation of the existing customer base that can be helpful with such retention strategies.

16
Product or product range

16.1   Importance of the product range
16.2   Hierarchy in the product range structure
16.3   Width and depth of product ranges
16.4   Structure of product categories
16.5   Product range structure according to the significance to the formula
16.6   Influence of the product range on the operation

The product range, in combination with the choice of the target group, is the most important marketing mix variable for retail. To some extent, this decision determines what one wants to offer as a retailer (the product range) and to whom (the target group or the choice of purchase moments) predominantly the choice for the other marketing mix variables: the choice of a very fashionable women's clothing range for the happy few almost automatically implies a location in an expensive shopping street, high prices, high operating level and a luxury store layout. The choice of a range of food and beverages for the daily purchase moment, almost automatically implies a location in the vicinity of the customers, a fixed layout of the store with fixed shelf positions, self-service and a high level of attendance. These subjects are discussed in this chapter.

16.1 Importance of the product range

Figure 16.1 shows the position of the product (or product range) in the strategic process.

FIGURE 16.1 The strategic process: the product (product range)

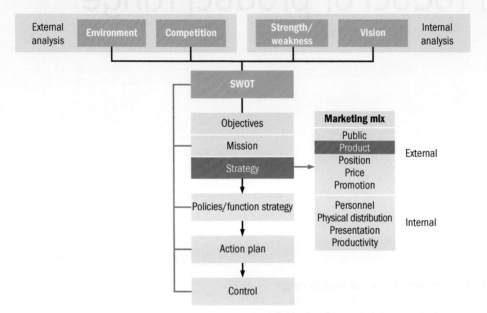

The product range (Verhage, 2010) is not only the most important marketing mix variable, but also one of the most difficult, in terms of policy formulation and implementation. First, because the product range image directly affects the positioning of the store formula. Secondly, because the product range needs to be continuously – as a result of changes in consumer demand – adjusted. Even in a relatively stable sector, such as that of food and beverages, we see that product ranges are entirely renewed within a period of four to five years (a product range loop of 0.2 to 0.25). In the fashion industry, this product range sales rate can even be as high as 6 to 8: in this sector, product ranges are sometimes entirely reconstituted once every one and a half to two months.

Because of the strategic importance of the product range as part of the formula, much attention was given to this marketing mix variable in the previous chapters. The developments in retail are discussed partly on the basis of the changing product range philosophy (from sector or product oriented to demand or sales relationship oriented product ranges). The classification of retail is partly discussed based on sorting per product range (daily/non-daily, convenience goods/shopping goods/specialty goods and goods categories). In the strengths and weaknesses analysis, the product range was discussed extensively, both from the perspective of return (goldmine and DPP) and from the perspective of the product range portfolio (ADM) and the operation of the branches.

Nevertheless, it is still necessary for the translation of the situation analysis in the policy, to once again pay attention to this part of the marketing mix. We specifically discuss a number of concepts associated with the product range sorting policy.

16.2 Hierarchy in the product range structure

Under *product range* we understand 'the totality of the number of different products or SKU's (*stock keeping units*) that a retailer offers'. The product range can be divided into *product range groups* or *sub product ranges*. These are collections of products that either contain the same consumer needs (such as the baby department in a department store, which contains clothing, furniture and baby toys), or are product related (the tools department in a builders market which contains saws, hammers and pliers). Here we see one of the dilemmas that occur in the product range policy. How do you organise the product range? And by extension, which purchasing organisation do you choose? And for which store presentation: demand relationship or product relationship?

There are no clear answers. Stores that focus on *high involvement fun shopping* will generally have a preference for an organisation in need categories. Stores that focus on *low involvement run shopping* will be more inclined to choose an organisation based on product relationship. Incidentally, all possible intermediate forms occur.

Determining the number of and the classification of the product range groups is very important for the image that the store evokes with the consumer. A consumer's first impression when entering a store is predominantly determined by what is offered. And once again, the first impression depends strongly on the logical classification, visibility and findability of the sub product ranges.

Product range groups or sub product ranges can be divided into *product groups*: parts of product range groups that are clustered from sales considerations (visibility or demand relationship for the consumer) or purchase considerations (corresponding suppliers). Thus the product group 'household textile' is often treated as a separate department in a supermarket. First, because the consumer expects to find these products together, secondly, because the technical characteristics of the product group (lower sales rate, other top-up techniques, other suppliers) makes this necessary.

Product groups are divided into *product types* or *product categories*, the lowest interpretation level of the consumer needs. Within the product range of a DIY market, we distinguish between the sub product ranges of tools, building materials, decorative products and electric appliances. Within the sub product range of decorative products, we distinguish between the product groups of paint, wall paper and curtains. Within the product group of paint, the product types can be classified in different ways: one can distinguish between high gloss, satin or matt. We can also distinguish between colours or price classes. Once again, the retailer is often faced with a dilemma. They need to determine, per product group, based on which selection criteria the consumer makes his choice. The selection criteria may vary per product type. Furthermore, the selection criteria may sometimes conflict with the need for clarity. In the abovementioned example of purchasing paint, it seems rather clear that the primary selection criteria will be

Product range

Product range groups

Sub product ranges

16

High involvement fun shopping

Low involvement run shopping

Product groups

Product types

Product categories

colour, or rather that this is usually the answer when we ask consumers how they choose paint. When following the consumer in his selection in the store, the situation seems to be entirely different: the primary selection criterion for the consumer does not appear to be colour, but rather the application: wall paint, lacquer or outdoor paint. Only then they will choose by colour. Placing together all variations of red in a shelf (interior/exterior, acrylic/latex, Histor/Sigma, matt/high gloss), leads to an extremely obscure selection for the consumer. The retailer often needs to find compromises.

Product variations

The lowest level in the product range is formed by the *product variations*: the number of different products that is offered within a product type. Within the product type of 'cat food', for example, one can choose between the products Whiskas salmon and Felix beef. It is at this level that the consumer ultimately comes to converting the original need into an actual product choice. Figure 16.2 shows an example of the structure of a product range.

FIGURE 16.2 Example of a structure of a range

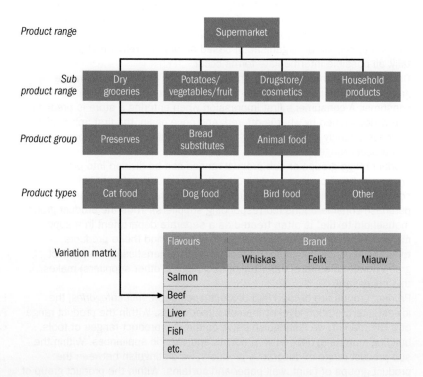

16.3 Width and depth of product range

In practice, it is not easy to consistently classify the product ranges into product range groups, product groups, product types and product variations. The distinction between a product range group and a product group is not always hard to make, just as the distinction between a product type and a product variation. It often seems that it is not as important. If only we agree on what belongs to groups and what belongs to types, then we know what we have and we can get started. On the one hand, the distinction between product range groups and product groups is particularly important, and on the other hand, product types and product variations. The first two (product range groups and product groups) in fact determine the *width of the product range selection*, the last two (product types and product variations) the *depth of the product range selection.*

Width of the product range selection

The width of the product range is generally defined as 'the number of different needs that the retailer covers for the consumer' and is determined by the number of product range groups and product groups.

Depth of the product range selection

The depth of the product range is generally defined as 'the choice that is offered within a specific need category' and is determined by the number of product types and variations.

The ratio between the width and the depth largely determines the type of selection (see figure 16.3). A store with a limited range (which caters for very few needs), but with a great depth (which offers many choices within the limited demand) may, as a whole, have an equally large product range as a store with a large range (many needs) but a limited depth (limited choice). In the first case we are dealing with a (super) specialist, in the second case with a parallelised operation (supermarket or department store). All intermediate forms may also exist.

FIGURE 16.3 The connection between width and depth of the product range and the selections of formulas

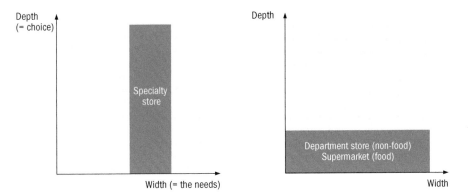

16.4 Structure of product categories

The technical structure of a product range must be completed from a product range philosophy on the level of product categories. A correct technical-administrative division of the product range would after all not mean that the structure is also transparent to the consumer. We will now discuss the pyramid position and significance of the private label.

16.4.1   Pyramid

Product categories are assembled to offer the consumer a selection within a sub product range. An important criterion is the value for money of what is offered. This is actually another important difference with manufacturers.

They will often focus their brand on clear value for money, while retailers within a product category will try to fill several value for money levels. For example, the Douwe Egberts brand represents a certain level of quality, the Kanis & Gunnink brand another. Within the retail sector, both brands appear on the shelf. When providing insight into this choice, we often use the so-called *selection pyramid* (see figure 16.4). The basic shape of the pyramid is a triangle, divided into three layers. The bottom layer reflects the basic package (often cheap with little added value), the middle layer concerns the actual 'formula package' (containing products which, in terms of value for money, are on the exact level that is intended with the formula) and the upper layer reflects the 'image package' (often high-quality, expensive products or brands, that are used to emphasise the quality image of the formula).

Selection pyramid

FIGURE 16.4 The selection pyramid

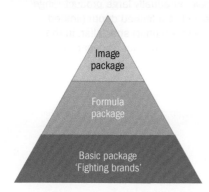

The operation of the pyramid can be illustrated using the brands structure of supermarket product groups. At the top of the pyramid, we find the so-called *A brands* and *premium brands*. For example, in the 'beer' product group, we have Grolsch and Carlsberg, in the 'coffee' product group we have Douwe Egberts. Due to the strong position of these brands, relatively low margins are made on these products: the premium brand image comes from the manufacturer and not from the retailer.

A brands
Premium brands

In the middle, we find the *B brands*: products of a very decent quality, but weaker in terms of brand image than the A-brands. In beer, for example, we find Amstel and in coffee, we find Van Nelle. The margin for the retailer is more attractive than with the A-brands. Therefore, retailers will generally try to promote these products, at the expense of the A-brands. The battle in the supply chain between strong manufacturers of A-brands and the retailer often takes place on the dividing line between the top and the middle of the pyramid.

B brands

At the bottom, we find the *C brands*, brands with a relatively low quality image, but cheap. These products are often used to improve the affordability-image of the retailer. These are fighting brands. They are used as weapons in the battle at the bottom of the supply chain, between retailers. Depending on the product range philosophy of the supply formula, the original pyramidal structure will vary. A discounter will generally focus on the structure at the bottom of the pyramid. A fun shopping department store such as de Bijenkorf will focus on the (top of the) middle layer

C brands

and the top of the pyramid. A company like Maison de Bonnetterie will focus specifically on the top of the pyramid.

The shape of the pyramid is also influenced by the product market. Markets of difficult products in which the high-involvement character is high, so that brands play an important role, will have a layout in which the upper and middle layer are strongly represented. An example is the hi-fi market. While markets of simple, low involvement products will often have a structure which focuses more on the lower side of the pyramid (see figure 16.5).

FIGURE 16.5 The product range pyramid in the high-involvement market for hi-fi

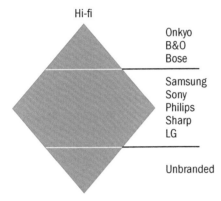

16.4.2 **Place and significance of the private label**

With the sorting per product range of a large number of retailers, the *private label* plays an important role. Private label include all brands that appear exclusively within the product range of a certain retailer or group of retailers. The reason for the popularity of private labels with the retailers is two-fold. On the one hand it is possible to distinguish between the private labels in terms of direct competitors, which can lead to customer loyalty. On the other hand, private labels also have advantages for retailers in terms of margin: the brand image premium need not be relinquished to the manufacturer, but can remain within the retail organisation. In recent years, private labels have increased in popularity, especially in the supermarket sector. The proportion of private label products in this sector is approximately a quarter of the total number of products. In addition, supermarket organisations are increasingly trying to enter the premium segment, with luxury private labels, such as Excellent by Albert Heijn, Exclusief by Jumbo or Superieur by Super de Boer. In parlance, private labels are often put in one box. Within private labels, however, we distinguish between at least three categories:

- *Generics/white brands*: these are 'unbranded' products, often in product categories where brand preference hardly plays an important role. It often involves *commodity products,* such as toilet paper and dishwashing brushes. The most important USP of these generics is the low price. The argument is often that the lack of promotion and the simple packaging make it possible to sell these products for less than the better known brands. Generics are therefore always at the bottom of the pyramid. They specifically compete with the C-brands and are mainly used as a weapon in a battle between retailers.

Margin notes: Private label · Generics/white brands

Fancy brands

- *Fancy brands*: fancy brands include the products that we only find at a certain retailer, but of which the name has no direct connection to the retailer. The lack of direct connection to the retailer often involves the fact that the retailer does not (yet) dare to make this connection, because its retail image is not favourable. Applying the store name could then lead to consumers hesitating about the expected quality. Using a fancy name may overcome this hesitation. Aldi initially grouped all its products under fancy brands. Only later, after Aldi's quality image had been anchored, did Aldi dare to introduce a large number of products under the brand name Aldi. The price level of fancy brands is usually the same as the level of the cheaper B brands and therefore located at the bottom of the middle part of the pyramid.

Store brands
Product lines

- *Store brands*: this includes products, usually organised in coherent *product lines*, in which there is a direct connection between the brand name and the store. Often (but not always), the store name is also the brand name and is therefore an important component in building the store image: the store as brand. This connection means that the store brand, in terms of quality, price and taste, must meet all requirements which the formula brings with it. From this consideration, the store brand is usually positioned at the top of the middle part of the pyramid and thereby competes directly with the A brands. More and more retailers are placing increasingly larger parts of their product range under their own store brand, in order to become more independent of their manufacturers. Examples of store brands are HEMA, Albert Heijn, The Body Shop, IKEA and ZARA. We provide two examples where the private label plays a role (examples 16.1 and 16.2).

The private label of Plus

EXAMPLE 16.1 NEW FORM OF PRIVATE LABELS

In 2007 the Ahold Coffee Company, the coffee roasting company of Ahold (mother company of amongst other Albert Heijn), introduced a new brand: puC. PuC is first of all a coffee pad machine (like a Senseo machine) that can also make cappuccino using special cups. The coffee machine can be purchased from Albert Heijn and C1000, but also from Blokker and Marskramer (both part of the Blokker group). But the puC brand is also found on the cappuccino cups and different types of coffee pads that are used in the machine, and these can also be purchased from AH, C1000, Blokker and Marskramer. The result is thus essentially a private label which, however, is offered by various formulas both inside and outside the Ahold group.

EXAMPLE 16.2 PRIVATE LABELS AT ALBERT HEIJN

Over the years, Albert Heijn has developed a wide range of private labels. The AH Basic brand has been part of the range for years, the result of a collaboration between a number of large European supermarket organisations. With the AH Basic product range, Albert Heijn wants to prove that one does not have to go to Aldi or Lidl for rock-bottom prices. The Albert Heijn private label is positioned next to the big brands. The products are of comparable quality, but just slightly cheaper. At the top of the choice pyramid, Albert Heijn has the premium label Excellent, with high quality products and a special culinary twist *(moment of indulgence)*. In addition, there is also a special private label variation, AH Biologisch [AH Organic]: products for which no fertiliser or chemical pesticides are used, free of chemical and synthetic supplements and produced in an animal friendly way. AH thereby covers the entire selection pyramid with four private label variations (see figure 1).

FIGURE 1 Selection pyramid private label variations AH

Opbouw private label portfolio	Albert Heijn	Voorbeeld pindakaas	
Premium PL	Excellent Om intens van te genieten		price index 367
Special PL	Biologisch Eerlijk en puur		price index 223
Regular PL	Albert Heijn AH kwaliteit altijd voordelig		price index 100
Discount PL	Voor de allerkleinste prijsjes		price index 62

Source: EFMI, 2006

16

Store brand becomes brand: Starbucks coffee is now also available on American supermarket shelves

Source: EFMI, 2006

16.5 Product range structure according to the significance to the formula

A distinction that is very relevant for the structure of the product range is that between core product range, secondary product range and additional product range. We will discuss this in more detail. We will also explore the roles of product range groups. Finally, we will discuss the connection with the assortment dominance matrix.

16.5.1 Core product range, secondary product range, additional product range

Core product range

Under *core product range* we understand that part of the product range that is absolutely necessary to maintain the formula image. The core product range is therefore the total number of SKU's that the consumer expects to at least find in the formula: it is the lower limit of the sorting per product range. A shoe store that does not include shoes in their product range will not be visited by shoe shoppers.

Secondary product range

The core product range is supplemented with the *secondary product range*: products that are not necessary for the primary formula (shoe store), but that can strengthen the formula because of their affinity with the core product range (good shoe store). In the example of the shoe store, it involves the service product package of shoelaces, shoe polish, insoles and shoe horns.

Additional product range

Finally, we also have the *additional product range*: products that have absolutely no significance to the formula, but that may be important for the success of the operation. These products will often produce an attractive return (profit increasing products, often found in the bottom right corner of the goldmine analysis discussed in paragraph 12.7) or promotional products which may (temporarily) increase the visitors index. Examples of the last category are the non-food product ranges of Aldi or Lidl and the range of bicycles or microwave ovens in an advertisement of a DIY store (see example 16.3).

EXAMPLE 16.3 ALDI AND KRUIDVAT

Aldi saves a space in every advertisement for a box in which they feature a varying selection of non-food products, at very competitive prices. These products are not part of Aldi's core product range, which, after all, consists of a limited selection of products in the area of storable food and beverages. Nor is it part of Aldi's secondary product range: the non-food products are often in no way related to the core product range.

Aldi uses this selection mainly to attract customer groups, which are not attracted by the formula, to the store in the hope that the occasional visit for 'non-branch related' products will lead to a repeat visit for the core product range. Aldi is especially successful in this: not only has this resulted in Aldi becoming a market leader in Germany in certain hardware groups (in the market for cameras, for example, Aldi functions as a *category killer* and, as a result, has since become market leader), but Aldi has also devel-

oped a gradual expansion of the target group of the poorer bottom layer of the population to include the total population.

Kruidvat is now operating in a similar strategy from similar considerations. Kruidvat was known as *drugstore/cosmetics discounter* and therefore operated at the bottom end of the market. In order to reach a portion of the top, which traditionally visited Etos or DA, Kruidvat developed a product range of highly discounted deals in the segment 'CD's with classical music'. They have been extremely successful and classical music lovers are no longer ashamed to admit that they have Bach collection consisting out of Kruidvat CD's. In the meantime, one can now buy laptops, DVD-players, camping accessories, deep-fryers and photo cameras from Kruidvat, depending on the applicable special offers.

At Kruidvat one can purchase many products that do not fall under the drugmetics-product range, such as laptops, DVD-players and CDs

16.5.2 Destination, preferred, convenience, seasonal destination and seasonal convenience

From the perspective of the product range structure, also known as category management (see sub-paragraphs 7.3.6 and 20.2.2), we look at the different roles that product range groups and products have within the groups. Based on this, we can define five roles: *destination, preferred, convenience, seasonal destination and seasonal convenience*. Products are classified into these category roles based on the importance to the consumer, importance to the formula and market opportunities.

Destination

Destination is a category in which the retailer wants to present himself according to his primary target group and will distinguish itself from the competition. The retailer wants to be the best in product range, promotion, pricing and merchandising and expects to score better than the fair share (compared to the market). A *destination* category gets more shelf space, promotional activities, has a wider range, but also gets more attention at the operational level (for example topping up). Examples of *destination* product ranges are wine at Albert Heijn and meat at C1000. The same applies for *seasonal destination* as for a *destination*, category, but the product range group only has a temporary character. Examples include special, luxury holiday product ranges at Albert Heijn (often from Excellent) or Plus (often of the luxury private label Appetit).

Seasonal destination

Preferred category

A *preferred category* provides for the daily needs of the consumer. In this category, the retailer wants to deliver a consistent quality and be competitive in the price aspect. This may involve a high promotional pressure. The product range is wide, but not complete. This category provides the largest part of the sales and the retailer wants to at least achieve its fair share. Examples of *preferred* categories are beer and cold drinks at C1000.

Convenience category

A *convenience category* makes it possible for customers to purchase all the necessary products in a single visit to the store, the so-called one-stop-shopping. The retailers' objective is to ensure that the primary target group can find all its daily groceries in one store, in which the retailer suffices with a minimal product range at non-competitive prices. Generally, these categories receive less attention in the area of purchasing, logistics, shelf room and promotional support. In that case the retailer does not expect to achieve his fair share. Examples include stationary and clothespins at most supermarket organisations. There are also *seasonal-convenience* categories: these are *convenience* groups that have a temporary nature. One example is the summer BBQ product range at C1000 or Plus.

16.5.3 Connection with the assortment dominance matrix

The classification into core, secondary and additional product range is partly consistent with the significance of the quadrants in the assortment dominance matrix (ADM) which is discussed in chapter 12. In addition, we must realise that the classification into core and secondary product ranges is used for the *ex ante* structure of the product range (the *target*-situation) while the assortment dominance matrix is rather used for the ex post observation of how consumers react to what is offered (the *1st* situation). We then see the following relationship: core product ranges are the essence of what is offered. Core product ranges should generate sufficient sales for a profitable operation and therefore often involves major market segments. In addition, they serve as a recognition for the consumer of the formula and should therefore – if we do it right – represent relatively higher sales than secondary or additional product ranges. The analogy with the *anchor product ranges* or *cherish groups* from the ADM are obvious: the anchor product ranges relate to large market segments, in which a higher than average market share is achieved. The *ex ante defined core product ranges would then preferably have to correspond with the ex post* established anchor product ranges.

Anchor product ranges

Cherish groups

We expect the *ex ante* defined secondary product ranges in the ADM *ex post* especially in the upper left quadrant. After all, the secondary product range often concerns (and certainly if the service product range is involved) relatively small market segments that exhibit demand relationships with the core product range. Therefore it should score above average in terms of market share, because they would have to follow in the core product range. Similarly, one would expect to find the additional product ranges, that are used to increase profit (not an essential part of the formula, often referring to uncompetitive and therefore relatively small markets), in the lower left quadrant. Additional product ranges that are used from the perspective of increasing the visitors index (many interested consumers therefore often large markets, and temporary offer from the supplier therefore a relatively low market share), will be found specifically in the lower right quadrant. Parallels can also be drawn in the product range classification according to *(seasonal) destination, preferred* and *(seasonal) convenience* with the assortment dominance matrix (ADM). The *destination* category is the image-enhancing group that one expects to find in the upper left quadrant: it is a category in which the retailer is specialised with a fair share that is significantly higher than one (the market share in this category is higher than the overall market share of the retailer). One expects to find the *preferred* categories in the upper right quadrant of the ADM: sales + recognition/cherish. The retailer draws the bulk of his sales from this and fulfils the daily needs of the consumer. The *convenience* categories can be both 'question marks' and 'opportunities', respectively the lower left and right quadrants, with the difference that they are not always considered by the retailer as question marks or opportunities. It can involve both large and the small markets, but the retailer usually has no ambition to increase the market share in these groups, given the function of the convenience product range.

16.5.4 Product range and no compromise game

The no compromise game-theory of Eysink Smeets, discussed in chapter 9, can also be applied to product ranges. The added value is compared on the horizontal axis from low to high. The price perception is compared on the vertical axis from low to high. In figure 16.6, we show the no compromise product range matrix. We can indicate, in the matrix, how the product ranges of retailers can be classified across the various levels. Here you can see where the different types of classifications of the products are positioned. In figure 16.7 we have plotted several products of Albert Heijn in the same matrix. It is clearly visible that an ever increasing part of the product range is filled by the retailers themselves.

FIGURE 16.6 The no compromise product range matrix

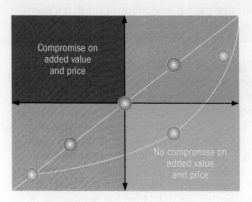

FIGURE 16.7 The no compromise product range matrix for AH

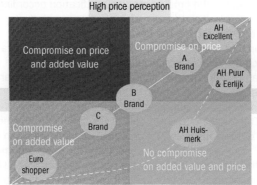

16.6 Influence of the product range on the operation

The choice for the size of the product range has a direct impact on the outcome of the operation of the retailer. The size of the product range determines the requirements that need to be placed on the surface of the store and thus to a large extent the level of the fixed costs (rent, layout). After all, product ranges that we cannot show you will not be sold: each SKU must have a place in the store (see figure 16.8).

Secondly, a comprehensive product range will automatically lead to high stocks and a relatively low sales rate. Thereby, the product range also has a direct impact on the level of the costs of the variable assets. It is therefore important to involve the impact thereof on the cost structure in every product range decision.

FIGURE 16.8 The relationship between product range size, sales rate and gross margin

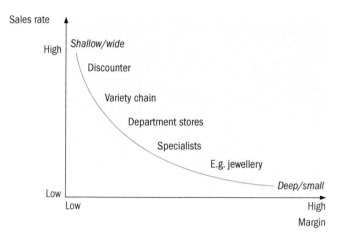

16

Summary

The P of product (or offered product range) is, in the modern concept of retailing as *demand satisfying process*, one of the most important marketing mix variables for retail. It is therefore that, even as result of the increasing product range sales rate, much attention should be paid to the technique of the product range structure.

We can consider this technical structure of the product range from various different perspectives:

- the level of detail: product range, sub product ranges, product groups, product variations;
- the quality construction: the product range pyramid, A brands and premium brands, B brands and C brands (fighting brands);
- the degree of specialisation: wide and shallow for parallelised, non-specialist suppliers, and small and deep for specialists;
- the degree of contribution to the store's image: private labels;
- the degree of contribution to the formula strength: core product range, secondary product range and additional product range;
- the degree of category role: destination, preferred, convenience, seasonal destination and seasonal convenience.

Especially the classification into core product range, secondary product range and additional product range appears to exhibit a consistency with the assortment dominance matrix (ADM) discussed in chapter 12.

The composition of the product range, finally, appears to be directly connected with a number of operational aspects such as sales rate, inventory costs and size of the store.

17
Location of the establishment

In this chapter, we discuss the location of the establishment, choice of the location, location theories: the macro approach, the store selection models: the micro approach and the marketing mix variable 'location' with existing branches.
We show the position of the 'location' element in the strategic process, and we discuss the so-called location theories or gravitation models.

17.1 The choice of location

Figure 17.1 shows where the 'location' element is positioned in the strategic process.

FIGURE 17.1 The strategic process: location of the establishment

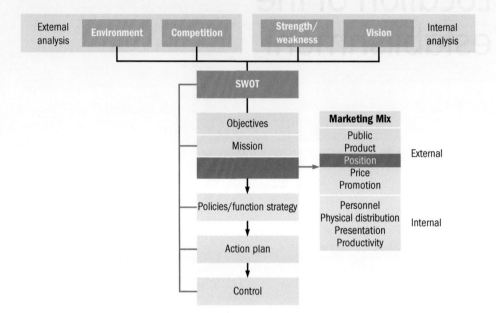

There is no subject on the field of retail that has been written about as much as the choice of location. This is also understandable, because before, when the function of retail solely concerned the distribution (redistribution), the choice of location was the most important decision that a retailer could make. There was a vertical price maintenance, which made the marketing mix variable 'price' barely manageable for the retailer, while the often product oriented product ranges were barely distinguishable from each other. Therefore, the choice of location is actually the only – and at least the most important – factor of the external marketing mix that could be influenced by the retailer himself. The choice of location directly affects the number of customers that visit the store and thereby the sales of the company.

The choice of location was also of great importance for the cost structure of the retailer. Concentration trends did not yet play a major role. Most of the stores were organisations with only one outlet. The labour costs were of relatively minor significance in that situation. Not only the wages were low, a large portion of the work was also performed by the owner and his family. The most important cost for a retailer was not, as currently, the labour costs, but the costs of renting or owning the store.

17

Today, the importance of the location in the marketing mix of the retailer is slightly less than in the past, though still large.

From the demand side, this is caused by the consumer having more demands from a store than just the proximity: the customer is sometimes willing to sacrifice the advantage of proximity of a store if there are other advantages (such as a wider product range, better service and lower prices) in return. Increased mobility strongly contributes to this.

From the supply side, the phenomenon plays a role in the development of the formula: it turns out that a good formula can develop autonomous attraction, reducing the direct dependence of the location.

Nevertheless, the choice of location remains important, even today, at least for the retailers in the *low involvement* segment, daily groceries range, in which the *convenience* aspect (proximity and accessibility) plays a major role. The choice of location, however, is relatively easy with these companies: make sure that you are as close as possible to the consumer. The choice of location for companies in the non-daily sector, however, in which many factors other than simply convenience are often important, is a much more complicated affair. Because this book was written to do justice to the non-food sector, it seems useful to pay attention to the developments in the field of location theories, even though the importance of the choice of location is decreasing in the overall marketing mix.

Figure 17.2 compares the shopping behaviour (demand side) and formula distinction (supply side) to each other. The classic P of position (location), in the sense of 'find the location which is surrounded by the most consumers' specifically applies in the lower left corner of the figure. In stores with very little formula distinction, but which are intentionally visited (upper left, DIY markets, furniture boulevards, garden centres) we see that a part of the importance of the P of position (location) is taken over by the P of promotion. In stores with a strong formula distinction, but with grocery-like behaviour, we see that they often seek locations that lie in high passer-by zones. This is where the P of position loses importance to the P of public. Finally: in the upper right corner (strong formula distinction and targeted purchasing behaviour), the importance of location is the least important. The product that these formulas put in the market for the target group is so strong, that the consumer is willing to overcome many barriers. The P of position therefore loses to the P of product. A condition for this is that there is parking (in the vicinity).

FIGURE 17.2 The declining importance of the P of position through the increased mobility and formula development

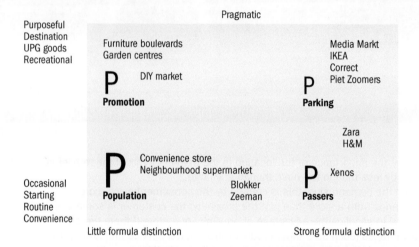

17.2 Location theories: the macro approach

Gravitation models

Most retail location theories (Graig, 1984) are, in some way, based on *gravitation models*, derived from the well-known Newton's law of gravity. We will discuss this in more detail. We discuss Reilly's law and Christaller's theory. Finally, we will discuss the hierarchy in the construction of retail facilities.

17.2.1   Gravitational models

Newton's law of gravity claims that two objects attract each other with a force that is directly proportional to the product of their masses, and inversely proportional to the square of their distance. Translated into retail: the attraction that a shopping area exerts on a consumer is positively influenced by the size of the selection and negatively by the distance from the consumer's home to the shopping area, a very recognisable situation in practice. Assuming that the selection is greater as the population in the immediate vicinity is larger, the simple gravitation models used, as approach of the environment of the selection, the population size of the city or the district. This could be an explanation of the distribution of stores (concentrations), in which only two variables played a role: (1) the size of the population and (2) the distance.

17.2.2   Reilly's law (1929)

The (too) simple gravitation law described in sub-paragraph 17.2.1 was subsequently differentiated by a number of writers, including William Reilly. The purpose of *Reilly's law of retail gravitation* (see figure 17.3) was primarily providing an explanation for the size of the catchment area of a store (concentration).

Reilly's law of retail gravitation

FIGURE 17.3 Reilly's law

City A
90,000
population

15 km

Point of indifference

5 km

City B
10,000
population

Source: Berman, Evans: *Retail management*

Reilly tried to find a point where consumers, given their place of residence, were indifferent in their choice between either one or the other store location. The analogy with Newton's gravitation law is again clear: Newton defined the *point of indifference* as the point where the attraction that two objects (in this case two store locations) exert on a third (in this case the consumer), is equal.

Point of indifference

The collection of all points of indifference collectively forms the demarcation of the catchment area of a store location. The law is expressed algebraically as:

$$D(ab) = d / (1 + \sqrt{Pb / Pa})$$

D = the distance from the boundary of the catchment area to the store
d = the distance between two store concentrations
Pb = the population of the city in which store concentration B
Pa = the population of the city in which store concentration A

Suppose two cities are 20 km apart. City A has a population of 90,000 residents and city B has a population of 10,000 residents. The border of the catchment area (the point of indifference) of city A lies at 15 km, that of city B at 5 km.

$$D(ab) = 20 / (1 + \sqrt{10 / 90}) = 15 \text{ km}$$

Although Reilly's law is basically the theoretical basis for the solution to one of the most difficult retail problems, namely determining the size of the catchment area, this model is too simple. In the first place, Reilly also assumes that the population size is a direct approach for the strength of the store selection. In practice, we often find that this is not true: some municipalities do not have enough stores, other have too many stores, not to mention the differences in the quality of the selection. In the second place, Reilly assumes that the influence of distance is the same, regardless of the product groups. Here too we observe that, in practice, this is a very simplified assumption: the distance elasticity to purchase a couch is much lower than to purchase daily groceries. Finally, Reilly's law explains to a certain extent – albeit on the basis of a strong simplification – the behaviour of consumers, but not the behaviour of retailers: why are retailers sometimes located somewhere else than according to the ideal solution offered by Reilly?

17.2.3   The central place theory of Christaller

Central place theory

Catchment area

Range

Threshold

In his *central place theory,* Christaller keeps in mind the selection aspects. In his theory, he uses a number of refinements that partially overcome the objections to be made against Reilly's model. In the first place, Christaller defines the concept of *catchment area* from two criteria. The first criterion is the concept of *range*, that is very similar to Reilly's definition of the catchment area. Under range, Christaller understands the distance that a consumer is still willing to travel to purchase a new product. So this is the catchment area, as determined from the demand side. The second criterion is the concept of *threshold*: the minimum population size that must be present to ensure that the retail operation runs profitable. This is the definition of the catchment area from the supply. Only if the range is greater than the threshold, a retail store will make sense.

A neighbourhood shopping centre in Utrecht

Translated into previously discussed models: the threshold actually comes down to the number of residents needed to achieve break-even sales. The threshold can be calculated by, using the gravitation model, calculating the number of customers ($VI \times C$ in the sales model from chapter 10) and multiplying this figure by the average ticket per store visit. The distance (in kilometres), where $\Sigma(CA \times VI \times C \times AT)$ = sales (break even), is then the threshold.

The philosophy behind determining the catchment area according to the two criteria systems of Christaller seems theoretical. In practice, his system is nevertheless widely used, albeit often in a pragmatic way. Especially chain stores apply threshold and range implicitly when determining the conse-quences of network saturation. Calculated based on the threshold, a new branch may signify quite a profitable addition to the establishment network. However, if the range is a great deal larger than the threshold, this may give rise to cannibalism within the establishment database. The new branch itself is profitable. However, because the catchment area (range) stretches into the area of the old branch and can therefore have a negative effect on the sales of the old branch (*cannibalisation*), the combined effect may lead to a negative effect on the returns for both branches together.

Cannibalisation

In the second place, Christaller adds the observation that the range (or the catchment area in the sense of Reilly) depends on the nature of the product that the consumer intends to purchase. For some products, consumers are willing to travel a great distance (such as couches and radio and TV equipment), for other products, even the smallest distance is too large (such as daily groceries).

The combination of various ranges per product category (the upper limit of the catchment area) and thresholds (the lower limit of the catchment area) then leads to a differentiated structure of the store selection. Product categories with a low range (the consumer does not want to travel great distances) and a low threshold (not many residents are needed to break even) will especially occur in neighbourhood shopping centres. Products with a large range and a high threshold end up in shopping centres with a supra-regional significance (often in the city centre). This differentiated structure led to the famous hierarchy of retail facilities, or the central place theory: the division into main shopping centres or city centres, district centres, community centres and neighbourhood stores (see figure 17.4).

FIGURE 17.4 The central place theory of Christaller

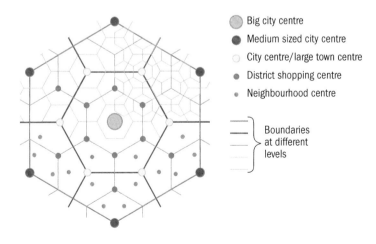

Big city centre
Medium sized city centre
City centre/large town centre
District shopping centre
Neighbourhood centre

Boundaries
at different
levels

17.2.4   The hierarchy in the structure of retail facilities

Building on the work of Christaller, Garner and Davies further structures
(Garner, 1966) the hierarchy of retail facilities. Garner relied on the assumption that stores with a high threshold, in the sense of Christaller, by definition
had to have a high *rent paying ability*, while companies with a low threshold
had to have a low rent paying ability.

**Rent paying
ability**

Due to their high rent paying ability, companies with a high threshold drive
companies with a low threshold (who can after all afford less rent) from the
city centre. This is also the reason why, at least in the perspective of Garner,
there are relatively few food companies within the city centre.

We will discuss the accessibility of the shopping area and the sustainability
of the hierarchy.

Accessibility of the shopping area

The resulting hierarchy of shopping areas (also applicable to meso level, for
example, within shopping centres) resulted in a concentric zoning of the
retail structure. The zoning in the form of concentric circles comes about
because Garner only used distance as an explanation for the rise of the
visitors index of consumers, given the selection. Davies has nuanced this
assumption: the consumer is not so much influenced by the distance to the
stores, but rather by the accessibility from the home address. Distance
does play a role, but so do other factors, such as traffic, infrastructure and
parking problems at the destination.

Accessibility

In Davies's vision, the variable 'distance' should be replaced by the factor
accessibility. The accessibility is not measured in kilometres, but rather in
time required. An increase in, for example, parking traffic in the city centre,
which means that it takes longer to find a parking space, affects the
accessibility and therefore the attractiveness of the city centre as a store
location. Similarly, the presence of a continuous direct connection could
mean that the accessibility, despite the fact that the distance is great, is

**Iso-distances
Isochrones**

still very good. The consequence of this distinction is that one no longer
defines the catchment areas in *iso-distances* but in *isochrones*: a collection
of points with an equal accessibility, measured in time, with regard to the
shopping centre (see figure 17.5).

Sustainability of the hierarchy

It is more and more apparent that the hierarchy of retail facilities, which has
long served as the basis for both the government policy on retail facilities
and the retailer's individual location policy, is no longer fully applicable. An
important reason for this is that in the current retail environment, the threshold is no longer fixed. Companies are able to influence their threshold (the
size of the catchment area in which break-even is applied) to a certain
extent. They also do that, since the release of the vertical price maintenance. In the old situation, where vertical price maintenance was allowed,
there was little or no difference in the price level of suppliers. It therefore
makes absolutely no sense to settle in cheaper, poorly accessible locations,
outside the hierarchy of retail facilities. Why, after all, would consumers

FIGURE 17.5 The difference between iso-distances and isochrones

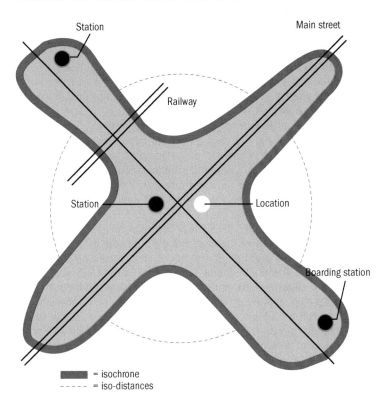

Station

Main street

Railway

Station

Location

Boarding station

= isochrone

= iso-distances

17

travel to a less attractive store location if they derive no benefit from it? After releasing the vertical price maintenance, it is possible to apply this price discrimination. From this situation, it is therefore attractive for suppliers to adjust their operation in such a way that a profit can still be made with lower sales prices. In other words, it is worth it, especially for price sensitive product categories, to lower the break-even point (and thereby the threshold). One of these methods is to lower the fixed costs, in other words, to find less expensive locations. The emergence of the original peripheral solitary retail, with its strong discount character, is therefore largely explicable. There is however another factor that plays a role in breaking the traditional hierarchy. All location theories discussed above are basically based on a homogenous selection in stores. This was also explainable for the traditional situation. After all, the selection between stores showed no excessive differences. In the current situation, however, we see more and more that the selection is not homogenous. In a sales channel, there are increasingly more differences between the suppliers as a result of a deliberate formula distinction, making it more a matter of a monopolistic competition than full competition. A very good formula, with a high autonomous appeal, it can therefore afford a less favourable location in terms of accessibility for the consumer. Examples thereof include IKEA, Piet Zomers and Radio Correct, companies that have independently developed supra-regional traction, without having to use the top regional attraction of the city centre.

The city centre, inner city and outer city
The developments of the environmental factors also affect the breaking of the hierarchy. As the accessibility of the current top of the hierarchy (the city centre) deteriorates, the inner city is losing appeal while the appeal of the peripheral locations is increasing. The shopping areas of many cities in Europe will shrink. Only the cities with a supra-regional function will jump the gun. The cities will see their urban shopping areas grow, if only for the fact that these cities will grow, but also because they attract many people every day to work, but also for shopping. In a country like the Netherlands this will be the four large cities, plus six to twelve other cities across the country. The other city centres will shrink in terms of store size, because we already have too many stores, while sales will stagnate and a part will be lost to the internet. Companies will disappear from the city centre and those that remain, or replace those that are leaving, will partly play a different role. More showrooms, outlets, will emerge in the city centre.

In recent decades, the inner city, the district centre or neighbourhood centres, have indeed taken over a part of the city function, but the momentum is very large and the question is whether all the centres will survive in the present form. The grocery shopping facilities will most likely survive just fine. Here, the supermarkets and drugstores are qualified best, for specialists it will really depend on their quality. For non-food retailers in the retail segment, it will be a tough fight. They will often not be able to handle the competition with the internet and the city centre. Pick-up opportunities will, however, develop in the inner city. These may be independent pick-up points where products that were purchased online can be collected in kiosks. While retailers of non-food products may also move towards this business. Fashion stores can also become pick-up points for websites that sell shoes, cosmetics and sporting goods, or convenience stores like Primera or Bruna may also enter this branch of sport.

The question is how long the local governments will be able to hold back the development of the peripheral locations. This attitude stems from the time when city centres were the main shopping areas. But with the surplus of stores on the one hand and the rise of online shopping on the other, new considerations will have to be made. These developments will translate into a shift of expenditures within the hierarchy. We expect that the outer city, which is often already full of empty furniture boulevards, will become the shopping areas for pick-up and experience. Products purchased online can be collected at easily accessible locations, where parking is a piece of cake and relatively cheap. We also expect that both pure players and traditional retailers, which are active online, will settle here. Not only can they have the products purchased online collected on these relatively low-cost retail metres, but they can also display the entire product range in a show-case environment.

The decision of the government to liberalise the distribution planning policy is not currently leading to a shift inside the hierarchy, but to a (further) breaking of the old traditional hierarchy.

17.3 Store selection models: the micro approach

The described location theories provide insight into how the macro structure of retail facilities is established. However, they hardly provide insight into the reasons why, out of the many alternatives, the consumer prefers a certain store or store concentration. The only consumer variables which are taken into account in the models is the distance or accessibility. The general dissatisfaction with this too simple assumption has led to the development of so-called *revealed-preference* models. However, it does not fit into the context of this book to provide a detailed explanation of these models, especially since such models are used more by scientists and policy officials in the government, than by the retailers themselves. Retailers are pragmatic people and prefer to take refuge in 'checklist methods', which, although partly based on the philosophy behind the *revealed-prefer-ence* models, are often greatly simplified.

Revealed-preference

17

17.4 The marketing mix variable 'location' for existing branches

The decision regarding the location is a long-term decision. After all, a lease is usually five to ten years, while the cost payback period of the establishment of a branch may amount to a very long period. This often means that we consider location more or less a fact for the marketing mix in the daily operation and thus exclude it from further consideration. This is unwise, especially chain stores on various locations, but certainly also for independent entrepreneurs. First, because every location may have been given specific characteristics that, to a certain extent, justify regionally different approaches. Second, because the environment is subject to rapid changes. This also applies in the area of outlets. Impoverishing or improving neighbourhoods and changes to the infrastructure may cause abrupt changes in accessibility, just as the introduction on parking regulations. Third, because, even for the most powerful chain store, it is almost never possible to have an ideal store in terms of size and shape at every location. Concessions are almost always required with this ideal. This also means that we will almost always have to make local adjustments to the concept. This is why the location, even for established companies and despite the long-term nature of the location decision, demand constant attention.
We will now look at the influence of the size of the catchment area.
This will be followed by the quality control of the existing establishment area.

17.4.1   Influence of the size of the catchment area
Especially for chain stores with many branches, it is not always feasible to determine the catchment area for each branch according to the methods described in the first part of this chapter. This is often not necessary. From experience with other branches, we are generally aware of where and in what catchment areas an operation may be profitable. In these cases, we usually use a simplified approach: the size of the population of the city or the district (figures often found in available statistics) is used as approach of the actual catchment area. This area is often divided into a 'primary

catchment area' (often arbitrarily defined as that area which generates 50% of the sales) and a 'secondary catchment area' (50% to 80% of the sales) and 'other' (from outside). The disadvantage of this simplification is that we cannot directly determine the expected sales: after all, the gravitation models teach us that the sales depends heavily on the distribution of the residents of the catchment area around the store, which cannot be determined in this way. Chain stores with many branches can circumvent this disadvantage by considering the link in their existing branches between the average expenditure per resident and the size of the catchment area, defined as the city or the district. In fact, this approach comes down to the condensation of the formula $S = CA \times VI \times C \times AT$ discussed in chapter 11 into two components: the catchment area CA and the average expenditure per consumer $VI \times C \times AT$. Generally this provides a context in which smaller communities or catchment areas show (very) high expenditures per resident of the catchment area, while low expenditures are detected in larger cities (see figure 17.6).

FIGURE 17.6 The relationship between the size of the city and the average ticket

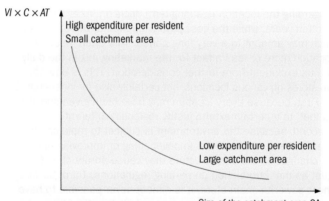

Size of the catchment area CA

If we know the relationship in figure 17.6 (in chain stores one can calculate this relationship from the analysis of the existing establishment base), then we can easily calculate the expected sales: multiply the number of residents of the city by the average ticket that goes with the size of the city. The negative relationship between the size of the catchment area and the expenditure per resident is caused by two factors:

Share of purchase
Share of wallet

- It can be assumed that, in smaller catchment areas, there is generally less competition. The *share of purchase* or *share of wallet* per resident will therefore be higher in smaller cities than in larger cities, where there is generally stronger competition.
- In smaller cities, the residents generally live much closer to the store than in larger cities. As a result of the function of accessibility, the average expenditure per resident in large cities will be lower than those in smaller cities.

The found correlation is universal: within this simplified methodology, we always find low expenditures per resident in large cities and high expenditures in small cities. However, the shape of the relationship could be different for each company, depending on the strength of the formula and depending on the range (Christaller) of the type of goods (see figure 17.7).

FIGURE 17.7 Two examples: Hubo (large competition, low range) and Prénatal (little competition, high range)

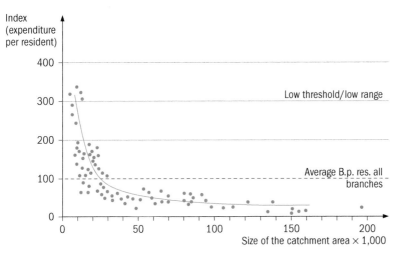

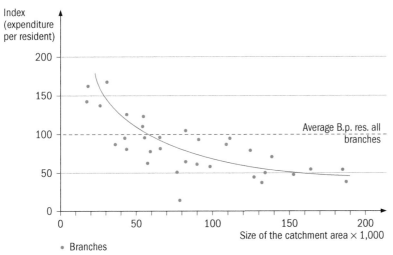

• Branches

17.4.2   Quality control of the existing establishment database

Chain stores are generally based on a uniform formula. This can basically lead to an equal size of the branches. However, there are several reasons why it is necessary to work with a different size per branch within an existing formula. We discuss the reasons below.

Adjustment of the branch size to the demand

The minimum size of a branch of a chain store is determined by the size of the core product range and the desired presentation. In fact, a branch of a chain store may never be smaller than this size. After all, if this is the case, one cannot sell the core product range and it would therefore be an incomplete formula.

Standard
space plan

The size and design of such a store, embodied in a floor plan, is known as the *standard space plan* (SSP). The standard space is not only directly relevant for the sale, because it indicates how the establishment should be set up, but also for the other two main functions of retail, namely purchasing and logistics. For the purchasing function, for example, because the standard space plan is the basis for the product range composition: as such, the standard space plan forms a barrier against the tendency of purchasing to continuously expand the product range. For the logistic function, the SSP forms the basis for the supply technique. After all, there should always be sufficient stock in the store to hold out until the next delivery. The SSP therefore indirectly determines the order frequency and the supply frequency. These two details form the basis for the logistics system.

For operation reasons we often need to deviate upwards from the standard space plan. In larger than average catchment areas, we will have to deal with a higher than average number of visitors ($CA \times VI$). This means that we will have to provide extra space for walking and moving around to accommodate the peak periods. Extension and expansion of the walking area will always affect the presentation of the product range and could therefore lead to adjustments in the standard space plan. In larger than average catchment areas we not only have more visitors ($CA \times VI$), but we will also, in absolute terms, have more customers. An equal percentage conversion as in the smaller catchment areas, leads to many more transactions in large catchment areas in absolute terms. In order to achieve this equal percentage conversion, we need more stock, especially for the product range components with a high sales rate. If we do not ensure this, the conversion will decrease, simply because the goods are sold out before the next delivery. In other words, we will lose customers. More stock, however, means more shelf space. More shelf space, means an adjustment of the standard space plan. This applies especially if the stock increase is not equally spread over the entire product range, for example with very different sales rates per range component.

Within an existing establishment database, we can measure to what extent the size of the stores is tailored to the size of the catchment area. After all, if we have applied the previous philosophy well, it should basically lead to a relatively small variation in the sales per metre per establishment. If not, it will lead to a very large variation. Because the costs of the sales area generally form the second largest cost for retail, it is important, in terms of returns, that a lot of attention is paid to this coordination (see figure 17.8).

FIGURE 17.8 Example of two formulas: good coordination and poor coordination of the size of the store in the catchment area

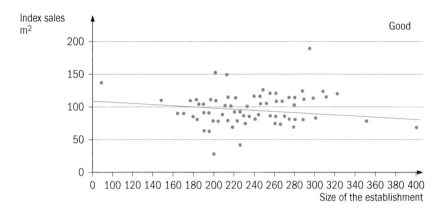

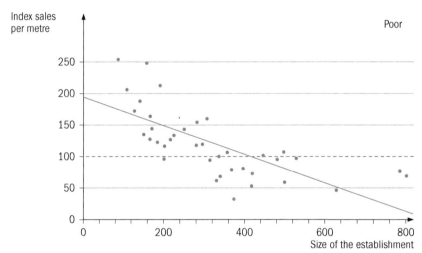

Formula differentiation within a chain

Collections of chain stores are not created in a matter of a day, but rather through a historical growth process. This means that, in the establishment database, we often deal with a large diversity. This is partly because formulas are developed over time, as a result of which older branches – in terms of size and location – do not always fit in the new formula. This is partly because it is virtually impossible to obtain the ideal situation at every location. If the requirements of the formula and the establishment charac-teristics are too far apart, it may be necessary to apply *formula differentia-tion* within the existing establishment database. Examples of such formula differentiation is Albert Heijn, that has divided its branches into different categories and two sub-formulas (XL and To Go), V&D, which now distin-guishes between the various company types in its branches, and HEMA, which has five different store types, based on location: home/mobile (internet store), high traffic, district shopping centre, city centre and big city.

Formula
differentiation

17

The selection processes that play a role in such formula differentiation can be structured using the location matrix (see figure 17.9). This matrix can be used to provide insight into the relationship between the size of the market area, the size of the store and the minimum required size of the core product range.

FIGURE 17.9 The location matrix

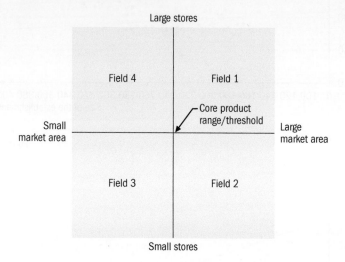

The zero point of the matrix on the vertical axis is defined by determining what the minimum floor surface of the store should be in order to bring the core product range under the attention of the consumer in the desired way. This is the lower limit of the store size, determined by the technical requirements that we must set to the presentation of the core product range. The zero point on the horizontal axis is formed by the threshold, the minimum size of the catchment area that is needed in order to work profitably. Four fields are therefore created, each of which have a different significance for optimising the establishment database.

- *Field 1*: large branches in large market areas. The stores are profitable and big enough to hold the core product range. There is no shortage of potential customers. There are two possible methods to use any excess space. We can use the excess space to improve internal processes, for example, by lowering the cost of the physical distribution. Large stores make it possible to hold a great deal of stock and therefore to use a low top-up frequency. We can also use the excess space to optimise the competitive position: further application of formula distinction with respect to the existing competition to increase the visitors index to the own store.
- *Field 2*: (too) small stores in large market areas. The store is profitable and there is no lack of customers. However, the core product range cannot all be placed on the shelves. There are three policy options:
  - We can expand the store by taking over adjacent stores or relocation. This is the best solution from formula management, but not always possible in practice.

- We can adjust internal processes, for example, by 'concentrating' the presentation techniques, making it possible to sell the entire core product range. Or by increasing the top-up frequency (from once a week to daily, for instance), thereby reducing the stock that is placed on the shelves and thus creating more space.
- If the first two options do not provide a solution, we may decide to make product range adjustments to optimise the return. We should then adjust the mix of the core product range for these branches in such a way that the high yielding products achieve a higher sales share than low yielding products. We can once again use the DPP or DAP systems discussed in paragraph 13.3.

- *Field 3*: (too) small stores in (too) small catchment areas. This actually refers to stores that do not (or no longer) fit in with the current formula policy. The first option is: close down. Again, this is not always an option, for example, when it involves long-term leases. The only option to reduce the loss, is to influence the visitors index. If there are only a few residents and the store is too small to hold the core product range, we at least select the products from the core product range that would lead to the scarcest consumers coming more often. This will often lead to adjustments in the direction of a convenience formula.
- *Field 4*: (too) large stores in small market areas. The stores are not profitable and there is a shortage of potential customers. We need to use the excess space to increase the attraction of the formula. This will often mean that we add additional product ranges to the core product range, with a large range (for which the consumer will want to travel greater distances), at low prices. In this way, we try to increase the size of the catchment area, and thus the support basis. If this is not possible, we may decide to make the store smaller (reducing the threshold through lower fixed costs) or to close it down.

Summary

Although the marketing mix variable 'location' has become relatively less important, the location decision remains an important one. First, because we are stuck to it for a long time and secondly because the establishment costs are the second most important cost entry for retail.

Theories on choosing the location have evolved over time, parallel to the changing role of retail, from very easy gravitation models (retail and distribution) to very advanced probabilistic models that are based on individual utility functions of consumers (retail as demand satisfying process). The advantage of these last models is that they give a good explanation of the behaviour of entrepreneurs and customers. The disadvantage is that they are difficult to manage in practice.

Retailers therefore usually resort to simple, experience based relationships when choosing locations. These relationships can usually, often without the retailer realising this, be traced back to the essence of the scientific location theories.

18
Price

In this chapter we discuss a number of important concepts and apply them specifically to retail, such as pricing strategy, pricing, pricing through global surcharge calculation, deviations from the global surcharge calculation, price image and adjustment of the price image.

We answer questions like: what position does the price hold in the strategic process? How is pricing determined? What do we understand under price elasticity? How does this system work and which aspects play a role? What is price image? When is adjustment of the price image desired and when is it necessary?

18.1 Pricing strategy

Figure 18.1 shows the position of the price in the strategic process.

FIGURE 18.1 The strategic process: price

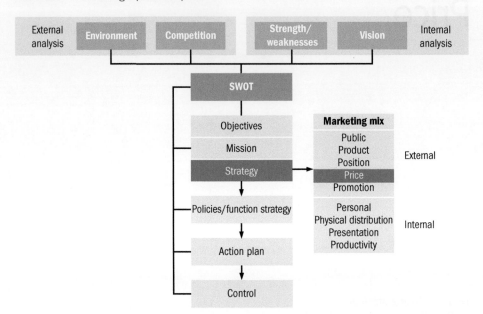

The Netherlands is a country of thrifty spenders. Price, but above all the price image, plays an important role in the consumers' decision to visit stores. Despite the fact that Dutch consumers say that the price is not the most important factor in choosing a store, we see in practice that they act as though the price is very important.

Retailers respond to this. Retail advertising, for example, is generally very promotion oriented. 'Was/now'-prices, price festivals and slogans like 'Extra specials this week' are found daily in advertisements. Price is also an easily and quickly applied variable for the retailer. The decision to temporarily reduce a price is made quickly and often generates extra sales. Price cuts are therefore a good weapon to compensate for setbacks in sales.

The danger of such a short term approach, is a development of a downwards price spiral, placing margins under pressure and endangering the long term profitability of the retailer. The art in using the marketing variable 'price' is therefore not to develop of a continuous stream of markdowns, but to develop a *pricing strategy*, in which long term profitability is guaranteed and which meets consumer expectations regarding the price level.

18.2 Pricing in the retail sector

Economic theory suggests that the *optimal price* for the supplier in terms of profit maximisation lies there where marginal costs (= the costs of the last added production unit) equals marginal revenue (= the revenue of the last added sales unit). To the right of the intersecting point of marginal costs and marginal revenues, we lose money on every added unit, to the left of the intersecting point, we are still making a profit (see figure 18.2).

FIGURE 18.2 Marginal costs and proceeds

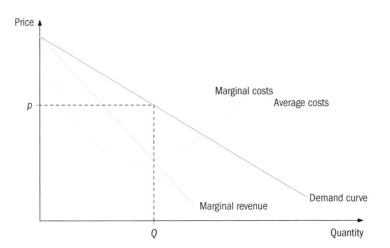

Such a theoretical way of pricing is difficult to apply in practice, even for non-retail companies. The approach requires a very significant amount of information. First, the shape of the demand curve needs to be known (the shape of the demand curve is determined by the price elasticity) and that is not always the case. In the second place, the shape of the cost curve needs to be known. And although that is often the case, it is only rarely used due to the complexity. For retailers, the application of the theory is even more difficult, because retail does not involve single product situations, but extensive product ranges. The elasticity of the demand (and thus the shape of the demand curve) may vary for every product within the product range. Application of the marginal cost rule is therefore virtually impossible for retail. Although price calculation using the micro-economic theory is not really an option for the retailer in practice, certain aspects from the theory are used. Specifically the concept of 'price elasticity', which determined the shape of the demand curve, is important.

Under *price elasticity* we understand the percentual change of the sales volume quantity (which is not the same as the sales) of a product due to a percentual change of the price.

In the form of a formula:

$$E = \frac{\text{Percentual change of quantity requested}}{\text{Percentual change of price}}$$

In general, price cuts will lead to an increase in sales, and vice versa. In other words, the price elasticity is usually negative. The price elasticity may vary significantly per product. Overall, we therefore usually use the following three categories:

Price elastic products
- We speak of *price elastic products* if the percentual change in the sales is larger than the percentual change in the price, so if $E < -1$. The increase in sales with a price cut then leads to an increase in sales, even with the new lower price. Price cuts therefore increase sales. Price increases reduce sales. Products with high price elasticity are ideally suitable to serve as special products for retail. Price elastic products often involve luxury goods for which many alternatives are available, with high average tickets, that is to say, a relatively high price compared to the income.

Price neutral products
- We speak of *price neutral products* if the percentual change in the sales is equally large as the percentual change in the price, so if $E = -1$. There is no harm done in using these products as special products, but it will not generate any profit. In terms of revenue, one could even say that it has a negative effect. After all, if the retailer has to pay for the price cut through margin sacrifice, he does not generate any profit: he generates the same sales, but at a lower margin.

Price-inelastic products
- We speak of *price-inelastic products* if the percentual sales change is smaller than the percentual price adjustment. In that case, price cuts result in a decrease of sales and price increases lead to an increase of sales. From the individual supplier, theoretically, these are products on which one could apply margin increases. These products would therefore not qualify for special products. Price-inelastic products, on the other hand, can be used to minimise the negative revenue effects of the promotions with other, price elastic products. Complementary products, for example, are often price-inelastic. It makes sense to run a special offer for tents during the holiday season. At that time, the demand for tents is undoubtedly more elastic than, for example, in the winter season. However, it makes no sense to place tent pegs or tent rubbers on sale. After all, these products have a 'necessary' character, with low average tickets. People buy them anyway if they are needed, regardless of the price. However, it does make sense to sell extra tent pegs, at a normal price, with every promotional tent. This is known as

Cross-selling
cross-selling with the aim of reducing the negative margin effects of the tent promotion. In electronics, this happens quite often when a Scart cable is sold with an LCD-TV. The *up-selling* is also often used, where

Up-selling
a gold plated cable is advised and sold instead of an ordinary Scart cable. Price-inelastic products often involve primary goods with low average tickets, for which there are very few substitutes in the market.

Real price elasticity is often difficult to measure. It is not true that retailers always know the exact price elasticity. Rather, there will be an overall impression on which products are price elastic and which are not. Yet retailers, especially retailers with many outlets, have the ability to experiment in the field in order to determine the price elasticity. By varying the prices in several geographically distinct market segments, we can get an impression of how the consumer responds to a different pricing, without any direct disastrous consequences for the overall level of return.

Although most retailers are to some extent influenced in their pricing by the price elasticity, it is very common for them – in contradiction to the theory – to still cut prices of price-inelastic products, and often with success. The reason for this it that, in addition to the '*real price elasticity*', which involves increasing the total sales in the market, there is also such a thing as '*unreal price elasticity*': an individual retailer that applies price cuts to inelastic products, will see his own sales grow at the expense of that of his competitors. The overall market size does not change (consumers will in totality not buy more of the same product), but rather the distribution of the sales (consumers choose other stores to purchase the same quantity of goods). Considering the range, we can illustrate the difference as follows: the real price elasticity results in responding to market developments, with the chance to build a lasting long-term market position. The unreal price elasticity leads to displacement marketing, with the chance of temporarily gaining market share, until the competition responds: this may result in a price war between retailers.

Real price elasticity

Unreal price elasticity

Reasoning from the demand, we can illustrate the difference as follows: the real price elasticity has to do with the price sensitivity of consumers (consumer will buy more, or more consumers will buy). The unreal price elasticity has to do with the cost awareness of consumers: they purchase differently. The effect of the unreal price elasticity actually forms a barrier that ensures that the theoretical possibility of profitable price increases on inelastic products, in practice, is very rare.

18.3 Pricing through global surcharge calculation

Although retailers are therefore aware of the backgrounds of the micro economic price theory and also act accordingly to some extent, the mere application of the theory for the pricing in retail is virtually excluded. In practice, the pricing therefore takes place in a much more pragmatic way, namely through *global surcharge calculation* (Verhage, 2010). We apply a fixed factor to the paid purchase price of the product, which should basically be enough to cover all costs, including the profit. We call this factor *surcharge factor* or the *calculation factor*. If this factor is determined separately for each product, it is known as *cost price calculation*. In retail, however, it is very laborious to allocate specific costs at product level due to the large numbers of products from which a product range may exist. Even though the information technology theoretically brings cost price calculation in retail within the range of possibilities, experience with DPP systems indicate that the practical applicability remains limited. We therefore generally apply global or uniform surcharge calculation in retail as the first step in the price strategy. The calculation factor is applied, without

Global surcharge calculation

Surcharge factor

Calculation factor

Cost price calculation

discrimination, to all products in a complete product range (uniform surcharge calculation) or a sub product range (differentiated surcharge calculation). Secondly, we determine if, in cases of exception, there is any reason to deviate from the resulting initial pricing.

The surcharge factor is determined in relation to the purchase price. A surcharge percentage of 100% corresponds with a calculation factor of 2. The purchase price is then multiplied by 2 in order to determine the sales price. A product that is bought in for €100, will be sold in the store for €200. This includes 19% VAT that the retailers collect from the consumer, for the government. The margin of this product (the gross profit as percentage of the sales price, in accordance with M in the formula $R = S \times M - C$) is then 34%. Similarly, a surcharge percentage of 50%, corresponding to a calculation factor of 1.5, leads to a margin of 17% (see table 18.1). Obviously, at first sight, the margins always seem to be very high, but we also have to take into account 19% VAT on non-food products and 6% VAT for many basic necessities.

TABLE 18.1 Example calculations of surcharge method

Purchase	Surcharge percentage (on purchase price)	Surcharge factor (× purchase price)	Sales price	Vat 19%	Sales price excl. VAT	Margin (of sales price, in %)
100	25	1.25	125	20	105	4%
100	50	1.5	150	24	126	17%
100	100	2	200	32	168	34%

The level of the surcharge factor is bound to limits. The lower limit of the surcharge factor is determined by the cost structure of the retailer. A retailer that cannot cover his costs from his surcharge, will not last long. The upper limit of the surcharge factor is determined by the market demand (consumers) and competition. A retailer who, with equal purchase prices, permanently applies a higher surcharge than the competition and/ or a higher surcharge than compared to what the consumer is willing to pay, will quickly be priced out of the market.

There are several possibilities to influence the surcharge factor within these limits. If a retailer, while maintaining his sales price level, is able to reduce his purchase prices, his surcharge factor will increase. Influencing the purchase prices is often related to the size of the retailer: the bigger, the more favourable purchasing conditions. This is why price aggressive mass merchandisers are often able, despite their low price level, to use very acceptable surcharge factors and margins and to achieve high profitability.

Another possibility is to develop a positive distinction by the consumers compared to the competition. If the consumer is willing to pay for this distinction, it will lead to the possibility to stretch the surcharge factor above the average that applies for the sector. Very unique formulas may even lead to a new, higher upper limit of the surcharge factor. This is why some relatively small niche players are sometimes more profitable in sales percentages than their larger colleagues. The connection to the Michael Porter philosophy discussed in chapter 9 is evident.

18.4 Deviations from the global surcharge calculation

In this paragraph, we discuss several reasons why one can or should deviate from the initial pricing through universal surcharge calculation at a later stage. This is illustrated in figure 18.3.

FIGURE 18.3 Price dimensions

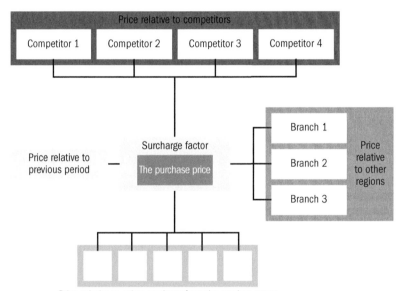

Source: Mc Goldrick, Mc Grawhill, 1987

18.4.1   The competitive aspect

Uniform surcharge calculation may lead to a pricing for certain products that is higher than that of the same products with the competition. If this is a key product for the sales and if the products determine the price image of the store (which means that the consumer is very price sensitive with regard to these products), we are forced to adjust the pricing of these products. Most consumers, either by a lack of information, or by limitations in cognitive capacity, only know a limited number of prices. Consumers often derive the price image of a store from the pricing of only a few products. Such price image determining products are known as *key items*. And it is the pricing of these key items that are important to the positioning of the own store compared to the competition.

Key items

Key items need to meet the following criteria:
- It should involve products of which the consumer knows the price. This often means that these are frequently purchased products (the repetitive aspects generate price recognition) or known brand products with a relatively high purchase price (the problem solving behaviour generates price recognition).
- It should involve products from the core product range. After all, it is precisely the pricing of the products from the core product range that determines the price image towards the public.
- The products should be comparable to that of the competitor. This condition also means that it will often involve basic products or known brand products. There is no point in comparing the price of a T-shirt with special printing, to that of a T-shirt of the competitor with a different print. It does however make sense to compare the basic unprinted white T-shirt of both suppliers.

The selection of the products that meet these requirements, results in a key-item list which can be used for price competitive research.

18.4.2 The geographic aspect

Basically, global surcharge calculation leads to all stores of a retail company using the same pricing. This certainly applies to a relatively small country like the Netherlands, where regional demand differences are limited and the distances are not so big that they result in very different distribution costs per region. In general, companies in the Netherlands will therefore use a central pricing. Also because the costs associated with the regional differentiation of prices, are very high. With the arrival of some new players and new formats and technology, this is subject to change. Media Markt has a business model with one managing partner per branch, who person-ally adjusts the pricing to the local competitors. In 2014 they even intro-duced the concept of dynamic pricing, which adjusts prices automatically in store. Or take Albert Heijn which applies different pricing with its To Go's, because the products have a different function on that spot. There are much larger differences abroad. That means that foreign retail companies often allow more freedom to local business managers to deviate from the central pricing. As more Dutch companies expand abroad, the problem of geographic pricing will thus become more important. Despite that we see, even within the Netherlands, that there are differences between geographi-cal areas that may require adjustments to the global surcharge calculation. In some areas we find much stronger and more price aggressive competi-tion than in other areas. Sometimes, this leads to the application of a regional surcharge factor that deviates from the central surcharge factor. Regional differences in demand may also result in certain product range components being provided with deviating pricing.

18.4.3 The time aspect

There are several reasons why one can or should temporarily deviate from the global surcharge calculation:

Price image
- *Maintenance of price image.* Some retailers try to maintain their price image with a constantly changing flow of offers. Lower than average surcharge factors are then taken into account beforehand for parts of the sales.

- *Influencing sales developments (temporary promotions)*. If such promotions are not co-financed by the suppliers (either by granting a bonus, or by temporarily reducing the purchase price), promotional prices will always be at the expense of the margin and will thus lead to a different surcharge percentage (later).
- *Markdowns*. Some products do not sell well. This kind of dead stock cannot remain in the store forever. First, because most stores lack the space, secondly because dead store stock leads to product range con- tamination. People often try to get rid of these products by marking them down. The result being that one accepts that the original surcharge factor is not achieved. The initial margin (or the inflow margin) is higher than the realised margin (or the sales margin). This phenomenon is very common in product groups with a strong fashion sensitive nature. One often sees that, for these groups, a higher than average surcharge factor is used on the entire product range in anticipation of this markdown risk.
- *Market developments*. The developments in the market may lead to the fact that we do not achieve the predetermined surcharge factor in practice, because we need to adjust ourselves to the market price level. This is the case in, for example, the market for personal computers. The development of new models is so fast that computers that were only purchased a few months ago, can no longer be sold at the original price, because they are outdated.

18.4.4   The product range aspect

The last and, from a strategic perspective, maybe even the most important aspect that may cause deviations from the global surcharge calculation, is the product range aspect. Consumers only rarely assess the price image of a store based on the absolute price comparison at product level (as indicated, a consumer only has one frame of reference for a limited number of products). The consumer' assessment is based mainly on the first impression of the price structure. In order to obtain a logical price structure, it may therefore be necessary for certain products in a sub product range, to deviate from the global surcharge calculation. Due to the strategic importance of this aspect, especially for the fashion and non-food sector, we will focus separately on this aspect below.

18.5 Price image

Under *price image* of a store, we understand the perception that consumers have on the price level applied by the store compared to the competition. In this paragraph we will first discuss the price perception versus the price level. We will then discuss the influence of the product range on the price image.

18.5.1   Price perception versus price level

The price image – or the impression that the consumer has of the price level – sometimes differs from the objective price level, determinable by price measurements (see figure 18.4).

FIGURE 18.4 Price perception and price level with electronics formulas

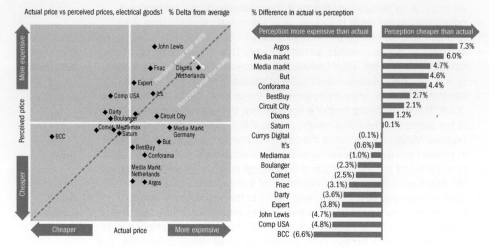

Source: *OC&C Strategy Consultant Consumer Surveys, store checks and analysis,* 2007

Conclusions:
- In the Netherlands, Media Markt is perceived as the cheapest and Dixons as the most expensive. At Dixons, the perceived price is just about equal to the actual price, Media Markt is perceived as being much cheaper than the actual price level.
- Expert is perceived as more expensive than Media Markt, while the actual price level of both electronic formulas is just about equal.
- BCC is actually the cheapest, but is not perceived as such. Media Markt is perceived as much cheaper, while the average (measured) price level is clearly higher than BCC.

On the left of figure 18.5, we see the price perception of consumers of Dutch supermarkets. Supermarkets that are perceived as cheap get a high score and vice versa. On the right we find the average price level of the product range, in which cheap is at the top and expensive is at the bottom.

Conclusions:
- Konmar and Hoogvliet are perceived as more expensive than the actual price level. Edah Lekker & Laag is also perceived as more expensive than the actual price level, but the difference here is much bigger.
- C1000, PLUS and Poiesz are perceived as cheap, while these chains are actually more expensive than the average price level in the market. Jan Linders is also very well reviewed on price level, while the price level is actually slightly below the average.

NB: The importance of at least a correct ratio between actual price and perceived price is supported mainly by the observation that two supermarket formulas that had a poor ratio between actual price and perceived price, have since disappeared: Konmar and Edah Lekker & Laag.

FIGURE 18.5 Price perception and price levels of supermarkets

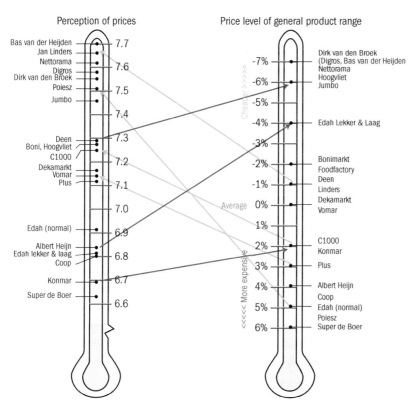

Source: *Processing based on the Consumentengids, 2006*

The problem is that, when choosing a store, consumers are guided more by the reputation than by objectivity. Stores with an unfairly high price image then have a problem: they are less likely to be included in the set store alternatives of the consumer, because the consumer does not trust their price level. In terms of the formula $S = CA \times VI \times C \times AT$, a poor price image therefore directly affects the visitors index. As a result, these stores are not able to prove that they are not expensive. After all, the objective perception that the high cost image deviates from reality, can only take place in the store. And if the people do not come to the store, it is impossible to provide that proof. Stores with a (justified or not) positive price image have an advantage: the likelihood that they appear on the list of store alternatives, is big. This is why most stores pay significant attention to developing and maintaining a positive price image (see example 18.1).

There are many factors that affect the price image of a store; sometimes they can be influenced by the company itself, sometimes they not cannot be influenced. Thus – completely beyond the control of the retailer – the arrival of a large discounter in a market may affect the price image of the existing suppliers, even if the actual price does not deviate. This happened, for example, in the construction world and the electronics industry. The arrival of very large German suppliers (customer's perception: large = cheap!)

EXAMPLE 18.1 PRICE WAR SUPERMARKET SECTOR – PRICE REDUCTION ROUNDS OF ALBERT HEIJN IN 2003

In mid 2003, the largest supermarket formula in the Netherlands – Albert Heijn – could see that its market share was declining.

While the economy was prosperous, Albert Heijn had increased its prices as such that, in 2003, their prices were as much as 15% higher than the price level of special formulas such as Dirk van den Broek and Nettorama. The price perception among customers of Albert Heijn had also increased significantly, so much so that they were even considering switching to another supermarket. To change the price image, Albert Heijn started reducing prices in 2003: this signalled the start of a price war in the supermarket sector in which almost all supermarket formulas participated. In fourteen rounds, Albert Heijn reduced prices by 8%. And not without success, as the market share recovered, indeed, Albert Heijn won a few percentages. Some other companies also won market share through the price war. The price war was fatal to at least one group: Laurus was forced to sell the Edah and Konmar formulas. All these supermarkets have since been sold and convert into other formulas. Laurus is now trading under the name Super de Boer.

Konmar and Edah have disappeared from the streetscape. Super de Boer was the only remaining formula in the Laurus-group, which was then renamed in Super de Boer N.V. and, after the takeover by Jumbo, also disappeared

like Hornbach and Media Markt resulted in the fact that existing suppliers like Praxis, Gamma, Expert and BCC had become more expensive in the price perception of the consumer.

An unbalanced assembled marketing mix may also affect the price image. A discounter in the P.C. Hooftstraat does not seem credible. The choice of the site makes consumers doubt whether the store is really that cheap.

The same applies if the store layout is too nice or too neat. This is why, for example, some stores plan 'clutter corners' in advance when renovating the store.

In the non-food sector, especially in the fashion sensitive segment, where brand perception is relatively small and where shopping has a comparative nature, the product range composition is of great importance for the price image.

18.5.2   Influence of the product range on the price image

The product range affects the price image in three ways, namely:

- through the general pricing, as discussed above;   **Pricing**
- through the applied price range: the percentage of the total price ranges   **Price range**
  present in the market, which are covered by the product range;
- through the price structure: the manner in which the price range applied   **Price structure**
  by the company, is completed.

The general pricing of the product range

The general pricing of the product range is determined from the selection by the used surcharge factor and the purchase price. The consumer will not be interested. The consumer will first look at the resulting price level and compare this to a kind of average perception. This average price perception of the store is compared to the average price perception of the market and (sometimes) to that of several competitors. Naturally the consumer does not actually use statistical analysis to calculate the averages. It is rather a kind of unconscious psychological processing of impression. Yet experience teaches us that this unconscious process does indeed have an influence. Market research shows that relative influence of the average price (in other words, an increase or decrease of the average price compared to the market price development) can directly influence the market share development. It is therefore very important for suppliers that they keep a close eye on the average price of a sub product range compared to the market, as first check point in the development of the price image.

It is important to keep track of two aspects. First, the absolute level of the average price. A company using an average price that is lower than that of the corresponding product range in the market, is more likely to be perceived by the consumer as being cheap, than a supplier who prices above the average market price. Secondly, the development of the relative price level over time. The consumer does not only look at the absolute price level, but especially at the relative price of the supplier in relation to the market or the competitor. It is therefore possible that a supplier may implement price reductions, giving him the idea that he is cheaper (which is also – from absolute figures – the case), but that his price image still deteriorates. For example, because the average prices in the market drop faster than his own price level (see table 18.2).

Influence of the price range of the product range

In addition to the average price level, the price range applied by the suppliers also affects the price image. The price range is actually a measure for the dispersion of the prices around the above discussed average price level. In general, we find that companies with a large price range, are perceived by consumers as being more expensive than companies with a smaller

TABLE 18.2 Example of reduction of the absolute price level of a supplier, leading to a poorer price image

	Average price in the market	Average price supplier X	Index with compared to the market
Period 1	€86.40	€110.20	€128*
Period 2	€86.80	€112.70	€130
Period 3	€82.20	€107.10**	€134***
Index in time (in %)	-5	-3	5

* Supplier X is relatively expensive.

** Supplier X reduces his prices.

*** However, because the market prices drop faster: increasing index X compared to market → strengthening high cost image.

price range. The reason of course is that the range downwards is limited by the cheapest price class (one cannot go much lower than 00.00), while the range to the top actually has no limit. A greater price range is therefore almost always characterised by its presence in the higher price ranges. And that leads to a high cost image. Table 18.3 gives an example of price range determination.

TABLE 18.3 Example of price range determination store 1 versus store 2 for winter coats, offered product range based on price category

Price class per product (in €)	Number of variations in store 1	Number of variations in store 2
0-20		
20-40		
40-60	3	
60-80	7	18
80-100	4	18
100-120	47	14 ← 120*
120-140	6	12
140-160	14 ← 160*	5
160-180		6
180-200	7	4
200-220	4	2
220-240	4	2

TABLE 18.3 Example of price range determination store 1 versus store 2 for winter coats, offered product range based on price category (continued)

Price class per product (in €)	Number of variations in store 1	Number of variations in store 2
240-260		
260-280		3
280-300	7	4
300-320		
> 320	1	20
Total number of SKU's	109	102

* ← gives median p

Source: Own market research

Despite the fact that the average price of store 2 is lower than that of store 1, there is still a reason to assume that the price image of store 2 is more expensive than that of store 1. This is because the price range of store 2 extends much further in the higher price ranges. After all, just look at the number of variations that are offered in the price class > 320.

Influence of the price structure of the product range
In addition to the average price level of the product range and the dispersion around the average (price range), the price of the product range compared to the market affects the expensive perception by the consumer.
Generally we can say that the price structure in the market is characterised by relatively low volume sales in the cheapest price ranges (the quality here is usually viewed negatively), large volumes in the lower and middle classes and small volumes in the highest price ranges. In terms of a graph, this means that the usual volume-price relation in the market would appear as that in figure 18.6a.

FIGURE 18.6a The usual price structure in the market

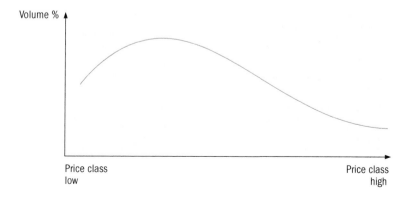

Volume %

Price class low

Price class high

How the actual price structure of the retailer relates to the market reference of the consumer, can have a major impact on the price image. Suppose the actual price structure of a retailer would appear as shown in figure 18.6b.

FIGURE 18.6b The price structure of an expensive supplier

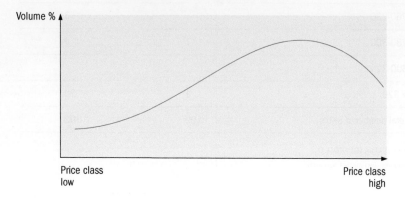

Volume %

Price class
low

Price class
high

The price competitive research based on key items that was conducted by this retailer, has shown that, for every comparable key item, his prices are lower than that of the competition. Yet his price image is worse than that of the competition. This appears to be the price structure. A comparison of the market price structure with the own price structure shows that there is an overrepresentation of sales in the highest price ranges. Within these price ranges it may well be that every product is cheaper than the competition. However, the fact that the success rate of the consumer (C in the formula $S = CA \times VI \times C \times AT$) is clearly higher in the expensive price ranges, automatically leads to an expensive image.

18.6 Adjustment of price image

Price is an easy to use and fast working marketing mix instrument for retail. The retail sector therefore often uses this instrument all along the line. The danger of using the price instrument for the short term, however, is the possibility of the development of a downward price margin spiral, a phenomenon that we often see occurring in times of stagnant retail expenditures. In practice, we see that the price instrument is often misused by the retail sector in the short term. This is dangerous, because short term price actions could have negative consequences on the carefully constructed price image constructed for the long term. This is especially important in sectors where there is a diffuse price image with little known prices and low brand experience (and we are talking about large parts of the retail sales, specifically in the fashion sensitive part or the non-food sector).
Adjustment of price image is quite a tedious process, as shown in example 18.2.

18

EXAMPLE 18.2 ADJUSTMENT OF A PRICE IMAGE: A PRACTICAL EXAMPLE FROM THE PAST

de Bijenkorf

De Bijenkorf has always been known as being expensive. The result was that the customer base of de Bijenkorf predominantly consisted of the higher income groups. The strategic reorientation which was aimed at also making de Bijenkorf accessible to the slightly lower income groups was therefore at risk of failing. A strategic adjustment of the price image of de Bijenkorf was therefore opted. This included a variety of measures, ranging from revising the presentation principles (basic products in the isle rather than the 'nicest' (= most expensive) products) to the development of a Bijenkorf House Collection. Part of the program, and certainly not the least important, was an adjustment of the price structure.

Step 1: analysis of average price level

They started with an analysis of the question of why the price image of de Bijenkorf was actually negative. Analysis of the average price level indicated that the average prices at de Bijenkorf were indeed slightly higher than in the market, but – especially taking into account the added value that de Bijenkorf provided – not so much that it would cause the negative price image. In several cases there was even a relevant price level below the market averages (see table 1).

Step 2: analysis price elasticity per sub product range

They then took a more detailed look at the relationship between the price sensitivity of the consumer and the actual price level. Thereby making the connection between the price level and the price elasticity. This time they did find a clear cause of the poor price image. By applying a uniform surcharge calculation on the product range, it appeared that some products (and precisely those products that were very price sensitive) came out more expensive than the market average. While other products (which turned out to be precisely the products for which consumers were less price sensitive)

deviated relatively little from the market average. The first measure that was taken was a differentiation of the uniform surcharge calculation. Price sensitive products were now calculated lower than non-price sensitive products (see figure 1).

Step 3: analysis of the price range

Finally, they examined the price range of a large number of products. Once again there was a possible explanation. In almost all cases, the price range of de Bijenkorf was much greater than that of its direct competitors. Additionally, it was thus decided to use a narrowing of the price range, in which the narrowing would have to take place especially from the top of the range (see table 2).

The findings resulted in the introduction of a monitoring tool for the implementation, in which price structure graphs were created every season for a large number of products, before the buyers left for the Far East. Based on these graphs, appointments were made on the adjustment of the price structure of the previous season. The price structure of year 1 clearly indicated that de Bijenkorf had missed opportunities in the price ranges in which the market showed the greatest volume. For year 2, it was therefore adjusted to this price class: in year 2 we see that the volume shifts to the most popular price class in the market.

The result of the adjustment is visible in table 3: de Bijenkorf is able to achieve an increase in volume in a declining market, leading to a significant gain in market share, both in volume and in sales. It may be noted that de Bijenkorf does this by reducing the average price, while the market shows an increase of the average price. This approach not only resulted in an attractive increase in sales, but most probably also had in a positive influence on the price image.

18

FIGURE 1 Price sensitivity of the consumer based on the price ratio of de Bijenkorf to the market

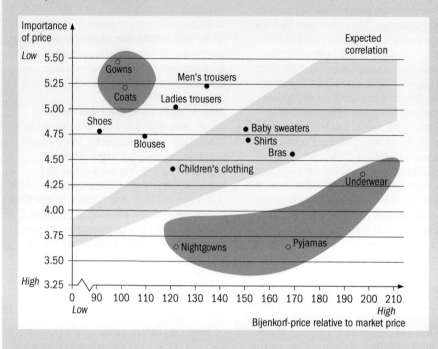

TABLE 1 Average price level of de Bijenkorf relative to the market

Market position of Bijenkorf	Average price	
Product	Market (in €)	de Bijenkorf (in €)
Women's wear		
Dresses	56.90	62.90
Skirts	39.00	46.30
Trousers	33.50	41.00
Blouses	26.00	27.90
Panties	2.19	4.60
Bras	9.00	14.75
Shoes	34.50	33.00
Pyjamas	17.70	29.70
General wear (ladies and girls)	4.70	7.00
Menswear		
Jackets	54.50	70.50

TABLE 1 Average price level of de Bijenkorf relative to the market (continued)

Market position of Bijenkorf	Average price	
Blazers, coats	104.75	93.00
Trousers	36.75	46.50
Shirts	18.30	26.00
Socks	2.40	4.40
Shoes	39.00	40.50
Baby clothing		
Sets	10.10	15.15
Blouses, sweaters, T-shirts	5.00	6.60
Children's wear		
Pants	19.40	25.25
Jackets	30.25	38.00

TABLE 2 Price Range Determination

Example: Dresses

Offered product range, based on price category

Percentage of sales

Price class per product (in €)	Bijenkorf	H&M	C&A	Claudia Sträter	Only
000-050		6			
050-100		44	15		33
100-150	5	31	29	12	67
150-200	13	11	51		12
200-250	9	3	3		
250-300	12	4	2	38	
300-350	24			7	
350-400	13			35	
400-450	9				
450-500	9				
500-550	5			7	

18

TABLE 2 Price Range Determination (continued)

Price class per product (in €)	Bijenkorf	H&M	C&A	Claudia Sträter	Only
550-600	1				
600-650					
650-700					
700-750					
> 750					
Median value	322	114	149	310	109
Total number of products	106	173	81	26	13

De Bijenkorf generally has a large selection of products and prices. The average Bijenkorf price level is usually at the top of the market, similar to a specialty store.

TABLE 3 Price structure

	Year 1	Year 2	
De Bijenkorf sales	19,755 pieces	22,810 pieces	
Market sales	1,450,000 pieces	1,390,000 pieces	
Market share	1.4%	1.6%	
The Bijenkorf sales	3,018 thousand	3,458 thousand	
Market sales	163,910 million	167,955 million	
Market share	1.8%	2.1%	
Average price			
• de Bijenkorf	152.75	151.60	−2
• Market	113.05	120.85	+20
Market share increases % in pieces per price class			

Summary

Price is a widely used (and often misused) instrument in the marketing of retail companies. Price is easy to use and leads to quick results in the short term. Price is also an important variable in the long term for 'lasting' profitability. It is therefore necessary to use a price strategy. The theoretically correct, microeconomic way of pricing appears to be inapplicable in retailing, due to the large quantities of products that are present in a retail product range. We therefore often use an easier methodology in retail, which is that of uniform surcharge calculation. Retrospectively we can then make adjustments to the sales prices, if it appears to be necessary for whatever reason. We need to distinguish between the actual pricing and the price image.
In practice, the consumer often believes that a certain seller is very cheap (price image), while objective research indicates that this is not the case (pricing). Building a positive price image is therefore of great importance for the price strategy. Stores with an actual low price level, but with a poor price image, will have a problem with the visitors index.
Price images are influenced by:
- the actual pricing;
- the price range of the product range;
- the price structure of the product range.

In addition, there may be other influencing factors that fall outside the direct influence of the price strategy. It seems possible, using fairly simple market research from available material, to make the three direct elements of a price strategy (pricing, price range and price structure) operational.

18

19
Promotion

In this chapter, we will discuss the aspect of communication within retail, whereby we further explain the following concepts: external promotion, communication methods, function of communication, objectives of retail communication, measurement of the effects of communication and the influence of loyalty programs.

We answer questions like: What is the position of promotion in the strategic process? Which communication methods are effective? Which resources can be used and what media is available? How do we measure the results and what is the effect of loyalty programs?

19.1 External promotion

In figure 19.1, we see the position of promotion in the strategic process.

FIGURE 19.1 The strategic process: promotion

Promotion	Under *promotion* (Floor and Van Raaij, 2008 and Franzen, 1983), we understand 'all activities of a company aimed at bringing the product that they supply to the attention of the public to promote sales of that product'. However, the term promotion is too simple for applications in retail. In retail, we distinguish between internal and external promotion.
Internal promotion	Under *internal promotion* we understand the promotional activities that take place within the store. They can be aimed at both the transaction (thus on direct sales effects by increasing the conversion and the average ticket of the consumers present in the store) and the attraction (on attracting visitors). We usually consider the internal promotion as a part of the store presentation. Therefore, we usually do not account internal promotion to the external marketing mix, but to the internal marketing mix.
External promotion	Under *external promotion* (which is the object of this chapter), we understand all promotional activities aimed at increasing the interest and purchase intention of the consumer in the catchment area of the store. The external promotion can also be aimed at increasing both attraction (indirect sales effects by increasing the flow of customers: *CA × VI*) and transaction (for example by influencing the visiting frequency and conversion through promotional advertising) (see figure 19.2). With industrial companies, which are often far from the consumer and have no direct contact with consumers, external promotion is one of the most important marketing mix variables.
Promotion mix	This sometimes goes so far that one can speak of using a *promotion mix*, instead of the marketing mix.

FIGURE 19.2 Connection internal/external, attraction/transaction

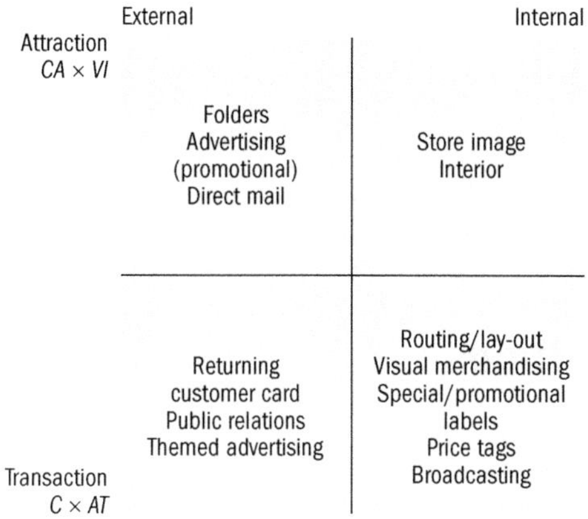

```
            External                      Internal
Attraction
  CA × VI
               Folders
               Advertising        Store image
               (promotional)        Interior
               Direct mail
       ─────────────────────────┼────────────────────────
                                 Routing/lay-out
               Returning         Visual merchandising
               customer card     Special/promotional
               Public relations        labels
               Themed advertising   Price tags
Transaction                      Broadcasting
  C × AT
```

This is not how it works in the retail, except for a number of strong sales oriented retailers. There are several important differences between retail promotion and industrial promotion. The most important is that, in retail, the external promotion is a derived instrument. It is makes very little sense to use promotion if all the other elements of the marketing mix are not in order. We may succeed in getting the consumer in the store once. But if he is disappointed, he will never return. This is also the cause of a number of marketing blunders in retail. A promotional campaign can be developed and implemented much faster than, for example, the conversion of hundreds of stores. Because of the restless nature of retailers, it does sometimes happen that the promotional campaign is already in motion, while the stores are not even ready yet. This means that the promises that are made outside of the store, cannot be fulfilled inside the store, which naturally leads to disappointed customers. It is extremely difficult and costly to convince a disappointed customer for the second time.

Due to the derived nature of external promotion in retail, we sometimes prefer to use the term *external communication*. In this vision, external communication is aimed at allowing the consumer to experience what the store represents and what he/she can expect from the store.

External communication

When it comes to promotion policy, we see significant differences between the policy in the industry and retail. The differences are further elaborated in table 19.1.

TABLE 19.1 Differences between industrial promotion/retail promotion

Retail	Industry
(Often) short term oriented	Longer term
Very dynamic and flexible	Outlining in campaign

TABLE 19.1 Differences between industrial promotion/retail promotion (continued)

Retail	Industry
Many products	One product(range)
Wide target group	Small target group
Local media	National media
Store oriented	Brand oriented

19.2 Communication methods

For the sake of convenience, the external promotion or external communication is often equated to advertising. However, this is too simple: admittedly, advertising costs are generally the most important part of the communication costs, but it is certainly not the only means of communication. There are retail companies that communicate extremely well with their customers, yet use virtually no advertising in the usual sense of the word. A common classification of the communication methods at a retailer's disposal, is that between 'paid and unpaid' on the one hand, and 'personal and impersonal' on the other (see figure 19.3).

FIGURE 19.3 Communication methods

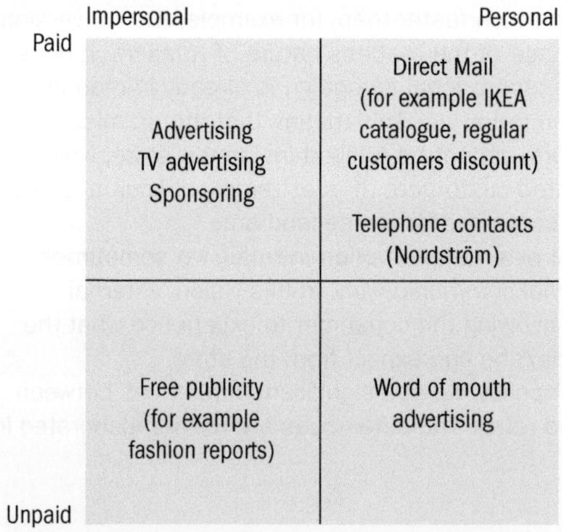

Source: Levy Weitz, *Retailmanagement*, page 397 (edited)

Figure 19.3 shows that there are several possibilities to communicate with customers. Advertising is only one of these possibilities, and sometimes not even the most important. The most important form of communication is often word of mouth advertising. We can only favourably initiate this form of communication when all elements of the marketing mix (product range, price, atmosphere, service) are in order and can be distinguished from the competition. Hence the statement that the most important means of communication in retail is the store (formula) and the external promotion is nothing more than a derived instrument. In the following paragraph, we will further discuss the changing customer journey and the consequences for our communication policy.

Even ZARA uses very little advertising

19.3   The new customer journey

Up to one or two decades ago, the search process of the consumer was specifically characterised by the marketing funnel. A model in which the consumer goes through the following phases to the analogy of the retail waterfall: known, consider, choose, purchase and returning (see figure 19.4). Marketers have the biggest impact on the beginning of the funnel, in particular in the phase in which familiarity plays a role. In this phase, the mass media is used to convey the message of where consumers can go. Marketers often think that they have much influence on the next phase, namely in the consideration. In this second phase, the marketers traditionally still have some influence. In the first phase, the Top Of Mind Awareness (TOMA) specifically plays a major role and, in the second phase, why one would need to consider a certain retailer. Fair is fair, in the second phase the elusive word of mouth advertising plays an extremely emphatic role. In the middle of the funnel, the marketer has very little to no influence. This starts with recommendations from acquaintances and runs on to recommendations from the personnel. However, in-store communication is a not to be underestimated marketing component, although the internet has placed this under pressure. At the end of the funnel, means of communication on the store floor and packaging play an important role. A consumer may have previously thought of what will be purchased where, but may still make a different purchase decision under the influence of the last minute stimuli in the store.

19

In terms of the retail waterfall, the attraction of the customer runs from the known phase, through the consider phase, all the way to the choosing phase of a store. The transaction and therefore the internal marketing mix runs from the choosing phase through the purchase phase. We cannot make a clear dividing line here. Obviously there will only be a transaction if the purchase is successful, but the choosing and purchase phases should both go well. In many cases the personnel factor plays a very important role in the internal marketing mix of a store. Although this is less the domain of the marketer, and more of operations and sales manager, personnel is a very important marketing factor within retail.

Retention refers to the returning customer. In other words, retention is related to the satisfaction of the customer. Customer satisfaction is an important measure for every marketer and should be measured regularly. Not in the least because acquiring new customers is much more expensive than retaining existing customers.

FIGURE 19.4 The marketing funnel

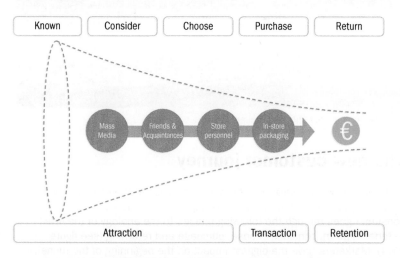

Source: Mooney, K. and Rollins, N. (2008). *The Open Brand* (own editing)

Social media, comparison sites and review sites on the internet have changed the search process of the consumer. This has also changed the shape of the funnel. The influence of internet based media in the centre of the funnel is so large that the funnel widens here rather than narrowing. We can no longer speak of the funnel, but must speak of the fish-shaped customer journey. Does this mean all traditional media has been written off? Not at all, but the mix of the media has changed drastically. This applies in particular to the combination of the media in every phase of the purchase process. Nowadays, marketers need to look much more at where, when and what media mix is used and for what purpose. Not only does this differ during the phases of the buying funnel, but also from sector to sector. Even within the retail sector, the differences are very large (see example 19.1).

Many more sources of information have been introduced which we can consult in the search process. In addition to the traditional media, such as newspapers, magazines, radio and television, the recommendations of friends and acquaintances have remained important. With the rise emergence of the internet, recommendations in the form of blogs, messages on communities, messages on forums and reviews have become even more important. Mooney and Rollins (2008) therefore converted the marketing funnel into a search process. This search process of consumers is characterised by creating, sharing and influencing. This resulted in the new customer-journey model, which has the shape of a fish (see figure 19.5). The customer journey starts more focused and narrow. Subsequently, the number of sources that consumers consult increases enormously. Twitter can be used to quickly scan what is said about a product, service or company. Facebook can also be consulted to see what friends think or say of a company, or it can be used to see how popular a brand is. Both channels remain on the surface and companies with a high TOMA often have many friends. In this phase we can also use comparison sites for product information, but also the websites of retailers themselves. Sites that compare and evaluate stores are impor-tant for the retail. The model is narrower at the tail of the fish, where consumers decide to make a purchase. The model then widens, because consumers will again create, share and influence. After the purchase, consumers will share their opinions and experiences on the product or the supplier. To do this, they use the channels that they used earlier to make an informed decision. This may be websites where they leave store reviews, but also sites of retailers to provide feedback on the products. In Mooney and Rollins's model, the wave movement of the fish continuously remains in position, because the end of a customer journey for one consumer could be the starting point for another consumer.

FIGURE 19.5 Customer journey model (fish model)

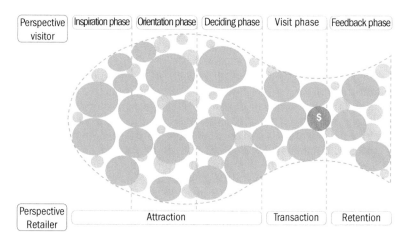

Source: Mooney, K. and Rollins, N. (2008). *The Open Brand* (own editing)

As with the marketing funnel, the principle with the fish shaped customer journey is that consumers go through various phases before they actually make a purchase. After one has decided to purchase a certain product, one then goes through the inspiration, orientation and purchase phase. The consumer can then choose to purchase through an offline or online channel. Finally, the after-sales phase is distinguished. This phase covers the activities undertaken by the consumer after purchasing the product. Even with this new customer journey, we once again find a connection with the retail waterfall and thus also with the retail monitor formula. This allows us to continue using the trusted models in the 'new world', while considering that new media should be added to our trusted marketing mix.

EXAMPLE 19.1 THE NEW CUSTOMER JOURNEY

The deployable communication mix requires constant attention of marketers at retailers. In 2010, Q&A Research & Consultancy launched a study into the new customer journey. The study is regularly repeated and performed in various sectors. In this example, we show the results that were collected in the spring of 2010. We have selected four sectors, namely: DIY markets, electronics, fashion and supermarkets.

Five main communication channels were used in the study: printing, internet, mass media (radio and television), people and stores. Each of these channels is then further broken down into underlying methods.

An initial rapid analysis shows (see figures 1 through 4), that the supermarkets still have a printing journey, in contrast to the electronics sector which has become a true internet journey. However, if we look at the chosen media mix of retailers, we must conclude that electronics retailers still fall back on the obvious means. The folder is still a widely used tool in the communication mix. If we look at the fashion sector, we can see that internet is indeed very important, but that printing is especially important in the inspiration phase and that, in the orientation phase, the store and the internet becomes more important and that printing decreases. In the

purchase phase, the store is the dominant means of communication.

The simple establishment of these interests of channels in the various phases in the purchase process are not enough. This means that printing should be used especially in the inspiration phase. This affects how this printing should look. Printing should inspire and encourage visiting the website or the store. The store should finally ensure that the purchase actually takes place. DIY markets also have an interesting customer journey. This consists of a combination of online and printing, in which the store plays an important role at the end of the journey. Even here it is important to carefully consider how printing and internet can be optimally connected as channels. Here, for example, the use of QR codes in the printing that refer to online content on the site could be of benefit. This step could obviously also take place in the store, where consumers can consult the online content through their telephone. The online content may consist of user reviews, but also from videos with explanations by employees of the DIY markets. In the DIY market sector, the store is very important at the end. The optimal utilisation of all means of communication in the mix can also contribute enormously to the conversion.

FIGURE 1 Customer journey electronics

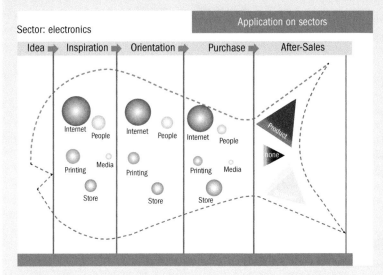

Source: Q&A Research & Consultancy 2010

FIGURE 2 Customer journey fashion

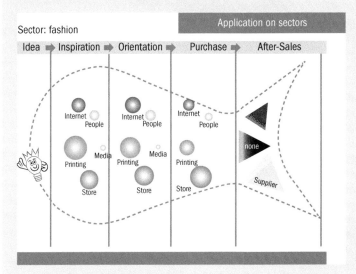

Source: Q&A Research & Consultancy 2010

Especially looking at electronics and DIY markets, we see that there are opportunities for retailers to respond to the feedback needs of consumers in terms of products.

FIGURE 3 Customer journey supermarkets

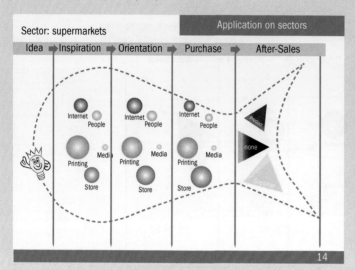

Source: Q&A Research & Consultancy 2010

FIGURE 4 Customer journey DIY markets

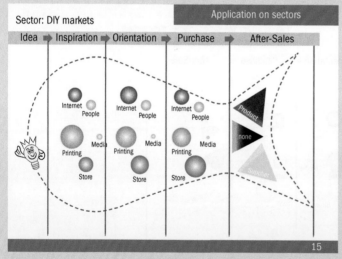

Source: Q&A Research & Consultancy 2010

In addition to the mix in means of communication that should be used in the various purchase phases, it is also interesting to understand whether there is a specific type of (communication) *channel loyalty*.

In figure 5, we expressed the channel loyalty for the various means of communication channels for the entire retail sector. This is the situation at the end of 2010. We should note that this is subject to change very quickly.

FIGURE 5 Channel loyalty

Channel loyalty				Customer journey	
Inspiration	Store	Internet	Printing	Media	People
	16%	32%	37%	3%	12%

⬇ ⬇ ⬇ ⬇ ⬇

Orientation	Store	Internet	Printing	Media	People
Stays	57%	77%	53%	10%	35%
Drops out	43%	23%	47%	90%	65%
Balance	9%	25%	20%	0%	4%

⬇ ⬇ ⬇ ⬇ ⬇

Purchase	Store	Internet	Printing	Media	People
Stays	88%	76%	65%	41%	33%
Drops out	12%	24%	35%	59%	67%
Balance	8%	19%	13%	0%	1%

Source: Q&A Research & Consultancy 2010

This means that a retail marketer should actually perform such a check for its own sector, every six months.
While printing is the most influential medium in the inspiration phase, we see that the loyalty for this medium rapidly decreases in the following phase. The differences between sectors are indeed great, but in general we can say that printing does a very good job to inspire consumers.
Per channel, redundancy takes place towards another channel in the next phase and people fall out.
On balance, however, online is a very strong channel and has a high loyalty (balance). It turns out that printing, which can be equated with the folders, is a very strong medium. This is actually one of the most powerful forms of mass media. Properly combining the internet, the folder and the store would eventually lead to the best communication mix for a retailer.

19.4 Function of communication

The communication process is structured from four components (see figure 19.6).
We already discussed the communication mix of the retailer and how this can be used as effectively as possible. Taking a step back, however, is gaining more insight into how communication works.
Let us therefore start with the *sender*. In practice this is often the retailer. But, in some cases, it may also be others, such as in the case of sector campaigns or joint manifestations of different retailers in shopping centre promotions. It must always be clear who the sender is.

Sender

FIGURE 19.6 Communication process

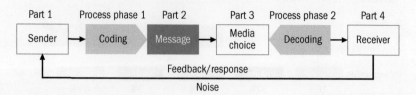

Source: Mazon, Meijer, Ezell, *Retailing*, page 502

This may seem obvious, but many mistakes are still made in this area: the sender is not mentioned at all, or without an address, or sometimes you only see the logo.

Message Coding

The second part of the communication system is the *message*. The process leadings to the formulation of the message, is known as *coding*: what do we want to say, using which texts, pictures and symbols? A message that is aimed at making it clear that the supplier is very inexpensive will use entirely different coding than a message that is aimed at indicating that the supplier delivers top quality. This coding may even extend to the selection of print material, for example, folders: a discounter will preferably choose cheap newspaper and an expensive clothes store will choose glossy material.

Means and media selection

The third phase is that of the *means and media selection*: which means of communication will be used to convey the message? Considering the high costs involved with external communication, this is a point which will receive significant attention, often more than the other phases, although it is basically just as important. The productivity of the medium as a carrier of the communication message is usually expressed in terms of cost per thousand contacts or mailboxes. A medium with a high circulation will be more expensive per communication expression than a medium with a low circulation. However, the costs may be lower per thousand. But this is only one side of the coin: apart from the productivity, effectiveness of the medium also plays a role. Not all means of communication are read equally well. A *special-interest* medium will be browsed more attentively than the local house-to-house magazine. Ultimately, not only the cost aspect is important, but also the quality aspects (the read range) of the medium. Given our discussion in the previous paragraph, we would even like to see a very well balanced communication mix when we speak of means of communication. It is important to consider not only the overall objective and message, but to also look at the phases of the purchasing process in which we would like to reach consumers. Every phase requires a different approach in terms of the means, in which the overall message may be the same, yet be tailored to the phase in the purchasing process.

Receiver

The last part of the system is the *receiver* (the target group). The message is interpreted by the receiver through a process of decoding. The more powerful the message, the coding and the medium is with the concept or the experience of the receiver, the easier the receiver will be able to decode the message. Knowledge of the attitudes, opinions and interests of the target group is extremely important in communication processes.

The process is described here in the form of a one-way traffic. It can be planned very thoroughly, but even then, as retailer, we do not know what effects the advertising has had. It is therefore important to get feedback or perform response measurements. How these measurements are performed, depends strongly on the desired effects. And the desired effects depend on the communication objectives.

19.5 Review marketing

We already indicated how important word-of-mouth advertising is for retailers. With the rapid development of the internet and especially the social component thereof, we are dealing with a new form of word-of-mouth advertising, or as the Americans like to say *Word of Mouse.*
Reviews are the new form of word-of-mouth advertising. This means that, as retailer as well as manufacturer, one should master this new form of marketing. Review marketing will develop into one of the most important marketing forms in the coming years.
That means that one should start thinking about how this marketing form will fit into the business processes. Certainly if we consider that today 41% of all store selections choice for online purchases are preceded by consulting one or more reviews. For physical store visits, this percentage is already 21%. In other words, one out of five consumers make their selections for a traditional store by consulting one or more reviews in advance. In 2015, we expect that this percentage for physical stores will rise to over 34%. In 2015, more than one out of three purchases in the physical retail will be based on a review and, in the internet world, this will even apply for almost half of all purchases. Significant difference to the traditional word-of-mouth advertising is that consumers today bow to the opinion of complete strangers.

Reviews are a great opportunity for retailers
Reviews are even more important for product choices. Studies conducted by ABN AMRO shows that almost 31% of Dutch people choose a product based on a review that they have read. For those that purchase products online, this percentage is even over 58%. In 2015, ABN AMRO expects that more than 41% of all product choices will be based on a review.
In 2012, about 80% of all product reviews were read on comparison sites, such as kieskeurig.nl and vergelijk.nl. This is not as surprising at the moment, since these sites still contain the most reviews. Incidentally, collecting reviews is no simple task for these parties. Most visitors to these sites are on the site because they wish to seek information and much less because they wish to share information.
This is no surprise, because consumers are visiting these sites early in the purchase cycle. Due to the many reviews on products, these sites will be on the top of the search results on search engines such as Google. The search engine is the starting point. However, retailers have a much better position when it comes to collecting product reviews. They have contact with consumers and can ask customers to write a review after several days or weeks, depending on the product group. This is where online retailers have an advantage, because they already have the customer's email address and this is also linked to the purchase. This method ensures that the customer is given a form of attention that is currently not happening. For quite a few purchases, of course, it is true that a customer's wish is coming true. There is nothing wrong with asking the customer how it pleases them.

Experience shows that the response percentages to the request to write a product review are reasonably good. As a rule, the customer has a chance to win back the entire or part of the purchase amount. The quality and authenticity of the reviews that are collected by a retailer are high and good. Placing such reviews on the site of a retailer contributes to consumers, who start an online search process, finding the retailer's website with many reviews much faster. If consumers find good and reliable information there, it is very likely that the purchase will eventually take place with this retailer.

Review marketing is the cheapest way for marketing companies. In fact, this method is thrown in the retailer's lap. Provided, however, that it fits into the business process in order to use it correctly within the own organisation. In our opinion, this is not difficult. Of course it is extra work and it is not something that retailers have always done, but it fits into the core of the primary business process of a retailer. A retailer derives its legitimacy from the fact the he makes prior choices for his customers. A retailer compiles a product range for his customers, to facilitate choosing and finding. A retailer does not show all available products, but rather chooses to compile the best selection for his customers. A retailer does not actually do much different when collecting reviews, perhaps adds another dimension. Actually, it is quite surprising that only a limited number of (physical) retailers use these opportunities and comparison sites, in particular, have assumed this function.

Moreover, it is possible for retailers to provide more added value by making it clear what type of customers have given certain reviews. Are these people who, like the customer, hold a certain opinion? This is what matters; relevance. A retailer can accomplish this much easier than a comparison site, since they generally do not work with a system in which only registered people can write a review.

Product reviews or supplier reviews

For reviews, it is important that the forum (medium) in which they can be found is regarded by consumers as being independent. Thus retailers (sites), especially if they offer brand products from different parties, are the ideal location for product reviews. Retailers are considered to be independent parties that make the product selection in order to facilitate the selection process of consumers. For some categories, however, consumers regard the retailer as a supplier who has an interest in the sale of certain products. Especially in the electronics industry. This is partly due to the commission method (which is still used in 2012). Consumers' product reviews, however, can also contribute to increasing objectivity. Ultimately, the reviews are returned to the store floor by placing them on the shelves with the products.

Because consumers are also looking for reviews of suppliers, it is also relevant for a retailer. These supplier reviews need to be collected on an independent forum. If this forum/platform is borne by consumers, retailers can report the score from this forum on their own website. This enables consumers to see at a glance what other consumers think of the relevant retailer. Again, relevance is all determining. If consumers then click on the general score, they will end up on the website of the forum, on the page of the relevant retailer. The user can then highlight an opinion that matches his or her own profile, whereby the score has maximum relevance.

19

It is not simply a question of doing the one and leaving the other. Product reviews are particularly relevant for retailers that offer brand products or products for which the perceived emotional or economic risk is big. Brands play a role, because these are often used in the search criteria. In this way, websites with many reviews on certain brands will be shown first. It is important that especially men search on product level. Higher economic risks are especially taken if products represent a higher value. Such as electronics, but this can also apply for other non-food goods, such as furniture. Emotional risks are equally important. They may appear softer, but we are talking in particular about whether you are going to buy the right product. Is this the right dress? Am I doing the right thing by purchasing this couch? This is more about the confirmation that consumers seek on whether they are making the right decision. That consumers will seek online help more frequently also has to do with the fact that the number of one person households will continue to increase. Moreover, this group has less time for purchases.

Who uses reviews

The expectation may be that especially the young generation of the so-called internet generation will use reviews. However, table 19.2 shows that reviews are used and written by everyone.

TABLE 19.2 Composition by age of reviewers on Wugly.nl

Age	Share
15-20	8%
21-30	21%
31-40	19%
41-50	23%
51-60	17%
61-70	10%
71 years and older	2%

Source: Wugly.nl December 2011

Actually, it is not surprising if we think a little more about reviews that the average user and writer of reviews is 42 years old according to review site Wugly.nl. Table 19.2 shows an age distribution of these reviews as of December 2011. Most of the users are between 21 and 50 years. These are busy careerists and the people just starting families. They do not have time to go through the entire process of searching for products and comparing suppliers, viewing them and then making a choice. It is much easier to follow the choice of others' who have already gone through the process and are satisfied.

Reducing search costs and increasing customer satisfaction

Consumers are always looking to reduce search costs, also known as transaction costs. From this theory it is therefore easy to establish that both the product and supplier reviews may contribute to reducing search costs. That retailer that is able to reduce the search costs of consumers in combination with offering the best results will rise in consumer preference. For product reviews, this means being current, working without censorship, being able to select based on profile and offering a decent range.

For supplier reviews, this means that the retailer should ensure that he is actively present on the various forums and is well-reviewed. A good review is ultimately realised in the store (online or offline) and therefore requires a good shopping process. The internal marketing mix should therefore be entirely in order. Supplier reviews may also help here.

A good review forum generally offers insight into all statistics, at a price. If these statistics are used to control the shopping process, the processes can be improved. It is important that the improvement is also visible on a forum. The retailer needs to do more than simply adjust; he should also actively participate in such forums. By informing consumers of the importance that such an organisation attaches to the customer's opinion and that the reviews are measured by independent forums, customers will share their opinions here. If the retailer emphasises that it will use customer opinions to continuously improve performances for its customers, the system will automatically work for the retailer. Ultimately, this means a better performance, a higher score and a greater chance of returning customers and attracting new customers. In an increasing displacement market, customer satisfaction is the best guarantee for success. If consumers can choose from different suppliers and have little time to devote to this, why would they opt for second best in future? If the information is available for the consumer, he/she will choose the best supplier. Better customer satisfaction will generally also result in more profitability.

19.6 Objectives of retail communication

As objectives of retail communication, we can distinguish:

Direct sales

- *Short term objectives: direct sales*. Short term objectives still include the majority of retail advertising. This has to do with the short term orientation of the retail sector, as discussed in paragraph 19.1. This is also the reason why retail advertising is often filled with products: retailers consider advertising space in the same way that they consider retail floor space. The sales per square centimetre of advertising space should preferably be as high as possible. This is why advertising companies are not always satisfied with retail customers. After all, retailers have much higher demands on the direct effect of advertising than, for example, industrial companies. They generally also try to measure this effect. The discussion about *accountability* of advertising is partly attributable to this phenomenon. Communication focused on direct sales is often highly price and product oriented.

Store traffic

- *Medium term objectives: store traffic*. Medium term objectives aim to increase the flow of visitors to the store, partly by increasing the visiting frequency of the existing customers, partly by attracting new visitors.

A clear example of *store traffic* communication is the non-food product range of Aldi.

- *Long term objectives: profiling the retail formula (store image).* The long term objectives are aimed at the constant increase of the interest within the catchment area (increasing visitors index: market penetration), but also at expanding the catchment area (market development). Examples of profiling advertising are Benetton and Hennes & Mauritz: it is not so much about the products that are offered, but rather the store personality.

  Store image

- *Profiling advertising*: this advertising always aims at anchoring the desired store image.

  Profiling advertising

An important distinction that is closely linked to the discussed communication objectives is that between thematic communication (aimed at anchoring the desired store image) and promotional communication (aimed at generating sales). Until recently, basically all the retail publicity was aimed at generating sales. Now, with the formula aspects of retail growing in importance, the subject of the communication is becoming increasingly more important. The rise in the number of retail formulas that only sells own brands increases this phenomenon even more. The store should be positioned as a brand. For a *brand image* you need a theme. Many retail formulas divide their communications budgets more and more in a balanced way between thematic and promotional communication.

19

19.7 Measurement of the effects of communication

We start by saying that practice shows that investments in *promotional communication* itself are very rarely paid back directly from the sales of the advertised products. This is logical, considering the small margins of retail and the high cost of advertising. An advertisement in a national newspaper, which easily costs more than €50,000, would, with a gross margin of 33%, need to generate €150,000 euro extra sales, in the advertised products alone, before there is any contribution to profitability. The consideration to advertise nevertheless is that the retailer hopes that customers who visit the store to purchase the advertised products will also purchase other products (at the full margin). However, this is very difficult to measure.

Promotional communication

The effects of promotional communication are primarily measured by changes in sales. This also forms the main problem with advertising effect measurement in the retail sector: how do we define the change of sales? In other words, how do we separate the additional sales resulting from the communication messages, from the non-related sales? Not only do we counter the influence of seasonal effects (which can be very big), but also the effects of occasional sound (which can be even bigger than seasonal effects). What is the weather like? How are the holidays? Is there an important game in the near future that may positively influence the sale of TV's, but which is very negative for other products? Although, in principle, there are statistical techniques to separate these kinds of effects, they are very rarely used in daily practice – partly due to the high frequency nature of retail communication – in retail. Only the largest companies can periodically perform this kind of analysis. In the daily routine one usually makes do this with rules of thumb. A product that is being advertised should generate a certain sales during the period, depending on the cost of the medium, before we can say that the advertising was successful. The analysis of whether this sales actually represents additional sales, is usually left aside.

Thematic advertising

Brand awareness survey

To measure the effects of *thematic advertising* retail uses three measurement instruments. The first instrument is simple *brand recognition research*. This method implies that, prior to commencement and following the completion of the theme campaign, people are simply asked which suppliers they know, for which a double question is often used. The spontaneous brand awareness is identified as 'the percentage of people that answer that they know the supplier without assistance'. Under assisted brand awareness, we understand 'the percentage of people that only recognise the supplier in the second instance'.

TOMA research

The second method is the *Top Of Mind Awareness (TOMA research)*: a slightly more advanced technique in which not only the name recognition is sought, but which also creates a ranking of the responses that are made. The result is a ranking of TOMA values. This list shows the order in which one thinks of stores when purchasing from certain product categories. The higher the TOMA value, the more like the supplier is to be included in the consumer's proposed store alternatives.

Image research

The third instrument is the image research. This is often a fairly extensive detailed consumer survey. Image research is costly and is therefore usually performed occasionally. The aim is to examine the extent to which the image that is pursued by the supplier, is actually experienced by the consumer and how this perception develops. Image research (before and after) is essential in repositioning approaches. It is actually the only method which we can use to verify whether the 'soft' targets of repositioning are achieved.

19.8 Influence of loyalty programs

Loyalty programs

Promotional approaches in retail almost always have somewhat of a 'shooting with buck-shot' character. The once more popular *loyalty programs* make it more and more possible to actually aim at a target. In the early nineties of the last century, loyalty programs were inseparable from retail. The prevailing thought was that it was cheaper to keep existing customers, than it was to acquire new customers. Customer Relationship Management (CRM) quickly became popular and almost every company had or started a CRM program.

A CRM program is based on a database which records a combination of customer details. In addition to transaction details, personal characteristics and interest are also included in a database. Through data mining, or analysis of the database, CRM makes it possible to make conclusions about the customer's needs. This is done to be able to respond to this with a tailored offer for the customer and therefore make this fuller. The combination of CRM and data collection in exchange for benefits results in a new boost of loyalty programs or saving systems.

Air Miles-like programs offer the opportunity, despite all privacy guarantees that had to be applied, to distinguish good customers from bad customers. This made it possible to develop certain special offers for good customers, on a limited basis.

However, after the promising start, loyalty programs have fallen from grace. The main reason for this is the unexpected complexity of managing the amount of customer information and consequential and disappointing results. Loyalty programs have only recently returned to the Netherlands as a sound marketing instrument. The two main reasons are, the further possibilities of today's information technology (web-based and web-enabled) and, the success of such programs in other countries, such as the Tesco Club card. An example of the resurrection of a loyalty system is the IKEA Family Card. After killing off the previous customer card, IKEA resurrected its loyalty system following the success of the IKEA Family Card abroad. At present, more retailers (whether or not behind the scenes) are busy resurrecting their loyalty programs.

One of the better loyalty systems in the Netherlands, at the moment, is the Albert Heijn Bonus card system. With this system, the customer basically gives permission to using his purchase data. Theoretically, it is then easier to develop special offers for a single customer. Theoretically, because the technical difficulties in processing the particularly large number of details are still far from being solved. Although Albert Heijn still uses the Bonus card system, it has slid from a theoretically advanced system for external promotion, to a more or less mundane discount system for internal promotion.

The idea behind the external promotions was the targeted approach of primary customers with personalised mailings. The aim was to increase the frequencies of visits and the average ticket. At this time, the bonus card is nothing more than an internal promotion agent with the aim of increasing the conversion and the average ticket of the customers present in the store.

In other countries, retailers are much further with the development of loyalty programs. The classic example is Tesco, as previously mentioned. Tesco differentiates its customer base into different segments, based on which profiles are formed. Customers receive appropriate offers based on their profile and their specific purchase behaviour. There is also a Tesco Club Card community, represented on the internet and in the various magazines (one for each profile).

With the Tesco Club Card, customers can save Club Card points in the store and in selected partner companies. Tesco also sends all card holders vouchers four times a year; these can be used in the store and online or with the Club Card Deals of the partner companies. In fact there is even a Tesco-web, which makes it much easier to aim at the target.

The resurrection of a loyalty system: the IKEA Family Card

19

Summary

In retail, notwithstanding the example in industrial promotion, we distinguish between external and internal promotion. External promotion is aimed at awakening the interest in the store. Internal promotion is aimed at increasing the number of transactions. Consistency with the monitor model that is discussed in chapter 11 is clear.

In practice, we often see that external promotion or communication is equated with advertising. However, there are many more ways in which we can interact with the consumer, varying from unpaid forms such as word-of-mouth advertising to paid forms such as sponsoring. We extensively discussed the new customer journey and the increasing importance of internet in our communication strategy. Since word-of-mouth advertising is just about the main form of communication in retail, internet with reviews, the new form of this advertising, offers a great opportunity. From this perspective, we discussed review marketing as the most important new form of marketing and advertising. For the purposes of retail promotion, we distinguish between short term objectives (direct sales), medium term objectives (store traffic) and long term objectives (store image). This classification is largely parallel to the distinction between thematic and promotional communication. Effects of promotional communication are difficult to measure due to the occurrence of various disturbances and sounds: seasons, the weather or events. We therefore often assume pragmatic standards to assess whether a certain promotional drive was successful. In order to measure the effects of the thematic communication, we can use various techniques, such as brand recognition research, TOMA research or image research. We see more and more that loyalty programs will play a role in the long term promotional efforts. Ultimately, this may lead to the return of one-on-one communication. Given the initial difficulties with processing the data, this will still take a while.

PART 6

Internal marketing mix

In this part we deal with the internal marketing mix: all instruments aimed at turning visitors into buyers and turning these buyers into 'full' buyers. The alignment of the internal market- ing mix variables react even more closely than that of the external marketing mix. The reason being that the components of the internal marketing mix not only influence each other mutually, but are sometimes also directly exchangeable. A change in the logistic system (for example more frequently deliveries = cost increase) makes a more efficient presentation (= lower costs) possible, because the necessary minimum is reduced. An improvement of the clarity of the presentation (which usually requires more room and thus increases the cost), making the findability of the products for the consumer better, will make it possible to use less personnel. This leads to lower personnel costs.

The internal marketing mix variables have a significant direct impact on the level of the variable costs (labour costs, presentation costs), much more than the external marketing mix variables, which strongly affect the fixed costs, such as rent. As a result, the search for the optimum mutual composition of the internal marketing mix is of great importance for the return. We intentionally use the concept 'optimal'. It may make sense to spend extra on one part of the marketing mix if this would create a more than proportional decrease in other costs (of extra revenue). Because the cost ratios constantly change, the composition of the internal marketing mix thereby becomes a continuous balancing of the optimal combination.

20
Personnel

The retail employee is central in this chapter: retailing is people's work. We will take a closer look at personnel management, personnel control, activities on the store floor, workforce and the planning thereof, and the influence of personnel costs on the returns. We answer questions like: what position does the personnel hold in the strategic process? What do we understand under personnel management and how do we give this form? Which organisational structures are found in retail? What features can we distinguish in this and how do these develop individually and relative to each other? What do we understand under HRM and how can we use this HRM knowledge and skills to achieve a high quality personnel management?

20.1 Retailing is people's work

Figure 20.1 shows the position of personnel in the strategic process.

FIGURE 20.1 The strategic process: personnel

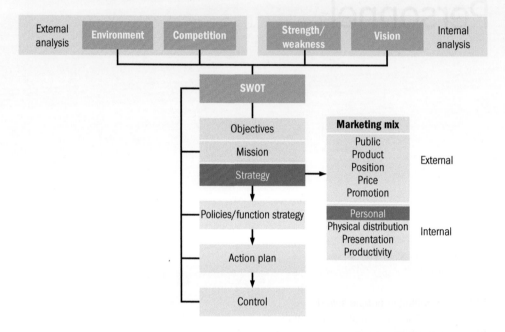

Retailing is people's work. Despite all the developments in automation and computerisation, which led to a considerable release of labour in the industry, the retail sector still needs people to do the work. Although there has been a constant effort in retail to reduce labour costs by increased process automation, but the possibilities for this are as yet more limited than in the industry. Shelves do not fill themselves, cash registers are still not fully automatic and customers still – even in self-service systems – need personal contact.

This is both the result of the effect of the scissors as discussed in chapter 6, as well as the reason why retail is one of the most important growth sectors from the perspective of job opportunities. In other words, retailing is labour intensive. Labour costs are the most important cost in the retail sector, at least in the Netherlands: an average of 50% of the margin in the retail sector is spent on labour costs.

The retail sector employs many people. Just in the goods sector of retail (the retail), the employment is about 630,000 people (of which more than 69% work in part time/flexible jobs), alone, and this number is still growing. Retail is therefore one of the largest employers in the Netherlands.

Employment in retail is also quite specific in nature. Many young people work here. 40% consists of employees younger than 24 years, while this is 15% in all other sectors. There are also many women (60%, in all other sectors 40%). Many people also work part time (60%). This enables retail to better respond to several *needs* of the working population than many other industries. Especially the need for flexible employment can be largely met in retail. The downside is that the staff sales in retail is very big, especially at the somewhat lower levels. Rates of 30% over a year are not uncommon. This means that the personnel management in retail is rather laborious. There is a constant and sizeable inflow and outflow. The personnel function then only has to ensure that the quality of the person-nel remains constant and complies with the requirements of the concept (refer to Labour Market Retail, EIM/HBD, 2003).

20.2 Personnel management in retail

Under *personnel management,* we understand a balanced compliance with the qualitative needs of the organisation with respect to the occupation of functions. Personnel management is not the same as personnel control. The latter means – given the chosen organisation form – using the person-nel as efficiently as possible.

Personnel management

The subjects in this paragraph are: the functions in retail, category manage-ment and human resources management.

20.2.1   Functions in retail

Consideration of the traditional *retail value chain* (see sub-paragraph 7.3.1) shows that we establish a significant deviation compared to the industry. Purchasing, which in many industrial companies has a relatively minor function and is often considered as the secondary function (Porter calls this function *procurement*), has a primary function in the retail. Purchasing in retail is equally important – and in the fashion sector maybe even more important – as the sales function. For small companies, where the func-tions are usually in hands of one person (namely the store owner), this will generally not pose a problem. However, in case the functions are sepa-rated, as with most business of chain stores, it delivers problems. This basically creates a kind of shared responsibility. And shared responsibility almost always leads to confusion. This causes many frictions in retail. The art of managing personnel in retail therefore focuses strongly on ensuring optimal conditions for the cooperation between purchasing and sales. Purchasing is therefore often held responsible for the success of the product range composition (measured with $S = MS \times MS$ – see chapter 12) and the (inflow) margin of the calculation (M). Sales are held responsible for the success of the store operation (measured with $S = CA \times VI \times C \times AT$ – see chapter 10) and the (store) costs C, including local markdowns. In terms of the previously used performance comparison, this can be repre-sented as follows:

Procurement

$$R = S \times M - C$$

Purchasing: responsible for *M* and *S* (where *S* is expressed as *MS* × *MS*). Sales: responsible for *C* and *S* (where *S* is expressed as *CA* × *VI* x *C* x *AT*).

20

Both areas of responsibility overlap each other through sales. This overlapping area is also where most of the friction occurs. It is a human trait, when things are not going well, to place the blame on others. It is obvious that when the returns are under pressure due to disappointing sales, the sales department will point an accusing finger towards the purchasing department.

They did not make the right purchases or they placed the margins too high. Conversely, purchasing will quickly accuse sales that they do not treat products properly in the store or that they lose sales by cutting too much in the costs. The problem is to keep these frictions to a minimum. The way to do this is to achieve a uniformity of views, in which a good strategy may be helpful. We can also reduce frictions by controlling the implementation, where we use a unique key-control variable, which is the same for both functions (see part 7).

20.2.2 Developments in the organisation structure: category management

In the majority of the larger retail companies, there is a separation of functions. A typical organisation structure of a traditional chain store is shown in figure 20.2.

Category
management
Divisional
organisation

In the new philosophy of *category management* (see sub-section 7.3.6), this division of responsibility is different. In category management, we do not assume a functional organisation, but a *divisional organisation*. The company is divided into separate *business units (categories)* which often consist of the consumer demand or group products related from operational issues. At the head of such business units, we find a category manager who is assisted by people with procurement expertise, people with sales expertise and people with logistics expertise. The category manager has the responsibility to optimise R for their own category in the formula $R = S \times M - C$.

The potential contradictions between the various functions are therefore at a much lower level in the organisation than in the old functional structure.

Intermediate forms between the old functional structure and the new category management structure also occur: one often sees that, although the final responsibility lies with the business units, functional experts still remain present. The result is a matrix-type organisation, where the divisions (the categories) have a lot of freedom, but where certain constraints are set.

The difference between a traditional functional organisation and the category management organisation is shown schematically in figure 20.3. Although every organisation may have differences in structure (a supermarket organisation will focus more on logistics and sales, a fashion chain more on purchasing), we generally still see the division between the commercial functions on the one hand (sales and purchasing) and the technical functions (administration, logistics, personnel) on the other hand. For very large companies, a separation is often also applied within the commercial functions. Purchasing and sales then fall under various managers, with a high probability of the troubles described above. Striking and illustrative of the changing function of the retail is the place that logistics occupies. Logistics used to be the absolute main function of retail.

FIGURE 20.2 Organisation structure

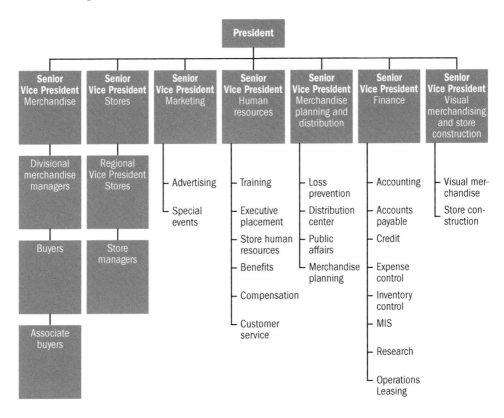

Source: Levy/Weitz, *Retail management*

FIGURE 20.3 The difference between a traditional functional organisation and the category management organisation

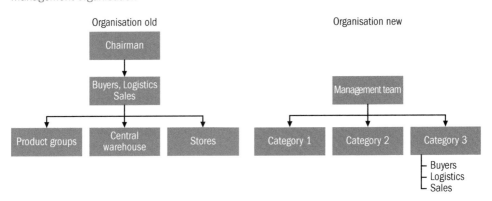

But in the new situation, logistics is more and more a function that is deemed equally important or even secondary to the other commercial functions. In some cases we see that even the distribution function is *outsourced* (contracted out).

The equalisation of the various functions does not mean that the workforce is thereby in proportion. The purchasing organisation and the logistics organisation are generally much, much smaller in scale than the sales organisation. Typically, depending slightly on the type of retail, the sales organisation consists of approximately 80% of the total workforce. From this perspective, it is therefore not surprising that sales is responsible for the management of the (variable) costs.

Finally, retailer organisations generally have a very flat structure. There are few retail organisations where we can distinguish more than four levels. On the sales organisation side, depending on the size of the company, the levels consist of:

- the management;
- regional managers or branch managers;
- branch managers or department managers;
- the sales staff.

On the purchasing organisation side, the levels consist of:

- the management;
- purchase leaders who are responsible for a number of related product range groups (for example hard goods such as toys, electronics and stationary);
- buyers who are responsible for a specific product range group (for example toys);
- *sub buyers* and/or buying assistants.

This means that the career lines in retail are short (with implications for the work pressure in the higher functions) and the *span of control* is fairly large, with implications for the work load of the higher functions.

20.2.3   Implications: the HRM matrix

The flat organisational structure of retail means that the personnel composition of retail is slightly different than in commercial branches where the organisational structure is deeper. This can be illustrated using the *human*

Human resources management matrix

resources management matrix (HRM matrix) (see figure 20.4). The HRM matrix was developed in order to evaluate the quality of the workforce and, if necessary, develop activities to improve this quality. The HRM matrix distinguishes between two dimensions: both the current performance of the employees, as well as the development potential of the employees. This in turn leads, as usual in portfolio like approaches, to four fields.

- A field that consists of employees who are currently performing well and

Stars

who also have opportunities for further growth. These are the *stars*, probably the future succession for the current management. The trick is to keep these people for the future.

- A field that consists of employees who are currently performing well, but who have little opportunities for further developments. These are the

Performers

performers that form the backbone of the organisation. The trick is to keep these people happy in their current function. Delegation of authority, *job satisfaction programs* and are good options.

- A field of employees who have not performed much (yet), but who

Potentials

are considered to be able to develop further: the *potentials*. Training programs and *job rotation* may be helpful here.

FIGURE 20.4 The human resources management matrix of Drenth

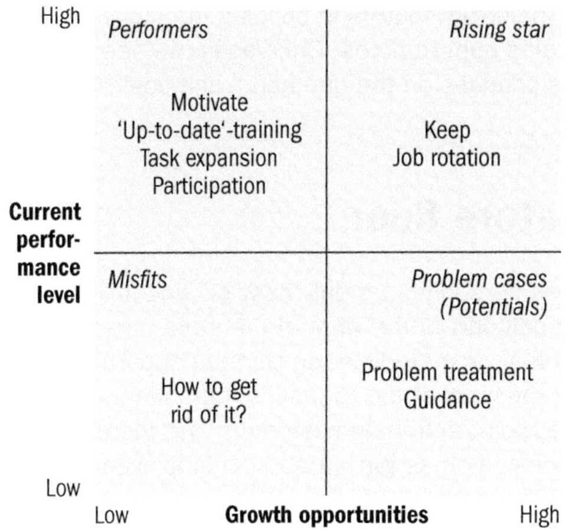

- Finally, there is a field that consists of the group of people who do not perform well and who show no potential for further development. This is actually the group of employees that one wants to get rid of. But this is not always possible.

In general we see that human resources managers strive to have as many as stars as possible in their database. After all, they measure their success based on the fact that they have a successor on standby for every important function. In retail, this is different. Given the flat organisational structure and the short career lines in retail, we should actually aim to keep as many as possible of these performers. After all, the star status can only be honoured by promotion in some cases. If a star is not promoted in due time, or at least confronted with a new challenge, he will disappear.
In that case we have educated and trained good employees for the competition! This is a terrible waste, from two perspectives: (1) the investment in the training has not generated any returns and (2) the competition is handed the expertise of the organisation on a silver platter. This is one of the reasons why we have the phenomenon of horizontal promotion in larger retailer organisations. This horizontal promotion is aimed at keeping the *stars* and *performers*. With *horizontal promotion* purchase managers (temporarily) go to sales and vice versa. In addition to the possibility of retaining good employees, this policy has an additional and very important advantage: this promotes the mutual understanding between the two major commercial functions. In the context of the previously discussed possible frictions between these functions, this is a significant gain.

Horizontal promotion

20.3 Personnel control

Under *personnel control* we understand – given the assignment of the functions – the optimal deployment of the personnel to keep cost as low as possible with the highest possible sales result. Considering the relatively heavy utilisation of the sales function, the focus of personnel control lies

Personnel control

20

mainly with the store personnel. The retailer is thereby confronted with a dilemma: on the one hand, the personnel forms the biggest cost and therefore any saving on personnel is favourable. On the other hand, the personnel is one of the most important factors in building the store image and thus greatly affects the sales opportunities. Once again we see a critical assessment of sales chances on the one hand, and cost efficiency on the other hand.

20.4 Activities on the store floor

It is a misconception that sales personnel are only busy serving the customers. Only a relatively small part of the work of the store personnel has to do with personal service. A time study in the German department store Kaufhof showed that, of the work of the 'front-line' personnel (thus only the personnel that were appointed to help customers and therefore not the personnel behind the scenes, such as the warehouse employees and administration), only 30% to 50% is actually spent on serving customers (see figure 20.5).

FIGURE 20.5 Time study summary Kaufhof

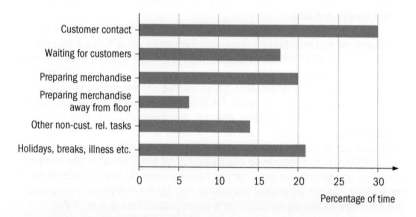

Percentage of time

It is debatable whether the modern consumer still has such a need for personal service. We can see that customers have an increasing need to be left alone while shopping. Personal service (in the sense of addressing the customer to make a purchase), when the customer has no need for the service, is rather seen as a 'dis-service' than as a service. Only if the customer really needs help, does he want to be assisted. And then preferably immediately! In practice, this means that the system of full service à la the TV series *Are you being served?* has just about disappeared in the 'better' specialty stores – which profiles on service. Personal service is replaced by systems of self selection and self service. With self selection we mean that the customer can make his or her own selection, but there is personnel available to solve problems and to 'assist'. With self service the customer does everything independently, except for payment at the cash register and even this may be one of the possibilities in the future. Albert Heijn has been

Self selection

Self service

experimenting with self-scanning shopping carts, and HEMA does the same with self-scanning cash registers. Practically this means that the store personnel are more and more concerned with *passive sales promotion* and only very partially with *active sales promotion*. Passive sales promotion is mainly about organising (and maintaining) the entourage in the store in such a way that the customer can find products undisturbed and easily. This in influenced by amongst other the presentation, layout of the store and the presence of goods. Sometimes, ensuring that these aspects of the store floor are correct, we need more 'hands' than with finishing with the customer in personalised service. This will be illustrated using the trinity analysis of both primary sectors of the retail in the Netherlands: the BV Supermarket Nederland and the BV Non-food Nederland (see figure 20.6).

Passive sales promotion

Active sales promotion

FIGURE 20.6 Trinity supermarket versus non-food 2010

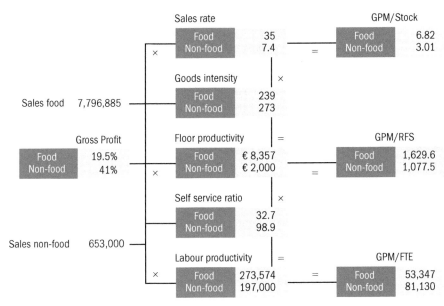

Source: HBD, Deloitte 2011, own editing

The charts were compiled based on the national accounts of retail in the Netherlands. The data therefore relates to the entire food sector and the entire non-food sector, both large and small companies. Looking at the charts, we see that the food sector, which mainly consists of companies which apply the self service system, display a self service ratio and a labour productivity that is much lower than that in the non-food, while the non-food sector generally applies a much more personalised service. Obviously, to ensure a good self service environment, it requires much more personnel deployment (especially behind the scenes) than one would initially expect.

20

20.5 Planning the workforce

Employees in retail work between 36 and 40 hours per week. Stores are generally open much longer. The Trading Hours Act of 1996 allows stores to be open maximum 14 hours per day, or 84 hours per week with a six day opening. This means that the operating time does not correspond with the opening time and that working schedules need to be used. With smaller retail companies, where only a limited number of employees are available, this may cause problems. This is why these smaller companies generally make relatively little use of the opportunities presented by the new trading hours act. Larger companies need to ensure a constant minimum occupation to keep the store open. With the resulting schedule, they will strive for the lowest possible cost. This again causes friction: when permanent employees work at 'unusual' times (late night shopping, Saturday and possibly Sunday), this is associated with significant surcharges. From this perspective, the retailer will seek to limit the input of permanent employees as much as possible. They will rather use temporary or auxiliary employees, for which there are no – or much lower – surcharges. The problem is that these 'unusual' times are often precisely the times when the customer flow is very large. With the result that precisely at these busy times, the workforce of expertly qualified permanent employees is very small. The trick is to make a schedule that achieves a balance between the desire to minimise costs and the desire to maximise service to the customer.

20.6 Maximum occupancy

In addition to the problem of maintaining the quality of the minimum capacity, an important aspect in personnel control is adapting the input of the personnel to fluctuations in demand. Customer flows are not constant over time. Variations occur on the hours of the day, on the days of the week, the weeks of the month and the months of the year (see figure 20.7).

These variations also vary depending on the sector of the retailer. In the fashion sector, for example, the customer pattern varies strongly during the week and per season. During the week, many customers come by for late night shopping and on Saturday. Each season there is a lot of interest at the start of the fashion season (in February and March for the summer season, and in September and October for the winter season). At supermarkets, the fluctuations are much stronger during the day and on a Saturday.

The most complicated pattern occurs at department stores. Not only do department stores exhibit a strongly fluctuating pattern during the day, but also during the week, with the fashion season (50% of the sales of department stores consists of clothing) and very strongly on holidays and peak moments such as Sinterklaas and Christmas. The occupancy pattern in a department store during the peak hours on the Saturday before Sinterklaas can be up to a thousand times higher than during off-peak hours on a Monday in January. Moreover, the occupancy patterns also vary during the year per department. In the fashion sector, the peak period falls in September, in the travel industry, this is in July.

Sales capacity planning

To meet these fluctuations, one can use a *sales capacity planning*: based on an analysis of the occupancy pattern, one determines the quantity

FIGURE 20.7 Graph of occupancy patterns: day, week

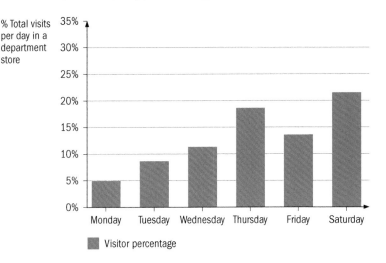

% Total visits per day in a department store

Visitor percentage

and the quality of the personnel deployment per department. The constantly required minimum capacity will then be filled as much as possible with permanent employees. They will try to fill the fluctuations during the day with part-time employees who have a contract for a fixed number of hours. The variations during the week are filled with auxiliary employees, while one will try to use temporary employees or *stand-by employees*: for the occasional peaks: more or less permanent employees who can be called up at times when extreme traffic is expected.

Stand-by employees

Summary

On the one hand, personnel forms the biggest cost in retail, which is why the retailer is continuously seeking labour-saving methods. On the other hand, it is one of the most important ways to influence the image of the store, which is why the retailer is constantly seeking to improve the quality of the personnel. Therefore, in retail, we distinguish between personnel management (the policy on personnel quality) and personnel control (the policy on the quantity of personnel).
Using the value chain of Michael Porter, we can clearly indicate which frictions occur between the functions in the retail. In particular, the friction between purchasing and sales is a deciding factor, especially since there is a degree of shared responsibility between these two functions.
Using the objective function discussed in chapter 6, we can explain this friction.
The objective function is: $R = S \times M - C$
- where purchasing is responsible for M and S (expressed as $S = MS \times MS$, or the ADM);
- where sales is responsible for C and S (expressed as $S = CA \times VI \times C \times AT$).

Personnel control focuses on the optimal deployment of quantity personnel. Precisely because patterns in retail can vary strongly in occupancy during the day, week and year, an adequate sales capacity planning using flexible

20

personnel is very important. Especially the slightly larger retail companies have used functional organisation to date (purchasing, sales, logistics). Due to the rapidly changing environment, there seems to be a certain degree of return to a divisional organisation currently (category management).

21
Physical Distribution

21.1   The physical distribution process
21.2   Inbound logistics
21.3   Goods management within the organisation
21.4   Outbound logistics: from store to consumer

In the past, physical distribution formed the essence of the retail, mainly the bridging of the imbalances of time (taking stock), location (from supplier to sales address) and quantity (breaking bulk) (for a detailed explanation of logistics, please refer to Buuron, 1995 and Van Goor and Ploos van Amstel, 1996 and for a more popular explanation, please refer to Goldratt and Cox, 1995). Although time, location and quantity are still part of the primary functions of retail, we can conclude the other two primary functions of retail, purchasing and selling, have become relatively more important. This does not mean physical distribution has become unimportant. On the contrary, goods that are not there at the right time cannot be sold. It means retail does not exclusively consist of the technical distribution of goods. In the current environment of retail, the physical distribution function forms part of an overall marketing system and should therefore be tailored to the demands that are set from the other primary functions. In fact, we can say the physical distribution function is taking on more of a role in connecting the purchasing and sales process in a flexible manner. In this context, we must consider the physical distribution as part of a marketing process rather than a technique. Therefore, in the current environment, not only is the technical management of the goods flow important, but also the speed of the process. And this applies both in terms of the commercial success and in terms of cost management. In a situation where the change in consumer behaviour is occurring faster and becoming more unpredictable, only the retailer that can get the desired goods in store quickly will survive. The fact that acceleration of the process also leads to lower inventory costs is a bonus. We discuss these subjects in this chapter.

21

21.1 The physical distribution process

Figure 21.1 shows the position of the physical distribution in the strategic process.

FIGURE 21.1 The strategic process: the physical distribution

Physical distribution

Under *physical distribution* (PD) we understand 'the process aimed at the physical flow of goods from manufacturer or supplier, through the store, to the consumer'. This process comprises of the logistics aspects of retail marketing. The purpose of the physical distribution is to achieve the maximum availability of the correct goods to the consumer, at the right time and at the lowest possible cost.

Physical distribution process

The physical distribution process includes three components:
1 the inbound logistics: from supplier to the store, whether or not through a central warehouse;
2 the management and processing of the goods within the store until the time of sale;
3 the outbound logistics: from the shelf to the consumer's home.

Information process

In parallel with the physical goods flow, but in the opposite direction, we find the *information process*. Any purchase by a consumer puts a flow of information in motion which should ultimately lead to the purchased product being fulfilled. The first signal (purchase) is registered by the checkout process. Orders are drafted based on the collective cash information (or in the 'old' situation, by periodically counting the stock in the store). Orders go to the central warehouse (if there is an in-house central storage function) or are converted into a direct order from the supplier.

In the current situation, where speed of replenishment is playing an increasingly bigger role, the collection of the information takes place increasingly more at the supplier level. The system of *continuous replenishment* means that information scanned at the checkout, is communicated to manufacturers online using Electronic Data Interchange (EDI).

Continuous replenishment

Described in this way, the PD process seems to be a relatively simple matter. The increased complexity of modern retailing, however, ensures the process is more complicated and the fulfilment of the PD function is an increasingly specialised discipline.

21

The increased complexity is caused by a number of factors. First, the transition from product orientation to demand orientation means the retailer is faced with more and more suppliers. The traditional grocer has to deal with only a limited number of suppliers of dry groceries. The modern supermarket, however, needs to deal with suppliers of fresh products and suppliers of household products. Each of these flows has their own characteristics. We often see that the process is divided into parallel sub-processes: slow-movers flows versus fast-movers flows, direct deliveries versus deliveries from the central warehouse and refrigerated transport versus un-cooled transport. In the fashion sector, this problem is further intensified, because the suppliers are often dispersed throughout the world. The effective smooth running of a supply flow from China requires different measures than acquiring goods from a supplier in Groningen.

Second, we can conclude that the actual transport of goods from the supplier to the store is causing more and more problems. An increase in the number of suppliers, with direct deliveries, leads to an increase in the number of trucks lined up in front of the store. This is one of the reasons why most large retail companies have their own *distribution centres* or warehouses. In these centres, deliveries by suppliers are redistributed and combined into grouped store orders. The store will now only have one truck in front of the door, with a large shipment, rather than countless vehicles with partial deliveries.

Distribution centres

Town centres also pose a problem. Due to increased congestion, it is becoming increasingly more difficult to supply the stores at predictable times. We often see deliveries need to take place either very early in the morning or even at night. This means the PD function in large retail companies is becoming more of a continuous operation, with irregular working hours. In the future, the congestion problem, especially for retail in the centres of large cities, will be even worse. Some larger municipalities have even setup *transfer areas*. These are transhipment centres at the edge of the city where shipments for various stores are transferred into smaller transport units that are easier to transport into the city. Finally, with the increasing volume of retail companies, the number of delivery addresses is also increasing. A company like Blokker has more than six hundred branches in the Netherlands alone. These branches are supplied from the central distribution centre, of which there are also more than 270 franchisees. Thus, the problem quickly becomes clear. Although the PD function in the current retail process is only one of the three primary functions, it remains a very important success factor.

Transfer areas

21

Those retailers, who are able to get the goods in store faster than the competition by using a sophisticated logistics system, have an enormous competitive advantage (see figure 21.2). Not only will they be able to reduce costs, but they will also be able to rapidly follow consumer trends. The PD will therefore continue to play a vital role in retail marketing.

FIGURE 21.2 Representation of the logistics system

As a result of the previously discussed chain reversal (from *product push* to *demand pull* – see paragraph 7.4), we see increasingly more merging of the process described above. This development is known as *supply chain management*. Activities that were traditionally performed within the central warehouse of the retail organisation (for example the store preparation), is increasingly being outsourced to the supplier. Likewise, there is a movement emerging where suppliers no longer supply to the central warehouse in bulk. They are increasingly delivering the goods already grouped per branch based on scanning information from branches that are placed online through EDI. All the retailer has to do is combine the partial shipments from various suppliers per branch into ready-made branch shipments. This is known as *cross docking*. Obviously, the supplier will try to negotiate a fee for these activities. This means the negotiations with the supplier are no longer just about the bare purchase price (as in the past), but the integration benefits that are to be achieved in the overall process from supplier to the store also factor in. In this process of *chain integration* one strives for a win-win situation. This requires a steady relationship with the supplier (*vendor relations, preferred suppliers*). In terms of organisation within the retail store, this means one should switch over from a functional purchasing organisation (purchasing should ensure a good margin: M in the formula $R = S \times M - C$) into a divisional category management organisation (the category manager should ensure the good R of his category). It is possible that it is decided to use a lower margin for the retailer if this leads to a more than proportional decrease in C. The development outlined here will not apply to all product categories that are maintained within retail. One may not necessarily need to maintain good vendor relations for worldwide available me-too-products. For high-quality, formula defining product ranges with a high out-of-stock risk, however, it will be necessary. Kraijlic summarises this in his purchasing product portfolio, where he compares the relative importance and cost of the product categories against the risk of non-delivery (see figure 21.3). The *me-too*-products then appear in the lower left corner of the matrix. These goods can simply be purchased through the purchasing department (who delivers the best at the lowest price). The *strategic products* (formula

Supply chain management

Cross docking

Chain integration

defining, with high *out-of-stock* risk) appears in the upper right corner.
These are the categories for which the partner *shipping* story applies.

FIGURE 21.3 Kraijlic's purchasing product portfolio

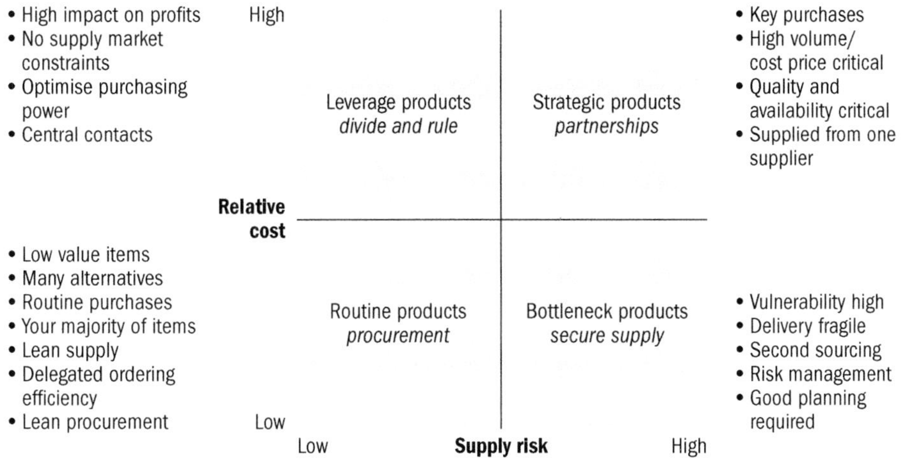

• High impact on profits
• No supply market
  constraints
• Optimise purchasing
  power
• Central contacts
	High
	
	Leverage products
	divide and rule
		Strategic products
		partnerships
			• Key purchases
			• High volume/
			  cost price critical
			• Quality and
			  availability critical
			• Supplied from one
			  supplier

Relative cost

• Low value items
• Many alternatives
• Routine purchases
• Your majority of items
• Lean supply
• Delegated ordering
  efficiency
• Lean procurement
	Routine products
	procurement
		Bottleneck products
		secure supply
			• Vulnerability high
			• Delivery fragile
			• Second sourcing
			• Risk management
			• Good planning
			  required

Low   **Supply risk**   High

21.2 Inbound logistics

In general, we can say the incoming flow of goods to the retailer is the
most difficult to master. The reason is that the organisation of this flow
can only partially be influenced by the retailer. It still depends on the
capabilities of the supplier. As a result, a large part of the activities
of the retailer in the PD is aimed at controlling the incoming flow as
much as possible. We discuss measuring the effectiveness of the
incoming flow and we discuss the supplier management.

21.2.1 Measuring the effectiveness of the incoming flow

The effectiveness of the incoming flow is measured by three variables.
First, the *delivery time*: the period that passes between placing the order   **Delivery time**
with the supplier and the moment the retailer receives the goods.
Second, the variable *delivery rate*: the percentage of the total number   **Delivery rate**
of order lines that are ordered and which are actually delivered with the
(first) supply. In situations where there is a continuous flow of goods in
terms of composition, this delivery rate will generally be high. Particularly
in the non-food sector, there is often talk of irregular flows arising from
varying seasons or variable production planning with the supplier. In
these cases, it often happens that certain items are not in stock, so the
delivery rate drops. Ultimately, this has implications for the availability of
the goods in the store. A rough rule of thumb that still applies in the
non-food retail, is 10% of undelivered products leads to 5% lost sales
(see table 21.1).

TABLE 21.1 Consumer response to out of stock situations

	Food (in %)	**Non-food** (in %)
Purchased replacement product	48	26
Did not purchase in visited store	52	74
• of which 'purchase later' at the same store	21	33
• of which purchase elsewhere	31	41 (lost sales)

Source: McGoldrick, 1990 (own editing)

The third variable is that of costs. The delivery conditions of the supplier often includes a specific mode of transport (for example by boat or train), respectively, certain conditions occur and the responsibility is transferred from supplier to receiver, such as *free on board* (FOB) or *cost, insurance, freight* (CIF). In some cases, however, it may be useful for the recipient to deviate from these conditions. For example, in the case of high quality goods, where the interest charges during transport may be high, it may make sense to consider air transport rather than boat transport. Something similar applies to shipments where the risks of the costs (lost revenue) of no-sales are greater than the additional cost of a faster mode of transport. The same applies for products that quickly go out of season.

The three variables are closely related to each other. A short delivery time may result in the delivery rate decreasing, because not all ordered products are present yet. Low transport costs may lead to an extension of the delivery time (boat transport is cheaper, but also much slower than air transport).

21.2.2   Vendor management

Vendor rating

To assess the quality of the supplier, larger retail companies are increasingly turning to *vendor rating*: a system where, looking at the 'scores' of every supplier, it is determined to what extent the requirements of the receiver are met. In addition to elements such as production quality, an important part of the vendor rating determines how the supplier cooperates in the solution of PD problems. The results of these analyses are often discussed with the relevant suppliers. This gives the suppliers better insight into the reasons why retailers are so demanding, while retailers will get a better understanding of the difficulties for the supplier. A platform is thereby created for improvement and further cooperation.

Figure 21.4 describes the chain reaction that occurs with a sudden expansion of consumers' demands. In January, there is a 10% increase in consumers' demands. With the slightest delay, this results in an 18% increase of orders by retailers from their wholesale dealers. This increase in the order quantity, in turn, leads to a 34% increase of factory orders by wholesalers to producers, resulting in a 50% expansion of the production planning.

FIGURE 21.4 The multiplier effect of an unexpected increase in retail sales of 10%

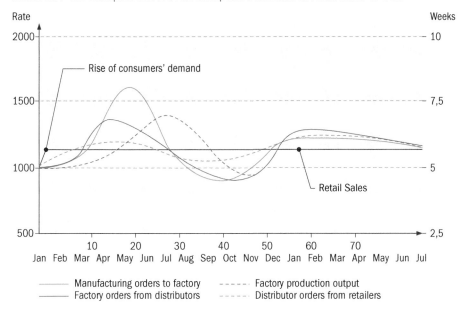

Rise of consumers' demand

Retail Sales

──── Manufacturing orders to factory	---- Factory production output
──── Factory orders from distributors	---- Distributor orders from retailers

The most extreme result of such a chain situation is the development of *sourcing*. With sourcing, the retailer no longer buys products from suppliers who have a good vendor rating and have proven to be able to participate in the overall chain, but rather with capacity to produce the products. Because the production capacity is reserved for the retailer, it is possible to wait up to the last minute with the final specification of the products. The flexibility of the sorting per product range is therefore considerably increased, while the *lead time* of the product development can be significantly shortened. That is a big advantage in situations where the consumers' demands undergo rapid changes. In fact, sourcing comes down to merging the logistics and the purchasing function within the *retail value chain*, and merging of the value chain of the producer and the retailer within the overall chain. Especially in the fashion industry, we see big international chains are increasingly moving from purchasing to sourcing. The Swedish Hennes & Mauritz, the American The Limited (including chains like Structure, Victoria's Secret and Express), the American GAP (including The Old Navy Store) and the Spanish ZARA are all using sourcing and are therefore able to follow fashion trends closely. As a result, they can achieve a very high sales rate. It is these vertically organised companies that are currently very successful.

It is clear such systems only make sense if there are very short, very quick and very active information systems. Modern information technology allows us to do this. *Point of sale* (POS), scanning and online connections with suppliers make it possible to supply customer information to the manufacturers practically simultaneously. *Automatic re-ordering*, rapid product development and rapid re-arrangement of the sourced production capacity are therefore made possible. This will result in a change of internal processes within the retail value chain, through which they will take on the form described in paragraph 7.4.

Sourcing

21

21.3 Goods management within the organisation

Goods that are received from the supplier often have to undergo
a number of transformations before they are ready to be placed on
the store shelves. Although, in context of the cooperation in the chain
discussed in paragraph 21.2, it occurs more frequently for suppliers to
perform activities that were previously carried out in the store, (this is
called *store ready supply*). Larger retail companies often perform such
centralised work in the distribution centre. In smaller companies, this
needs to take place in the store. The activities comprise of:

Store ready supply

- checking the delivered quantities;
- finishing defect reports;
- unpacking and repacking the goods;
- pricing or readying the goods for scanning;
- transport to the branches for supplies to the central distribution
  centre;
- sorting the goods in the branches for store presentation;
- stocking the shelves, respectively presentation.

Although each of these activities is not very difficult, the process-
alignment of this work is complicated. This is especially true since our
customers should preferably not notice any of this. It is highly annoying
to a customer if, while shopping, he has to create a path through the
empty boxes or stock carts blocking the aisle. The store floor is there
for the convenience of the customer and not for the efficiency of the
replenishment process. We measure the effectiveness of the internal
goods management on the period between receiving the goods from the
supplier and the time at which the goods are sold. The measurement we
use in retail is the sales rate. We discuss this concept in more detail
below. We also look at the various aspects of stock control, especially
the optimisation thereof.

21.3.1 The concept of sales rate

Sales rate

The *sales rate* is defined in its simplest form as 'sales divided by
inventory'. A sales rate of 12 means, on average, the goods are present
in the organisation for a month. With a sales rate of 24, this is two
weeks and, with a sales rate of 3, this is four months. However, we need
to be careful with the interpretation of the concept of 'sales rate'. Some
companies value the stock at purchase value (*at cost*) and other companies at market value (*at retail value*). Some companies define sales
excluding VAT, others including VAT. Some calculate it at inflow value
(before markdowns) and in other cases it is valued against cash register
sales (after markdowns). Franchise organisations calculate the sales
rate at delivery value (only including the fee for the franchise organisation) and in other cases at consumer value, where the margin for the
retailer is also included in the base value. Each of these methods leads
to a different figure for the stock sales rate, although the same amounts
of goods are always processed in a period of time.

At cost

At retail value

It is therefore important to assess the sales rate according to which
method is used to measure. This will not cause big problems for the
internal comparison. It is understood, once we have chosen a particular
basis for measurement, this basis must be applied consistently. The
development of the sales rate, in which ever way it is measured, always

provides insight into the development of the internal efficiency of goods management. But if we use the sales rate as benchmark variable, thus compare the efficiency between various companies, we have to be especially careful.

21.3.2   Influence of seasonal movements on the calculation of the sales rate

In situations that involve a continuous and stable sales pattern, it is generally sufficient for the calculation of inventory to be measured at any given time. After all, if the sales pattern is stable – with adequate control – the inventory will be equal all of the time. However, in cases where it involves a pronounced seasonal pattern in demand, the measurement of time is of great influence. We can no longer use sufficient time measurements of the inventory levels, but should work with moving average inventory levels. Example 21.1 may be able to explain this.

EXAMPLE 21.1 STOCK OF CHRISTMAS PRODUCTS

A department store has an annual sales of €10 billion in Christmas products. With the inventory balance sheet on the 1st of February (retail companies often have a fiscal year that runs from the 1st of February to the 31st of January, so they close after the year-end sales, when the stock is at its lowest) the complete inventory appears to have been sold. The sales rate according to the simple method on the balance sheet date is then infinite (€10 billion / 0).

In order to have enough stock to be able to realise this sales of €10 billion, however, it already had to be available in August of the previous year. In other words, for six months, from February through July of the previous year, there was no stock of Christmas decorations. For four months, from August through November, the entire stock was present. For the month of December, half of the stock was present, considering that during this month, the stock is sold out completely and for January there was no stock. The weighted average sales on annual basis was then 2.7. And that is quite different from infinity. Table 1 explains the calculation.

The weighted average stock is:
$(6 \times 0 + 4 \times 10 + 1 \times 5 + 1 \times 0) / 12 =$ 3.75 million

The weighted average sales rate is:
$10 / 3.75 = 2.7$

TABLE 1 The calculations of the weighted average sales rate (at market value)

Month	Stock	Sales
February	0	0
March	0	0
April	0	0
May	0	0
June	0	0
July	0	0
August	10 million	0
September	10 million	0
October	10 million	0
November	10 million	0
December	5 million	10 million
January	0	0

21.3.3   Aspects of stock control

When treating stock control in retail, it makes sense to distinguish between the flow of goods with a stable and constant character and the flow of goods with irregular seasonal patterns, as in large parts of the fashion and non-food sector. In the first case, the consumers' demand is easy to predict and we can manage the stock based on the sales developments in the store.

Pull methods   In this case we speak of *pull methods*: the *trigger* for the stock control is the sales development in the store and thus ultimately the consumers' demand. In the second case, where a constant fluctuation of product ranges occur and where one cannot know in advance whether a certain product will be successful, and the sales personnel often do not know the product in

Push methods   advance, we must resort to *push methods*: the goods are 'pushed' into the store and, only once this is done, we do find out whether or not the products are successful. In this case, the trigger for stock control is formed by the activities of the purchasing department.

21.3.4   Optimisation of the stock control with continuous goods flows: pull methods

Both primary objectives of the PD, specifically maximum availability for the consumer (expressed in sales), at minimum cost for the company (expressed in the level of stock) are incorporated in the sales rate as a measure for the effectiveness of the internal goods management. The combination of maximising on the one hand and minimising on the other hand has always resulted in a process of optimisation. The same applies in the PD: maximum availability for the consumer leads to extremely high inventory costs, minimum inventory costs leads to an extremely low availability. Somewhere in between is the optimal ratio between sales and stock. In determining this optimum, we use the concepts of 'economic order size' (or it's reciprocal: the 'optimal order frequency') and 'minimum stock'.

Minimum stock

Minimum stock   Under *minimum stock* we understand the stock necessary to bridge the sales during the period between the order by the retailer and the delivery by the manufacturer. Maintaining this minimum stock should mean the consumer, except for changes in the normal purchasing pattern, never loses out. The minimum stock also determines the minimum order frequency and the minimum order size. It is now clear why retailers are so set on rapid delivery times in the view of incoming goods flow. After all, speeding up the delivery cycle reduces the minimum amount of stock to be maintained and thereby the cost of stock in proportion to the reduction in delivery time. The minimum stock has no safety margin. There is only need for one thing to go wrong in the supply and the availability of the products, for the consumer to no longer be guaranteed. This is why retailers often strive for a certain amount of overstock or buffer stock. When determining the buffer stock, the costs play an important role.

Optimal order size

Every order that goes out the door is accompanied by costs, both for the retailer (such as carrying out the order, receiving the goods and distribution within the organisation) and for the supplier (such as order picking and transport). The relationship between the average order size and the total costs associated with the completion of the orders, progresses as in

FIGURE 21.5 Optimal order size

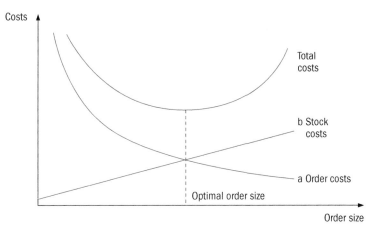

curve a in figure 21.5. The higher the average order size (or the less frequently an order is placed), the lower the order costs per unit product. However, the relationship is not linear, but asymptotic. A low order frequency (or high average order size) is, however, associated with high inventory costs (interest and space). The relationship between the average order size and the total inventory costs progresses as in curve b in figure 21.5. This relationship will generally be linearly increasing. The *optimal order size* can now be determined by checking where the sum of the costs for maintaining and ordering inventory, is the lowest (see figure 21.5).

Optimal order size

If the optimal order size is lower than the minimum stock, the retailer will always seek to maintain the minimum order frequency. If the optimal order size is higher than that corresponding to the minimum stock, the retailer will try to make use of this situation for incorporating a safety margin: the buffer stock.

21.3.5 Optimisation of the stock control with discontinuous goods flows: push methods

The stock control with discontinuous flows and flexible sorting per product range varies significantly from that of the continuous flows. The problem is not so much determining the optimal order size per supplier, but determining the optimal purchase quantity per product. The retailer can determine the optimal order size with continuous flows based on the actual sales development, in other words, afterwards. This is not possible when determining the optimum purchase quantity with discontinuous flows. He must anticipate how the market will behave and how successful the product will be. Considering the fact that discontinuous flows often involve fashion product ranges, which are developed far in advance (in the summer of year X, the preparations for the summer collection of year X + 1 are made), this is a very uncertain affair. With stock control, the aim is to get the maximum sales from the product while simultaneously having as little as possible residual stock at the end of the season. In contrast to the continuous flows, it therefore does not involve an optimisation between availability and costs, but between availability and the risk of residual stock.

21

This is why, especially within the fashion sector of retail, lead-time reduction (shortening the period between the order and the delivery) has become of paramount importance. Therefore, in discontinuous flows of goods it is important to determine the minimum stock, reduce the risk of residual stock and adjust this in time. Risks are minimised if the period between order and delivery is shortened.

Determining the minimum stock

The stock planning with discontinuous flows starts with a budgeting of sales based on the estimated growth in demand. Based on previous experiences with successes, failures and assessments of the purchasing regarding the future market development, the retailer drafts a marketing plan. Based on this, he can draft a purchasing plan. This purchasing plan is then based on the expected seasonal pattern and converted into a *goods receipt planning*. This is a schedule of partial deliveries that should lead to the present stock being adjusted as much as possible during the term of the product range to the expected fluctuations in demand, without involving a very high over-stock. Due to the unpredictability of the demand, a lot can go wrong in this process. For example, a container can get lost in route and deliveries can be made too late or too early. Therefore, it is important to include a certain level of flexibility in the goods receipt planning.

Goods receipt planning

Restricting the risk of residual stocks: OTB

When production planning of discontinuous, strongly fluctuating flows is determined far in advance, it is almost impossible to cancel ordered products, unless very big mistakes were made by the supplier. In this, an order is a one-off binding contract, rather than a type of delivery arrangement. Products that do not appear to be successful after the first partial delivery still need to be purchased. On the other hand, the purchasing department will do their best to repurchase products that are unexpectedly successful and therefore sell out quickly, during the season. This means there is a kind of automation that can lead to an increase of stock. Products that do not sell remain unsold and products that do sell are repurchased. To prevent automation which leads to an explosion of the stock size, we use the control system called Open To Buy (OTB).

OTB-system

Basically, the *OTB-system* is very simple: on the basis of the goods receipt planning derived from the budget planning, the already placed orders are deducted. The balance shows what may still be repurchased according to the budget. This is known as the OTB limit. In practice, this is more complicated. In order to anticipate the commercial dynamics, the retailer makes constant changes during the budgeting period. Departments that exceed the budget in terms of sales (and are therefore unexpectedly successful), the limit is adjusted upwards to prevent no-sales later on in the season. For departments that do not run as expected, the limit is adjusted downwards to prevent non-saleable residual stocks.

Adjustments during the lifetime of the product range

It is clear the risks associated with discontinuous flows are significantly higher than with continuous flows. With continuous flows, an incorrect order most of the time leads to a temporary reduction in sales rate. But the sales rate will restore itself in time. Or it leads to a relatively small missed sales, because the products are usually in stock at the supplier level. With discontinuous flows, an incorrect order always leads to difficult to repair situations. Too much of an order leads to residual stocks that will probably not be sold the following year, given the rate of things going out of demand. An order that is too small leads to missed sales, which – given the lead time of the production process – can probably never be recovered.

The risk associated with too much of an order leads to the need for very rapid identification of 'bad buys', so one can quickly start with corrections, either by *merchandise management* (redistribution of goods over branches), or by disposing of the product through markdowns. Markdown losses should generally be taken as soon as possible, first because the initial markdown is the smallest and therefore the least expensive, second because the interest costs of residual costs may be substantial.

Merchandise management

The risk associated with too little of an order leads to, in addition to the need for rapid identification, the need for the sourcing and supply chain management discussed in paragraph 21.1. Only if one has access to production capacity with willing suppliers, one can adjust quickly. Process-oriented means retailers strive to redirect the ratio between the previously classified production capacity and still sub divisible production capacity (in the old purchasing methods often 70/30) to a ratio that is closer to 30/70. In other words, the OTB limit which, in the old situation, would only amount to 30% of the expected sales at the start of the season would have to increase to 70% in the new methodology.

FIGURE 21.6 The implications of uncertainties: the trumpet of doom

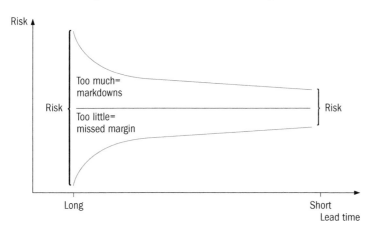

Shortening the time between order and delivery
Figure 21.6 describes the risk a retailer runs when purchasing discontinuous, often fashion sensitive, goods flows. This involves two different risks. In the first place the retailer runs the risk the products he should actually have purchased, have not been purchased. For example, because he did not follow a trend this obviously leads to missed sales. This risk has increased in recent years, driven by the fast changing consumer demands and shorter lasting trends. It is clear the risks increase significantly if the orders have to be placed further in advance and the risks decrease as the lead time becomes shorter. Secondly, the retailer runs the risk the goods he has ordered are not or are no longer in demand when they are delivered to the store because the trend has passed. The goods still need to be sold at some point, otherwise the pipeline will fill up and one will have an outdated

product range policy. This means the goods need to be marked down, which results in a loss of margin. It is clear this risk can be reduced significantly as one is better able to shorten the period between ordering and delivering.

21.4 Outbound logistics: from store to consumer

We currently pay very little attention to the outgoing flow. Retailers assume consumers that have purchased something in their stores, will organise their own transport home. For the vast majority of categories of goods it is not a problem and consumers expect nothing more. But there are types of goods or purchase situations where this may form a problem. This relates to heavy or large products such as furniture, products requiring installation, like washing machines and televisions, but also purchasing a large quantity of groceries at once. In such cases, the retailer should provide *after sales service*, such as a courier service (privately managed or contracted), installation service, or availability of delivery vans or *caddy services*. The latter form of after sales service is used in American supermarkets, for example, where groceries are packed at the cash register and assistance is given in transporting the groceries to the car. The costs associated with such services may be rather significant. Nevertheless, it is important one does not forget the outgoing flow in the development of the logistics system, as customers may become irritated (see example 21.2).

After sales service

Caddy services

Our products can be taken home immediately

EXAMPLE 21.2 PRAXIS

DIY store, Praxis, devotes much attention to the comfort of shopping for its customers. Given the bulky products that are sold in DIY stores, they developed special shopping carts, which large slabs of wood and thick bundles of boards can be moved easily.
The aisles were kept wide so shoppers would have enough space to move freely. However, after making the purchase,

customers would take the shopping carts into the parking area to load the purchased goods into their cars and often leave them behind in the parking area. As a result, new customers sometimes could not find a shopping cart and retrieving the shopping carts required extra personnel costs to be made. In order to avoid this problem, Praxis – in site of reducing costs – placed poles at the exit which the shopping carts could not pass.

After checking out, customers needed to leave their shopping carts outside, unattended, while they pulled up their cars. Only then could they load the goods into their vehicle. There is no need in pointing out this caused severe irritation with their customers. The poles have since been removed and the problem has been solved by implementing a type of deposit system, as used in supermarkets.

21

Summary

The physical distribution, parallel to the changing role of retail, has developed from the primary function within the distribution process to one of the three primary functions, with the main task to smoothly connect the other two primary processes: purchasing and sales. The logistic processes are an increasing part of an integrated marketing system, rather than solely a cost. The process is divided into three parts: the incoming flow, management within the organisation and the outgoing flow. The incoming flow still causes quite a few problems for the retailer. This is why more and more retailers introduce supplier management. The ultimate result of supplier management is the development of sourcing: collectively planning the production capacity for the retailer, in cooperation with the manufacturer. First of all, this leads to an increase of flexibility in the sorting per product range and secondly, this leads to an acceleration of deliveries.
The concept of sales rate plays an important role in managing the goods within the organisation. The sales rate is influenced significantly by the optimal order size or the minimum order frequency. It is important to keep a close eye on the differences between stable product ranges (*pull methods*) and strongly varying product ranges (*push methods*). In the first instance, the optimisation serves mainly to minimise the inventory costs. In the second instance, mainly to minimise the risk of residual overstock. The open to buy system plays an important role here.

22
Presentation

Co-Author: Chantal Riedeman

In this chapter on presentation, we will further discuss the concept of presentation, the process of the store layout, store design, the 'layout plan', layout, departmental layout, shelf layout, goods presentation and in-store promotion.

We will answer questions like: What position does the presentation hold in the strategic process? What is the process of store layout? What do we understand about store design?

22.1 The concept of presentation

Figure 22.1 shows the position of presentation in the strategic process.

FIGURE 22.1 The strategic process: presentation

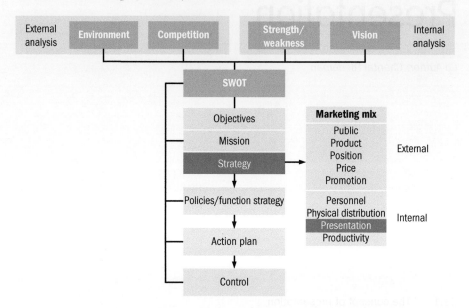

Presentation
Presentation includes all activities aimed at translating the strategy, commercial objectives and the retail formula (the store concept) into the optimal shopping experience (for a better understanding of the store layout aspect, see Underhill, 1999). In this scenario, the P of presentation consists of much more than just preparing goods for sale through shelf design or showcasing. This chapter deals with the shopping experience in a broad sense. In fact, we talk about the outward appearance of our strategy, translated into the shopping environment. Actually, we can say the shopping environment fulfils the function of the packaging strategy and the store concept. A nicely packaged product, which does not contain a good product (in other words, is not supported by a strategic approach), will eventually fail. At the same time, a good product that is sold in poorly designed packaging will be difficult to sell to consumers. In short, every aspect of the retail formula should be perfectly matched. Shopping experience and presentation form an essential part of the strategy and should, considering the enormous competition of online shopping, play a much more important role in the physical store operation. In many stores, from chain stores to independent entrepreneurs, the P of 'presentation' often does not receive the attention and resources that are so desperately needed.

22.2 Personal sales versus self-service

The most important question a retailer should ask himself is this: can the sales representatives always assist every shoppers with their purchases?

If the answer to this question is no, it indicates they expect a large percentage of their shoppers are able to help themselves. Stores need to be fitted accordingly but we can conclude they often are not or are inadequately fitted to assist shoppers with their purchases. This logically leads to consumer questions and confusion which disrupts the shopping and purchasing process of the consumer.

Many stores and retail organisations are heavily focused on efficiency, largely because of the surplus of stores and margin pressure. As retailers cut down on their personnel costs, training and shopping experience, the potential customers will need to become more independent shoppers. However, the shopping environment is often still insufficiently organised. In such shopping environments, it is not possible to structurally generate additional sales since that requires an adjustment of the environment or change in terms of personnel.

Stores that are 100% focussed on *personal sales* need a store that is commercially optimised. Consumers today are shopping more independently than ever, partly because they have familiarised themselves with the stores and products online prior to walking into the store. They want to look around first, pottering and poking, and it is late in the purchasing process they start looking for additional help. At that moment, it is important for the stores' 'salesperson' to be prepared to help the customer. The first impressions and experiences with the store determine whether the visitor will remain in the store, if he will start looking around, possibly be open for advice and eventually end up making a purchase. In the case of a full-service concept, we can also ask an important question: do all visitors always want to be helped immediately by a salesperson? As indicated already, this is no longer always the case today. For a large percentage of the consumers, this implies the traditional established full-service concept no longer lives up to the needs of many consumers.

Personal sales

The non-optimal store experience, even in the case of a *full-service concept* that is not adapted to today's needs, leads to a distortion of the shopping and purchasing process. Consumers subconsciously feel 'forced' to turn to a salesperson, although they would prefer to make the decision themselves. The latter usually happens at the end of the shopping process.

Full-service concept

Self-service ratio or floor utilisation rate
We already discussed the pressure of personnel costs in chapter 20. In economically difficult times, the need for cutbacks is one of the few adjustable factors. Cutbacks in personnel mean, the number of employees in a store is lower than before, while the work load simultaneously increases. The salespeople therefore spend a large portion of their time, carrying out the following processes: tidying up, cleaning, mark-downs, stocking up the shelves, counting, promotions, filing and new shelf-designs and so on. As a result, they have too little time left to still help their potential customers with their purchasing.

A good indicator of a store's *self-service level* is the self-service ratio discussed in chapter 20. The higher the factor, the higher the level of self-service of the visitors.

Self-service level

The self-service ratio is a model-based reflection of reality. We have just seen that reality is often more convoluted in practice than in theory. Theoretically, there could be five employees working over 200 square metres of retail floor space, which results in a self-service ratio of 40. However, if only two of the five salespeople are available to actually help the

22

customers, because the other employees have to take care of other tasks, the actual self-service ratio quickly changes to 100. The full-service concept of this retailer discussed earlier may be ambitious with a self-service ratio of only 40, but the reality is another factor 2.5.

With this reality in the back of our minds, from a commercial perspective, the store can no longer exclusively be seen as a 'nice presentation place' (location/presentation). From a commercial perspective, it is essential to view the store and to design it as an independent sales instrument.

It is unfortunately an illusion for many stores that the salesperson plays the most important role in the sales process. In reality, it appears the consumer is mostly left to carry out his shopping process on his own. When the store formula is still largely aimed at personal sales, but this is not realised because of the limited availability of professional and client friendly employees, it is time for a change in the shopping environment. Retailers should purposefully design stores as largely self-service stores, in which the transaction power of the store itself needs to be optimised.

EXAMPLE 22.1 IKEA

IKEA is a perfect example of a success formula that works because the store concept is built entirely around the needs of the consumer, and not vice versa. Most stores are built around the products. When there is a product range, which hopefully has a target audience, there is a location. The location is designed based on the product range, forcing the consumer (the targeted audience) to find their way to the product, resulting in the sale.

IKEA does the exact opposite and thereby proves to be successful worldwide. Their method is based on universal customer needs and is based on universal shopping and purchasing behaviour.

People do not buy more with children dangling at their side, when they are hungry or thirsty, or need to go to the restroom. No one stays in a store to pensively consider purchasing a very expensive item if you are constantly in the spotlight of 'greedy' salespeople. Hence the success of IKEA's Smaland, which is a free children's play area in their stores where parents can leave their children while they shop. Additionally, consumers in general are not really able to come up with all possible product combinations, so the store is furnished with purchasing suggestions. Consumers are forgetful, so there are 'posts' every few metres with sales aids, shopping lists and pencils. Consumers are wise and preferably do not take a bag immediately, let alone a complete shopping cart, so you find these every few metres, throughout the store. Consumers want to feel and try, so you can touch and try EVERY product at IKEA. Each product has a display model, possibly even a few, in strategic places within the store. In short, the IKEA store concept was literally developed by paying extremely close attention to the needs and shortcomings of consumers. IKEA helps their visitors in every possible way to increase their purchases.

The store should therefore be designed from the perspective of the customer, and that starts with attention to the little details. Consumers expect they will easily find the promotional products from the flyer or advertisement in the store. They expect the featured products to be presented as the main display or in the immediate vicinity of the displays. Consumers expect matching products to be lying, hanging or standing together and products to be priced clearly. In short, they expect shopping will be easy and convenient.

Unfortunately, reality is often a lot more hectic. Clothing presented on display, is difficult to find in the store. Products are not priced clearly. Promotions and conditions are unclear. The fitting rooms cannot be found, are small, often filthy, not enough hooks to hang the items, you must often also wait a long time and you may only take a limited number of items in at a time. The average bookstore does not have an information booth where you can quickly look for information on the book you want independently. It seems an impossible task to make a store customer ready. In the next paragraph, we will first take a brief look at the five steps for setting up a store in which a customer can find his own way.

22.3 **The store layout process**

The store layout process (for a better understanding of the store layout aspect, see Underhill, 1999) consists of several steps and comprises of the total process of determining the store design, the most commercial layout plan, the ideal layout, the departmental plan, shelf layout and the most commercial and effective location for in-store-communication.

Step 1 Store design
Under store design, we understand the spatial interpretation of the store formula and the strategy. The idea is to create an atmosphere and spatial experience that would amplify the store formula for the intended customer. The intended target audience, the intended positioning in the market and the price level have an immediate influence on store design. The consumer's sensory perceptions are very important in store design. What does the potential customer see, hear, feel, smell and experience in-store? An important part of store design is the development of the store concept. Which colours, materials and forms represent the best interpretation of the formula and the strategy? As an example, we can assume Aldi and Albert Heijn would need different materials, colours and an alternative light plan in order to create their desired ideal shopping experience. Store design is often contracted to a special internal department or to an external design/project agency.

Step 2 The layout plan
A layout plan is a rough, sketch drawing of the available space based on the intended product range. It is important to properly implement results from SWOT, goldmine and fair-share analyses done earlier into the layout plan. Which products and/or product groups are the so-called anchors, image builders, concerns, sales makers to allocate a specific number of square metres just to the anchors or just the goldmines in order for these product group(s) to realise their sales.

In short, based on research and analysis (where are we now?) and the strategy (where are we heading?), we determine the strategic distribution of the square metres and strategic classification of the store.

Space allocation plan

How much space will be *allocated* to each department and why?
At the same time, there is typically too little space to be able to optimally accommodate the entire desired product range in the store. The secret here is to find the ideal balance. The consumer does want the feeling of a huge selection, but he is actually specifically looking for the best solution. Retail has always been a business of choice; reducing the search costs for the consumer is and remains central in everything we do. Presenting the best solution is the (physical) retailer's most important and most distinctive task.

When developing a complete new store design, the layout plan is an important part of the briefing for the design department or the external design agency.

The layout plan must regularly be critically analysed (preferably every quarter) and adjusted if needed; simply because the market changes at a fast pace. New products, trends and companies are added every day. In short, to be successful and above all, to be able to remain successful, it is essential to ensure every day the shopping environment ties in perfectly with the current demands and needs of the consumer.

Step 3 The layout
The purpose of the layout is to repurpose the most commercial layout plan based on research and determined on strategy, into a logical and simultaneously inviting store layout. The first and maybe the biggest challenge for stores are to attract relevant visitors. But the second and certainly no less important challenge is to entice as many visitors as possible to stay in the store as long as possible, to see as much as possible of the store (in other words see as many products as possible) and to spend as much as possible.

An important question a retailer should ask himself is: what is the anticipated duration of a visit to the store? The answer to this question largely determines the physical store layout.

Store targeted at a commercial purpose
We can imagine the potential AH to Go customers would like to rush through the store as quickly as possible. Then it is not such a good idea to make too many 'pleasant' aisles in the store, lined with nice products the customer would maybe like to purchase. The AH to Go-store is furnished optimally to accommodate focussed customers who require maximum speed, comfort and efficiency.

On the contrary, it is a good idea to ensure in a consumer electronics or fashion store, that there is in fact much to experience and discover. Visitors of an electronics store want to first see, hear and feel before they consider the purchase. In short, there should be a lot to experience. The sensory experience is also the most powerful distinctive differentiator compared to the internet.

With a purchase that is associated with a major financial risk, it is important to give the consumer quiet time and the opportunity to consider his purchase at leisure. A comfortable quiet corner in the store or a cafe can be a perfect solution. For example, a coffee corner with good coffee, or a restaurant such as that of IKEA offers a quiet space for the consumer to consider their purchase. In this tranquil environment, one can also make new suggestions to the customer for new future purchases. In the IKEA restaurant, everything you see is from IKEA. The same applies for the

HEMA restaurant. And at electronics companies like BCC or Media Markt, it's not only the coffee that offers a new impulse, but the tablets or laptops that can be used here too.

Media Markt-Saturn convinces potential customers with the largest range and a powerful low price perception, but the market proposition is practically impossible for all other consumer electronics stores. So instead of even trying to compete on price and product range, they can look for other distinctive ways of enticing their visitors.

Fashion stores, especially for ladies, should have much to be discovered. It is therefore not a good idea to make everything clearly visible at a glance. If all products were made visible at a glance, many visitors would feel they have seen it all from the entrance, and turn around.

In short, there is a tension between the shopping and purchase behaviour of the consumer on the one hand, and the strategy and commercial objectives on the other hand. The commercial objectives must be obvious in the store. At the same time, the shopping environment must be optimally furnished, aimed at the specific shopping and purchasing behaviour of the consumer. Only in this way can we achieve our commercial ambitions on the store floor.

The strategy, the commercial objectives, the market proposition, the location, store formula and possible marketing efforts collectively determine the *occupancy pattern* of the store. Choosing a specific routing system is essential to determine the ideal store layout. Stores with a high customer flow will have to apply other space planning criteria than stores with an extremely low customer flow. We must also keep in mind that the occupancy pattern will fluctuate constantly during the year, the month, the week and even during the day. This fluctuation applies to every store. **Occupancy pattern**

It is important to develop a *semi-flexible layout* where the expansion of existing or introduction of new product groups and fixed 'flex'-metres for promotional products placement can be considered in advance. The shift in product range over the holidays is commonly known. Other, perhaps important products or even complete product groups are then removed temporarily from the product range, at the expense of the Christmas range. The same applies for promotional displays that will afterwards often still have to be fitted into the already developed layout. It is often not the most commercial, and certainly not the most attractive solution. In addition, one must consider the *physical distribution systems*. The retailer could choose to reduce the size of the departments or products/product groups with a higher sales rate and fulfillment frequency than smaller departments with a lower fulfillment frequency. From a commercial perspective, he will then have to consider if he should not actually make the departments/product groups with a high sales rate larger. Obviously there is a big demand and this demand can relatively easily generate more sales. So it is important to continue looking at the so-called *space-elasticity of demand*. In general, this applies: the larger the department, the higher the expenditure per customer. **Semi-flexible layout** **Physical distribution systems** **Space-elasticity of demand**

It could also be true it is more effective for certain products and product groups, from a logistics point of view, to locate them closer to the warehouse.

In short, before drafting a proper and optimal commercial layout, one must consider all possible factors. Despite all logistic and commercial concerns, sometimes the conflicting store and purchasing process of consumers must be the most important point of the plan because they will ultimately determine whether or not more money ends up in the cash register.

The layout of the store must be the perfect commercial and spatial translation of the layout plan, and must connect seamlessly with the needs of the consumer.

Layout types

Depending on the needs, we can distinguish between several different layout types. It is important to slow down or even stop visitors by trying to captivate the consumer's attention. This can be done with adding new products to the product range, but also with price promotions, seasonal specials and matching communication and new solutions. You can also draw the consumer's attention by offering inspirational ideas.

Before we determine the layout type, we must look at the following important aspects that largely determine the final success of the store and it must be included directly in the planning:

- *Stopping force in the street/the display*: what is the walk-by/drive-by frequency of the average consumer? In other words, how often must we refresh the stopping force of our store? What competition do we have in the area and how often do they refresh their stopping force?
- *Entrance*: once we have slowed down the consumer, thanks to our enormous stopping force on the street, and we enticed them inside with our display, it is obviously important to wet the visitor's appetite for more, as quickly as possible. The entrance is the first real introduction for the visitor to the store and he must ultimately be assisted towards making the purchase.
- *Viewing angles*: consumers are just not able to see everything at once so they first 'scan' a shopping environment to see if they like something. If they see something that draws their attention and literally draws them in, they will proceed to walk deeper into the store. This depends on the viewing angles. Have we designed the store in such a way the consumer can look further into the store and see over stands and shelving in the first sections of the store? A store needs layering in the structure and this must be supportive of the consumer's shopping experience. This helps in attracting customers. But seen from a logistics and economical point of view, this is less attractive because the entrance's metric space is actually the most expensive and in this case we will see the least goods here. Goods also cannot be stacked up to two metres high, because it reduces visibility of the rest of the store.
- *Hot spots*: nowadays, the product ranges at many stores are large and extensive because of the increase in scale that has taken place. Thus, it is hardly possible for consumers to get to know the full product range during a single visit to the store. This means it is even more important the store will take the lead and show as many parts of the product range that can be found elsewhere in the store and place them in areas where everyone passes by. In these hot spots or stop spots, storekeepers are able to display part of the product range or a single product. In the store, these areas are often used for promotional product presentations.

Step 4: design per department
Only after determining the most commercial layout plan, the layout,
naming the viewing angles and hot and stop spots, is it time to actually
fill up the rest of the space. All products that form the product range
must be located within the space specified in the layout plan and the
layout. Within it, one must start from the specific store behaviour of the
store's targeted audience. How does the customer search and shop?
Based on product type? Size? On colour? Is it 'run' or 'fun' shopping?
Or both? And then, what applies for which product group?
It is important to find the ideal balance between the commercial
objectives and logistic efficiency on the one hand, and the overview and
enticement value of the store on the other hand. On the one hand, we
want to make it as simple as possible for the consumer to find the
product type as soon as possible (overview), on the other hand we want
to entice them with other products (temptation).

Step 5: product presentation or merchandising
This is the most important phase: the commercial objectives, the
strategy, everything has to come together perfectly in the final store
environment, because it must all lead to the final transaction. The
previous phases serve to bring (as many as possible) visitors in and to
keep them inside as long as possible, to get them to stop often and to
offer them as many purchase ideas as possible. The actual product
presentation should live up to all high expectations and lead to the final
transaction.
We must also consider the *internal promotion*, an aspect that is becoming   **Internal**
increasingly more important in merchandising. Internal promotion is the   **promotion**
practical translation of the shopping experience. It is the oil that
lubricates the shopping and purchasing process and makes the products
attractive, bringing them to the attention of the consumer. *Visual mer-*
chandising and *internal communication* by means of *signage* and *displays*   **Visual**
are samples of internal promotion.   **merchandising**
                                                                                   Internal
                                                                                   communication
The classification of the five steps mentioned above is furthermore not
set in stone. The various steps will regularly intertwine. It is, however,
important to constantly continue to distinguish the various steps and to
constantly give attention to the various steps, both during the planning
and development of a new store concept and during the operation of an
existing store.
It is useful in almost all cases to entirely re-plan the stores every once
in a while; to take another look at the strategy and commercial objectives, at the layout plan, the layout, the actual anchors and goldmines,
at the distribution of square metres, the stopping force in the street,
the viewing angles and interpretation of the hot spots and stop spots.
And also to look at the shelf layout and in-store communication, step
by step.

FIGURE 22.2 Design of the exterior view and entrance

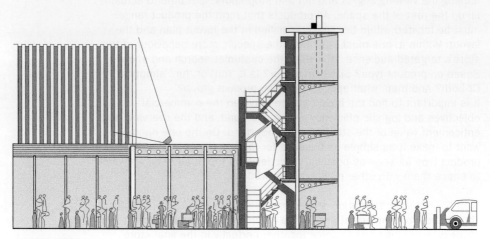

SIDE ELEVATION

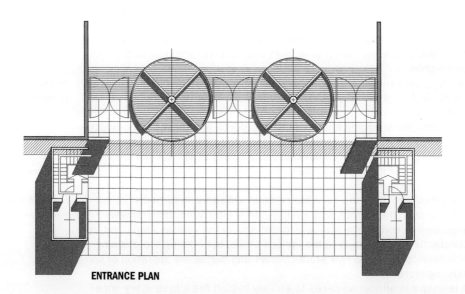

ENTRANCE PLAN

The frequency depends on the size of the stores and the type of products, but should definitely be included in the activity planning. We often see the bigger picture gets distorted and the commercial objectives get increasingly more difficult to achieve over the long(er) term by constantly focussing on the new deployment of new collections, releasing new themes, promotions and folders and customising the shelf layout.

It is clear from this statement, the presentation in the broader sense must link directly to all elements of the marketing plan. Every change in the marketing plan will then theoretically also have consequences for the presentation: the presentation in a broader sense forms the integration of all elements of the marketing mix.

The examples we use below to explain the process, were derived from a design for an English superstore (see figure 22.2).

22.4 Store design

The store design forms the connecting link between the external marketing mix and the internal marketing mix. It should attract a passer-by through the first impression of the store and confirm expectations for targeted visitors, even before the visitor has really gone through the selection. The visitor must get the feeling this is really the store where he will be able to succeed in his shopping effort.

Components of the store design for the outside are:
- location;
- facade;
- logo or brand image;
- entrance;
- overall stopping force;
- display.

Components of the store design for the inside are:
- interior design style;
- material use;
- lighting;
- ceilings;
- colorways;
- layout;
- use of viewing angles;
- use of hotspots and stop spots;
- use of in-store communication/promotion;
- general signing.

22.4.1   Stopping force in the street

When we go and stand in a random place in a shopping centre, we see an enormous amount of store signs, flags and company names. The challenges for the retailer are to stand out with his store (formula) amongst all the *noise*. That is the first thing one has to consider carefully: standing out in the landscape.

In recent years, the 'traffic' has withered tremendously in shopping centres. According to City Traffic the average *footfall,* the number of passers-bys in a street, in the Netherlands, has declined by about 5% between 2007 and 2010. There are other agencies that even speak of a 10% or more decrease in the same period. It is therefore immensely important to entice as many passers-bys as possible to enter the store. When there are less passers-bys but the numbers that enter the retailer's store remains the same or increases, it implies a profit for the retailer. Initially, it is not important what a retailer does as long as it is something that stands out and slows people down to focus their attention on the store. It can be a board hanging at an odd angle like Scotch & Soda, or putting semi-naked surf dudes outside the door, in good and bad weather, as with Abercrombie & Fitch. It could be the smell of fresh bread or sweets wafting around, as in a candy store in New York or creating a spectacular display with real models, as with the Society Shop. A retailer must create a stopping force on the street.

Footfall

22

22.4.2   The display

The display plays an important role in creating a stopping force. Yet, many retailers still do not see the importance of a (stopping) force display. Changing the display once every three months is obsolete. Just creating a 'nice display' is also no longer enough anymore, simply because every store tries to do at least that much. We can only create the maximum stopping force in two ways:

- *A spectacular presentation in the display*: just filling an entire display 'ordinarily' with 89 pairs of shoes from the product range ensures relatively little stopping force. We strive to achieve maximum stopping force. So, go crazy. Stand out and only use one colour in the display of ten different pairs, or only display red pumps and only the left shoe, but make it a hundred.
- *Change the display regularly*: the ideal frequency for the type of store depends on the location and the 'walk-by' frequency of the consumers. It is very important people realise the consumers became spoilt thanks to the rapidly changing displays of formulas like H&M, ZARA and Vero Moda. Consumers are accustomed to constantly receiving new stimuli. Consumers must be given a reason to come back inside. Especially, if the store sells baby baths, dining room chairs, vehicles, printers or globes. Again, surprise the consumer through regular change.

22.4.3   The entrance

Once we have slowed down the consumer, thanks to the stopping force on the street and we enticed them to come inside with our display, it is important to guide the visitor to the intended target, as soon as possible. First, the visitor must get used to the new environment, the level of light, the temperature. We must assume the visitor will not see anything in that first metre of the store and continues to enter the store as quickly and as far in as possible. It is now important to give the visitor enough time to acclimatise, but also to slow down or to 'stop' and to get him in a buying mood. That must happen immediately in the entrance.

Amuse bouche   The primary function of an *'amuse bouche'* (literally; entertainment for the mouth) in a good restaurant is to arouse our appetite with a tasty little appetiser. The entrance to every store has exactly the same function. To wet the 'buying appetite' of the visitors, one must first get their attention. The most commercial and most effective interpretation differs per store(concept) and is strongly dependent on the type of store (full-service or largely self-service) and the target group/potential, prospective customer. The shopping and purchasing process must literally start at the entrance. It is important to start the shopping and purchasing process with an accessible and attractive presentation of low-threshold products that are interesting for 99% of the visitors. This can be a dishwashing brush (IKEA), or even an attractively styled display figure with the presented products directly next to it. The most important aspect, apart **Entrance** from the tantalising *entrance presentation* is the store should make sales **presentation** aids available immediately (shopping baskets, bags et cetera). The shopping process has started!

22.5 The layout plan

The layout plan is aimed at establishing a rough positioning of the departments that will lead to a comprehensible unity of space between the
stores' departments for the consumer. Drawing up a layout plan is specifically important in large-scale stores, especially if they have a wide product
range (for many different consumer needs). Examples of such stores are
large supermarkets, warehouses and hypermarkets. By creating
a comprehensible unity (often indicated by the English term *logical
adjacencies*) one ensures the store becomes more logical for the consumer and the departments are easier to find.

**Logical
adjacencies**

Drawing up a layout plan seems easier than it is. It is obviously important
for a hyper store to position all hardware together, separate from fashion
and food. The reason being the consumer's shopping and purchasing
behaviour differs for each of these categories: hardware is often purposefully purchased based on product, food is a targeted purchase and fashion is often purchased based on an actual intent to purchase the type of
product, but the actual decision to buy takes place on the store floor.
So how do we position these main groups in the store? Fashion first, then
hardware and food? Or should it actually be the other way around? And
how do we organise the departments within the main groups? In fashion,
is it first the underwear and then the outerwear? Or should it actually be
the other way around? Do we position the men's, ladies and children'
sock departments together? Or do we split them up: men's socks with
the men's clothing and so on? Practice has proven that it works much better

FIGURE 22.3 First step: sequence 'families' and determining the logical adjacencies

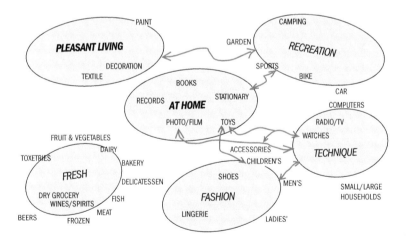

22

FIGURE 22.4 Where are the fixed points?

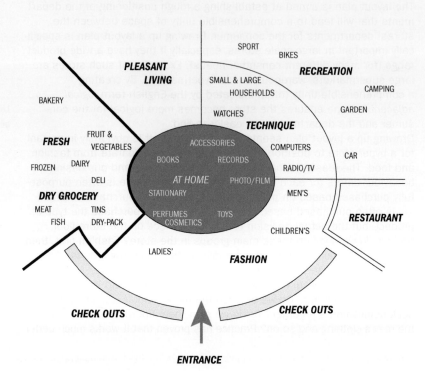

FIGURE 22.5 How do we fit this into the shape of the building?

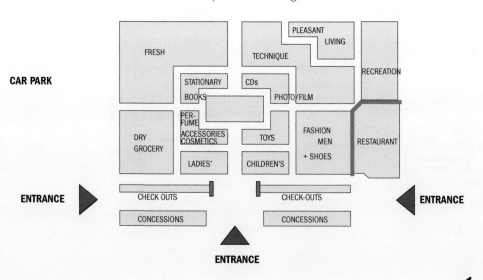

1

to place underwear the specific fashion department; lingerie with ladies fashion, children's underwear with children's fashion. This way, the consumer will find it whether it was planned or not, and it is easier to 'add it to the purchase'. We fill in the layout plan based off a framework. This framework is designed based on the extent of the store, the shape of the store and a number of fixed points, like the entrance, the exit, the goods arrival and the processing and finishing area (see figures 22.3 through 22.5).

22.6 Layout

Once the layout plan is drafted, it must be converted to a *layout*. The layout is actually a floor plan of the store in which the flow pattern is defined, as well as the space allocated to the various groups of goods. We will discuss the layout forms and the space allocation.

Layout

22

22.6.1   Layout forms

The two main store layout forms are the *grid layout* and the free flow layout. Intermediate forms will also occur, the most important one being the 'loop layout'.

A grid layout is characterised by a straight, parallel layout of the shelves. It is an efficient way to layout a store, but not really beneficial for the consumer's fun shopping feeling. We use grid layouts especially for run shopping and convenience stores like supermarkets and discounters. Grid layouts are often accompanied by a forced store routing. Recently, however, we see these companies try to overcome the rigidity of the grid layout by implementing 'islands' within the grid layout.

Originally, 'run shop stores' like supermarkets, DIY markets and discounters (Gamma, Makro et cetera) experienced it was becoming more and more difficult to satisfy visitors with a grid layout and to entice customers to buy new or impulse products, simply because they do not or barely see it. This form of store layout helps the visitors to shop as quickly as possible, and to literally run through the store. The number of stores with a purely grid layout is reducing day by day, also because of pressure from manufacturers who would like to influence the shopping and purchasing behaviour to their advantage. Convenience stores also want to slow their visitors down as much as possible by creating as many stopping forces as possible 'along the way'.

The *free flow layout* is characterised by an un-structured store routing. The consumer can reach any part of the store directly and poke around wherever he wants to, in any random order. We often use free flow layouts in fun shopping environments, fashion environments and it is often accompanied by idea generating presentations. The bigger the store becomes, the more difficult it is for the consumer to (continue to) determine his direction using a free flow layout. The consumer quickly becomes disoriented in a store, because he is busy shopping. The bigger the store, the bigger the risk that disorientation will disturb the shopping and purchasing process.

Loop layouts are an in-between form. The sections are connected by a main traffic path to which all departments are localised. The loop is not a forced store routing (you can deviate from it if you wish), but it's more like a suggested way of making your way through the store. Originally, it was typically warehouses that often used loop layouts, but today you see it in

Grid layout

Free flow layout

Loop layouts

FIGURE 22.6 Example grid-lay-out, free flow lay-out, loop lay-out

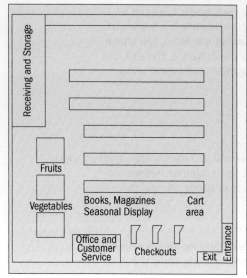

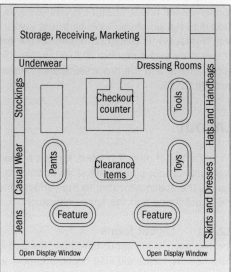

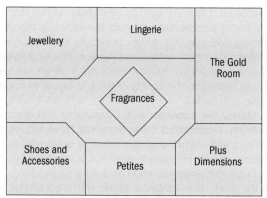

more and more store types; from a supermarket to a fashion boutique on the corner. The purpose of this layout is to confront the customer with as many departments as possible during his visit to the store.

Figure 22.6 shows what the various layout forms look like.

22.6.2 Walking speed

Various research projects have shown the longer people walk right through a store, the faster people will be walking. It is important to include this detail in a store layout. The earlier quoted lost sales research, shows approximately 3% of all purchases in non-food are made on impulse. These are therefore products that were not necessarily on the shopping list, but of which the consumer decided on the spot he wanted to buy the product. A part of the sales is therefore determined by the impulses the store passes on to the customer.

Highway

A really long 'highway' or even an athletic track in the store ensures the consumers will continue to build up speed, and will cost sales. Simply

because the faster the consumers will be walking, the less they will see.
And if you do not see something, you cannot buy it.
It is important to slow down as many visitors as possible, as often as
possible and to entice them to stop in the store. The ideal average store
speed of the potential customer depends on the type of store: the average
speed in a supermarket will be much faster than in a fashion store. In
a supermarket, this even varies per department.
That is why we should work with different walkways and equipment, even
within a store. In the supermarket, we want consumers to walk quietly and
discover at the beginning of the fresh produce department, guiding them
efficiently through the dry groceries.
The ideal *store speed* creates tension because, what is it the customer
wants? It is important to determine the limits and to slow the consumer
down as much as possible, getting him to actually stop, without most of
the consumers seeing it as a disruption of the shopping process.

Store speed

22.6.3   Viewing angles
To entice visitors to go as 'deep' as possible into the store, it is important
to create the best viewing angles and then to make good use of it. Viewing
angles can be used effectively to increase the walking speed or, if needed,
to slow it down by making the walkway longer or shorter.
Stores like IKEA are established entirely based on as many possible viewing
angles and on slowing down and stopping their visitors. IKEA allows most of
its visitors to entice themselves into becoming a customer.

22.6.4   Hot spots
There are two types of hot spots:
- Automatic hot spots: these are the hot spots that arise naturally at
  the end of all viewing angles. These are the places everyone sees.
  Commercially, they may be the most important spots. These locations
  offer great sales opportunities. It is important to know all the hot spots
  well and to keep them stocked up with the correct products. It
  is commercially desirable to renew the hot spots regularly and to stock
  them with new items. The frequency depends on the *visit frequency*
  of the average customer to this store.

FIGURE 22.7 Viewing angles of the visitor

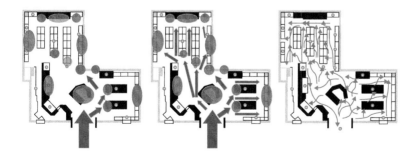

- *Created hot spots, or stop spots*: the retailer creates these himself along the (main) path. The content changes regularly and depends on the season and the moment of the day, week, month or year. The goal is to slow the visitors down and to focus their attention on one of the products they otherwise would not have seen.

Based on the viewing angles of the visitor, starting from the doormat, we first identify the hot spots and stop spots. By filling these places optimally, we ensure optimal appeal through the entire store. That leads to the most optimal flow of customers through the entire store.

22.6.5   Space allocation

An important part of the layout is the space allocation per product range component. In doing so, we have to deal with the following aspects:
- standard space plan (SSP);
- adjustment of the SSP to the occupancy patterns and sales patterns;
- adjustments due to the occupancy pattern;
- adjustments due to the sales pattern;
- adjustments to the seasonal sales pattern.

Standard space plan

Standard space plan

The *standard space plan* (SSP) is the commercial basis of the actual product presentation and should ideally only be drawn up after the ideal store layout has been defined. The standard spatial plan was perhaps the most important tool in a product oriented market, but because the power shifted more to the demand side and the market is more demand oriented, it is important to first ensure the consumer is slowed down as much as possible, stopped and enticed. This process requires valuable square metres (creating the necessary extra stop spots for example), and it is essential to realise as many opportunities to slow the consumer down as possible to result in the most possible transactions. So the ideal layout should first be determined.

In addition, practice shows us every day most stores have too little space to show all its products properly. In short, if one was to start with the SSP at a too early stage, you will never succeed in creating sufficient stopping force; simply because all the space will already be filled to capacity.

The SSP is very numerical and abstract: one divides the store and allocates a number of available square metres to certain products and/or product groups based on the following criteria:
- the desired dominance per department (core product ranges);
- the profitability per department (DPP-aspects);
- the physical distribution system (minimum stock);
- the sales rates.

It is important to take the maximum availability of the goods for the consumer into account and to strive towards optimal profitability as a whole. Various software packages are available for supermarkets, such as Space-Man, with which we can design the standard space plan using computers. Space-elasticity is also kept in mind in these software programmes.

Space management system

More and more 'merchandise' packages are also developed for non-food stores. Nike, for example, works with a *space management system* in which both their products and their stores are represented three-dimensionally.

Nike employees (buyers, store planners, vision merchandisers et cetera) can design all their stores virtually with a single push of a button. We see this method being used more frequently because it quickly makes it clear whether you will be able to 'manage' with the given square metres. But we also see many stores still end up establishing a SSP using a trial-and-error system. Unfortunately, we can also conclude many retailers still are not creating a SSP at all.

Adjustments
Because of local circumstances, we must often deviate from the average standard space plan.

Adjustments because of the occupancy pattern and type of visitor
Some stores attract more visitors than other stores, and some stores have extreme peaks and lows in their *visitor numbers*. We must take into account specific needs of the intended customer group. For example, it is understandable the importance of width and length of the walkways in a baby's and children's department. At Prénatal, for example, the walkways are expected to be much wider than an 'ordinary' department or product group. After all, the specific target group of this store usually visits the store with a pram. Saturdays are often the busiest days and we may even have two-way traffic on most of the paths. In short, we need to keep this in mind.

Visitor numbers, during both low and *peak moments*, and the specific needs of visitors, determine the width and the length of the aisles. The number of visitors also determines the number of cash registers and the necessary space per cash register. It goes without saying that widening or lengthening the aisles has direct consequences for both the total space of the store and for the length of the shelves.

Adjustments due to the sales pattern
The occupancy pattern influences the customer's freedom of movement and through the expansion of the walking space, indirectly influences the shelf space. The sales pattern, on the contrary, directly influences the shelf space. A store that has a sales rate that is twice as high as the average store, but is just as often supplied, will have to stock the shelves on average twice as much in order to guarantee availability of the goods for the customer. We can then choose between maintaining or adjusting the SSP. If we opt for maintaining, there will be a need for an increase in stocking frequency. If we opt for a length-wise adjustment, the shelves remain the same depth, but more of each product is forward facing (the shelves become longer). If we opt for a width-wise adjustment, the shelves remain the same length, but we use deeper shelves. No matter the choice, everything affects the total interpretation of the square metres. A longer shelf may result in a higher (or maybe even too high) average store speed. Deeper shelves may result in the aisles becoming too narrow for the target group. On Saturday, for example, it will be impossible for parents with a pram to pass each other. They will then skip certain aisles, which ultimately will cost sales. In short, it is and remains important, at all times, to always pursue the ideal store layout.

Visitor numbers

Peak moments

22

Adjustments to the seasonal pattern of the sales
Especially for stores with a wide product range that show deviating
seasonal patterns for the various components (such as department-like
stores), we cannot suffice with one SSP for the entire year. We need to
prepare separate SSPs per period. At the very least, one SSP for the
winter season and one for the summer. But we see increasingly more
often that we need more than two SSPs per year. It is also important for
such companies to keep the classification of the store as flexible as
possible.
Figure 22.8 has abandoned the straight forward layout of figure 22.5.
Various solutions were adopted for each department. A grid layout was
chosen for the supermarket and the household department. A free flow
layout was selected for recreation, technology and fashion, and a loop
layout for the drugstore. The old layout plan is however still recognisable.
In the convenience section, it is clear to see the option fell on a maximum efficiency and speed store. The aisles are long and are not inter-
rupted, and there is no specific attention to the content of the hot spots,
nor are there specific stop spots. On the contrary, we see the recreation
Pinball department is clearly arranged more like a *'pinball machine'*. The
machine 'grocery' section is an efficient circuit where the customer can go
shopping without any restraints.

FIGURE 22.8 The final lay-out of the English hyper store

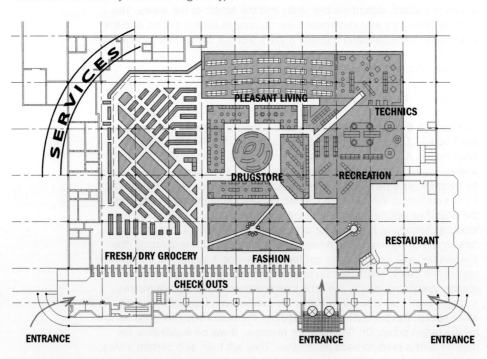

22.7 Departmental layout product presentation/ shelf layout

It is important to realise practically no store can take on the unlimited product range of online stores. Unless the 'unlimited offer' proposition (Media Markt, DIY stores, super XL-supermarket) can be somewhat fulfilled, a store should opt for a different and distinctive 'approach path'. The choice may then fall on the best/coolest/most inspiring/most convenient/ straightforward product range, or stand out with the absolute best solution for the consumer's preference. For this, some difficult choices have to be made. This is where things often go wrong for retailers.

The suggestion of a lot of choices on the store floor can provide a lot of stopping force, but ultimately this does not necessarily lead to the desired high conversion. Simply because consumers will not be able to choose.

If the layout of the store is finally determined, the square metres are allocated, the most important viewing angles and hot spots and stop spots are determined, it is time to literally furnish the departments. In fact, we need to follow the same process here as for the master plan for the total store, on a more detailed level. There is only one very important step that is added, optimising the transaction power of the department.

The commercial and attractive design of the department and the attractive presentation of the goods is an extremely important phase in the store layout process, simply because this phase leads to the final transaction. This is the moment where the consumer will decide whether or not to buy, so any potential purchasing objection should be removed. Here it is also important we realise there is a major change going on from a product oriented market to a demand oriented market. The consumer can choose from a huge range of providers and chose the one that best suits his needs. He opts for the store that offers the best solution.

Creating a proper shelf layout and preparing a good, logical and attractive classification is no longer sufficient. It is important to help the consumer to succeed in his entire purchasing need, as quickly as possible. The consumer has the power and is therefore no longer willing to go through too much trouble for his purchase(s).

Designing a department is mainly a matter of logical thinking. Always start with the needs of the customer. How can we ensure the consumer easily succeeds as quickly as possible?

Examples of common sense at the department level:
- Is the consumer here looking for *paint*? Then we should make room in the paint shelf for the basic requirements (tape, gloves), preferably in more than one place on the shelf, so the consumer will not forget this in his purchasing process and/or ends up buying it elsewhere at a later stage.
- Is the consumer here looking for *coffee or tea*? Then we should make room in the coffee and tea shelf for 'the biscuit of the week', especially since research has proven more and more consumers avoid the 'sweets and biscuits' aisle on purpose.
- Is the consumer here looking for *children's wear* for his/her children? Remember there are not that many children who find shopping fun. Nobody will be buying (more) with a nagging child in the vicinity. So make sure the children will be able to have fun while the parents are choosing clothing.

22

- Is the consumer here looking for *wooden logs*? Then we should make sure this display is in the vicinity of the shopping carts. Give the visitors a reason to choose a shopping cart instead of a shopping basket.
- Does the consumer enter the store with a *stroller or walker*? Make sure there is plenty of room to move, also in case of a large flow of visitors.
- Is the consumer here looking for *cartridges*? Then we should make sure the print paper (preferably in large quantities) is lying next to it.

22.8 In-store promotion

Chapter 19 made an explicit distinction between internal and external promotion. This distinction is made because the approach of internal and external promotion is quite different, though both ultimately focus on increasing the sales. External promotion is primarily aimed at establishing the attraction of the store ($CA \times VI$). Internal promotion is primarily aimed at establishing the transaction in the store ($C \times AT$).

If we assume the presentation in the narrower sense is also aimed at making it as easy and as enjoyable as possible for the customer to realise the transaction, there really would not be a reason to distinguish between presentation and *in-store promotion*. The distinction is somewhat artificial and, in practice, we see the approaches are getting mixed up.

In-store promotion

If there is any distinction, it can be defined as follows. The presentation aims to create transactions of planned purchases. In-store promotion is aimed at generating more transactions than only the planned purchases. We will discuss the rediscovery and the forms of in-store promotion below. Visual merchandising will receive extra attention.

'Rediscovering' in-store promotion

The rediscovery of the in-store promotion as a separate part of the marketing mix, probably has more to do with the retail environment than with the retailer itself. In-store promotion has existed as long as there have been stores in which goods have been presented. In the current marketing environment, we have to recognise there has been a growing concentration in the retail sector. This phenomenon plays a role especially in the food sector. Fewer and fewer formulas are left to serve the ever increasing groups of consumers. A company like Albert Heijn (the largest advertiser in the Netherlands) is known by virtually the entire Dutch population, while 80% of Dutch housewives visit (or have visited) Albert Heijn. Albert Heijn has an unprecedented high market share of almost 35%. A further increase in the market share by attracting new customers is therefore becoming more and more difficult. In such a situation, it is less meaningful for Albert Heijn to spend very high amounts to attract the remaining 20% of the Dutch population who have not visited Albert Heijn, especially since this 20% is probably unreachable. Promotions could perhaps be used a lot more profitable for retention strategies within the store (for example Air Miles, focussed on preserving and maintaining the visitors index of existing fixed customers) or on efforts to make the customer experience 'fuller' (such as promotions in the store and displays). Advertising agencies then notice, to their horror, one of the biggest spenders of advertising costs is reorganising the application of their promotional budget. More is spent on in-store promotion, often carried out by the retailer itself (whether or not in cooperation with the supplier) and less on external promotion (in other words sales by advertising agencies). This explains the sudden revival of attention to in-store promotion 'in the world'.

22.9 Visual merchandising

A special form of in-store promotion is created by *visual merchandising*. Visual merchandising is actually an intermediate form between 'ordinary' presentation techniques and in-store promotion. This method is aimed at showing goods in conjunction with each other. The purpose of visual merchandising is presenting the goods as attractively as possible, in order to realise as much sales as possible. The term 'attractive' may lead to some confusion. A huge stack of boxes with sets of cookware can also be attractive (bulk presentation). It is all about making the presentation attractive for the consumer.

Visual merchandising is thus making the presentation of the products as attractive as possible. Topping up the shelves, straightening things and mirroring in supermarkets is also visual merchandising. An additional purpose of visual merchandising is establishing cross-over selling. For example, by not only displaying skirts, but the matching blouses and sweaters in combination, one hopes the consumer will purchase not just one, but multiple articles of clothing. Visual merchandising is often used in fashion-sensitive product ranges, but it is becoming more common in other product ranges as well.

There are many forms of visual merchandising. We can group and present the products in many different ways; for example on brand, colour, size, season, theme, and material, on activity, time of use, on price or on type of product.

We should then choose the type of presentation. Here one must think of a bulk presentation (lots), a cascading presentation (from low to high), a pyramid presentation (low-high-low) or a museum presentation (few products in an otherwise empty space).

With the presentation of clothing, an important choice is which articles do we hang 'sideways' (shoulder presentation) and which articles we hang 'facing'. By hanging articles sideways, we can have more products per square metre and the sales per square metre could thus be increased. However, consumers (both men and women) buy faster with 'facing' presentations, which is good for both the circulation speed and for the sales per square metre. But hanging everything facing to the front is also not as 'exciting' or attractive and therefore not good for circulation speed and sales per square metre.

Then a choice must still be made between hanging and lying. Hanging takes up more space, but once again, it is better for the circulation speed and lying basically takes up less space, but, depending on the presentation, is less commercial. In short, it is also a matter of finding the right balance, and making the correct commercial choices. In which way(s) do we sell the most?

Visual merchandising

22

22.9.1   Displays

Displays

Every retailer applies visual merchandising in a greater or lesser degree, which can take on many forms. The most applied form is that of product deals using *displays*. This happens in both the food and the non-food sector. Displays are temporary presentation areas, on which actual products are presented – whether or not at special prices. Many retailers in the food sector, for example, have fixed main displays on which the 'deals of the week' are placed in the spotlight (main displays). Other forms of displays are:

- Island displays: special areas, whether in aisles, or on a special promotional floor which can be approached from various sides (in the latter we speak of 'promotional areas').
- Shelf displays: special areas in the shelf on which the attention is focused on through signage.
- Checkout displays: the space right before the checkout, where the customer – while waiting to pay – can still be drawn to products; checkout displays are often 'the golden sales metres'.

These checkout displays can lead to negative shopping experiences as seen from example 22.2.

EXAMPLE 22.2 IN-STORE PROMOTION

In-store promotion is typically short term directed sales promotion. In-store promotion is always aimed at getting consumers to buy more than they were planning on when they entered the store. The danger of this approach is the customer may feel cheated after visiting the store. 'You always spend more than you intended to' is not an experience that encourages customer loyalty and a repeat visit.

Feargall Quinn, a remarkable Irish supermarket entrepreneur who is known globally for his client focused approach, explains in his book Crowning the customer why he has completely done away with checkout displays, despite the fact these displays were especially profitable. During one of his frequent branch visits, he noticed women with young children were very stressed at the checkout. The reason was while waiting at the checkout, the children became whiny when confronted with a display of sweets. Actually, the young mothers were forced to buy something expensive to keep their children calm. He decided to test something by removing all the candy displays at one of the checkouts in the store and noticed the majority of woman with young children chose this checkout lane to pay for their groceries, even if the waiting periods at this checkout were longer than normal. His conclusion was, although the checkout displays provided a need, which was apparent from sales per metre, it appeared in practice the checkout displays could lead to negative shopping experiences and therefore to unhappy customers. Since then, there are no more checkout displays in Quinns's supermarkets and the young mothers appear to be over-represented in Quinns's customer database. They would rather drive two supermarkets further than be confronted with the risk of blackmail by their children.

The importance of in-store promotions is relatively large. A study within the DIY sector conducted by Q&A Research & Consultancy commissioned by POPAI (the organisation for in-store promotions) into the point of purchase, gave the following results. Only one in seven visitors of a DIY store has a shopping list for the purchase of DIY products. Almost 60% of the visitors of a DIY store have no brand preference when they walk into the store. Of the consumers that purchased something in the store, depending on the category, 12% to 20% did this based on a promotion they saw in store. What is more important, whether one plans a purchase in advance or in the store?

With respect to in-store decisions, we distinguish between four decision levels:

- *Specifically planned*: the purchase was planned on brand level.
- *Generally planned*: the purchase was only planned up to product level. The brand choice occurs in the store.
- *Substitute*: the purchase was planned through brand level, but one decides on the spot to purchase a different brand.
- *Unplanned*: one purchases a product without mentioning it during the entry interview.

Specifically planned
Generally planned
Substitute
Unplanned

The majority of all 'generally planned', 'substitute' and 'unplanned'-purchases compared to the total number of purchases, is the in-store decision level.

From the previously cited study, it appears the in-store decision level within DIY is less than 77%. This means the use of in-store communication is extremely important in this sector. It generally appears the in-store decision level in retail is between 65% and 80%. This is also the explanation for the enormous attention from narrow casting, the use of (interactive) screens in stores. The retailer hopes this will tempt the consumer to buy. Depending on the sector and the correct use of this technology, it may contribute to the desired purchases. Especially manufacturers in fast-
moving retail environments (drugstores or supermarkets), or in brand environments (electronics, sports or DIY) will be interested in using this. After all, the customer decides at the point of purchase. For retailers, this is not as exciting because at the point the purchase is eventually made, they will only earn slightly more if they aim for up-selling or cross-selling. But this is especially interesting for manufacturers, because the brand preferences were, in many cases, only made inside the store.

It is generally important with the presentation and with in-store promotion, in particular, to position the displays and signage correctly. Figures 22.9a through 22.9d indicate how, in the case of a supermarket, you can define the signage and display locations. The customers' 'tendency to look to the right' is clear. Not only is the consumer inclined to always follow the route through the store clockwise, but he also directs attention to the right (see the arrows). This does not apply to countries where traffic has a left sided orientation.

FIGURE 22.9a The layout of the supermarkets

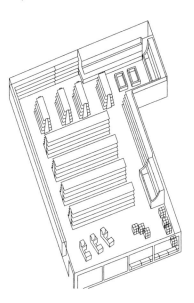

FIGURE 22.9b The analysis of the flow of pedestrian traffic within the layout

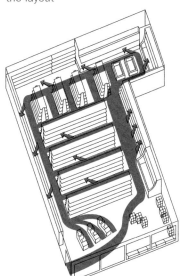

FIGURE 22.9c Based on the flow of pedestrian traffic, we can now indicate the problem zones (the circles)

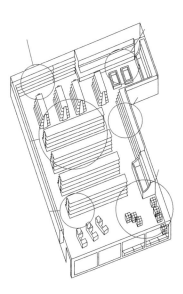

FIGURE 22.9d Using signage and promotional locations, one can now try to divide the attention for the products in the store more regularly

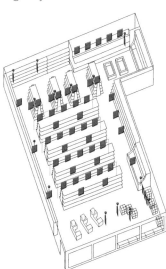

22.9.2 Sensory merchandising

Growing neuro-marketing research shows the term 'visual merchandising' is actually no longer complete. In order to entice the consumer in a physical store to consider making a purchase or to make an actual purchase, a positive sensory experience is necessary. Retailers such as Rituals, Simon Lévelt and IKEA owe a large part of their success to the fact they allow their consumers to taste, touch, smell and try. There are currently **Sensory merchandising** a large number of developments relating to *sensory merchandising*. Many studies have been done on the subject, books have written and conferences have been held – in short there is an entire industry in development. And above all, in the daily practice, many tests and other *scent marketing* **Scent marketing** practices have already been implemented. The American Abercrombie & Fitch is known for its huge success with the use of their own 'scent' in their stores and on their products. In short, merely stimulating the eyes of the consumer is no longer enough to create a distinction.

22

FIGURE 22.10 Development of department design fashion: the final layout of the department and the micro translation into presentations

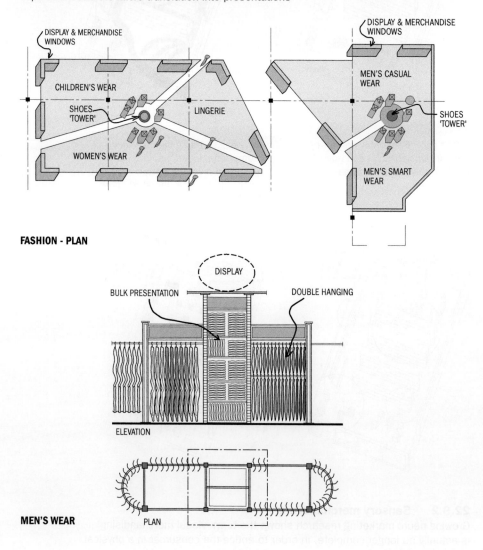

Being able to offer a sensory experience is becoming more and more of an opportunity for physical retailers to be distinguished from competitors, both online and offline with relative ease.

22.9.3   Cross merchandising and move merchandising

The further and more conscious application of *cross merchandising* could be an important means of distinction with regard to the internet. We see that web based stores like H&M, Koelkast.nl and Bol.com have applied this type of visual merchandising with immense success. After all, with a new dress, you also need new shoes and with a new refrigerator, you also need an ice block holder, fridge cleaner and thermometer.

Probably the cheapest method of visual merchandising is move merchandising. Take your business for a walk. Surprise, inspire, seduce and create cheer by having the products move through the store. At H&M, they have turned this form of visual merchandising into an art. Every day the collections are moved through the store, not to relocate, but to sell these collections. If we walk through an H&M store, we always see employees working with the 'new' products. This often means new attention for already existing merchandise stocks. Based on new visual merchandise proposals from the head office, the mannequins are provided with 'new' outfits and the tables and furniture are equipped with accompanying products. In this way, H&M gives new stimuli to the visitor so he always sees the 'new items'. New products, or new combinations, generate sales.

Cross
merchandising

22

Summary

Under the term 'presentation in the broad sense', we understand all activities aimed at translating a desired store concept into the actual store layout. It is the culmination of the strategic approach.
In the process of store layout, we deal with the following phases:
- store design;
- layout plan;
- store layout;
- department design;
- departmental layout (presentation in narrow sense).

We have explained the process of store layout and improved some of the components of the process. We concluded the chapter with the subject of visual merchandising.

PART 7

Control

In this part, we deal with the control of the implementation. We will especially look at how we can use the analysis instruments discussed previously, with the control of the implementation process. We thus get a consistent set of instruments: we can use the same instruments that we use for the analysis, for the control of the process.

This part also connects to the P of productivity that is yet to be discussed.

The reason why this P is included so explicitly in the retail marketing mix, is because of the relatively low average profitability, at least in the Dutch retail goods.

Minor changes in the operation can then make the difference between profit and loss. Any modification or change in the marketing mix variables would therefore actually still need to be tested against the influence that it actually has on the cost or productivity. This is something that is often forgotten in the very intensive processes with which strategies are associated. Productivity is therefore basically a derivative marketing mix variable. This part will extensively deal with the productivity using the control system. Finally, the concluding chapter will illustrate the relationship between the instruments discussed in this book and the central objective formula ($R = S \times M - C$).

23
Control of the implementation

This chapter focuses on control of the implementation process. We discuss subjects like the control system, control variables and consistency within the process. We answer questions like 'What is the role of productivity in the strategic process'? How do we set up an effective control system and which variables play a role in this? What is the effect of strategic analysis on the chosen variables?

23

23.1 Control system

FIGURE 23.1 The strategic process: control and productivity

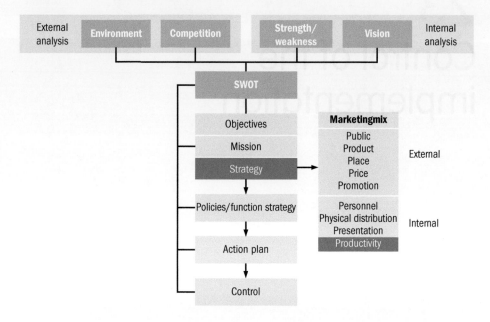

Control

By *control* we understand all activities aimed at making and keeping the strategic change process manageable and measurable. Although retailing seems to be a simple matter in theory, the previous chapters have made it clear that this is not the case in practice. Choices have to be made on an ongoing basis between long-term and short-term approaches, or between managing costs or stimulating sales. A multitude of decisions need to be made every day. And each of these decisions can affect other parts of the process. How do you keep an eye on the overall strategy in such an environment? And how do you ensure that there is no deviation from the bigger, strategic picture? The use of a control system plays an important role in the implementation of strategy. The basis for such a control system should be a

Key control
variables

set of *key control variables*: criteria which we can use to measure whether actions taken actually bear results. And which, when the results are inadequate, can help us manage corrective action.

23.2 Control variables to be used

When designing the control system, it is important to keep the number of control variables as low as possible – perhaps as low as a single, key variable which is applicable to all functions in the company. When using multiple control variables it is indeed tempting to define separate control variables for each sub-function. This can, however, lead to unwanted difficulties in implementation. Using a control variable such as 'margin development' for purchasing and 'sales development' for sales can lead to inconsistencies – for instance: an increase in margin may lead to a reduction of sales. It is better to define a more comprehensive variable that can be affected by both purchasing and sales. We often then arrive at a 'key control variable', related in some way to profitability or contribution, and perhaps linked to a fixed optimisation factor. The benefit of choosing such a profit-related variable is also that it reflects the reality of retail. In fact, the variable represents the profit contribution factor R in formula $R = S \times M - C$, and therefore includes sales, margin and cost effects. However, just one control variable is not always sufficient. Sometimes we have to add derived variables. However, these derived variables should be considered more as instruments than objectives. They are always linked to the 'key variable' and do not function as objectives themselves. The achievement of a higher margin without an increase in profit is, for instance, not the intention.

We discuss, below, how environment and problem formulation affect the chosen variables.

23.2.1   Influence of the environment

Choice of *control variables* may vary, depending on the environment. In the current German retail environment, for example, one is often inclined to use profit contribution or sales per employee as control variable. The reason is that, of the three production factors (labour, retail floor space and stock), floor space – especially since the fall of the Berlin Wall – is abundantly available and the interest rate is not high, but labour costs are relatively high and inflexible. It then makes sense to measure effectiveness of activities by changes in the productivity of the most scarce or most expensive factor – in this case the labour factor. In contrast, several years ago, when interest rates were extremely high (approximately 15%) in England, one would have chosen for optimisation of the stock factor. Retail floor space was not scarce and labour costs in England were very low compared to the mainland. In such a situation it is clear that effectiveness could be measured by the stock sales rate: the higher the sales, the lower the inventory and interest costs and, therefore, the bigger the profit.

In the Netherlands the situation is different: labour costs, although the biggest cost factor, are relatively flexible (partly due to the high incidence of part time labour) and interest rates are not high, but retail floor space is extremely scarce and inflexible. In good times, we cannot get enough of it, while in bad times you cannot give floor space away. As a result, there is a tendency to measure effectiveness of activities by their influence on profit per unit of floor space. Incidentally, this is not written in stone: the Netherlands is not immune from environmental influences on control variables. Changes in the Trading Hours Act (deregulation of opening times) could result in a control variable no longer being defined, exclusively, as 'contribution per unit of space' but rather as 'contribution per unit of space per hour of trading'. Similarly, the reverse chain (already discussed above), with its accompanying acceleration of lead time, could lead to GMROI playing an ever more important role as control variable.

Control variables

23.2.2   Influence of problem formulation

The results of strategic analysis also have a direct effect on the selection of variables. Although the key variables will mostly be a measure of the development of profitability, the sub-variables can be heavily influenced by other problems detected in developing the strategy. A company in which the problem may be characterised as 'sales is decreasing across the range', will be

23

inclined to use the development of market share as a control. However, a
company in which the problem is described as 'overall sales is still growing,
but sales in existing stores is declining', will be inclined to use sales per
metre on a like for like basis (i.e. in existing stores) as sub-variable. Finally,
a company without sales problems – on neither a total nor like for like basis
– will be much more inclined to find a solution on the cost side and thus to
define sub-variables in terms of cost or productivity. The lesson to be learnt
here is: try to define a core key control variable – and then link sub-variables
to it as required by the strategically-detected problems and the environment.

23.3 Consistency within the process

As we work through the overall, strategic process (as we have done in this
book), we use techniques and models that make use of only a few, core
numbers:
- DAP and DPP (discussed in chapter 13) involved profitability per unit of
  space.
- For the assortment dominance matrix (chapter 12), we used market size
  and market share.
- Monitor analysis (chapter 11) involved the visitors index, conversion and
  sales receipts.
- The trinity-analysis (chapter 13) used stock efficiency, floor efficiency and
  labour efficiency.

Strategic audit   The results of such a *strategic audit* will generally be discussed throughout
the organisation. This means that one has used several key indicators,
based on the analysis, to express the problem and that these indicators are
current and meaningful within the organisation. It is recommended that the
same indicators are used for the control variables as were used in the
strategic audit, in order to achieve a direct and consistent connection
between the results of the strategic audit and the required corrective action.
The following sub-paragraphs will accordingly focus on the application, for
control purposes, of the models explained in this book.

23.3.1 Consistency in time
Performing a strategic audit and developing a (new) strategy, although often
more time consuming than people think, usually takes no more than a few
months. However, implementing the strategy and the action plans derived
from it may take many years.
This means that we also have to continue to work with the same control
variables for many years. And also that the definition of these control
variables must remain constant over time. In practice this may cause some
problems for retailers. These problems are caused, on the one hand, by the
pursuit of accuracy and, on the other, by the skill and ingenuity of people in
the organisation itself.

23.3.2 Resourcefulness of the organisation
Every strategic analysis is based partly on an analysis of the environment.
We often use external information for this, for example from Statistics
Netherlands (CBS) or from external market research agencies. It is not
uncommon that external data series are rebased, because the new basis is
more 'accurate'. This creates a problem in relation to control. After all, if a

recalibration of the CBS statistics were to indicate that, according to new methods, the size of a certain market segment is smaller than it was according to the old methods, and if the control variable were expressed in market share, then this market share objective may be achieved more quickly under the new method, without involving any actual improvement in the way the business functions. In such a case, you need to adjust the standardisation of the control variables. This kind of adjustment is often inevitable when dealing with external sources. Unfortunately we often see changes occur in internal indicators during control periods. The guideline here is, 'better to be wrong and consistent than to be right in an unmanageable situation' – i.e. maintain consistency, unless there is no alternative but to adjust the variables.

23.3.3   Level variables versus dynamic variables

Discussions often arise when the control variable is made up of components that cannot be influenced by the relevant personnel themselves. A tendency to question allocation arises. Notable examples include the amount of allocated rent in the case of department stores (the rent allocated to the fourth floor is lower than that of the ground floor), or the calculated share of overheads.

These discussions about allocation can be endless and they generally draw attention away from the essential issues. Furthermore: the development shown by the control variable is relevant – not its level at commencement. An 'incorrect' starting point is therefore not particularly important.

The solution can be sought in two areas:

- Separate definition of the control variable for each level in the organisation – so as to include only costs and revenues that are manageable at that level. For management, the overhead forms a part of the control variable – for the man on the floor, it does not. The disadvantage of this approach is that the set of control variables grows in proportion to the number of levels. The advantage is that development of the variable can be influenced the same way at each level.
- Definition of the control variable in terms of 'targeted improvement'. Only changes relative to the previous period are looked at. Costs and revenues that are the same for both periods (as in the case of lease and/or overhead allocation), will cancel each other out.

A very significant advantage of the latter approach is that the control acquires a dynamic character and becomes independent of the starting level. The control variable is now defined in terms of relative improvement. Reducing the loss of an unprofitable department is now just as valuable as improving the profits of an already thriving department.

This approach fits the realities of retailing. Profit can often vary across the broad assortments carried in retail outlets. 'Problem children' and 'goldmines' can often appear side by side.

Both are necessary for the overall consumer proposition. Addressing the problem by simply eliminating the problem children is not the solution. Customers will not understand why a DIY market sells wood and paint (gold mines), but not cement, plaster or stones (problem children). If we want to focus the formula on customer needs, we need to accept the presence of problem children to a certain extent. The criteria for this decision is that the average level of profitability must be sufficient to ensure viability of the

23

FIGURE 23.2 Profitability of a department store: two ways to improve average profitability

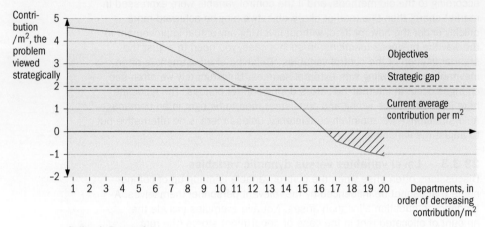

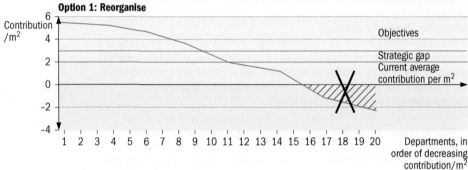

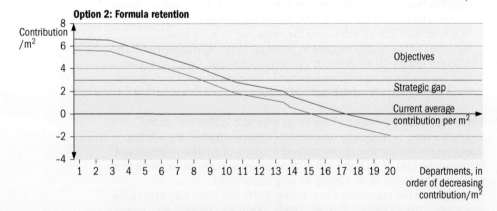

company. This average can be affected by both reducing the losses of poorly performing departments and by improving profits of thriving departments. The upper part of figure 23.2 illustrates the problem: the departments are arranged in order of decreasing contribution per metre. Departments 16 to 20 appear to make a negative profit contribution. The average profit is reflected by the *present average* line. However, this profit is insufficient. We actually want to achieve the average profit indicated by the *targeted average* line. A *strategic gap* should therefore be bridged.

The middle and bottom parts of figure 23.2 show two methods for bridging this strategic gap:
- Reduce headcount in all unprofitable departments and reduce the product range. Disadvantage: the proposition to the consumer is more limited (see option 1 in figure 23.2).
- Retain the formula and ensure that every department becomes more profitable. In bridging the strategic gap, reducing loss in unprofitable departments is just as important as improving the profitability of thriving departments (see option 2 in figure 23.2).

Summary

Control includes 'all activities aimed at making and keeping the strategic change process manageable and controllable'. It is recommended that control be implemented using only a few variables in order to prevent the development of conflicting sub-objectives. These variables also need to have a certain degree of familiarity within the organisation in order to accelerate the process. Choice of control variables often depends on the environment in which the retailer operates, as well as on the results of the SWOT analysis.
The control variables to be chosen should meet the requirements of consistency, both within the process (the same variable for different components) and in time (the base should preferably not be changed during implementation).
Given the often large number of product categories found in retail (often with different levels of profitability), it is preferable to define the control variable in terms of 'targeted improvements'. Reducing the loss of an unprofitable department may contribute just as much to achieving the overall objective as increasing the profit of a thriving department.

24
Control instruments

We can perform strategic audits using the analysis models explained above – and we can control the implementation of a change in strategy. This requires some adjustment to the models. We will illustrate these approaches in the following paragraphs.

24.1 Control of the strategic process

Figure 24.1 shows the position of control in the strategic process.

FIGURE 24.1 Strategic process: control

The example at the end of the previous chapter (figure 23.2) essentially shows the far-reaching consequences of a strategic choice. Although this is an old example (the figure reflects the strategic reorientation of de Bijenkorf in the eighties), it illustrates the problems that can occur in the control of strategy change processes. These problems also occur nowadays. The change process that is currently seen at V&D, for example, follows the same lines as those illustrated in figure 23.2. De Bijenkorf suffered significant losses in the early eighties. This was the result of an ambitious investment program in the preceding years, in combination with a growing recession which came unexpectedly for many. Within a year consumer expenditure on durable consumer goods, especially in the more expensive segment on which de Bijenkorf focuses, dropped by 30%. Investments could not be made profitable in this environment. New investment in expansion, in order to realise *economies of scale,* was impossible. Sale of the loss-making Bijenkorf organisation was seriously considered, but did not appear to be an option. Recovery had to be achieved using existing resources and current floor space.
The choice was:
- Dispose of all unprofitable departments and branches and continue on a limited basis, but with profitable departments. Essentially, this meant that de Bijenkorf would cease to function as a department store of national significance and would continue as a major, regional fashion retailer (option 1 in figure 23.2).

- Continue as a department store, with profit coming from improvements within the existing floor space (option 2 in figure 23.2).

The second alternative was chosen. The consequence of this decision was that the effectiveness of activities undertaken would no longer be measured in terms of overall sales development, but in terms of profitability per metre. Every metre within de Bijenkorf would have to produce more or lose less. Determining the minimum 'improvement standard' was simple: the existing loss was divided by the number of available sales metres. To determine whether this standard was met (i.e. to control implementation), it was necessary to determine profit per metre in the starting situation for every department in every branch of the store. This required a DAP model, to determine the profit contribution per department, per branch and per metre. Fortunately, the internal information system of de Bijenkorf was such that preparation of this DAP model could proceed without major problems.

We will now discuss the influence of change in the control variable, the further implementation of change and DAP as black box.

24.1.1   Influence of change in the control variable

Although the approach described above seems simple, it resulted in a *culture shock* within the business. There had never been a shortage of square metres in de Bijenkorf. The available space was more than adequate to sell the product range. Previously, the control variable had only been overall sales development, independent of the number of metres required. In the new situation square metres were made 'artificially' scarce and the use of every square metre had to be optimised. The *mind shift* required to engage this may be illustrated with reference to figures 24.2a and 24.2b.

Figure 24.2a describes the development of the men's fashion department in the situation prior to the strategic *turnaround*: it was a healthy department. Both sales and profit contribution were on the increase. At that time de Bijenkorf was losing sales overall and losses were increasing, so this department was a 'star'. After the introduction of the new control variables (contribution per metre instead of overall sales) the conclusion appeared to be entirely different.

Figure 24.2b describes the development of the men's fashion department based on the new control variables: we now see both sales and profit contribution decreasing on a per square metre basis. The reason is clear: the department was thriving, so more metres were added to it. As a result, development per metre became negative. In fact, in the old situation, the men's fashion department was a goldmine, while in the new situation it became a problem child. Under the new approach the men's fashion department contributed to the increasing losses of de Bijenkorf, a conclusion that was rather difficult for the responsible manager to accept.

Mind shift

Turnaround

24.1.2   Further implementation

It was decided to use a department of a branch as the lowest unit of control. This meant that, since de Bijenkorf had approximately forty departments and six branches, 240 DAPs had to be calculated each period.

24

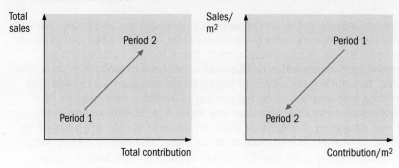

This was laborious and inconvenient, but it had to happen. A very robust and simple presentation of the model was selected in order to prevent an overload of information. This took the form of simple graphs, which showed at a single glance what was going on in the department. Given the dynamic nature of the control, it was chosen only to illustrate the change and to express this in terms of the previous, corresponding period. We will now look at where this approach led and its effects on communication.

Interpretation
The approach led to a simple graph, on which four possible vectors of change could be displayed. The results from the previous period, both sales per metre and DAP per metre, were set at 100. The department's development was then viewed against this base.
Development was shown by means of an arrow (see figure 24.3).

FIGURE 24.3 Interpretation of possible developments

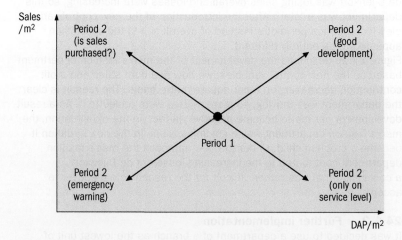

If the arrow points to the upper right corner (both sales and DAP increasing per square metre), then the department is basically contributing to achievement of the strategic objective: improvement of profit per square metre. The only point then open for discussion is whether the extent or rate of contribution improvement is sufficient.

If the arrow points to the lower right corner (DAP increases per square metre, but sales decreases per square metre), then the department also contributes to the strategic objective. But some comments need to be taken into account: did we perhaps increase prices? What does this mean for our market position in the long term? Did we perhaps lower costs too much? What does this mean for *service levels* over time? If the arrow points to the upper left corner, we receive a warning signal. In the previous situation, one would probably have been quite pleased. After all, sales has increased. But in the new situation this development is unacceptable. DAP has decreased, despite increased sales. We are either 'purchasing' sales (for example, through price cuts), or the costs are out of control.

Finally, if the arrow points to the lower left corner, this is the ultimate warning signal: the department is not contributing to the strategic objective in any way. This could be caused by unfavourable market circumstances. In which case we need to consider reducing the department's area and using the released square metres for other, better-performing departments. The other possibility is that the department is inadequately managed. This aspect must therefore be changed.

The mechanism therefore not only functions to control the effectiveness of the measures taken, but also as a warning system during the process. Departments for which the arrows point in the right direction do not need very much attention. Departments for which the arrows point in the wrong direction, need to be examined, in which case the direction of the arrows provide the first indication to the solution. It appears that the system not only works as control mechanism, but also contributes to management of the change process.

Communication between branches

The results of the DAP analyses were discussed, per period, with all involved parties – with purchasing as well as sales, with store manager as well as departmental manager. These discussions did not take place in a reproachful atmosphere but rather in a solution-building one. Solutions were agreed. The extent to which these solutions were applied and resulted in improvement became the subject of a follow-up meeting. Management looked specifically at the development of DAP (R in the formula $R = S \times M - C$). The relevant departmental managers were required to indicate how they would achieve a possible improvement of R by manipulating S, M or C. As departmental managers in branch 1 could also see the results achieved by the departmental manager in branch 2, there was also an internal learning process: managers asked themselves why things were going well in one branch and not in another. This benchmark-like situation was accompanied by a certain degree of internal competition, which was certainly also beneficial.

Communication between purchasing and sales

In chapter 20 we also discussed the ever-present friction in retail companies between purchasing and sales. This was present to a significant degree in the old Bijenkorf. Since the DAP control variable was applied in the same way to both purchasing and sales, a common basis for discussion arose. Additionally, the DAP system enabled them to some extent to distinguish between 'central problems' and 'branch problems'. Figure 24.4a reflects the development of DAP for a single department across four

24

24

branches. It is clear that things are not going well in this department: although sales has increased, DAP decreased – and the same applies for each of the four branches. It is therefore logical to conclude that this is a central problem, which is more likely to be resolved through better central purchasing than individually via the four separate branches.

FIGURE 24.4a Diagnosis: central problem

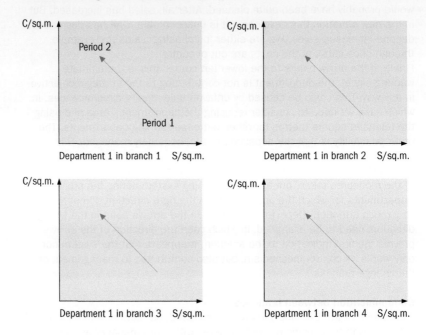

Figure 24.4b shows a different picture: all arrows point in different directions. There seems to be a branch problem. The manager of the department in branch 4, who claims that the poor development of his branch is caused by purchasing, can now immediately be confronted with the fact that the manager in branch 2 is doing well, with the exact same product range. The manager of the department in branch 4 is therefore well advised to learn from his colleague.

Although the DAP control model has not eliminated all the frictions between purchasing and sales, it has contributed to making friction easier to discuss and to working together to find a solution. Friction is no longer counter-productive.

24.1.3 DAP as black box

Use of the control variable 'DAP/m^2', as in the example of de Bijenkorf, is based on the *black box* philosophy: the development of a single variable is examined, without determining which factors influence the development of this variable. The development of corrective measures is left to the individuals involved. Advantage of this application is that there is a robust and transparent signalling and management system. The disadvantage is that the causes of the problem are not directly exposed. To achieve this, the problem must be more closely described. The choice here is between

FIGURE 24.4b Diagnosis: branch problems

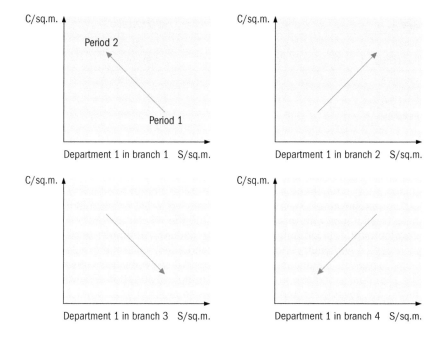

providing all materials used in DAP calculations to the managers (thus running the risk of information overload), or supplementing the DAP system with additional control systems (such as the trinity model) which reveal underlying causes. We will mainly focus on the latter aspect in the following paragraphs.

An intermediate form, between the *DAP-system* and the trinity model, is control using the break even mechanism. Table 24.1 identifies the development of the break-even point and the resistance level per branch.

DAP system

TABLE 24.1 Control using the break even model

Branch 1	Period 1	Period 2	Index
Sales	€5,887,321	€5,818,485	0.99
Margin	30.2%	30.3%	1.00
Fixed costs	€745,5740	€656,784	0.88
Var. costs	14.1%	15.0%	1.07
B.E. sales	€4,622,936	€4,301,429	0.93
Resistance	21.5%	26.1%	1.21

TABLE 24.1 Control using the break even model (continued)

Branch 2	Period 1	Period 2	Index
Sales	€2,599,581	€2,772,185	1.07
Margin	25.4%	26.5%	1.04
Fixed costs	€144,562	€303,956	2.10
Var. costs	10.4%	11.4%	1.09
B.E. sales	€965,263	€2,016,104	2.09
Resistance	62.9%	27.3%	0.43

In branch 1 we see that, despite sales stagnation (the index is 0.99), the break even point decreases (index 0.93) and resistance increases (index 1.21). The cause seems to be the reduction of fixed costs. In the old situation where sales was the main driving force, one would not have been happy with this development. In the new situation, the development is favourable. The opposite happens in branch 2: the sales increases significantly and the margin increases, while the break even point increases significantly and resistance decreases. The reason is the significant increase in fixed costs. In the old situation this would have been favourable, but not in the new situation.

24.2 Opening the black box: the trinity model

While direct assortment profitability indicates how profitability develops but does not clearly indicate how this is caused, the trinity model indicates what is going on in the operation without being directly linked to the level of profitability. Both systems therefore complement each other. DAP uses a black box approach to show profit development. The trinity model opens the black box and shows the causes of this development.

The trinity model focuses mainly on explaining developments in the operation. This model is strongly focused on stores. The trinity model is therefore especially useful for control purposes where branch operation plays a role, i.e. it is especially relevant in those situations where sales development is not the immediate problem, but rather cost control. This model is less suitable for applications to control market position.

In the following paragraph we discuss the use of the trinity model as a benchmarking tool.

24.2.1   Using the trinity model as a benchmarking tool

Trinity model

In the discussion on internal analysis we mainly explained the *trinity model* from a strategic point of view: which strengths and weaknesses arise in relation to operation of the company as a whole? If, based on the implementation of the model, we have identified the weak points and have drafted action plans for improvement, we can then use the model to control the effectiveness of such improvement measures. There is a frequent need for information on the progress of development per branch. This means that we need to refine the analysis to branch level. This refinement will generally not cause any problems. The data for the interpretation of the model at company level are generally derived from the branches themselves. Disaggregation to the level of the individual branch should therefore not be a problem.

24.2.2 Comparison at absolute level (benchmarking between branches)

Figure 24.5 is an example of a trinity analysis of a branched organisation with five branches in the discount retail environment. Overall company figures are also given. By comparing the performance of the branches with the figures for the overall company we get information on the performance of individual branches. We should take into account the fact that the trinity model does not use the sales of a branch as an explanatory variable, while the sales does have an impact on the key indicators in the model. There may be more explanations for the differences between indicators per branch than is immediately visible from the model. For example, if a branch has too much retail floor space (RFS) in a market segment that is too small, all efficiency variables may be lower than average. The example in figure 24.5 clearly shows differences in performance per branch.

Branch 1
Branch 1 plays a leading role in all respects compared to the average performance of the company as a whole: high stock efficiency (1.26 compared to 0.81 for the overall company), high floor efficiency (1,040 compared to 705) and high labour efficiency (41,025 compared to 35,249). This is because the margin is higher than average and all productivity variables are extremely favourable. Obviously branch 1 has no need for extra attention at the moment. However, it is striking that this branch has a very low self-service ratio, compared to the average (39.5 compared to 50 in total). The profitability of this branch may be improved with better staffing.

Branch 2
Branch 2 also performs better than average on all efficiency variables, although not as impressively as branch 1. However, a comparison with the variables of branch 1 shows that branch 2 has a relatively high goods intensity. The input data shows that, with a sales that amounts to half of that of branch 1 and a RFS that is two thirds the size of branch 1, goods intensity is 20% higher than that of branch 1. Improvement of stock control in this branch should be examined.

Branch 5
Branch 5 performs far below average in all respects: all efficiency variables are significantly below the average of the total organisation. An important cause is undoubtedly the especially low sales level (see the input at the bottom of the chart). This branch is apparently situated in a poor catchment area.

24

24

FIGURE 24.5 Trinity model with five branches

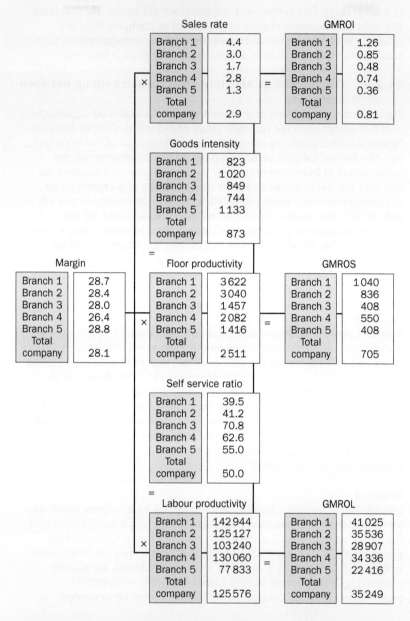

Sales rate		GMROI	
Branch 1	4.4	Branch 1	1.26
Branch 2	3.0	Branch 2	0.85
Branch 3	1.7	Branch 3	0.48
Branch 4	2.8	Branch 4	0.74
Branch 5	1.3	Branch 5	0.36
Total company	2.9	Total company	0.81

Goods intensity	
Branch 1	823
Branch 2	1 020
Branch 3	849
Branch 4	744
Branch 5	1 133
Total company	873

Margin		Floor productivity		GMROS	
Branch 1	28.7	Branch 1	3 622	Branch 1	1 040
Branch 2	28.4	Branch 2	3 040	Branch 2	836
Branch 3	28.0	Branch 3	1 457	Branch 3	408
Branch 4	26.4	Branch 4	2 082	Branch 4	550
Branch 5	28.8	Branch 5	1 416	Branch 5	408
Total company	28.1	Total company	2 511	Total company	705

Self service ratio	
Branch 1	39.5
Branch 2	41.2
Branch 3	70.8
Branch 4	62.6
Branch 5	55.0
Total company	50.0

Labour productivity		GMROL	
Branch 1	142 944	Branch 1	41 025
Branch 2	125 127	Branch 2	35 536
Branch 3	103 240	Branch 3	28 907
Branch 4	130 060	Branch 4	34 336
Branch 5	77 833	Branch 5	22 416
Total company	125 576	Total company	35 249

This is exactly when management of the operation becomes extremely important. Consideration of the figures shows a failing, in particular, of stock management in this branch: the goods intensity is the highest of all branches and the sales rate is the lowest of all branches. Improving stock control is therefore very necessary. The combination now revealed (low sales rate and high goods intensity), will almost certainly lead to problems in the future. The combination of a high goods intensity and a low sales rate points to 'ageing' of the stock. In such a situation, dead stock is bound to increase. The result may be the need for significant sacrifices in margin in order to get rid of 'contaminated' stock via markdowns in the next year.

24.2.3 Comparison of development over time: implementation control

More important than the direct comparison of absolute figures (no matter how useful!), is the comparison of branch development. Does every branch contribute equally to achieving the strategic objective? To this end it is more practical to work with 'improvement' than with absolute figures, partly because the absolute figures can be influenced by various – even external – factors that cancel each other out in the comparison. The application is basically no different from the application of a dynamic, *direct assortment profitability* model, as discussed in chapter 13: one sets the performance of the branch in the previous corresponding period at 100 and then compares the current period's performance. When a variable is below the 100 index, this signifies deterioration. When a variable is above 100, it signifies an improvement compared to the previous period.

FIGURE 24.6 The development of the ten branches (indexed to previous year)

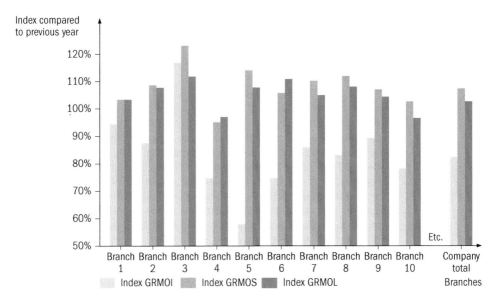

Figure 24.6 shows the development of ten branches – as an example of a company with a large number of branches. Due to the number of branches a table format was used, rather than the usual presentation of this model. As a result the figures are less clear. The final presentation of the relevant results of the involved branches is also done differently, namely in the form of bar diagrams.

The example describes the situation of a rapidly expanding branch organisation. The overall growth in sales was excellent. The strategic analysis, however, shows that sales on a like for like basis had been stagnating for several years and had even started to decline.

24

This basically meant that the company was trying to escape its fate in a headlong rush towards the future – and failure: the formula had weakened, but this was not evident in the results as it was disguised by expansion. However, if the expansion were to come to an end (in a small country like the Netherlands this can happen very easily), the inherent weakness of the concept would then very quickly lead to a dramatic situation in terms of profit development. This primary conclusion led to an action plan being drawn up, designed to achieve a reversal in the development of sales per square metre on like for like basis. This led to a comprehensive program which addressed, among other things: product range renewal and expansion, 'concentrating' presentation and correction of price levels. In short, all elements of the marketing mix were examined and, where necessary, corrective measures were introduced. The effects of this for the operation, after implementation of the program, were:

- sales per metre in the branches would need to increase (broader and better assortment);
- the sales rate might decrease (wider and deeper assortment in the same retail floor space, leading to a higher goods density);
- labour productivity should increase (higher sales with only a slight increase in personnel).

The margin should at least remain at the same level, but hopefully increase slightly as a result of the new assortment. Expressed in trinity control variables, namely GMROI (stock efficiency), GMROS (floor efficiency) and GMROL (labour efficiency), this meant that GMROI could decrease, GMROS should increase significantly and GMROL should show a slight increase.

- Table 24.2 clearly shows how the various branches contribute to this process. We measured the first period after the branches were renovated. The bottom line of table 24.2, reflecting the development across the total company, shows that the expectations of management were broadly met: GMROI decreased (index 82), GMROS increased (index 107) and GMROL also increased (index 102). At branch level we see that this result was achieved because most of the branches exhibited the same behaviour, but to varying degrees. Branch 3 is an exception with regard to the GMROI: in this, the GMROI increased in comparison to the previous period by index 116. Further consideration shows that this branch was reduced in size during renovation (index square metres 87). Here too, however, there is a relative increase in the stock: index 92, with an index RFS of 87.

Branch 4 needs further attention: the approach seems to be failing in this branch. In this case, GMROS and GMROL appear to be decreasing instead of increasing. Consideration of the input shows that here, contrary to the other branches, there is no increase in sales after renovation (index 98). Why is this? Is there additional competition? Or were the renovations not performed properly?

TABLE 24.2 Trinity data table

Name / Year	Margin	Sales	FRS	Stock	FTE	Sales rate	Sales cm²	Sales FTE	Goods intensity	Self service ratio	Control variables		
											GMROI	GMROS	GMROL
Branch 1	102%	100%	100%	108%	100%	93%	100%	100%	108%	100%	94%	102%	102%
Branch 2	103%	115%	108%	137%	110%	84%	106%	105%	127%	98%	86%	110%	108%
Branch 3	102%	105%	87%	92%	95%	114%	121%	111%	106%	92%	116%	123%	113%
Branch 4	102%	98%	106%	134%	104%	73%	92%	94%	126%	102%	75%	94%	96%
Branch 5	102%	102%	100%	180%	105%	57%	102%	97%	180%	95%	58%	104%	99%
Branch 6	106%	137%	137%	194%	131%	71%	100%	105%	142%	105%	75%	106%	111%
Branch 7	100%	110%	100%	127%	105%	87%	110%	105%	127%	95%	87%	110%	105%
Branch 8	103%	111%	102%	138%	105%	80%	109%	106%	135%	97%	83%	112%	109%
Branch 9	104%	110%	98%	129%	100%	85%	112%	110%	132%	98%	89%	117%	114%
Branch 10	102%	101%	101%	133%	107%	76%	100%	94%	132%	94%	77%	102%	96%
Etc.													
Company total	102%	105%	100%	131%	105%	80%	105%	100%	131%	95%	82%	107%	102%

24

Branch 5 also requires further attention: even though the GMROS increases and the GMROL remains pretty much the same, the GMROI is decreasing significantly (index 58 compared to the average in the total company index 82).

Consideration of the input shows that the stock level in this branch has increased significantly: the stock index is at 180 compared to 131 across the entire company. It is clear that more attention should be given to stock control in this branch.

24.3 Consistency between variables

Given the problem, the most important key control variable in this case was the development of profit contribution per square metre in existing branches. Management exercised control mainly in the manner described in paragraph 24.2. They did however indicate what was expected in terms of development in the sub-variables at branch level. We therefore see, in this case, that the trinity model was used as sub-system of the total control system and focussed on variables that could be influenced by the branches. A system was therefore also developed on the sales side, by which it was possible to measure actual strategic variables at a high level (the like for like contribution per square metre) while, at operational level, variables measured were those that could be influenced directly by the individuals involved, and which were consistent with the overall objective.

24.4 Control of sales development and market position: ADM, fair-share and monitor analysis

DAP models

Using *direct assortment profitability models* (DAP models) we are able to make implementation of the strategic approach controllable and manageable, where it concerns the overall variable. The trinity model can be used when it comes to the overall objective, supplemented by control of the development of the operation. Sales development plays an important role in both models: *ceteris paribus,* positive sales development will always influence the key control variables favourably. However, there are situations in which information purely on the overall development is not enough, but where the quality of sales also plays a role. We cannot assess quality of sales based on DAP models or trinity models. In these cases we need to make adjust-

ADM

ments to the *assortment dominance matrix* (ADM) or the monitor analysis in order to make the developments manageable.

24.4.1   ADM

Suppose that we use the strategic ADM analysis to conclude that sales is indeed reasonable, but that the composition of the assortment positioning is becoming less favourable. Such an example has already been discussed in chapter 12 (see figure 24.7).

FIGURE 24.7 ADM of a men's fashion store for two different years

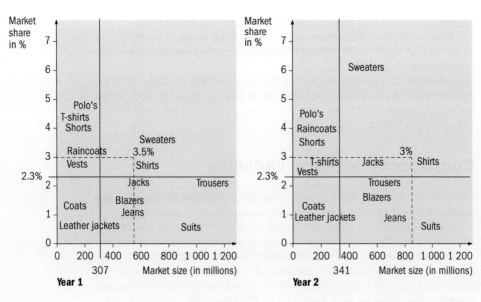

We will use the same example to explain how development of the product range portfolio can be managed, based on ADM. The ADM of figure 24.7 deals with the development of a men's fashion store, which seemingly had no problems with the sales development. In four years' time, sales grew by 10%. This matched the growth of the overall market. On average, the company was therefore able to maintain its market share. But the way in which growth was achieved gave rise to some concerns: the company was losing market share in large, growing markets and gaining market share in shrinking, small markets. In short, market share was gained mainly in markets that were not interesting to the competition. And the quality of sales was declining. This conclusion was drawn by comparing two, annual ADMs. This was a rather cumbersome affair.

If we come to the conclusion that it is necessary to improve the quality of sales, we can convert the ADM into a control instrument. Also in this case, for control purposes, measurement of dynamics is more important (and easier to interpret) than comparison of absolute levels. After all, in this case, quality improvement of sales should be measured by determining whether market share has been gained in growing markets. The actual size of the market and the actual value of the market share itself are less important: assessing the effectiveness of the measures is about the dynamics and not about dimensions like big/small or high/low.

By indexing the data of two consecutive periods, we get a 'dynamic ADM'. The performance in the previous period per product range component is set at 100. If all market shares remain equal and all markets remain stable with regard to size, then all assessments for the new period will be located at this centre point. This exercise, for the relevant men's fashion store, was illustrated in figure 24.8. The period under comparison is the two years following the realisation that something was wrong with the quality of the sales. The product range improvement program that was implemented during this period would lead to a reversal.

FIGURE 24.8 A dynamic ADM for a men's fashion store

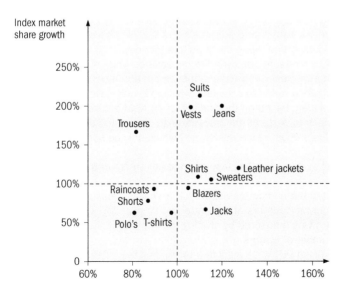

24

**Fair share
analysis**

The graph clearly shows that the objective was, generally, successfully attained: the quadrant 'growing market/growing market share' now contains seven product range groups, some of which are in relatively large markets (jeans, shirts, sweaters and suits). Things seem to be going rather well. Although the development of jackets is a concern. This is a rather large market, in which the company used to perform reasonably well. The approach that was effective for the other groups was apparently not effective for this group. Recalibration of the marketing plan seems in place. A simplified form of the use of ADM as a control instrument can be found in the *fair share analysis*. As discussed in chapter 12, we can use fair share analysis as an indication of relative market share, or as measure of the extent to which a branch differs from the average of the overall enterprise. The V&D example illustrated in that chapter is actually an application of fair share analysis as a control instrument.

24.4.2   Using monitor analysis as a control instrument

**Monitor
analysis**

ADM is well suited for measuring development in the product range portfolio, but is not suitable for determining how sales is generated from the perspective of the customer in the store. If the identified problems lie in the attractiveness of the store or the effectiveness of the store as a sales machine, we should resort to the monitor analysis ($S = CA \times VI \times C \times AT$). By once again taking the figures from the corresponding period in the previous year and indexing the figures of the same period in the current year, we arrive at an explanation of sales development from a customer behaviour perspective, especially if we maintain this measure over a longer period. As an example, let us look at the development of sales in an interior decorating business. This company was very successful for a long time, but at a certain moment sales growth started to decline. Analysis, using the customer monitor, indicated that this was not caused by the store becoming less attractive, as the visitors index (the number of visitors) still showed considerable increase. The cause of the decline of sales growth was mainly that conversion was relatively low compared to the competition and had also declined. In any event, conversion declined more quickly than the increase in the number of visitors. It therefore seemed that the 'outside image' of the store was not in line with what we encountered on the inside. After all, the formula was able to attract visitors, but was increasingly unsuccessful in converting these store visitors into buyers. It was decided to develop several measures designed to increase conversion – such as presentation improvements, more personnel on the floor and adjustment of price level. In addition to these activities, which may only have a short term effect, it was decided, based on the findings of an ADM analysis, to make significant changes to parts of the product range. The expectation was that the effects of this product range adjustment would only be noticeable in the longer term.

A simple control system was developed for measurement of the short term effects.

- Development in the number of visitors ($CA \times VI$) was measured by applying electronic counters at the entrance.
- Conversion (C) was measured by dividing the number of checkouts by the measured number of visitors.
- The average ticket (AT) was calculated by dividing the sales by the number of checkouts.

This case was, once again, about determining whether there were any changes in the control variables. And, once again, the control was based on changes measured against previous periods. The measurements took place over a number of consecutive periods, including the period in which the short term measures were implemented. The result was presented in the form of several graphs. The effect of interference (weather, holidays) was neutralised by calculation of the moving average. The graphs (figures 24.9a to 24.9d) reflect an image of the moving average during the execution of the promotional program.

24

FIGURE 24.9a Development of moving average during the short-term approach: visitor numbers (CA × VI)

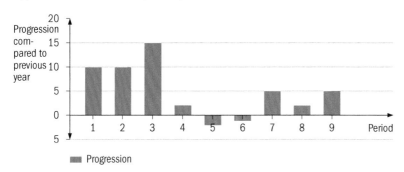

FIGURE 24.9b Development of moving average conversion, C

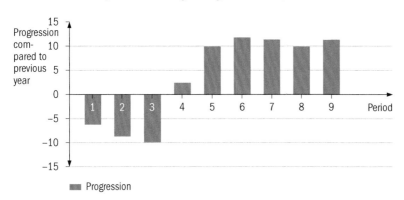

It is clear that there was a gradual change in development during the period. During the restructuring period (period 1, 2 and 3), the number of visitors continues to rise (clearance effect?) and the conversion percentage and checkout amount continues to drop. After completion of the renovations and once more personnel had been deployed, we gradually see the number of visitors stabilise and even decline slightly in certain periods. But the conversion increases significantly, just as the checkout amount. The measures taken have clearly resulted in fewer 'window shoppers' and bargain hunters, while the proportion of 'good' customers has increased, as a result of which checkout values also increased. The core customer proposition has improved.

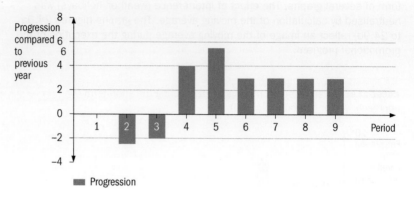

FIGURE 24.9c Moving average checkout amount (sales receipt) AT

FIGURE 24.9d Result: sales development

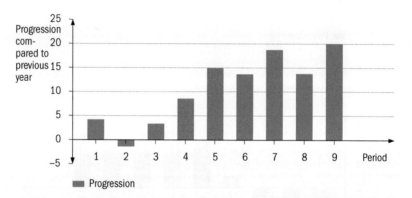

A warning is in order: as regards measurements over time using the customer monitor, take into account that there is a connection between growth in the number of visitors and conversion growth. We almost always see that an increase in the number of visitors is accompanied by a reduction in conversion, and vice versa. The reason is that an increase in the number of visitors often means that one has attracted new customers, who do not yet know the store. The probability that they will succeed in completing their purchase is lower than in the case of visitors who already know what they can expect in store. Conversely, declining visitor numbers often mean that the least loyal customers are the first to stay away. The remaining customer base **Core customers** consists of a larger proportion of *core customers* who have higher conversion. For popular, new companies it is even possible that all variables develop positively. This was the case in the first years after the launch of H&M. In general, however, we rarely find that both the number of visitors and conversion increase in existing companies. The point is therefore that the changes in the number of visitors and in the conversion ratio are beneficial to each other.

24.5 Integration and consistency of the process

The strategic process was explained on the basis of the objective formula $R = S \times M - C$. We have seen that this objective formula is actually nothing more than a model-based representation of the break even mechanism.

A pincer effect lurks in the background: The phenomenon that, in terms of trend, the nominal increase in costs is almost always higher than the nominal increase in sales, *ceteris paribus*. This is why sales growth plays an important role in retailing. The objective of the strategy is to optimise profit (R). This requires that the factors on the right side of the objective formula are manipulated simultaneously. Altering one of the factors will affect the other two factors. We can interpret the objective formula from the short term perspective. In such a case, we are operating tactically. We can also interpret the objective formula from the long-term perspective. We are then busy with strategy. In retail, the final result of a strategy is a retail formula.

The most important and difficult variable in the objective formula is the S of sales. This should be interpreted in the long-term as 'stable growth off an existing base'. Only if these conditions (stable, growth, an existing base) are met, can we be sure of escaping a pincer effect in the long-term. Survival of the formula is possible.

Sales growth is possible in several ways: market penetration (selling more of an existing product to existing target groups), market development (approaching new target groups with the existing product), product development (developing new products for an existing target group) and diversification (new market and new product).

In line with the philosophy on which this book was based, diversification is not dealt with here. After all, diversification essentially relates to starting a new company from scratch, while this book is mainly based on an existing operation. However, the other methods of sales growth are treated, using two models: the ADM and the monitor models. Consistency between the methods of growth and the two models is reflected in figure 24.10.

The fact that retail really should pay close attention to growth strategies (influencing S) does not relieve us of the obligation to properly monitor both the cost and margin side of the operation.

The reason is that returns in the Dutch retail environment are quite low. In retailing in the Netherlands, we cannot and should not consider marketing as only influencing sales. We should always ask ourselves whether we can also influence profitability. And that means that every market strategic approach should be accompanied with an analysis of possible costs (C) and proceeds (M). The consistency is reflected in figure 24.11.

24

24

FIGURE 24.10 Consistency between growth strategies and instruments

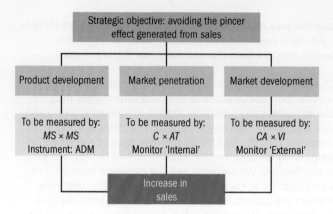

After having determined, based on the mentioned consistencies, which elements of the operation need to be improved (the SWOT), we use the marketing mix to develop the necessary corrective measures. The marketing mix is a coherent set of formula principles which should lead to the definition of a concept that provides added value to the consumer. The added value or the exchange benefit should always be considered in relation to the existing competition.

FIGURE 24.11 Consistency between the profit formula and the instruments

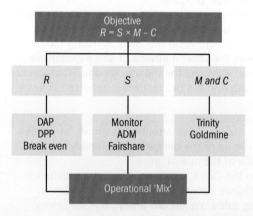

The marketing mix in retail is two-fold: on the one hand designed to attract visitors (attraction), on the other hand designed to convert visits into purchase behaviour (transaction). In the interpretation of the marketing mix we should always take into account the problems encountered in the strategic audit and the influence that each of the marketing mix variables may have on the objective formula. The consistency is reflected in figure 24.12.

FIGURE 24.12 Consistency between profit formula and the marketing mix

	S	×	M	–	C	=	R
Public (target groups)							
Product (product range)							
Position							
Price							
Promotion							
Personnel							
Presentation							
Physical distribution							
Productivity							
Total							

Finally, we get to the control of the implementation. Given the large amount of interference that occurs from the daily operation, it is important in strategic retail approaches to consistently determine whether the long-term objective will be met. It has been found that the instruments that we can use to identify a strategic problem can largely also be used for control. This completes integration and consistency: the analysis of the problem and the control of implementation are actually part of one and the same process.

Summary

In the development and implementation of actual control, it is recommended to link to the findings of the strategic audit. A situation in which the models that are used in the pre-analysis are also used for the implementation of control, is the clearest solution for the organisation. In this chapter, based on a large number of practical examples, we explained how we can convert the analysis instruments explained in this book, into control instruments. Finally, we illustrated the consistency between the instruments discussed in this book and the central objective formula ($R = S \times M - C$).

Literature

Alsem, K.J. (2001). *Strategische marketingplanning*. Groningen: Noordhoff Uitgevers.

Amit, R. & Zott, C. (2001). Value creation in e-business. *Strategic Management Journal*, 22, 493-520.

Bradach, J.L. (1998). *Franchise Organisations*. Boston: Harvard Business Review Press.

Buuron, P.M.A. (1995). *Retail informatietechnologie*. Amsterdam: VU Uitgeverij.

Coase, R.K. (1934). The Native of the Firm. *Economica*, December, p. 386-405.

Dreesmann, A.C.R. (1968). Patterns of evolution in retailing. *Journal of retailing*, Spring.

Eysink Smeets, H. (2011). *Porn for Bankers*. Amsterdam: Short Circuit Publishing B.V.

Floor, J.M.G. & Raaij, W.F. van (2008). *Marketingcommunicatiestrategie*. Houten: Stenfert Kroeze.

Franzen, G. (1983). *Waar het in retailreclame om draait*. Voordracht BvA.

Garner, B.J. (1966). *The Internal Structure of Retail Nucleations*. Northwestern University Studies in Geography, No. 12, Department of Geography Evanston, Illinois.

Goldratt, E.M., Cox, J. & G. Marka, G. (1995). *Het doel*. Houten: Spectrum.

Goor, A.R. van & Ploos van Amstel, M.J. (1996). *Fysieke distributie, Denken in toegevoegde waarde*. Houten: EPN.

Graig, C.S. et al. (1984). Models of the retail location process. *Journal of retailing*, Spring.

Grembergen, W. van & Amelinckx, I. (2002). *Measuring and managing e-business projects through the Balanced Scorecard*, Proceedings of the 35th Hawaii International Conference on System Sciences, HICSS, Maui.

Haasloop Werner, W & Quix, F. (2010). Van e-commerce naar e-strategy. *Tijdschrift voor Marketing*, September.

Hendry, J. (1990). The problem with Porter's generic strategies. *EMJ*, 8, 4, December.

Hollander, S.C. (1966). Notes on the retail accordeon. *Journal of retailing*, nr. 42.

Kind, R.P. van der (1998). *Retail & Marketing*. Deventer: Kluwer.

Kind, R.P. van der & Quix, F.W.J. (2008). Onderzoek winkelkeuzecriteria.

Lusch, R.E. (1986). The new algebra of high performance retail management. *Retail control*, 1986, 54, 7.

Maronick, T. J. & Walker, B. J. (1975). *The dialectic evolution of retailing* in Proceedings: Southern Marketing Association, Barnett Greenberg (ed.). Atlanta: Georgia State University.

McGoldrick, P.J. (1990). *Retailmarketing*. New York: McGraw Hill.

McNair, M.P. (1958). *Significant trends and development in the post war period*. Pittsburg: University of Pittsburg Press.

Mooney, K. & Rollins, N. (2007). *The Open Brand. When push comes to pull in a web made world*. Berkeley: New Riders.

Munneke, H. (1998). Category Management en ECR in Kind, R.P. van der (1998). *Retail & Marketing*. Deventer: Kluwer.

Porter, M.E. (1985). *Competitive advantage: creating and sustaining superior performance*. New York: Free Press.

Quix, F. (1996). Conversie Franchise. Rijksuniversiteit Groningen.

Quix, F. & Terra, J. (2011). *Crosschannel Retail*, ABN AMRO.

Quix, F. & Terra, J. (2010). *Re'structure*, HBD en CBW-MITEX.

Quix, F. & Van Wulfen, G. (1996). Ernst & Young.

Quix F., Bakker, B. & Lewis, A. (2010). *Lost Sales*. Q&A Research & Consultancy.

Quix, F., Terra, J., Hamann, E. & Wortel, C. (2011). *Het nieuwe winkelen*, Hoofdbedrijfschap Detailhandel.

Raaij, W.F. van & Antonides, G. (1999). *Consumentengedrag*. Den Haag: Lemma.

Reichheld, F.F. (2003). The one number you need to grow. *Harvard Business Review*, December.

Reijnders, W.J.M. (1994). *Prestaties van netwerken in de detailhandel*. Houten: Stenfert Kroese.

Rogers, E.E.M. (2003). *Diffusion of innovations*. New York: Free Press.

Scott, S. (2008). The Contribution Revolution. *Harvard Business Review*.

Strauss, W. & Howe, N. (1992). Generations. Hammersmith Perennial.

Underhill, P. (1999). *Why we buy, The science of shopping*. New York: Simon & Schuster.

Verhage, B.J. (2010). *Grondslagen van de marketing*. Groningen: Noordhoff Uitgevers.

Weinberg, B.D., Parise, S. & Guinan, P.J. (2007). Multichannel marketing: mindset and program development. *Business Horizons,* 50, 385-394.

Williamson, O.E. (1975). *Markets and Hierarchies*. New York: Free Press.

Index

For Product Safety Concerns and Information please contact our EU
representative GPSR@taylorandfrancis.com Taylor & Francis Verlag GmbH,
Kaufingerstraße 24, 80331 München, Germany

Printed and bound by CPI Group (UK) Ltd, Croydon, CR0 4YY
08/05/2025
01864465-0001